Sequels in Children's Literature

ALSO BY VICKI ANDERSON

Cultures Outside the United States in Fiction (1994)
Immigrants in the United States in Fiction (1994)
Native Americans in Fiction (1994)
Fiction Sequels for Readers 10 to 16, 2d ed. (1998)

AND FROM MCFARLAND

Sequels in Children's Literature

*An Annotated Bibliography
of Books in Succession or with
Shared Themes and Characters, K–6*

Vicki Anderson

McFarland & Company, Inc., Publishers
Jefferson, North Carolina, and London

Many thanks to the many children's librarians
who helped me, especially those in Phoenix

British Library Cataloguing-in-Publication data are available

Library of Congress Cataloguing-in-Publication Data

Anderson, Vicki, 1928–
    Sequels in children's literature : an annotated bibliography of
books in succession or with shared themes and characters, K–6
/ Vicki Anderson.
      p. cm.
    Includes index.
    ISBN 0-7864-0285-7 (sewn softcover : 50# alkaline paper) ∞
    1. Children's stories—Bibliography. 2. Children's stories.
English—Bibliography. 3. Sequels (Literature)—Bibliography.
I. Title.
Z1037.A542   1998
[PN1009.A1]
016.80883'0083—dc21
                                           97-51207
                                               CIP

Manufactured in the United States of America

McFarland & Company, Inc., Publishers
  Box 611, Jefferson, North Carolina 28640

Table of Contents

Introduction

There is a great abundance of sequel (succession) books published, especially in picture books and easy readers. This creates a need for a way to access these books for optimum use.

As I worked as a librarian over the years it occurred to me that I needed a complete list of these books for several reasons—to answer requests for "another one about..."; to keep my collection of them annotated; to assure that I purchased the needed titles in any series to make reader's guidance programs more flexible, and so on.

When working with readers it is important to do a follow-up when they come back asking for "another one like it." If it is a sequel and you know it, your job is made easier. When introducing a book, knowing it has a follow-up or companion book can help "sell" it.

We've all had the experience of finding ourselves with book one or book three of a trilogy and having never bought book two. We've also found ourselves trying to help a patron select a good book not knowing it was part of a trilogy and so offer book three before book one. Or not realizing that even though the title is quite different one book really is about the same character as another book. So in these situations and in any reader's guidance service knowing instantly what is a sequel and where in a sequence a particular title belongs is important.

In some cases even though the most important factor may not be where in the sequence it belongs, it is important to know it is part of a series of books about a specific person or animal.

There is really no simple way to identify sequel books. The review journals do not al-ways identify them as such. The catalog cards do not always do so. Even the book jacket, which is usually read after purchase, frequently doesn't.

The present book offers a key to these considerations; it deals with a wide range of sequels. It is intended to help librarians and readers sort out these sequels in any book collection.

The selection is as broad as I could make it. Since selectivity is never completely objective anyway, I chose to include almost everything I could find. Therefore appropriateness, type and availability, and not the quality of writing, were listed as criteria.

The contents include books with literary value, as well as ones with easy readability, or that are high in popularity, or which attract the reluctant reader. There are many, of course, that challenge the true reader.

This book has a broad coverage. It includes stories about ethnic groups, families, sports, humor, animals, birds, fish, etc. You should be able to find the proverbial well-rounded collection within these sequels, just as you would find in your collection overall.

The titles selected range from pre-school through sixth grade. I have not put a great deal of emphasis on age group levels since experience has taught me that all readers are individuals and as such are not necessarily ready for the same book at the same time. Each child's taste in books, current interest, social maturity, reading ability or listening skills are different from those of other readers and listeners of the same age.

In her book *Sequences, An Annotated Guide*

to Children's Fiction in Series, Susan Roman states: "Series of fiction may or may not show an elaboration of character and plot through the individual titles. Within series there are stories that are more closely related to one another. These are sequences. Sequences do show this development of character and plot through each novel in the series. A sequel is a series title with the same character as those in an earlier book. Often they may have only superficial unity."

In this collection a sequel is a book that can stand alone and be read and enjoyed by itself, but is also one of several books written about the same main character following a similar theme. Sometimes it is developmental and sometimes not. The books selected can be said to simply have a common thread reappearing in each book; sometimes a minor character in one book becomes a major character in another and visa versa. Sometimes they cover different members of the same family or different generations of the same family; sometimes they all go to the same school, or live in the same neighborhood. Sometimes the character grows and matures through the books and sometimes they remain the same throughout all the books. These books are considered sequels because they have the same character in each book and continue the theme of an earlier work. This book is not about series or sequences, it is about sequels.

Series do not always come with series titles and even if they do the titles do not necessarily represent sequels or sequences. What this book does is connect stories related by having a common character. Some of them do not need to be read in order, but if the reader identifies with the character, the library collection needs to reflect all other books with that character.

This list contains about 7500 titles arranged alphabetically by author. As in most any list of books, there are titles both included and excluded that users of this book may wonder about. I repeat: I included all I could find within the age group and the time frame established. I'm sure there are more titles.

Some of the books listed herein may be out of print but since out of print books are still found on library shelves, or can be obtained on interlibrary loan, I didn't consider that important and have included them because of their value or interest and because readers should not miss them. I included all titles I could determine were still being checked out to readers or have a historical reason to be included. When some books have proven to have long term popularity, especially in a sequel, it is best to keep them and all their companions on the shelves as long as readers are using them.

This list is not intended solely as a selection guide. It can be used to put identifying labels on the spines of these books indicating that it is part of a sequel and what part it is. In this way both librarian and readers would know which books are part of a larger group and which of them comes first.

It can be used to check the collection and see if it contains all volumes of a set.

It can be used as a promotional device to introduce sequel books to your readers. We know that if a reader comes back for book two or three we probably have captured another reader.

Each series is grouped by author. A series may have a definite progression to the storyline from book to book or the stories may be quite independent from one another. If there is a discernible chronology to the story, then the books will appear in the order of the story.

There are several instances of prequels, that is, books written after the series was started or completed but giving background or earlier information about characters or situations in the series. They are noted as such in the annotation.

If the stories do not have a progression, then the publication date determines the order in which the books appear under the author's name.

Please note that an author may have written more than one series. Each new series will repeat the author's name.

Brief bibliographic information is given. The publishers are given in short form (for example, Harper for Harper and Row Publishing Company). The full names and addresses are easily available in the many other publications, such as *Books in Print* and *Children's Catalog*. Some of the books have been published outside the United States but have been widely distributed in the United States.

The annotations were gleaned from the books themselves, the book jackets, the catalog cards, the review journals and any other source I could find.

In some cases there is one annotation for two or more titles if they are quite similar or the title is indicative of the subject and an annotation is not needed.

In a few cases where many books are in a sequel or series, I have not individually annotated each one but have given a sample annotation as a guide.

There is a title index giving the entry number in this book. There is also an appendix listing series by grade level, to differentiate the picture books (k–3) from the easy readers (2–5) from the novels (4–6) from the more challenged reader (5–8).

This book grew out of a need to know my collection better and keep readers interested once they found a book they liked. I hope this bibliography helps you in *your* mission to help kids become enthusiastic readers!

The Bibliography

1. Abels, Harriette S., *Forgotten World* (Crestwood, 1979) k–3. A malfunctioning engine forces the EM 88 to land on an uncharted asteroid which bears a strange resemblance to Earth.

2. ____. *Green Invasion* (Crestwood, 1979) k–3. Vigorous weeds from another galaxy will kill the crops grown for Earth on an Astro–orb and threaten to destroy the entire agricultural station.

3. ____. *Silent Invaders* (Crestwood, 1979) k–3. An army of humanoids threatens to blow up any colony whose inhabitants will not vacate.

4. ____. *Meteor from the Moon* (Crestwood, 1979) k–3. When the headquarters Astro-orb goes out of orbit, the members of spaceship EM 88 try a daring plan to put it back in place.

5. ____. *Medical Emergency* (Crestwood, 1979) k–3. The commander of the EM 88 is stricken with what may be the first case of smallpox in several centuries.

6. ____. *Planet of Ice* (Crestwood, 1979) k–3. The crew of emergency spaceship EM 88 is sent to rescue a colony from Venus when increasingly cold temperatures begin to freeze the life support systems.

7. ____. *Unwanted Visitors* (Crestwood, 1979) k–3. The crew of emergency spaceship EM 88 discovers that the mysterious object that they have been sent to investigate is a vehicle for a group of amorphous blobs fleeing from their galaxy.

8. ____. *Strangers on NMA* (Crestwood, 1979) k–3. The theft of nickel ingots from asteroid NMA-6 provides a puzzling mystery until members of spaceship EM 88 step in to investigate

9. ____. *Mystery on Mars* (Crestwood, 1979) k–3. While visiting the Mars colony, the crew of the emergency spaceship EM 88 help to rescue miners trapped by an earthquake and discovers some unusual inhabitants deep in the mountain.

10. Abrahams, Anthony. *Polonius Penguin Learns to Swim* (Watts, 1963) k–3. Polonius Penguin left his South Pole home by ship because of his inability to swim. Timmy, the son Rufus, the sailor, became Polonius' best friend and taught him to swim. Polonious returned to his family.

11. ____. *Polonius Penguin and the Flying Doctor* (Watts, 1966) k–3. Polonius Penguin is a jolly bird. He goes back to his friend Timmy in London from the boring old South Pole and it is an attack of appendicitis that inspires the means of transportation.

12. ____. *Polonius Penguin Comes to Town* (Watts, 1978) k–3. A penguin who can't swim and doesn't want to learn is befriended by a sailor and enthusiastically adapts to life in London, in spite of an appendix operation performed by Hippocrates Hippopotamus.

13. Adams, Laurie. *Alice and the Boa Constrictor* (Houghton, 1983) 4–6. After learning in science class that boa constrictors make wonderful pets, Alice saves her money until she has enough to buy Sir Lancelot.

14. ____. *Who Wants a Turnip for President Anyway?* (Bantam, 1987) 4–5. Peaches and Turnips are trying to get their candidate to win the fifth grade presidency. Alice of the Peaches thinks she is going to win. But there is some switching of sides and Alice loses the election because of "dirty politics."

15. ____. *Alice Whipple, 5th Grade Detective* (Houghton, 1988) 4–6. Alice, 10, suspects her art teacher of being a thief and smuggler of art objects. Her friend helps her crack this case.

16. ____. *Alice Whipple in Wonderland* (Bantam, 1989) 4–5. Alice, a fifth grader, is involved in discovering who is attempting to sabotage a school play. She tries out for several parts in the play. Since she has no talent, she doesn't get the parts but does solve the mystery.

17. ____. *Alice Whipple for President* (Bantam 1990) 4–6. Alice is running for fifth grade class president and her opponents are up to nasty tricks in order to win.

18. ____. *Alice Whipple Shapes Up* (Houghton, 1991) 4–6. Unathletic Alice tries to shape up to join the soccer team at her private school. It is hard work for a husky girl.

19. Adams, Pam. *Mrs. Honey's Glasses* (Child Play, 1994) k–3. Mrs. Honey interacts with her grandchildren, as they look for her missing glasses in totally inappropriate places.

20. ____. *Mrs. Honey's Dream* (Child Play, 1994) k–3. Mrs. Honey and her cat each dream different segments of their adventure with pirates.

21. Adams, Ruth. *Mr. Picklepaw Popcorn* (Lothrop, 1965) k–3. Mr. Picklepaw grew 29½ bushels of popcorn. One hot day his popcorn began to pop, raising the roof and Mr. Picklepaw high in the air. He was rescued by a helicopter and children had popcorn to eat for weeks to come.

22. ____. *Mr. Picklepaw's Puppy* (Lothrop, 1970) k–3. Although his puppy is more a hindrance than a help on the farm, Mr. Picklepaw finds it difficult to get along without him.

23. Adamson, Jean. *Topsy and Tim Go Pony Trekking* (Blackie, 1972) k–3. Topsy and Tim are always five years old. The events in these books cover sore throats, church clocks, planting seeds, going to the doctor and the dentist, visits from Granny, going to football games, having their hair washed, being invited to tea, going pony-trekking, meeting multi-ethnic friends and practicing gymnastics.

24. ____. *Topsy and Tim at the Football Match* (Blackie, 1972) k–3. Topsy and Tim are delighted at the chance of going to support the Blues at a football match.

25. ____. *Topsy and Tim Go Safely* (Blackie, 1972) k–3. This story teaches road safety.

26. ____. *Topsy and Tim Visit the Dentist* (Blackie, 1972) k–3.

27. ____. *Topsy and Tim's ABC* (Blackie, 1981) k–3. This series started in the 1960s, but is being reissued. Mummy and Dad cope with holidays, travel sickness, librarians, police, football crowds, pets, hair washing, having friends in for tea, pony trekking and visits to Belgium.

28. ____. *Topsy and Tim's Counting* (Blackie, 1981) k–3. "Six pork sausage sizzling in a pan. Three went Pop and the rest went Bang." A counting book.

29. ____. *Topsy and Tim Go to Playschool* (Blackie, 1981) k–3.

30. ____. *Topsy and Tim's Birthday* (Blackie, 1981) k–3.

31. ____. *Topsy and Tim's New Pet* (Blackie, 1981) k–3.

32. ____. *Topsy and Tim Can Help Birds* (Blackie, 1982) k–3. Topsy and Tim design a bird table. A blue titmouse takes over the nest box they have watched their dad put up.

33. ____. *Topsy and Tim's Garden* (Blackie, 1985) k–3. "They don't look like much now, but they will grow nicely if you look after them," the garden center man said. "They" refer to sunflower seeds.

34. ____. *Topsy and Tim Go to the Doctor* (Blackie, 1985) k–3. Topsy and Tim have sore throats. The reader learns about doctors and surgery.

35. ____. *Topsy and Tim Tell the Time* (Blackie, 1985) k–3. A story designed to uncover the mysteries of the clock face.

36. ____. *Topsy and Tim's New Friends* (Blackie, 1988) k–3. Topsy and Tim meet some young Asians.

37. ____. *Topsy and Tim Can Play Party Games* (Blackie, 1985) k–3.

38. ____. *Topsy and Tim in the Farmyard* (Blackie, 1988) k–3.

39. ____. *Topsy and Tim Stay with a Friend* (Blackie, 1988) k–3.

40. ____. *Topsy and Tim at the T.V. Studio* (Blackie, 1988) k–3.

41. Adler, C.S. *Goodbye, Pink Pig* (Putnam, 1985) 5–8. Amanda would rather live in the fantasy world of her imagination than go to her new middle school, where the custodian is the grandmother she has never met.

42. ____. *Help, Pink Pig* (Putnam, 1990) 5–8. Moving to Los Angeles to live with her mother, a lonely girl, Amanda, escapes the boredom and torment of a neighborhood bully by entering a fantasy world with her magical toy pig.

43. ____. *Split Sisters* (Macmillan, 1986) 5–8. Case, ll, and Jen, 14, face a separating family. Case stays with her stepfather and Jen with her mother. The parents try again to make a go of it.

44. ____. *One Sister Too Many* (Macmillan, 1989) 5–8. Case and her sister Jen face growing up: first dates, baby-sitting and the usual family problems.

45. Adler, David A. *My Dog and the Key Mystery* (Watts, 1982) k–3. Jennie's dog, who is good at solving mysteries, helps her friend Susan find her lost house key.

46. ____. *My Dog and the Knock Knock Mystery* (Holiday, 1985) k–3. Jennie's dog, who is good at solving mysteries, helps her friend Billy discover the source of the mysterious knocking at his house.

47. ____. *My Dog and the Green Sock Mystery* (Holiday, 1986) k–3. Jennie's dog solves the mystery of the disappearing objects at her friend Andy's house.

48. ____. *My Dog and the Birthday Mystery* (Holiday, 1987) k–3. With the help of her dog, Jennie spends her birthday investigating a bicycle theft and wondering why no one seems to remember it is a special day for her.

49. Adler, David A. *Cam Jansen and the Mystery of the Stolen Diamonds* (Viking, 1980) 3–5. A fifth grader, Cam, with a photographic memory, and her friend Eric, help solve the mystery of the stolen diamonds.

50. ____. *Cam Jansen and the Mystery of the U.F.O.* (Viking, 1980) 3–5. Ten-year-old Cam, possessor of a photographic memory, and her friend, Eric, investigate what seems to be a brief appearance of U.F.O.'s.

51. ____. *Cam Jansen and the Mystery of the Dinosaur Bones* (Viking, 1981) 3–5. When she notices some bones missing from a dinosaur skeleton exhibited in the museum, Cam, a young girl with a photographic memory, tries to discover who has been taking them and why.

52. ____. *Cam Jansen and the Mystery of the Television Dog* (Viking, 1981) 3–5. A fifth grader, Cam, uses her photographic memory, and with help from her friend, Eric and his twin sister, solve the mystery of Poochie, a famous canine television star.

53. ____. *Cam Jansen and the Mystery of the Gold Coins* (Viking, 1982) 3–5. While using her photographic memory to find her missing science fair project, Cam accidentally locates two valuable gold coins.

54. ____. *Cam Jansen and the Mystery of the Babe Ruth Baseball* (Viking, 1982) 3–5. Cam uses her photographic memory to identify the person who stole a valuable autographed baseball.

55. ____. *Cam Jansen and the Mystery of the Circus Clown* (Viking, 1983) 3–5. Fifth grader Cam Jansen uses her photographic memory to help find a pickpocket at the circus.

56. ____. *Cam Jansen and the Mystery of the Monster Movie* (Viking, 1984) 3–5. Cam, a fifth grader, uses her photographic memory with help from her mother and her friend Eric, to find a missing reel of a monster film they go to see.

57. ____. *Cam Jansen and the Mystery of the Carnival Prize* (Viking, 1984) 3–5. When fifth grader Cam notices that the prizes for the most difficult game at the school carnival are rapidly disappearing, she uses her amazing memory to investigate.

58. ____. *Cam Jansen and the Mystery at the Monkey House* (Viking, 1985) 3–5. Fifth grade sleuth, Cam Jansen, uses her photographic memory to solve a monkey smuggling mystery at the city zoo.

59. ____. *Cam Jansen and the Mystery of the Stolen Corn Popper* (Viking, 1986) 3–5. Fifth grade sleuth, Cam Jansen, uses her photographic memory to catch a thief during a department store sale.

60. ____. *Cam Jansen and the Mystery of Flight 54* (Viking, 1989) 3–5. Cam Jansen and her friend Eric go to the airport to meet Cam's Aunt Molly who has just arrived from France, but before they can say "bonjour," a young French girl has disappeared.

61. ____. *Cam Jansen and the Mystery of the Haunted House* (Viking, 1992) 3–5. Cam and her friend Eric, chase the thief of Aunt Katie's wallet through an amusement park, and find themselves involved in another case requiring their special detective skills.

62. ____. *Cam Jansen and the Chocolate Fudge Mystery* (Viking, 1993) 3–5. When Cam Jansen and her friend Eric uncover a mystery while selling fudge door-to-door to raise money for the local library, Cam uses her photographic memory to foil a crime.

63. ____. *Cam Jansen and the Triceratop Pops Mystery* (Viking, 1995) 3–5. Cam and Eric visit the mall and look for music by the Triceratop Pops Group. All the CD's disappear from the music store. Cam solves the mystery and brings the thief to justice.

64. Adler, David A. *Jeffrey's Ghost and the Leftover Baseball Team* (Holt, 1984) 3–5. Jeffrey discovers a ghost in his new home. He and his sister are on a baseball team made up of kids not otherwise chosen. Jeff's ghost, Bradford, helps them win many games.

65. ____. *Jeffrey's Ghost and the Fifth Grade Dragon* (Holt, 1985) 3–5. Jeffrey, Laura and Bradford, the ghost are in school and cause some obvious problems. They all write a report on an old schoolhouse.

66. ____. *Jeffrey's Ghost and the Ziffel Fair Mystery* (Holt, 1987) 3–5. Jeffrey, Laura and their friend, Bradford the ghost, attend a local fair where they investigate some strange goings-on when it comes to winning prizes.

67. **Adler,** David A. *Fourth Floor Twins and the Fish Snitch Mystery* (Viking, 1985) 2–4. Two sets of twins suspect their neighbors of wrong-doings when they observe the strange behavior of the couple's nephew.

68. ____. *Fourth Floor Twins and the Fortune Cookie Chase* (Viking, 1985) 2–4. Two sets of twins receive a message in a fortune cookie, warning them to beware of a man in a blue hat.

69. ____. *Fourth Floor Twins and the Disappearing Parrot Trick* (Viking, 1986) 2–4. Two sets of twins launch a wild chase when the "disappearing parrot" in their school talent show magic act really does disappear.

70. ____. *Fourth Floor Twins and the Silver Ghost Express* (Viking, 1986) 2–4. Two sets of twins catch a thief while tracking down a missing suitcase in a train station.

71. ____. *Fourth Floor Twins and the Skyscraper Parade* (Viking, 1987) 2–4. When a famous sculpture is stolen from the museum, two sets of twins team up to track down the thief.

72. ____. *Fourth Floor Twins and the Sand Castle Contest* (Viking, 1988) 2–4. In an extraordinary day at the beach, after winning a sand castle contest, two sets of twins resolve the mystery of the disappearance of a rich woman's dog.

73. **Adler,** Susan S. *Meet Samantha, An American Girl* (Pleasant, 1986) 3–5. In 1904, Samantha, nine, an orphan living with her wealthy grandmother, and her servant friend, Nellie, have a midnight adventure when they try to find what has happened to the seamstress who left her job.

74. ____. *Samantha Learns a Lesson* (Pleasant, 1986) 3–5. Samantha is determined to help nine-year-old Nellie, attending school for the first time, with her schoolwork and learns a great deal about what it is like to be a poor child and work in a factory.

75. **Adshead,** Gladys. *Brownies–Hush* (Oxford, 1938) k–3. A story about the Brownies who helped an old man and woman with their work; when the old couple rewarded them, they vanished forever.

76. ____. *Brownies–It's Christmas* (Oxford, 1955) k–3. When the Brownies finish trimming the tree of

Old Grandmother and Old Grandfather, they are greeted with a very special surprise, which makes it a happy Christmas for all.

77. ____. *Brownies–Hurry* (Walck, 1959) k–3. Brownies again help Old Grandfather and Old Grandmother and receive a glorious spring surprise.

78. ____. *Brownies–They're Moving* (Oxford, 1970) k–3. When Old Grandmother and Old Grandfather decide to move to a new laborsaving home, the brownies help them pack.

79. ____. *Where Is Smallest Brownie?* (Walck, 1971) k–3. After being lost and chased by a cat, Smallest Brownie realizes it was a mistake to go exploring by himself early in the morning.

80. ____. *Smallest Brownie and the Flying Squirrel* (Walck, 1972) k–3. When a flying squirrel tries to look after a curious little Brownie, they both get into trouble.

81. Ahlberg, Janet. *Jolly Postman* (Little, 1986) k–3. A story that tells about the postman's delivery route on one particular day.

82. ____. *Jolly Christmas Postman* (Little, 1991) k–3. Jolly Postman delivers Christmas cards to several famous fairy-tale characters such as Big Bad Wolf, Cinderella and the Three Bears.

83. ____. *Jolly Pat Letter Wallet* (Little, 1993) k–3. A story in which fairy-tale characters correspond with each other via letters delivered by the bicycle–riding postman—Goldilocks to the Three Bears and the Queen of Hearts to Little Jack Horner.

84. Aitken, Amy. *Ruby* (Bradbury, 1979) k–3. Anything is possible for Ruby. She decides to be an author or an artist or a movie star or maybe even president of the United States.

85. ____. *Ruby, the Red Knight* (Bradbury, 1983) k–3. Ruby, imagining herself as a Knight of the Round Table, accepts King Arthur's challenge to solve the mystery of the disappearing realm. She comes across giants, dragons, and wizards in the course of her quest.

86. Albeck, Pat. *Ben and His Toys* (Methuen, 1970) k–3. A picture book of excellent drawings of toys.

87. ____. *Ben in the Kitchen* (Methuen, 1970) k–3. A picture book of all the things one may find in a kitchen. Good for identification.

88. ____. *Ben at the Shop* (Methuen, 1970) k–3. A picture book with clear concise pictures of everyday things.

89. ____. *Ben in the Garden* (Methuen, 1970) k–3. A picture book of clear drawings of things one finds in the garden.

90. Albright, Molly. *Room of Doom* (Troll, 1989) 4–6. Chaos erupts when 12-year-old Missy has all her friends help her redecorate her room at the same time a famous designer is "doing" her neighbor Stephanie's house.

91. ____. *Fright Night* (Troll, 1989) 4–6. Missy accepts a challenge from Stephanie to spend Halloween night with her dog in a haunted house.

92. ____. *Mascot Mess* (Troll, 1989) 4–6. Missy and her classmates scramble to turn their pets into the best candidate for the soccer team mascot.

93. ____. *Video Stars* (Troll, 1989) 4–6. Disaster stalks Missy's attempts to make the best videotape of self and family for a class assignment until her actress-grandmother comes to the rescue.

94. Alderson, Sue Ann. *Bonnie McSmithers, You're Driving Me Dithers* (Tree Frog, 1974) 2–4. A little girl is driving her mother out of her mind.

95. ____. *Hurry Up Bonnie* (Tree Frog, 1976) 2–4. Bonnie, a pre-schooler is still bringing up mother as she teaches her mother what's important in a walk "to get the paper": fire sirens, shiny screws and busy ants. Bonnie rides on her mother's back all the way home.

96. ____. *Bonnie McSmithers Is at It Again* (Tree Frog, 1981) 2–4. Every time Bonnie accomplishes something on her own she remarks in rhyme to her mother. Her mother is tolerant even when Bonnie makes a mess.

97. Alexander, Barbara. *Little Bigalow Story* (Oak Tree, 1985) k–3. In the world of T.J.'s and Katie's imagination, Bigalow, the pantry mouse, begins a new life as he takes a ride on a helium-filled balloon.

98. ____. *Mysterious Disappearance of Ragsby* (Oak Tree, 1985) k–3. In the world of T.J.'s and Katie's imagination, a favorite teddy bear is kidnapped by a lonely monster.

99. ____. *Muddle-Mole and His Exploding Birthday Party* (Oak Tree, 1985) k–3. In the world of T.J.'s and Katie's imagination, a friendly mole throws a birthday party for himself.

100. ____. *Furnace for Castle Thistlewart* (Oak Tree, 1985) k–3. In the world of T.J.'s and Katie's imagination, a homeless dragon finds shelter in a basement of a castle and provides heat for its inhabitants.

101. Alexander, Lloyd. *Illyrian Adventure* (Dutton, 1986) 5–8. On a visit to a remote European kingdom in 1872, a fearless 16-year-old orphan and her guardian research an ancient legend and become enmeshed in a dangerous rebellion.

102. ____. *El Dorado Adventure* (Dutton, 1987) 5–8. Vesper stops a canal from being built because it would destroy the homeland of an Indian tribe. Again evil Helvitius is foiled. This time by a volcano eruption.

103. ____. *Drakenberg Adventure* (Dutton, 1988) 5–8. Vesper tangles with Dr. Helvitius, her number one enemy. He is looking for an art treasure.

104. ____. *Jedera Adventure* (Dutton, 1989) 5–8. Vesper Holly and her faithful guardian, Brinny, travel to the remote country of Jedera where they brave many dangers trying to return a valuable book borrowed many years ago by Vesper's father.

105. ____. *Philadelphia Adventure* (Dutton, 1990) 5–8. In 1876, on the eve of the Centennial Exposition in Philadelphia, Vesper Holly and her friends clash yet again with the archfiend Dr. Helvitius, whose evil schemes plunge them into danger.

106. Alexander, Martha. *Blackboard Bear* (Dial, 1969) k–3. A story of how an imaginative little boy gets even with the big boys who won't let him play with them.

107. ____. *And My Mean Old Mother Will Be Sorry, Blackboard Bear* (Dial, 1972) k–3. A little boy's adventures in the forest with his friend, Blackboard Bear, come to an end when he decides home is more comfortable than a cave.

108. ____. *I Sure Am Glad to See You, Blackboard Bear* (Dial, 1976) k–3. Little Anthony's bear is immensely helpful when he has to deal with other children who are teasing, selfish, or bullying.

109. ____. *We're in Big Trouble, Blackboard Bear* (Dial, 1980) k–3. Anthony's bear learns hard lessons about leaving other people's things alone.

110. ____. *You're a Genius, Blackboard Bear* (Candlewick, 1995) k–3. Blackboard Bear helps a small boy build a spaceship for a trip to the moon, but when the boy packs so many supplies that there is no room for him, the bear goes alone.

111. Alexander, Martha. *When the New Baby Comes, I'm Moving Out* (Dial, 1979) k–3. Oliver is going to be a big brother, and doesn't like the idea one bit.

112. ____. *Nobody Asked Me If I Wanted a Baby Sister* (Dial, 1971) k–3. Resenting the attention and praise lavished on his new baby sister, Oliver tries to give her away to several people in the neighborhood.

113. ____. *I'll Be the Horse If You Will Play with Me* (Dial, 1975) k–3. It is hard to be in the middle with brothers too old or too young to play with ... or are they?

114. ____. *Where's Willy?* (Candlewick, 1993) k–3. Willy hides from his older sister Lily in a paper bag.

115. ____. *Willy's Boot* (Candlewick, 1993) k–3. Lily and her little brother Willy clean up the room, but then Willy undoes their work in his search for his boot.

116. ____. *Lily and Willy* (Candlewick, 1993) k–3. As Lily and her younger brother Willy play together, whatever Lily's doll does, Willy's teddy bear wants to do too.

117. ____. *Good Night Lily* (Candlewick, 1993) k–3. Lily reads a bedtime story to her younger brother Willy, who shares it with his teddy bear, who in turn reads it to Lily's doll.

118. Alexander, Sue. *Witch, Goblin and Sometimes Ghost!* (Pantheon, 1976) 3–5. Goblin has friends who will help him even when he is afraid, forgetful, or even grumpy.

119. ____. *More Witch, Goblin and Ghost Stories* (Pantheon, 1978) 3–5. Witch, Goblin and sometimes Ghost are friends. They support one another, have adventures and learn from each other.

120. ____. *Witch, Goblin and Ghost in the Haunted Woods* (Pantheon, 1981) 3–5. Goblin, Ghost and Witch look for buried treasure, go swimming, play a game, hear a story and get lost in a snowstorm.

121. ____. *Witch, Goblin and Ghost's Book of Things to Do* (Pantheon, 1982) 3–5. Three friends show how to write a rebus, play a game, write in secret code, put on a play and perform a magic trick.

122. ____. *Witch, Goblin, and Ghost Are Back* (Pantheon, 1985) 3–5. Five short stories about Witch, Goblin and Ghost.

123. Alexander, Sue. *World Famous Muriel* (Little, 1984) 3–5. Asked to tightrope walk for the Queen's birthday party, Muriel arrives to discover that all the decorative paper lanterns have disappeared and that her detecting skills are needed too.

124. ____. *World Famous Muriel and the Scary Dragon* (Little, 1985) 3–5. Muriel is asked by the King to rid the kingdom of a terrible dragon.

125. ____. *World Famous Muriel and the Magic Mystery* (Little, 1990) 3–5. World Famous Muriel earns her reputation again when, with the help of numerous peanut butter cookies, she finds the Great Hocus Pocus after he disappears in the middle of rehearsing for his magic show.

126. Alexander, William. *Ghost of Sharkly Manor* (Troll, 1990) 4–6. A story about five foster children, the Clues Kids, aged from eight to twelve. One is Vietnamese and one Afro–American. They live with a retired police chief, Chief Klink, and his wife.

127. ____. *Case of the Funny Money Man* (Troll, 1990) 4–6. The Clues Kids, five foster children living with Chief Klink and his wife, suspect their new neighbors of being counterfeiters.

128. ____. *Case of the Gumball Bandit* (Troll, 1990) 4–6. The Clues Kids, five foster children living with Chief Klink and his wife, suspect that jewel thieves are stashing their diamonds in gumball machines.

129. ____. *Case of the Pizza Pie Spy* (Troll, 1990) 4–6. While searching for a bike thief, the Clues Kids, five foster children living with Chief Klink and his wife, investigate the suspicious activities at a local pizza parlor.

130. Aliki. *Keep Your Mouth Closed, Dear* (Dial, 1966) k–3. A young crocodile swallows everything from a can of baby powder to his father's hat until the day he helps his mother tidy up the house with the vacuum cleaner.

131. ____. *Use Your Head, Dear* (Greenwillow, 1983) k–3. Follows the activities of a young crocodile who insists on getting things wrong.

132. Allan, Mabel E. *Wood Street Group* (Methuen, 1970) 4–6. A West Indian boy is the leader of the Wood Street Group, the Liverpool boy's band.

133. ____. *Wood Street Secret* (Methuen, 1970) 4–6. Ben and Cherry make friends with the Wood Street Gang and enter an abandoned house. A storm traps them inside. They are rescued by starting a fire.

134. ____. *Wood Street Rivals* (Methuen, 1971) 4–6. This time their junior pop group's future is threatened when a rival gang smashes Julian's guitar.

135. ____. *Wood Street Helpers* (Methuen, 1973) 4–6. The Liverpool gang finds a useful way of enjoying their summer vacation by taking over the local junkshop for its crotchety old owner while he is in the hospital.

136. ____. *Away from Wood Street* (Methuen, 1975) 4–6. The three O'Donnell children are forced to move from Wood Street to a cheaper house. Their father is a sailor who has been injured and can't work. Mayo gets in trouble but his sister saves him. Bridget makes friends with the girl next door.

137. ____. *Wood Street and Mary Ellen* (Methuen, 1979) 4–6. Mary Ellen does not like living and working in a pub. Neither does her mother and she moves away leaving Mary Ellen and the Wood Street gang to set up, clean up, produce snacks and wash up. Mary Ellen's mother finally comes home.

138. ____. *Strangers in Wood Street* (Methuen, 1981) 4–6.

139. ____. *Growing Up in Wood Street* (Methuen, 1982) 4–6.

140. Allan, Mabel E. *Goodbye to Pine Street* (Abelard, 1982) 4–6. A group of boys and girls are in their last year at Pine Street School. Mr. Shaw falls on the ice and his place is taken by someone who has new ideas; a school magazine, a concert, and a new garden. Samantha outwits the school bully, Bert.

141. ____. *Pine Street Problem* (Abelard, 1981) 4–6. The Almond House gang, plus Reg Delton, their old enemy, stand up to Bert who is still a bully. Bert tries to burn Pine Street School. He fails and is somewhat reformed.

142. ____. *Friend at Pine Street* (Abelard, 1984) 4–6. Samantha, member of the Almond House gang, is alone at Pine Street School. All her friends went on to an upper grade school but because she is only nine she is left behind. She goes on museum and library visits, talks with old Mr. Crump, forages for a fancy dress and is locked out on the roof chasing the family cat. Life seems unfair.

143. ____. *Pride of Pine Street* (Blackie, 1985) 4–6. Samantha thought up a "crazy carnival" as a farewell celebration to her old school building. She wins a scholarship to a "posh" school but chooses to go to Ash Grove.

144. Allan, Mabel E. *Crumble Lane Adventure* (Methuen, 1983) 4–6. The Crumble Lane children undertake a project during the summer vacation to find out something about the history of the place where they live. Who are those two mysterious people camping in the courtyard of Highbeck Hall?

145. ____. *Trouble in Crumble Lane* (Methuen, 1985) 4–6. A young man and wife remodel an old mansion as a museum. But vandalism, inverted snobbery, rivalries, and jealousies pervade the town and all is not well.

146. ____. *Crumble Lane Captives* (Methuen, 1986) 4–6. It is winter at Highbeck Hall and the children are snowed in. Food is short, heat is inadequate and there is the fear of an intruder.

147. ____. *Crumble Lane Mystery* (Methuen, 1987) 4–6. William and Lynne recruited the five children from Crumble Lane to begin work on empty Highbeck Farm. They camp on the high fellside, find a secret tunnel from the Hall and learn of an 18ᵗʰ century legend of lost treasures.

148. Allard, Harry. *Stupids Step Out* (Houghton, 1974) k–3. A sublimely silly family at their outing.

149. ____. *Stupids Have a Ball* (Houghton, 1978) k–3. The Stupid family celebrates the children's awful report cards by inviting their relatives to a costume party.

150. ____. *Stupids Die* (Houghton, 1981) k–3. The Stupid family think they are dead when the lights go out.

151. ____. *Stupids Take Off* (Houghton, 1989) k–3 In an attempt to avoid a visit from Uncle Carbuncle, the Stupids fly off in their airplane and visit several other relatives who are just as stupid as they are.

152. Allard, Harry. *Miss Nelson is Missing* (Houghton, 1977) k–3. The kids in room 207 take advantage of their teacher's good nature until she disappears and they are faced with a vile substitute.

153. ____. *Miss Nelson is Back* (Houghton, 1982) k–3. When their teacher has to go away for a week, the kids in Room 207 plan to "really act up."

154. ____. *Miss Nelson Has a Field Day* (Houghton, 1985) k–3. The notorious Miss Swamp reappears at the Horace B. Smedley School, this time to shape up the football team and make them win at least one game.

155. Allen, Jeffery. *Mary Alice, Operator #9BI* (Little, 1975) k–3. When an efficient duck, who gives the time over the telephone, gets sick, other animals, believing the job to be easy, try to take her place.

156. ____. *Mary Alice Returns* (Little, 1986) k–3. Mary Alice, the duck who is an efficient and conscientious telephone operator, attempts to track down an anonymous caller in distress.

157. Allen, Joy. *Boots for Charlie* (Hamilton, 1975) k–3. It is hard to be a younger brother, especially when you get his cast offs. Charlie gets a new pair of boots for his very own. He dirties them and tries to clean them up and ruins them. He is satisfied to have his brother's cast off ones.

158. ____. *Move for Charlie* (Hamilton, 1978) k–3. A story to allay the trauma and real fears of childhood, such as a sense of insecurity about moving. Charlie accepts the change bravely.

159. ____. *Cup Final for Charlie* (Puffin, 1985) k–3. Charlie, now a middle child, is quite willing to forego his Saturday match to accompany his godfather, Uncle Tim, to Wembley to watch Arsenal and West Han play. Although he falls in the canal, he doesn't disgrace himself and swims back to shore to be given a change of clothes—an Arsenal strip—as a birthday present.

160. ____. *Adventure for Charlie* (Hamilton, 1986) k–3. Charlie, nine, heard a new boy being teased at school about his Scottish accent. He not only stands up for him but also gets him picked for the football team where he scores a goal. The two small boys become friends.

161. ____. *Computer for Charlie* (Hamilton, 1987) k–3.

162. ____. *Stick to It, Charlie* (Hamilton, 1989) k–3.

163. ____. *Sport's Day for Charlie* (Hamilton, 1990) k–3.

164. ____. *Look Out Charlie* (Hamilton, 1993) k–3. Charlie's class visits Farm Park. He is late to school, plays games with his friends, finds some animals and rides in a police car.

165. Allen, Judy. *Dim Thin Ducks* (Walker, 1991) k–3. Both books in this series show a picture of life on a new city farm, seen through the eyes of Kate, a small girl whose perky common sense conceals a timid streak.

166. ____. *Great Pig Sprint* (Walker, 1991) k–3. Kate stands her ground as a rather young helper at an inner-city farm.

167. Allen, Laura. *Rollo and Tweedy and the Case of the Missing Cheese* (Harper, 1983) 2–4. Two detective mice travel to Paris and back in search of a valuable missing cheese.

168. ____. *Where is Freddy?* (Harper, 1986) 2–4. Famous mouse detective Tweedy and his assistant Rollo investigate the case of wealthy Mrs. Twombly's missing grandson.

169. ____. *Rollo and Tweedy and the Ghost at Dougal* (Harper, 1992) 2–4. Lord Dougal, mouse detective Tweedy, and his friend Rollo are called in to catch a ghost that is haunting a Scottish castle. A sneeze helps them solve the mystery.

170. Allen, Judy. *Mrs. Simkin's Bed* (Morrow, 1976) k–3. Mrs. Simkin finds a pig under the bed and she wants to find the owner. The pig has no owner, so they name it Maras and install her in their pet filled home. 46 pigs show up and it is time to sell the bed.

171. ____. *Mr. Simkin's Grandma* (Morrow, 1986) k–3. A little old lady turns up on Mr. Simkin's doorstep and insists that she is his grandma. The Simkin's try everything to get rid of her but she won't go until grandpa turns up and grandma stalks out.

172. ____. *Mrs. Simkin and the Very Big Mushroom* (Morrow, 1986) k–3. A suburban couple who find a giant mushroom in their garden use it as a unique breakfast-umbrella to the fury of their next door neighbor. It becomes a tourist attraction and when it breaks, the couple makes mushroom soup, which they share with everyone.

173. ____. *Mrs. Simkin and the Magic Wheelbarrow* (Morrow, 1989) k–3. "When I sit in it I don't feel like Mrs. Simkin anymore. I feel like a queen."

174. Allen, Linda. *Lionel and the Spy Next Door* (Morrow, 1980) 3–5. Lionel obsessed with the idea of becoming a spy, becomes convinced a mysterious new neighbor has something to hide.

175. ____. *Lionel, the Lone Wolf* (Morrow, 1988) 3–5. Lionel wants to be a private investigator. He uses disguises and develops stalking stratagems.

176. ____. *Lionel* (Piccolo, 1991) 3–5. Lionel now wants to be a bodyguard. He might even end up guarding the Queen. Lionel, his older sister who is skeptical, and grandpa round out the story.

177. Allen, Pamela. *Mr. McGee* (Nelson, 1987) k–3. Mr. McGee lives under a tree and is transformed into a human balloon. He enjoys floating but a bird's beak sends him to earth.

178. ____. *Mr. McGee Goes to Sea* (Hamilton, 1992) k–3. It rains so much when Mr. McGee is having tea he floats away to sea, with his umbrella and teapot. They both are useful in his journey before he lands back home.

179. ____. *Mr. McGee and the Blackberry Jam* (Hamilton 1993) k–3.

180. Allison, Rosemary. *Travels of Ms. Beaver* (Women's, 1973) k–3. Ms. Beaver goes to the desert frontier but likes home best.

181. ____. *Ms. Beaver Travels East* (Women's, 1978) k–3.

182. ____. *Ms. Beaver Goes West* (Women's, 1983) k–3. Ms. Beaver visits the west coast to prevent widespread decimation of trees by a logging company.

183. Albert, Lou. *Emma Swings* (Whispering Coyote, 1991) k–3. Emma, four, plays on a swing suspended from a tree, pumping higher and higher till she flies over the trees and into the sky ... until her mother's voice brings her back.

184. ____. *Emma Lights the Sky* (Whispering, 1991) k–3. Emma spends her evening fixing and replacing fallen stars as a nighttime adventure.

185. ____. *Emma's Turn to Dance* (Whispering Coyote, 1991) k–3. Emma finally gets a chance to take dancing lessons, just like her older sister.

186. ____. *Emma and the Magic Dance* (Whispering Coyote, 1991) k–3. When she is in bed at night, Emma sinks down to a mysterious world of beasts' underground, where she joins their nightly dance and feast and shows herself to be the greatest dancer of all.

187. Ambrus, Victor. *Dracula* (Oxford, 1980) k–3. Dracula is in poor straits. He must avoid his creditors by pretending to be dead. But Igor the butler, Nora Rock the cook and Sweet William the gardener along with Auntie Elizabeth and Uncle Vlad welcome visitors. Then a Hollywood talent scout finds him and he becomes famous and can afford a bat shaped swimming pool.

188. ____. *Dracula Late Night T.V. Show* (Crown, 1992) Fang and Dracula set up their own satellite T.V. station. They show "This Is Your Life," "Miss Marbles Investigates" and a Renta Fang youngster drama.

189. ____. *Count, Dracula* (Crown, 1992) k–3. Dracula counts the "pets" in his castle, including two skeletons, five wolves and ten ghosts.

190. ____. *What Time Is It Dracula?* (Crown, 1992) k–3. Dracula tells time throughout the day so that he doesn't miss his appointment with the dentist.

191. Amerman, Lockhart. *Guns to the Heather* (Harcourt, 1963) 5–8. Jonathan, known as Posy, accepts a job as tutor for twins of Dr. Sarx, who is really a mad scientist.

192. ____. *Cape Cod Casket* (Harcourt, 1964) 5–8. Jonathan is pursued because of his foreign agent father. The hunt is a dangerous one. He is kidnapped but escapes. He finds his father and they hunt the hunters.

193. Anderson, Alasdair. *Chewy Toffee Man* (Dobson, 1977) K–3. Fifi, the singer, is accompanied by Figgy Bellringer when her orchestra doesn't appear. The audience doesn't like it. They go to Chewy Toffee Man's house. Robbers steal the toffee and the adventure begins.

194. ____. *Last Toffee in the World* (Dobson, 1980) k–3. A story of the adventures of the Chewy Toffee Man, who eats nothing but toffee (if he eats ordinary food he breaks out in large purple lumps which hum). He goes to Shangri-La and discovers people who wear kilts and turbans.

195. ____. *Billy and Blaze* (Macmillan, 1936) 2–4. Billy, a little boy who loves horses more than anything in the world, has a horse named Blaze.

196. ____. *Blaze and the Gray Spotted Pony* (Macmillan, 1936) 2–4. Tommy, Billy's young neighbor, dreams of nothing but horses and ponies. With the help of Billy and his pony Blaze, Tommy's wish comes true—a certain beautiful gray spotted pony of his own.

197. ____. *Blaze and the Forest Fire* (Macmillan, 1938) 2–4. Billy and Blaze discover a forest fire. Billy knows he must warn the farmers. Blaze carries Billy quickly to the nearest farmhouse. This involves the jumping of fences and ditches and makes an exciting ride.

198. ____. *Blaze Finds the Trail* (Macmillan, 1950) 2–4. The story of Billy and a wonderful ride with Blaze—through the woods, getting lost, a storm and a wild dash home.

199. ____. *Blaze and Thunderbolt* (Macmillan, 1955) 2–4. Billy and Blaze were spending the summer on a ranch in the West. They make friends with the wild black horse, Thunderbolt.

200. ____. *Blaze and the Mountain Lion* (Macmillan, 1959) 2–4. Billy and Blaze find a little calf stranded on a narrow ledge, chased there by a mountain lion. Billy is able to lasso the calf and, with Blaze's help, draw him up over the ledge to safety. When the mountain lion is captured, Billy and Blaze receive a new lasso for their bravery.

201. ____. *Blaze and the Indian Cave* (Macmillan, 1964) 2–4. Adventure story of Billy and his pony Blaze on a camping trip to an old Indian cave.

202. ____. *Blaze and the Lost Quarry* (Macmillan, 1966) Two boys spend a happy day exploring with their ponies.

203. ____. *Blaze Shows the Way* (Macmillan, 1969) 2–4. Billy and his friend Tommy enter their ponies in the pairs jumping contest.

204. ____. *Blaze Finds Forgotten Roads* (Macmillan, 1971) 2–4. Billy and Blaze take every right turn and venture deep in the woods where they find an old powder horn and arrowheads. They have lunch by a waterfall. As it grows dark Blaze finds the way home.

205. Anderson, Gerry. *VIP* (Armada, 1968) 4–6. Leading character in both these books is father Unwin, no ordinary Vicar but a top secret service agent who, with his assistant, has such gadgets as a minimizer able to reduce people to a mere two feet.

206. ____. *Secret Service: The Destroyer* (Armada, 1969) 4–6.

207. Anderson, Lena. *Bunny Bath* (Farrar, 1986) k–3. Bunny is awakened by the boy coming in from the cold. Bunny helps him take off articles of clothing and when the boy is undressed they plunge into the tub to relax.

208. ____. *Bunny Party* (Farrar, 1987) k–3. A youngster awakens at a small table and finds a large white rabbit making preparations for a party for two—item by item. It ends with the boy and bunny sharing food and conversation.

209. ____. *Bunny Story* (Farrar, 1987) k–3. A child brings objects to cheer a bunny. He brings a kitten, a puppy, a piglet, a mouse, a frog, a lamb and an owl. Finally he brings a baby bunny who needs to be tucked in bed.

210. ____. *Bunny Surprise* (Farrar, 1990) k–3. Bunny and his little friend introduce toddlers to the contents of brightly wrapped and beribboned packages.

211. ____. *Bunny Box* (Farrar, 1991) k–3. A small boy is ready for bed, but is crying. His bunny mother gives him a box of toys but nothing helps until he finds a friend's blanket at the bottom of the box.

212. ____. *Bunny Fun* (Farrar, 1991) k–3. A mother rabbit and her child and a small boy spend the day fishing and swimming. They play with a boat, eat lunch then blow up and use an inner tube.

213. ____. *Bunny Outing* (R & S, 1991) k–3. Bunny takes his friends fishing, but, of course, they don't keep their catch.

214. ____. *Bunny Toys* (R & S, 1991) k–3. Bunny has a whole box of toys to keep the little boy entertained, but only one works.

215. Anderson, Lena. *Stina* (Greenwillow, 1989) k–3. On a visit to her grandfather's house by the sea. Stina goes outside to see a storm but is frightened by it until grandfather finds her and shows her the best way to watch a storm is together.

216. ____. *Stina's Visit* (Greenwillow, 1991) k–3. Stina and her grandfather visit an old sailor on his birthday.

217. Anderson, Mary. *F*T*C* Superstar* (Atheneum, 1976) 5–8. Freddie, the cat, is stagestruck. His friend Emma helps teach him the tricks of the trade. He starts making commercials. But does he really want fame?

218. ____. *F*T*C* and Company* (Atheneum, 1979) 5–8. Freddie, the cat, and Emma rid a theater of ghosts and start a theatrical company of their own. But the building is to be wrecked.

219. Anderson, Mary. *Matilda Investigates* (Atheneum, 1973) 4–6. Matilda wants to be a detective. She buys a microscope and her brother helps her find a crow that is trained to steal things.

220. ____. *Matilda's Masterpiece* (Atheneum, 1977) 4–6. A $50,000 Degas painting is stolen. After two blundering attempts Matilda finds the thief.

221. Andreus, Hans. *Stories of Mr. Bumblemoose* (Abelard, 1971) k–3. Mr. Bumblemoose is a very eccentric schoolteacher who performs magic at will.

222. ____. *Mr. Bumblemoose Flying Boy* (Abelard, 1972) k–3. Mr. Bumblemoose has adventures with a ghost, a new blackboard and a boogie-woogie fiddle.

223. ____. *Mr. Bumblemoose and the Glad Dog* (Abelard, 1972) k–3. Mr. Bumblemoose, the eccentric schoolmaster, owns Learned Cat.

224. ____. *Mr. Bumblemoose Buys a Motorcar* (Abelard, 1973) k–3. Mr. Bumblemoose buys a car; finds a bird in his garden; argues with his class; and treads the edge of fantasy with his talking animals.

225. ____. *Mr. Bumblemoose and the Laughing Record* (Abelard, 1974) k–3. More adventures of this schoolmaster/inventor. This time a self-activating surprise camera and mole glasses play a role.

226. ____. *Mr. Bumblemoose Goes to Paris* (Abelard, 1975) k–3. Mr. Bumblemoose is the stout benevolent teacher. He builds a swimming pool and visits Paris. He takes magic and science in his stride. He succeeds in inventing an artificial sun.

227. ____. *Mr. Bumblemoose Omnibus* (Abelard, 1978) k–3. Mr. Bumblemoose is a teacher; kind and

talented, especially in magic; but also has the ability to talk to cars and blackboards, to undusted park benches and to help ghosts.

228. Andrews, Jean. *Flying Fingers Club* (Gaullaudet, 1988) 3–5. Two boys are close friends even though one of them is deaf.

229. ____. *Secret in the Dorm Attic* (Gaullaudet, 1990) 3–5. While visiting his friend Matt on the campus of his special school for the deaf, Donald, nine, discovers something strange going on in the attic of Matt's dorm and becomes involved in the theft of a priceless necklace from a nearby museum.

230. ____. *Hasta Luego, San Diego* (Kendall Green, 1991) 3–5. Disabled Donald and his deaf friend Matt are kidnapped by crooks who have stolen rare cockatoos from the San Diego zoo. His older sister is involved in a Hispanic boy's abuse by his father.

231. Anfousse, Ginette. *Rosalie's Battles* (Yearling, 1995) 2–4. A fight ensues among children from different ethnic backgrounds in a schoolyard. Rosalie learns to show more respect for the feelings of others.

232. ____. *Rosalie's Catastrophes* (Yearling, 1996) 2–4. Rosalie is adopted by seven aunts. Two aunts worry about her eating habits, with opposite views; two aunts worry about her attitudes, with opposite views. This causes a lot of trouble but also a lot of love.

233. ____. *Rosalie's Big Dream* (Yearling, 1996) 2–4. A story about tap-dancing, dreams and friendship.

234. Anglund, Joan W. *Brave Cowboy* (Harcourt, 1959) k–3. Little Cowboy shoots rattlesnakes off his bedpost, drags home a bear along with Mommie's groceries, and races on his bicycle to warn the stagecoach that a bridge is out.

235. ____. *Cowboy and His Friend* (Harcourt, 1961) k–3. Little Cowboy has an imaginary friend, Bear. Bear is always with him; in the bath, playing football, whatever happens Bear is there.

236. ____. *Cowboy's Secret Life* (Harcourt, 1963) k–3. In his imagination Little Cowboy lives a life in which knights and dragons, ferocious lions and adventures of every kind are masterfully met and dealt with.

237. ____. *Cowboy's Christmas* (Harcourt, 1972) k–3. Relates the young cowboy's activities as he prepares for Christmas.

238. Anholt, Catherine. *Truffles in Trouble* (Little, 1987) k–3. Truffles is full of ideas for how to be a good little pig—but soon discovers that being good isn't as easy as he thought.

239. ____. *Truffles Is Sick* (Little, 1987) k–3. Although he has to stay in bed and take the most awful tasting medicine, Truffles the pig discovers that being sick has its advantages.

240. Antrobus, John. *Ronnie and the Haunted Rolls Royce* (Robson, 1982) 3–5. The story of a good natured and rather put upon ghost, and an impecunious Count called Jeffery de String who has a large and varied collection of ... string.

241. ____. *Ronnie and the Great Knitted Robbery* (Robson, 1982) 3–5. Ronnie goes into a high rise, which is deserted from the 12th floor up (except for an old woman on 19). She is a witch who captures Ronnie in her oven. He has adventures back in time.

242. Appiah, Sonia. *Amoko and the Efua Bear* (Macmillan, 1989) k–3. Amoko, a little girl living in Ghana, takes her favorite teddy bear everywhere that she goes and is broken hearted when she thinks he's lost.

243. ____. *Amoko and the Party* (Macmillan, 1991) k–3. The story tells of a party and Amoko's role in it.

244. Appleton, Victor. *Tom Swift and His Submarine Boat* (Grosset, 1910) 5–8. Tom Swift, boy inventor, science fiction pioneer started in 1910, ending in 1941 with book 41. He lived with his inventor father and housekeeper, Mrs. Baggert. Together they face patent thieves, the town bully. In 1991 Pocket Books began to publish up-dated stories using the same characters.

245. ____. *Tom Swift and His Motor Boat* (Grosset, 1910) 5–8. Tom begins a new adventure on the day he purchases a damaged motorboat at auction and is threatened by a bully. He coaches his girlfriend, Mary, and helps her win a race in her boat, *Dot*.

246. ____. *Tom Swift and His Airship* (Grosset, 1910) 5–8. The young inventor builds an airship, makes a trial trip and experiences a smash-up in mid-air.

247. ____. *Tom Swift and His Motor Cycle* (Globe, 1910/1992) 5–8. Having longed for a motorcycle, bright ingenious Tom Swift, gets one unexpectedly.

248. ____. *Tom Swift and His Electronic Electroscope* (S & S, 1910) 5–8.

249. ____. *Tom Swift Among the Diamond Makers* (Grosset, 1911) 5–8.

250. ____. *Tom Swift and His Wizard Camera* (Grosset, 1912) 5–8. Tom invented a new kind of moving picture camera—a small light one, worked by electricity—a regular wizard camera. Tom toured the world in his airship and filmed exotic nature: an elephant stampede, a fight between lions, an avalanche, a jungle fire, a volcano and an earthquake.

251. ____. *Tom Swift and His Great Searchlight* (subtitled *On the Border for Uncle Sam*) (Grosset, 1912) 5–8.

252. ____. *Tom Swift and His Big Tunnel* (subtitled *The Hidden City of the Andes*) (Grosset, 1916) 5–8.

253. ____. *Tom Swift and His Flying Boat* (subtitled *The Castaways of the Giant Iceberg*) (Grosset, 1923) 5–8.

254. ____. *Tom Swift and His Talking Pictures* (subtitled *The Greatest Invention on Record*) (Grosset, 1928) 5–8.

255. ____. *Tom Swift and His House on Wheels* (subtitled *A Trip to the Mountain of Mystery*) (Grosset, 1929) 5–8.

256. ____. *Tom Swift and His Giant Magnet* (subtitled *Bringing Up the Lost Submarine. A story with a touch of science fiction.)* (Grosset, 1932) 5–8.

257. ____. *Tom Swift and His Electric Runabout* (Grosset, 1992) 5–8. Tom Swift and his rival, the bully Andy Foger, are in a big electric car race. As Tom constructs his electric racer he discovers he gets more than he bargained for.

258. ____. *Tom Swift and His Space Solatron* (Amereon) 5–8.

259. ____. *Tom Swift and His Triphibian Atomicar* (Amereon) 5–8.

260. Appleton, Victor. *Motion Picture Chums' First Venture* (Grosset, 1913) 5–8. Pep, Randy and Frank start a neighborhood storefront movie house. They named it Wonderland. The story describes the appearance of and the cost of operating a movie house before World War I.

261. ____. *Motion Picture Chums' at Seaside Park* (Grosset, 1913) 5–8. Pep, Randy and Frank open another movie house in Seaside Park, New Jersey. They named this one Wonderland, too, so they could reuse the sign from their first theater. They added electric fans to keep the theater cool and also added updated equipment. They showed a comedy, an airship specialty and a romance.

262. ____. *Motion Picture Chums' New Ideas* (Grosset, 1914) 5–8. Pep, Randy and Frank now open a theater in a large city, Boston. Here they show educational films. They added a piano and a pipe organ and showed four shows a day, two in the afternoon and two at night.

263. ____. *Motion Picture Chums' Outdoor Exhibition* (Grosset, 1914) 5–8. Pep, Randy and Frank start an outdoor movie theater called the Airdrome. It was at an amusement park in Palisades.

264. ____. *Moving Picture Boys* Subtitled: *Perils of a Great City Depicted* (Motion picture production) (Grosset, 1913) 5–8.

265. ____. *Moving Picture Boys in Earthquake Land* (subtitled: *Working Amid Many Perils* (Volcanoes and Earthquakes)) (Grosset, 1913) 5–8.

266. ____. *Moving Picture Boys on the Coast* Subtitled: *Showing Up the Perils of the Deep* (California Mystery) (Grosset, 1913) 5–8.

267. ____. *Moving Picture Boys and the Flood* (subtitled: *Perilous Days on the Mississippi* (Floods)) (Grosset, 1914) 5–8.

268. ____. *Motion Picture Chums' Series* (Grosset, 1914) 5–8. There were three other volumes of this series: *On Broadway; At the Fair* and *War Spectacle*. Nothing but their titles is known. *On Broadway* was referred to in another book but nothing but the titles are known about the others. The series is a good representation of early movie theaters.

269. Appleton, Victor. *Tom Swift: The Astral Fortress* (S & S, 1981) 4–6. Tom and his friends are captured by David Luna. Forced to install a space drive in Luna's "Astral Fortress," the friends try to escape. But Luna escapes, too.

270. ____. *Tom Swift: Terror on the Moons of Jupiter* (S & S, 1981) 4–6. Tom and his friends build a robot on their way to Jupiter. They discover a space probe and alienate a military officer.

271. ____. *Tom Swift: City in the Stars* (S & S, 1981) 4–6. Tom designs a spaceship, makes friends with a computer expert and a hot tempered, red–headed girl.

272. ____. *Tom Swift: War in Outer Space* (S & S, 1981) 4–6. Tom and his friends go to rescue Skree from Chutans. Tom has all he needs to explore space possibilities.

273. ____. *Tom Swift: Alien Probe* (S & S, 1981) 4–6. Tom and his friends are back on Earth. The officer steals the probe and gives it to their rival. They rescue the probe and learn its secret before it is destroyed.

274. ____. *Terror on the Moons of Jupiter* (Carousel, 1981) 4–6. Tom and his friends Ben and Anita travel with their new robot, Aristotle, to the moons of Jupiter where they encounter a sinister rival. Tom is in conflict with the jealously ambitious naval officer Burt Foster.

275. ____. *Tom Swift: Rescue Mission* (S & S, 1982) 4–6. A distress call brings Tom, Ben, Anita and Aristotle to a planet overrun by robots. They want to destroy all organic life. But Aristotle, a robot, saves the day and Tom rescues everyone.

276. ____. *Tom Swift: Ark Two* (S & S, 1982) 4–6. Disaster and the disappearance of a space station causes Tom Swift to go to the water planet Equilla. He almost gets killed and his archenemy David Luna has returned.

277. ____. *Tom Swift: Gateway to Doom* (S & S, 1983) 4–6. Tom Swift, aboard the science survey ship *Hawking*, discovers unusual sunspot activity indicating the sun will soon explode, destroying all life in the solar system.

278. ____. *Invisible Force* (S & S, 1983) 4–6. Tom and his friends enter a new dimension where ruthless Molvaarians rule an alien universe with an iron hand.

279. ____. *Tom Swift: Crater of Mystery* (S & S, 1983) 4–6. Tom, Anita and Ben Walking Eagle and Aristotle the robot go through space and face exploding suns and other threats of nuclear destruction.

280. ____. *Tom Swift: Chaos on Earth* (Wanderer, 1984) 4–6. When a terrible plague descends upon Earth, Tom Swift and his friends have to find a cure in time to save the human race.

281. ____. *Planet of Nightmares* (Wanderer, 1984) 4–6. Mr. Swift takes several guests, Tom and his friends, to a mining planet owned by his company, but what began as a vacation becomes a nightmare.

282. ____. *Tom Swift: Cave of Ice* (S & S, 1992) 4–6. Tom is off to Alaska to find a valley of gold. Andy tries to beat Tom out of the prize.

283. ____. *Tom Swift: Quantum Force* (Pocket, 1993) 4–6. Tom invents a personal force field that allows him to walk unmugged in the bad parts of town.

284. Arden, William. *Three Investigators and the Mystery of the Moaning Cave* (Random, 1968) 4–6. While vacationing on a California ranch, three boys decide to investigate strange wails that come from a mysterious cave where a famous outlaw disappeared.

285. ____. *Three Investigators and the Mystery of the Laughing Shadow* (Random, 1969) 4–6. Three boys try to solve another mystery involving a gold Indian amulet and a weird laughing shadow that appeared to them in the night.

286. ____. *Three Investigators and the Secret of the Crooked Cat* (Random, 1970) 4–6. Because they are present when a mysterious man steals a prize at the carnival, the three investigators are launched on another adventure.

287. ____. *Three Investigators and the Mystery of the Shrinking House* (Random, 1972) 4–6. The three investigators solve a case involving an international gang of art forgers.

288. ____. *Three Investigators and the Secret of Phantom Lake* (Random, 1973) 4–6. This mystery involves an Oriental chest, a sunken ship and a strange dual identity.

289. ____. *Three Investigators and the Mystery of the Dead Man's Riddle* (Random, 1974) 4–6. Three investigators go on a high stakes treasure hunt to restore a fortune to the rightful heirs.

290. ____. *Three Investigators and the Mystery of the Dancing Devil* (Random, 1976) 4–6. This time the three investigators search for a stolen art statue. There is an alive life-size version of the statue and sinister villains.

291. ____. *Three Investigators and the Mystery of the Headless Horse* (Random, 1977) 4–6. When three junior detectives search for a valuable old Spanish sword lost since the Mexican War, the headless statue of a horse yields a clue.

292. ____. *Three Investigators and the Mystery of the Deadly Double* (Random, 1978) 4–6. Jupe is mistakenly kidnapped. He is not the son of the African leader. The blackmailers must be uncovered and both Jupe and Ian saved.

293. ____. *Three Investigators and the Secret of Shark Reef* (Random, 1979) 4–6. The story centers around Shark Reef #1, an offshore drilling rig. Ecology, demonstrators, saboteurs and sunken subs are part of the mystery.

294. ____. *Three Investigators and the Mystery of the Purple Pirate* (Random, 1982) 4–6. Modern day pirates are encountered while searching for a legendary pirate treasure. Each of the three investigators solves the mystery in their own way.

295. ____. *Three Investigators and the Mystery of the Smashing Glass* (Random, 1984) 4–6. A series of car windows are shattered and the three investigators want to know why and by whom. There is also the missing double eagle coin.

296. ____. *Three Investigators and the Mystery of Wrecker's Rock* (Random, 1986) 4–6. The three investigators take pictures of a family reunion and are embroiled in a gold hunt and insurance scam.

297. ____. *Three Investigators and the Mystery of Hot Wheels* (Random, 1989) 4–6. Mystery and music intertwine as the three investigators try to find the connection between a car-theft ring and a Latin rock band.

(For other books about the "Three Investigators," *see* Arthur, Robert; Brandel, Marc; Carey, M.V.; Stine, Megan; West, Nick.)

298. Ardizzone, Edward. *Little Tim and the Brave Sea Captain* (Oxford, 1936) k–3. A factual description of life at sea with five-year-old Tim as the hero.

299. ____. *Tim to the Rescue* (Oxford, 1949) k–3. Ginger is the unfortunate ship's boy who borrows the third mate's hair-restorer and finds to his alarm that it works only too well. Tim comes to the rescue in the teeth of a gale.

300. ____. *Tim and Charlotte* (Oxford, 1990) k–3. Tim and Ginger rescue Charlotte from the sea. Charlotte, who was very rich, came to live with Tim and Ginger.

301. ____. *Tim in Danger* (Oxford, 1953) k–3. When their friend, Ginger, runs away to sea, Tim and Charlotte get hired aboard a cargo ship. Charlotte helps with the cooking and Tim as a chore boy. They run into a storm, ram another ship and find Ginger.

302. ____. *Tim All Alone* (Oxford, 1957) k–3. Tim returns home to find his house shut up and no one there. What happens to him—on land and sea-before he is finally reunited with his family is told.

303. ____. *Tim and Lucy Go to Sea* (Walck, 1958) k–3. When Tim, Lucy, Mr. Grimes and an unwilling Mrs. Smawley go to sea in the *Evangeline*, their smooth sailing is interrupted by some shipwrecked sailors.

304. ____. *Tim's Friend Towser* (Walck, 1962) k–3. Tim and his friend Ginger, cabin boys on the S.S. *Royal Fusilier* find a stowaway puppy and manage to save him from the dog-hating captain.

305. ____. *Tim and Ginger* (Walck, 1965) k–3. How two young friends manage to survive a frightful night on the stormy sea after becoming stranded in their boat.

306. ____. *Tim to the Lighthouse* (Walck, 1968) k–3. Tim and his friends set out on a stormy night to see why the lighthouse is dark. They find the keeper unconscious, and they switch on the light in time to guide a ship safely by. They help capture two villainous wreckers.

307. ____. *Tim's Last Voyage* (Walck, 1973) k–3. Tim and Ginger run into trouble when they sail as deck hands on the *Arabella*.

308. ____. *Ship's Cook Ginger* (Macmillan, 1978) k–3. Tim and his friend Ginger are allowed to stay aboard Captain McFee's ship. Tim mans the wheel and saves the ship when the crew gets ill. Ginger works as the ship's cook for the same reason.

309. Argent, Kerry. *Wombat and Bandicoot* (Little, 1990) k–3. Presents the adventures of Wombat and Bandicoot as they learn the bonds of friendship, spend a glorious day at the beach, relish the thrill of hiding, and share a picnic with good friends.

310. ____. *Happy Birthday, Wombat* (Little, 1991) k–3. Bandicoot and his friends set up a surprise birthday party for Wombat.

311. Arkle, Phyllis. *Railway Cat* (Hodder, 1983) 2–4. Alfie, the cat, is a railway cat and could probably look after the station as well as either Hack or Fred, whose duty it really is. He saves lives when a train crashes and he is a footwarmer for an old lady.

312. ____. *Railway Cat and Digby* (Hodder, 1984) 2–4. Hack, the guard, has a dog, Digby. The Stationmaster has a cat, Alfie. Digby is entered in a local show and Alfie teases him into taking unwanted exercise. Then Alfie wins a prize and drinks milk from a silver cup.

313. ____. *Railway Cat's Secret* (Hodder, 1985) 2–4. Alfie leaves the station in disgust as it is being scrubbed and painted in preparation for a royal visit. He finds a new friend and because he later attracted the attention of the royal children he finds his new friend a home.

314. ____. *Railway Cat and the Horse* (Hodder, 1987) 2–4. Alfie, the cat, and Hack watch Rex, the rocking horse, be restored. They suspect someone will try to steal it and even after careful watch it is stolen. Alfie howls and the thieves are caught in their hiding place.

315. Armitage, Ronda. *Lighthouse Keeper's Catastrophe* (Deutsch, 1977) k–3. Mr. and Mrs. Grinling take care of the lighthouse. One day he locks himself out of the tower, unable to get to the light that will help ships in a coming storm. But Mrs. Grinling finds a way to get him in.

316. ____. *Lighthouse Lunch* (Dutton, 1986) k–3. Mr. Grinling's wife sends him lunch every day by means of a wire that runs from their cottage to the lighthouse. A problem arises when seagulls attack the basket and eat the food. Finally they come up with a solution.

317. ____. *Lighthouse Keeper's Rescue* (Deutsch, 1990) k–3. Mr. Grinling is getting old and a younger man is hired to replace him. But a whale is beached and Mr. and Mrs. Grinling try to save it. This attracts the attention of the village and Mr. Grinling is hired back part-time.

318. ____. *Lighthouse Keeper's Picnic* (Deutsch, 1995) k–3.

319. Arneson. *Zorro and the Pirate Raiders* (Bantam, 1986) 5–8. Zorro, the mysterious masked rider, fights for justice in old California. Captain Ramor and his pirate raider kidnap the daughter of a wealthy caballero to use her to trap Zorro.

320. ____. *Zorro Rides Again* (Bantam, 1986) 5–8. Zorro clears his name when an imposter wearing a mask and carrying a whip begins to terrorize the country.

321. Arnosky, Jim. *Mouse Numbers and Letters* (Harcourt, 1982) 2–4. A mouse encounters ten groups of objects to be counted during a visit to the beach and then constructs the letters of the alphabet from twigs.

322. ____. *Mouse Writing* (Harcourt, 1983) 2–4. A pair of skating mice trace out the letters of the cursive alphabet on ice.

323. Artes, Dorothy. *Rich and Po: Village Detectives* (Windswept, 1987) 4–6. Po and Rich want to be detectives and are helped by Po's uncle, Chris.

324. ____. *Rich and Po, Special Agents 5* (Windswept, 1988) 4–6. Po, Rich and Po's uncle, Chris, go to New York. They dodge enemy agents to deliver vital plans to the United Nations.

325. Arthur, Robert. *Three Investigators and the Secret of Terror Castle* (Random, 1964) 4–6. The three investigators look for a haunted house. They look at the home of a former movie star and run into ghosts and a well-kept secret.

326. ____. *Three Investigators and the Mystery of the Stuttering Parrot* (Random, 1964) 4–6. This is a case of missing parrots brought from Mexico who have learned to speak. In their speech is the secret to the mystery that the three investigators must solve.

327. ____. *Three Investigators and the Mystery of the Whispering Mummy* (Random, 1965) 4–6. Jupiter, Pete and Bob, the three investigators, won the use of a car and driver and are making good use of it.

328. ____. *Three Investigators and the Mystery of the Green Ghost* (Random, 1965) 4–6. The three investigators become entangled in the theft of a string of rare pearls and a fraudulent scheme involving family inheritance when they try to solve the mystery of a ghost's appearance in the old Green Mansion.

329. ____. *Three Investigators and the Mystery of the Vanishing Treasure* (Random, 1966) 4–6. Jupiter, Pete and Bob, the three investigators, are involved in a baffling museum robbery and almost end up in the Middle East.

330. ____. *Three Investigators and the Secret of Skeleton Island* (Random, 1966) 4–6. The three investigators are assisted by a Greek youth as they search for clues to a mysterious theft on an island once inhabited by pirates.

331. ____. *Three Investigators and the Mystery of the Fiery Eye* (Random, 1967) 4–6. Three junior detectives solve a mystery involving a collection of old antique busts, a legacy, a strange letter and a red ruby.

332. ____. *Three Investigators and the Mystery of the Silver Spider* (Random, 1967) 4–6. Three junior detectives travel abroad to solve a mystery involving a silver spider and a political plot that endangers the life of a young prince.

333. ____. *Three Investigators and the Mystery of the Screaming Clock* (Random, 1968) 4–6. This time the mystery concerns a strange clock that screams. The three investigators must find out how and why.

334. ____. *Three Investigators and the Mystery of the Talking Skull* (Random, 1969) 4–6. An old trunk involves the three investigators with dangerous criminals seeking a cache of stolen money.

(For other books about the "Three Investigators," *see* Arden, William.)

335. Asch, Frank. *Sand Cake* (Parents, 1978) k–3. Papa Bear uses his culinary skills and a little imagination to concoct a sand cake.

336. ____. *Moon Bear* (Scribner, 1978) k–3. Worried that the moon is growing smaller each night, Bear decides to do something about it.

337. ____. *Popcorn* (Parents, 1979) k–3. Sam Bear invites his friends to an impromptu Halloween party and asks them to bring a treat.

338. ____. *Bread and Honey* (Parents, 1981) k–3. Ben paints a picture of his mother, with a little help from Owl, Rabbit, Alligator, Elephant, Lion and Giraffe.

339. ____. *Happy Birthday, Moon* (Prentice, 1982) k–3. A little bear wants to give the moon a birthday present.

340. ____. *Mooncake* (Prentice, 1983) k–3. Bear builds a rocket to take him to the moon so he can taste it.

341. ____. *Moongame* (Prentice, 1984) k–3. During the game of hide-and-seek, Moon hides behind a cloud, leaving his friend Bear very worried.

342. ____. *Bear Shadow* (Prentice, 1984) k–3. Bear tries everything he can think of to get rid of his shadow.

343. ____. *Bear's Bargain* (Prentice, 1985) k–3. Bear and Little Bird try to help each other achieve impossible ambitions.

344. ____. *Goodbye House* (Prentice, 1986) k–3. Just before leaving with his family for the move to their new home, Little Bear says goodbye to all his favorite places in and around his old house.

345. ____. *Skyfire* (S & S, 1988) k–3. When he sees a rainbow for the first time. Bear thinks that the sky is on fire and he is determined to put out the skyfire.

346. ____. *Milk and Cookies* (Parents, 1992) k–3. While spending the night at Grandfather's house, Baby Bear dreams of feeding milk and cookies to a dragon.

347. ____. *Moondance* (Scholastic, 1993) k–3. Bear fulfills his dream of dancing with the moon.

348. ____. *Moonbear's Canoe* (Little Simon, 1993) k–3. Animals ask for a ride down the river. All goes well until a moose comes aboard.

349. ____. *Moonbear's Friend* (Little Simon, 1993) k–3. This story shows the difference between Bear and Little Bird—size, diet, sleeping habits, etc.

350. ____. *Moonbear's Books* (Little Simon, 1993) k–3. A book of opposites.

351. Asch, Frank. *Little Devil's 1 2 3* (Scribner, 1979) k–3. Humorous illustrations introduce the numbers 1 through 25.

352. ____. *Little Devil's ABC* (Scribner, 1979) k–3. Humorous illustrations of little devils and their activities introduce the alphabet.

353. Asch, Frank. *Pearl's Promise* (Delacorte, 1984) 4–6. With her brother in the clutches of a python in a pet shop, Pearl, a mouse, goes through hair-raising adventures to rescue him.

354. ____. *Pearl's Pirates* (Delacorte, 1987) 4–6. Led by the plucky Pearl, a small band of mice set sail in a model ship and brave the dangers of Frog Island in search of a lost pirate treasure.

355. Asher, Sandy. *Teddy Teabury's Fabulous Fact* (Dell, 1985) 5–8. Teddy lives in Thistledown, Missouri, and builds up a tourist trade by proving the town has more gerbils than people.

356. ____. *Ted Teabury Peanutly* (Dell, 1989) 5–8. Teddy, in sixth grade, has many adjustments to make. Much is expected of him. Teachers expect perfection. Little Jake worships him and Corky threatens him.

357. Asimov, Janet. *Norby Finds a Villain* (Walker, 1987) 4–6. Jeff and his mixed-up robot Norby travel backwards and forwards in time and find themselves prisoners on an alien planet in another universe.

358. ____. *Norby and Yobo's Great Adventure* (Walker, 1989) 4–6. When Jeff and his robot Norby accompany Admiral Yobo to prehistoric times so the admiral can do family research, the trip turns into a dangerous adventure.

359. ____. *Norby Down to Earth* (Walker, 1989) 4–6. Jeff leaves the space academy with his mixed-up robot Norby. The two of them head back to Earth to help Jeff's brother unravel a mystery involving zapped robots and stolen computer parts.

360. ____. *Norby and the Oldest Dragon* (Walker, 1990) 4–6. Jeff Wells and his personal robot Norby find adventure when they travel to planet Jamyn and attend the Grand Dragon's birthday party.

361. ____. *Norby and the Court Jester* (Walker, 1991) 4–6. While visiting the toy and game fair on planet Izz, Jeff and Norby search for a missing robot and the villain responsible for sabotaging the planet's computer system.

362. Asuka, Ken. *Toto Visits Mystic Mountain* (Garrett, 1989) k–3. Toto Squirrel and his friends go to mystic mountain to pick magic flowers.

363. ____. *Smile for Toto* (Garrett, 1990) k–3. Toto the squirrel pretends to be a photographer for the other animals.

364. ____. *Toto in Trouble* (Garrett, 1991) k–3. A small squirrel walks to his aunt's house dressed as a girl after getting soaked crossing the river.

365. Attenberger, Walburga. *Who Knows Little Man* (Random, 1972) k–3. Little Man takes a stroll in the rain, goes swimming, catches a fish for dinner and goes to bed.

366. ____. *Little Man in Winter* (Random, 1972) k–3. Little Man puts on his heavy clothes, goes sledding, rescues Katrina who has fallen through the ice and takes her home for hot soup.

367. Auel, Jean. *Clan of the Cave Bear* (Crown, 1980) 5–8. In the early days of humanity Ayla gave birth to a malformed child. She was told to kill it because that was the way things were done. She refused and knew that only tragedy could come from her decision.

368. ____. *Earth's Children* (Crown, 1980) 5–8. Ayla lived millions of years ago. As her known world is destroyed she must learn to survive as more than an animal. The lion and the Clan both play a role in her survival.

369. Augarde, Steve. *Barnaby Shrew Goes to Sea* (Deutsch, 1978) k–3. Barnaby Shrew packs up and tries to run away to sea. First he has to find a vessel that will take him. He sees a sign that a shrew is needed as cabin boy. He goes abroad and is hired. But the ship is in disarray.

370. ____. *Barnaby Shrew, Black Dan and the Mighty Wedgwood* (Deutsch, 1979) k–3. In port for a holiday, the crew of the *Pied Piper* tangle with Black Dan the Pirate and his fearsome parrot, Tough Eric.

371. Averill, Esther. *Cat Club or, the Life and Times of Jenny Lin* (Harper, 1944) k–3. Contains: "Cat Club"; "Jenny's First Party"; "When Jenny Lost Her Scarf"; "Jenny's Adopted Brothers"; "How the Brothers Joined the Cat Club."

372. ____. *School for Cats* (Harper, 1947) k–3. Jenny runs away from a school in the country where she was sent when her owner went away. She thinks better of it and returns and makes friends.

373. ____. *Jenny's First Party* (Harper, 1948) k–3. Jenny, Captain Tinker's small, shy black cat, wears her beautiful red scarf as she sets out to have some fun with her two friends, Pickles and Florio. They arrive at a party in someone's backyard.

374. ____. *Jenny's Moonlight Adventure* (Harper, 1949) k–3. Jenny braves Halloween demons on Mulligan Street to visit a sick friend.

375. ____. *When Jenny Lost Her Scarf* (Harper, 1951) k–3. Jenny not only recovers her favorite red scarf but is acclaimed by the Fire Department and the Cat Club for her spirit of unselfishness.

376. ____. *Jenny's Adopted Brother* (Harper, 1952) k–3. Jenny faces several important tests when two stray cats take over her favorite spots in the master's home.

377. ____. *How the Brothers Joined the Cat Club* (Harper, 1953) k–3. Jenny Linsky, a lovable little black cat, overcame selfish sentiments to make her new brothers, Edward and Checkers, members of the Cat Club.

378. ____. *Jenny's Bedside Book* (Harper, 1954) k–3. While Jenny recovers from the flu her brother, Checkers and Edward and friends come to entertain her. They tell her stories.

379. ____. *Jenny's Birthday Book* (Harper, 1954) k–3. Jenny Linsky, the little black cat, celebrates her birthday at a party in the park with her friends.

380. ____. *Jenny Goes to Sea* (Harper, 1957) k–3. Jenny and her adopted brothers, Checkers and Edward, and their master are on their way around the world on the ship *Sea Queen*. In one port they have their fortune told by a cat who reads paws.

381. ____. *Fire Cat* (Harper, 1960) k–3. One day Pickles, a young cat, chased another cat up a tree. Then Pickles couldn't climb down so Mrs. Goodkind, his only friend, called the fire department. Joe the fireman took Pickles back to the firehouse where he learned to be a fire cat. Pickles got a chance to be a hero.

382. ____. *Hotel Cat* (Harper, 1969) k–3. Relates the rise of Tom, the hotel cat, from catcher of mice in the cellar to successful upstairs cat in charge of the hotel's guest cats.

383. Avery, Gillian. *Ellen's Birthday* (Lodestar, 1971) 3–5. In the 1850s the Earl of Pembroke forbade villagers to gather wood on his land. But Ellen wanted to bake her birthday cake and needed fuel.

384. ____. *Ellen and the Queen* (Lodestar, 1975) 3–5. A young girl dreams of meeting Queen Victoria. Her wish comes true in an amusing way.

385. Avery, Gillian. *Maria Escapes* (S & S, 1992) 5–8. While living with her sole living relative, an uncle in Oxford, 11-year-old Maria shares an eccentric tutor with the boisterous Smith brothers and enjoys unusual outings and adventures in the English countryside.

386. ____. *Maria's Italian Spring* (S & S, 1993) 5–8. When her latest guardian dies, a 12-year-old English girl is relieved when a distant cousin offers her a home in Italy.

387. Awdry, W. *Tank Engine Thomas Again* (Random, 1949) k–3.

388. ____. *Troublesome Engines* (Random, 1950/1985) k–3.

389. ____. *Toby the Tram Engine* (Random, 1952/1991) k–3. A stout gentleman comes to the rescue when Toby the Tram Engine's line is about to be closed down.

390. ____. *Gordon the Big Engine* (Random, 1953) k–3.

391. ____. *Duck and the Diesel Engine* (Random, 1958/1987) k–3.

392. ____. *Thomas the Tank Engine's Storybook* (Random, 1963/1993) k–3. All about Thomas and his friends: Thomas Peoragon, Trust Thomas; Donald's Duck; Edward, Trevor and the really useful party; also the stories "Scarf for Percy"; "Trouble with Mud"; "No Jokes for James"; "Henry's Forest"; "Diesel Does It Again"; "Time for Trouble."

393. ____. *Thomas the Tank Engine* (Windmill, 1970) k–3.

394. ____. *Thomas, Percy and the Post Train* (Random, 1972) k–3. Thomas and Percy show that they can deliver the mail on time in any weather, even when it's too windy for Harry the Helicopter to fly.

395. ____. *Thomas Christmas Party* (Random, 1985) k–3. Mrs. Kyndley arranges a Christmas party for Thomas. A heavy snow falls and Thomas is fitted with a snowplow to bring Mr. & Mrs. Kyndley, who are marooned, to the party.

396. ____. *James and the Troublesome Trucks* (Random, 1985) k–3. The red engine pits his strength and cunning against his rebellious tail.

397. ____. *Trouble for Thomas* (Random, 1989) k–3. Thomas the Tank Engine learns about the dangers of fishing, traveling in the snow and how to pull freight cars.

398. ____. *Thomas Gets Tricked* (Random, 1989) k–3. Thomas the Tank Engine learns not to tease the big engines and pulls his first passenger train.

399. ____. *Meet Thomas the Tank Engine and His Friends* (Random, 1989) k–3. Sir Topham Hatt, in charge of all the railway engines on the island of Sodor, introduces the various engines and the freight cars they pull, describing the personality of each.

400. ____. *Happy Birthday, Thomas* (Random, 1990) k–3. Thomas the Tank Engine thinks that all the other engines are too busy to help him celebrate his birthday, but he is in for a surprise.

401. ____. *Thomas's ABC Book* (Random, 1990) k–3. An alphabet book featuring Thomas the Tank Engine and his friends.

402. ____. *Breakfast Time for Thomas* (Random, 1990) k–3.

403. ____. *Thomas the Tank Engine: Colors* (Random, 1991) k–3.

404. ____. *Thomas the Tank Engine: Counts to Ten* (Random, 1991) k–3.

405. ____. *James the Red Engine* (Random, 1991) k–3.

406. ____. *Thomas the Tank Engine: Shapes and Sizes* (Random, 1991) k–3.

407. ____. *Thomas and the Hide-and-Seek Animals* (Random, 1991) k–3. When Thomas the Tank Engine gets in trouble with animals along the line, Toby the Tram Engine tries to help him.

408. ____. *James and the Foolish Freight Cars* (Random, 1991) k–3. James the Red Engine successfully pulls some foolish freight cars and earns the respect of Sir Topham Hatt.

409. ____. *Percy Runs Away* (Random, 1991) k–3. Percy, a good friend of Thomas the Tank Engine, panics and runs away when he almost causes an accident in the train yard.

410. ____. *Thomas Breaks the Rules* (Random, 1991) k–3. When Thomas the Tank Engine gets in trouble with the police, Toby the Tram Engine comes to his aid.

411. ____. *Thomas and Trevor* (Random, 1991) k–3. Trevor, a traction engine, is happy that he can be useful when he helps Thomas with his work at the harbor.

412. ____. *Diesel's Devious Deed* (Random, 1992) k–3. Diesel causes no end of trouble among the engines when he arrives at Thomas the Tank Engine's train yard.

413. ____. *Thomas Gets Bumped* (Random, 1992) k–3. When unavoidable accidents cause Thomas the Tank Engine to call upon the help of Bertie the School Bus, Thomas worries that he will lose all his passengers.

414. ____. *Cow on the Line* (Random, 1992) k–3. Sir Topham Hatt's railroad engines discover that respect for the rules and for each other pays off in the end.

415. ____. *Thomas Goes Fishing* (Random, 1992) k–3. Thomas is embarrassed at the uncomfortable outcome when he goes fishing.

416. ____. *Thomas and the Freight Train* (Random, 1992) k–3.

417. ____. *Percy, the Small Engine Takes the Plunge* (Random, 1992) k–3.

418. ____. *Thomas the Tank Engine and the Tractor* (Random, 1992). k–3

419. ____. *Thomas the Tank Engine's Noisy Engine* (Random, 1993). k–3

420. ____. *Wave Hello to Thomas* (Random, 1993) k–3.

421. ____. *Tell the Time with Thomas* (Random, 1993) k–3.

422. ____. *Thomas and the School Trip* (Random, 1993) k–3. Attempting to hurry through his work so he can give some school children a ride, Thomas the Tank Engine must overcome a series of obstacles.

423. ____. *Percy's Promise* (Random, 1993) k–3. Percy braves a storm to keep his promise to get children home from the beach.

424. ____. *Duck Takes Charge* (Random, 1993) k–3. With the help of Sir Topham Hatt, Duck and Percy find a way to stop the other engines in the train yard from ordering them about.

425. ____. *Gordon and the Famous Visitor* (Random, 1993) k–3. When a famous visitor comes to the station, Gordon becomes jealous and risks his dome to get attention.

426. ____. *James in a Mess* (Random, 1993) k–3. Sir Topham Hatt's railroad engines, Harold the Helicopter and Bertie the School Bus learn about good manners and hard work.

427. ____. *Toby's Tightrope* (Random, 1994) k–3. Although the train engines learn social lessons, their improved behavior is often based on fear of their owner.

428. ____. *Midnight Ride of Thomas the Tank Engine* (Random, 1994) k–3. Thomas the Tank Engine, on a midnight run to take toys to the children's hospital, has an accident and must rely on some new friends to help him complete his task.

429. ____. *Surprise, Thomas* (Random, 1994) k–3.

430. ____. *New Tracks for Thomas* (Random, 1994) k–3.

431. ____. *Thomas and the Helicopter Rescue* (Random, 1995) k–3.

432. ____. *Thomas the Tank Engine and the Great Race* (Random) k–3.

433. ____. *Thomas Visits a Farm* (Random) k–3.

434. ____. *Tracking Thomas the Tank Engine and His Friends* (Random) k–3.

435. Ayars, James. *Basketball Comes to Lonesome Point* (Viking, 1952) 4–6. A sports story of a good teacher who enjoys his students. He aids and abets their schemes for a team and uniforms with all the trimmings.

436. ____. *Track Comes to Lonesome Point* (Dutton, 1973) 4–6. The seven boys in Lonesome Point junior high decide to form a track team even though the only qualified coach is a girl their own age.

437. "B.B." *Forest of Boland Light Railway* (Methuen, 1969) 2–4. Tales of gnomes and leprechauns. All the basic magic stuff: railways, small funny creatures, snug dwelling holes, potions, courage, villainy and retribution.

438. ____. *Lord of the Forest* (Children's, 1975) 2–4. The lord of this forest is its natural king, the oak tree, planted in 1272 and still standing in 1944. People weave their way in and out of its life in uncomplicated procession as do animals and lower forms of life.

439. ____. *Wizard of Borland* (Methuen, 1977) 2–4. The wicked wizard works magic which destroys the peasants' livelihood and temporarily robs the wizard of his daughter, Helda. She later outwits the magician upon whom a dragon wreaks vengeance.

440. "B.B." *Bill Badger and the Wandering Wind* (Methuen, 1981) 3–5. A stay-at-home badger takes over a canal barge and with Izzybizzy the hedgehog, takes money to a distant bank.

441. ____. *Bill Badger's Winter Cruise* (Methuen, 1981) 3–5. Bill Badger and Izzybizzy's barge is held in the ice and they face a cheerless Christmas. Mr. Parker, the fox, helps change their situation.

442. Baba, Noboru. *Eleven Hungry Cats* (Carolrhoda, 1988) k–3. Eleven very hungry cats are determined to catch the big fish that sometimes sings lullabies to himself.

443. ____. *Eleven Cats and a Pig* (Carolrhoda, 1988) k–3. Eleven cats and a pig contend for possession of an abandoned house, as well as a new house which they build together.

444. ____. *Eleven Cats in a Bag* (Carolrhoda, 1988) k–3. Eleven naughty cats learn the importance of obeying the instructions on signs after an encounter with a monster.

445. ____. *Eleven Cats and Albatrosses* (Carolrhoda, 1988) k–3. Eleven hungry cats with a yen for roasted bird follow an albatross home to meet his family and find themselves with too much albatross to handle.

446. Babbitt, Natalie. *Devil's Storybook* (Farrar, 1974) 4–6. Ten stories recount the Devil's exploits, successes and failures, in Hell and in the world above. About the Devil's often unsuccessful inventions to add to his collection.

447. ____. *Devil's Other Storybook* (Farrar, 1987) 4–6. The further exploits of the Devil in his own realm and in the world above are recounted in ten more tales.

448. Baker, Alan. *Benjamin and the Box* (Lippincott, 1977) k–3. Benjamin Hamster is curious about the contents of a box he cannot open.

449. ____. *Benjamin Bounces Back* (Lippincott, 1978) k–3. Shortsighted Benjamin Hamster goes through a door with a sign he can't read and experiences some unusual adventures.

450. ____. *Benjamin's Dreadful Dreams* (Lippincott, 1980) k–3. Benjamin, a hamster, is sleepless and hungry. He falls into a collection of fireworks and everything explodes. But then he wakes up and is back in his own bed.

451. ____. *Benjamin's Book* (Lothrop, 1982) k–3. A hamster in glasses tries to eradicate a pawprint from a clean white page.

452. ____. *Benjamin's Portrait* (Lothrop, 1987) k–3. Benjamin the hamster tries to paint his portrait and gets some unexpected results.

453. ____. *Benjamin's Balloon* (Lippincott, 1990) k–3. Benjamin blows up a balloon and begins a travel adventure that causes him a certain amount of worry.

454. Baker, Alan. *Gray Rabbit's 1 2 3* (Kingfisher, 1994) k–3. Rabbit has great wads of colorful clay that she keeps molding into different lively animals—eight rumpeting, trumpeting elephants; nine spotted, dotted bugs; ten squeaking, peeking mice—which at the end of the day left one weary, bleary rabbit fast asleep.

455. ____. *White Rabbit's Color Book* (Kingfisher, 1994) k–3. Rabbit finds three tubes of paint and proceeds to bathe in each of the colors, making all the colors of the rainbow—and a big mess in the process.

456. ____. *Black and White Rabbit's ABC* (Kingfisher, 1994) k–3. Rabbit is trying to make a present for his mom. He works his way through all sorts of trouble (and the alphabet) before finishing his beautiful present.

457. ____. *Brown Rabbit's Shape Book* (Kingfisher, 1994) k–3. Rabbit is trying to blow up different shaped balloons and has all sorts of tiring adventures.

458. ____. *Gray Rabbit's Odd One Out* (Kingfisher, 1995) k–3. A rabbit sorts through and groups all his stuff in order to find his favorite book. In each grouping, one item doesn't belong and this leads to the next sorting.

459. Baker, Barbara. *Digby and Kate* (Dutton, 1988) 3–5. Six episodes in the friendship of Digby the dog and Kate the cat, who enjoy each other's company even when they have differences in areas as catching a mouse or fixing lunch.

460. ____. *Digby and Kate Again* (Dutton, 1989) 3–5. Digby the dog and Kate the cat share four adventures: hunting, bicycling, letter writing and raking the leaves.

461. Baker, Elizabeth. *Tammy Camps Out* (Houghton, 1958) 2–4. On her first camping trip in the White Mountains, Tammy, eight, learned how to cut a blaze and to build a cooking fire. She also showed her family how resourceful she could be in an emergency.

462. ____. *Tammy Climbs Pyramid Mountain* (Houghton, 1962) 2–4. Tammy and her father add Harold to their Pyramid Mountain climbing party. In the thunderstorm Harold proves he knows how to get along out-of-doors.

463. ____. *Tammy Goes Canoeing* (Houghton, 1966) 2–4. Tammy is in Algonquin Park to find a discarded deer antler. She leads her father and brother into various difficulties until she finds it.

464. ____. *Tammy Camps in the Rocky Mountains* (Houghton, 1970) 2–4. During a Rocky Mountain camping trip Tammy's enthusiastic picture-taking becomes frustrating for her father and brother, and dangerous to her.

465. Baker, Leslie. *Third Story Cat* (Little, 1992) k–3. A house cat longs to visit the park across the street. She "escapes" her comfortable apartment, meets a streetwise cat, and is given a tour that is hair-raising and an encounter that sends her home.

466. ____. *Antique Store Cat* (Little, 1992) k–3. Alice doesn't take "no" for an answer when she starts prowling through the treasures of a nearby antique store.

467. Baker, Margaret. *Shoe Shop Bears* (Ariel, 1965) 3–5. Boots, Slippers and Socks are teddy bears that live in a shoe shop. A crisis occurs when old Mr. Shoehorn retires and the new owner decides to get rid of the bears. At night the bears discuss what to do with Hobson the cat and others.

468. ____. *Hannibal and the Bears* (Farrar, 1966) 3–5. Now living in a real home, with the Trinkey family, Boots, Slippers and Socks set out to rescue some discarded toy animals who have been sent to the rubbish heap. Among them is Hannibal, a once magnificent old elephant on wheels.

469. ____. *Bears Back in Business* (Farrar, 1967) 3–5. The three bears go on a new adventure in a wider world. They become aware of thieves as they help apprehend them and then live happily with Polly.

470. Balch, Glenn. *Wild Horse* (Crowell, 1948) 4–6. In southwestern Idaho Ben and Dixie fight to save a black stallion from capture for the rodeos.

471. ____. *Lost Horse* (Crowell, 1950) 4–6. Ben and Dixie help their family and their horses. Their divided loyalty also meshes and helps them to understand things better.

472. ____. *Midnight Colt* (Crowell, 1952) 4–6. Ben and Dixie buy their first race horse and name him Peck o' Trouble. They slowly train him and sell him at a profit.

473. ____. *Wild Horse Tamer* (Crowell, 1955) 4–6. Ben and Dixie's wild stallion, King, has disappeared and they must go look for him.

474. ____. *Horse in Danger* (Crowell, 1960) 4–6. Dixie and Ben of Tack Ranch defend their wild stallion, King, against charges of raiding the neighbor's herds.

475. Balch, Glenn. *Horse of Two Colors* (Crowell, 1969) 4–6. Two Indian boys escape from the Spanish, each with a horse. They head for their village but only one boy makes it. The dead boy's horse is carrying a foal.

476. ____. *Spotted Horse* (Crowell, 1961) 4–6. A follow-up story to *Horse of Two Colors* about the life of the boy who brought the horse back to his village and of the devoted horse.

477. Balian, Lorna. *Humbug Witch* (Abingdon, 1964) k–3. There was this little witch. Its commands were always ignored. Its magic potions never exploded. This thing called "witch" got discouraged. It took off its long black dress...and then the unexpected happened.

478. ____. *Humbug Rabbit* (Abingdon, 1974) k–3. Father Rabbit's reply of "Humbug" to the idea that he is the Easter Bunny doesn't spoil Easter for his children or Granny's grandchildren.

479. ____. *Bah! Humbug?* (Abingdon, 1977) k–3. Two children set a trap for Santa Claus but only one of them manages to see him.

480. ____. *Humbug Potion* (Abingdon, 1984) k–3. A homely witch is delighted to find a secret recipe for beauty but it is written in a code that the reader must help her decipher by learning the letters of the alphabet.

481. Ball, Brian. *Look Out, Duggy Dog* (Hamilton, 1985) k–3. Duggy Dog is a cheerful dog who gets his head stuck in a yellow watering can. It enables him to scare off the nasty big dog who keeps Duggy's

friend out of the Big Field where they want to play chase.

482. ____. *I'm Lost Duggy Dog* (Hamilton, 1987) k–3.

483. ____. *Hop It Duggy Dog* (Hamilton, 1989) k–3. A story about the various interruptions Duggy Dog has in his attempts to get to sleep before he actually lands in a muddy pond.

484. Ball, Brian. *Jackson's House* (Hamilton, 1975) 2–4. Jackson is a tomcat who takes advantage of Marilyn, the next door kitten. They pose as strays at a big house. They make mischief at the village shop. In both places they get good meals.

485. ____. *Jackson's Friend* (Hamilton, 1975) 2–4. Jackson, the cat, is puzzled by Oscar the parrot. Oscar says he is a bird but Jackson has his doubts. Oscar takes on Bodger the dog and wins.

486. ____. *Jackson and the Magpies* (Hamilton, 1979) 2–4. Jackson is a cat whose job is to chase thieving magpies from the milk and cream left unattended on the doorstep of Field House Road. He has a friend Marilyn, a white kitten.

487. Ball, Duncan. *Emily Eyefinger* (S & S, 1992) 3–5. Having been born with an extra eye on the end of her finger, Emily finds that it comes in very handy in many unusual situations.

488. ____. *Emily Eyefinger, Secret Agent* (S & S, 1993) 3–5. A young girl feels different from everyone else because she has an eye on the end of one finger, but it comes in handy on occasion, such as when she is helping catch a spy.

489. ____. *Emily Eyefinger and the Lost Treasure* (S & S, 1994) 3–5. The further adventures of a young girl who has an extra eye on the end of one finger, which comes in handy when she helps to save the reputation of a famous artist and discovers a lost treasure from ancient Egypt.

490. Ball, Duncan. *Selby's Secret* (Angus, 1986) 4–6. Selby discovered his talking gift by chance while watching television, but decides to hide it from his owners, lest he stop being treated like a pet and find himself living a "dog's" life.

491. ____. *Selby Screams* (Angus, 1991) 4–6.

492. ____. *Selby Speaks* (Harper, 1997) 4–6. Selby the talking dog continues his exploits and adventures while still attempting to keep his skills secret.

493. Balter, Lawrence. *What's the Matter with A.J.?* (Barron, 1989) 3–5. The arrival of a new baby in the family affects big brother A.J., who responds with jealousy and unpredictable outbursts of anger.

494. ____. *A.J.'s Mom Gets a New Job* (Barron, 1990) 3–5. When A.J.'s mother decides to take a job outside the home, he is upset and attempts to adjust to the new arrangements and his new role in the family.

495. Balter, Lawrence. *Sue Lee's New Neighborhood* (Barron, 1989) k–3. A little girl faces the anxieties of moving, trading old friends and familiar places for unfamiliar rooms and a new neighborhood.

496. ____. *Sue Lee Starts School* (Barron, 1991) k–3. Worried about starting at a new school, Sue Lee feels lonely and scared but soon discovers that her natural traits and talents make her very popular with her new classmates.

497. Bang, Betsy. *Old Woman and the Red Pumpkin* (Macmillan, 1975) k–3. A retelling of an Indic folktale in which a skinny old woman outwits the jackal, bear and tiger who want to eat her.

498. ____. *Old Woman and the Rice Thief* (Greenwillow, 1978) k–3. Retells a traditional India tale in which an old woman outwits a rice thief.

499. Banks, Lynne Reid. *Indian in the Cupboard* (Doubleday, 1981) 4–6. Omni has three presents: a magic cupboard, a key to lock it and a tiny plastic Indian, Little Bear. The Indian comes to life and must have his needs met.

500. ____. *Return of the Indian* (Doubleday, 1986) 4–6. A year after he sends Little Bear, his Indian friend, back into the magic cupboard, Omni decides to bring him back only to find that he is close to death and in need of help.

501. ____. *Secret of the Indian* (Doubleday, 1989) 4–6. A story about Omni and his magic cupboard. He and his friend Patrick must risk grownups discovering their secret when they find themselves in need of a friend's toy plastic doctor to save wounded people from the dangerous world of the Old West.

502. ____. *Mystery of the Cupboard* (Doubleday, 1993) 4–6. Omni remains cautious of the dangers of "playing" with the cupboard, but he is pleased when all the plastic characters come to life. A history of the cupboard and its magical key.

503. Banner, Angela. *Ant and Bee and ABC* (Watts, 1950) 3–5. A story of how Ant and Bee first meet and learn the alphabet in the process of investigating a sort of glorified Lost Property Office.

504. ____. *1, 2, 3 with Ant and Bee* (Heinemann, 1958) 3–5. Kind Dog is in this book with a nice story line. One can learn to count, write and read numbers. And Ant is "sad in bed."

505. ____. *Around the World with Ant and Bee* (Kaye, 1960) 3–5. A sort of infant's geography book.

506. ____. *More and More Ant and Bee* (Heinemann, 1961) 3–5. Alphabetical story about Ant and Bee and Kind Dog.

507. ____. *Ant and Bee and Kind Dog* (Kaye, 1963) 3–5. Ant and Bee set out with a dog friend to track down a smell which they never find. An alphabetical story.

508. ____. *Happy Birthday with Ant and Bee* (Heinemann, 1964) 3–5. Designed to teach children the days of the week, but also covers good behavior at birthday parties. Talks about presents, games, prizes and balloons. It is Kind Dog's birthday.

509. ____. *Ant and Bee and the Rainbow* (Heinemann, 1966) 3–5. A story about the range of colors.

510. ____. *Ant and Bee Time* (Watts, 1969) 3–5. Ant and Bee participate in many of the zoo games.

511. ____. *Ant and Bee and the Secret* (Heinemann, 1970) 3–5. Every time Bee calls him stupid, Ant runs away to a secret place and won't tell Bee where it is.

512. ____. *Ant and Bee and the Doctor* (Heinemann, 1971) 3–5. First Bee has a cold, then Ant comes down with the mumps. They are confined to the house. They keep occupied even though they are invalids.

513. ____. *Ant and Bee Go Shopping* (Heinemann, 1972) 3–5. A story crammed full of details of a shopping trip.

514. Barber, Antonia. *Satchelmouse and the Dinosaur* (Barron, 1987) k–3. Sarah meets a real dinosaur with the help of her friend, a mischievous mouse, and his magic trumpet.

515. ____. *Satchelmouse and the Doll's House* (Barron, 1990) k–3. Sarah wants to be the little girl in the white dress but her satchelmouse friend makes her the kitchen maid. When she returns to the classroom dollhouse she teaches the girl in the white dress the lesson she just learned.

516. Bargar, Gary. *What Happened to Mr. Forester?* (Clarion, 1981) 4–6. Louis is an underdog and needs to develop his self–confidence. He likes to write and a friendly teacher helps. That teacher turns out to be homosexual and is fired from his job.

517. ____. *Life. Is. Not. Fair.* (Clarion, 1984) 4–6. Dewitt moves into an all white neighborhood next door to Louis. Louis befriends him, aware of the social liability he will be.

518. Barklem, Jill. *Winter Story* (Philomel, 1980) k–3. The winter activities of the mice of Brambly Hedge are highlighted by a Snow Ball.

519. ____. *Spring Story* (Philomel, 1980) k–3. Follows the activities of the Brambly Hedge community of field mice on a spring day as they prepare a surprise picnic for Wilfred's birthday.

520. ____. *Summer Story* (Philomel, 1980) k–3. Despite some unexpected developments, the summer wedding of mice Poppy and Dusty goes off beautifully.

521. ____. *Autumn Story* (Philomel, 1980) k–3. A well-to-do little mouse, exploring on her own, experiences both pleasant and frightening adventures before she is safely home again.

522. ____. *Sea Story* (Philomel, 1980) k–3. Brambly Hedge mice Poppy, Dusty, Primrose and Wilfred set sail for the sea and find it's not all easy sailing.

523. ____. *Big Book of Brambly Hedge* (Philomel, 1981) k–3. The further adventures of the Brambly Hedge community of field mice.

524. ____. *Secret Staircase* (Philomel, 1983) k–3. Quite by accident, the young mice, Primrose and Wilfred, find a secret staircase in the Old Oak Palace which leads them to a magnificent surprise.

525. ____. *High Hills* (Philomel, 1986) k–3. Inspired by an old song, young mouse Wilfred uses a trip into the hills as an opportunity to look for gold and explore unknown country.

526. ____. *Four Seasons of Brambly Hedge* (Philomel, 1990) k–3. Contains: "Spring Story"; "Summer Story"; "Autumn Story"; "Winter Story." Four stories that follow the activities of the Brambly Hedge community of field mice through the four seasons.

527. ____. *Through the Hedgerow* (Philomel, 1993) k–3. The mice of Brambly Hedge are celebrating a birthday. Blackberries are picked for jam and jellies. Mrs. Crustybread is baking a cake. Mrs. Apple is recording events in her diary.

528. ____. *World of Brambly Hedge* (Philomel, 1993) k–3. Follows the activities of a community of field mice through the year. (Same as *Through the Hedgerow,* entry 527.)

529. ____. *Poppy's Babies* (Putnam, 1995) k–3. Mrs. Crustybread is making a special cake. Mrs. Toadflax is hanging curtains and Lady Woodmouse is laying out new quilts. It is all for Poppy now that she has three new babies.

530. Barracca, Debra. *Adventures of Taxi Dog* (Dial, 1990) k–3. Follows the day in the life of a dog befriended by a New York City taxi driver.

531. ____. *Maxi, the Hero* (Dial, 1991) k–3. The further adventures of Maxi, the dog, who rides with Jim in his taxi and becomes a hero when he chases and catches a thief.

532. ____. *Taxi Dog Christmas* (Dial, 1992) k–3. Maxi and Jim the taxi driver gladly interrupt their Christmas celebration to lend Santa a hand.

533. ____. *Maxi, the Star* (Dial, 1993) k–3. Maxi and Jim take their taxi cross-country so that Maxi can do a screen test for Doggie Bites.

534. Barron, T.A. *Heartlight* (Philomel, 1991) 5–8. Kate and her astrophysicist grandfather are bound together by a deep relationship. Kate is lonely and misunderstood at school, and grandfather is absorbed in a laboratory. Together they journey across the galaxy on a quest to save our solar system from annihilation.

535. ____. *Ancient One* (Philomel, 1992) 5–8. Kate continues her time-traveling journeys, this time in Oregon while visiting Great-Aunt Melanie, who is trying to save a forest from logging. Kate finds herself caught up in mysteries, which she must unravel in order to save the lives of the forest.

536. ____. *Merlin Effect* (Putnam, 1994) 5–8. Kate is in Mexico with her dad. He is doing research in finding the Merlin cup. The cup might be in a sunken ship in the bottom of a whirlpool. Kate is sucked into the whirlpool and she and her dad must be saved.

537. Barry, Margaret. *Boffy and the Teacher Eater* (Collins, 1971) 2–4. Boffy, six, is a genius who can fly a jet plane safely to Morocco and back, but he knows little about Father Christmas.

538. ____. *Boffy and the Mumford Ghosts* (Harrap, 1974) 2–4. Boffy, a bespectacled boy-genius, rearranges the living accommodations of a houseful of noisy ghosts and sets up a giant dinosaur theft.

539. Barry, Margaret. *Tommy Mac* (Collins, 1972) 2–4. The Liverpool boys get involved with a tramp who sets up house in Tommy's gang headquarters.

540. ____. *Tommy Mac Battles On* (Viking, 1974) 2–4. The Mac family are urban dwellers with the problems of inner city life.

541. ____. *Tommy on Safari* (Viking, 1975) 2–4. Tommy Mac and his gang live among the worker's class in Liverpool.

542. Barry, Margaret. *Woozie* (Harrap, 1973) 2–4. Woozies are a kind of unique creatures that only appear once in a decade or so. Children found a pet and beg to be allowed to keep it.

543. ____. *Woozie Gets Lost* (Harrap, 1973) 2–4. A variation of "getting caught in a factory assembly line" joke. Here Woozie gets lost in an ice cream parlor.

544. ____. *Woozie Goes to School* (Harrap, 1973) 2–4.

545. ____. *Woozie on Television* (Harrap, 1974) 2–4. Big Woozie and six little woozies create havoc in the television studio.

546. Barry, Margaret. *Witch of Monopoly Manor* (Harrap, 1974) 2–4. Simon's inconvenient friend has now leased a dilapidated mansion. The witch got the needed money when she found a diamond tiara. Simon and his friends visit the witch and are served strange sandwiches.

547. ____. *Simon and the Witch* (Collins, 1976) 2–4. Simon's witch is normal most of the time but when Simon wants something done, like turning the school gardener into a frog, the witch comes out. George is the witches' cat and when she forgets to feed him he eats pages and gets into mischief.

548. ____. *Return of the Witch* (Collins, 1978) 2–4. Simon's witch turns a lion tamer into a pork pie and then a bad egg. The witch's anti-social behavior drives away Simon's unpleasant Aunt Maud. She catches a smuggling pleasure boatman and has many other adventures.

549. ____. *Witch on Holiday* (Fontana, 1984) 2–4. A grumpy witch is uncontrollable and unpredictable. She gets Simon in all sorts of scrapes: on a school trip to Boulogne with the witch speaking fluent French and on the school camping holiday with the witch ensconced in a huge marquee.

550. ____. *Witch VIP* (Collins, 1987) 2–4. Simon's life is disrupted by a witch and George, his moth-eaten cat. The witch takes over his school and plays havoc as a baby-sitter.

551. ____. *Simon and the Witch in School* (Collins, 1988) 2–4.
552. ____. *Witch and the Holiday Club* (Collins, 1989) 2–4. Simon is a schoolboy. His best friend is Witch. The witch vows never to return to school but instead embarks on a plan to populate Valdini's cafe with customers. This is done but not before vying with Lady Fox-Custard, her arch enemy.

553. Barry, Margaret. *Maggie Gumptron* (Collins, 1981) 2–4.
554. ____. *Maggie Gumptron Flies High* (Collins, 1981) 2–4. Maggie is a doll. Her friends are Pinky Dar and Polly. They live in an attic next door to toy soldiers. Seven different episodes about them all, especially Polly.

555. Baskin, Leonard. *Hosie's Alphabet* (Viking, 1972) 3–5. A full-page illustration of a creature for each letter of the alphabet, including a bumptious baboon, furious fly, ghastly garrulous gargoyle and quintessential quail.
556. ____. *Hosie's Aviary* (Viking, 1979) 3–5. Text and pictures portray a variety of birds.
557. ____. *Hosie's Zoo* (Viking, 1981) 3–5. Animal portraits and animal poetry.

558. Bassett, Lisa. *Clock for Beany* (Dodd, 1985) k–3. Beany Bear is not quite sure he likes the clock he received for his birthday.
559. ____. *Beany and Scamp* (Dodd, 1987) k–3. Just as Beany Bear is ready for his long winter's nap, friend Scamp Squirrel asks his help in searching for his misplaced winter nut supply.
560. ____. *Beany Wakes Up for Christmas* (Putnam, 1988) k–3. Scamp Squirrel gets everything ready for Christmas to surprise Beany when he wakes up for the occasion.

561. Baum, L. Frank. *Wonderful Wizard of Oz* (Holt, 1900/1982) 4–6. After a cyclone transports her to the land of Oz, Dorothy must seek out the great wizard in order to return to Kansas.
562. ____. *Land of Oz* (Children's, 1904/1985) 4–6. An account of the further adventures of the Scarecrow and the Tin Woodsman. Tip and his creation, Jack Pumpkin, run away to Oz where they save the city after it is captured by girls.
563. ____. *Ozma of Oz* (Morrow, 1907/1981) 4–6. A storm blows Dorothy to the land of Ev where lunches grow on trees. She meets Scarecrow, Tin Woodsman, and the Cowardly Lion, and Princess Ozma. Together they set out to free the Queen of Ev and her ten children.
564. ____. *Dorothy and the Wizard of Oz* (Morrow, 1908/1984) 4–6. During a California earthquake Dorothy falls into the underground Land of the Manaboos where she again meets the Wizard of Oz.
565. ____. *Road to Oz* (Morrow, 1909/1991) 4–6.

Dorothy and her friends follow the enchanted road to Oz and arrive in time for Ozma's birthday party.
566. ____. *Emerald City of Oz* (Rand, 1910/1979) 4–6. Dorothy's aunt and uncle get acquainted with Oz after they lost their farm and Ozma invites them to live with her.
567. ____. *Patchwork Girl of Oz* (Ballantine, 1913/1990) 4–6. A boy, a patchwork girl, and a glass cat go on a mission to find the ingredients for a charm which will transform some people turned to marble statues back into people.
568. ____. *Tik-Tok of Oz* (Reilly, 1914/1980) 4–6. Introduces Ann Soforth, Queen of Dogaboo, whom Tik–Tok, the clockwork man, assists in conquering the Nome King.
569. ____. *Scarecrow of Oz* (Ballantine, 1915/1980) 4–6. The adventure of Trot and Cap'n Bill take them to Oz where they help solve the problem of Pom, whose true love's heart has been turned to ice by witches.
570. ____. *Rinkitink in Oz* (Ballantine, 1916/1980) 4–6. The perilous quest of Prince Inga of Pingaree and King Rinkitink in the magical isles that lie beyond the borderland of Oz.
571. ____. *Lost Princess of Oz* (Ballantine, 1917/1980) 4–6. The long search for a thief and the things he stole: all the magic in Oz as well as Princess Ozma, its ruler.
572. ____. *Tin Woodsman of Oz* (Ballantine, 1979) 4–6. Dorothy tries to rescue the Tin Woodsman and Scarecrow from the giantess who has changed them into a tin owl and a teddy bear and is using them for playthings.
573. ____. *Glinda of Oz* (Ballantine, 1985) 4–6. The Sorceress and Wizard of Oz attempt to save Princess Ozma and Dorothy from the dangers which threaten them when they try to bring peace to two warring tribes.
574. ____. *Little Wizard Stories of Oz* (Schocken, 1985) 4–5. Six tales of the further adventures of Dorothy and Toto, Ozma, Tik-Tok, Jack Pumpkinhead, the Tin Woodsman and other characters from the land of Oz.
575. ____. *Giant Horse of Oz* (Ballantine, 1985) 4–6. Trot from California and Benny, a living stone statue from Boston, join a giant horse in Ozian adventures involving a monster sea serpent.
576. ____. *Gnome King of Oz* (Ballantine, 1985) 4–6. Unsuspectingly, Peter, a boy from Philadelphia, assists the wicked Gnome King in escaping from the island where he has been banished and who is now determined to reclaim his former kingdom and ravage Oz.
577. ____. *Jack Pumpkinhead of Oz* (Ballantine, 1985) 4–6. A Philadelphia lad returns to Oz and joins forces with Jack Pumpkinhead to rescue Ozma and the Emerald City from conquest.
578. ____. *Marvelous Land of Oz* (Morrow, 1985) 4–6. Tip and his creation, Jack Pumpkin, run away to Oz, where they save the city after it is captured by girls.

579. Baum, L. Frank. *Kidnapped Santa Claus* (Bobbs, 1904) 2–4. Unhappy because Santa has been spreading too much contentment among the children, the five Demons devise a plan to kidnap him.

580. _____. *Life and Adventures of Santa Claus* (Dutton, 1976) 2–4. Relates Santa's life, from childhood to old age and immortality, mentioning such adventures as those with the friendly wood nymphs and the wicked Awgwas.

581. Baum, Susan. *Gear Bear's Good Morning* (Grosset, 1988) k–3. Gear Bear is busy every morning from the time he wakes up till he goes out to play.

582. _____. *Goodnight, Gear Bear* (Grosset, 1988) k–3. Gear Bear tries a variety of ways to make himself sleepy one night when he just can't get to sleep at bedtime.

583. Baumgart, Klaus. *Anna and the Little Green Dragon Step Out* (Disney, 1992) k–3. Anna's little green dragon comes out of his picture book and plays around her room during the night, or was it just a dream?

584. _____. *Anna and the Little Green Dragon* (Hyperion, 1992) k–3. During breakfast a little green dragon comes out of Anna's box of cornflakes and makes a mess on the table.

585. _____. *Where Are You, Little Green Dragon?* (Hyperion, 1993) k–3. Anna's little green dragon has a new adventure inside the refrigerator.

586. Bawden, Juliet. *Good Teddy* (Bannon, 1987) k–3. Teddy Bear helps around the house by making his bed, clearing the table, taking out the garbage, just as any good young child would.

587. _____. *Poor Teddy* (Bannon, 1987) k–3. Teddy is caught in the bushes, stung by a bee, sick with the measles, stuck with a toothache and drenched by the rain.

588. _____. *Naughty Teddy* (Barron, 1987) k–3. Teddy Bear does some naughty things around the house—being sloppy, scribbling on the wall, not sharing—behaving much as any young child might at times.

589. Bawden, Nina. *Keeping Henry* (Dell, 1988) 4–6. Henry is a baby squirrel found by Charlie. He thinks of humans as trees to be leapt upon, explored and used for foot storage. The reader learns of Henry's diet and sleeping habits. He is mischievous and magical.

590. _____. *Henry* (Dell, 1990) 4–6. Evacuated to the English countryside during World War II, a fatherless family tries to raise a baby squirrel that also lost its home.

591. Bayley, Nicola. *Patchwork Cat* (Knopf, 1981) k–3. When Tabby's patchwork quilt was thrown out, she sets out to retrieve it. A nice ending to this comforting story.

592. _____. *Elephant Cat* (Knopf, 1984) k–3. A cat imagines what it would be like to be an elephant—that is, until bathtime comes.

593. _____. *Polar Bear Cat* (Knopf, 1984) A cat imagines what it would be like to be a polar bear and live on the ice.

594. _____. *Crab Cat* (Knopf, 1984) A cat imagines what it would be like to be a crab living by a pool at the seashore.

595. _____. *Parrot Cat* (Knopf, 1984) A cat imagines what it would be like to be a parrot and live in the jungle.

596. _____. *Spider Cat* (Knopf, 1984) k–3. A cat imagines what it would be like to be a spider—spinning, eating, and playing in the garden.

597. _____. *Copycats* (Knopf, 1992) Contains: "Parrot Cat";. "Elephant Cat"; "Polar Bear Cat"; "Crab Cat"; "Spider Cat."

598. Baynton, Martin. *Fifty Saves His Friend* (Crown, 1986) k–3. Fifty the Tractor pulls carts and logs all day, but when someone is in danger he proves he is a good friend too.

599. _____. *Fifty and the Fox* (Crown, 1986) k–3. Fifty the Tractor helps softhearted Wally get rid of a fox that is scaring the chickens.

600. _____. *Fifty Gets the Picture* (Crown, 1987) k–3. Fifty the Tractor gives the farm hand Wally some assistance in his chores so that he will have time to finish painting Fifty's portrait.

601. _____. *Fifty and the Great Race* (Crown, 1987) k–3. Fifty the Tractor must win the race at the annual fair or risk being scrapped for junk.

602. Beatty, Patricia. *Nickel Plated Beauty* (Morrow, 1964) 5–8. When the Kimball's old stove began to rust away, Whit, the oldest of seven children, ordered a new one C.O.D. All the children had to raise money to earn the price of this elegant new stove.

603. _____. *Sarah and Me and the Lady from the Sea* (Morrow, 1989) 5–8. Marcella's family is at their summer home because of financial distress. They learn to subsist on less and yet have adventures. The reader also learns more about what happened to the Kimballs.

604. Beck, Martine. *Wedding of Brown Bear and White Bear* (Little, 1990) k–3. A brown bear sees a white bear on the skating rink. He gets to know her and court her. He proposes marriage by letter and she accepts. They wed and dance the night away.

605. _____. *White Bear's Secret* (Little, 1991) k–3. The couple resides in a mountain chalet. An avalanche destroys their house, slightly injuring them both. Villagers come to help rebuild. White Bear is expecting a baby they will name Balibar.

606. _____. *Rescue of Brown Bear and White Bear* (Little, 1991) k–3. After a snowy mishap, Brown Bear and White Bear welcome spring and the arrival of their baby cub, Balibar.

607. Belden, Wilanne. *Mind-Call* (Atheneum, 1981) 5–8. Tallie has ESP. She dreams of what is about to happen. She is alone except for the cat, and manages to pack and to get on Paul's sailboat just before the tidal wave strikes. Others join her to fight evil.

608. ____. *Mind-Hold* (Harcourt, 1987) 5–8. Carson, 12, and Caryl, 10, have telepathic powers and have mental battles with each other. They are seeking their father after a devastating earthquake.

609. ____. *Mind-Find* (Harcourt, 1988) 5–8. Laurel, 13, who has ESP, spends time with a neighboring family with psychic powers. She uses her powers to save some children during a storm.

610. Bemelmans, Ludwig. *Madeline* (Viking, 1987) k–3. Madeline, smallest and naughtiest of the 12 little charges of Miss Clavel, wakes up one night with an attack of appendicitis.

611. ____. *Madeline's Rescue* (Viking, 1953) k–3. This is the story of a canine who saved little Madeline from the waters of the Seine.

612. ____. *Madeline and the Bad Hat* (Viking, 1956) k–3. Madeline is back again. The "bad hat" is the Spanish ambassador's little boy who, prodded by Miss Clavel's little girls, finally reforms.

613. ____. *Madeline and the Gypsies* (Viking, 1959) k–3. Twelve little girls in two straight lines visit a carnival, but only 11 return because Madeline is with the gypsies.

614. ____. *Madeline in London* (Viking, 1961) k–3. Madeline and her schoolmates go to London to visit the son of the Spanish ambassador. They attend his birthday party and give him, as their present, a horse that has been retired from Her Majesty's forces.

615. ____. *Madeline's Christmas* (Viking, 1985) k–3. With everyone else in bed sick with a cold on Christmas Eve, it is up to Madeline to run the school and she finds a remarkable helper in a rug-selling magician.

616. Bentley, Anne. *Grogg's Have a Wonderful Summer* (Deutsch, 1980) k–3. Because they can't afford to go to the seashore, Mr. Grogg puts sand, water and a beach hut in the back yard.

617. ____. *Grogg's Day Out* (Deutsch, 1981) k–3. The Grogg family build a bicycle for four and head for the country. They fix a farmer's sick tractor, have a fine afternoon visiting the farm, ending with tea, and then happily go home.

618. Berenstain, Michael. *Dwarks* (Bantam, 1983) 2–4. The Dwarks are a family of small, furry creatures like possums/humans. They live in a car at the dump. They raid garbage cans for food. One day a human takes the car with the Dwarks still inside.

619. ____. *Dwarks Meet Skunk Momma* (Bantam, 1984) 2–4. Dwarks are funny creatures with many adventures.

620. ____. *Dwarks at the Mall* (Bantam, 1985) 2–4. Dwarks are a small furry, fun-loving family who live in a cozy old car in a junkyard. Every night they disguise themselves as possums and raid the house of humans for their favorite food—garbage. One day Mama Dwark takes her family to a mall.

621. Berenstain, Stan. *Big Honey Hunt* (Beginner, 1962) k–3. Papa Bear tries to teach Small Bear how to find honey in a tree.

622. ____. *Bike Lesson* (Beginner, 1964) k–3. Small Bear wants to ride his new bike, but Father Bear wants even more to show him a few pointers. As a result, the young bear doesn't get to ride.

623. ____. *Bears' Picnic* (Beginner, 1966) k–3. In searching for a nice spot to have a picnic, Papa Bear leads his family from one disaster to another.

624. ____. *Bear Scouts* (Beginner, 1967) k–3. The further adventures of the Bear family also include information on holidays, weather and the seasons.

625. ____. *Bears' Vacation* (Beginner, 1968) k–3. The bear family goes to the seaside for its vacation and Dad tries to teach his son the rules of water safety.

626. ____. *Bears on Wheels* (Random, 1969) k–3. When the Bear Scouts go camping, Papa Bear goes along because he is sure he knows more than the guidebook.

627. ____. *Bears' Christmas* (Beginner, 1970) k–3. In his usual bungling way, Papa Bear teaches his son how to ski, sled and skate, using the things Santa brought for Christmas.

628. ____. *Bears in the Night* (Random, 1971) k–3. Bear cubs go on a rampage after being put to bed. Seven bears sneak out of bed, through the window, and across the dark countryside to investigate the source of a noise.

629. ____. *Berenstains' B Book* (Random, 1971) k–3. Big, brown bear, blue bull and beautiful baboon, only encounter objects or meet people whose names begin with the letter "B."

630. ____. *Bears' Almanac* (Beginner, 1973) k–3. The further adventures of the Bear family also include information on holidays, weather and the seasons.

631. ____. *Berenstain Bears' New Baby* (Random, 1974) k–3. Small Bear outgrows the bed his father made him when he was a baby—and none too soon.

632. ____. *Bear Detectives: Case of the Missing Pumpkin* (Beginner, 1975) k–3. The Bear family don their detective gear and try to solve the mystery of the missing prize pumpkin.

633. ____. *Bears' Nature Guide* (Random, 1975) k–3. On a nature walk Papa Bear introduces animals, plants and other beauties and wonders of the earth.

634. ____. *Berenstain Bears' Counting Book* (Random, 1976) k–3. While skating together, the Berenstain Bears introduce the numbers one through ten.

635. ____. *Berenstain Bears' Science Fair* (Random, 1977) k–3. Papa Bear teaches Small Bear and Sister about machines, matter and energy and helps them prepare projects for a science fair.

636. ____. *Berenstain Bears and the Spooky Old Tree* (Beginner, 1978) k–3. One by one, three brave little bears have second thoughts about exploring the interior of a spooky old tree.

637. ____. *Berestain Bears Go to School* (Random, 1978) k–3. Sister Bear, nervous about entering kindergarten, overcomes her fears when she discovers that school is really fun.

638. ____. *Berenstain Bears and the Missing Dinosaur Bone* (Beginner, 1980) k–3. The three Bear detectives and their dog Snuff, search for a dinosaur bone that is missing from the Bear museum. It turns out that Snuff has buried the bone; and the mystery is solved.

639. ____. *Berenstain Bears' Christmas Tree* (Random, 1980) k–3. During the Bears' search for a Christmas tree they are reminded of what Christmas is all about.

640. ____. *Berenstain Bears' Moving Day* (Random, 1981) k–3. The Bear family decides it is time to move to a larger house.

641. ____. *Berenstain Bears Visit the Dentist* (Random, 1981) k–3. Sister and Brother get some needed dental attention.

642. ____. *Berenstain Bears and the Sitter* (Random, 1981) k–3. Brother and Sister Bear are not happy with the idea of Mrs. Grizzle for a baby-sitter, but they find her drawstring bag very intriguing.

643. ____. *Berenstain Bears Go to the Doctor* (Random, 1981) k–3. Dr. Grizzly gives the Berenstain cubs a regular check-up.

644. ____. *Berenstain Bears in the Dark* (Random, 1982) k–3. When Brother Bear brings a spooky book from the library, bedtime and the dark becomes ominous and threatening to Sister Bear.

645. ____. *Berenstain Bears Go to Camp* (Random, 1982) k–3. The Berenstain cubs enjoy day camp, although they are dubious about the end-of-season pow-wow and sleep-out at the top of Skull Rock.

646. ____. *Berenstain Bears Get in a Fight* (Random, 1982) k–3. Mama Bear is called upon to put a halt to a minor disagreement between Brother and Sister Bear that has turned into major warfare.

647. ____. *Bear's Holiday* (Beginner, 1982) k–3.

648. ____. *Berenstain Bears and the Messy Room* (Random, 1983) k–3. The entire Bear family becomes involved in an attempt to clean and organize the cubs' messy room.

649. ____. *Berenstain Bears' Trouble with Money* (Random, 1983) k–3. Brother and Sister Bear learn important lessons about earning and spending money.

650. ____. *Berenstain Bears and the Truth* (Random, 1983) k–3. Brother and Sister Bear learn how important it is to tell the truth after they accidentally break Mama Bear's most favorite lamp.

651. ____. *Berenstain Bears Meet Santa Bear* (Random, 1984) k–3. Sister Bear enjoys Christmas preparations, especially getting her list ready—but on Christmas morning she realizes what Christmas is all about.

652. ____. *Berenstain Bears and Too Much TV* (Random, 1984) k–3. Concerned that the family is spending too much time in front of the television and neglecting the other activities, Mama Bear decides that there will be no more television watching for a week.

653. ____. *Berenstain Bears and the Dinosaurs* (Random, 1984) k–3. Brother Bear's interest in dinosaurs swells to the point where he is driving his whole family crazy.

654. ____. *Berenstain Bears and the Neighborly Skunk* (Random, 1984) k–3. When the Bears' new neighbor turns out to be a skunk, they have some reservations, which Mr. Skunk soon dispels.

655. ____. *Berenstain Bears Learn About Strangers* (Random, 1985) k–3. The Berenstain Bear cubs learn not to be overly friendly with strangers and give their rules for dealing with them.

656. ____. *Berenstain Bears and Too Much Junk Food* (Random, 1985) k–3. Mama Bear starts a campaign to convince her family that they are eating too much junk food.

657. ____. *Berenstain Bears Forget Their Manners* (Random, 1985) k–3. Mama Bear comes up with a plan to correct the Bear family's rude behavior.

658. ____. *Berenstain Bears on the Moon* (Beginner, 1985) k–3. Two Berenstain bears and their pup take a rocket ship to the moon.

659. ____. *Berenstain Bears and the Trouble with Friends* (Random, 1987) k–3. Lonely without friends her age to play with, Sister Bear is delighted when a new little girl cub moves into the house down the road.

660. ____. *Berenstain Bears, No Girls Allowed* (Random, 1986) k–3. Annoyed that Sister Bear always beats them at baseball and other "boy" type activities, her brother and the other male cubs try to exclude her from their new club.

661. ____. *Berenstain Bears' Trouble at School* (Random, 1986) k–3. When Brother Bear returns to school after being out sick, he get into a mess that gets worse and worse until Gramps gives him some advice.

662. ____. *Berenstain Bears Go Out for the Team* (Random, 1986) k–3. Brother and Sister Bear are such good baseball players that Papa Bear decides they should try out for the Bear Country Cub League.

663. ____. *Berenstain Bears and Too Much Birthday* (Random, 1986) k–3. Sister Bear is distressed that things don't go quite right at her birthday.

664. ____. *Berenstain Bears and the Bad Habit* (Random, 1986) k–3. With the help of her family, Sister Bear breaks her habit of biting her nails.

665. ____. *Berenstain Bears Get Stage Fright* (Random, 1986) k–3. Sister Bear worries about her lines in the school play while Brother Bear has no fear. Guess who forgets the lines during the performance.

666. ____. *Berenstain Bears and the Week at Grandma's* (Random, 1986) k–3. When Brother and

Sister Bear get left with their grandparents for a whole week, they had a better time than they expected.

667. ____. *Berenstain Bears on the Job* (Random, 1987) k–3. Two young bears speculate on all the things they could grow up to be including a bus driver, farmer, scientist, singer and computer programmer.

668. ____. *Berenstain Bears and the Missing Honey* (Random, 1987) k–3. Sister Bear, Brother Bear, Cousin Freda and his hound Snuff search for the thief who stole Papa Bear's blackberry honey.

669. ____. *Berenstain Bears and the Big Road Race* (Random, 1987) k–3. Papa Bear and his family watch as the little red car competes in a race against the big, orange, yellow, green and blue cars.

670. ____. *Berenstain Bears Blaze a Trail* (Random, 1987) k–3. Bumbling Papa Bear tries to help the Bear Scouts earn their merit badges in hiking.

671. ____. *Berenstain Bears and the Bigpaw Problem* (Random, 1988) k–3. Brother and Sister Bear are upset when their friend Bigpaw is arrested for being too big and clumsy.

672. ____. *Berenstain Bears Ready, Set, Go* (Random, 1988) k–3. The Bear family engage in competitive sports events while demonstrating to the reader the comparison of adjectives.

673. ____. *Berenstain Bears and the Ghost of the Forest* (Random, 1988) k–3. Papa Bear's attempt to scare a band of young campers by telling them about ghosts in the woods comes to an unexpected conclusion with a double ghost lesson.

674. ____. *Berenstain Bears and the Double Dare* (Random, 1988) k–3. Brother Bear feels excited about joining Too-Tall Grizzly's gang until the members dare him to steal one of Farmer Ben's juicy watermelons.

675. ____. *Berenstain Bears Get the Gimmies* (McKay, 1988) k–3. Gran and Gramps come up with a plan to help selfish Brother and Sister Bear get rid of a bad case of the galloping greedy gimmies.

676. ____. *Berenstain Bears and the Bad Dream* (Random, 1988) k–3. After viewing a scary movie about the Space Grizzlies, Brother Bear has a nightmare.

677. ____. *Berenstain Bears and Too Much Vacation* (Random, 1989) k–3. The Bear family experiences one mishap after another when they vacation in the Great Grizzly Mountains.

678. ____. *Berenstain Bears and the Slumber Party* (McKay, 1990) k–3. Lizzy Bruin's slumber party becomes even wilder when Too-Tall Grizzly and his friends decide to attend uninvited.

679. ____. *Berenstain Bears and the Prize Pumpkin* (Random, 1990) k–3. Mama Bear's reminders about the true meaning of Thanksgiving are left in the dust as the spirit of competition takes over and Papa Bear and the cubs begin a campaign to win first prize in the Thanksgiving pumpkin contest.

680. ____. *Berenstain Bears' Trouble with Pets* (Random, 1990) k–3. Brother and Sister Bear learn that a new puppy is not a plaything, but a responsibility.

681. ____. *Berenstain Bears Don't Pollute (Anymore)* (Random, 1991) k–3. Brother and Sister Bear learn about oil leaking into streams, dirty smoke pouring into the air and refuse collecting in lakes.

682. ____. *Berenstain Bears' Trick or Treat* (Random, 1991) k–3. The Berenstain Bear cubs have an adventure on Halloween night that proves Mother's adage, "Appearances can be deceiving."

683. ____. *Berenstain Bears at the Super-Duper Market* (Random, 1991) k–3.

684. ____. *Berenstain Bears Are a Family* (Random, 1991) k–3.

685. ____. *Berenstain Bears and Too Much Pressure* (Random, 1992) k–3. Members of the Bear family commit themselves to so many time-consuming activities that the resulting stress brings on a crisis and makes them admit that there are only so many hours in a day.

686. ____. *Berenstain Bears and the Trouble with Grown-Ups* (Random, 1992) k–3. Nagging parent bears and heedless cubs switch roles to show each other the difficulties of being grown-ups and children.

687. ____. *Berenstain Bears Accept No Substitutes* (Random, 1993) k–3. When a new substitute teacher comes to Bear Country School, the cubs learn that appearances can be deceiving.

688. ____. *Berenstain Bears and the Bully* (Random, 1993) k–3. When she takes a beating from the class bully, Sister Bear learns a valuable lesson in self-defense and forgiveness.

689. ____. *Berenstain Bears and the Female Fullback* (Random, 1993) k–3. Bothered by the fact that boys and girls are treated differently in the extracurricular activities at Bear Country School, Queenie McBear decides to get some changes made.

690. ____. *Berenstain Bears and the Wheelchair Commando* (Random, 1993) k–3. Harry, a new student at Bear Country School who is disabled and uses a wheelchair, has trouble making friends until the others discover that he is really very much like them.

691. ____. *Berenstain Bears and the New Girl in Town* (Random, 1993) k–3. Brother Bear's budding romance with Squire Grizzly's niece helps bring about an end to the fierce feud between the Grizzly and Bear clans.

692. ____. *Berenstain Bears and the Nerdy Nephews* (Random, 1993) k–3. Brother and Sister Bear don't realize the problems they will face when they agree to help Professor Actual Factuba's super-smart nephew fit in at school.

693. ____. *Berenstain Bears and the Red-Handed Thief* (Random, 1993) k–3. Mr. Dweebish, the new teacher at the Bear Country School, tries to explain to the class bully how democracy works.

694. ____. *Berenstain Bears and the Drug Free*

Zone (Random, 1993) k–3. Brother and Sister Bear try to solve the mystery of how illegal drugs are getting into their school.

695. ____. *Berenstain Bears Gotta Dance* (Random, 1993) k–3. With the help of Sister's ballet teacher, Brother Bear conquers his fear of dancing and can ask his favorite girl cub to the school dance.

696. ____. *Berenstain Bears on the Road* (Random, 1993) k–3.

697. ____. *Berenstain Bears and the Terrible Termite* (Random) k–3. Papa bear becomes the first victim of Raffish Ralph's termite insurance scam, but Brother and Sister Bear save the woodpile.

698. ____. *Berenstain Bears and the Coughing Catfish* (Random) k–3. Papa and the cubs go fishing and get a lesson in ecology and water pollution.

699. Beresford, Elizabeth. *Wombles* (Meredith, 1969) 5–8. The adventures of the Wombles who live underground and collect the things that untidy humans leave behind.

700. ____. *Wombles at Work* (Penguin, 1973) 5–8. The Wombles are back in Hyde Park coping with the litter left after a pop concert. A Russian womble called Omsk and a trained swan called HooBoo are added to the story.

701. ____. *Wombles in Danger* (Puffin, 1973) 5–8. The Wombles, who tidy up Wimbledon Common, plan a dangerous rescue when one of them is left outside with a human in the vicinity.

702. ____. *Wombles to the Rescue* (Benn, 1975) 5–8. Why is cousin Botany from Australia looking over the Mere through a tube? Great-Uncle Bulgaria is off to America taking Bungo with him. What is Madame Cholet's new recipe?

703. ____. *Wombling Free* (Benn, 1978) 5–8. The Wombles are aware of air and water pollution and litter. MacWomble comes from Loch Ness in his clockwork car to help in the conservation effort.

704. ____. *Snow Womble* (Benn, 1975) 5–8.

705. ____. *Wombles Book* (Puffin, 1975) 5–8.

706. ____. *Wombles Go Round the World* (Benn, 1980) 5–9. The Wombles of Wimbledon Common are sent on a trip around the world to write a new chapter in Womble history based on their own adventures. Orinoco, Bungo, Tomsk and Willington travel by balloon to visit America, Tokyo, Tibet and Australia.

707. ____. *Wombles Make a Clean Sweep* (Puffin, 1975) 5–8.

708. ____. *Invisible Wombles* (Benn, 1991) 5–8.

709. ____. *Wandering Wombles* (Benn, 1991) 5–8.

710. ____. *MacWombles Pipe Band* (Benn, 1992) 5–8.

711. ____. *Wombles of Wimbledon* (Puffin) 5–8.

712. Bergman, Thomas. *Thomas Till Three* (Kestrel, 1984) k–3. Thomas pees on the floor while putting Teddy on the pot. He fights with his friends.

713. ____. *Thomas's First 300 Days* (Kestrel, 1984) k–3. Thomas will soon have a baby brother or sister.

This book comforts the child who is anxious about this event.

714. Bergstrom, Gunilla. *Alfie Atkins and the Monster* (Farrar, 1979) k–3. Alfie's bad conscience over hitting a smaller boy creates a monster under his bed, which keeps him from sleeping at night.

715. ____. *Alfie Atkins and the Secret Friend* (Farrar, 1980) k–3. Alfie and his imaginary friend are making a pretend train. But by borrowing dad's pipe for a "chimney" Alfie realizes he is in serious trouble when the pipe disappears.

716. ____. *Who's Scaring Alfie Atkins?* (Farrar, 1987) k–3. Alfie must deal with a premonition that something is rustling and breathing heavily. He tries the rhyme his father taught him but the ghost won't go away.

717. ____. *You Have a Girlfriend, Alfie Atkins* (Farrar, 1988) k–3.

718. ____. *Alfie Atkins Doesn't Play with Girls* (Farrar, 1988) k–3. Alfie likes his friend Milly because she does not act the way he thinks girls always behave, whispering and laughing and playing dumb games, but he does worry about what his other male friends will think of him if he spends time with her.

719. ____. *Is That a Monster, Alfie Atkins?* (Farrar, 1989) k–3.

720. Berna, Paul. *Clue of the Black Cat* (Pantheon, 1965) 4–6. The Thiriet family lived in a small apartment. They were conned out of 10,000 francs with only a black cat as a lead to the criminals. Bobby and his friends actually catch the culprits.

721. ____. *Mule of the Expressway* (Pantheon, 1967) 4–6. Bobby Thiriet and his friends are interested in a lost and injured mule. Why does someone want to buy him at a high price? He was being used by crooks.

722. Berridge, Celia. *Hannah's New Boots* (Scholastic, 1992) k–3. A little girl is enthralled by her new boots which she wears everywhere she goes.

723. ____. *Hannah's Temper* (Scholastic, 1992) k–3. As one thing after another goes wrong for her, a toddler becomes increasingly bad-tempered.

724. Beskow, Elsa. *Peter in Blueberry Land* (Merrimack, 1894) k–3. Peter is seeking cranberries and blueberries for his mother's birthday. He meets king of Blueberry Land who makes Peter small and takes him to Blueberry Land where he meets Mrs. Cranberry and her daughters. He returns to proper size and goes home.

725. ____. *Peter and Lotta's Christmas* (Merrimack, 1947) k–3. The Christmas customs of a century ago in forest and homestead, with Christmas Goat. Aunt Lavender tells a tale of an enchanted prince.

726. ____. *Adventures of Peter and Lotta* (Merrimack, 1931) k–3. Peter and Lotta find a home for some kittens, they ride the bear in the circus in their borrowed clothes, lose their way in the woods and bathe in the brook. They still live with aunts Green, Brown and Lavender.

727. Bethancourt, T.E. *New York City Too Far from Tampa Blues* (Holiday, 1975) 5–8. Tom has adjustments to make as he tries for a corner shoeshine job. He and friend Aurelio form a group and perform for money. They even cut a record.

728. ____. *T.H.U.M.B.B.* (Holiday, 1983) 5–8. Tom and Aurelio sign up for the school band and form a marching band complete with cheerleaders and march in the St. Patrick's Day parade. The Hippest Underground Marching Band in Brooklyn.

729. Blanchi, John. *Bungalo Boys: Last of the True Rangers* (Bungalo, 1987) 2–4. Bungalo brothers, Little Shorty, Curly, Rufus and Johnny Red, riding trees instead of horses, apprehend the Beaver Gang, a group of beavers who wrestle trees.

730. ____. *Bungalo Boys III* (Bungalo, 1990) 2–4. The home hockey team, Granny and the Bungalo Boys take on three penguins and three bears.

731. Biegel, Paul. *Dwarfs of Nosegay* (Blackie, 1979) k–3. The dwarfs of Nosegay collect honey from the purple heather on the moorlands. A swarm of bees invade their territory. Peter goes to see the queen for help. The dwarfs and bees work out a solution.

732. ____. *Fattest Dwarf of Nosegay* (Blackie, 1980) k–3. Virgil is like a golf ball. He tries to get to a mirror to see how fat he really is. He has many adventures, some dangerous and frightening.

733. ____. *Virgil Nosegay and the Cake Hunt* (Blackie, 1981) k–3. Virgil is inquisitive and ventures into the world of humans. He wants to find a cake for Ianto Gnome's 1000th birthday. He stows away in Andy's picnic basket and was taken to school to be studied and flown to a palace. He finally escapes back home and with the cake!

734. ____. *Virgil and the Hupmobile* (Blackie, 1983) k–3. Virgil, the dwarf, sets off to meet rich Uncle Frederick but falls into the hands of thieves. He escapes in a Hupmobile and finds himself in a toy department. He just misses his uncle several times as Virgil is caught and rescued. They finally meet and Virgil finds Uncle Frederick a bore.

735. ____. *Virgil Nosegay's Wellington Boots* (Blackie, 1984) k–3. Jasper finds Virgil, the dwarf, and must save him from the trouble he gets into. A tale of goodies and badies held together with humor and imagination.

736. Biegel, Paul. *Little Captain* (Dent, 1971) 3–5. Little Captain comes from nowhere, lives alone, follows no rules. He patches up his boat; to make a propeller he melts down pennies and pours the stuff in a propeller-shaped hole in the sand.

737. ____. *Little Captain and the Pirate* (Blackie, 1980) 3–5. Little Captain must return seven treasure chests to their rightful owner. Scurvy-Boots, the pirate, stole them. Little Captain tries to deliver the

chests but the owner is now dead and the treasure must be delivered to his children.

738. Billam, Rosemary. *Fuzzy Rabbit* (Random, 1984) k–3. As Fuzzy Rabbit's mistress gets other newer toys, he begins to feel neglected and unloved.

739. ____. *Fuzzy Rabbit in the Park* (Random, 1985) k–3. Ellen takes Alpaca Rabbit to visit her friend Mary and her dog, Beetroot. Alpaca rides on Beetroot's back, but when the dog rushes out he takes the toy rabbit with him. Alpaca falls off and has adventures. But Beetroot finds and rescues him.

740. ____. *Fuzzy Rabbit and the Little Brother Problem* (Random, 1988) k–3. Both Ellen and her toy rabbit, Alpaca, try to avoid Ellen's rambunctious baby brother, Robert.

741. ____. *Fuzzy Rabbit Saves Christmas* (Random, 1991) k–3. Ellen and Robert leave Fuzzy Rabbit under the tree on Christmas Eve and he is thus on hand to save the holiday when Santa falls asleep in their sitting room.

742. Binnamin, Vivian. *Case of the Planetarium Puzzle* (Silver, 1990) k–3. The "Fantastic Fifteen" solve the puzzle of the strange salad the planetarium teacher has left for them.

743. ____. *Case of the Snoring Stegosaurus* (Silver, 1990) k–3. When Miss Whimsy's third grade class goes to the museum to see dinosaurs they investigate a snoring stegosaurus.

744. ____. *Case of the Anteaters Missing Lunch* (Silver, 1990) k–3. Miss Whimsy's "Fantastic Fifteen" visit the zoo and discover what happened to the anteater's lunch.

745. ____. *Case of the Mysterious Mermaid* (Silver, 1990) k–3. On a class visit to the aquarium, Miss Whimsy's 15 students search for a missing mermaid.

746. Binzen, William. *Alfred the Little Bear* (Doubleday, 1970) k–3. Alfred, a stuffed toy bear, goes exploring.

747. ____. *Alfred Goes House Hunting* (Doubleday, 1974) k–3. Tired of living in the playroom, a teddy bear goes in search of a home outdoors.

748. ____. *Alfred Goes Flying* (Doubleday, 1976) k–3. Alfred and his cousin Huckleberry are stuffed toy bears who build an airplane out of a tin can, a funnel and a piece of flashlight. They parachute to an island in Goose Lake.

749. Bird, Kenneth. *Dog Called Himself* (Macdonald, 1986) 4–6. Himself is the dog of an Irish tinker, Timothy. Both can converse intelligently. Himself is kidnapped by a villain called Von Tripp who wishes to make large sums of money by putting the dog on stage.

750. ____. *Stardom for Himself* (Macdonald, 1970) 4–6. Himself is a talking dog owned by an Irish tinker, Timothy. He escapes the clutches of a circus man only to find out he is morally blackmailed into doing an American T.V. commercial. He goes to America and catches a crook and makes money for an orphanage.

751. ____. *Himself in a Yellow Balloon* (Macdonald, 1971) 4–6. Evil triumphs for a rather long time, but the hero escapes and the good are rewarded in the end.

752. ____. *Himself and Macafferly's Queen* (Macdonald, 1969) 4–6. The Irish tinker, Timothy and Himself are in winter quarters in a castle where various adventures befall them all.

753. ____. *Himself and the Fake Santas* (Macdonald, 1970) 4–6. Charles Egan, the circus manager crosses Himself's path again; the monastery is hard up for money as usual and is helped by Kerry Crusher, a former bruiser.

754. ____. *Not a Word for Himself* (Macdonald, 1973) 4–6. Timothy Hogan, a tinker, is the owner of Himself an ex-circus dog that talks himself into trouble especially when an anti-animal widow aims to marry the tinker.

755. ____. *Himself and the Rooney Rebellion* (Macdonald, 1975) 4–6. Himself, a talking dog, Timothy, the tinker, and Mulligan the mule never get into serious trouble, however....

756. ____. *Himself and the Kerry Crusher* (Macdonald, 1976) 4–6. Himself is involved with a pop group looking for a "new sound." He howls to the music. Himself and Kerry Crusher, a wrestler, raise money for the church.

757. ____. *Himself and Tomorrow Ogre* (Macdonald, 1979) 4–6. Himself and his master Timothy meet a robot called Cass and an automatic bathroom presents problems.

758. ____. *Himself and the Golden Ghost* (Macdonald, 1980) 4–6. Himself, a talking dog, concerns himself with the eventual capture of two bullion thieves. Timothy, his master, buys a derelict cottage which turns out to be haunted.

759. ____. *Himself Beats the Bill* (Macdonald, 1996) 4–6. Himself stows away to Spain, is caught by the police and rescued by Tobias Twinkerton, manufacturer of Meaty Munch dog food. Himself gets as far as to make a speech in the House of Commons defeating the bill aimed at reducing the dog population.

760. Biro, Val. *Gumdrop Story of a Vintage Car* (Follett, 1966) k–3. Even as a wreck, Gumdrop, an antique jalopy, is appealing to one car buff who puts him together again.

761. ____. *Gumdrop and the Farmer's Friend* (Follett, 1967) k–3. Gumdrop, an Austin Clifton Twelve-four of 1926 and Farmer's Friend, a Fowler traction engine of 1903, prove mutually helpful in stopping two car thieves.

762. ____. *Gumdrop on the Move* (Follett, 1969) k–3. Gumdrop, a 1926 vintage Austin Healy Twelve-four, wasn't good enough for any of the various people who bought it until it finally returned to Mr. Oldcastle, its original owner.

763. ____. *Gumdrop at the Rally* (Follett, 1969) k–3. Gumdrop, an antique automobile, came in last in the vintage car rally but he certainly wasn't a loser.

764. ____. *Gumdrop Goes to London* (O'Hara, 1971) k–3. Gumdrop, the antique automobile, is invited to appear on BBC. But he encounters bandits. He blocks their escape route just as the 3 o'clock show begins and three million people watch the capture.

765. ____. *Gumdrop Finds a Friend* (Follett, 1973) k–3. When Mr. Oldcastle's vintage car Gumdrop is adopted by a small black dog, it becomes implicated in a smuggling operation.

766. ____. *Gumdrop and the Steamroller* (G. Stevens, 1976) k–3. Mr. Oldcastle's smart old car, has a near calamity with a steamroller.

767. ____. *Gumdrop on the Brighton Run* (Hodder, 1976) k–3. Gumdrop plans to join the Brighton Run for veteran cars. On his way there he picks up a bus load of Senior Citizens, the president of the club, a T.V. crew, a steam roller, a Model A—and arrives in grand style.

768. ____. *Gumdrop Posts a Letter* (Children's, 1976) Gumdrop, the antique car, helps catch the post office van so that Mr. Oldcastle, his owner, can mail an important letter.

769. ____. *Gumdrop Has a Birthday* (Follett, 1977) k–3. On the occasion of Gumdrop's fiftieth birthday, Mr. Oldcastle, enroute to buy a birthday cake, picks up some kind neighbors and disaster ensues.

770. ____. *Gumdrop Gets His Wings* (Follett, 1979) k–3. Mr. Oldcastle suffers many mishaps while trying to make Gumdrop the best looking and safest vintage car on the road.

771. ____. *Gumdrop and the Secret Switches* (Follett, 1981) k–3. Horace, the cocker spaniel, discovers secret switches that cause the vintage car Gumdrop to do things no other 1926 Austin Healy Twelve-four has ever done before.

772. ____. *Gumdrop Finds a Ghost* (Follett, 1980) k–3. At Mildew Manor, Gumdrop discovers a real ghost for the owner who has wanted one.

773. ____. *Gumdrop in Double Trouble* (Follett, 1982) k–3. With an ailing car full of children, Mr. Oldcastle pursues a thief into the midst of a children's fancy dress competition.

774. ____. *Gumdrop and Horace* (Hodder, 1982) k–3. Horace, the dog, stampedes through the market and enrages the shoppers.

775. ____. *Gumdrop at Sea* (Hodder, 1983) k–3. Mr. Oldcastle transports the Bumblebus family to the seaside in Gumdrop. The extra weight hurts Gumdrop's engine. Mr. Oldcastle fears a long search for another one but Horace the dog finds a replacement.

776. ____. *Gumdrop Has a Tummy Ache* (Hodder, 1984) k–3. Mechanical defects are interpreted in human terms.

777. ____. *Gumdrop's Magic Journal* (Knight, 1984) k–3. Gumdrop, the classic car, finds itself in a land where invented folk tales still exist.

778. ____. *Gumdrop Is the Best Car* (G. Stevens,

1984) k–3. Mr. Oldcastle's friends try to convince him that his vintage car Gumdrop is no good and should be replaced by a new one like theirs.

779. _____. *Gumdrop and the Great Sausage Caper* (G. Stevens, 1985) k–3. Disobeying orders to stay with the vintage car Gumdrop, Horace, the puppy, faces an angry crowd and a mean bulldog after finding some sausage.

780. _____. *Gumdrop and the Farmyard Caper* (G. Stevens, 1985) k–3. Mr. Oldcastle, his vintage car Gumdrop and his puppy, Horace, have an outdoor adventure in which Horace chases all the farm animals and meets a hungry fox.

781. _____. *Gumdrop Floats Away* (G. Stevens, 1985) k–3. At high tide, Mr. Oldcastle's puppy Horace floats away in his vintage car Gumdrop.

782. _____. *Gumdrop Catches a Cold* (G. Stevens, 1985) k–3. When Gumdrop, a vintage car, catches a cold, Mr. Oldcastle is concerned by his sneezing and wheezing and must save him from falling apart.

783. _____. *Gumdrop at the Zoo* (G. Stevens, 1985) k–3. A sick camel at the zoo leaves the children without rides, unless Gumdrop the vintage car can save the day.

784. _____. *Gumdrop and the Monster* (Hodder, 1985) k–3. There are some subtle social comments in this story of Gumdrop and Mr. Oldcastle.

785. _____. *Gumdrop on the Farm* (Hodder, 1985) k–3.

786. _____. *Gumdrop Goes Fishing* (Hodder, 1985) k–3.

787. _____. *Gumdrop Races a Train* (G. Stevens, 1986) k–3. Gumdrop has a race with his old friend, a green steam engine.

788. _____. *Gumdrop Gets a Life* (G. Stevens, 1986) k–3. While giving everyone a ride, Gumdrop the vintage car, gets stuck in the creek and needs help himself.

789. _____. *Gumdrop and the Dinosaur* (Hodder, 1988) k–3. Gumdrop travels with Dan and Dan's grandfather to prehistoric times where they find Topsy whose skeleton (Triceratops) is in a local museum. Gumdrop kills a dangerous Tyrannosaur and is made an honorary Dinosaur before he leaves.

790. _____. *Gumdrop and the Pirates* (Hodder, 1991) k–3.

791. _____. *Gumdrop's Merry Christmas* (Hodder, 1992) k–3. Gumdrop needs a new starter motor. Mr. Oldcastle gives his neighbor Mr. Bumblebus a lift to the village where he goes to a Christmas party. He went shopping and when he came back for Mr. Bumblebus he was given a lift to Father Christmas, and he gives Gumdrop a new starter motor as a present.

792. _____. *Gumdrop and the Bulldozer* (Hodder, 1992) k–3. Gumdrop helps get petitions against a highway being built. He saves the day by getting stuck on the soft muddy ground of the park. Down the hole where he is stuck appears an ancient vase full of old coins. It proves that the land intended for the road is of ancient importance and must be preserved.

793. _____. *Gumdrop Goes to School* (G. Stevens, 1986) k–3. When Mr. Oldcastle takes his vintage car Gumdrop to school to show to the students, one of them tries to go for a ride without permission.

794. Bishop, Bonnie. *Ralph Rides Away* (Doubleday, 1979) 3–5. When Mr. and Mrs. Muggs take their pet parrot Ralph on a picnic, he embarks on an exciting adventure.

795. Bissett, Bill. *Adventures of Yak* (Methuen, 1973) k–3.

796. Bjork, Christina. *Linnae in Monet's Garden* (Farrar, 1987) 2–4. Teaches children about the art and life of the impressionist painter Claude Monet through the tale of a little girl's love affair with his paintings.

797. _____. *Linnea's Almanac* (Farrar, 1989) 2–4. Mr. Bloom and Mr. Brush help Linnea celebrate the seasons. October is maple leaves and June is wildflowers.

798. _____. *Linnea's Windowsill Garden* (Farrar, 1992) 2–4. An illustrated introduction to plants and how they grow with information on creating a home garden.

799. Black, Christopher. Set in the year 2525, readers and sidekick Robot 2-Tor are involved in galactic action. In the following books they ward off armies of androids and space pirates; solve mysteries and basically save the world from destruction.

800. _____. *Android Invasion* (Dell, 1984) 5–8.

801. _____. *Dimension of Doom* (Dell, 1985) 5–8.

802. _____. *Lost Planets* (Dell, 1985) 5–8.

803. _____. *Moons of Mystery* (Dell, 1985) 5–8.

804. _____. *Cosmic Fun House* (Dell, 1985) 5–8.

805. _____. *Planets in Peril* (Dell, 1985) 5–8.

806. _____. *Weird Zone* (Dell, 1985) 5–8.

807. _____. *Galactic Raiders* (Dell, 1985) 5–8.

808. _____. *Exploding Suns* (Dell, 1986) 5–8.

809. _____. *Haunted Planets* (Dell, 1986) 5–8.

810. Blacker, Terence. *Ms. Wiz Spells Trouble* (Arch, 1991) 3–5. Something's weird about the new teacher at Public School 101—and it's not just her green eyes, black nail polish, and the rat she keeps up her sleeve.

811. _____. *In Control, Ms. Wiz?* (Arch, 1991) 3–5. Ms. Wiz is back again with plans to help her student friends prevent a nearby library from being closed down.

812. _____. *You're Under Arrest, Ms. Wiz* (Arch, 1991) 3–5. Lizzie Thompson is looking for her mysteriously missing cat and only the magical Ms. Wiz can help her.

813. Blackman, Malorie. *Girl Wonder and the Terrific Twins* (Dutton, 1991) 3–5. In the following books, the plans that Maxine, the Girl Wonder, and her younger brothers, the Terrific Twins, come up with usually means trouble for their mother.

814. ____. *Girl Wonder's Winter Adventures* (Dutton, 1993) 3–5.
815. ____. *Hurrican Betsy* (Dutton, 1993) 3–5.
816. ____. *Girl Wonder to the Rescue* (Dutton, 1994) 3–5.
817. ____. *Betsy Biggalow, the Detective* (Dutton, 1994) 3–5.
818. ____. *Betsy Biggalow Is Here* (Dutton, 1994) 3–5.

819. Blackwood, Mary. *Derek the Dinosaur* (Carolrhoda, 1987) k–3. While his Mesozoic contemporaries are out in the snow gobbling each other up, little green Derek sits cozily inside, knitting himself sweaters and shawls in preparation of the coming Ice Age.
820. ____. *Derek the Knitting Dinosaur* (Carolrhoda, 1987) k–3. Derek, a little green dinosaur, is somewhat worried that he likes to stay home and knit instead of acting like his ferocious brothers, but the onset of cold weather allows his knitting to become useful.

821. Blair, Anna. *Arthur the White House Mouse* (Media, 1975) k–3. There is a good old mouse who saves the little mice from traps.
822. ____. *Harrah for Arthur* (Media, 1983) k–3. Cousin Achille has a piece of paper needed by the president for his Washington's birthday speech.

823. Blake, Jon. *Roboskool* (Blackie, 1990) 4–6. A story of a futuristic school run by robots. The teachers enforce a routine of punishment, duty and fear.
824. ____. *Roboskool—The Revenge* (Blackie, 1992) 4–6. A story of a futuristic school run by robots. There is a need for the reader to be familiar with computer language.

825. Blake, Quentin. *Lester and the Unusual Pet* (Collins, 1975) 3–5. A strange, stick-like dragonesque creature who wanders about with his ally Otto avenge themselves on a dwarf called Nose with the help of a creature with a round head and two small feet.
826. ____. *Lester at the Seaside* (Collins, 1976) 3–5. Lester and his friend Otto and flop-eared Lorna find the pleasures of sea and sand.
827. ____. *Adventures of Lester* (Collins, 1978) 3–5. The adventures of Lester, Otto and flap-eared Lorna. They live by the Boots-&-Shoe tree. They organize their own Olympic games of cake weight guessing and throwing the Welly.

828. Blance, Ellen. Monster is a giant—purple, kind but not too clever. He bakes cookies, learns to ride a bike, and takes lessons in house building from Lady Monster. The following 20 books are about monster & Lady Monster in everyday activities.
829. ____. *Monster Goes to School* (Bowmar, 1973) k–3. At school Monster learns about time, drawing a clock with pictures that represent his day.
830. ____. *Monster on the Bus* (Bowmar, 1973) k–3.
831. ____. *Monster and the Magic Umbrella* (Bowmar, 1973) k–3.
832. ____. *Monster Has a Party* (Bowmar, 1973) k–3.
833. ____. *Monster Comes to the City* (Bowmar, 1973) k–3.
834. ____. *Monster at School* (Bowmar, 1973) k–3.
835. ____. *Monster Goes to the Museum* (Bowmar, 1973) k–3.
836. ____. *Monster Cleans His House* (Bowmar, 1973) k–3.
837. ____. *Monster Goes to the Zoo* (Bowmar, 1973) k–3.
838. ____. *Monster Looks for a Friend* (Bowmar, 1973) k–3.
839. ____. *Monster Looks for a House* (Bowmar, 1973) k–3.
840. ____. *Monster Buys a Pet* (Bowmar, 1976) k–3.
841. ____. *Monster Goes Around the Town* (Bowmar, 1976) k–3.
842. ____. *Monster Goes to the Beach* (Bowmar, 1976) k–3.
843. ____. *Monster Gets a Job* (Bowmar, 1976) k–3.
844. ____. *Monster and the Toy Sale* (Bowmar, 1976) k–3.
845. ____. *Monster Goes to the Circus* (Bowmar, 1976) k–3.
846. ____. *Monster Goes to the Hospital* (Bowmar, 1976) k–3.
847. ____. *Monster and the Surprise Cookie* (Bowmar, 1976) k–3.
848. ____. *Monster and the Mural* (Bowmar, 1976) k–3.

849. Blance, Ellen. *Monster Meets Lady Monster* (Bowmar, 1973) k–3.
850. ____. *Lady Monster Help Out* (Atheneum, 1976) k–3. Monster is a giant—purple, kind but not too clever. He bakes cookies, learns to ride a bike, and takes lessons in house building from Lady Monster.
851. ____. *Lady Monster Has a Plan* (Bowmar, 1976) k–3. Monster and the little boy decide to build a special house for their many animals but they are unsuccessful until Lady Monster helps out.
852. ____. *Monster, Lady Monster and the Bike Ride* (Bowmar, 1976) k–3.

853. Bland, Edith. *Wouldbegoods* (Coward, 1901) 5–8. The Bastable children want to do something nice for someone every day but these good intentions sometimes go awry.
854. ____. *Story of the Treasure Seekers* (Coward, 1987) 5–8. The Bastable children see the family and their house go downhill since the death of their mother. They hold a meeting and decide to raise needed money.
855. ____. *New Treasure Seekers* (Coward, 1962) 5–8. Continues the tales of Oswald, Dora, Dickey,

Alice, Noel and H.O. Bastable, who first appeared in *The Treasure Seekers*.

856. ____. *Bastables* (Watts, 1966) 5–8. Contains "Story of the Treasure Seekers" and "Wouldbe-goods."

857. Bland, Edith. *Five Children and It* (Random, 1959) 5–8. Psannead is a sand fairy whom a group of children find. He makes their lives exciting but it also confuses them.

858. ____. *Phoenix and the Carpet* (Random, 1960) 5–8. An accident with fireworks meant a new nursery carpet. When it arrives it was far from new but rolled in it was a strange egg. Anthea, Robert, Cyril and Jane have magical adventures.

859. ____. *Story of the Amulet* (Coward, 1984) 5–8. Five children travel back in time in search of the missing half of an amulet found in a Bloomsbury junk-shop. Their brief view of Atlantean civilization ends in a narrow escape from a tidal wave.

860. Blathwayt, Benedict. *Tangle and the Firesticks* (Knopf, 1987) k–3. When a tiny mischievous creature is banished from his homeland, he returns a hero after meeting a human and acquiring some firesticks.

861. ____. *Tangle and the Silver Bird* (Knopf, 1989) k–3. Tiny Tangle and his friend Burt accidentally take a ride on an airplane and have many adventures in a strange countryside before returning home.

862. Blaustein, Muriel. *Bedtime, Zachary* (Harper, 1987) k–3. Mr. and Mrs. Tiger have a hard time convincing their energetic cub, Zachary, to go to bed at night until they change roles and let him pretend to be the parent.

863. ____. *Play Ball, Zachary* (Harper, 1988) k–3. Zachary, the tiger cub, is good at art and reading and not good at sports, but he proves to his athletic father that they can still do things together.

864. ____. *Make Friends, Zachary* (Harper, 1990) k–3. Zachary, the tiger cub, gets into trouble when he plays with other children until his cousin Alfie joins him on a camping trip, and he finds having a friend is not so bad.

865. Blume, Judy. *Otherwise Known as Sheila the Great* (Dutton, 1972) 3–5. Peter finds out that Sheila is afraid of bugs, bees, water, noises, and more.

866. ____. *Tales of a Fourth Grade Nothing* (Dutton, 1972) 3–5. Peter is the younger brother of Fudge. Among other things Fudge swallows Peter's pet turtle. Peter has a friend in Sheila.

867. ____. *Superfudge* (Dutton, 1980) 3–5. Fudge's life is a mess. He moves from New York to New Jersey. He gets a baby sister called Tootsie. And he doesn't like either event.

868. ____. *The Pain and the Great One* (Bradbury, 1984) 4–6. A six-year-old (The Pain) and his eight-year-old sister (The Great One) see each other as troublemakers and the best loved in the family.

869. ____. *Fudge-A-Mania* (Dutton, 1990) 4–6. Pete describes the family vacation in Maine with the Tubmans, highlighted by the antics of his younger brother, Fudge.

870. Bly, Stephen. *Crystal's Blizzard Trek* (Cook, 1986) 5–8. Crystal, 14, her trusty horse, Caleb, her boyfriend and her Indian girlfriend solve a mystery.

871. ____. *Crystal's Solid Gold Discovery* (Cook, 1987) 5–8. Crystal finds a burlap bag buried in a pasture. This leads her and her father to foil a would-be swindler.

872. ____. *Crystal's Rodeo Debut* (Cook, 1987) 5–8. Crystal and her friend Betsy Jo find a novel that leads them to a cache of gold buried in a local valley in 1902.

873. ____. *Crystal's Grand Entry* (Cook, 1987) 5–8. Crystal, 14, solves mysteries. She and her Indian friend, Gabrielle and her boyfriend and her horse Caleb help each other with the clues they find.

874. ____. *Crystal's Mill Town Mystery* (Cook, 1987) 5–8. Taffy is vain and cloying. Her diary is stolen and eventually recovered. In her diary she reveals her lack of friends and some of her ugly thoughts. She gains friends in the process of getting her diary back.

875. ____. *Crystal's Perilous Ride* (Cook, 1987) 5–8. Crystal, 14, overcomes an obsession with her hair when she unwittingly becomes involved in a robbery at the rodeo.

876. Blyton, Enid. *Day with Mary Mouse* (Hodder, 1979) k–3. A story of a doll's house family with the usual domestic mishaps. Mary Mouse cares for Pip, Roundy and Melia. She also helps Daddy and Mummy.

877. ____. *Mary Mouse and Her Bicycle* (Hodder, 1979) k–3.

878. ____. *Mary Mouse and the Doll's House* (Ravette, 1988) k–3.

879. ____. *Mary Mouse on Holiday* (Ravette, 1988) k–3.

880. Blyton, Enid. *Secret Seven and the Circus Adventure* (Children's, 1950/1972) 4–6. The Secret Seven help apprehend a thief who works at the circus.

881. ____. *Secret Seven and the Tree House Adventure* (Children's, 1951/1972) 4–6. When a mistreated boy takes refuge in their tree house, the Secret Seven are determined to find out who he is hiding from.

882. ____. *Secret Seven Get Their Man* (Children's, 1953/1972) 4–6. In search of an activity for their secret society, the Secret Seven begin "shadowing" people and uncover a ring of dognappers.

883. ____. *Secret Seven and the Case of the Stolen Car* (Children's, 1954/1972) 4–6. The Secret Seven go after car thieves after two of their members disappear in a stolen car.

884. ____. *Secret Seven and the Hidden Cave Adventure* (Children's, 1955/1972) 4–6. When they move their meeting place to a hidden cave, the Secret Seven stumble across evidence in a mailbag robbery.

885. _____. *Secret Seven and the Grim Secret* (Children's, 1956/1972) 4–6. Seven friends are determined to find out who is occupying the big house that is supposed to be closed up while the owners are in Europe.

886. _____. *Secret Seven and the Missing Girl Mystery* (Children's, 1957/1972) 4–6. Accused of stealing, a girl runs away from a private school but is found and cleared by the Secret Seven.

887. _____. *Secret Seven and the Case of the Music Lover* (Children's 1958/1972) When seven young friends attempt to help a family whose house is burned down, they discover the family's plight is worse then they had expected.

888. _____. *Secret Seven and the Bonfire Adventure* (Children's, 1959/1972) A thief in town nearly spoils the Secret Seven's celebration of Guy Fawkes Day.

889. _____. *Secret Seven and the Old Fort Adventure* (Children's, 1960/1972) 4–6. With the help of a telescope and two interfering non–members, the Secret Seven recover some valuable paintings and capture the gang who stole them.

890. _____. *Secret Seven and the Case of the Missing Medals* (Children's, 1962/1972) The Secret Seven search for valued war medals stolen from an old general.

891. _____. *Secret Seven and the Case of the Old Horse* (Children's, 1963/1972) 4–6. The Secret Seven help a lame horse, assist in capturing horse thieves, and find a good job for an unhappy old man.

892. _____. *Secret Seven and the Case of the Dog Lover* (Children's, 1972) 4–6. When their own club dog becomes one of many missing from the neighborhood, the Secret Seven begin a search for the dog thief.

893. _____. *Secret Seven and the Mystery of the Empty House* (Children's, 1972) 4–6. Seven children and a dog find a stolen racehorse after some late night adventures with thieves.

894. _____. *Secret Seven and the Railroad Mystery* (Children's, 1972) 4–6. The Secret Seven, rivaled by the Famous Five, find a make-believe mystery turns into a real one and a train robbery is foiled.

895. Boegenhold, Betty. *Pippa Mouse* (Knopf, 1973) 3–5. Six stories about a little mouse and her animal friends in the woods.

896. _____. *Here's Pippa Again* (Knopf, 1975) 3–5. Six further adventures of Pippa Mouse and her animals friends.

897. _____. *Pippa Pops Out* (Random, 1979) 3–5. Four stories relate the further adventures of Pippa Mouse and her animal friends.

898. _____. *Hurray for Pippa* (Knopf, 1980) 3–5. More adventures of Pippa Mouse and her animal friends.

899. Bondal, Susi. *Bobby the Bear* (North-South, 1986) k–3. Two stories in which two stuffed toys swear undying devotion to each other.

900. _____. *Harry the Hare* (North-South, 1986) k–3. Harry is plunged into disaster when a dog rips his cottontail away, but he feels safe later when he is in bed with his owner.

901. Bond, Felicia. *Poinsettia and Her Family* (Crowell) k–3. Poinsettia thinks the house they live in is much too small for a family of nine pigs.

902. _____. *Poinsettia and the Firefighters* (Crowell, 1984) k–3. Lonely and afraid of the dark in her new room, Poinsettia Pig is comforted when she discovers that fire fighters are awake and keep watch during the night.

903. Bond, Michael. *Paddington's Lucky Day* (Random, 1973) k–3.

904. _____. *Paddington at the Station* (Houghton, 1982) k–3.

905. _____. *Paddington Does It Himself* (Houghton, 1982) k–3.

906. _____. *Paddington and the Knickerbocker Rainbow* (Putnam, 1984) k–3. Despite bad weather, Paddington and the Brown family have a very pleasant outing at the beach.

907. _____. *Paddington at the Zoo* (Putnam, 1984) k–3. Paddington makes six sandwiches to take on an outing to the zoo, where he reluctantly gets rid of them without eating a single one.

908. _____. *Paddington's Art Exhibition* (Putnam, 1985) k–3. After going to an outdoor art exhibition, Paddington decides to paint some pictures for an exhibition of his own. He thinks his paintings would look good if displayed in frames.

909. _____. *Paddington at the Fair* (Putnam, 1985) k–3. The Browns take Paddington to Hampstead Fair where he samples various amusement rides.

910. _____. *Paddington's Clock* (Houghton, 1986) k–3. Paddington gets up at 8 o'clock, cooks with Mrs. Brown, naps, writes postcards, drinks tea and goes to bed. A concept of time.

911. _____. *Please Look After This Bear* (Caedmon, 1986) k–3. Paddington Bear arrives at Paddington Station from deepest, darkest Peru and is taken home by the Brown family.

912. _____. *Paddington at the Airport* (Houghton, 1986) k–3. Paddington has a new experience at the airport. But can he handle this?

913. _____. *Paddington Cleans Up* (Putnam, 1986) k–3. Paddington wreaks havoc in the name of "spring cleaning" while Mrs. Brown is out.

914. _____. *Paddington at the Palace* (Putnam, 1986) k–3. Crowds of people prevent Paddington from seeing the Changing of the Guard at Buckingham Palace, but a special honor comes his way instead.

915. _____. *Paddington and the Christmas Shopping* (Caedmon, 1986) k–3. Paddington is befriended by a millionaire as he shops at a fancy London department store.

916. ____. *Paddington Posts a Letter* (Hutchison, 1986) k–3. Another adventure of Paddington Bear. These are published as board books and are intended for the very young children.
917. ____. *Paddington and the Marmalade Maze* (Houghton, 1988) k–3.
918. ____. *Paddington Turns Detective* (Houghton, 1991) k–3.
919. ____. *Paddington's Colors* (Viking, 1991) k–3. Paddington does his spring cleaning. He puts a red blanket in the washer. He adds a white sheet. The now pink sheet is hung to dry. But gray clouds threaten rain so Paddington pulls out his black umbrella, and so it goes.
920. ____. *Paddington on the River* (Houghton, 1991) k–3.
921. ____. *Paddington's Picnic* (Houghton, 1993) k–3.
922. ____. *Paddington Meets the Queen* (Houghton, 1993) k–3. Paddington's efforts to meet the Queen of England land him in some unusual sections of Buckingham Palace and the Tower of London.
923. ____. *Paddington Rides On* (Houghton, 1993) k–3. Paddington creates havoc when he decides to be a cowboy.

924. Bond, Michael. *Tales of Olga da Polga* (Macmillan, 1971) 3–5. Olga is a guinea pig with a funny imagination. She tells her fellow animals stories of great interest.
925. ____. *Olga Meets Her Match* (Hastings, 1973) 3–5. Olga, the guinea pig, matches her wits with Boris, another guinea pig who tells more outlandish tales than Olga.
926. ____. *Olga Makes a Wish* (EMC, 1977) 3–5. A guinea pig in a pet shop hopes to be chosen as a pet in a good home.
927. ____. *Olga Counts Her Blessings* (EMC, 1977) 3–5. Olga takes time to count the good things she has in her new home.
928. ____. *Olga Takes a Bite* (EMC, 1977) 3–5. The family cat's introduction to Olga the guinea pig proves to be painful.
929. ____. *Olga Makes Her Mark* (EMC, 1977) 3–5. Olga wonders how to let her new family know her name.
930. ____. *Olga Makes a Friend* (EMC, 1977) 3–5. Olga is introduced to a charmer named Boris.
931. ____. *Olga Carries On* (Hastings, 1977) 3–5. Olga is a guinea pig who fights a fire and sets a trap for an uninvited guest.
932. ____. *Olga's New Home* (EMC, 1977) 3–5. Olga is delighted when she is chosen to be a birthday present and leaves the pet shop to live in a hutch of her own.
933. ____. *Olga Takes Charge* (Viking, 1982) 3–5. Who will win a "sponsored Squeak?" Who will be knocked unconscious by a falling mulberry? Olga, the beautiful and accomplished guinea pig.
934. ____. *Complete Adventures of Olga da Polga* (Delacorte, 1983) 3–5. Olga, an imaginative guinea pig, keeps all her animal friends captivated with her stories and adventures.

935. Bond, Michael. *J.D. Polson and the Liberty Head Dime* (Mayflower, 1981) 4–6. J.D. Polson is a Texas armadillo who comes to New York and finds an 1894 Liberty Head dime. He goes to Get Ahead Advisors, Inc., and winds up president of the United States.
936. ____. *J.D. Polson and the Dillogate Affair* (Mayflower, 1981) 4–6. J.D., the armadillo, finds himself as president of the United States. His grand gesture is giving the United States back to the Red Indians.
937. Bond, Michael. *Paddington Bear* (Random, 1972/1992) k–3. Mr. and Mrs. Brown discover the now famous marmalade-loving, hat-wearing little bear from darkest Peru in London's Paddington station. A new edition, re-illustrated and adapted from Paddington's first adventures.
938. ____. *Padding at the Circus* (Houghton, 1973) k–3. In this adventure, Paddington Bear goes to the circus and ends up as part of the trapeze act.
939. ____. *Paddington Goes Shopping* (Collins, 1973) k–3. Paddington Bear's first visit to a new supermarket almost turns into a comic disaster, but instead he wins a prize.
940. ____. *Paddington's Garden* (Random, 1973) k–3. Paddington is given his own garden but doesn't know what to plant. He gets construction workers to help him design his garden.
941. ____. *Paddington's Storybook* (Houghton, 1974) k–3. Ten short stories featuring the inquisitive bear with a passion for marmalade sandwiches.
942. ____. *Paddington Goes to School* (Houghton, 1974) k–3. Paddington finds he must attend school but his antics turn school life topsy-turvy.
943. ____. *Paddington at the Seaside* (Houghton, 1975) k–3. Paddington Bear's visit to the beach takes a comic turn when he innocently interrupts a Punch and Judy show.
944. ____. *Paddington at the Tower* (Houghton, 1975) 4–6. When Paddington Bear visits the Tower of London, his suitcase full of marmalade sandwiches causes unexpected trouble.

945. Bond, Michael. *Here Comes Thursday* (Lothrop, 1967) 3–5. Thursday, an orphan mouse, who is to be adopted as the 20th child of the Cupboardosites arrives in their organ loft by balloon and this flight plays an unexpected part in saving the family grocery business.
946. ____. *Thursday Rides Again* (Lothrop, 1969) 3–5. The quiet country vacation of Thursday, the mouse, and his adopted family is interrupted when they are kidnapped by a strange gang and taken to France.
947. ____. *Thursday Ahoy* (Lothrop, 1970) 3–5. Thursday and family, Harris and Baron Munchen outfit and launch a showboat. They are piloted into

a penal colony. Thursday escapes and rescues the others.
948. ____. *Thursday in Paris* (Lothrop,) 3–5.

949. Bonfils, Bolette. *Peter's Package* (Crocodile, 1994) k–3. Peter is a bug-eyed, buck-toothed bunny. He receives a package containing a hot air balloon. Peter and Duck soar away, land in a desert and escape from a lion.
950. ____. *Peter Joins the Circus* (Crocodile, 1994) k–3.

951. Bonsall, Crosby. *Case of the Hungry Stranger* (Harper, 1963) 3–5. In this story all the club members set out to find the culprit who has taken the missing blueberry pie.
952. ____. *Case of the Cat's Meow* (Harper, 1965) 3–5. Snitch, Wizard, Skinny and Tubby, the same four private eyes who appeared in *Case of the Hungry Stranger* now solve the mystery of the puzzling disappearance of Snitch's cat Mildred.
953. ____. *Case of the Dumb Bells* (Harper, 1966) 3–5. Skinny, Wizard, Snitch and Tubby get involved in the mystery of crossed wires which cause doorbells to ring.
954. ____. *Case of the Double Cross* (Harper, 1980) 3–5. Marigold concocts a mystery that finally gets her and her friends into the boys' private eye club.
955. ____. *Case of the Scaredy Cats* (Harper, 1984) 3–5. A story of the events that occurred after the girls take over the boys' club house.

956. Boon, Emilie. *Peterkin's Wet Walk* (Random, 1984) k–3. Peterkin's walk with his friends becomes dangerous when the rain begins and they must rely on the help of a friendly mushroom and deer.
957. ____. *Peterkin Meets a Star* (Random, 1984) k–3. A child plucks a star from the sky and takes it home for his own; but the star is not happy in its new environment.
958. ____. *It's Spring, Peterkin* (Random, 1986) k–3. While enjoying the sights and sounds of a beautiful spring day with his animal friends, Peterkin helps a baby bird in distress.
959. ____. *Peterkin's Very Own Garden* (Random, 1987) k–3. Peterkin plants his own very first garden, but all the hungry animals want to share in the harvest.

960. Boon, John. *High Street Witch* (Hodder, 1986) k–3. Bronwen keeps witch supplies but tends to mix up her stock. When a farmer asks for help with his corn, he ends up with foot remedies. When a man asks for help with hair on his head, he gets apples growing there.
961. ____. *High Street Witch at the Zoo* (Hodder, 1988) k–3. Bronwen is a witch in a shop on High Street. She is called in to search for a snake missing from the zoo. Her instructions are misinterpreted and

exceeded, modified or ignored. The result is confusion.

962. Booth, Esma. *Kalena* (Longman, 1954) 5–8. Kalena is to be married to the chief's son, but the wedding is delayed and she is delighted. She pursues an education, meets a medical student and is no longer interested in the chief's son.
963. ____. *Kalena and Sana* (McKay, 1962) 5–8. A young African woman marries a doctor. She is an educated person and there is conflict between the old and the new ways, especially among the educated youth.

964. Bos, Burney. *Meet the Molisons* (North-South, 1995) k–3. Members of the Molison family exchange birthday presents, have a bike race, go camping and enjoy other activities.
965. ____. *Leave it to the Molisons* (North-South, 1995) k–3. A family of moles turns the most everyday events, such as washing dishes, wallpapering the living room, and visiting a museum, into remarkable events.
966. ____. *More From the Molisons* (North-South, 1995) k–3. A family of moles turn everyday events such as grocery shopping, ice-skating or painting their house into extraordinary occurrences.

967. Boshell, Gordon. *Captain Cobwebb and the Crustaks* (Harper, 1966) 3–5. The uncle of David and Toby introduces them to an undersea world where they do battle with an evil crab-like Crustaks.
968. ____. *Captain Cobwebb's Cowboys* (Macdonald, 1969) 3–5. Another adventure for David and Toby Green from Dingle Down village. This time they are in the Wild West where they meet a great variety of characters.
969. ____. *Captain Cobwebb* (Macdonald, 1973) 3–5. Toby and David, bored on a dull day at home, are spirited off to search for buried treasure with the aid of a map, a boat that travels through the air and a talking gorilla. They must defeat pirate Captain Morgan and locate the inland cave.
970. ____. *Captain Cobwebb's Adventures* (Macdonald, 1973) 3–5. Fun, thrills for David, Toby and Uncle Septimus and Mr. Stretch.
971. ____. *Captain Cobwebb and the Chinese Unicorn* (Macdonald, 1976) 3–5. Two boys and their uncle set out to save the Yeti and Sacred Unicorn. They meet wicked people, bandits and all sorts of dangers.
972. ____. *Captain Cobwebb and the Mischief Man* (Macdonald, 1977) 3–5. Toby and his brother David overthrow the Mischief Man who planned to create such chaos everywhere that he would be in command once the government relinquished power. The boys and Captain Cobwebb must overthrow the Mischief Man who is a stuffed Guy Fawkes come to life.
973. ____. *Captain Cobwebb and the Magic Drops* (Macdonald, 1979) 3–5. David and Toby are aboard

an invisible bus with Count Dolo. Captain Cobwebb sends Porcus, a flying pig, to guide the boys but he fails and the boys are caught by Count Dolo. They escape by using the Count's magical drops which turns them into a dog and an owl.

974. ____. *Captain and the Amazing Cloud* (Macdonald, 1980) 3–5. The adventures of David and Toby Green: a threat of world enslavement through a powerful drug, an island of battling Old English sheepdogs, a poison-compound, Count Birottini whose dirty scheme has got to be stopped.

975. Bouma, Paddy. *Bertie at the Dentist's* (Bodley, 1987) k–3.

976. ____. *Bertie Visits Granny* (Bodley, 1987) k–3.

977. ____. *Bertie in the Bag* (Bodley, 1988) k–3. It is Thomas' first day at his new school. He takes Bertie, his toy hippo, with him. He doesn't know anyone. Bertie begins to explore and unexpected things happen. Thomas meets Tim and then Thomas decides he doesn't need Bertie at school.

978. Bourgeois, Paulette. *Franklin in the Dark* (Scholastic, 1987) k–3. A turtle afraid of small dark places, and therefore of crawling into his shell, asks a variety of animals for advice, only to find out that each has a fear of its own.

979. ____. *Hurry Up, Franklin* (Scholastic, 1991) k–3. Even though he is very slow and has many distractions on the way, Franklin, the turtle, manages to get to Bear's house just in time for a special event.

980. ____. *Franklin Fibs* (Scholastic, 1992) k–3. Franklin, the little turtle, discovers that boasting to his friends can lead to problems. After a great deal of anxiety, Franklin realizes his mistake.

981. ____. *Franklin Is Lost* (Scholastic, 1992) k–3. Franklin wanders off while playing hide-and-seek with his friends.

982. ____. *Franklin Is Bossy* (Scholastic, 1994) k–3. Franklin, the turtle, learns that he cannot always be the leader or always have his way.

983. ____. *Franklin Is Messy* (Scholastic, 1994) k–3. Franklin's room is so messy he can't even find his favorite toys until his parents propose a solution.

984. Boyd, Lizi. *Willy and the Cardboard Boxes* (Viking, 1991) k–3. With the help of his imagination and a lot of empty boxes at his father's office, Willy flies into a colorful world where the boxes become a boat, horse, fire truck and more.

985. ____. *Sweet Dreams, Willy* (Viking, 1992) k–3. Not wanting to sleep at bedtime, Willy goes in search of others still awake, thus beginning adventures in the night world with birds, fish, the moon and the stars.

986. Boyle, Constance. *Story of the Little Owl* (Barron, 1985) k–3. Little Owl's lost teddy bear turns up in the park, next to a woman who plans to give it to her granddaughter.

987. ____. *Little Owl and the Weed* (Barron, 1985) k–3. Little Owl takes such good care of the weed growing in the doormat by the kitchen door that it soon becomes impossible to get in or out of the house.

988. ____. *Little Owl and the Tree House* (Barron, 1985) k–3. Little Owl gets his own tree house and then is flooded out of it.

989. ____. *Little Owl's Favorite Uncle* (Barron, 1985) k–3. Little Owl decides to be an actor when he grows up, like his Uncle Horace.

990. Bradford, Ann. *Mystery of the Live Ghosts* (Children's, 1978) k–3. Five children visit a haunted mansion on Halloween night and are confronted by the mystery of the live ghosts.

991. ____. *Mystery of the Missing Raccoon* (Children's, 1978) k–3. Five youngsters discover who is repeatedly letting a friendly raccoon out of his cage at the zoo.

992. ____. *Mystery in the Secret Club House* (Children's, 1978) k–3. Upon entering their secret clubhouse, five youngsters discover they have had a mysterious visitor.

993. ____. *Mystery of the Missing Dogs* (Children's, 1980) k–3. Barry's friends help him look for his missing dog and in the process uncover a dog-snatching ring.

994. ____. *Mystery at Misty Falls* (Children's, 1980) k–3. While at summer camp the five children from Maple Street solve the mystery of disappearing jewelry.

995. ____. *Mystery of the Square Footsteps* (Children's, 1980) k–3. While walking along the beach, five children find a set of strange, square footprints that lead them to a robot.

996. ____. *Mystery of the Blind Writer* (Children's, 1980) k–3. When a tape recorder is stolen from a blind writer, five children help him search for the thief.

997. ____. *Mystery at the Treehouse* (Children's, 1980) k–3. When televisions were stolen from their neighborhood, five children keep watch for the thief from their tree house.

998. ____. *Mystery of the Midget Clown* (Children's, 1980) k–3. When Steve, the midget, fails to show up for his job as clown at the circus, five children set out to find him.

999. Bradford, Jan. *Caroline Zucker Meets Her Match* (Troll, 1990) 4–6. When their mother's job takes her away overnight, Caroline and her younger sisters find themselves stuck with Mrs. Gladstone, a strict baby-sitter, whom the girls suspect is a witch.

1000. ____. *Caroline Zucker and the Birthday Disaster* (Troll, 1990) 4–6. Caroline, eight, is upset when she learns that she and her younger sister Vickie must share a birthday party.

1001. ____. *Caroline Zucker Makes a Big Mistake* (Troll, 1990) 4–6. After insisting that the redecoration of her bedroom include wallpaper with lavender daisies and yellow roses, Caroline, nine, changes her mind but cannot figure out what to do about her colorful mistake.

1002. ____. *Caroline Zucker Helps Out* (Troll, 1990) 4–6. Caroline, nine, receives unexpected help from her two younger sisters in her plans to earn her own spending money, but their efforts end up creating a big problem for the entire family.

1003. ____. *Caroline Zucker Gets Her Wish* (Troll, 1990) 4–6. Caroline makes exciting plans for her third grade class's participation in the school fair and tries to convince her mother to let her dress in a more attractive manner.

1004. ____. *Caroline Zucker Gets Even* (Troll, 1991) 4–6. Caroline and her best friend Maria plot to outwit Duncan, the most obnoxious boy in their third grade class.

1005. Bradman, Tony. *Dilly Goes to the Dentist* (Viking, 1987) 2–4. Dilly the dinosaur is scared of his first visit to the dentist, but the dentist knows how to make him relax.

1006. ____. *Dilly the Dinosaur* (Viking, 1987) 2–4. Relates the adventures of a young mischievous dinosaur.

1007. ____. *Dilly Tells the Truth* (Viking, 1988) 2–4. Dilly, the naughty little dinosaur, comes down with the measles, decides to tell the exact truth regardless of repercussions, holds his own Dinolympics in the back yard, and gets lost on a family outing.

1008. ____. *Dilly's Muddy Day* (Viking, 1988) 2–4.

1009. ____. *Dilly and the Tiger* (Viking, 1988) 2–4.

1010. ____. *Dilly: Worst Day Ever* (Viking, 1989) 2–4.

1011. ____. *Dilly and the Horror Movie* (Viking, 1989) 2–4. A mischievous young dinosaur goes to nursery school for the first time, gets a scare from a horror movie and has other adventures.

1012. ____. *Dilly the Angel* (Viking, 1990) 2–4.

1013. ____. *Dilly Goes on Holiday* (Viking, 1991) 2–4.

1014. ____. *Dilly the Dinosaur, Superstar* (Viking, 1991) 2–4.

1015. ____. *Dilly and the Swamp Lizard* (Viking, 1991) 2–4. Dilly goes to a museum and a gym club. He introduces his girlfriend and swamp lizard. His swamp lizard was a prize in the pet show, where Dilly causes chaos.

1016. ____. *Dilly Speaks Up* (Viking, 1991) 2–4. Dilly and his older sister go shopping. He is under her control and she decides what he will wear, answers for him when he is spoken to and hurries him away from his friends at the mall. Finally she relents and peace is restored.

1017. ____. *Dilly Goes to School* (Viking, 1992) 2–4.

1018. Bradman, Tony. *Adventure on Skull Island* (Barron, 1990) 4–6. Relates the exciting adventures of Jim and Molly who live with their pirate parents, the Bluebeards, on a pirate ship, *Good Ship Saucy Sally*. They tangle with Cap'n Swagg and his crew.

1019. ____. *Bluebeards: Mystery at Musket Bay* (Barron, 1990) 4–6. Villainous Cap'n Swagg and his crew are back—and they are out to trick the Bluebeard family again.

1020. ____. *Peril at the Pirate School* (Barron, 1990) 4–6. Young Molly and Jim are sent to Miss Prudence Proper's Academy for Pirate Pupils. But very soon Jim is in danger.

1021. Braithwaite, Althea. *Jeremy Mouse* (Rourke, 1974) k–3. Jeremy Mouse decides to explore the garden near his country house.

1022. ____. *Jeremy the Mouse and Cat* (Merrimack, 1981) k–3. Jeremy Mouse drops an apple on a sleeping cat who then keeps him cornered in a hole in a tree, until called for dinner.

1023. ____. *Jeremy Mouse Was Hungry* (Macmillan, 1981) k–3. Hungry Jeremy eats too many blackberries before dinner, then falls into a stream while reaching for more.

1024. Braithwaite, Althea. *Smith the Lonely Hedgehog* (Dinosaur, 1970) k–3. A story of the friendly relationships of two hedgehogs.

1025. ____. *Smith and Matilda* (Dinosaur, 1971) k–3. Two hedgehogs, living in a nice home, are about to have a baby.

1026. Braithwaite, Althea. *Victoria and the Flowerbed Children* (Dinosaur, 1970) k–3. An introduction to Victoria, a little girl with a vivid imagination.

1027. ____. *Victoria and the Balloon Keeper* (Dinosaur, 1971) k–3. A story about a little girl riding a rocking horse up into the sky.

1028. Braithwaite, Althea. *Desmond Meets a Stranger* (Rourke, 1970) k–3.

1029. ____. *Desmond at the Carnival* (Rourke, 1971) k–3. Desmond the Dinosaur restores two escaped lions to willing captivity by asking them about the grievances and getting them redressed.

1030. ____. *Desmond Goes Bathing* (Rourke, 1977) k–3. When Desmond's kind hostess loses her punt pole, he can of course, help out with his tail.

1031. ____. *Desmond and the Strangers* (Rourke, 1977) k–3. Desmond meets the president of the United States.

1032. ____. *Desmond Goes Boating* (Rourke, 1977) k–3. Desmond takes a ride in a punt. He rescues some passengers from a disabled boat and as a reward gets free passes to ride the boat.

1033. ____. *Desmond and the Fancy Dress Party* (Rourke, 1981) k–3. Desmond the dinosaur is invited to a costume party and decides to go as a dragon.

1034. ____. *Desmond the Dusty Dinosaur* (Rourke, 1981) k–3. Desmond moves to a new town but can't fit into his new bathtub or shower to get clean.

1035. ____. *Desmond Goes to New York* (Rourke, 1981) k–3. At the prime minister's invitation Desmond goes to the United States to see New York City and tell the people there about Great Britain.

1036. ____. *Desmond Goes to Scotland* (Rourke, 1973) k–3. Desmond goes to Scotland for his vacation and swims with the Loch Ness monster.

1037. ____. *Desmond and the Monsters* (Rourke, 1976) k–3. While on holiday, Desmond, a dinosaur, helps the townspeople to contain monsters on a rampage.

1038. Brand, Christianna. *Nurse Matilda* (Gregg, 1964) 4–6. The incorrigible Brown children, who devour nannies, nursemaids and governesses, finally meet their match.

1039. ____. *Nurse Matilda Goes to Town* (Dutton, 1968) 4–6. The adventures of the many Brown children the second time Nurse Matilda comes to take care of them. The mischievous children get better and better while Nurse Matilda becomes less and less ugly.

1040. ____. *Nurse Matilda Goes to the Hospital* (Brockhampton, 1975) 4–6. Nurse Matilda looks after the naughty Brown children. Nurse Matilda soon reforms them. The children are in the hospital by mistake and they cause havoc and pandemonium. While recovering at the seaside they have a sequence of riotous calamities.

1041. Brande, Marlie. *Nicholas* (Adapted by Streatfeild, Noel) (Follett, 1968) k–3. Nicholas creates a playmate for himself, and together with his dog, they become tiny an have a day of exciting adventures.

1042. ____. *Sleepy Nicholas* (Follett, 1970) k–3. Nothing anyone tried seemed to wake up sleepy Nicholas in the morning.

1043. Brandel, Marc. *Three Investigators and the Mystery of the Kidnapped Whale* (Random, 1983) 4–6. A stranded pilot whale needs to be rescued. It disappears from its makeshift pool. The three investigators find it and discover it is being used to find a sunken ship.

1044. ____. *Three Investigators and the Mystery of the Two-Toes Pigeon* (Random, 1984) 4–6. Jupe, Bob and Pete are in charge of a carrier pigeon. He is spirited away and replaced by another and they discover a group of ingenious thieves.

1045. ____. *Three Investigators and the Mystery of the Rogue's Reunion* (Random, 1985) 4–6. The reunion of a group of child movie stars plunges the three young detectives into a case of theft, kidnapping and false identify.

(For other books about the "Three Investigators," *see* Arden, William; Arthur, Robert; Carey, M.V.; West, Nick.)

1046. Brandenberg, Franz. *Leo and Emily* (Green-willow, 1981) 3–5. Leo and Emily make a trade that helps them to put on a magic show.

1047. ____. *Leo and Emily's Big Ideas* (Greenwillow, 1982) 3–5. Leo's and Emily's three big ideas involve the garden shed, the scare and flags for sale.

1048. ____. *Leo and Emily and the Dragon* (Greenwillow, 1984) 3–5. Leo and Emily pack their rucksacks and hike in search of a dragon.

1049. ____. *Leo and Emily's Zoo* (Greenwillow, 1988) 3–5. When Leo and Emily decide to open their own zoo and charge admission, they encounter a few problems, but their families find a unique way to run disaster into success.

1050. Brandenberg, Franz. *Aunt Nina and Her Nephews and Nieces* (Greenwillow, 1983) k–3. When Aunt Nina gives a birthday party for her cat, the guests receive surprise presents.

1051. ____. *Aunt Nina's Visit* (Greenwillow, 1984) k–3. Aunt Nina's six kittens disrupt a puppet show given by her nieces and nephews.

1052. ____. *Aunt Nina, Goodnight* (Greenwillow, 1989) k–3. When Aunt Nina's nephews and nieces spend the night, they find a multitude of excuses for not going to bed right away.

1053. Brandon, Brunsic. *Luther* (Eriksson, 1969) 2–4. Luther is a charming little black boy with racial pride and feelings of dignity and justice.

1054. ____. *Luther Haps* (Eriksson, 1971) 2–4. More adventures with little Black Luther as he copes with everyday life.

1055. Brandreth, Gyles. *Ghost at No. 13* (Viking, 1985) 4–6. A boy is constantly overshadowed by his achieving older sister. However, when a ghost comes to spend the holidays in his room it gives him an idea for a school project that is bigger and better than anything sister Susan could manage.

1056. ____. *Hiccups at No. 13* (Viking, 1987) 4–6. A story of a boy who develops a prolonged case of the hiccups, with results which are suitably disruptive and, in the end, surprisingly positive.

1057. Breinburg, Petronella. *My Brother Shawn* (Crowell, 1973) k–3. A story about a small boy's first day at nursery school. He is bewildered and tearful when his mother leaves him. Finally he is happy to be left there.

1058. ____. *Shawn Goes to School* (Crowell, 1973) k–3. Shawn's first day at school is described by his older sister. He had been looking forward to this first day but now he panics and cries. He is comforted and begins a small smile.

1059. ____. *Doctor Shawn* (Crowell, 1975) k–3. A little boy and his sister play at being doctor and nurse. It got a little messy when the cat knocked over the doll's crib and Shawn served banana pills.

1060. ____. *Shawn's Red Bike* (Crowell, 1976) k–3. Because his mother can't afford to buy the new red bicycle in the shop window, Shawn saves all the money he earns to buy it for himself.

1061. Breinburg, Petronella. *Sally Ann's Umbrella* (Bodley, 1975) k–3. A story of the West Indian children living in a mixed community.
1062. ____. *Sally Ann in the Snow* (Bodley, 1977) k–3. Sally Ann learns not to be afraid of tobogganing.
1063. ____. *Sally Ann's Skateboard* (Bodley, 1979) k–3. A story of being forced to disobey an order and doing something dangerous on a skateboard.

1064. Brennan, Joseph. *Gobo and the River* (Holt, 1985) 2–4. While trying to rescue Wembley when he falls in the river, Gobo accidentally knocks himself out and floats away to distant places he has never seen before.
    (For additional books on the Fraggles, Boober, Gobo, Mokey, Red or Wembley, *see* Calder, Lyn; Calmenson, Stephanie; Gilkow, Louise; Gilmour, H.B.; Grand, Rebecca; Muntean, Michaela; Perlberg, Deborah; Stevenson, Jocelyn; Teitelbaum, Michael; Weiss, Ellen; Young, David.)

1065. Brenner, Barbara. *Lion and Lamb* (Bantam, 1989) 3–5. Lamb sees through the fierce reputation of her friend Lion and recognizes him for the gentle pussycat he really is.
1066. ____. *Lion and Lamb Step Out* (Bantam, 1990) 3–5. Follows the adventures of two best friends, Lion and Lamb.

1067. Brenner, Barbara. *Five Pennies* (Knopf, 1963) k–3. Shows Nicky's plight and how it was resolved by a stray puppy, after he had spent all five pennies of the money he saved for a new pet, for supplies and housing.
1068. ____. *Nicky's Sister* (Knopf, 1966) k–3. Nicky, an only child, was jealous when a baby sister was born. He wanted a hamster. When the town bully spoke unkindly to the baby, Nicky decides to be a big brother.
1069. ____. *Beef Stew* (Random, 1990) k–3. Nicky has permission to bring a friend home for a dinner of beef stew. However, he can't persuade anyone to come home with him.

1070. Brenner, Barbara. *Mystery of the Plumed Serpent* (Knopf, 1972) 4–6. Elena and Michael are involved in a gang of thieves trying to smuggle Aztec treasures.
1071. ____. *Mystery of the Disappearing Dogs* (Knopf, 1982) 4–6. Elena and Michael are looking for dognappers. Elena is captured and rescued.

1072. Brent, Stuart. *Strange Disappearance of Mr. Toast* (Viking, 1964) 3–5. When they arrive at their summer home, mother, father and six children realize that Mr. Toast, their golden retriever, is not with them. Can he be lost?

1073. ____. *Mr. Toast and the Woolly Mammoth* (Viking, 1966) 3–5. The Brent family unearths the bones of a prehistoric animal. Their exploration trip starts out calmly but a landslide tosses them to the bottom of a quarry where Mr. Toast, a golden retriever, finds the bones.
1074. ____. *Mr. Toast and the Secret of Gold Hill* (Lippincott, 1970) 3–5. A family's gentlemanly dog accompanies them on a treasure hunt and is an indispensable member of the expedition.

1075. Brent-Dyer, E.M. *School at the Chalet* (Chambers, 1925) 4–6.
1076. ____. *Coming of Age at the Chalet School* (Collins, 1958/1982) 4–6. Joey Maynard is now a famous author but still untidy. She attends a reunion at her former school.
1077. ____. *Redheads at the Chalet School* (Collier, 1965) 4–6. This episode concerns Flavia who must change her name and is strictly forbidden to have anything to do with strangers.
1078. ____. *Chalet Girls in Camp* (Collins, 1969) 4–6.
1079. ____. *Genius at Chalet School* (Collins, 1969) 4–6.
1080. ____. *Prefects of the Chalet School* (Collins, 1970) 4–6.
1081. ____. *Carola Storms the Chalet School* (Collier, 1977) 4–6.
1082. ____. *Leader in the Chalet School* (Collins, 1985) 4–6. Shows how two dominant personalities effect a certain term. The new girl is called Jack and is determined to make her mark. She disrupts discipline with jokes and experiments. Len, oldest of the triplets, restores balance.
1083. ____. *Chalet School Wins the Trick* (Collins, 1985) 4–6. These events take place in the neighborhood not at the school. Jealousy and idle malice builds to a campaign of abuse and sabotage which causes trouble, especially to Josette.
1084. ____. *Chalet School Triplets* (Armada, 1986) 4–6. The family ties and camaraderie of the schoolgirls, carry no hint of sexuality.
1085. ____. *Lavendar Leigh at Chalet School* (Collins, 1991) 4–6.

1086. Brett, Jan. *Trouble with Trolls* (Putnam, 1992) k–3. While climbing Mount Baldy, Treva outwits some trolls who want to steal her dog.
1087. ____. *Christmas Trolls* (Putnam, 1993) k–3. When Treva investigates the disappearance of her family's Christmas things, she finds two mischievous trolls who have never had a Christmas of their own.

1088. Brett, Simon. *Three Detectives and the Missing Superstar* (Scribner, 1986) 4–6. The disappearance of Britain's leading rock star begins an investigation by the three detectives.
1089. ____. *Three Detectives and the Knight in Armor* (Scribner, 1987) 4–6. Stewie of the three de-

tectives, encounters a knight in armor near Scale-thorpe Castle. The crime is replacing armor with fiberglass replicas.

1090. Bridwell, Norman. *Clifford's Puppy Days* (Scholastic, 1989) k–3. Prequel. Recounts the antics of big, lovable Clifford when he was a very small puppy.

1091. ____. *Clifford Gets a Job* (Scholastic, 1965) k–3. Because he eats so much Mother and Dad say they must get rid of Clifford. Clifford gets a job as a side show attraction at the circus. He couldn't jump through the hoop or do other things a little dog can do so he left and went to a farm to round up cows and pull a wagon but he was too big and destructive. But in the end he caught some robbers and was paid in dog food.

1092. ____. *Clifford Takes A trip* (Scholastic, 1966) k–3. Clifford was left behind when Emily and her parents went on vacation. But Clifford missed them and sniffed his way to where they were. On the way he encountered a disabled truck, wet cement, traffic jams and a toll bridge. But he found Emily just in time to save her from a Mama bear.

1093. ____. *Clifford's Halloween* (Four Winds, 1967) k–3. Clifford, Emily's big dog, loves the holidays. He gets to blow his horn on New Year's Eve, wear a costume on Halloween, and much more.

1094. ____. *Clifford's Tricks* (Scholastic, 1969) k–3. A competition between Bruno, the new dog next door and Clifford. Clifford is only bigger and louder but in the end he saves the girls next door from drowning.

1095. ____. *Clifford, the Small Red Puppy* (Scholastic, 1972) k–3. Clifford begins life as a very small puppy, but once he starts growing into a very large red dog there seems no limit to his potential size.

1096. ____. *Clifford's Riddles* (Scholastic, 1974) k–3.

1097. ____. *Clifford's Good Deeds* (Scholastic, 1975) k–3. Clifford is a large shaggy dog whose efforts to be helpful result in comic mishaps.

1098. ____. *Clifford Goes to Hollywood* (Scholastic, 1980) k–3. Clifford goes to Hollywood and stars in a movie, but he decides he would rather stay home with Emily than live in Hollywood.

1099. ____. *Clifford's ABC* (Scholastic, 1983) k–3. Clifford romps among the 26 letters of the alphabet.

1100. ____. *Clifford's Christmas* (Scholastic, 1984) k–3. Clifford, the big red dog, and his friends celebrate Christmas and even get to meet Santa Claus.

1101. ____. *Clifford's Family* (Scholastic, 1984) k–3. Emily and Clifford visit the city. Clifford met his mother who hardly knew him, he'd grown so big. He went to visit a brother who was a rescue dog at the fire station, a sister who was a guide dog for the blind, another sister who was a farm dog and then his father who lived with a lot of kids.

1102. ____. *Clifford's Kitten* (Scholastic, 1984) k–3.

1103. ____. *Clifford's Pals* (Scholastic, 1985) k–3.

1104. ____. *Clifford at the Circus* (Scholastic, 1985) k–3. Clifford displays a host of talents when the circus comes to town.

1105. ____. *Count on Clifford* (Scholastic, 1985) k–3. Activities at a birthday part for Clifford, the big red dog, provide opportunities for counting balloons, presents and other objects from one to ten.

1106. ____. *Clifford and the Grouchy Neighbors* (Scholastic, 1985) k–3. Clifford is so huge that five children can ride on his back. He can pull up trees with his bare paws. No wonder the neighbors get grouchy.

1107. ____. *Clifford's Halloween* (Scholastic, 1986) k–3. Clifford was a very scary ghost last Halloween and Emily wonders what he should be this year.

1108. ____. *Clifford's Manners* (Scholastic, 1987) k–3. Clifford, the big red dog, offers some advice on basic good manners.

1109. ____. *Clifford's Birthday Party* (Scholastic, 1988) k–3. Clifford, the big, lovable, red dog, celebrates his birthday.

1110. ____. *Clifford, the Big Red Dog* (Scholastic, 1988) k–3. Emily Elizabeth describes the activities she enjoys with her very big, very red dog and tells how they care for each other.

1111. ____. *Where Is Clifford?* (Scholastic, 1989) k–3.

1112. ____. *Clifford's Happy Days* (Scholastic, 1990) k–3. A story showing just how much fun Clifford the dog really is.

1113. ____. *Clifford, We Love You* (Scholastic, 1991) k–3. When Clifford, the big red dog, is feeling sad, Emily Elizabeth and her friends do everything they can think of to cheer him up.

1114. ____. *Hello, Clifford with a Puppet* (Scholastic, 1991) k–3.

1115. ____. *Clifford the Small Red Dog, Follows His Nose* (Scholastic, 1992) k–3. When Clifford was a puppy he accidentally went off with the pizza deliveryman and had to follow his nose to find his way back home.

1116. ____. *Clifford's Thanksgiving* (Scholastic, 1993) k–3. Clifford pays a holiday call on his mom. He encounters a Clifford balloon at the Macy's Thanksgiving Parade.

1117. ____. *Clifford the Fire House Dog* (Scholastic, 1994) k–3.

1118. ____. *Clifford's First Easter* (Scholastic, 1995) k–3.

1119. Bridwell, Norman. *Clifford's Peekaboo* (Scholastic, 1991) k–3. The reader may guess where a small red puppy is hiding at each turn of the page.

1120. ____. *Clifford's Bedtime* (Scholastic, 1991) k–3. Clifford the small red puppy exasperates his mother by thinking of many ways to postpone bedtime.

1121. ____. *Clifford's Animal Sounds* (Scholastic, 1991) k–3. Clifford the small red puppy meets a variety of animals and discovers what kinds of sounds they make.

1122. ____. *Clifford's Bathtime* (Scholastic, 1991) k–3. A small red puppy doesn't want to take a bath, but finds it very enjoyable after all.

1123. ____. *Clifford Counts Bubbles* (Scholastic, 1992) k–3. Clifford the small red puppy counts from one to ten while playing with bubbles.

1124. ____. *Clifford's Noisy Day* (Scholastic, 1993) k–3. Clifford the small red puppy takes a walk in his neighborhood and hears all kinds of new sounds.

1125. Bridwell, Norman. *Witch Goes to School* (Scholastic, 1965) k–3. A normal day at school becomes special when the witch comes for a visit and uses her magic.

1126. ____. *Witch Next Door* (Scholastic, 1966) k–3. The new neighbor next door is not what the children expected—she's a witch. But the children find she is a friendly, helpful witch and they love her. When other children insult her she casts a gracious spell.

1127. ____. *Witch's Christmas* (Scholastic, 1986) k–3.

1128. ____. *Witch Grows Up* (Scholastic, 1987) k–3. The story of the witch next door. Her parents are kind but punish her when she is bad. Food flies in her mouth; her sandbox is a desert; her pool has an octopus and her bed tucks her in.

1129. ____. *Witch's Vacation* (Scholastic, 1987) k–3.

1130. Briggs, Raymond. *Father Christmas* (Puffin, 1973) k–3. Santa Claus hates wintry weather.

1131. ____. *Father Christmas Goes on Holiday* (Coward, 1975) k–3. Father Christmas visits France. Scotland, and Las Vegas while on his annual vacation.

1132. Bright, Robert. *Georgie* (Doubleday, 1944) k–3. Georgie was the friendly ghost who lived in the Whitakers' attic and haunted their house.

1133. ____. *Georgie to the Rescue* (Doubleday, 1956) k–3. Georgie, the friendly little ghost, goes on a trip to the city with the family whose house he haunts and rescues his friend, the owl, from captivity in the city zoo.

1134. ____. *Georgie's Halloween* (Doubleday, 1958) k–3. Georgie, the ghost, almost wins a prize for the best costume at the Halloween party.

1135. ____. *Georgie and the Robbers* (Doubleday, 1963) k–3. Georgie was too gentle to scare anyone until the night when thieves ransacked the house and Georgie knew this time he must be a big scary ghost.

1136. ____. *Georgie and the Magician* (Doubleday, 1966) k–3. When the barn burns down, the neighbors plan a benefit to rebuild it. Mr. Whittaker's scheduled to do magic tricks but his wand has lost its magic power. Georgie, Herman, the cat, and Miss Oliver, the owl, come to the rescue.

1137. ____. *Georgie and the Noisy Ghost* (Doubleday, 1971) k–3. Fortunately for the Whittakers and the noisy ghost in the beach cottage they rent for the summer, their personal quiet ghost Georgie comes along on the vacation.

1138. ____. *Georgie Goes West* (Doubleday, 1973) k–3. On a trip West, Georgie, the ghost, and his friends help to foil horse thieves.

1139. ____. *Georgie's Christmas Carol* (Doubleday, 1975) k–3. Back home in New England, Georgie, the little ghost, helps make Christmas a little merrier for everyone.

1140. ____. *Georgie and the Buried Treasure* (Doubleday, 1979) k–3. Georgie, the ghost, tries to discourage his neighbor from digging for buried treasure.

1141. ____. *Georgie and the Ball of Yarn* (Doubleday, 1983) k–3. Georgie, the ghost, and his rabbit friends help a little girl retrieve a lost ball of yarn.

1142. ____. *Georgie and the Baby Birds* (Doubleday, 1983) k–3. Georgie, a kind and helpful ghost, relocates a family of robins when the wind destroys their nest.

1143. ____. *Georgie and the Runaway Balloon* (Doubleday, 1983) k–3. When a field mouse gets carried away by a helium-filled balloon, Georgie, the ghost, plans a rescue.

1144. ____. *Georgie and the Little Dog* (Doubleday, 1983) k–3. With the help of a kindly ghost, an overprotected little dog that is never taken outside by its owner gets to go for a walk.

1145. Brimmer, Larry. *Country Bear's Good Neighbor* (Orchard, 1988) k–3. Country Bear borrows all the ingredients for a cake from his neighbor and then gives her the cake as a present.

1146. ____. *Country Bear's Surprise* (Orchard, 1991) k–3. Trying to find out why his birthday has been forgotten, Country Bear persists in interrupting the activities of what appears to be a secret club.

1147. Brinckloe, Julie. *Gordon Goes Camping* (Doubleday, 1975) 3–5. When he is finally ready to go camping, Gordon has to add one more thing to his supplies—a friend to help him carry them.

1148. ____. *Gordon's House* (Doubleday, 1976) 3–5. Five stories featuring the antics of Gordon the bear and his animal friends.

1149. Brinsmead, Hesba. *Longtime Passing* (Angus, 1971) 4–6. A story of the Truelana family of Australia. Five children live with mother and father. There are aunts and uncles. It is both funny and grim as they eke out a living by shooting rabbits and planting potatoes.

1150. ____. *Christmas at Longtime* (Angus, 1985) 4–6. Teddy lives at Longtime. She waits for Christmas when the children come home from school and college. Christmas day is celebrated. A nice story about life in New South Wales.

1151. Brisley, Joyce. *Milly-Molly-Mandy Stories* (McKay, 1928/1976) 3–5. Thirteen adventures with Millicent Margaret Amanda including those in which she spends a penny, goes blackberry picking, and makes a cozy.

1152. ____. *More of Milly-Molly-Mandy* (McKay, 1929/1976) 3–5. Thirteen more adventures of Milly-Molly-Mandy, among them having her photo taken, going to the movies, and going to the sea.

1153. ____. *Further Doings of Milly-Molly-Mandy* (McKay, 1932/1976) 3–5. Milly-Molly-Mandy's adventures include thatching a roof, camping out and motoring.

1154. ____. *Milly-Molly-Mandy and Billy Blunt* (McKay, 1967) 3–5. Nine adventures with Milly-Molly-Mandy and Billy Blunt including those in which they go excavating, ride a horse and have American visitors.

1155. ____. *Milly-Molly and Mandy Again* (McKay, 1977) 3–5. Milly-Molly-Mandy gets a new dress, participates in a wedding and acquires a playful duck.

1156. ____. *Milly-Molly-Mandy and Company* (McKay, 1977) 3–5. The adventures of a little English girl and her friends as they play dress–up, cook dinner, and take part in a film being made in their village.

1157. Brisson, Pat. *Your Best Friend, Kate* (Bradbury, 1989) 4–6. Kate's letters to her best friend back home chart her family's trip through the South and back up through Kentucky, Ohio, and Pennsylvania and reveal her true affection for her brother even though they fight.

1158. ____. *Kate Heads West* (Bradbury, 1990) 4–6. In a series of letters to her relatives and friends, Kate describes her trip through Oklahoma, Texas, New Mexico and Arizona with her best friend, Lucy and Lucy's parents.

1159. ____. *Kate on the Coast* (Macmillan, 1992) 4–6. Kate's letters to her best friend back home chronicle her family's move to the Pacific Northwest and their travels in Washington, Alaska, Canada, Oregon and Hawaii.

1160. Brittain, Bill. *Wizards and the Monster* (Harper, 1994) 4–6. Two young children discover their substitute teacher Mr. Merlin is King Arthur's magician. Simon wants to be a magician. Becky yearns to fight a monster. Instantly they are in a castle's great hall where each wish is fulfilled.

1161. ____. *Mystery of the Several Sevens* (Harper, 1994) 4–6. This time Simon, Becky and Merlin travel to fairyland where seven dwarfs are in trouble. Through solving a riddle, Simon outwits a witch and rescues the dwarfs.

1162. Brock, Emma. *Mary Makes a Cake* (Knopf, 1964) 3–5. Mary, nine, wants to learn to cook. Mother and Grandmother see her through the trials and triumphs of a birthday cake for Grandmother.

1163. ____. *Mary on Roller Skates* (Knopf, 1967) 3–5. Mary broke her ankle roller-skating and tries to skate and ride a bicycle in a cast. It heals before she goes to camp.

1164. ____. *Ballet for Mary* (Knopf, 1973) 3–5.

Mary has an uncanny ability to make things happen without any effort on her part and is devoted to ballet.

1165. Broeger, Achim. *Bruno* (Morrow, 1975) 4–6. Amazing things keep happening to Bruno: a dinosaur comes to dinner, snowmen and statues talk to him, and in one day he meets 42 doubles.

1166. ____. *Bruno Takes a Trip* (Morrow, 1978) 4–6. A little man, lacking funds to accept an invitation to visit friends, prepares himself and his pet raven in an addressed crate and are put aboard the baggage car. After the visit all his friends post themselves back to Bruno's.

1167. Brook, Judy. *Tim Mouse* (Lothrop, 1968) k–3. When some of his old friends are trapped in a cornfield which is being cut, a little mouse flies to their rescue in a red balloon.

1168. ____. *Tim and Helen Mouse* (Lothrop, 1970) k–3. This episode finds Tim married and much put upon by his charming young bride, who develops a mania for dressmaking.

1169. ____. *Tim Mouse and Father Christmas* (Lothrop, 1971) k–3. Tim Mouse has two children. He finds a Father Christmas cake decoration lying in the snow and takes it home. They know nothing about Christmas. But their visitor tells them all about it and they like it.

1170. ____. *Tim Mouse and the Major* (Lothrop, 1973) k–3. A mouse meets a toy soldier who trains the mice and forms an army.

1171. ____. *Tim Mouse Goes Down the Stream* (Lothrop, 1975) k–3. When Willy Frog is captured by fierce river rats, Tim Mouse sets sail on his little raft to the rescue.

1172. ____. *Tim Mouse Visits the Farm* (Lothrop, 1977) k–3. Tim Mouse and his friend, the hedgehog go to Barleybeans Farm for milk but succeed only in frightening the six cows over the hills and far away.

1173. Brook, Judy. *Noah's Ark* (Watts, 1973) 2–4. The Noah family rescues animals all over the world when the flood comes and returns them afterwards to their own countries.

1174. ____. *Mrs. Noah and the Animals* (Watts, 1978) 2–4. A 20th century Noah, dressed in contemporary clothes, Mrs. Noah gives the animals hot water bottles to comfort them. When they get noisy she feeds them to quiet them down.

1175. ____. *Mr. Noah's ABC* (Watts, 1979) 2–4. Mr. Noah is a farmer. The animals in the ark dance and leap to form letters of the alphabet.

1176. Brooke, Leslie. *Johnny Crow's Garden* (Warne, 1951) k–3. A story of a crow and all the animals in his garden.

1177. ____. *Johnny Crow's Party* (Warne, 1907) k–3. Johnny Crow plies rake and hoe to improve his garden. The other animals all come to his party and leave with a hearty vote of praise.

1178. ____. *Johnny Crow's New Garden* (Warne, 1935) k–3. Johnny Crow invites all his animal friends to visit his new garden.

1179. Brown, Jeff. *Flat Stanley* (Harper, 1964) 2–4. Stanley was crushed to a half-inch thickness when a bulletin board fell on him. He has numerous adventures, like traveling to California in an envelope, and hanging in a museum to trap art thieves—until his brother restores him.

1180. ____. *Stanley in Space* (Harper, 1991) 2–4. An American president personally phones Flat Stanley and invites him to take a trip in space as their ambassador to Tyrra. The Tyrrans are Liliputians and are no threat. Stanley finds a way to help them recover their economy which was devastated by destroyed vegetation.

1181. Brown, Laurie. *Rex and Lilly Playtime* (Little, 1995) k–3. Dinosaur siblings Rex and Lilly play at various activities.

1182. ____. *Rex and Lilly Family Time* (Little, 1995) k–3. Contains "Happy Birthday Mom," "Robot Bob," "Best Pet."

1183. Brown, Marc. *Arthur's Nose* (Little, 1976) k–3. Unhappy with his nose, Arthur visits the rhinologist to get a new one.

1184. ____. *Arthur's Eyes* (Little, 1979) k–3. His friends tease Arthur when he gets glasses, but he soon learns to wear them with pride.

1185. ____. *Arthur's Valentine* (Little, 1980) k–3. Arthur's wrong guess about the identity of the secret admirer sending him valentine messages leads to teasing, but later clues allow him to get his due.

1186. ____. *True Francine* (Little, 1981) k–3. Francine has a tough choice to make: protect her new best friend or tell the truth.

1187. ____. *Arthur's Halloween* (Little, 1982) k–3. Arthur finds everything about Halloween scary, including his little sister's costume, his morning snack and the big house on the corner.

1188. ____. *Arthur Goes to Camp* (Little, 1982) k–3. Arthur is not looking forward to Camp Meadowcroak, and when mysterious things start happening there, he decides to run away.

1189. ____. *Arthur's Thanksgiving* (Little, 1983) k–3. Arthur finds his role as director of the Thanksgiving play a difficult one, especially since no one will agree to play the turkey.

1190. ____. *Arthur's April Fool* (Little, 1983) k–3. Arthur worries about remembering his magic tricks for the April Fool's Day assembly and about Blinky's threats to pulverize him.

1191. ____. *Arthur's Christmas* (Little, 1984) k–3. Arthur puts a lot of time, effort and thought into his special present for Santa Claus.

1192. ____. *Arthur's Tooth* (Little, 1985) k–3.

Arthur, tired of being the only one in his class who still has all his baby teeth, waits impatiently for his loose tooth to fall out.

1193. ____. *Arthur's Teacher Trouble* (Little, 1986) k–3. Arthur, a third grader, is amazed when he is chosen to be in the school spellathon.

1194. ____. *Arthur's Baby* (Little, 1987) k–3. Arthur isn't sure he is happy about the new baby in the family, but when his sister asks for his help in handling the baby, Arthur feels much better.

1195. ____. *Arthur's Birthday* (Little, 1989) k–3. Their friends must decide which party to attend when Francine schedules her birthday party for the same day as Arthur's birthday party.

1196. ____. *Arthur's Pet Business* (Little, 1990) k–3. Arthur begins an earnest quest for a dog. His foray into the business world becomes quite an adventure for himself, his family and friends.

1197. ____. *Arthur Meets the President* (Little, 1991) k–3. When Arthur learns he has to recite his winning essay on television he is terrified, but D.W., his sister, saves the day.

1198. ____. *Arthur Babysits* (Little, 1992) k–3. Arthur's experience baby-sitting for the terrible Tibble Twins is as challenging as he expected, but he finally gets control by telling them a spooky story.

1199. ____. *Arthur's Family Vacation* (Little, 1993) k–3. Arthur is unhappy about going on vacation with his family, but he shows them how to make the best of a bad situation when they end up stuck in a motel because of rain.

1200. ____. *Arthur's New Puppy* (Little, 1993) k–3. Arthur's new puppy causes problems when it tears the living room apart, wets on everything and refuses to wear a leash.

1201. ____. *Arthur's Chicken Pox* (Little, 1994) k–3. Arthur, the aardvark, catches chicken pox a week before he is supposed to go to the circus.

1202. ____. *Arthur's Television Trouble* (Little, 1995) k–3. When Arthur sees an advertisement for the Amazing Doggy Treat Timer, he decides to earn enough money to buy it for his dog, Pal.

1203. ____. *Arthur's Computer Disaster* (Little, 1997) k–3. Arthur's mother leaves home for work and tells Arthur not to touch the computer. But the lure of the computer game Deep Dark Sea is too much. Just as Arthur and his friends are about to uncover the mystery of the deep, the computer keyboard crashes to the floor. What to do?

1204. Brown, Marc. *D.W. Flips* (Little, 1987) k–3. D.W., Arthur's self–assured little sister, discovers that lots of practice eventually helps her master the new routine in her gymnastics class.

1205. ____. *D.W., All Wet* (Little, 1988) k–3. D.W. bosses her brother Arthur into carrying her on his shoulders at the beach because she maintains that she hates the water, until she gets a big wet surprise.

1206. ____. *Roll Over D.W.* (Little, 1990) k–3.

1207. ____. *D.W. Rides Again* (Little, 1993) k–3.

D.W. graduates from a tricycle to her first two-wheeler and under Arthur's careful guidance learns the basics of bicycle safety.

1208. ____. *D.W. Thinks Big* (Little, 1993) k–3. Even though her brother says she is too little to help with the upcoming wedding. D.W. proves she is just the right size when disaster strikes during the ceremony.

1209. ____. *D.W., the Picky Eater* (Little, 1995) k–3. D.W. is Arthur the aardvark's little sister. She won't eat anything with eyes, never liver, and not many vegetables. She hates spinach, or so she thinks. She has to stay home when the family eats out.

1210. Brown, Michael. *Santa Mouse Meets Marmaduke* (Putnam, 1978) k–3. Bad Marmaduke Mouse impersonates and debunks Santa Claus. Santa Mouse retaliates angrily and they fight. The real Santa Claus appears, lectures them both and then forgives. The reformed Marmaduke receives his own Santa suit as a present.

1211. ____. *Santa Mouse* (Putnam, 1984) k–3. A mouse brushed his teeth and washed his paws. My goodness, no one gives a gift to Santa Claus. So he gives Santa some cheese and Santa reciprocates.

1212. ____. *Santa Mouse, Where Are You?* (Putnam, 1988) k–3. A slight tale of one of Santa's little helpers.

1213. Brown, Myra. *First Night Away from Home* (Watts, 1960) k–3. Stevie was so excited about spending the night at David's that he almost forgot to pack his pajamas. Mother helped him to remember everything.

1214. ____. *Pip Camps Out* (Golden Gate, 1966) k–3. A small loving account of the sort of things that might happen to any child who spends a summer night sleeping out in his own garden. It is lonelier and scarrier than he thought. But Pip's father joins him and it is a perfect adventure.

1215. ____. *Pip Moves Away* (Golden Gate, 1967) k–3. On moving day, Pip and his best friend watch the movers at work loading the van, and then at the new house Pip meets a boy with whom he investigates the neighborhood.

1216. Brown, Roy. *Undercover Boy* (Anderson, 1979) 5–8. Chips looks for his dog, Mitzi, and gets involved with a gang of teenaged dropouts. They are helping Larson, a jewel thief, escape the country. Chips acts as an undercover agent and gets into the gang. He steals the escape plans.

1217. ____. *Chips and the Crossword Game* (Anderson, 1979) 5–8. Chips delivers newspapers for Mr. Nuggett to earn money for hi-fi equipment. Chips is assisted(?) by his pet Labrador Mitzi. Chips and his friends look for a bicycle thief. Their only clue is a half-finished crossword puzzle. The leader of the thieving gang is Mr. Nuggett.

1218. ____. *Chips and the Black Moth* (Anderson, 1982) 5–8. Chips and his dog, Mitzi, get involved with a private plane and a horsebreeding establish-

ment. Why is security so heavy? Who are the stable girls? Why are unintentional trespassers fired on?

1219. ____. *Chips and the River Rat* (Anderson, 1982) 5–8. Chips, Regan's teenage son, meets a white-faced boy in a ruined church. He asks Chips for supplies and a sleeping bag. Chips complies but it is a trap. He is without his dog, Mitzi or his friend, a girl named George.

1220. Brown, Roy. *Chubb on the Trail* (Abelard, 1977) 3–5. Chubb of Scotland Yard is a basset hound, now retired but still solving crimes. A humorous look at Scotland Yard where Chubb will win out.

1221. ____. *Chubb to the Rescue* (Abelard, 1978) 3–5. Chubb is a basset hound who did police work. He is retired and now lives with Mr. Peacock. Together they rescue a baby who was thought to be kidnapped, thwart a gang of stray dogs and chase away some mice.

1222. ____. *Chubb Catches a Cold* (Anderson, 1980) 3–5. Chubb, the super sleuth dog, operates to protect the Princess of Glockenstein on her one night stop from London to Dover. The climax is a storm in a dog basket.

1223. Brown, Ruth. *Greyfriar's Bobby* (Dutton, 1995) k–3. A gardener tells of the devoted dog who lingered near his master's grave from 1858 until his own death in 1872 and who won the affection of an entire town in Scotland.

1224. ____. *Ghost of Greyfriar's Bobby* (Dutton, 1996) k–3. A boy and his sister find a fountain named after a dog, Bobby. They are invited to see his grave and hear his tale. The tale unfolds: Old Jock owns Bobby and Bobby is devoted to him. When Old Jock dies the dog keeps vigil by his grave for 14 years.

1225. Browne, Anthony. *Willy the Wimp* (Knopf, 1984) k–3. A young chimpanzee, tired of being bullied by the suburban gorilla gang, decides to build up his muscles so he won't be a wimp anymore.

1226. ____. *Willie the Champ* (Knopf, 1985) k–3. Not very good at sports or fighting, mild-mannered Willy nevertheless proves he's the champ when the local bully shows up.

1227. ____. *Willy and Hugh* (Knopf, 1991) k–3. Willy, the chimpanzee, is lonely until he meets Hugh Jape in the park, and the two become friends.

1228. Browne, Anthony. *Bear Hunt* (Atheneum, 1980) k–3. Hunters after a bear are constantly outwitted as Bear takes his pencil and draws his way out of each situation.

1229. ____. *Little Bear Book* (Doubleday, 1988) k–3. As Bear walks in the forest, with pencil in hand, he meets several grumpy forest dwellers and knows what to do for them.

1230. ____. *Bear Goes to Town* (Doubleday, 1989) k–3. Bear takes a walk in town and uses his magic pencil to rescue his new animal friends from an evil man in black.

1231. Browne, Anthony. *I Like Books* (Knopf, 1988) k–3. A young chimp declares his love for all kinds of books, from funny books and scary books to songbooks and strange books.

1232. ____. *Things I Like* (Knopf, 1989) k–3. A young chimp enumerates favorite playtime activities, from painting and riding a bike to paddling in the sea and partying with friends.

1233. Bruna, Dick. *Miffy* (Price, 1975) k–3. Mr. and Mrs. Rabbit's wish to have a baby is granted by an angel.

1234. ____. *Miffy at the Seaside* (Follett, 1970) k–3. An inquisitive bunny goes through the sounds and smells around him.

1235. ____. *Miffy at the Zoo* (Follett, 1970) k–3. Miffy and her devoted family spend a day at the zoo.

1236. ____. *Miffy in the Snow* (Follett, 1970) k–3. Miffy, a rabbit, makes a snowman and builds a house for a bird with frozen feathers.

1237. ____. *Miffy's Birthday* (Price, 1971) k–3. Title tells all.

1238. ____. *Miffy in the Hospital* (Methuen, 1976) k–3. Relates Miffy's experiences in the hospital.

1239. ____. *Miffy's Dream* (Methuen, 1979) k–3. Miffy meets a playmate from another land in her dream.

1240. ____. *Miffy at the Beach* (Methuen, 1980) k–3.

1241. ____. *Miffy Goes to School* (Price, 1984) k–3. Miffy, a baby rabbit, has her first adventure at school.

1242. ____. *Miffy at the Playground* (Price, 1984) k–3. Miffy the rabbit goes to the playground with her parents.

1243. ____. *Miffy Goes Flying* (Price, 1984) k–3. Miffy's uncle takes her for a ride in his airplane.

1244. ____. *Miffy's Bicycle* (Price, 1984) k–3.

1245. Bruna, Dick. *Snuffy and the Fire* (Two Continent, 1975) k–3. After Snuffy alerts the firemen to a fire in the yellow house, he becomes their mascot.

1246. ____. *Snuffy* (Two Continent, 1975) k–3. Snuffy the dog locates Mrs. Pockelton's lost child.

1247. Brunhoff, Jean de. *Story of Babar* (Random, 1933/1960) k–3. Babar ran away from the jungle and went to live in a house with a lady who lived in Paris. His cousins Arthur and Celestine came to visit and Babar returned with them, and once there he was chosen king of the jungle.

1248. ____. *Travels of Babar* (Random, 1934/1961) k–3. Babar and Celeste have many adventures as they travel around the world.

1249. ____. *Babar the King* (Random, 1935/1986) k–3. After making peace with the rhinoceros, King Babar and Queen Celeste plan a model city and live happily with their friends and subjects in the country of elephants.

1250. ____. *Zephir's Holiday* (Random, 1937/1993) k–3.

1251. ____. *Babar at Home* (Random, 1938) k–3. In Celesteville it is duly proclaimed that the royal household is expecting a happy event and that it will be announced by the firing of a cannon. It fires three times and Flora, Pom and Alexander are born.

1252. ____. *Babar and His Children* (Random, 1938) k–3. Everyone rejoiced when Queen Celeste's triplets were born. They were named Pam, Flora and Alexander. As they grew up, they had mishaps and adventures but help always turned up in the nick of time.

1253. ____. *Babar and Father Christmas* (Random, 1941) k–3. A story of the adventures of the elephant king, Babar, during his search for Father Christmas and what happened when he was found.

1254. ____. *Babar and Zephir* (Random, 1942) k–3. Zephir, the monkey goes home for the holidays, where he is able to rescue Princess Isabelle.

1255. ____. *Babar and the Rascal Arthur* (Random, 1946) k–3. A story of Cousin Arthur's stolen ride on a plane and his rescue by Babar.

1256. ____. *Babar's Picnic* (Random, 1959/1967) k–3. Babar's children pack their Indian suits and go on a picnic, meet some savages, help to capture a wild boar and have exciting adventures during the rain.

1257. ____. *Babar's Visit to Bird Island* (Random, 1952) k–3. The elephant royal family pays a visit to the Bird King and Queen.

1258. ____. *Babar's Fair* (Random, 1954) k–3. In honor of Celesteville a great fair is held with appropriate seating for all animals. Alexander is in danger of drowning but is rescued by the little green duck.

1259. ____. *Babar and the Professor* (Random, 1957) k–3. Life in Celesteville gets a pick-me-up with a visit from the Old Lady and her brother, Professor Grifaton.

1260. Brunhoff, Jean de. *Serafina the Giraffe* (World, 1961) k–3. Serafina planned to bake a banana-flour cake for her grandmother's birthday. Her friends Patrick the rabbit, Hugo the kangaroo, Beryl the frog and Ernest the crocodile were happy to help.

1261. ____. *Serafina's Lucky Find* (World, 1962) k–3. The animals' boat renovating project runs aground when the rabbit, the frog and the crocodile prefer play to work and Serafina the giraffe discovers she knows nothing about sailing a boat once it is ready to go.

1262. ____. *Captain Serafina* (World, 1963) k–3. An adventure of the giraffe, Serafina, and her friends, Ernest the crocodile, Hugo the kangaroo, Beryl the frog and Patrick the rabbit. They are off in a boat for a picnic on the beach.

1263. Brunhoff, Laurent. *Babar's Castle* (Random, 1962) k–3. King Babar, Queen Celeste and their family move into Castle Bonnetrompe. Alexander, a child elephant, knows that the castle has an underground passage so the children go looking for it.

1264. ____. *Babar Comes to America* (Random, 1965) k–3. Babar finally has come to America. His adventures in what is, to him anyway, a strange land are related.

1265. ____. *Babar Loses His Crown* (Random, 1967) k–3. The red suitcase in which Babar has his crown is exchanged for one with a flute, and since he can't wear a flute, he and his family chase after the man they think has the crown.

1266. ____. *Babar's Moon Trip* (Random, 1968) k–3.

1267. ____. *Babar's Birthday Surprise* (Random, 1970) k–3. Queen Celeste decides to surprise King Babar with a statue of himself for his birthday but has a difficult time keeping it a secret.

1268. ____. *Babar Visits Another Planet* (Random, 1972) k–3. Babar and his friends are kidnapped and taken to another planet, a friendly, floating planet.

1269. ____. *Babar and the Secret Planet* (Random, 1973) k–3. Babar is kidnapped and carried off to a planet inhabited by space elephants. He manages to return his party safely to Celesteville, but not without lots of adventure and some frights.

1270. ____. *Babar Bakes a Cake* (Random, 1975) k–3. Babar puts his cake in the oven. Arthur is going to make the icing. The children keep the birthday girl out of the kitchen. Babar lets the cake burn and they all go to the bakery for a new cake. Celeste is delighted and blows out all the candles.

1271. ____. *Babar to the Rescue* (Random, 1975) k–3. Babar and Arthur have a mission to fly medical supplies to 22 isolated mountain climbers. Arthur loses his balance and parachutes out. He lands near the plane and gets back to the city.

1272. ____. *Babar's Concert* (Random, 1975) k–3. A typical story of Babar and his family. This time they are involved in a concert assisted by a monkey on the violin.

1273. ____. *Babar's Christmas Tree* (Random, 1975) k–3. They locate, set up and decorate a tall Christmas tree. Only to have Zephir, the monkey, swing wildly down from the top.

1274. ____. *Babar's Bookmobile* (Random, 1975) k–3.

1275. ____. *Babar and the Wully-Wully* (Random, 1975) k–3. Wully-Wully almost causes a war between the elephants and the rhinos, who both want the lovable creature as a pet.

1276. ____. *Babar Saves the Day* (Random, 1976) k–3. Babar convinces Kawak the parrot not to run away following an argument, but to return to Olala's singing group.

1277. ____. *Babar Learns to Cook* (Random, 1978) k–3. After Babar and Celeste watch him on television, Truffles, the most famous chef in Celesteville, comes to the palace to give cooking lessons.

1278. ____. *Babar's Mystery* (Methuen, 1978) k–3. Thievish crocodiles and their rhino boss play havoc at Celesteville-at-Sea till Babar and his family, helped by the old lady, bring them to justice.

1279. ____. *Babar the Magician* (Random, 1980) k–3. Babar takes magic lessons and puts on a show for his family and friends.

1280. ____. *Babar's ABC* (Random, 1983) k–3. The residents of Celesteville present the letters of the alphabet, accompanied by words and sentences for each letter.

1281. ____. *Babar's Book of Color* (Random, 1984) k–3. Pom, Flora, Alexander and Arthur go to Babar's studio and learn about mixing and using colors.

1282. ____. *Meet Babar and His Family* (Random, 1985) k–3. Babar and his family enjoy a variety of activities during each of the year's seasons.

1283. ____. *Babar and the Ghost* (Random, 1981/1986) k–3. The ghost of the Black Castle follows Babar and his family and friends back to Celesteville.

1284. ____. *Babar's Counting Book* (Random, 1986) k–3. Babar's three children go for a walk and count what they see.

1285. ____. *Babar's Little Girl* (Random, 1987) k–3. The arrival of a new baby, Isabelle, creates much excitement in Babar's family, particularly after she learns to walk and gets lost in the mountains.

1286. ____. *Babar's Friend Zephir* (Random, 1988) k–3. A story about a little monkey, home from school in Celesteville and how he was helped by a mermaid in his rescue of the monkey princess.

1287. ____. *Babar's Little Circus Star* (Random, 1988) k–3. Unhappy because she is the smallest in the family, Isabelle discovers that being little has its advantages when she is asked to perform in the circus.

1288. ____. *Babar Goes Camping* (Random, 1991) k–3.

1289. ____. *Babar and the Doctor* (Random, 1991) k–3.

1290. ____. *Babar the Pilot* (Random, 1991) k–3.

1291. ____. *Babar's Battle* (Random, 1992) k–3. Discord between the elephants and the rhinoceroses threaten to lead to war, but King Babar has a plan of his own.

1292. ____. *Babar's Car* (Random, 1993) k–3. A book with four wheels giving the appearance of a car.

1293. ____. *Rescue of Babar* (Random, 1993) k–3. With the help of her animal friends, little Isabelle rescues her father, King Babar, from the land of the lost elephants.

1294. Brunhoff, Laurent. *Bonhomme* (Pantheon, 1965) k–3. Emilie first sees Bonhomme, the little animal with the horn on top of his head, through her telescope—and it is love at first sight for both of them.

1295. ____. *Bonhomme and the Huge Beast* (Random, 1975) k–3. Emilie and her imaginary friend Bonhomme tell each other stories and go looking for the strange beast Randolphe. They have small adventures with Huge Frog and Stone Horse.

1296. Brustlein, Janice. *Little Bear's Sunday Breakfast* (Lothrop, 1958) k–3. The adventures of a bear who goes into a house and makes himself at home pretty much as Goldilocks did at the Three Bears residence. Then he discovers that Goldilocks lives there.

1297. ____. *Little Bear's Pancake Party* (Lothrop,

1960) k–3. The story of a greedy little bear who tries to have a pancake party but doesn't realize that the pancakes have to be cooked. This problem is finally solved with the help of some other smarter animals.

1298. ____. *Little Bear's Christmas* (Lothrop, 1964) k–3. Little Bear woke up early from his winter sleep. All the houses were lit up and doors had wreaths tied with red ribbons. Little Bear had never seen anything like this before. It was his first Christmas Eve.

1299. ____. *Little Bear Marches in the St. Patrick's Day Parade* (Lothrop, 1967) k–3. In return for being allowed to wear a green hat, march in the parade and beat the drum, Little Bear stops the rain with his magic umbrella.

1300. ____. *Little Bear's Thanksgiving* (Lothrop, 1967) k–3. When Little Bear receives an invitation for Thanksgiving dinner he is afraid he will sleep through it, but the other animals promise to wake him in time.

1301. ____. *Little Bear Learns to Read the Cookbook* (Lothrop, 1969) k–3. Little Bear can't do many of the things the other animals do so he learns to do something they can't.

1302. ____. *Little Bear's New Year's Party* (Lothrop, 1973) k–3. Little Bear gives a New Year's party and welcomes more guests than he invited.

1303. Buchanan, Heather. *Emily Mouse's First Adventure* (Dial, 1985) k–3. Emily Mouse leaves her family's teapot home and finds adventure in the house beyond.

1304. ____. *Emily Mouse Saves the Day* (Dial, 1985) k–3. The patchwork jackets Emily Mouse makes for her brothers saves their lives.

1305. ____. *Emily Mouse's Garden* (Dial, 1986) k–3. Emily runs into the garden chasing her two baby brothers. Seeing the flowers inspire her to plant her own garden.

1306. ____. *Emily Mouse's Beach House* (Dial, 1987) k–3. Emily leaves her family in its teapot home, travels to the beach, builds a sand castle and meets George when he rescues her family from her collapsed house.

1307. Buchanan, Heather. *George Mouse's First Summer* (Dial, 1985) k–3. With a wagon he builds in his secret workshop, Little George Mouse saves his family's store of acorns from squirrels.

1308. ____. *George Mouse Learns to Fly* (Dial, 1985) k–3. George Mouse, who has dreamed of flying off to adventure, builds himself a flying machine.

1309. ____. *Matilda Mouse's Patchwork Life Jackets* (Methuen, 1985) k–3. The colorful jackets that Matilda Mouse made for her twin brothers prove useful when hungry Harriet, the cat, pays a visit.

1310. ____. *Matilda Mouse's First Adventure* (Methuen, 1985) k–3. A young mouse leaves her comfortable teapot home to go exploring in the kitchen and finds a ladybug stranded in the sink.

1311. ____. *Matilda Mouse's Garden* (Children's, 1986) k–3. Matilda Mouse longs to have a little garden of her own—and finally manages to do so.

1312. ____. *Matilda Mouse's Shell House* (Children's, 1986) k–3. Matilda Mouse sets off to find adventure, only to have a brush with death and be rescued by a mouse named George who asks her to marry him.

1313. ____. *George Mouse's Riverboat Band* (Dial, 1987) k–3. George builds a boat and the family floats down the river playing musical instruments that he also made.

1314. ____. *George Mouse's Caravan* (S & S, 1987) k–3. George in a gaily striped suit builds a boat, sundry musical instruments and an ingenious caravan.

1315. ____. *George Mouse's Covered Wagon* (Dial, 1987) k–3. George builds a wagon out of logs, tin cans and a plastic juice bottle. His sisters paint designs on the side, make patchwork curtains and sleeping bags out of an old glove and then take off for a holiday at sea.

1316. ____. *George and Matilda Mouse and the Doll's House* (S & S, 1988) k–3. George and Matilda Mouse get married and find the perfect home in an abandoned dollhouse.

1317. ____. *George and Matilda Mouse and the Floating School* (S & S, 1990) k–3. After a scary encounter with the cat, a class of mice finds a safer location for its school.

1318. ____. *George and Matilda Mouse and the Moon Rocket* (S & S, 1992) k–3. When the smoke from fireworks blots out the moon, George and Matilda, thinking the moon is lost, set out by rocket to search for it.

1319. Buckeridge, Anthony. *Jennings Goes to School* (Goodchild, 1950) 4–6. Jennings' first term at Linbury Court School. He attempts to deal with a stowaway discovered in a crate of bananas. That stowaway is a spider that he keeps in a jar; he wonders if he should feed it bananas.

1320. ____. *Our Friend Jennings* (Puffin, 1958) 4–6. Untouched by current controversies about the state of education, Linbury Court School still flourishes and so does its most famous pupil, Jennings.

1321. ____. *Jennings as Usual* (Goodchild, 1969) 4–6. Jennings makes his first appearance at Linbury Court Preparatory School. A schoolboy hero whose adventures any child can identify with. Jennings himself supplies a self-igniting, self-fueling imagination, quick, resourceful but flawed thinking, whose logical consequences are more flawed thinking and more rash acts.

1322. ____. *Take Jennings for Instance* (Goodchild, 1969) 4–6. Jennings and Form III join the Natural History Club.

1323. ____. *Typically Jennings* (Goodchild, 1971) 4–6.

1324. ____. *Best of Jennings* (Goodchild, 1973) 4–6. Stories of the misadventures of boarding school life, with Jennings as a good/bad boy getting into naughty scrapes but always with the best of intentions.

1325. ____. *Just Like Jennings* (Goodchild, 1980) 4–6. The usual dormitory feasts and daily muddles. There is a fine analysis of an aborted discourse in a geography lesson that goes too well and a letter "Dear Sir: I hope you are well and having weather...."

1326. ____. *Jennings and Darbishire* (Goodchild, 1986) 4–6. Darbishire is Jennings' less spirited but seldom daunted ally. He is the clergyman's son, bespectacled but as silly and excitable as himself.

1327. ____. *Jennings' Diary* (Goodchild, 1986) 4–6.

1328. ____. *Jennings' Little Hut* (Goodchild, 1986) 4–6.

1329. ____. *Jennings' Report* (Goodchild, 1990) 4–6.

1330. ____. *Jennings Again* (Goodchild, 1991) 4–6. The boys and staff undertake to keep Linbury Court School green. Headmaster is in charge. Jennings and his friends get into scrapes and are pursued by the housemaster. Jennings is still as work prone as ever.

1331. ____. *Jennings* (Macmillan, 1992) 4–6.

1332. Buckley, Helen. *Grandfather and I* (Lothrop, 1959) k–3. A child considers how Grandfather is the perfect person to spend time with because he is never in a hurry.

1333. ____. *Grandmother and I* (Lothrop, 1961) k–3. A child considers how Grandmother's lap is just right for those times when lightning is coming in the window or the cat is missing.

1334. Buckley, Helen. *Where Did Josie Go?* (Lothrop, 1962) k–3. A story that shows all the places in Josie's house where she might be hiding while she plays the game of hide-and-seek. Where Josie is finally found makes a surprising ending.

1335. ____. *Josie and the Snow* (Lothrop, 1964) k–3. A story of Josie's day in the snow when her brother, her father and her mother come along to play too. First they bundle up, then getting out the skis and sleds and the Whee-eee. Even falling down is fun.

1336. ____. *Josie's Buttercup* (Lothrop, 1967) k–3. Buttercup is a bouncy, jouncy, pouncy dog whose favorite escapade is chasing butterflies.

1337. Buckley, Helen. *Little Boy and the Birthdays* (Lothrop, 1965) k–3. A young boy learns that remembering other people's birthdays is as pleasant as having others remember his.

1338. ____. *Wonderful Little Boy* (Lothrop, 1970) k–3. No one except Grandmother seems to understand what it is to be the smallest in the family.

1339. Bucknall, Caroline. *One Bear All Alone* (Dial, 1985) k–3. Relates the activities of one to ten bears during a busy day.

1340. ____. *One Bear in the Picture* (Dial, 1987) k–3. Though he wants to look his best for the class photograph, Ted Bear finds it very hard to stay clean.

1341. ____. *One Bear in the Hospital* (Dial, 1991) k–3. Ted Bear breaks his leg and undergoes an overnight stay in the hospital.

1342. Budhill, David. *Snowshoe Trek to Otter River* (Dial, 1976) 4–6. Three short stories relate the adventures of 12-year-old Daniel and his friend Seth while camping in the woods alone together.

1343. ____. *Bones on Black Spruce Mountain* (Dial, 1978) 4–6. Seth and Daniel's camping trip to a lonely mountaintop becomes a journey into a painful past that Daniel must confront.

1344. Bullock, Kathleen. *Surprise for Mitzi Mouse* (S & S, 1989) k–3. Mitzi, a young mouse, resents the presence of her new sister Fifi until she comes to like having her around.

1345. ____. *Friend for Mitzi Mouse* (S & S, 1990) k–3. Mitzi Mouse, four, hurts her younger sister's feelings by ignoring her and spending all her time with her new best friend, the girl next door.

1346. Bunting, Eve. *Day of the Dinosaurs* (EMC, 1975) k–3. When one of them pulls the lever on the museum's dinosaur display, three children are transported back to a prehistoric dinosaur land.

1347. ____. *Death of a Dinosaur* (EMC, 1975) k–3. Carmen, Joe and Riley go back through time once more to witness the end of the dinosaurs.

1348. ____. *Dinosaur Trap* (EMC, 1975) k–3. Joe and Riley go back to dinosaur land determined to bring back Carmen who stayed behind on their last trip.

1349. ____. *Escape from Tyrannosaurs* (EMC, 1976) k–3. Joe and two friends go back 150 million years. Using the museum dinosaur displays they have discovered are time machines, the three children enter dinosaur land, after escaping from the Tyrannosaurs.

1350. Bunting, Eve. *Skateboard Four* (Whitman, 1976) 3–5. Feeling threatened by a new boy who wants to join his club, Morgan, leader of the Skateboard Four, discovers the importance of being a responsible leader.

1351. ____. *Skate Patrol* (Whitman, 1980) 3–5. Two boys skate and sleuth through the park near their apartment complex. They observe a very suspicious man and believe him to be the Creep Thief, who robs senior citizens.

1352. ____. *Skate Patrol Rides Again* (Whitman, 1982) 3–5. Milton and James, the skate patrol, figure out the surprising identity of the culprit who has been stealing pets from their apartment building.

1353. ____. *Skate Patrol and the Mystery Writer* (Whitman, 1982) 3–5. Handwriting analysis and some fast roller-skating help Milton and James close in on the vandal who's been defacing their apartment building with red paint.

1354. Bunting, Eve. *Robot People* (Children's,

1978) 3–5. Magnus, one of two robots programmed to work in an underground nuclear operation, possesses a hatred for all humans and forms goals of which the scientists are unaware.

1355. ____. *Robot Birthday* (Dutton, 1980) 3–5. Pam and Kerry receive a useful but rather unusual birthday present from their mother.

1356. Bunting, Eve. *Karen Kepplewhite Is the World's Best Kisser* (Clarion, 1983) 5–8. Karen, 13, wants to kiss the boy she has a crush on but a new girl, Star, threatens to take the attention of all the boys. Mark and Karen share their feelings.

1357. ____. *Janet Hamm Needs a Date for the Dance* (Clarion, 1986) 5–8. Star and Karen are friends and have dates to the dance. Janet has to invent a date, but she finds her dishonesty brings complications.

1358. Burch, T.R. *Shane McKellar and the Face at the Window* (Heinemann, 1980) 4–6. Shane, Sam and Rags, a dog, are criminal fighters. They are supported by Nan and Mumps, Shane's grandparents.

1359. ____. *Shane McKellar and the Treasure Hunt* (Heinemann, 1980) 4–6. Shane and his friend Sam are able to frustrate nasty men who are lawbreakers. They have the help of Rags, Shane's dog, and the support of Nan and Mumps, Shane's grandparents.

1360. Burgess, Thornton. *Mother West Winds' Neighbors* (Little, 1968) k–3. Fifteen tales of Johnny Chuck, Sammy Jay and Jimmy Skunk and the other animals and birds of the Green Meadows.

1361. ____. *Mother West Wind's Children* (Little, 1985) k–3. Tales that explain why Danny Meadow Mouse has a short tail, why Reddy Fox has no friends, and other stories about the residents of the Green Meadow.

1362. ____. *Old Mother West Wind* (Holt, 1990) k–3. The adventures of Peter Rabbit, Johnny Chuck, Reddy Fox, the Merry Little Breezes and all their companions in the fields, the woods and the streams.

1363. Burman, Ben. *High Water at Catfish Bend* (Messner, 1952) 4–6. The animals went to New Orleans on a shantyboat to try to get the mayor and the Army engineers to build some levees at Catfish Bend. But the mayor refused to do anything until Doc Raccoon changed his mind.

1364. ____. *Seven Stars for Catfish Bend* (Funk, 1956) 4–6. This is the story of how the idyllic peace of Catfish was suddenly shattered by the arrival of the enemy, the hunters, in an invasion more terrible than the worst Mississippi flood.

1365. ____. *Blow a Wild Bugle for Catfish Bend* (Taplinger, 1967) 4–6. Coyotes threaten to destroy the peaceful life of the animals at Catfish Bend.

1366. ____. *Three from Catfish Bend* (Harrap, 1067) 4–6. Three stories told by a local raccoon about animal politics and dramas in the Mississippi Swamp.

1367. ____. *Owl Hoots Twice at Catfish Bend* (Puffin, 1974) 4–6. A city slicker fox joins the animals' community at Catfish Bend and becomes dictator.

1368. ____. *High Treason at Catfish Bend* (Vanguard, 1977) 4–6. The further adventures of the residents of Catfish Bend.

1369. ____. *Strange Invasion of Catfish Bend* (Vanguard, 1980) 4–6. Relates the adventures of Catfish Bend animals as they go on a quest that leads them first to the Okefenokee Swamp and then to the terrible blizzards of the Yukon.

1370. ____. *Thunderbolt at Catfish Bend* (Weiser, 1984) 4–6. When the young animals at Catfish Bend make it clear they'd like to take over, the older animals sadly leave to look for a better place to live in Australia and India.

1371. Burningham, John. *Come Away from the Water, Shirley* (Crowell, 1977) k–3. Shirley's adventures at the beach are interspersed with familiar parental warnings.

1372. ____. *Time to Get Out of the Bath, Shirley* (Crowell, 1978) k–3. During her bath Shirley is off on a series of imaginative adventures about which her mother tidying up the bathroom has no idea. While mother talks on and on Shirley meets a knight in a castle, a royal family and goes to a jousting match.

1373. Burningham, John. *Colors* (Sainsbury, 1985) k–3. A young child and dog romp through nursery characters (dragon, snowman, witch), everyday objects (balloon, umbrella, sofa) and fantasy adventures (chased by a tiger, encountering a hippo and training frogs), identifying colors, numbers and opposites.

1374. ____. *1 2 3* (Crown, 1985) k–3. A counting book that follows ten children as they clamber up into a big tree, until they are surprised by a final climber.

1375. ____. *Opposites* (Crown, 1985) k–3. Introduces the concept of opposites through labeled pictures of a boy interacting with a thin pig and a fat one, a hot dragon and a cold snowman, and other creatures and situations.

1376. Burningham, John. *Mr. Gumpy's Outing* (Holt, 1971) k–3. A rabbit, cat, dog, sheep and others go along for a ride with Mr. Gumpy. They squabble and tip over the boat and land themselves in the drink.

1377. ____. *Mr. Gumpy's Motor Car* (Crowell, 1976) k–3. Mr. Gumpy's human and animal friends squash into his old car and go for a drive—until it starts to rain.

1378. Butterworth, Oliver. *Enormous Egg* (Little, 1956) 5–8. Nate is helping a chicken hatch a super deluxe egg.

1379. ____. *Narrow Passage* (Little, 1973) 5–8. Nate, 13, is asked to go to France in search of prehistoric man. He meets Nicole and they discover a cave with drawings and a man!

1380. Byars, Betsy. *Golly Sisters Go West* (Harper, 1987) 2–4. May-May and Rose, the singing, dancing Golly Sisters, travel west by covered wagon, entertaining people along the way.
1381. ____. *Hooray for the Golly Sisters* (Harper, 1990) 2–4. In continued adventures, May-May and Rose take their traveling road show to more audiences.
1382. ____. *Golly Sisters Ride Again* (Harper, 1994) 2–4. The Golly Sisters, May-May and Rose, share further adventures as they take their traveling show through the West.

1383. Byars, Betsy. *Burning Question of Bingo Brown* (Viking, 1988) 4–6. Bingo worries about freckles, mixed sex conversations, his girlfriend, Melissa and bully "Rambo" who lives next door. His teacher has girlfriend problems and a motorcycle accident.
1384. ____. *Bingo Brown and the Language of Love* (Viking, 1989) 4–6. Bingo has no phone privileges because of a large telephone bill. Melissa has moved and Rambo is no longer a threat but life is still a tangle with a baby brother on the way.
1385. ____. *Bingo Brown, Gypsy Lover* (Viking, 1990) 4–6. A sixth grade boy deals with the prospect of a new baby brother and a long-distance love relationship.
1386. ____. *Bingo Brown's Guide to Romance* (Viking, 1992) 4–6. Bingo Brown's work on his definitive "Guide to Romance" hits a snag when his long distance girlfriend Melissa returns unexpectedly from Oklahoma.

1387. Byars, Betsy. *Not-Just-Anybody Family* (Delacorte, 1986) 4–6. Pap, the head of the family and the children's grandfather, is arrested for disturbing the peace. Junior, the youngest child, attempts to fly off the roof. Their mother is away as a trick rider on the rodeo circuit. Maggie and Bern must hold the family together.
1388. ____. *Blossoms Meet the Vulture Lady* (Delacorte, 1986) 4–6. Junior disappears and his family panics. Meanwhile he has trapped himself in his cage and can't escape. He is rescued by Mad Mary.
1389. ____. *Blossoms and the Green Phantom* (Delacorte, 1987) 4–6. The Blossom family help get Junior's newest invention, a flying saucer, off the ground. Will his father be proud? Pap falls into a dumpster and can't get out. Vern does not want his friends to meet his family.
1390. ____. *Blossom Promise* (Delacorte, 1987) 4–6. Two weeks of rain has swollen the river. Pap remembers another river rising, and has a heart attack. Vern is launching a raft.

1391. ____. *Wanted ... Mud Blossom* (Delacorte, 1991) 4–6. Convinced that Mud is responsible for the disappearance of the school hamster that he was taking care of for the weekend, Junior Blossom is determined that the dog should be tried for his "crime."

1392. Byers, Irene. *Tim and Tiptoes* (Hodder, 1975) 3–5. Tim rescues a carrier pigeon attacked by a cat in a town park. The bird is wounded but kept safe. He is aided by a pet shop owner and he persuades his parents to keep it. He later trains it to be an outstanding pigeon.
1393. ____. *Tiptoes and the Big Race* (Hodder, 1979) 3–5.

1394. Byfield, Barbara. *Haunted Spy* (Doubleday, 1969) 3–5. A spy retires expecting to lead a quiet life in a comfortable old castle but the ghost of a former owner has other plans for him.
1395. ____. *Haunted Churchbell* (Doubleday, 1971) 3–5. Sir Roger, the master spy, seeks shelter from a blizzard in a village where he is confronted with the mystery of a ghost wolfpack and a churchbell that rings by itself.
1396. ____. *Haunted Ghost* (Doubleday, 1973) 3–5. The castle ghost has to find the link between a roast beef dinner, a factory whistle, and an old forgotten well before he figures out what has been haunting him.
1397. ____. *Haunted Tower* (Doubleday, 1976) 3–5. A retired spy and his ghost friend reluctantly become involved with the case of Crown Prince Brulph who disappears on the eve of his coronation.

1398. Byrne, Donn. *Meet Captain Luki* (MEP, 1986) 5–8. These four stories are about two children and their friend Captain Luke, from outer space.
1399. ____. *Captain Luke and the Green Planet* (MEP, 1986) 5–8.
1400. ____. *Captain Luke and the Sea People* (MEP, 1986) 5–8.
1401. ____. *Captain Luke and the Red Robots* (MEP, 1986) 5–8.

1402. Calder, Lyn. *Gobo and the Prize From Outer Space* (Holt, 1986) 2–4. Arguing over who gets to use the bicycle they hope to win in a contest, five friends in Fraggle Rock have a terrible fight and stop speaking to each other.
    (For additional books on the Fraggles, Boober, Gobo, Mokey, Red or Wembley see Brennan, Joseph; Calmenson, Stephanie; Gilkow, Louise; Gilmour, H.B.; Grand, Rebecca; Muntean, Michaela; Perlberg, Deborah; Stevenson, Jocelyn; Teitelbaum, Michael; Weiss, Ellen; Young, David.)

1403. Calmenson, Stephanie. *Waggleby of Fraggle Rock* (Holt, 1985) k–3. Boober befriends a cave creature with some very destructive habits—and some lovable ones, too.

(For additional books on the Fraggles, Boober, Gobo, Mokey, Red or Wembley see Brennan, Joseph; Calder, Lyn; Gilkow, Louise; Gilmour, H.B.; Grand, Rebecca; Muntean, Michaela; Perlberg, Deborah; Stevenson, Jocelyn; Teitelbaum, Michael; Weiss, Ellen; Young, David.)

1404. Cameron, Ann. *Stories Julian Tells* (Pantheon, 1981) 2–4. Stories of Julian's life which include getting into trouble with his younger brother, Huey, planting a garden, what he did to try to grow taller, losing a tooth and finding a new friend.

1405. ____. *More Stories Julian Tells* (Knopf, 1986) 2–4. More episodes in the life of Julian including a bet with his best friend Gloria, a secret project, and what happens when his brother Huey decides to be Superboy.

1406. ____. *Julian's Glorious Summer* (Random, 1987) 2–4. When his best friend, Gloria, receives a new bike, seven-year-old Julian spends the summer avoiding her because of his fear of bikes.

1407. ____. *Julian Stories* (Random, 1988) 2–4. Two black boys, Huey and his younger brother, involved in childish pranks and misunderstandings. A good father-son relationship.

1408. ____. *Julian, Secret Agent* (Random, 1988) 2–4. When Julian, his little brother Huey and their friend Gloria decide to be "crime busters," they find themselves in one adventure after another.

1409. ____. *Julian, Dream Doctor* (Random, 1990) 2–4. Julian and Huey try to find the perfect birthday gift for Dad with amusing results.

1410. Cameron, Anne. *Raven Returns the Water* (Harbour, 1988) k–3. Recounts how Raven, the trickster, saves the earth from drought after Frog has swallowed the world's water.

1411. ____. *Raven and Snipe* (West Coast, 1992) k–3. Raven is a well-known trickster; she is naughty, beguiling her trusting friends and gobbling their shares of the hard-won food. At last their patience exhausted and their bellies empty, Puffin, Cormorant, Snipe and her other victims teach her a much-needed lesson about sharing.

1412. ____. *Raven Goes Berrypicking* (West Coast, 1992) k–3.

1413. Campbell, P. *Koala's Spring Cleaning* (Methuen, 1972) k–3. Michael, a friend of Fred and Stanley, disguises himself as Uncle Lloyd and amuses himself with a bit of do-it-yourself.

1414. ____. *Koala Party* (Methuen, 1972) k–3. Fred and Stanley are Koala bears. Michael is their wicked friend. He disguises himself as a parcel in order to get at the party food first.

1415. Campbell, Hope. *Why Not Join the Giraffes?* (Norton, 1968) 5–8. Suzie's brother is the leader of a combo, the Giraffes. The whole family is unconventional. Suzie's new love is "straight." What to do?

1416. ____. *Meanwhile Back at the Castle* (Norton, 1970) 5–8. Suzie now lives on an island her father bought. But they turn this into an independent sovereign with their usual non-conformity.

1417. Campbell, Rod. *Buster's Morning* (Berdick, 1984) k–3. Buster, a round-faced toddler in a blue stretchy has fun uncovering everyday objects and animals such as the washer, cupboard, birdhouse, and so on.

1418. ____. *Buster's Afternoon* (Berdick, 1984) k–3. Buster, a round-faced toddler in a blue stretchy frolics in the afternoon peeking under leaves and flowers in the garden.

1419. ____. *Buster's Bedtime* (Barron, 1986) k–3. A picture of Buster's bedtime routine. One can stroke the furry cat, pull the wooly blanket over Buster and can see oneself in his mirror.

1420. ____. *Buster Keeps Warm* (Barron, 1988) k–3. A little boy puts on warm clothing for his winter activities.

1421. ____. *Buster Gets Dressed* (Barron, 1988) k–3. Describes various articles of clothing as Buster gets dressed. Turning each half page adds another piece of clothing to the illustration of Buster.

1422. Carey, M.V. *Three Investigators and the Mystery of the Flaming Footprints* (Random, 1972) 4–6. When an eccentric local artist disappears suddenly, the three investigators look into the matter.

1423. ____. *Three Investigators and the Mystery of the Singing Serpent* (Random, 1972) 4–6. The three investigators get involved with witchcraft when they try to rescue a woman from the influence of snake worshippers.

1424. ____. *Three Investigators and the Mystery of Monster Mountain* (Random, 1973) 4–6. The three young sleuths solve a case of double identity while investigating the legend of Monster Mountain.

1425. ____. *Three Investigators and the Secret of the Haunter Mirror* (Random, 1974) 4–6. A story of looking for the truth about an ancient mirror thought to be haunted by a magician. Jupiter, Pete and Bob get involved in a mugging and a kidnapping.

1426. ____. *Three Investigators and the Mystery of the Invisible Dog* (Random, 1975) 4–6. Jupiter, Pete and Bob help solve a haunted mystery but then a crystal dog is missing and they encounter poisoning, ransom notes, etc. This story has a touch of the supernatural the others didn't.

1427. ____. *Three Investigators and the Mystery of the Death Trap Mine* (Random, 1976) 4–6. The three investigators, aided by their friend, Allie, try to untangle the unusual circumstances surrounding an abandoned mine.

1428. ____. *Three Investigators and the Mystery of the Magic Circle* (Random, 1978) 4–6. A fast moving, exciting, absorbing realistic story of witch-craft.

1429. ____. *Three Investigators and the Mystery of the Sinister Scarecrow* (Random, 1979) 4–6. A living scarecrow and killer ants are two of the obstacles encountered by three heroes in this fast paced adventure.

1430. ____. *Three Investigators and the Mystery of the Scar-Faced Beggar* (Random, 1981) 4–6. A wallet dropped by a scar-faced beggar sets the three investigators on the trail of bank robbers.

1431. ____. *Three Investigators and the Mystery of the Blazing Cliffs* (Random, 1981) 4–6. The sighting of a UFO leads the three investigators to uncover a bizarre confidence game.

1432. ____. *Three Investigators and the Mystery of the Wandering Cave Man* (Random, 1982) 4–6. Three young sleuths investigate the disappearance of a caveman's bones from a museum and undercover skullduggery at a science foundation.

1433. ____. *Three Investigators and the Mystery of the Missing Mermaid* (Random, 1983) 4–6. A statue of a mermaid proves to be a vital clue when the three investigators set out to trace a missing child.

1434. ____. *Three Investigators and the Mystery of the Trail of Terror* (Random, 1984) 4–6. While accompanying Pete's inventor grandfather to New York where the old man plans to sell his new invention, the three investigators find themselves in the middle of a dangerous spy case.

1435. ____. *Three Investigators and the Mystery of the Creep-Show Crooks* (Random, 1985) 4–6. The three investigators tangle with a couple of shady producers of horror films when they try to track down a runaway teenager.

1436. ____. *Three Investigators and the Mystery of the Cranky Collector* (Random, 1987) 4–6. When a book collector disappears, the three investigators break into his computer files searching for clues, and undercover his mysterious past.

1437. ____. *Three Investigators and the Case of the Savage Statue* (Random, 1987) 4–6. By making the correct decisions, the reader helps the three investigators in defeating a killer cult, whose members have kidnapped a ransom victim to get their hands on a valuable statue.

(For other books about the "Three Investigators," *see* Arden, William; Arthur, Robert; Brandel, Marc; West, Nick.)

1438. Carley, Wayne. *Percy the Parrot Strikes Out* (Garrard, 1971) k–3. The White Sons and the Jets have trouble at the game with their mascots—a noisy parrot and a large dog.

1439. ____. *Percy Parrot Passes the Puck* (Garrard, 1973) k–3. Percy the Parrot goes to the hockey arena to do a live commercial but spoils it by playing dead after consuming Crunchy Delicious Bird Seed. He recovers, escapes and helps his team win by dropping feathers.

1440. ____. *Percy the Parrot Yelled Quiet* (Garrard, 1974) k–3. When Percy tells all the other animals in the pet store to be quiet, Mrs. Gray decides he is the quiet pet she needs.

1441. Carlson, Dale. *Perkins the Brain* (Doubleday, 1964) 3–5. When he realized that he's not the oldest, tallest, smallest, fastest or anything special in his new neighborhood, Perkins, nine, decides to be the brainiest.

1442. ____. *House of Perkins* (Doubleday, 1985) 3–5. Perkins the Brain and his friends try to build a tree house, convert it into a ground house and then find it after it mysteriously disappears.

1443. Carlson, Nancy. *Harriet and the Roller Coaster* (Carolrhoda, 1982) k–3. Harriet accepts her friend George's challenge to ride the frightening roller coaster, and finds out that she is the brave one.

1444. ____. *Harriet and the Garden* (Carolrhoda, 1982) k–3. Harriet feels terrible until she confesses to trampling on a neighbor's garden and ruining a prize dahlia.

1445. ____. *Harriet and Walt* (Carolrhoda, 1982) k–3. Harriet decides that her little brother Walt isn't as big a pest as she once thought he was.

1446. ____. *Harriet's Recital* (Carolrhoda, 1982) k–3. Harriet overcomes her stage fright and dances successfully and proudly at her ballet recital.

1447. ____. *Harriet's Halloween Candy* (Carolrhoda, 1982) k–3. Harriet learns the hard way that sharing her Halloween candy makes her feel much better than eating it all by herself.

1448. Carlson, Nancy. *Loudmouth George and the Fishing Trip* (Carolrhoda, 1983) k–3. Loudmouth George, a rabbit who brags about catching the biggest fish even though he had never been fishing, is embarrassed by the size of the fish he finally does catch.

1449. ____. *Loudmouth George and the Cornet* (Carolrhoda, 1983) k–3. George's cornet playing is too much for both his family and the band.

1450. ____. *Loudmouth George and the Big Race* (Carolrhoda, 1983) k–3. George brags, procrastinates, and offers excuses instead of training for the big race—much to his later embarrassment.

1451. ____. *Loudmouth George and the Sixth-Grade Bully* (Carolrhoda, 1983) k–3. After having his lunch repeatedly stolen by a bully twice his size, Loudmouth George and his friend Harriet teach him a lesson he'll never forget.

1452. ____. *Loudmouth George and the New Neighbors* (Carolrhoda, 1983) k–3. When a family of pigs moves in next door, the rabbit, George, wants nothing to do with them. But finally he gives in and finds out they aren't so bad after all.

1453. Carlson, Nancy. *Bunnies and Their Hobbies* (Carolrhoda, 1984) k–3. Describes the many activities bunnies like to spend time on after a "long day at work."

1454. ____. *Bunnies and Their Sports* (Viking, 1987) k–3. Reveals bunnies involved in jogging, swimming and exercising at the gym.

1455. Carlson, Nancy. *Louanne Pig in the Talent Show* (Carolrhoda, 1985) k–3. No-talent Louanne's spirits droop as her friends prepare for the talent show, but then she is called upon to perform in a very special way.

1456. ____. *Louanne Pig in Witch Lady* (Carolrhoda, 1985) k–3. Louanne Pig is befriended by an old woman she always believed to be a witch.

1457. ____. *Louanne Pig in Making the Team* (Carolrhoda, 1985) k–3. Though she plans to try out for cheerleading, Louanne pig helps her friend Arnie try out for football, with surprising results.

1458. ____. *Louanne Pig in the Mysterious Valentine* (Carolrhoda, 1985) k–3. When she receives a valentine from a secret admirer, Louanne Pig tries to find out who sent it.

1459. ____. *Louanne Pig in the Perfect Family* (Carolrhoda, 1985) k–3. Louanne thinks she wants to be part of a big family until she spends a weekend with her friend George and his five sisters and four brothers.

1460. Carlson, Nancy. *Arnie and the Stolen Markers* (Viking, 1987) k–3. After spending his allowance at Harvey's Toy Shop, Arnie steals a set of markers and suffers the consequences of his action.

1461. ____. *Arnie Goes to Camp* (Viking, 1988) k–3. Arnie is sure that he won't survive summer sleepaway camp; but when he arrives he is surprised to find that camp is not at all what he expected.

1462. ____. *Arnie and the New Kid* (Viking, 1990) k–3. When an accident requires Arnie to use crutches, he begins to understand the limits and possibilities of his new classmate, who has a wheelchair.

1463. Carlson, Natalie. *Marie Louise and Christophe* (Scribner, 1974) k–3. A snake constantly plays tricks on his best friend, a mongoose, until he causes them both to get into serious trouble.

1464. ____. *Marie Louise's Heyday* (Scribner, 1975) k–3. Marie Louise baby-sits for five possum children and, while finding it an exhausting experience, realizes it is not without rewards.

1465. ____. *Runaway Marie Louise* (Scribner, 1977) k–3. Marie Louise, the brown mongoose, runs away after her mother spanks her for being naughty.

1466. ____. *Marie Louise and Christophe at the Carnival* (Scribner, 1981) k–3. Anxious to attend the carnival celebration in the village Marie Louise and Christophe go to the Witch Toad to get appropriate disguises so that no one would realize they are a mongoose and a snake.

1467. Carlson, Natalie. *Spooky Night* (Lothrop, 1982) k–3. A witch's black cat who wishes to become a family pet must perform one last bit of magic before he can be free.

1468. ____. *Spooky and the Ghost Cat* (Lothrop, 1985) k–3. On Halloween night, Spooky, a black cat, rescues a ghost cat from a witch to whom he once belonged.

1469. ____. *Spooky and the Wizard's Bats* (Lothrop, 1986) k–3. Spooky, formerly a witch's cat, is plagued by bats sent by a wizard and thinks of a plan to outwit him.

1470. ____. *Spooky and the Bad Luck Raven* (Lothrop, 1988) k–3. Cats, Spooky and Snowball, sabotage the witches' Sabbat Race, creating chaos never before seen at the event.

1471. ____. *Spooky and the Witch's Goat* (Lothrop, 1989) k–3. Two cats protect their catnip bed from the "witch's goat" at great cost to the goat.

1472. Carlstrom, Nancy. *Jesse Bear, What Will You Wear?* (Macmillan, 1986) k–3. Rhymed text and illustrations describe Jesse Bear's activities from morning to bedtime.

1473. ____. *Better Not Get Wet, Jesse Bear* (Macmillan, 1988) k–3. Jesse Bear is admonished not to get wet under a variety of tantalizing circumstances, until finally he receives permission in his own wading pool.

1474. ____. *It's About Time, Jesse Bear* (Macmillan, 1990) k–3. From early morning to bedtime, rhymes present the activities of Jesse Bear as he dresses, plays, eats, and gets ready for bed.

1475. ____. *How Do You Say It Today, Jesse Bear?* (Macmillan, 1992) k–3. Rhymed text and illustrations describe Jesse Bear's activities from January to December.

1476. Carpenter, Humphrey. *Mr. Majeika* (Viking, 1984) 2–4. A new teacher, a former magician, floats into school very late on a magic carpet. He annoys the head teacher but amuses Harris, the class show-off.

1477. ____. *Mr. Majeika and the Music Teacher* (Viking, 1986) 2–4. The music teacher is a witch and one of the teachers is a white wizard. The end of term concert is a contest between witch and wizard with spells flying everywhere.

1478. ____. *Mr. Majeika and the Haunted Hotel* (Viking, 1987) 2–4. Mr. Majeika is a teacher at St. Barty's. He takes his class on a visit to Hadrian's Wall, staying at a hotel called "The Green Banana." The hotel is haunted, and there are many adventures, enhanced by Mr. Majeika being a magician.

1479. ____. *Mr. Majeika and the School Play* (Viking, 1991) 2–4.

1480. ____. *Mr. Majeika and the School Book Week* (Viking, 1992) 2–4. Mr. Majeika, a wizard, gets well-known children's book characters to wander into one another's stories.

1481. ____. *Mr. Majeika and the Dinner Lady*

(Viking, 1992) 2–4. A good portrayal of ghosts, witches and wizards.

1482. ____. *Mr. Majeika and the School Inspector* (Viking, 1993) 2–4.

1483. Carrick, Carol. *Lost in the Storm* (Seabury, 1974) k–3. Christopher must wait out a long, fitful night before searching for his dog lost during an island storm.

1484. ____. *Dark and Full of Secrets* (Clarion, 1984) k–3. Christopher drifts too far away from shore while snorkeling in the pond, then panics when he can't touch bottom. His dog comes to his rescue.

1485. ____. *Left Behind* (Clarion, 1988) k–3. Christopher gets lost on the subway during an excursion to the aquarium and is afraid he'll never be reunited with his class.

1486. Carrick, Carol. *Patrick's Dinosaurs* (Clarion, 1983) k–3. When his older brother talks about dinosaurs during a visit to the zoo, Patrick is afraid, until he discovers they all died millions of years ago.

1487. ____. *What Happened to Patrick's Dinosaurs?* (Clarion, 1986) k–3. Fascinated with dinosaurs, Patrick invents an imaginary explanation of why they have become extinct.

1488. Carrick, Donald. *Harald and the Giant Knight* (Clarion, 1982) k–3. When a group of knights decide to use his father's farm for their spring training, Harald and his family must take desperate measures to get the troublesome knights off their land.

1489. ____. *Harald and the Great Stag* (Clarion, 1988) k–3. When Harald, who lives in England during the Middle Ages, hears that the Baron and his royal guests are planning to hunt the legendary Great Stag, he devises a clever scheme to protect the animal.

1490. Carris, Joan. *When the Boys Ran the House* (Lippincott, 1982) 5–8. Four brothers run the house while mother is ill and father is away. They are helped by a strange visiting nurse. The bees, the cat, the food, the secret room all make a hilarious story.

1491. ____. *Pets, Vets and Marty Howard* (Lippincott, 1984) 5–8. Marty wants to be a vet and gets a part-time job in an animal hospital. He learns about saving and having puppies. He also learns about death and neglect.

1492. Carroll, Ruth. *Beanie* (Oxford, 1953) 2–4. Beanie, six, lives in the Great Smoky Mountains. He went for a walk in the woods on his birthday, with his new puppy and his toy gun. What happened when he met a bear and lost his puppy makes the story.

1493. ____. *Tough Enough* (Oxford, 1954) 2–4. Beanie's family thought the puppy was a real nuisance until Tough Enough had a chance to prove his worth during a flash flood.

1494. ____. *Tough Enough's Trip* (Oxford, 1956)

2–4. Beanie Tatum and Tough Enough, his dog, have a wonderful time collecting all sorts of pets on a trip to the Coastal Plains.

1495. ____. *Tough Enough's Pony* (Oxford, 1957) 2–4. When the Tatum family visits an island off the coast of North Carolina, Tough Enough finds a wild pony that has been lamed. Through Beanie's care and Tough Enough's devotion the pony is made well again.

1496. ____. *Tough Enough and Sassy* (Oxford, 1958) 2–4. The Tatum family has come on hard times. The children had to find some way to earn money, or Pa might have to sell their pony Sassy. Ma's project of making "woods pretties" to sell to tourists is a great success. But it is Sassy who saves the day and gives a happy ending.

1497. ____. *Tough Enough's Indians* (Oxford, 1960) 2–4. The Tatums are fleeing the worst fire they have ever seen. Beanie and his brothers and sisters, Sassy and Tough Enough ended up lost until Tough Enough put his nose to the ground and sniffed them right into the back yard of an Indian family.

1498. ____. *Runaway Pony, Runaway Dog* (Walck, 1963) 2–4. Tough Enough, a dog, and Sassy, a pony, journey together back to the Tatum's house in the Smoky Mountains after escaping from strangers.

1499. Cartlidge, Michelle. *Teddy Trucks* (Lothrop, 1981) k–3. Driver, Gerry, easily distracted from his work and always running late, puts in a long day of work for Teddy Trucks, but finished in time for tea.

1500. ____. *Dressing Teddy* (S & S, 1983) k–3.

1501. ____. *Teddy's House* (S & S, 1986) k–3. Teddy sees a window, a clock, a cupboard, a crib, a telephone and many other things in his house.

1502. ____. *Teddy's Dinner* (S & S, 1986) k–3.

1503. ____. *Teddy's Toys* (S & S, 1986) k–3.

1504. ____. *Teddy's Garden* (S & S, 1986) k–3.

1505. ____. *Teddy's Birthday Party* Puffin, 1986. k–3

1506. ____. *Teddy's Holiday* (Puffin, 1987) k–3.

1507. ____. *Teddy's Friends* (S & S, 1992) k–3. A day with Teddy and his friends and family. He plays with trains, makes a tent, has lunch and plays outside.

1508. ____. *Good Night Teddy* (Candlewick, 1992) k–3. After playing in the bath, Teddy goes to bed with his favorite toys.

1509. ____. *Teddy's Christmas* (S & S, 1986) k–3. A simple story about Christmas—buying presents, talking to Santa, trimming the tree, sharing Christmas dinner.

1510. Cartlidge, Michelle. *Mouse's Diary* (Dutton, 1982) k–3. A mouse dresses and acts like a little girl. She goes to school, takes ballet lessons, plays and quarrels with her brother. She keeps journal entries about her busy days.

1511. ____. *Mouse Work* (Dutton, 1983) k–3. Mice work in the post office, at dressmaking, at bakeries, a launderette and in a garage. Mice are shopping, bi-cycling, motoring and going to work.

1512. _____. *Bear's Room: No Peeping* (Willowisp, 1986) k–3. A mouse family wants to join Bear in his rooms. But Bear won't let them in. He is busy cook-ing, painting and building. Then he makes a wel-come sign and invites the mice in for a party and rides the seesaw he made just for them.

1513. _____. *Mouse's Christmas Tree* (Puffin, 1986) k–3.

1514. _____. *Little Mouse Makes Sweets* (Dutton, 1987) k–3. Little Mouse is taught to make pepper-mint creams and chocolate fudge.

1515. _____. *House for Lily Mouse* (Prentice, 1987) k–3. Forced to leave her old home, Lily Mouse searches far and wide until she finds a new home that is just right for a little mouse.

1516. _____. *Mouse House* (Dutton, 1990) k–3. Shows the unexpended and elaborate dwelling places of mice.

1517. _____. *Mouse Time* (Dutton, 1991) k–3.

1518. _____. *Mouse in the House* (Dutton, 1991) k–3.

1519. _____. *Mouse Theater* (Dutton, 1992) k–3. A troupe of theater mice travel from town and put on a different play each night.

1520. _____. *Baby Mice at Home* (Dutton, 1992) k–3.

1521. _____. *Mouse Letters* (Dutton, 1993) k–3. Six tiny letters to "Dear Friend" are inserted in envelopes attached to pages throughout text.

1522. _____. *Mouse Birthday* (Dutton, 1994) k–3. This book has flaps that reveal presents to Mouse, in-cluding books from his brother and a tea set from his aunt.

1523. Cartlidge, Michelle. *Bear in the Forest* (Dut-ton, 1991) k–3. Illustrations with one-word labels name the creatures that Bear sees in the forest and everywhere else he goes.

1524. _____. *Bears on the Go* (Dutton, 1992) k–3.

1525. Caryl, Jean. *Bones and the Black Panther* (Funk & Wagnalls, 1963) 4–6. Bones' determination to own a Black Panther, an expensive bicycle, leads him to shining shoes, losing weight and other money-raising projects. He gets his bike but it is soon stolen and another adventure begins.

1526. _____. *Bones and the Smiling Mackerel* (Funk & Wagnalls, 1964) 4–6. Chubby Boniface is still on a diet, but this time while at Camp Crescendo.

1527. _____. *Bones and the Pointed House* (Funk & Wagnalls, 1968) 4–6. Bones gives up a successful social and school life when his family moves to a new neighborhood and a unique "pointed house." He determines to revolt by wearing sweatshirts, long hair and a dirty face to the new school.

1528. Caseley, Judith. *Molly Pink* (Greenwillow, 1985) k–3. Molly Pink sings "as clear as a bell," but only when her family is not watching her.

1529. _____. *Molly Pink Goes Hiking* (Greenwillow, 1985) k–3. While hiking with her family, Molly learns not to judge people by their size.

1530. Casey, Winifred. *Henrietta, the Wild Woman of Borneo* (Four Winds, 1975) k–3. Henrietta lives in a state of total inadequacy, especially in relation to her pretty, perfect older sister. Hurricane-haired and high-spirited, she sets out to return to Borneo, whence she believes she came.

1531. _____. *Henrietta and the Day of the Iguana* (Four Winds, 1978) k–3. Henrietta is sure she wants an iguana as a pet until she sees one.

1532. _____. *Henrietta and the Gong from Hong Kong* (Four Winds, 1981) k–3. While visiting her grandparents, Henrietta learns that she's not the only one to have problems with behaving. Her grand-mother tells her about her own mother's problems and pains of growing up.

1533. Cass, Joan. *Cat Thief* (Abelard, 1961) k–3. A story about two stolen cats who were rescued from a thief by various neighborhood cats who banded to-gether to help them.

1534. _____. *Cat Show* (Abelard, 1962) k–3. A trip to the cat show almost proves disastrous for Siamese Sarah and her kittens. But Arabella, the alley cat, her kittens and other back-street friends come to the res-cue.

1535. _____. *Cats Go to Market* (Abelard, 1969) k–3. The cats of River View Road loved market day, es-pecially the fish stall of Mrs. Matilda Gubbins.

1536. _____. *Cats' Adventure with Car Thieves* (Abelard, 1971) k–3. A couple of crooks with designs on Mr. Humber's new sports car are scared off by the caterwauling with which Arabella and her friends rouse the neighborhood and the growls of the five lit-tle tabbies, hidden under the car's tarpaulin.

1537. Cass, Joan. *Milly Mouse* (Abelard, 1975) k–3. Milly Mouse can't button her new green cardigan and her brothers and sisters won't wait for her. But she learns from the human world how such things are managed successfully.

1538. _____. *Milly Mouse and the Measles* (Abelard, 1976) k–3. There is an epidemic of the dreaded mouse measles and Mrs. Mouse decides to have her family immunized. Milly finds it is not too terrible to get an injection.

1539. _____. *Persistent Mouse* (Abelard, 1983) k–3. Albert Henry was a pet mouse and followed his mas-ter on a cruise where he found a lady mouse and dis-appeared. He later returns to his master with a wife and six baby mice.

1540. Cass, Joan. *Witch and the Naughty Princesses* (Hodder, 1978) 2–4. Molly and Florid like to bewitch royalty. Molly kidnaps the badly behaved Royal twins, Stella and Bella, whose conduct is greatly im-proved after two months working as housemaids to their captors.

1541. ____. *Witches' Lost Spell Book* (Hodder, 1980) 2–4. Molly, an unwilling and inefficient witch, wanders off her path and discovers the headquarters of the Nightshades, a band of witches who have stolen the spellbook belonging to Molly's friends.

1542. ____. *Trouble Among the Witches* (Hodder, 1983) 2–4.

1543. ____. *Witch's School* (Hodder, 1985) 2–4. The Nightshades, failures of witch school, are Elusive Elaine, Arrogant Alice and Tempestuous Teresa. They hope to find jobs in the village but....

1544. ____. *Witch of Witchery Wood* (Hodder, 1985) 2–4. This witch is a dotty old crone armed with a tatty spellbook, an ill-mannered cat and an aging broomstick with a will of its own. Her plans to waylay the princess go awry, while the princess herself is mistakenly metamorphosed into another black cat.

1545. Cates, Emily. *Ghost in the Attic* (Bantam, 1990) 5–8. Dee and Louisa try to reunite Louisa with the spirits of the rest of her family. There are four members and two of them are found in this book.

1546. ____. *Ghost Ferry* (Bantam, 1991) 5–8. Dee, a 13-year-old, lives in a remote Maine Island. She is bored and lonesome until she meets a ghost who lived there 100 years ago.

1547. Caveney, Sylvia. *Little Zip's Zoo Counting Book* (Pelham, 1977) k–3. This counting book is about buns. Zip's rambling tale of an ordinary trip to the zoo and simple subtraction from ten.

1548. ____. *Little Zip Dressing Up* (Pelham, 1978) k–3. Little Zip loves to dress up. He rises and jumps on his faithful cat Podger. After breakfast Zip becomes a bus conductor, then an astronaut, a doctor, a fireman, a tiger and a ghost. Poor Podger must go along with these antics and indignities.

1549. ____. *Little Zip and the Water Book* (Pelham, 1979) k–3. Little Zip loves water but his cat Podger doesn't. He walks in the rain carrying Podger. Podger only likes water with fish in it.

1550. ____. *Little Zip's Night-time Book* (Pelham, 1982) k–3. Little Zip tries to tell cat Podger what he has learned about the movement of Earth, Sun, and Moon. There are owls, badgers and bats and a few night-working humans. Finally, Zip dreams.

1551. Cazet, Denys. *Saturday* (Bradbury, 1985) 3–5. Although Barney's day begins badly, Grandpa and Grandma soon find ways to make it all right again.

1552. ____. *Sunday* (Bradbury, 1988) 3–5. Barney, the dog, spends a busy Sunday with his grandparents and their animal neighbors, attending a church breakfast, playing bingo and fighting a stubborn washing machine.

1553. Cebulash, Mel. *Spring Street Boys Go All Out* (Children's, 1982) 2–4. Mike, the teen champion of Al's Pool Room, gets a chance to play the Masked Marvel and possibly win $500.

1554. ____. *Spring Street Boys Team Up* (Children's, 1982) 2–4.

1555. ____. *Spring Street Boys Hit the Road* (Children's, 1982) 2–4.

1556. ____. *Spring Street Boys Settle a Score* (Children's, 1982) 2–4.

1557. Cebulash, Mel. *Ruth Marini of the Dodgers* (Lerner, 1983) 5–8. Ruth, 18, was the star of her high school baseball team and the Los Angeles Dodgers think she may be good enough to become professional baseball's first female player.

1558. ____. *Ruth Marini, Dodger Ace* (Lerner, 1983) 5–8. This is a story of the first woman to play major league baseball.

1559. ____. *Ruth Marini, World Series Star* (Lerner, 1985) 5–8. Ruth, professional baseball's first female player, fights the rumor that a serious midseason injury has ended her short career.

1560. Chaikin, Miriam. *How Yossi Beat the Evil Urge* (Harper, 1983) 3–5. A young Chassidic boy, Yossi, finds that his inability to concentrate on his studies may result in his being sent away from his family and home.

1561. ____. *Yossi Asks the Angels for Help* (Harper, 1985) 3–5. When he loses the Hanukkah money he planned to use for presents for his sister and parents, Yossi prays to the angels for help.

1562. ____. *Yossi Tries to Help God* (Harper, 1987) 3–5. Inspired by his rabbi's teaching that doing a good deed makes an angel, Yossi follows a plan that backfires and almost cost him his two best friends.

1563. ____. *Feathers in the Wind* (Harper, 1989) 3–5. Yossi learns the Rabbi's lesson about not speaking in an evil tongue firsthand when he tries to repair the damage done by a joke gone sour.

1564. Chalmers, Mary. *Throw a Kiss, Harry* (Harper, 1958) k–3. Harry was a kitten who got himself in real trouble. And it all came from disobedience. He climbed a tree, then a house, and he couldn't get down. The fire department came to the rescue—and Harry quite enjoyed his role.

1565. ____. *Take a Nap, Harry* (Harper, 1964/1991) K–3. Since he does not yet feel sleepy enough to take his nap, Harry the cat helps his mother bake a cake.

1566. ____. *Be Good, Harry* (Harper, 1967) k–3. When Harry's mother goes to visit a sick friend, Harry takes all his toys and goes to stay with someone else for the first time.

1567. ____. *Merry Christmas, Harry* (Harper, 1977) k–3. Harry the cat is delighted when Santa Claus brings him his Christmas wish.

1568. ____. *Come to the Doctor, Harry* (Harper, 1981) k–3. Harry kitten learns that a trip to the doctor is nothing to fear.

1569. Chambers, John. *Finder* (Atheneum, 1981)

5–8. A dog found Jenny when she arrived at Fire Island for the summer. The dog belonged to another boy. Jenny and her friend Lauren came upon a mystery and a kidnapping.

1570. ____. *Snowdown of Apple Hill* (Atheneum, 1982) 5–8. Jenny and her brother, Bill, run into the Quarry gang of robbers and murderers. They are looking for the loot that was hidden there 12 years ago.

1571. ____. *Fire Island Forfeit* (Atheneum, 1984) 5–8. Jenny and her brother, Bill, and her girlfriend, Lauren, investigate a mystery of Fire Island. Lione, a model is murdered. She is the same girl that gave Lauren a box with keys in it.

1572. Chappell, Audrey. *Surprise for Oliver* (Blackie, 1989) k–3. A story of Oliver, a small boy who loses his favorite toy (an octopus) at nursery school. A book full of surprises, not only for Oliver.

1573. ____. *Outing for Oliver* (Blackie, 1990) k–3. A nursery school outing to a farm: the bus trip, the friendly farmer and his wife, the many animals and the unexpected (the caretaker's dog and the piglets born).

1574. Charbonnet, Gabriella. *Competition Fever* (Skylark, 1996) 4–6. Kelly is given stiff competition from newcomer Maya, who is Russian. She is also Kelly's stepsister! They must cooperate for the good of the team. But can they?

1575. ____. *Split Decision* (Skylark, 1996) 4–6. Monica is tall for her age. She is the tallest girl on the gymnastic team. She finds a kitten and takes care of it. She starts to volunteer at a veterinarian's office. Should she give up gymnastics?

1576. ____. *Bully Coach* (Skylark, 1996) 4–6. Kelly, Maya and the gymnastic team are happy that a new coach is coming. The new coach is both harsh and cruel. The team plans a mutiny. They don't need him, do they?

1577. ____. *Balancing Act* (Skylark, 1996) 4–6. Maya wants to be friendly with her classmates, including Kelly. She finds out about American customs as she tries to become "American."

1578. Charles, Donald. *Letters from the Calico Cat* (Children's, 1974) k–3. Calico Cat shows the reader the letters of the alphabet.

1579. ____. *Count on Calico Cat* (Children's, 1974) k–3. A counting book depicting the contents of Calico Cat's garbage can including six shoes, seven rags and eight wires.

1580. ____. *Calico Cat Looks Around* (Children's, 1975) k–3. This book deals with shapes. Each two-page spread has "sidewalk squares" or "rectangle windows."

1581. ____. *Fat, Fat Calico Cat* (Children's, 1977) k–3. After suffering from eating the wrong kinds of food, Calico Cat discovers the benefits of a proper diet.

1582. ____. *Calico Cat Meets Bookworm* (Children's, 1978) k–3. Bookworm introduces a bored Calico Cat to exciting books available at the library.

1583. ____. *Time to Rhyme with Calico Cat* (Children's, 1978) k–3. Calico Cat and Shaggy Dog compose rhymes such as "There's a rose on my nose."

1584. ____. *Shaggy Dog's Animal Alphabet* (Children's, 1979) k–3. Shaggy Dog presents a rhymed alphabet of animals.

1585. ____. *Shaggy Dog's Tall Tale* (Children's, 1980) k–3. Shaggy Dog tells Calico Cat what happens to him when he fell into a deep puddle on a rainy day.

1586. ____. *Calico Cat at School* (Children's, 1981) k–3. Calico Cat spends a day at school.

1587. ____. *Calico Cat at the Zoo* (Children's, 1981) k–3. Calico Cat visits various animals in the zoo, characterizing them as big, proud, funny and many other adjectives.

1588. ____. *Calico Cat's Exercise Book* (Children's, 1982) k–3. Calico Cat demonstrates various exercises to his class of mice.

1589. ____. *Shaggy Dog's Halloween* (Children's, 1984) k–3. Shaggy Dog tries on all sorts of costumes to go to a party. But none will do. Calico Cat suggests that they go as each other.

1590. ____. *Calico Cat's Year* (Children's, 1984) k–3. Rhymed text and illustrations describe the characteristics of each of the four seasons.

1591. ____. *Calico Cat Looks at Shapes* (Children's, 1986) k–3. Text and illustrations introduce a variety of shapes.

1592. ____. *Calico Cat Looks at Colors* (Children's, 1986) k–3. Calico Cat demonstrates the colors of the rainbow during his adventures with a mouse, a bird, and a snake.

1593. ____. *Shaggy Dog's Birthday* (Children's, 1986) k–3. Shaggy Dog's many animal friends give various excuses for not attending his party, while actually planning a birthday surprise for him.

1594. Charnas, Suzy. *Bronze King* (Houston, 1985) 5–8. When Valentine starts noticing odd things are vanishing from New York City, she unknowingly summons a wizard from Sorcery Hall who enlists her help in his fight against a dreaded monster of darkness.

1595. ____. *Silver Glove* (Bantam, 1988) 5–8. Valentine lives in New York with her divorced mother. Her grandmother, living in a rest home, has just disappeared. There are good and bad sorcerers, a wicked psychologist and a magic carpet ride.

1596. ____. *Golden Thread* (Houston, 1989) 5–8. Bosanka, an alien witch from another world, wants Valentine, a New York City teenager, to use her magical powers to help Bosanka return home.

1597. Chase, Catherine. *Mouse in My House* (Dandelion, 1979) k–3. A little girl misses the mouse her mother forces to leave the house, but one day the door is left open.

1598. ____. *Baby Mouse Learns His ABCs* (Dandelion, 1979) k–3. Baby Mouse learns the alphabet by mastering one letter each day.

1599. ____. *Baby Mouse Goes Shopping* (Nelson, 1981) k–3. Baby Mouse goes shopping for different items at a variety of stores.

1600. Chell, Mary. *Slimtail's Picnic* (Black, 1979) k–3. The Slimtails are little brown mice. They have a pet weevil named Edwin. They live on Barleybag Avenue along with Tom Noddy the cat and other neighbors.

1601. ____. *Mrs. Slimtail Goes Shopping* (Black, 1979) k–3.

1602. ____. *Slimtails' New House* (Black, 1979) k–3.

1603. ____. *Edwin's Adventures* (Black, 1979) k–3.

1604. Chenault, Nell. *Parsifal the Poddley* (Little, 1960) k–3. Poddleys are odd creatures, one foot high. They wear pith helmets and white nightgowns. Each is assigned to take care of a lonely child until he finds a friend. Parsifal is assigned to Christopher.

1605. ____. *Parsifal Rides the Time Wave* (Little, 1962) k–3. Parsifal comes to help Colin who is in the hospital recovering from injuries suffered when he and his dog were hit by a car. A trip through time to Scotland and Robert Bruce, whose dog Colin meets, make it easier for him to accept the death of his own dog.

1606. Chevalier, Christa. *Spence Makes Circles* (Whitman, 1982) k–3. Spence acquires a moustache and an odd-looking haircut when he throws himself into an independent art project.

1607. ____. *Spence and the Sleepy Time Monster* (Whitman, 1984) k–3. A monster really does come to Spence's room when the lights go out, but this time he captures it himself.

1608. ____. *Spence Isn't Spence Anymore* (Whitman, 1985) k–3. Spence disguises himself as somebody else for a while, but when his mother does the same, he finds it upsetting, and decides it's also good to be oneself.

1609. ____. *Spence and the Mean Old Bear* (Whitman, 1986) k–3. Angry at his mother, Spence draws a mean old bear who comes to life to take her away and then Spence is sorry.

1610. ____. *Spence Is Small* (Whitman, 1987) k–3. Spence finds he is too short to perform some tasks but just the right size to help his mother do others.

1611. Childs, Rob. *Soccer at Sanford* (Blackie, 1980) 4–6.

1612. ____. *Sandford on the Run* (Blackie, 1982) 4–6.

1613. ____. *Sanford on Tour* (Blackie, 1983) 4–6. Gary, a football player is temperamental due to troubles at home. The story describes football games with

authority and understanding. Gary and his friends play April Fool's Day tricks.

1614. ____. *Sanford in to Bat* (Blackie, 1987) 4–6. Chris Webster, the young hero of this story, is obsessed by his chosen sport and acts out his assumed superiority to the point where he angers his friends and teachers and gets dropped from the team.

1615. Chorao, Kay. *Magic Eye for Ida* (Seabury, 1973) 2–4. Running away because she feels ordinary and ignored, Ida meets a palmist who helps her find a special talent of her own.

1616. ____. *Ida Makes a Movie* (Seabury, 1974) 2–4. Ida is troubled when the judges of the Children's Film Making Contest award her movie first prize, but completely misinterprets the plot.

1617. ____. *Ida and Betty and the Secret Eggs* (Clarion, 1992) 2–4. Vacationing in the country, Ida, a spunky kitten, becomes jealous when an older kitten makes friends with Ida's best friend, Betty.

1618. Chorao, Kay. *Molly's Moe* (Seabury, 1976) k–3. Through a process of systematic deduction, Molly finds not only her lost stuffed dinosaur Moe, but also lots of other things she's misplaced.

1619. ____. *Molly's Lies* (Seabury, 1979) k–3. Challenged by a classmate on the first day of school, Molly stops making up stories and admits her fears.

1620. Chorao, Kay. *Oink and Pearl* (Harper, 1981) 2–4. Presents the adventures of two piglets, Pearl and her little brother Oink.

1621. ____. *Ups and Downs with Oink and Pearl* (Harper, 1986) 2–4. Piglet Oink concocts an unusual birthday present for his sister Pearl, helps her escape from a witch, and ignores her advice on a mail-order movie projector.

1622. Chorao, Kay. *Kate's Box* (Dutton, 1982) k–3. Kate hides in a box when cousin Otto comes to visit.

1623. ____. *Kate's Car* (Dutton, 1982) k–3. A misunderstanding about Kate's desire for a "car" is resolved by a family friend.

1624. ____. *Kate's Quilt* (Dutton, 1982) k–3. Kate's disappointment over receiving a quilt instead of a doll changes as a night grows cold and scary.

1625. ____. *Kate's Snowman* (Dutton, 1982) k–3. Kate plans to incorporate certain family traits into her snowman.

1626. ____. *George Told Kate* (Dutton, 1987) k–3. George delights in misleading his sister, Kate, about the difficulty of cleaning his room, going to school, and the possibility of moving to a new home.

1627. Christelow, Eileen. *Henry and the Red Stripes* (Clarion, 1982) k–3. A small brown rabbit finds a very good reason for not painting red stripes on his fur.

1628. ____. *Henry and the Dragon* (Clarion, 1984) k–3. At bedtime Henry Rabbit is sure he sees a shadow of a dragon on his bedroom wall even though his parents can find no evidence of it.

1629. Christelow, Eileen. *Jerome and the Baby-sitter* (Clarion, 1985) k–3. Mrs. Gatoman's nine frisky little pranksters put Jerome, their baby-sitter, through his paces.
1630. ____. *Jerome and the Witchcraft Kids* (Clarion, 1988) k–3. Jerome Alligator's skill is put to the test of Halloween night when he baby-sits Mrs. Witchcraft's two devilish kids, Lucy and Lucifer.

1631. Christelow, Eileen. *Five Little Monkeys Jumping on the Bed* (Clarion, 1989) k–3. A counting book in which, one by one, the little monkeys jump on the bed only to fall off and bump their heads.
1632. ____. *Five Little Monkeys Sitting in a Tree* (Clarion, 1991) k–3. Five little monkeys sitting in a tree discover, one by one, that it is unwise to tease Mr. Alligator.
1633. ____. *Don't Wake Up Mama* (Clarion, 1992) k–3. Five little monkeys wake up with the sun. Today is their mama's birthday and they are going to bake her a cake. They'll have to measure the flour, mix in the eggs and get it in the oven without waking Mama.

1634. Christian, Mary. *Sebastian (Super Sleuth) and the Hair of the Dog Mystery* (Macmillan, 1982) 3–5. A clever dog helps his owner solve a case involving a missing Gypsy necklace, an evil curse, and a kidnapped, larcenous cat.
1635. ____. *Sebastian (Super Sleuth) and the Crummy Yummies Caper* (Macmillan, 1983) 3–5. The world's greatest four-legged detective goes underground, posing as an ordinary dog in order to foil a dognapping at a local dog show.
1636. ____. *Sebastian (Super Sleuth) and the Bone to Pick Mystery* (Macmillan, 1983) 3–5. While investigating a case of breaking and entering at the local museum the canine detective uncovers a fraud involving dinosaur bones.
1637. ____. *Sebastian (Super Sleuth) and the Secret of the Skewered Skier* (Macmillan, 1984) 3–5. While on a ski trip to the Frozen Dreams resort, Sebastian, dog detective, and his master, John, run into a case of jewel theft.
1638. ____. *Sebastian (Super Sleuth) and the Santa Claus Caper* (Macmillan, 1984) 3–5. Dog detective Sebastian goes undercover as Santa Claus to unravel a mystery at a department store.
1639. ____. *Sebastian (Super Sleuth) and the Clumsy Cowboy* (Macmillan, 1985) 3–5. Dog detective Sebastian goes on an enforced vacation to a seemingly haunted dude ranch.
1640. ____. *Sebastian (Super Sleuth) and the Purloined Sirloin* (Macmillan, 1986) 3–5. Dog detective Sebastian is on the trail of auto thieves and also tries to retrieve his stolen sirloin.
1641. ____. *Sebastian (Super Sleuth) and the Stars-in-His-Eyes Mystery* (Macmillan, 1987) 3–5. Myste-

rious attacks on Chummy the Wonder Dog lead canine detective Sebastian to go underground as a stunt performer in the making of Chummy's new movie.
1642. ____. *Sebastian (Super Sleuth) and the Egyptian Connection* (Macmillan, 1988) 3–5. Dog detective Sebastian helps his master find a shipment of stolen Egyptian artifacts that is being smuggled into the country.
1643. ____. *Sebastian (Super Sleuth) and the Time Capsule Caper* (Macmillan, 1989) 3–5. Dog detective Sebastian investigates the disappearance of the contents from a rich family's 60-year-old time capsule.
1644. ____. *Sebastian (Super Sleuth) and the Baffling Big Foot* (Macmillan, 1990) 3–5. Sebastian the dog and his detective master search for Big Foot and other suspects when a guest is attacked by something "big and hairy" at the Sasquatch Inn.
1645. ____. *Sebastian (Super Sleuth) and the Mystery Patient* (Macmillan, 1991) 3–5. Dog detective Sebastian helps his master protect a mystery patient at City hospital at a time when an attempted coup has just occurred in a nation friendly to the United States.
1646. ____. *Sebastian (Super Sleuth) and the Impossible Crime* (Macmillan, 1992) 3–5. When a painting disappears into thin air before a crowd of guests, the police chief promises results within 48 hours. It's Sebastian to the rescue. He sniffs out the culprit and saves his human's reputation.
1647. ____. *Sebastian (Super Sleuth) and the Copycat Crime* (Macmillan, 1983) 3–5. While speaking at a crime conference, bumbling detective John Quincy Jones is aided by his capable canine in solving the mystery of two missing manuscripts.
1648. ____. *Sebastian (Super Sleuth) and the Flying Elephant* (Macmillan, 1994) 3–5. Sebastian the canine sleuth comes to the aid of detective John Q. Jones to solve the mystery of the missing circus elephant.

1649. Christian, Mary. *Goosehill Gang and the May Basket Mystery* (Concordia, 1977) k–3. Pete decides the family next door are "wierdos" because they never speak, but learns along with the other members of his gang that the family is not weird but handicapped.
1650. ____. *Goosehill Gang and the Mystery of the Runaway House* (Concordia, 1977) k–3. In solving the mystery of the runaway house, the Goosehill gang starts a project that benefits the children of their neighborhood.

1651. Christian, Mary. *Penrod's Pants* (Macmillan, 1986) 3–5. Despite Penrod Porcupine's sometimes exasperating behavior, he and Griswold Bear remain good friends.
1652. ____. *Penrod Again* (Macmillan, 1987) 3–5. The adventures of two friends who sometimes argue, but really love and support each other.
1653. ____. *Penrod's Party* (Macmillan, 1990) 3–5.

Presents the amusing adventures of two friends Griswold Bear and Penrod Porcupine.

1654. ____. *Penrod's Picture* (Macmillan, 1991) 3–5. Penrod Porcupine gives Griswold Bear a picture he has drawn and Griswold used it to cover a hole in his wall. Penrod buys an out of date magazine, plants weeds unsuccessfully and has a garage sale.

1655. Christian, Mary. *Green Thumb Thief* (Whitman, 1982) k–3. Deke and Snitch, the Undercover Kids, track down a plant thief with the help of a tiny dog and some far-reaching disguises.
1656. ____. *Undercover Kids and the Museum Mystery* (Whitman, 1983) k–3. Deke and Snitch find out who's stealing priceless relics from the Egyptian exhibit at the museum.

1657. Christian, Mary. *Mysterious Case Case* (Dutton, 1985) 2–4. Boy detectives Fenton and Gerald and their rival Mae Donna find their sleuthing talents severely tested when they tangle with a bank robber.
1658. ____. *Phantom of the Operetta* (Dutton, 1986) 2–4. Intrepid detectives Fenton and Gerald and their rival Mae Donna try to discover who or what is haunting the local Civic Theater.
1659. ____. *Merger on the Orient Expressway* (Dutton, 1986) 2–4. Fenton P. Smith and Gerald Grubbs the Determined Detectives, investigate a case of construction bidding which has made Fenton's mother look like she's being disloyal to her firm.
1660. ____. *Maltese Feline* (Dutton, 1988) 2–4. Fenton P. Smith and Gerald investigate a suspected kidnapping after finding a note containing a plea for help tucked inside a cat's collar.

1661. Christian, Mary. *Swamp Monsters* (Dial, 1983) 2–4. A duo of young swamp monsters who are convinced that children are make-believe, find themselves in a school with real children and a substitute teacher.
1662. ____. *Go West, Swamp Monsters* (Dial, 1985) 2–4. Four young swamp monsters put on cowboy clothes and go in search of the wild, wild West.

1663. Christian, Mary. *Mystery of the Missing Scarf* (Milliken, 1989) 4–6. A multi-ethnic group of boys and girls, the Sherlock Street Detectives, solve minor mysteries. This one centers around a homemade weather vane.
1664. ____. *UFO Mystery* (Milliken, 1989) 4–6. A multi-ethnic group of boys and girls, the Sherlock Street Detectives, solve minor mysteries. In this edition they work with a telescope.
1665. ____. *Pet Day Mystery* (Milliken, 1989) 4–6. A multi-ethnic group of boys and girls, the Sherlock Street Detectives, solve minor mysteries. The main emphasis in this one is on information about animal habits.
1666. ____. *North Pole Mystery* (Milliken, 1989) 4–6. A multi-ethnic group of boys and girls solve

minor mysteries. In this episode they work with a homemade compass.
1667. ____. *Mystery of the Message from the Sky* (Whitman, 1992) 4–6. Four children (two blonde, one Hispanic and one Afro-American) make up the Sherlock Street Detectives. They focus on a balloon coated in chili pepper, a silver disk like cat's eyes that falls from the air with a partially destroyed role.
1668. ____. *Mystery of the Fallen Tree* (Whitman, 1992) 4–6. There are four children (two blonde, one Hispanic and one Afro-American) in the Sherlock Street Detectives. They discover who destroyed a sapling and make arrangements for it to be replaced.
1669. ____. *Mystery of the Polluted Stream* (Milliken, 1992) 4–6. The four children (two blonde, one Hispanic and one Afro-American) of the Sherlock Street Detectives hunt for all possible polluters responsible for a fish kill.

1670. Christopher, Matt. *Dog That Stole Football Plays* (Little, 1980) 3–5. Mike listens while his telepathic dog transmits the opposing team's signals. When Harry, the dog, gets sick the team must win without that kind of "cheating."
1671. ____. *Dog That Called the Signals* (Little, 1982) 3–5. During a football game, Harry, the dog calls plays from the home of the sick coach.
1672. ____. *Dog That Pitched a No-Hitter* (Little, 1988) 3–5. Mike's telepathic dog, Harry, is sending his usual signals but Mike's pitching is so bad they must try another plan.
1673. ____. *Dog That Stole Home* (Little, 1993) 4–6. When his telepathic dog Harry is grounded for nipping another dog, Mike wonders how he'll ever make it through the baseball game without his advice and encouragement.

1674. Christopher, Matt. *Johnny Long Legs* (Little, 1970) 4–6. Johnny was tall with long legs but he was being outplayed by shorter members of the basketball team. Why?
1675. ____. *Johnny No Hit* (Little, 1977) 4–6. Threatened with a beating if he hits against Roy's pitching, Johnny almost loses a ball game for his team.

1676. Christopher, Matt. *Kid Who Only Hit Homers* (Little, 1972) 4–6. When a mysterious man promises to make him a great player, Sylvester accepts and begins a phenomenal home–run streak.
1677. ____. *Return of the Home Run King* (Little, 1992) 4–6. Sylvester meets an ex–baseball player, Cheeko, who offers him a few pointers and his game improves. But Sylvester suspects Cheeko and his own ability to play.

1678. Christopher, Matt. *Team That Couldn't Lose* (Little, 1967) 4–6. A young, inexperienced football team discovers that its beginner's luck is due to a series of mysterious but successful plays anonymously sent to their coach.
1679. ____. *Team That Stopped Moving* (Little,

1975) 4–6. A new baseball team gets some supernatural help from a concerned wizard.

1680. Churchill, David. *It, Us and the Others* (Heinemann, 1979) 5–8. When Andy goes fishing, there is something nasty at the bottom of the river. It communicates by tugging on the fishing line. Andy wants to help return it to the strange dimension from which it has become exiled. Jill, a handicapped girl, is Andy's friend and helps in the adventure. She is rewarded by a tandem bike ride with Andy.

1681. ____. *Silbury Triangle* (Heinemann, 1979) 5–8. Steve and Jo on a UFO hunt see a mysterious object emerging from Silbury Hill and inform the police. Then the objects form themselves into a huge flower and disappear. Steve decides this was a signal for friendliness.

1682. Clare, Helen. *Five Dolls in the House* (Prentice, 1965) 4–6. The dolls are Vanessa, the bossy one; Jane, the helpful one; Jacqueline, the foreign paying guest; Lupin, who wears her happy vest and Amanda, the pretty one. And, of course, the monkey who lived on the roof.

1683. ____. *Five Dolls in the Snow* (Prentice, 1967) 4–6. Elizabeth makes herself small and visits the five dolls in their doll house when it snowed, for a train ride, during a garden party and other special occasions.

1684. ____. *Five Dolls and the Monkey* (Prentice, 1967) 4–8. Elizabeth visits her dollhouse, turning herself into Mrs. Small and enters the lives of the dolls.

1685. ____. *Five Dolls and the Duke* (Prentice, 1968) 4–6. More adventures with Elizabeth, who can grow small enough to join her five dolls in their dollhouse. Here, the Duke of Cranberry, supposedly the father of one of the dolls, arrives for a visit.

1686. ____. *Five Dolls and Their Friends* (Prentice, 1968) 4–6. A story of Elizabeth Small and the tenants of her doll's house.

1687. Claret, Maria. *Melissa Mouse* (Barron, 1985) k–3. Every month Melissa Mouse's magic cupboard gives her a piece of advice, which is reinforced by her friends' behavior.

1688. ____. *Melissa Mouse's Birthday Surprise* (Barron, 1987) k–3. This story shows how Melissa Mouse uses her magic cupboard's advice about the birthday party.

1689. Clark, Margaret. *Barney and the UFO* (Dodd, 1979) 4–6. Tibbo of the U.F.O. wants to take Barney in his spacecraft. Barney feels unwanted and is tempted to go but he finds he is loved and Tibbo leaves promising to return.

1690. ____. *Barney in Space* (Dodd, 1981) 4–6. Rokell, a deranged Gark, decides that Barney is an enemy of his planet. Barney is trapped but released before a trip to the moon for a showdown.

1691. ____. *Barney on Mars* (Dodd, 1983) 4–6. Tibbo returns to Earth to warn Barney about a flood. He goes to Mars with Tibbo to rescue his dog, Alfie.

But the Garks say they rescued him and he is theirs but gives him back in the end.

1692. Clarke, Pauline. *Return of the Twelve* (Coward, 1963) 4–6. Max, eight, plays in the attic with twelve odd-looking toy soldiers who tell him their secret that they once belonged to the famous Bronte children and now want to get back to the family home, which has become a museum.

1693. ____. *Twelve and the Genii* (Coward, 1977) 4–6. Fantasy has entered the lives of the Morley family, though, at first, only the youngest, Max, knows about it; it is the possession of the toy soldiers which are really alive.

1694. Cleary, Beverly. *Dear Mr. Henshaw* (Morrow, 1983) 4–6. In his letters to his favorite author, Leigh, ten, reveals his problems in coping with his parents' divorce, being the new boy in school, and generally finding his own place in the world.

1695. ____. *Strider* (Morrow, 1991) 4–6. In a series of diary entries, Leigh tells how he comes to terms with his parents' divorce, acquires an abandoned dog and joins the track team.

1696. Cleary, Beverly. *Ellen Tebbits* (Morrow, 1951) 4–6. Ellen, a third grader, gets her wish for a best friend. Austine lives nearby, goes to the same school and, like Ellen, must wear winter underwear.

1697. ____. *Otis Spofford* (Morrow, 1953) 4–6. Otis is a mischievous, impudent, class clown. He is a show–off and a pest, but still likable. He and Ellen Tebbits tangle often.

1698. Clevin, Jorgen. *Jacob and Joachim* (Benn, 1969) 2–4. Jacob and Joachim live at #14 Flower Road. Joachim tells Jacob what he wants for his birthday. Jacob looks after him, wraps his present and packs his school lunch (Jacob and Joachim are the same as Johnny and Pete).

1699. ____. *Jacob and Joachim's Rescue Service* (Benn, 1972) 2–4. Jacob is a small boy and Joachim is an elephant. They have a rescue service. They tackle anything from putting out forest fires to helping old ladies with their shopping.

1700. ____. *Pete's First Day at School* (Random, 1973) k–3. Pete, an elephant, lives with Johnny who watches over him. It is a question and answer child participation book.

1701. ____. *Peter the Mouse* (Random, 1973) k–3.

1702. ____. *Jacob and Joachim on Holiday* (Benn, 1974) 2–4. Jacob and his friend Joachim the elephant decide to go on a vacation by a game of chance.

1703. ____. *Pete and Johnny to the Rescue* (Random, 1974) k–3. Johnny and his elephant friend Pete form a rescue squad to return an escaped canary, to cheer up hospital patients, and to otherwise help the people of their town.

1704. Clewes, Dorothy. *Mystery of the Scarlet Daffodil* (Coward, 1953,) 5–8. Peter, 16, and the five other Hadley children try to find out who stole the rare scarlet daffodil before the flower show. The gardener? A gypsy boy? The Maid?

1705. ____. *Mystery of the Blue Admiral* (Coward, 1954) 5–8. The Hadley children recover a stolen painting which reveals the hiding place of a buried treasure.

1706. ____. *Mystery of the Jade–Green Cadillac* (Coward, 1958) 5–8. The Hadley children in Vienna are followed by a Cadillac because Bobbie looks like the son of a Hungarian refugee.

1707. ____. *Mystery of the Lost Tower Treasure* (Coward, 1960) 5–8. The Hadley children look for a long lost treasure in the Tower of London and find a boy who tells about an attempt to steal the crown jewels.

1708. ____. *Mystery of the Singing Strings* (Coward, 1961) 5–8. A famous violinist hides a piece of music and the Hadley children want to find out why.

1709. ____. *Mystery of the Midnight Smugglers* (Coward, 1964) 5–8. Three youngsters are embroiled in a plot that defied solution, a plot that unravels clue by clue—from a gold watch to a blind organist, from a lobster fisherman to a trick chimney.

1710. ____. *Roller Skates, Scooter and Bike* (Coward, 1966) 5–8. The adventures of three children as they look for a missing scooter and a racing bicycle.

1711. Clewes, Dorothy. *Secret* (Coward, 1956) 4–6. Kay and Rory find a garden, build a rabbit hutch and use it as a secret place but a classmate finds out and wants to use it his own way.

1712. ____. *Old Pony* (Coward, 1960) 4–6. Kay and Rory want to rescue the old milk pony that is being replaced by a truck. How do you care for a secret pony?

1713. ____. *Hidden Key* (Coward, 1961) 4–6. Rory and Kay take over a grocery store to help Mr. Marsden but they do more harm than good with their good intentions.

1714. Clewes, Dorothy. *Runaway* (Coward, 1957) 3–5. Penny moves to a new town where she knows no one. She wants to run away to the city but she meets the postman and the milkman. She then finds an important letter which she and Maxwell return to the colonel.

1715. ____. *Hide-and-seek* (Coward, 1960) 3–5. Penny's day on the farm is different from what she imagined. The farm is not a play-land but a very busy place with lots to do.

1716. ____. *Holiday* (Coward, 1964) 3–5. Penny visits an English seaport with her friend, Maxwell. They are invited aboard a boat. They are accidentally bound across the channel for France. They have a wonderful adventure.

1717. Clifford, Eth. *Flatfoot Fox and the Case of the Missing Eye* (Houghton, 1990) 2–4. Fox uncovers the thief who stole Fat Cat's glass eye.

1718. ____. *Flatfoot Fox and the Case of the Nosy Otter* (Houghton, 1992) 2–4. Mrs. Chatterbox asks Flatfoot Fox to find her missing son.

1719. ____. *Flatfoot Fox and the Case of the Missing Whooo* (Houghton, 1993) 2–4. Flatfoot Fox deals with distractions from Silly Goose, Pushy Peacock and Cranky Worm as he tries to find out what happened to Mournful Owl's whooo.

1720. ____. *Flatfoot Fox and the Case of the Bashful Beaver* (Houghton, 1995) k–3. Although Flatfoot Fox is fairly certain that he knows who stole Bashful Beaver's buttons, the smartest detective in the world allows his assistant Secretary Bird, to try to solve the case.

1721. Clifton, Lucille. *Some of the Days of Everett Anderson* (Holt, 1970/1987) k–3. Nine poems about a boy who likes to play in the rain, is not afraid of the dark and sometimes feels lonely.

1722. ____. *Everett Anderson's Nine Month Long* (Holt, 1970/1987) k–3. A small boy and his family anticipate the birth of their newest member.

1723. ____. *Everett Anderson Christmas Coming* (Holt, 1971/1991 k–3. Relates, in verse, the excitement and joy of a young boy anticipating, as well as celebrating, Christmas in the city.

1724. ____. *Everett Anderson's Year* (Holt, 1974) k–3. Chronicles, in verse, the month-to-month activities of seven-year-old Everett Anderson throughout the seasons of the year.

1725. ____. *Everett Anderson's Friend* (Hold, 1976) k–3. Having eagerly anticipated the new neighbors, a boy is disappointed to get a whole family of girls.

1726. ____. *Everett Anderson's 1–2–3* (Holt, 1977) k–3. A small boy's mother considers remarriage, he considers the numbers one, two, and three—sometimes they're lonely, sometimes crowded, but sometimes just right.

1727. ____. *Everett Anderson's Goodbye* (Holt, 1983) k–3. Everett Anderson has a difficult time coming to terms with his grief after his father dies.

1728. Clymer, Eleanor. *Horatio* (Atheneum, 1968) 3–5. Horatio, the cat, is quite disgruntled when his owner starts to bring other pets into the house. He runs away to get some peace but finds his troubles just beginning.

1729. ____. *Leave Horatio Alone* (Atheneum, 1974) 3–5. Upset at being left alone with Mrs. Casey's other pets, Horatio the cat leaves home only to get involved with something even more upsetting—a baby.

1730. ____. *Horatio's Birthday* (Atheneum, 1976) 3–5. Finding the house too quiet after Mrs. Casey's other pets grow up and leave home, Horatio begins to mope until he finds a way to remedy the situation.

1731. ____. *Horatio Goes to the Country* (Atheneum, 1978) 3–5. Everything about the farm visit was awful, until Horatio the cat explored the beauties of a meadow at night.

1732. ____. *Horatio Solves a Mystery* (Atheneum,

1980) 3–5. Horatio is not concerned about the missing items around the house until it is his catnip tiger that is missing. Then he goes on the prowl for the culprit.

1733. Coatsworth, Elizabeth. *Bob Bodden and the Good Ship Rover* (Garrard, 1968) 2–4. Having smashed his huge ship into the South Pole, Bob Bodden decides to leave it behind to be mistaken for a new continent.

1734. ____. *Bob Bodden and the Seagoing Farm* (Garrard, 1970) 2–4. Homesick for the Maine farm where he grew up, Captain Bob sets up a farm on his ship.

1735. Coatsworth, Elizabeth. *Grandmother Cat and the Hermit* (Macmillan, 1970) 2–4. On an exploring trip up an arroyo, a young boy and his cat discover the well-hidden home of a hermit who is the friend of all the animals.

1736. ____. *Grandmother Cat* (Atheneum, 1971) 2–4. Dave and his crusty old cat walk through California country. They make friends with a hermit who lives with animals as his friends; he has barley and vegetables as his diet.

1737. Cohen, Barbara. *R My Name is Rosie* (Lothrop, 1978) 5–8. Rosie lives in a hotel her mother owns and runs. She is fat and lonely with few friends. She dreams about another life as compared with real life.

1738. ____. *Innkeeper's Daughter* (Lothrop, 1979) 5–9. Rachel is Rosie's older sister. Their mother runs a hotel. There is a fire and a valuable painting is saved. The money is used to rebuild the hotel.

1739. Cohen, Barbara. *Christmas Revolution* (Lothrop, 1987) 4–6. Emily is Jewish and protests the school's Winter Concert. There is a vandalism problem that Emily and her sister correct.

1740. ____. *Orphan Game* (Lothrop, 1988) 4–6. Sally, Emily and their friends play a game of being orphans and running away from a cruel home. Miranda, an adopted cousin is spoiling the fun.

1741. Cohen, Barbara. *Molly's Pilgrim* (Lothrop, 1983) k–3. Told to make a doll like a pilgrim for a Thanksgiving school display, Molly's Jewish mother dresses the doll as she herself dressed before leaving Russia to seek religious freedom—much to Molly's embarrassment.

1742. ____. *Make a Wish, Molly* (Doubleday, 1994) k–3. Molly, who recently emigrated with her family from Russia to New Jersey, learns about birthday parties and who her real friends are.

1743. Cohen, Dan. *Mystery of the Faded Footprint* (Carolrhoda, 1979) 2–4. Two sisters, Ruthann and Polly, assist their police officer friend in following clues to find who stole a wallet.

1744. ____. *Mystery of the Marked Money* (Carolrhoda, 1979) 2–4. Two young girls help solve a case of fraud involving marked bills.

1745. ____. *Mystery of the Locked Door* (Carolrhoda, 1979) 2–4. Two sisters help Officer Greenwood locate a coin stolen from a valuable collection.

1746. ____. *Case of the Missing Poodle* (Carolrhoda, 1979) 2–4. A poodle disappears from a dog show and sisters Ruthann and Polly help Officer Greenwood find the dognapper.

1747. ____. *Mystery of the Missing Ring* (Carolrhoda, 1980) 2–4. Polly and Ruthann help Officer Greenwood identify the thief who made off with Lefty Pearson's World Series ring.

1748. ____. *Mystery of the Mellareller Elephant* (Carolrhoda, 1980) 2–4. When a valuable piece of art disappears from a museum, Ruthann and her sister Polly help Officer Greenwood solve the mystery.

1749. ____. *Case of the Spanish Stamps* (Carolrhoda, 1980) 2–4. Two girls are on vacation in Mexico City with their parents. A thief steals two Spanish stamps during a stamp show.

1750. ____. *Case of the Supermarket Swindle* (Carolrhoda, 1980) 2–4. Polly and Ruthann inadvertently provide a crucial clue in a mystery involving disappearing groceries.

1751. Cohen, Miriam. *Tough Jim* (Macmillan, 1974) k–3. The first grade's costume party is interrupted by the third grade bully.

1752. ____. *Jim Meets the Thing* (Greenwillow, 1981) k–3. The only one in first grade afraid of the Thing, Jim overcomes his fear on the playground.

1753. ____. *Jim's Dog Muffins* (Greenwillow, 1984) k–3. When Jim's dog is killed, the other first graders experience with him his natural reactions to death.

1754. Colbert, A. *Amanda Has a Surprise* (Macmillan, 1971) k–3. An account of a small girl's rowing boat outing with her father. She finds magic and joy in all she views.

1755. ____. *Amanda Goes Dancing* (Macmillan, 1972) k–3. Amanda's father takes her on his bicycle to dancing class; they buy fruit and flowers in the marketplace, Amanda puts a coin in a collection box and she sees a wedding.

1756. Cole, Babette. *Nungu and the Hippopotamus* (McGraw, 1978) k–3. A young African boy living in a remote village where water is scarce goes on a journey to make a river reappear.

1757. ____. *Nungu and the Elephant* (McGraw, 1980) k–3. A young African boy living in an area that hasn't had rain for two years befriends a clumsy elephant that wanders into the village and discovers he is one of the three animals responsible for making rain.

1758. Cole, Joanna. *Magic School Bus at the Water Works* (Scholastic, 1986) k–3. Ms. Frizzle, the strangest teacher in school, takes her class on a field trip to the waterworks, everyone ends up experiencing the water purification system from the inside.

1759. ____. *Magic School Bus Inside the Earth* (Scholastic, 1987) k–3. On a special field trip in the magic school bus, Ms. Frizzle's class learns firsthand about different kinds of rocks and the formation of the earth.

1760. ____. *Magic School Bus Lost in the Solar System* (Scholastic, 1990) k–3. On a special field trip in the magic school bus Ms. Frizzle's class goes into outer space and visits each planet in the solar system.

1761. ____. *Magic School Bus Inside the Human Body* (Scholastic, 1990) k–3. A special field trip on the magic school bus allows Ms. Frizzle's class to get a first hand look at major parts of the body and how they work.

1762. ____. *Magic School Bus on the Ocean Floor* (Scholastic, 1992) k–3. On another special field trip on the magic school bus, Ms. Frizzle's class learns about the ocean and the different creatures that live there.

1763. ____. *Magic School Bus in the Time of the Dinosaur* (Scholastic, 1994) k–3. A trip to a dinosaur dig turns into a time-travel journey through the past with Ms. Frizzle and her class of students.

1764. ____. *Magic School Bus Plants Seeds* (Scholastic, 1995) k–3. The class's garden is to be featured in a magazine, but one of the plots is empty. Ms. Frizzle shrinks the bus to the size of a ladybug and the class is off and flying to find a plant for it.

1765. ____. *Magic School Bus Gets Baked in a Cake* (Scholastic, 1995) k–3. Ms. Frizzle's class learns about kitchen chemistry.

1766. ____. *Magic School Bus in the Haunted Museum* (Scholastic, 1995) k–3. A book about sound, acoustics and physics as observed by Ms. Frizzle and her class.

1767. ____. *Magic School Bus Inside a Hurricane* (Scholastic, 1995) k–3. The Magic School Bus goes up in a hurricane from start to finish, from edge to eye; Arnold falls in the ocean, and on the fashion front, the forecast is for Bees.

1768. ____. *Magic School Bus Hops Home* (Scholastic, 1995) k–3. Wanda turns the entire classroom into a comfortable new home for her pet frog, Bella. When Bella jumps out an open window, Wanda learns to rethink her idea of what a frog needs.

1769. ____. *Magic School Bus Inside the Haunted House* (Scholastic, 1995) k–3. The class is thrilled about their upcoming concert at the Sound Museum...until they discover that the spooky mansion is more of a thrill than they bargained for.

1770. ____. *Magic School Bus Plays Ball* (Scholastic, 1995) k–3.

1771. ____. *Magic School Bus Meets the Rot Squad* (Scholastic,) 1995. k–3

1772. ____. *Magic School Bus Gets Ants in Its Pants* (Scholastic, 1995) k–3.

1773. ____. *Magic School Bus Gets All Dried Up* (Scholastic, 1995) k–3.

1774. ____. *Magic School Bus Blows Its Top* (Scholastic, 1995) k–3. Ms. Frizzle's class is having a hard time putting together a giant globe of the world. A piece is missing...an island so new it hasn't been discovered yet. And the Friz knows where to find it. Before they know it, the kids are beneath the ocean's surface exploring an underworld volcano.

1775. ____. *Magic School Bus Explores the Ocean* (Scholastic, 1995) k–3.

1776. ____. *Magic School Bus Gets Eaten* (Scholastic, 1995) k–3. A trip to the ocean becomes a search for the connection between Arnold's soggy shoe full of pond scum and Keesha's tuna fish sandwich. The bus shrinks and travels through the ocean food chain, getting eaten along the way.

1777. ____. *Magic School Bus Goes to Seed* (Scholastic, 1995) k–3.

1778. ____. *Magic School Bus Inside Ralphie* (Scholastic, 1995) k–3.

1779. ____. *Magic School Bus Inside a Beehive* (Scholastic, 1996) k–3. Ms. Frizzle's class is off on another wild field trip that teaches readers about bees and honey while providing plenty of laughs.

1780. ____. *Magic School Bus Gets Lost in Space* (Scholastic, 1996) k–3. When Ms. Frizzle's class gets lost while on a field trip in outer space, Arnold's know-it-all cousin Jane may be the only one who can save them.

1781. Cole, Joanna. *Clown-Arounds* (Parents, 1981) k–3. The Clown-Around family enters a contest, which promises a big surprise for the winner.

1782. ____. *Clown-Arounds Have a Party* (Parents, 1982) k–3. The funniest family in town pulls some of their best high jinks to cheer up homesick Cousin Fizzy.

1783. ____. *Get Well Clown-Arounds* (Parents, 1983) k–3. A wacky family thinks that they have become very sick when they look in a mirror and see green spots.

1784. ____. *Clown-Arounds Go on Vacation* (Parents, 1984) k–3. The Clown-Around family has some misadventures on its way to visit Uncle Waldo.

1785. ____. *Sweet Dreams, Clown-Arounds* (Parents, 1993) k–3. After an exciting and busy day, the Clown-Around family has trouble getting Baby to go to bed.

1786. Cole, Michael. *Bod's Apple* (Follett, 1967) k–3. Chubby Bod is amazed when the apple he tosses up fails to come down. Aunt Flo, Frank the postman and other friends wait with him till at last...

1787. ____. *Bod's Dream* (Follett, 1967) k–3. Bod has a dream about strawberries with cream and all the next day he can think of nothing else.

1788. ____. *Bod and the Cherry Tree* (Follett, 1967) k–3. Bod teaches Aunt Flo that everything happens to cherry trees for a reason.

1789. ____. *Lot of Bod* (Follett, 1978) k–3. Six stories about Bod: one about a kite which gets mixed up with a helicopter; one on the beach where poor Aunt Flo finds that collecting shells can be hazardous as the tide comes in. And others where Bod meets dogs of all sizes and shapes until he finds the right one to play with.

1790. ____. *Bod's Present* (Follett, 1975) k–3. Aunt Flo does not flinch when she receives four identical hats for Christmas.

1791. ____. *Bod in the Park* (Follett, 1975) k–3.

1792. ____. *Bod and the Birds* (Follett, 1975) k–3.

1793. Cole, Michael. *Kate and Sam's Tea* (Methuen, 1971) k–3. Kate and Sam have ideas about what their mother is going to provide for tea. They include caravan cake, rainbow juice and fish and chips. They got jelly, meringues and fuzzy orange. Just what they wanted!

1794. ____. *Kate and Sam* (Methuen, 1971) k–3. Kate and Sam are brother and sister. They have mild fantasies and off they go but come back to reality, usually in time for bed.

1795. ____. *Kate and Sam Go Out* (Methuen, 1971) k–3.

1796. ____. *Kate and Sam's New Home* (Methuen, 1971) k–3. Shows the children inside a bird's nest, a rabbit hole, a goldfish bowl, and a great curly snail shell.

1797. ____. *Kate and Sam's Pet* (Methuen, 1971) k–3.

1798. Cole, Michael. *Gran Knits* (Blackie, 1983) k–3. Puppet–Gran demonstrates a happy contrast between white hair and eccentric enterprise. Her cheerful grin and floral apron are seen in some very ungrandmotherly scenes.

1799. ____. *Gran Camping* (Blackie, 1983) k–3. A stout, untidy granny is a contest between white hair and eccentric enterprises. These eight books cover, among other things, goatkeeping, hang-gliding and pet-keeping, amateur paleontology and television appearances. She is still willing to take on new experiences and happy to share them with Jim, her grandson.

1800. ____. *Gran Gliding* (Blackie, 1983) k–3. Gran is trying her hand at hang-gliding.

1801. ____. *Gran's Old Bones* (Blackie, 1983) k–3. Gran is an amateur paleontologist.

1802. ____. *Gran's Good News* (Blackie, 1983) k–3. The stout untidy granny is still open to new experiences and happy to share them with Jim, her grandson. Whether as television star, amateur paleontologist, hang-glider, or keeping of exotic pets.

1803. ____. *Gran's Goats* (Blackie, 1983) k–3. Gran is a goat keeper for Huddley pool.

1804. ____. *Gran's Pets* (Blackie, 1983) k–3. Gran is a collector of exotic pets.

1805. ____. *Gran's Game* (Blackie, 1983) k–3.

1806. Coleman, L. *Wilberforce and the Whale* (Blackie, 1973) 3–5. Wilberforce can talk; he goes on a diet and wears a Tam O' Shanter.

1807. ____. *Wilberforce and the McMonster* (Blackie, 1979) 3–5. Wilberforce gets a message to see his Aunty Barbacle at once. On the way he finds out that a mad professor wants to take her prisoner. Wilberforce turns into McMonster with a plan to save Aunty but the plan backfires and Aunty saves her nephew Wilberforce.

1808. Coles, Alison. *Mandy and the Train Journey* (EDC, 1984) k–3. Mandy has her first train journey alone.

1809. ____. *Mandy and the Hospital* (EDC, 1984) k–3. Mandy has to visit the hospital because of a cut on her knee, which requires stitches.

1810. ____. *Mandy and the Dentist* (EDC, 1986) k–3. Mandy fears going to the dentist for the first time because she needs a filling. But all goes well for her.

1811. Coles, Alison. *Michael's First Day at School* (EDC, 1985) k–3. Michael is anxious about his first day at school.

1812. ____. *Michael in the Dark* (EDC, 1985) k–3. Michael is afraid of the dark. When the light is turned on the ghostly shapes are seen as normal objects.

1813. ____. *Michael and the Sea* (EDC, 1986) k–3. Michael is able to conquer his fear of water with the help of his parents.

1814. Collier, James. *Teddy Bear Habit* (Norton, 1967) 5–8. George knows that at 12 he shouldn't depend on his teddy bear but when his father gives it away he tries to recapture it leading to an unexpected adventure.

1815. ____. *Rock Star* (Four Winds, 1970) 5–8. A young boy who loves music finds that even though he enjoys Rock he must study music seriously if he is to become a great musician.

1816. ____. *Rich and Famous* (Four Winds, 1975) 5–8. George is now 13 and plays the guitar. A record company makes an offer and George sees himself as a star. But he must contend with agents, television and advertising people.

1817. Colman, Hila. *Diary of a Frantic Kid Sister* (Crown, 1973) 5–8. Sarah and Didi are sisters. Sarah wants to write and slowly grows less dependent on her sister and becomes her own person.

1818. ____. *Nobody Has to Be a Kid Forever* (Crown, 1976) 5–8. Sarah kept a diary about school, parent problems, sister's romance and her own sexual awareness.

1819. Colman, Hila. *Rachel's Legacy* (Crown, 1979) 4–6. Ellie's mother, Rachel, tells of life in New York for Jewish immigrants during the Depression. Her two sisters took different paths to success. Ellie is like her mother.

1820. ____. *Ellie's Inheritance* (Crown, 1979) 4–6. Ellie, Rachel's daughter, lives with her father. She starts to follow the dressmaking business of her mother and has several romances.

1821. Colver, Anne. *Bread-and-Butter Indian* (Holt, 1964) 2–4. Barbara befriends an Indian who rescues her when she is kidnapped by his tribe in Pennsylvania, in 1783.

1822. ____. *Bread-and-Butter Journey* (Holt, 1964) 2–4. A family moves west in 1784 and they walked with packhorses. Barbara learns that home is where friends are, not the possessions they may own.

1823. Colver, Anne. *Borrowed Treasure* (Knopf, 1958) 4–6. Molly-O and Pip are friends; they want to own a horse. A farmer lends them a horse for the winter. They call it Borrowed Treasure.

1824. ____. *Secret Castle* (Knopf, 1960) 4–6. Pip and Molly-O solve a mystery with the Boldt castle in the Thousand Islands where they are vacationing. Old gift books in the library are the clues.

1825. Cone, Molly. *Mishmash* (Houghton, 1962) 4–6. Mishmash, a dog, moved like a cyclone into Pete's heart, his new house, the neighbor's garden and life was never the same. Mishmash introduced Pete to everyone in his new town.

1826. ____. *Mishmash and the Substitute Teacher* (Houghton, 1963) 4–6. Mishmash is a friendly black dog who creates a mishmash of everything for Pete, his friends, and their substitute teacher Miss Dingley.

1827. ____. *Mishmash and the Sauerkraut Mystery* (Houghton, 1965) 4–6. Mishmash has been sent to a kennel while Miss Patch is in Europe. Pete, Mishmash's former owner, is taking care of Miss Patch's lawn. Mishmash escapes and comes home. Someone stole six cases of sauerkraut. Is it Mishmash?

1828. ____. *Mishmash and Uncle Looey* (Houghton, 1968) 4–6. A dog that seems to have an imaginary playmate causes no end of trouble in the neighborhood.

1829. ____. *Mishmash and the Venus Flytrap* (Houghton, 1976) 4–6. As the owner of a Venus Flytrap, Miss Patch becomes suspicious when her dog Mishmash disappears.

1830. ____. *Mishmash and the Robot* (Houghton, 1981) 4–6. Mishmash falls in love with a robot and they both mysteriously disappear after a supermarket is burglarized.

1831. ____. *Mishmash and the Big Fat Problem* (Houghton, 1982) 4–6. When Mishmash the dog becomes overweight, Pete and Wanda try hypnosis and an exercise routine to get him slim again.

1832. Conford, Ellen. *Case for Jenny Archer* (Little, 1988) 3–5. After reading three mysteries in a row, Jenny becomes convinced that the neighbors across the street are up to no good and decides to investigate.

1833. ____. *Job for Jenny Archer* (Little, 1988) 3–5. Convinced that her parents are poor because they refuse to get her a horse or a swimming pool, Jenny, nine, follows her own path to making money including a plunge into real estate that puts her own house on the market.

1834. ____. *Jenny Archer, Author* (Little, 1989) 3–5. Stymied by an assignment to write her autobiography, Jenny decides to enhance her life story by using her considerable imagination.

1835. ____. *What's Cooking, Jenny Archer?* (Little, 1989) 3–5. Follows the comic mishaps of Jenny Archer as she goes into business preparing lunches for friends at school.

1836. ____. *Jenny Archer to the Rescue* (Little, 1990) 3–5. After perfecting her first aid skills, Jenny is disappointed in not finding anyone to rescue and decides to invent her own emergencies.

1837. ____. *Can Do, Jenny Archer* (Little, 1991) 3–5. Attempting to win a can-collecting contest, the winner of which will direct a class movie, Jenny risks losing her best friend.

1838. ____. *Nibble, Nibble, Jenny Archer* (Little, 1993) 3–5. Jenny Archer is excited about making a television commercial for a new snack food, until she discovers that the food she liked so much was meant for gerbils.

1839. ____. *Get the Picture, Jenny Archer* (Little, 1994) 3–5. Jenny lets her imagination run away with her when she decides to enter a photography contest and starts taking "candied," that is candid, pictures around her neighborhood.

1840. Conrad, Pam. *I Don't Live Here!* (Dutton, 1984) 3–5. Nicki, eight, believes she will never be happy in the large old house her family has moved to, even if it does have a gazebo in the yard.

1841. ____. *Seven Silly Circles* (Harper, 1987) 3–5. Nicki is embarrassed about the circles left on her face while playing with a rubber arrow, but supportive parents and friends help her forget her problems during the fun and commotion of a leaf-raking party.

1842. Cook, Ann. *Robot Comes to Stay* (Dell, 1982) k–3. The little girl tells how she uncovers Robot in a junkyard, takes him home, fixes him and becomes his friend.

1843. ____. *Robot in Danger* (Dell, 1982) k–3. Involves the little girl and the Robot in the high-tech adventure of watering a living room jungle of hanging plants which drip on rustable Robot.

1844. ____. *Robot Saves the Day* (Dell, 1982) k–3. Robot saves the day for the neighborhood kids by helping them train for the big "Track Meeting" and coming to the rescue when the stadium clock breaks down.

1845. ____. *Robot and the Flea Market* (Dell, 1982) k–3. Robot's idea for spring cleaning of the neighborhood kids' messy rooms is a kids' flea market where they will sell their old toys, hats, books. The sale is a success but everyone's room is full again with new "stuff."

1846. _____. *Robot Goes Collecting* (Dell, 1982) k–3. After visiting a collector's fair Robot and the little girl look for things to collect. The little girl looks for balls and Robot collects junk—a broken umbrella, squashed tin cans, etc. He makes them into a "little Robot."

1847. _____. *Robot Visits School* (Dell, 1982) k–3. Robot has his calculating mechanism repaired and helps the children tabulate the results of their survey about the suitability of the cafeteria food. They print and distribute these results.

1848. Coolidge, Susan. *What Katy Did* (Puffin, 1983) 3–5. A classic story, sometimes thought of as one of the first books for children. Katy is a tomboy and because she misbehaved, had a tragic accident. (A reissue of an 1872 printing.)

1849. _____. *What Katy Did Next* (Dell, 1965/1989) 3–5. More adventures of Katy, an early tomboy in children's stories. (A reissue of an 1873 printing.)

1850. _____. *What Katy Did at School* (Little, 1939/1985) 3–5. Katy and her sister Clover dread being sent away to boarding school, but discover that being away from home isn't so bad after all. (A reissue of an 1873 printing.)

1851. Coombs, Patricia. *Dorrie's Magic* (Lothrop, 1962) 2–4. Dorrie, a child witch, who didn't want to clean her room, looked for a potion that would do the task for her.

1852. _____. *Dorrie and the Blue Witch* (Lothrop, 1964/1980) 2–4. Shrinking powder enables young Dorrie the witch to capture the bad blue witch and win the first prize for witch catching.

1853. _____. *Dorrie's Play* (Lothrop, 1965) 2–4. Dorrie, the little witch, has turned her talents to producing a play with the help of her cat, Gink. All goes well until Dorrie cuts up what she thinks is an old cloth but which is her mother's costume for the ball.

1854. _____. *Dorrie and the Weather-Box* (Lothrop, 1966) 2–4. Hoping to make picnic weather, Dorrie, the little witch, meddles with her mother's magic. To her dismay, she accidentally conjures—and then has to weather—a unique storm.

1855. _____. *Dorrie and the Witch Doctor* (Lothrop, 1987) 2–4. Witch Dorrie resolves to be good during her Aunt Agra's visit. But Aunt Agra is not pleased with anything. The witch doctor tries to cure grumpy old Aunty of her bad temper.

1856. _____. *Dorrie and the Wizard's Spell* (Lothrop, 1968/1974) 2–4. Dorrie's hat is always crooked and her socks never match. She is a little witch and her mother is the big witch.

1857. _____. *Dorrie and the Haunted House* (Lothrop, 1970/1980) 2–4. During her search for shelter from a storm, a little witch unknowingly saves all witches and wizards from being turned into weathervanes, toads and park benches.

1858. _____. *Dorrie and the Birthday Eggs* (Lothrop, 1971) 2–4. Magic spells and the birthday theme combine in this story of Dorrie and her adventures.

1859. _____. *Dorrie and the Goblin* (Lothrop, 1972) 2–4. Dorrie rescues the Short High Sorcerer from a goblin spell and ensures the success of her mother's tea and magic show.

1860. _____. *Dorrie and the Fortune Teller* (Lothrop, 1973) 2–4. It seems doubtful that even Dorrie can save Witchville when a wizard forecloses a mortgage and a fortune-teller behaves suspiciously.

1861. _____. *Dorrie and the Amazing Magic Elixir* (Lothrop, 1974) 2–4. Left in charge of an elixir that will make one spell-proof, Dorrie, the little witch, foils the Green Wizard's attempt to steal it.

1862. _____. *Dorrie and the Witches' Trip* (Lothrop, 1975) 2–4. A bad witch creates a double for Dorrie after locking her in the bathroom. Her mother suspects something because the double is too neat.

1863. _____. *Dorrie and the Halloween Plot* (Lothrop, 1976) 2–4. Dorrie foils a plot to kidnap the Great Sorceress.

1864. _____. *Dorrie and the Dreamyard Monsters* (Lothrop, 1977) 2–4. Dorrie helps convert fierce monsters into lovable friends.

1865. _____. *Dorrie and the Screebit Ghost* (Lothrop, 1979) 2–4. Dorrie calls forth a playful witch companion who likes Big Witch's magic ring.

1866. _____. *Dorrie and the Witchville Fair* (Lothrop, 1980) 2–4. Bad-tempered Old Irontoes is up to something at the Witchville Fair and only Dorrie suspects.

1867. _____. *Dorrie and the Witches' Camp* (Lothrop, 1983) 2–4. Big Witch, Dorrie's mother, is turned into a robot by Morzo, the Magician of Machines.

1868. _____. *Dorrie and the Museum Case* (Lothrop, 1986) 2–4. With the help of her cousin Cosmo, Dorrie, the little witch, thwarts the scheme of Giblett the Enchanter on the opening day of the Witchville Museum.

1869. _____. *Dorrie and the Pin Witch* (Lothrop, 1989) 2–4. Dorrie suspects that the evil Pin Witch is responsible for the witches' angry behavior on the day of the Witches' Ball.

1870. _____. *Dorrie and the Haunted Schoolhouse* (Lothrop, 1992) 2–4. Dorrie the little witch goes to school where she and Dither, a fellow student, cause chaos when they mix up some spells.

1871. Cooney, Caroline. *Face on the Milk Carton* (Bantam, 1990) 5–8. A photograph of a missing girl on a milk carton leads Janie to a search for her real identity.

1872. _____. *Whatever Happened to Janie* (Delacorte, 1993) 5–8. The members of two families have their lives disrupted when a teenage girl who had been kidnapped 12 years earlier discovers that the people who raised her are not her biological parents.

1873. Cooney, Caroline. *Cheerleader* (Scholastic, 1991) 5–8. Alther will do anything to be popular even if it means sacrificing her friends to a vampire who lives in the center of her house. She must keep providing the vampire with the souls he desires.

1874. ____. *Return of the Vampire* (Scholastic, 1992) 5–8. Devnee is plain looking and it bothers her. In her new home she shares a tower room with a vampire. The vampire grants her wish to be beautiful, smart and athletic, but at the cost of these traits from three other girls.

1875. ____. *Vampires Promise* (Scholastic, 1993) 5–8. A group of six teenagers is spending the night in an abandoned building. Randy is their leader. The vampire promises that five may go free and they must choose whom the victim will be. How will they decide?

1876. Cooper, Clare. *Black Horn* (Hodder, 1981) 5–8. Simon is a reluctant wizard living in Wales. He finds himself responsible for sending Cafall, King Arthur's great wolfhound, back to the netherworld from which he has accidentally been summoned. He is helped by a girl and an old witch, Miss Blodwen Immanuel. He manages to overcome the evil Twn Cymylan and restore the equilibrium.

1877. ____. *Wizard Called Jones* (Hodder, 1985) 5–8. Simon is a wizard with second sight. He is responsible for returning King Arthur's hound who has strayed into the twentieth century. But he gains confidence while facing monsters, heavy mists and spells.

1878. Cooper, Gale. *One Unicorn* (Dutton, 1981) k–3. A unicorn repeatedly appears to princess Alicia until she loses her childhood innocence.

1879. ____. *Unicorn Moon* (Dutton, 1984) k–3. A princess searches for the meaning of true love in order to break the spell over a young man she sees constantly in her dreams.

1880. Cooper, Ilene. *Winning of Miss Lynn Ryan* (Morrow, 1987) 5–8. No matter how hard she tries, Carrie fails to impress her attractive, new fifth grade teacher who favors the more popular class members and ignores and criticizes Carrie and her new friend Luke, the class nerd.

1881. ____. *Queen of the Sixth Grade* (Morrow, 1988) 5–8. After helping her supposedly best friend found the sixth grade's secret club, Robin accidentally gets on her wrong side and discovers how bossy and cruel Veronica really is.

1882. ____. *Choosing Sides* (Morrow, 1990) 5–8. Jonathan doesn't want his father to think he's a quitter, but middle school basketball—under the lash of a gung-ho coach—is turning out to be anything but fun.

1883. ____. *Mean Streak* (Morrow, 1991) 5–8. Having alienated her best friend Robin, Veronica, 11, has no one to turn to for sympathy and support when it appears that her divorced father might remarry.

1884. ____. *New Improved Gretchen Hubbard* (Morrow, 1992) 5–8. "Hippo Hubbard" of the sixth grade, Gretchen, slims down but feels uncomfortable receiving compliments and attention from her classmates.

1885. Cooper, Ilene. *Frances Dances* (Knopf, 1991) 4–6. As she takes ballet lessons and participates in a school play, a timid fourth grader confronts her fears and learns a lesson about friendship.

1886. ____. *Frances and Friends* (Knopf, 1991) 4–6. Frances is crushed when a new girl threatens to come between her and her best friend Polly, until an incident helps her realize that best friends don't have to do everything together.

1887. ____. *Frances Four-Eyes* (Random, 1991) 4–6. A shy fourth grader becomes more assertive as she dances the lead role in a recital, suggests a community project in class, and starts to wear her new glasses.

1888. Cooper, Ilene. *Trick or Trouble* (Viking, 1994) 5–8. Lia makes four friends at summer camp, but when they come to her house in Maple Park, at Halloween, she worries that they will discover that she is not so popular in her seventh grade class.

1889. ____. *Worst Noel* (Viking, 1994) 5–8. Feeling out-of-place when she visits her father's new family, Kathy decides to spend Christmas with the close knit family of Erin, one of her friends from summer camp.

1890. ____. *No-Thanks Thanksgiving* (Viking, 1996) 5–8. The Holiday Five-Kathy and her friends from summer camp—share a disastrous Thanksgiving weekend in New York City.

1891. Cooper, Jilly. *Little Mabel* (Granada, 1980) k–3. Mabel, runt of the litter, is half purebred police dog and half mongrel. She overcomes her diffidence and becomes socially acceptable when she saves her owners from fire.

1892. ____. *Little Mabel's Great Escape* (Granada, 1981) k–3. Mabel and her mongrel dad are sent to the kennels while the Thompson's are on vacation. Unhappy at the Stalag Wolf Home, they dig their way out, helped by friendly underground moles and by Mabel's police dog mother.

1893. ____. *Little Mabel Wins* (Granada, 1982) k–3. Little Mabel, a ginger mongrel, asks her dad and a cat "What Is Crufts?" (a dog show). Her dad takes her but mongrels aren't allowed to compete. Little Mabel causes havoc among the other dogs but maintains her own good behavior.

1894. Cooper, Margaret. *Solution: Escape* (Walker, 1980) 5–8. Set in the 21st century, Stefan finds out he is a clone and is part of the scheme to control the government. Evonn is his look-alike. They both try to escape. But to where?

1895. ____. *Code Name: Clone* (Walker, 1982) 5–8.

While trying to find their "father" Evonn and Stefan reach America in 2060. They flee capture in the tunnels of New York City. Guard dogs, agents and drugs are all used to try to capture them.

1896. Corbett, Scott. *McGoniggle Great Grey Ghost* (Little, 1975) 2–4. McGoniggle and Ken try to locate and claim a $50.00 prize attached to Gray Ghost, a publicity balloon. They stumble upon the balloon but it is attached to a third floor gutter. They do recover the prize but give it away.

1897. ____. *Great McGoniggle's Key Play* (Little, 1976) 2–4. While collecting money for charity in front of the supermarket, two boys inadvertently become involved in a jewel theft.

1898. ____. *Great McGoniggle Rides Shotgun* (Little, 1977) 2–4. Mac and Ken accept a ride from a nervous stranger and find themselves involved in a robbery.

1899. ____. *Great McGoniggle Switches Pitches* (Little, 1980) 2–4. With Kilroy High's victory hanging in the balance, Mac McGoniggle calls a surprising pitch in the championship game against Gunther High.

1900. Coren, Alan. *Arthur the Kid* (Little, 1977) 2–4. Arthur the kid, ten, takes over an outlaw gang and changes their lives forever.

1901. ____. *Arthur's Last Stand* (Little, 1977) 2–4. Arthur, ten, employs an unusual technique to save the garrison at Fort Moccasin from an Indian attack.

1902. ____. *Railroad Arthur* (Little, 1977) 2–4. Arthur, ten, must not only solve a series of train robberies but must clear his own name of suspicion.

1903. ____. *Buffalo Arthur* (Little, 1978) 2–4. In response to a newspaper ad, Buffalo Arthur, ten, searches for a ring of cattle rustlers.

1904. ____. *Lone Arthur* (Little, 1978) 2–4. The owners of the Yellow Seafood Restaurant engage the services of a ten-year-old sleuth to track down some thieves.

1905. ____. *Klondike Arthur* (Little, 1979) 2–4. It takes a ten-year-old bard to reform Grizzly Wilkinson, the meanest prospector in the Klondike gold fields.

1906. ____. *Arthur and the Bellybutton Diamond* (Little, 1979) 2–4. Arthur, our hero, in his impeccably polite and never priggish way, out Sherlocks Mr. Holmes and, among other exploits, recovers a manuscript by Gilbert and Sullivan.

1907. ____. *Arthur and the Great Detective* (Little, 1979) 2–4. Arthur joins forces with Sherlock Holmes to solve a shipboard robbery.

1908. ____. *Arthur v. the Rest* (Robson, 1981) 2–4. Arthur helps Lower Sloatmumbling, a village, by organizing a cricket match between it and Upper Sloatmumbling, to help it regain confidence in itself.

1909. ____. *Arthur and the Purple Panic* (Parkwest, 1983) 2–4. Arthur helps his neighbor Sherlock Holmes find out who is painting the monuments of London purple. The painter is using a hot air balloon to paint these towering monuments.

1910. Cosgrove, Stephen. *Morgan and Me* (Creative, 1978) k–3. A young princess with a penchant for postponing activities learns not to procrastinate.

1911. ____. *Morgan Morning* (Price, 1982) k–3. A young horse's curiosity leads him into mortal peril and a new existence.

1912. ____. *Morgan and Yew* (Price, 1983) k–3. A sheep wishes for a horn like his unicorn friend has, but it costs him more than he can bear.

1913. ____. *Morgan Mine* (Rourke, 1984) k–3. A princess without a playmate tries to capture a unicorn with tricks and pouts, but finds that friendliness and patience are more effective.

1914. ____. *Misty Morgan* (Rourke, 1987) k–3. A princess regrets her selfish behavior when her friend Morgan the unicorn disappears.

1915. Cosgrove, Stephen. *Sleepy Time Bunny* (Price, 1984) k–3. Bunny takes a bath, listens to a story and gets a bedtime snack. It is a warm family story of a bedtime ritual.

1916. ____. *Bunny goes to Market* (Price, 1984) k–3. Bunny goes to market to see all the food. He gets to ride in the cart and picks out his favorite cookies.

1917. Costa, Nicolette. *Missing Cat* (Grosset, 1984) k–3. Molly and her cat, Tom, are best friends. Tom is upset when Molly goes out with her mother, leaving him alone at home. When Molly comes home, Tom is nowhere to be found.

1918. ____. *Dressing Up* (Grosset, 1984) k–3. Molly and her pet cat, Tom, do everything together, not always to Tom's liking.

1919. ____. *Molly and Tom, Birthday Party* (Grosset, 1984) k–3. Molly and her pet cat, Tom, learn about birthdays and birthday parties.

1920. Costa, Nicolette. *New Puppy* (Macmillan, 1985) k–3. Even though Billy's father thinks his new puppy is sometimes naughty, Billy thinks he is just perfect. Bob causes disaster with a little pull of the tablecloth.

1921. ____. *Grown-up Dog* (Macmillan, 1985) k–3. As a grown-up dog, Bob has many duties including fetching the newspaper, walking Billy to school, helping with the shopping, and visiting his dog friends.

1922. ____. *Clever Dog* (Macmillan, 1985) k–3. Billy's sheep dog, Bob, is so clever he can catch a biscuit in his mouth and fetch a ball.

1923. ____. *Naughty Puppy* (Corgi, 1986) k–3. Bob is the mischievous puppy and Billy is his owner. Bob gets into the chocolate cake and milk.

1924. ____. *Baby Puppy* (Corgi, 1986) k–3.

1925. Couffer, Jack. *Galapagos Summer* (Putnam, 1975) 3–5. A father and son relate their experiences of exploring Galapagos Islands.

1926. ____. *African Summer* (Putnam, 1976) 3–5. A photographer and his son record the family's adventures in Kenya where the father is filming a television series.

1927. ____. *Canyon Summer* (Putnam, 1977) 3–5. A father and son relate their summer experiences exploring the Arizona canyon country and living one day in the ancient way of the Anasazi Indians.

1928. ____. *Salt Marsh Summer* (Putnam, 1978) 3–5. Describes the wildlife of a southern California salt marsh and the efforts of dedicated individuals to save it and its surrounding area from encroaching "civilization."

1929. **Counsel,** June. *Dragon in Class Four* (Faber, 1984) 3–5. A dragon takes up residence in a nursery school where, despite an occasional accident, he proves a useful and enjoyable character

1930. ____. *Dragon in Spring Term* (Faber, 1988) 3–5. Scales, the dragon, has moved out of the classroom to a storeroom. He leaves messages on the class computer. Two children discover these while practicing their computer skills. They contact Scales and another adventure begins.

1931. ____. *Dragon in Summer* (Faber, 1990) 3–5. The class is to perform St. George and the Dragon. Scales appears but in his version the dragon kills St. George.

1932. **Cousins,** Lucy. *Maisy Goes to Bed* (Little, 1990) k–3. It's time for Maisy to go to bed. First she drinks her bedtime drink, then she has to brush her teeth, wash her hands, and put on her pajamas. There's lots to do.

1933. ____. *Maisy Goes Swimming* (Little, 1990) k–3. A story of Maisy as she gets ready to go swimming.

1934. ____. *Maisy Goes to the Playground* (Little, 1992) k–3. By pulling tabs on each page the reader can interact with a little mouse enjoying herself at the playground.

1935. ____. *Maisy Goes to School* (Little, 1992) k–3. By lifting flaps and pulling tabs the reader shares a young mouse's experiences at school.

1936. **Coville,** Bruce. *Space Brat 1* (Pocket, 1992) 2–4. Although bratty Blork is good at throwing tantrums, even a megatantrum can't save his pet Toonoobie when it is taken by the Big Pest Squad.

1937. ____. *Space Brat 2: Blork's Evil Twin* (Pocket, 1993) 2–4. On a class field trip to the Museum of New Inventions, bratty Blork is pulled inside a copy machine which creates his evil twin.

1938. ____. *Space Brat 3: Wrath of Squat* (Rocket, 1994) 2–4. Space brat Blork, Moomie, Peevik, Appus Meko and their pets are captured by the dread Squat and taken to his planet Snarf.

1939. ____. *Space Brat 4: Planet of the Dips* (Pocket, 1995) 2–4. It is all Blork can do to contain his temper when the spaceship he captains goes into a Whoopee Warp that draws it 14 squintillion miles off track to the planet of the Dips. Lunk, Blork's dog-like pet plays an important role.

1940. **Coville,** Bruce. *My Teacher Is an Alien* (Pocket, 1989) 5–8. Susan Simmons can tell that her new substitute teacher is really weird. But she doesn't know how weird until she catches him peeling off his face and realizes "Mr. Smith" is really an alien.

1941. ____. *My Teacher Glows in the Dark* (Pocket, 1991) 5–8. When Peter Thompson discovers that his newest teacher glows in the dark, he's flying away from Earth in a spaceship full of aliens and there's no one he can call.

1942. ____. *My Teacher Fried My Brains* (Pocket, 1991) 5–8. The first day of seventh grade was probably the worse day of Duncan Dougal's life. He knows that things are really bad when he finds an alien's hand in a dumpster and then gets plunged into an alien brain fryer.

1943. ____. *My Teacher Flunked the Planet* (Pocket, 1992) 5–8.

1944. **Coville,** Bruce. *Ghost in the Third Row* (Bantam, 1987) 4–6. An old theater, a 50-year-old murder, a ghost, a romance, sabotage and an inquisitive heroine provide the basis for this mystery about an attempt to stop the production of a play about the murder of a famous actress by an actor who was in love with her.

1945. ____. *Ghost Wore Gray* (Bantam, 1988) 4–6. Nina, a sixth grader, and her friend Chris go to a haunted inn. They are curious about the ghost of the Confederate soldier. The ghost provides clues on how to find his hidden treasure.

1946. ____. *Ghost in the Big Brass Bed* (Bantam, 1991) 4–6. The ghost of a little girl is looking for her father and the father's ghost is looking for his daughter. There is a lost painting and an antique house. Nina and Chris are resourceful and courageous as they unravel the secret of the identity of the villain.

1947. **Coville,** Bruce. *Sarah's Unicorn* (Lippincott, 1979) 2–4. Although she tries to keep her friendship with Oakhorn a secret, Sarah's wicked aunt finds out and is determined to rob the unicorn of his magic.

1948. ____. *Sarah and the Dragon* (Lippincott, 1984) 2–4. When Sarah is kidnapped by a dragon and taken to his castle in the clouds, it is up to her friend Oakhorn, the Unicorn, and her Aunt Mag to rescue her.

1949. **Craft,** Ruth. *Fancy Nancy* (Young Lions, 1987) k–3. Nancy, five, is curious about her world. She decides never to be "just plain Nancy" when asked her name.

1950. ____. *Fancy Nancy in Disguise* (Collins, 1990) k–3. Nancy decides that she really should be someone else.

1951. Craig, Helen. *Mouse House, 1 2 3* (Knopf, 1978) k–3. Humorous scenes of mice using paint, balloons, rope, wood and other things to form numbers.
1952. ____. *Mouse House, ABC* (Knopf, 1982) k–3. Humorous scenes of mice using paint, balloons, rope, wood and other things to form letters.
1953. ____. *Mouse House Months* (Knopf, 1982) k–3. Humorous pictures of a tree through its annual cycle followed by a scene appropriate to each month.

1954. Craig, Helen. *Susie and Alfred in the Night of the Paper Bag Monsters* (Knopf, 1985) k–3. Susie and Alfred, two pigs, are dreaming up Halloween costumes. They decide to be monsters with paper-bag faces. They get paint all over each other and get mad. That night each costume is so fierce that they scare each other.
1955. ____. *Susie and Alfred in the Knight, the Princess and the Dragon* (Knopf, 1985) k–3. Susie and Alfred, two pigs, see a picture of a pig knight saving a pig princess from a dragon. Susie wonders if Alfred would save her. She finds out that he will.
1956. ____. *Welcome for Annie* (Knopf, 1986) k–3. Susie and Alfred plan a naughty welcome for their new neighbor, Annie, but when their plan backfires they discover that Annie is very much a kindred spirit.

1957. Craig, Karl. *Emanuel and His Parrot* (Oxford, 1970) k–3. A Jamaican background story about a native boy and his scarlet and blue parrot, Rico.
1958. ____. *Emanuel Goes to Market* (Oxford, 1971) k–3. Detailed Jamaican scenes and realistic pictures enmeshed in a slight story.

1959. Crayder, Dorothy. *She, the Adventuress* (Atheneum, 1973) 5–8. Maggie is the adventuress. She is going to Italy to see an aunt. She has many adventures as the unattended minor on an Italian liner.
1960. ____. *She and the Dubious Three* (Atheneum, 1974) 5–8. Maggie arrives in Italy. She saw a couple with a baby as she takes the train to Venice. She thinks the baby is kidnapped. She finds the real father after searching the canals and back alleys of Venice.

1961. Cressey, James. *Palava Parrot* (Black, 1977) k–3. Parrot is captured by sneaky hunters. It dominates the household where it goes to live. It tracks down burglars and intensifies the chase and ends up with its own greenhouse built as a reward.
1962. ____. *Pet Parrot* (Prentice, 1979) k–3. A humorous tale of how a pet parrot helps out around the house.

1963. Cresswell, Helen. *Ordinary Jack* (Macmillan, 1977) 5–8. Jack is the only ordinary boy of the talented and eccentric Bagthorpe family. He concocts a scheme to distinguish himself as a prophet with ESP.

1964. ____. *Absolute Zero* (Macmillan, 1978) 5–8. Members of the talented and eccentric Bagthorpe family channel their energies into slogan writing contests and taking labels off cans of food. Zero, the pet dog, can't sniff dog bones.
1965. ____. *Bagthorpes Unlimited* (Macmillan, 1978) 5–8. The competitive Bagthorpes join forces in a rare display of solidarity when Grandma organizes a family reunion. They plan zany incidents to annoy the rest of the relatives.
1966. ____. *Bagthorpes Vs. the World* (Macmillan, 1979) 5–8. The Bagthorpes contend with father's attempts to be self–sufficient. Because he mistakenly thinks they are poor, he wants them to raise their own food and keep animals.
1967. ____. *Bagthorpes Abroad* (Macmillan, 1984) 5–8. This time the Bagthorpes are on vacation in Wales, but in a haunted house where they want to learn more about ghosts. One incident after another happens to make life chaotic.
1968. ____. *Bagthorpes Haunted* (Macmillan, 1985) 5–8. Still on vacation in the haunted house, the Bagthorpes try to contact the ghost living there.
1969. ____. *Bagthorpes Liberated* (Macmillan, 1989) 5–8. Upon returning from a vacation, the members of the Bagthorpe family find chaos as a tramp takes over their house, their maid disappears, and the demonic Cousin Daisy arrives with her pet goat.
1970. ____. *Bagthorpes Triangle* (Faber, 1993) 5–8. Joseph O'Toole, an Irish tramp has moved into Unicorn House during the Bagthorpe's holiday in Wales. He drank Mr. Bagthorpe's whiskey and disappears. The Bagthorpes search for him and one by one they too disappear…The Bagthorpe Triangle.

1971. Cresswell, Helen. *Rug Plays Ball* (Benn, 1969) 2–4. Rug is a talking teddy bear but says nothing in this story.
1972. ____. *Rug and the Picnic* (Benn, 1969) 2–4. Rug, a talking teddy bear, has a limited vocabulary: "I like picnics;" "Go away rain."

1973. Cresswell, Helen. *Two Hoots* (Crown, 1978) k–3. A little owl's daytime search for a mouse will bring him a big surprise tomorrow.
1974. ____. *Two Hoots and the Big Bad Bird* (Crown, 1978) k–3. Big Hoot and Little Hoot are convinced that there is a big bad bird in the woods waiting to eat them up.
1975. ____. *Two Hoots in the Snow* (Crown, 1978) k–3. Two silly owls discover that things are not always what they appear to be.
1976. ____. *Two Hoots Go to the Sea* (Crown, 1978) k–3. Two owls discover they prefer living in the woods rather than by the sea.
1977. ____. *Two Hoots Play Hide-and-Seek* (Crown, 1978) k–3. Little Hoot tries to interest his owl friends in a game of hide-and-seek.
1978. ____. *Two Hoots and the King* (Crown, 1978) k–3. The two Hoots request the gift of wisdom from

a small yellow bird they are convinced is the king of the sun.

1979. Cresswell, Helen. *My Aunt Polly* (Wheaton, 1980) k–3. It rains cats and dogs. The milkman is a duck. The vicar's wife is a real angel. Polly's niece takes everything her Aunt Polly says literally.

1980. ____. *My Aunt Polly by the Sea* (Wheaton, 1981) k–3. Aunt Polly tells her niece that it was raining cats and dogs. The little girl pictures mewing cats and barking dogs. They spend a day at the beach where Aunt Polly's niece literally believes every word.

1981. ____. *Secret World of Polly Flint* (Macmillan, 1984) k–3. Polly Flint, a girl who sees things other people can't, finds herself involved with the "time gypsies" of Grimstone, inhabitants of a lost village who have become trapped in a time not their own.

1982. Cresswell, Helen. *Meet Posy Bates* (Macmillan, 1992) 3–5. The adventures and misadventures of a little girl, Posy Bates, who desperately wants a dog or cat for a pet.

1983. ____. *Posy Bates and the Bag Lady* (Bodley, 1993) 3–5. Posy, thoughtful and inventive, is willing to learn from experience, learns to live dangerously and survive. She continues to turn Fred, her baby brother, into a genius. She also transforms the henhouse into a home for the bag ladies.

1984. ____. *Posy Bates Again* (Macmillan, 1994) 3–5. Posy Bates and her stray dog Buggins seem to get into nothing but mischief no matter how good their intentions are.

1985. Cresswell, Helen. *Jumbo Spencer* (Lippincott, 1963) 3–5. Jumbo announces to his gang that they are going to improve the village single-handed. He schemes and devises plans that beautify the town. They also build a recreation center. Change brings happier times.

1986. ____. *Jumbo and the Big Dig* (Lippincott, 1968) 3–5. Jumbo turns his attention to archaeology which is more rewarding than digging in the garden.

1987. Cretan, Gladys. *Lobo* (Lothrop, 1969) 2–4. Because it seems a long way to the end of his tail when he looks at himself, Lobo can't understand why everyone thinks he is the smallest dog in the neighborhood. Then through a heroic act he finds that "bigness" is sometimes more than a matter of size.

1988. ____. *Lobo and Brewster* (Lothrop, 1971) 2–4. Since Lobo, a small dog, tries diligently to guard the family from monsters, he feels defeated and rejected when the family brings their own monster—a Manx cat—into the house.

1989. Crofford, Emily. *Matter of Pride* (Carolrhoda, 1981) 4–6. This loving family tries to buy a cow so their youngest child could have milk. Meg,

ten, has an encounter with a brutal neighbor. Both she and her mother show courage.

1990. ____. *Stories from the Blue Road* (Carolrhoda, 1982) 4–6. Meg, 11, lives on a cotton plantation during the Depression. The family weathers hard times with fun and dignity, a pet dies, a friend is ostracized, the adults have problems and the dilemma of disobedience vs. independence comes up.

1991. Cross, Gilbert. *Mystery at Loon Lake* (Atheneum, 1986) 4–6. Jeff and his brother Nguyen discover a tunnel in the lake that is being used by art smugglers. They are discovered and try to escape.

1992. ____. *Terror Train!* (Atheneum, 1987) 4–6. Jeff and Nguyen are involved in a disappearance of a passenger on a train they are riding. They cleverly bring the criminal to justice.

1993. Cross, Peter. *Trouble for Trumpets* (Random, 1984) k–3. Just as the Trumpets, summer creatures who live in a world of warmth and sunshine, prepare to hibernate, the Grumpets, winter creatures who live in the dark, frozen mountain, prepare to take over their land.

1994. ____. *Trumpets in Grumpetland* (Random, 1985) k–3. Livingstone the lute-player and the beautiful Kim are brought together by their love of musk, while fierce Havoc the Grumpet and his Grumpicats are repelled by the Trumpets and the Borderers.

1995. Culliford, Pierre. *Astrosmurf* (Random, 1982) k–3. Smurfs are little blue people: Brainy, Lazy, Greedy, Grouchy and Little. Little Smurf dreams of becoming an Astrosmurf but becomes severely depressed after his carefully constructed rocket fails to take off.

1996. ____. *Smurf Cake* (Random, 1982) k–3. Smurfs are trying to retrieve an egg from the hen house so the baker can finish his cake.

1997. ____. *Smurf in the Air* (Random, 1982) k–3. Concerns one who tries to fly with the aid of feathers, an umbrella, a witch's broom and a mixed drink. When it finally works he can't get back down.

1998. ____. *Smurfic Games* (Random, 1982) k–3. Verbs, nouns and adjectives are changed into "smurf" words. "He's going to Smurf in alive"; "As Smurf as Mud."

1999. ____. *Wandering Smurf* (Random, 1982) k–3. Sad Smurf yearns to travel but when he does, he gets scared and wants to go home again.

2000. ____. *Fake Smurf* (Random, 1982) k–3. A wizard who hates the Smurfs because they are so nice, transforms himself into a small Smurf and tries to cause an accident, but he injures himself instead. He is rescued by the Smurfs and returns to his normal shape and color but stays Smurf small. He hates it.

2001. ____. *King Smurf* (Random, 1982) k–3. Who will become King Smurf when Papa Smurf temporarily leaves the village? Smurf makes careless campaign promises to win the election. His victory goes to his head and a revolt is plotted.

2002. ____. *Romeo and Smurfette* (Random, 1979) k–3. Contains 13 different Smurf stories.

2003. Cumberiege, Vera. *Shipwreck* (Follett, 1974) k–3. A story about a young boy who witnesses a disaster at sea and the efforts to effect a rescue.

2004. ____. *Trapped by the Tide* (Follett, 1977) k–3. A story of the more sensible child saving some less sensible (silly) children caught by an incoming tide.

2005. Cunliffe, John. *Farmer Barnes and the Bluebell* (Deutsch, 1966) k–3. A tale of the havoc caused in a village by a runaway cow.

2006. ____. *Farmer Barnes Buys a Pig* (Deutsch, 1968) k–3. A little boy wants a pig for his birthday but none of the ones his father shows him seems to be right.

2007. ____. *Farmer Barnes and the County Fair* (Deutsch, 1971) k–3. Farmer Barnes takes his family in his newly painted donkey cart to the County Fair. Bluebell, the cow, doesn't win a prize and Little John and Baby Candy are disappointed. But they win a prize in a competition they didn't enter—the Donkey Cart Competition.

2008. ____. *Farmer Barnes and the Goats* (Deutsch, 1971) k–3. When his troublesome goats get into a quarry, Farmer Barnes has to find some way to get them out.

2009. ____. *Farmer Barnes Goes Fishing* (Deutsch, 1972) k–3. This is a story of a fishing trip where the catch, though unexpected, is varied and useful.

2010. ____. *Farmer Barnes and the Snow* (Deutsch, 1974) k–3. An ordinary but enjoyable description of a family forced to eat food purchased for neighbors, when the Land Rover gets stuck in the snow.

2011. ____. *Farmer Barnes Fells a Tree* (Deutsch, 1977) k–3. Farmer Barnes has a new power chain saw. He prunes trees and hedges but wants to fell a tree. When the tree falls it blocks the road, destroys a wall and brings down telephone wires.

2012. ____. *Farmer Barnes and the Harvest Doll* (Deutsch, 1977) k–3.

2013. ____. *Farmer Barnes's Guy Fawkes Day* (Deutsch, 1978) k–3. John and Candy, living with their farm family, are given timely warning about the dangers of fireworks when a rocket destroys their tree house.

2014. Cunliffe, John. *Postman Pat and the Mystery Thief* (Deutsch, 1981) k–3. Postman Pat and his black cat, Jess, stop for a picnic near Thompson's farm. A hen steals his van keys and flies into a tree with them. When he climbs up he finds a hoard of shiny treasures that the "magpie hen" has stolen, including Mrs. Thompson's wedding ring.

2015. ____. *Postman Pat's Secret* (Deutsch, 1982) k–3. This story concerns Postman Pat's birthday secret. It is mysteriously discovered by the whole vil-

lage. Pat and Jess return after the day's delivery with a van full once more.

2016. ____. *Postman Pat's Treasure Hunt* (Deutsch, 1982) k–3. Postman Pat and his cat Jess deliver the mail. He looks for Katy's missing birthday doll. He finds other missing items and discovers the doll, Sarah Ann, in the Mobile Grocery van and returns it to Katy.

2017. ____. *Postman Pat's Foggy Day* (Deutsch, 1983) k–3.

2018. ____. *Postman Pat's Three Wishes* (Deutsch, 1984/1990) k–3. Postman Pat wishes he could fly like a bird, climb a tree like a squirrel and swim like a fish—and he almost does.

2019. ____. *Postman Pat's Tractor Express* (Deutsch, 1984) k–3. Postman Pat sees sheep trampling on a cottage garden, delivers a new mail order catalog for Granny and a registered letter for the Intake Farm.

2020. ____. *Postman Pat and His Village* (Deutsch, 1984) k–3.

2021. ____. *Postman Pat's Thirsty Day* (Deutsch, 1984) k–3.

2022. ____. *Postman Pat Goes Sledging* (Deutsch, 1985) k–3. Postman Pat is determined that the mail must get through and when Peter Fogg's tractor, converted into a makeshift snow plow, cannot clear a path for him he delivers a parcel by sledge.

2023. ____. *Postman Pat's A, B, C Story* (Deutsch, 1986) k–3.

2024. ____. *Postman Pat's 1, 2, 3 Story* (Deutsch, 1986) k–3.

2025. ____. *Postman Pat's Letters on Ice* (Deutsch, 1986) k–3.

2026. ____. *Postman Pat's Breezy Day* (Deutsch, 1986) k–3.

2027. ____. *Postman Pat's Messy Day* (Deutsch, 1987) k–3.

2028. ____. *Postman Pat and Christmas Puddings* (Deutsch, 1987) k–3.

2029. ____. *Postman Pat's Day in Bed* (Deutsch, 1987) k–3.

2030. ____. *Postman Pat's Safari* (Deutsch, 1987) k–3.

2031. ____. *Postman Pat Makes a Splash* (Deutsch, 1987) k–3.

2032. ____. *Postman Pat's Wet Day* (Deutsch, 1987) k–3.

2033. ____. *Postman Pat's Rainy Day* (Deutsch, 1987) k–3.

2034. ____. *Postman Pat Plays for Greendale* (Deutsch, 1987) k–3.

2035. ____. *Postman Pat and the Greendale Ghost* (Deutsch, 1988) k–3.

2036. ____. *Postman Pat's Christmas Tree* (Deutsch, 1989) k–3. Postman Pat involves everyone in an English town in the preparations for a Christmas Fair to raise money for children in the local hospital.

2037. ____. *Postman Pat Gets Fat* (Deutsch, 1990) k–3.

2038. ____. *Postman Pat's Lost Hat* (Deutsch, 1991) k–3. Postman Pat looks everywhere for his hat. He looks in his bed, the bath and in the refrigerator. He finds a mouse, a spider and a nail.

2039. ____. *Postman Pat and the Letter Puzzle* (Deutsch, 1991) k–3.

2040. ____. *Postman Pat Wins a Prize* (Deutsch, 1992) k–3.

2041. ____. *Postman Pat Makes a Present* (Deutsch, 1992) k–3. Pat realized that he had not bought his mother a gift. He and his cat, Jess, try to find some ideas for a present. Granny Dryden suggests he make something himself. So he bakes a cake for his mother and another of his own family.

2042. ____. *Postman Pat and the Toy Soldiers* (Deutsch, 1993) k–3.

2043. Cunliffe, John. *Mr. Gosling and the Runaway Chair* (Deutsch, 1978) k–3. Mr. Gosling's daughter Sara points out the ornate chair that a sad man is pushing toward their antique shop. He wants to trade the chair to replace the one his wife lost. The wife then chases both Mr. Gosling and her husband.

2044. ____. *Mr. Gosling and the Great Art Robbery* (Deutsch, 1979) k–3. Mr. Gosling, an antique dealer, and his daughter Sara are taking a parcel by train to a customer and it becomes mixed up with another package.

2045. Curry, Jane. *Mindy's Mysterious Miniature* (Harcourt, 1970) 4–6. Willie with his erratic "Reducer" shrinks houses and people. Mindy and Mrs. Bright are shrunk to miniature size and meet seven other people who were living this way for 45 years. Mindy helps everyone escape.

2046. ____. *Lost Farm* (Harcourt, 1974) 4–6. Willie was an inventor. With his erratic "Reducer" he shrinks a whole mountain farm along with its three inhabitants and the livestock. "Trashbin" dies unmourned but Granny and her grandson Pete learn to cope with the situation.

2047. Curtis, Philip. *Mr. Browser and the Brain Sharpeners* (Anderson, 1981) 4–6. Extraterrestrial beings attempt to sharpen the brains of a school class they wish to develop their new planets. One child resists.

2048. ____. *Mr. Browser and the Comet Crisis* (Anderson, 1981) 4–6. Aliens, in the shape of three very, very ordinary humans emerge from the sea. They seek anonymity before they take over the world. The alien boy's downfall is his expertise at marbles, which gives the game away.

2049. ____. *Mr. Browser Meets the Burrowers* (Anderson, 1981) 4–6. Mr. Browser and the children are of Chivvy Chase School. The Burrowers appear to young Selwyn and tells him that if they go on with their digging for oil all buildings will be sucked below the earth. Then Mr. Browser disappears, a chimney collapses and a large monument sways.

2050. ____. *Mr. Browser and the Museum* (Anderson, 1985) 4–6. Mr. Browser's class is spirited away to an alien environment where they are "curiosities" for the inhabitants of that planet. How to get home again? The children's ingenuity promises the answer.

2051. ____. *Mr. Browser and the Mini-Meteorites* (Anderson, 1983) 4–6. Mr. Browser is a teacher at Chivvy Chase School. A metal object, magnified by sunrays, explodes and makes everyone feel happy. A friend of Mr. Browser is making happiness pills so Mr. Browser goes to see him. Aliens are planning to take over the planet by brainwashing everyone into happiness.

2052. ____. *Mr. Browser and the Space Maggots* (Anderson, 1989) 4–6. An alien race of Space Maggots has a weapon to destroy the Earth. Three children investigate the disappearance of the native reservation warden. He left a note suggesting he has been kidnapped by the Space Maggots.

2053. ____. *Mr. Browser Meets the Mind Shrinkers* (Knopf, 1991) 4–6.

2054. Curtis, Philip. *Invasion of the Comet People* (Knopf, 1981) 4–6. Spiky discovers that his new friend Jason and his parents are an outer-space family from Halley's comet and that their plans pose grave danger to the Earth.

2055. ____. *Invasion from Below the Earth* (Knopf, 1981) 4–6. The Burrowers, an underground civilization, depend on oil for their energy needs. Selwyn and his teacher try to avoid war between the humans and the Burrowers over oil depletion.

2056. ____. *Invasion of the Brain Sharpeners* (Knopf, 1981) 4–6. Michael is the only one who outsmarts the Brain Sharpeners, who have captured the minds of others in school. The aliens brainwash their victims into studying so they can colonize a planet with Earthlings.

2057. ____. *Revenge of the Brain* (Anderson, 1982) 4–6. Mr. Salt of Chivvy Chase School is returned to Earth. He is to kidnap his Class 8 children to be brain-sharpened and used to develop a new planet. Their plans are thwarted by Michael and Spiky and Mr. Salt's brain is permanently affected.

2058. ____. *Beware of the Brain Sharpener* (Anderson, 1984) 4–6. The Brain Sharpeners kidnap the Chivvy Chase School choir. They can freeze the human body and numb the human mind. These aliens are concerned about the weapon being developed on Earth.

2059. ____. *Bewitched by the Brain Sharpeners* (Knopf, 1987) 4–6.

2060. Cushman, Doug. *Aunt Eater Loves a Mystery* (Harper, 1987) 3–5. Aunt Eater loves mystery stories so much that she sees mysterious adventures wherever she looks.

2061. ____. *Aunt Eater's Mystery Vacation* (Harper,

1992) 3–5. A mystery loving anteater has a chance to solve several mysteries during her vacation at the Hotel Bathwater.

2062. Cutts, David. *Pinocchio and the Puppet Show* (Troll, 1982) k–3. Pinocchio, a mischievous puppet carved from a talking piece of wood, sells his new spelling book to buy a seat at a puppet show.
2063. ____. *Pinocchio Meets the Cat and Fox* (Troll, 1982) k–3. Pinocchio is tricked into planting his gold coins in the Field of Miracles by the evil Cat and Fox.
2064. ____. *Pinocchio Goes to School* (Troll, 1982) k–3. In the village of Busy Bees, Pinocchio resolves to work hard, obey, and tell the truth, so that he can become a real boy.
2065. ____. *Pinocchio and the Great Whale* (Troll, 1982) k–3. Pinocchio saves his father and himself when they rediscover each other in the stomach of a great whale, and then shows his good heart by toiling away in order to care for his sick father and the Fairy.

2066. Cuyler, Margery. *Freckles and Willie* (Holt, 1986) k–3. Freckles, the dog, is Willie's best friend until a little girl who doesn't like dogs moves in across the street.
2067. ____. *Freckles and Jane* (Holt, 1990) k–3. Jane dislikes her friend Willie's dog Freckles, until Freckles defends her from a big, mean dog.

2068. Dahl, Lucy. *Matilda* (Viking, 1996) 2–4. Matilda is very bright and has a good angel, the librarian, Mrs. Phelps. Nasty Miss Trunchbull was her headmistress. Matilda manages to expose Miss Trunchbull as the criminal she was. She also restores Miss Honey, the nice teacher.
2069. ____. *Matilda's Movie Adventure* (Viking, 1996) 2–4. Matilda, the book–loving, naughty girl has more misadventures with her neglectful parents and cruel school headmistress.

2070. Dallas, Ruth. *Children in the Bush* (Methuen, 1969) 3–5. Stories about a family in pioneer New Zealand.
2071. ____. *Big Flood in the Bush* (Methuen, 1972) 3–5. Jean, eight, tells of the flood in New Zealand in 1891. It is told in the first person.
2072. ____. *Holiday Time in the Bush* (Methuen, 1983) 3–5. Helen and Jean are going to a picnic with new dresses but Sophie only has a new hat. A visit to the seaside has never been done before. And a leg of lamb is brought for dinner so a rooster's life is saved.

2073. Dana, Maggie. *No Time for Secrets* (Troll, 1986) 4–6. When 13-year-old Kerry takes a job as companion to a handicapped girl whose mother runs a stable, she knows she eventually will have to deal with a past incident that has made her want to stay away from the horses she once loved.

2074. ____. *Jumping into Trouble* (Troll, 1988) 4–6. Kerry enjoys her job as live-in companion to a handicapped girl and helper at a horse stable until a jealous neighbor tries to force her out of her position.
2075. ____. *Racing for the Stars* (Troll, 1988) 4–6. Determined to earn money to buy her own horse, Kerry tries out for a part in a film to be made at the Timber Ridge Riding Stable where she lives with her friend Holly and her mother.
2076. ____. *If Wishes Were Horses* (Troll, 1988) 4–6. Kerry rescues a mistreated horse from a grisly fate and trains her for the upcoming horse show, unaware that the horse may be stolen.

2077. Dann, Colin. *Fox's Feud* (Hutchinson, 1985) 5–8. Fox has a feud with a rival fox, Scarface, who plays dishonestly and viciously. The other animals band together and destroy him.
2078. ____. *Fox Cub Bold* (Magna, 1986) 5–8. Bold, a fox cub, leaves home in search of adventure and freedom. He is shot by a hunter and almost blinded. Shadow the badger, Robert the crow and Rollo the mastiff help Bold survive the winter.

2079. Dann, Colin. *Animals of Farthing Wood* (Nelson, 1979) 5–8. A variety of animals cross a river, dodge a vicious dog, escape a fox and cross a freeway to get to White Deer Park. Each animal contributes to the trip.
2080. ____. *Animals of Farthing Wood: The Continuing Story* (Nelson, 1979) 5–8.
2081. ____. *Siege of White Deer Park* (Magna, 1987) 5–8. White Deer Park is upset by a cunning predator. Animals are being killed and eaten. Stopping this may be impossible as everything is tried.
2082. ____. *Battle for the Park* (Hutchinson, 1992) 5–8. The veterans of Farthing Wood defend their territory against an invasion of rats.
2083. ____. *Further Adventures of Farthing Wood* (Nelson, 1994) 5–8.

2084. Danziger, Paula. *Everyone Else's Parents Said Yes* (Delacorte, 1989) 5–8. Matthew cannot resist the temptation to play practical jokes on his older sister and all the girls in his class at school, so by the time of the big party for his eleventh birthday they have all declared war on him.
2085. ____. *Make Like a Tree and Leave* (Delacorte, 1990) 5–8. Matthew, a sixth grader, gets into trouble at home and at school, spars with his older sister, and helps save an elderly friend's property from the hands of a developer.

2086. Danziger, Paula. *Amber Brown Is Not a Crayon* (Putnam, 1994) 4–6. Amber is a spunky, opinionated third grader, who is devastated by the impending move of her best friend, Justin.
2087. ____. *You Can't Eat Your Chicken Pox, Amber Brown* (Putnam, 1995) 4–6. Amber survived third grade with her best friend Justin. She goes to Lon-

don to stay with her Aunt Pam. She expects to go to see her father, but chicken pox strikes and she is bedridden.

2088. ____. *Amber Brown Wants Extra Credit* (Putnam, 1996) 4–6. Amber is not working to the best of her ability and she's in trouble with her teacher and her mom. She's got a half-finished book report in a garbage bag in her closet, which she vows to think about…tomorrow, unless working on it means she doesn't have to meet her mother's new boyfriend.

2089. Dauer, Rosamond. *Bullfrog Grows Up* (Greenwillow, 1976) 3–5. A family of mice raises a card-playing, bath-taking tadpole who, as a bullfrog, begins to eat alarming amounts.

2090. ____. *Bullfrog Builds a House* (Greenwillow, 1977) 3–5. Not wanting to forget any important items in his new house, Bullfrog seeks the advice of Gertrude. Upon completion he finds he has overlooked one thing.

2091. ____. *Bullfrog and Gertrude Go Camping* (Greenwillow, 1980) 3–5. When Bullfrog and Gertrude go camping, they take an unlikely member into their family circle.

2092. Davidson, Amanda. *Teddy's First Christmas* (Holt, 1982) k–3. Teddy climbs out of a big red box under the tree to enjoy some Christmas Eve adventures.

2093. ____. *Teddy at the Seashore* (Holt, 1984) k–3. A lonely teddy bear gets a surprise visit to the beach.

2094. ____. *Teddy's Birthday* (Holt, 1985) k–3. A teddy bear gets letters, a cake, presents, and a surprise party on his birthday.

2095. ____. *Teddy's Favorite Food* (Holt, 1985) k–3. Teddy eats meals and snacks and enjoys food at any time. He identifies all the food on his plate.

2096. ____. *Teddy's Wash Day* (Holt, 1985) k–3. Teddy enjoys messing in and around water.

2097. ____. *Teddy Goes Outside* (Holt, 1985) Little bear's playtime activities are matched to the weather: if hot and sunny he plays at the beach; if it is cold he plays in the snow.

2098. ____. *Teddy Cleans the House* (Holt, 1985) k–3. Teddy is a fuzzy, smiling teddy bear. He tells of cleaning house and what a big job it really is.

2099. ____. *Teddy Goes Shopping* (Holt, 1985) k–3. Teddy goes to all the stores and sees what they sell. In the end he decides not to spend his money but puts it in a bank.

2100. ____. *Teddy in the Garden* (Holt, 1986) k–3. When Teddy loses his favorite hat to a mischievous dog, he and his friends begin a digging search that uncovers a number of interesting objects.

2101. ____. *Teddy's Christmas Cut Out* (Holt, 1987) k–3.

2102. Davies, Andrew. *Marmalade Atkins* (Crown, 1982) 2–4. A humorous story about the worst girl in the world, dotty nuns and spacemen.

2103. ____. *Marmalade Atkins in Space* (Crown, 1982) 2–4. Marmalade Atkins is not a nice girl and she stays bad throughout the story. Even her parents want her to be as far away as possible. They want to send her to an improving school.

2104. ____. *Educating Marmalade* (Crown, 1983) 2–4. Marmalade, a bad girl, is destructive in both Dartmoor and Albert Hall schools. She demolishes the headmistress, the social worker, a nanny, a dog trainer and prison thugs.

2105. ____. *Marmalade and Rufus* (Crown, 1983) 2–4. The adventures of a very naughty little girl and her similarly behaved talking donkey.

2106. ____. *Marmalade Atkins' Dreadful Deeds* (Crown, 1983) 2–4. Marmalade and Rufus, the talking donkey, visit and perform in a nightclub, take part in a steeplechase and wreck a nativity play.

2107. ____. *Marmalade Hits the Big Time* (Crown, 1985) 2–4. The "worst girl in the world" and her friend Rufus, the world's worst donkey, move to London. After storming the Ritz and demolishing Dinosaur Hall they leave Mr. Atkins stranded on top of Nelson's Column, and more.

2108. ____. *Danger—Marmalade at Work* (Crown, 1985) 2–4.

2109. Davies, Hunter. *Come on, Ossie* (Bodley, 1986) 4–6. Ossie is sassy to his mother, but the story reflects realistic family situations.

2110. ____. *Ossie Goes Supersonic* (Bodley, 1987) 4–6. Ossie, 12, puts on his granddad's army belt and becomes 18! He beats Steve at snooker, stands in for Agony Uncle on a radio phone-in program and joins Queen Mother on a trip in the Concorde.

2111. Davies, Hunter. *Flossie Teacake's Fur Coat* (Bodley, 1982) 2–6. A nine-year-old English girl fulfills some of her life-long ambitions when she dons a magical coat and becomes eighteen years old.

2112. ____. *Flossie Teacake—Again* (Bodley, 1984) 4–6. Flossie, ten, tries on her sister's fur coat and becomes a grown up. She runs a hair salon, goes to a pop concert, does some doctoring and goes baby-sitting.

2113. ____. *Flossie Teacake Strikes Back* (Bodley, 1985) 4–6. Flossie, ten, is transformed each time she puts on her big sister's fur coat. She goes shopping, goes dancing, and tells fortunes, mostly as a glamorous grown-up.

2114. Day, Alexandra. *Good Dog, Carl* (Green Tiger, 1985) k–3. Lively and unusual things happen when Carl, the dog, is left in charge of the baby.

2115. ____. *Carl Goes Shopping* (Farrar, 1989) k–3. Carl, the family dog, is left in charge of the baby while his owner goes to the upstairs level in a shopping center. Carl and the baby have a wonderful time exploring the lower level.

2116. ____. *Carl's Christmas* (Farrar, 1990) k–3. A

family's faithful dog and the baby left in his charge share an adventure-filled Christmas Eve.

2117. ____. *Carl's Birthday* (Farrar, 1991) k–3. Carl, a rottweiler, along with baby, Mom and Dad, celebrate his birthday, in an unusual way.

2118. ____. *Carl's Afternoon in the Park* (Farrar, 1991) k–3. Carl, the rottweiler, in charge of a baby and a puppy, takes advantage of Mom's absence to lead them on a wild romp through the park.

2119. ____. *Carl's Masquerade* (Farrar, 1992) k–3. Carl, a large dog, and the baby in his charge fit right in when they follow Mom and Dad to a PTA masquerade.

2120. ____. *Carl Goes to Day Care* (Farrar, 1993) k–3. Carl, the rottweiler, takes charge when things take an unexpected turn at the day care center he is visiting.

2121. ____. *Carl Makes a Scrapbook* (Farrar, 1994) k–3. Carl, the rottweiler, and the toddler in his care glue items in a scrapbook.

2122. Day, Alexandra. *Frank and Ernest* (Scholastic, 1988) k–3. An elephant and a bear take over a diner and find out about responsibility and food language.

2123. ____. *Frank and Ernest Play Ball* (Scholastic, 1990) k–3. An elephant and a bear take over the management of a baseball team for one night and learn about cooperation, responsibility and baseball lingo.

2124. ____. *Frank and Ernest on the Road* (Scholastic, 1994) k–3. While making a delivery for a friend, an elephant and a bear become familiar with the experiences and language of truck drivers.

2125. Dean, Karen. *Maggie Adams, Dancer* (Avon, 1980) 5–8. Maggie, 14, has a friend with anorexia, another has a domineering stage mother. She wants to continue studying ballet while her father wants her to do something else. All ends well.

2126. ____. *Mariana* (Avon, 1981) 5–8. Mariana is a young dancer, daughter of a ballerina from Russia and a Mexican father. The father wants to keep Mariana away from dancing; the mother wants her to have a career in dancing and both parents want her to stay away from Adam, a piano student.

2127. ____. *Between Dances* (Avon, 1982) 5–8. Maggie does not get the lead in the ballet company but it goes to her friend Lupe. Maggie's boyfriend is away at college and she misses him. She is later offered the lead and chooses dance over marriage.

2128. De Beer, Hans. *Little Polar Bear* (North-South, 1987) k–3. While hunting with his father, a young polar bear drifts out to sea and ends up in a jungle where a friendly hippopotamus helps him return home.

2129. ____. *Ahoy There, Little Polar Bear* (North-South, 1988) k–3. When a young polar bear is caught in a fishing net that brings him to the city, the friendly ship's cat helps him return home.

2130. ____. *Little Polar Bear Finds a Friend* (North-South, 1990) k–3. Lars, the little polar bear, is captured and loaded on a plane for the zoo. Lars and the other caged animals break free. A little brown bear named Bea and a walrus join Lars on his journey home.

2131. ____. *Little Polar Bear and the Brave Little Hare* (North-South, 1992) k–3. Lars the polar bear teases his friend Hugo the hare for being afraid of everything, until the day they get lost in the snow.

2132. DeClements, Barthe. *Five-Finger Discount* (Delacorte, 1989) 4–5. Jerry, ten, tries to adjust to his new school and make new friends but he is determined to keep secret the fact that his father is serving time in the local prison for being a thief.

2133. ____. *Monkey See, Monkey Do.* (Delacorte, 1990) 4–6. Jerry's adored father seems unable to stay out of jail, causing the sixth grader anguish at home and at school.

2134. Del Rey, Lester. *Outpost to Jupiter* (Holt, 1963) 4–6. There is an outbreak of the plague on Granymede that brings about a meeting between the humans living there and the alien creatures.

2135. ____. *Runaway Robot* (Westminster, 1975) 4–6. Rex, a robot, is Paul's companion on Granymede. They become inseparable and when it is time to go back to Earth, Paul refuses to part with him.

2136. Delacre, Lulu. *Nathan and Nicholas Alexander* (Scholastic, 1987) k–3. Nathan, the elephant, hears a noise coming from his toy chest. He looks there and discovers a small mouse named Nicholas Alexander. Although Nathan is uneasy at first, they agree to be friends.

2137. ____. *Nathan's Fishing Trip* (Scholastic, 1988) k–3. Nicholas Alexander, the mouse, is taking Nathan on a fishing trip. All the gear and food is ready. Nathan is not a good fisherman and causes chaos, but he does catch a fish with his trunk. When it is time to cook and eat the fish Nathan decides to let the fish go and he and Nicholas Alexander eat their sandwiches.

2138. ____. *Time for School, Nathan* (Scholastic, 1989) k–3. Nathan wants to go to his first day of school by himself but Nicholas Alexander follows him into the classroom. When he sees Nathan in school he is jealous and afraid of being left out. But Nathan not only makes new friends, he keeps his old one.

2139. ____. *Nathan's Balloon Adventure* (Scholastic, 1991) k–3. Nathan, the elephant and Nicholas Alexander, the mouse, set out for a balloon ride. Henri, the balloon owner, is hesitant because of Nathan's weight, but he relents. Later, when the balloon runs out of fuel in mid-flight, Nathan inflates the balloon with his trunk.

2140. DeLage, Ida. *Farmer and the Witch* (Gerrard, 1966) 3–5. The Old Witch casts a spell and mixes magic brews to bewitch the barnyard animals and the farmer's crop. The farmer finally chases the witch away and uses her cloak for a scarecrow.

2141. ____. *Weeny Witch* (Garrard, 1968) 3–5. Because she is afraid of spiders, instead of capturing the night fairies in a web, Weenie Witch rescues one. She discovers she is not really a witch but a long lost child of the night fairies.

2142. ____. *Old Witch Goes to the Ball* (Garrard, 1969) k–3. After she is mistaken for someone else at the Halloween Ball and consequently loses the prize for best costume, the angry old witch plans her revenge.

2143. ____. *Old Witch and the Ghost Parade* (Chelsea, 1978) k–3. Old Witch faces a turnabout when she gets scared herself.

2144. ____. *Old Witch and Her Magic Basket* (Chelsea, 1978) k–3. Old Witch enlivens a sick child's Halloween.

2145. ____. *Old Witch and the Dragon* (Chelsea, 1979) k–3. Old Witch outwits a dangerous dragon and saves an endangered town for one hundred years.

2146. ____. *Old Witch Finds a New House* (Chelsea, 1979) k–3. Old Witch magically constructed a house in one day; she saves a woodcutter who then rewards her.

2147. ____. *Old Witch Gets a Surprise* (Garrard, 1981) k–3. The Old Witch is not impressed with the wizard's flying invention, a hot-air balloon. She does agree to a ride but brings along her broom as security. And that's a good thing because the wizard can't steer the balloon out of a storm.

2148. ____. *Old Witch and the Crows* (Chelsea, 1983) k–3. When King Crow had to stay up all night protecting his flock from an owl, Old Witch comes up with a plan to help him get some sleep. Pasting crow feathers onto an old black cloak, she disguises herself as a giant crow and frightens the owl, which is never seen again.

2149. ____. *Old Witch's Party* (Chelsea, 1991) k–3. The Old Witch posts a sign at the school inviting children to a Halloween party. The children follow her to a cave where there are spiders, rats, bats and rattlesnakes.

2150. ____. *Old Witch and the Wizard* (Chelsea, 1991) k–3. The wizard offers to trade his magic cat to Old Witch for her secret brew recipe. She says no, but her cat and the wizard like each other and have three black kittens. After trying to get rid of them, Old Witch discovers they have magic power and decides to keep them.

2151. ____. *Old Witch and the Snores* (Chelsea, 1991) k–3. The Old Witch must eliminate a troublesome bear from her cave because he snores. She offers to make a giant some of her magic stew if he will get rid of the bear for her.

2152. DeLage, Ida. *ABC Pirate Adventure* (Garrard, 1977) k–3. The A to Z adventures of a rollicking crew of pirates who are searching for treasure.

2153. ____. *ABC Fire Dogs* (Garrard, 1977) k–3. Fearless dogs fight and prevent fires from A to Z.

2154. ____. *ABC Pigs Go to Market* (Garrard, 1977) k–3. When this pig family goes to market, they buy everything from A to Z.

2155. ____. *ABC Halloween Witch* (Garrard, 1977) k–3. An alphabet book featuring a witch and her Halloween preparations such a bubbling brew, Magic spells and an enchanted toad.

2156. ____. *ABC Christmas* (Garrard, 1978) k–3. The alphabet is presented as a family of children makes preparations for Santa Claus on Christmas Eve.

2157. ____. *ABC Santa Claus* (Garrard, 1978) k–3. Santa Claus prepares for his Christmas Eve journey with a last minute check of details from A to Z.

2158. ____. *ABC Easter Bunny* (Garrard, 1979) k–3. The Easter bunny makes deliveries to children in the city and in the country, all in alphabetical order.

2159. ____. *ABC Triplets at the Zoo* (Garrard, 1980) k–3. The ABC triplets take an alphabetical walk through the zoo with the 26 letters highlighted by animals' names and zoo adventures.

2160. DeLage, Ida. *Witchy Broom* (Garrard, 1969) 3–5. When her broom breaks down, the old witch borrows an ordinary one from a nearby farm but forgets to take the magic out when she returns it.

2161. ____. *What Does a Witch Need?* (Garrard, 1971) 3–5. The little dog cannot replace the witch's dead cat but he finds his own way to be of use to her.

2162. ____. *Beware, Beware! A Witch Won't Share* (Garrard, 1972) 3–5. The wrath of a selfish witch changes the attitude of a farmer and his wife toward the gypsies.

2163. DeLage, Ida. *Bunny Ride* (Garrard, 1975) k–3. Young bunnies envy their friends whose mothers carry them to the store. When they finally arrive at the store Mother Bunny buys a wagon so they can ride home.

2164. ____. *Bunny School* (Garrard, 1976) k–3. Four little bunnies hop off to bunny school where they learn about all the dangers that rabbits face.

2165. ____. *Am I a Bunny?* (Garrard, 1978) k–3. A brown Bunny thinks he is a rat, a cat, a squirrel and a frog, until he meets some other brown bunnies.

2166. Delton, Judy. *Brimhall Comes to Stay* (Lothrop, 1978) 3–5. Bear welcomes the arrival of his cousin Brimhall to live with him, but Brimhall's eccentric habits soon tax Bear's hospitality.

2167. ____. *Brimhall Turns to Magic* (Lothrop, 1979) 3–5. Brimhall learns enough magic to make a rabbit appear in a hat, but not enough to make him vanish.

2168. ____. *Brimhall Turns Detective* (Carolrhoda, 1983) 3–5. Huge footprints in the snow cause Brimhall the bear to try to identify and trap the "monster."

2169. ____. *Birthday Bike for Brimhall* (Carolrhoda, 1985) 3–5. Brimhall receives a bicycle for his birthday but is ashamed to admit that he doesn't know how to ride it.

2170. ____. *No Time for Christmas* (Carolrhoda, 1988) 3–5. While planning to give surprise Christmas gifts to each other, Bear and Brimhall come to a realization about the meaning of Christmas.

2171. Delton, Judy. *Back Yard Angel* (Houghton, 1983) 4–6. Although ten-year-old Angel loves her little brother Rags dearly, care of him weighs heavily on her young shoulders.

2172. ____. *Angel in Charge* (Houghton, 1985) 4–6. Mom goes on vacation leaving Angel and Rags in care of Alyce who goes to the hospital and leaves them alone.

2173. ____. *Angel's Mother's Boyfriend* (Houghton, 1986) 4–6. Angel, ten, finds plenty to worry about when she learns that her mother's new boyfriend is a clown.

2174. ____. *Angel's Mother's Wedding* (Houghton, 1987) 4–6. Angel is worried because her mother does not seem to be making any preparation for her upcoming wedding.

2175. ____. *Angel's Mother's Baby* (Houghton, 1989) 4–6. Angel, 12, has adjusted to her mother's remarriage and she and her younger brother, Rags, now live in the perfect family, until she discovers that her mother is going to have another baby.

2176. Delton, Judy. *Pet for Duck and Bear* (Whitman, 1982) k–3. Duck and Bear find out that the best gift to give a friend is not necessarily the very thing you'd like yourself.

2177. ____. *Duck Goes Fishing* (Whitman, 1983) k–3. Disaster-prone Duck joins Owl and Fox on their fishing trip.

2178. ____. *Bear and Duck on the Run* (Whitman, 1984) k–3. Duck tries to get Bear to join him in running everyday, but Bear is very uncooperative.

2179. ____. *Elephant in Duck's Garden* (Whitman, 1985) k–3. After trying many stratagems to remove the elephant in Duck's garden, Bear and Duck discover that the simplest approach is sometimes best.

2180. Delton, Judy. *My Mom Hates Me in January* (Whitman, 1977) k–3. A little boy finds it is the winter blues and not his behavior that makes his mother impatient in January.

2181. ____. *My Mom Made Me Go to Camp* (Delacorte, 1990) k–3. Archie's negative feelings about camp change after he catches a fish.

2182. ____. *My Mom Made Me Go to School* (Delacorte, 1991) k–3. Archie hates the idea of his first day in kindergarten and everything connected with it, but he ends up going and finds it tolerable.

2183. ____. *My Mom Made Me Take Piano Lessons* (Doubleday, 1993) k–3. Archie's complaints about his piano lessons cutting into his playtime subside

when his schoolteacher presents the opportunity for Archie to become a star.

2184. Delton, Judy. *Rabbit Finds a Way* (Crown, 1975) k–3. After turning down tempting food offerings from other friends, Rabbit discovers Bear can't always be counted on to bake carrot cake on Saturdays.

2185. ____. *Rabbit Goes to Night School* (Macmillan, 1988) k–3. Using his newly acquired magic to do a hat trick, Rabbit accidentally produces another rabbit instead of the expected handkerchief and acquires a new friend.

2186. ____. *Hired Help for Rabbit* (Macmillan, 1988) k–3. Overwhelmed with housework, Rabbit decides to get help in cooking, cleaning and gardening.

2187. Demarest, Chris. *Lunatic Adventure of Kitman and Willy* (S & S, 1988) k–3. Kitman and Willy's adventures take them into space, where they dislodge the moon and several stars from their places and have to think of a way of putting them back.

2188. ____. *Kitman and Willy at Sea* (S & S, 1991) k–3. Kitman and Willy find themselves on a remote island where a sinister someone is trapping all the animals, until Kitman and Willy beat him at his own game.

2189. Denim, Sue. *Dumb Bunnies* (Blue Sky Press, 1994) k–3. Adventures of the Dumb Bunnies, a rabbit family that does everything without rhyme or reason.

2190. ____. *Dumb Bunnies Easter* (Blue Sky, 1995) k–3. It's December 24th, and the Dumb Bunnies are celebrating the holidays in their own ridiculous way.

2191. ____. *Make Way for Dumb Bunnies* (Blue Sky, 1996) k–3. Dumb Bunnies have a very active day, during which they do many things backwards or wrong.

2192. Dennis, Lynne. *Raymond Rabbit's Early Morning* (Dutton, 1987) k–3. Raymond Rabbit hops out of bed and begins the day, only to discover that it is too early to be up and everyone else is still sleeping.

2193. ____. *Raymond Rabbit Goes Shopping* (Dutton, 1988) k–3. Raymond Rabbit's shopping trip with his mother brings him unexpected excitement when he suddenly finds himself following a different adult instead of his mother.

2194. Dennis, Wesley. *Flip* (Viking, 1941) k–3. Flip, a colt, likes to imitate everything his mother does. But he could not imitate her jump across a stream, no matter how hard he tried. One day he fell asleep and dreamed he had wings and could fly over anything.

2195. ____. *Flip and the Cows* (Viking, 1942) Flip, the colt, was terrified of cows and when he found himself in a field with a whole herd of them he need to free himself of his fear forever..

2196. ____. *Flip and the Morning* (Viking , 1951/1977) k–3. Flip, the colt, is an early riser and in doing so disturbs all the other animals.

2197. De Paola, Tomie. *Bill and Pete* (Putnam, 1978) k–3. When William Everett Crocodile is chosen to be a suitcase, his talking toothbrush becomes his salvation.
2198. ____. *Bill and Pete Go Don the Nile* (Putnam, 1987) k–3. Little Willie Everett Crocodile and his friend Pete take a class trip to a Cairo museum where they encounter a jewel thief.

2199. De Paola, Tomie. *Strega Nona* (Prentice, 1975) k–3. Strega Nona can cure a head cold, help girls get husbands and cure warts. She can also make pasta by singing a magic song. Her houseboy starts to make pasta, but doesn't know how to stop it.
2200. ____. *Strega Nona's Magic Lessons* (Harcourt, 1982) k–3. Big Anthony disguises himself as a girl in order to take magic lessons from Strega Nona.
2201. ____. *Merry Christmas, Strega Nona* (Harcourt, 1986) k–3. Big Anthony plans a surprise Christmas party for Strega Nona.
2202. ____. *Strega Nona Meets Her Match* (Putnam, 1993) k–3. A rival puts Strega Nona out of the healing business until Big Anthony's assistance inadvertently sabotages the newcomer in his usual well-meaning way.

2203. De Paola, Tomie. *Katie, Kit and Cousin Tom* (S & S, 1986) k–3. A story focusing on the problem of facing a bully.
2204. ____. *Katie and Kit at the Beach* (S & S, 1986) k–3. Big sister Katie helps Kit overcome his fears and enjoys their excursion. Then Little Kit returns the favor, and teaches big sister that you can have fun in the rain.
2205. ____. *Katie's Good Idea* (S & S, 1986) k–3. Kit's problem is that his legs aren't long enough to reach the pedals of his new tricycle.
2206. ____. *Katie, Kit and the Sleepover* (S & S, 1987) k–3. Kit has forgotten his pajamas; a helpful Grandpa quickly takes care of that.

2207. Derleth, August. *Mill Street Irregulars: Special Detectives* (Duell, 1959) 5–8. Instead of a summer of fishing, a mystery at a farm is solved by the boys who also learn about proper detecting equipment.
2208. ____. *Ghost of Black Hawk Island* (Duell, 1961) 5–8. Steve and Sim are camping when they see the ghost of an Indian. They investigate and solve the mystery and also recover the stolen necklace.
2209. ____. *Irregulars Strike Again* (Duell, 1964) 5–8. Steve and Sim, the Mill Street Irregulars, catch some deer hunting out of season.

2210. Derwent, Lavinia. *Macpherson in America* (Burke, 1965) 4–6. Macpherson visits America, especially New York. He visits a ranch and goes to a barbecue.
2211. ____. *Macpherson Sails the Seas* (Burke, 1966) 4–6. Macpherson takes his ailing Grandma (an old sea dog) on a voyage to the sea aboard the *Indian Queen*. Macpherson's adventures are funny.
2212. ____. *Macpherson on the Farm* (Burke, 1967) 4–6. Macpherson and two friends, one of them a near delinquent orphan, are given an unexpected holiday on a farm. The farmer and his wife eventually adopt the orphan.
2213. ____. *Macpherson's Lighthouse Adventure* (Blackie, 1977) 4–6. Macpherson is on a seaside vacation where he is tending his grandpa and coping with Aunt Janet. He meets a junk man, a lighthouse keeper and his old friend Maisie Murphy.
2214. ____. *Macpherson's Skyscraper* (Burke, 1979) 4–6.
2215. ____. *Macpherson's Caravan* (Blackie, 1980) 4–6. Macpherson, his grandfather, friend Maisie and Snowy the kitten go on a caravan tour. They meet a traveling zoo and take part in a cowboy movie.
2216. ____. *Macpherson's Highland Fling* (Burke, 1980) 4–6. Macpherson is invited to visit Lord Provost. He tells the villagers that an old tenant is not a witch but a lonely octogenarian, crippled with rheumatism. A picture of the Highland Games and life in Scotland.
2217. ____. *Macpherson's Island* (Smith, 1980) 4–6. When Grandpa falls ill, Miss Peacock persuades him to stay with her cousin in a castle on the coast. The castle is haunted; there are caves to be explored and a donkey to ride.
2218. ____. *Macpherson's Mystery Adventure* (Blackie, 1982) 4–6. Macpherson goes to London with Maisie and Grandpa. Macpherson becomes a friend of Billy-Boy; he sees Scotland Yard and saves a theater from fire.

2219. Derwent, Lavinia. *Song of Sula* (Gollancz, 1976) 4–6. Magnus lives with Gram and is a good artist. His friend, the duke, is becoming famous for his Sula symphony.
2220. ____. *Return of Sula* (Canongate, 1985) 4–6. A story about the dour, self-contained climate of a remote Scottish island as seen through the eyes of one of its young inhabitants.
2221. ____. *Sula* (Canongate, 1988) 4–6. Magnus lives on Sula, a small island. He likes animals and gets away from home, school and chores to observe, draw and be with the seals, birds, sheep and goats, but the new teacher, Mr. Murray, changes his life.
2222. ____. *Boy from Sula* (Trafalgar, 1989) 4–6.

2223. Devlin, Wende. *Cranberry Thanksgiving* (Four Winds, 1980) k–3. Grandmother almost loses her secret recipe for cranberry bread to one of the guests she and Maggie invite to Thanksgiving dinner.

2224. ____. *Cranberry Christmas* (Four Winds, 1980) k–3. Mr. Whiskers faces a gloomy Christmas until Maggie and her grandmother help him straighten out his house and find the deed to the nearby pond.

2225. ____. *Cranberry Halloween* (Four Winds, 1982) k–3. On Halloween night the people of Cranberryport almost lose the money they have raised to build a new dock.

2226. ____. *Cranberry Mystery* (Four Winds, 1985) k–3. Maggie and Mr. Whiskers go in search of thieves who are stealing many valuable old things in Cranberryport.

2227. ____. *Cranberry Valentine* (Four Winds, 1986) k–3. Maggie, her grandmother, and the sewing circle make Cranberryport a brighter place for Mr. Whiskers when they send him secret valentines.

2228. ____. *Cranberry Birthday* (Four Winds, 1988) k–3. On his birthday, Mr. Whiskers has one calamity after another until the residents of Cranberryport step in to save the day.

2229. ____. *Cranberry Easter* (Four Winds, 1990) k–3. Events at Easter time convince Seth, owner of Cranberryport's general store, that he is needed in town and should change his plans to retire and leave.

2230. ____. *Cranberry Summer* (Four Winds, 1992) k–3. When the circus moves on from Cranberryport and leaves a donkey behind, Maggie and Mr. Whiskers try to find the money to feed her. Through their hard work at the Fourth of July celebration, they are able to provide a home for the donkey.

2231. ____. *Cranberry Autumn* (Four Winds, 1993) k–3. When Grandmother and Maggie help organize an antique sale in Cranberryport, Mr. Whiskers feels useless until he helps Grandmother make a big profit.

2232. Devlin, Wende. *Old Black Witch* (Ency Brit, 1963) k–3. Nicky and his mother's efforts to turn an old New England house into a tearoom are hampered by the old witch who haunts the place, until they learn how well she cooks.

2233. ____. *Old Witch and the Polka-Dot Ribbon* (Parents, 1970) k–3. When the kitchen is finally empty, Old Witch makes her own magic nut cake to enter in the carnival's contest.

2234. ____. *Old Witch Rescues Halloween* (Parents, 1972) k–3. Old witch uses her magic to overcome Mr. Butterbean's edict against Halloween.

2235. DeWeese, Gene. *Dandelion Caper* (Putnam, 1986) 5–8. Having rescued many stranded "tourists" from outer space, Walter and his friend Kathy are unprepared for the evil aliens they meet in an abandoned house and the strange cat with unusual powers that comes to their rescue.

2236. ____. *Calvin Nullifier* (Putnam, 1987) 5–8. A 12-year-old's intergalactic friend Dandelion helps his engineer father repair a space probe to Uranus and provides the rest of the family with a space adventure.

2237. Dexter, Patricia. *Emancipation of Joe Tepper* (Nelson, 1977) 4–6. Joe's alcoholic mother dies and he manages by getting a part-time job. The social worker wants to put him in a foster home but he is declared "emancipated" because he can support himself.

2238. ____. *Arrow in the Wind* (Nelson, 1978) 4–6. Benton resents his father for wanting a divorce. They may lose their home and must scrape for a living. Fancy, their dog, and Joe Tepper, a "stray" child draw the family together after a flash flood.

2239. Deyneka, Anita. *Tanya and the Border Guard* (Cook, 1973) 5–8. A story of Tanya's desire to own a Bible in religion repressed Russia. She is befriended by Gregori, a Russian soldier who shares his faith with her.

2240. ____. *Alexi and the Mountain Treasure* (Cook, 1982) 5–8. Alexi and Tanya find a note sent by Anwar's grandfather. He wants to visit their Russian village to give his family a treasure before he dies. The children make the dangerous trip to meet him and learn of the treasure.

2241. Dickens, Frank. *Great Boffo* (Cape, 1973) 3–5.

2242. ____. *Boffo and the Great Air Race* (Cape, 1977) 3–5. Boffo is in a great air race. There are crooked chimneys and a tasty snack set out at the side of the airplane.

2243. ____. *Boffo* (Parents, 1978) 3–5. William and Lucy don't want to drink their milk. Uncle Boffo then talks about the Great Motorcycle Race where his rival Rudy puts nails in his path. He fills his two flat tires with milk from an obliging cow. The milk turns to butter and seals the holes and he is racing again and wins.

2244. Dickens, Frank. *Albert Herbert Hawkins, Naughtiest Boy in the World* (Doubleday, 1978) k–3. The naughtiest boy in the world skips school to find out if spacemen are afraid of mice.

2245. ____. *Albert Herbert Hawkins and the Space Rocket* (Doubleday, 1978) k–3. A little boy with a mouse in his school bag sneaks into a launching site and releases the mouse which causes confusion; someone pushes the button to launch the now unmanned rocket.

2246. Dickens, Monica. *House at World's End* (Doubleday, 1970) 4–6. Tom is the responsible elder brother, Carrie is an animal lover, especially horses, Em, a younger sister, is practical and Michael is the youngest. They are cared for by an aunt and uncle while their parents are away. They run away and fend for themselves. All is resolved in the end.

2247. ____. *Spring Comes to World's End* (Heinemann, 1971) 4–6. The Fieldings' teenagers use their battered remote old farmhouse for a refuge for neglected horses. Money and ways to earn it are constant problems.

2248. ____. *World's End in Winter* (Heinemann, 1971) 4–6. The Fielding children come to the rescue of little Priscilla, confined to a wheelchair by injury to her spinal cord, and teach her to ride a pony.

2249. ____. *Summer at World's End* (Heinemann, 1972) 4–6. While on a voyage around the world with their gypsy-like father the children rescue many animals from "evil" people, even research scientists.

2250. Dickinson, Mary. *Alex's Bed* (Deutsch, 1980) k–3. To give Alex more space to play in his room, Alex's mother figures out how to raise his bed up near the ceiling.

2251. ____. *Alex and the Baby* (Deutsch, 1982) k–3. Alex doesn't like the girl baby his mother is looking after. His mother is not so sure she likes looking after her when noise and confusion reign. But the baby's mother comes to collect her and mother says she's glad to have a big boy like Alex.

2252. ____. *Alex's Outing* (Deutsch, 1983) k–3. Alex and his friends go to the country for a picnic. He sees cows, gets stuck in the mud, picks blackberries and gets tired and dirty. But his mother isn't cross. She bathes him and puts him to bed.

2253. ____. *New Clothes for Alex* (Deutsch, 1984) k–3. Alex hates going shopping for clothes with his mother but finally finds something that he likes.

2254. ____. *Alex and Roy: Best Friends* (Deutsch, 1982) k–3. When Roy comes over to play. Alex hides in his room until he realizes Roy is having a good time without him.

2255. Dickinson, Mary. *Jilly, You Look Terrible* (Dutton, 1986) k–3. Jilly tries out her mother's make-up. She is the center of attention at the wedding reception.

2256. ____. *Jilly Takes Over* (Deutsch, 1987) k–3. Jilly puts her mother, who has a tummy ache, to bed and then makes a huge sandwich for herself and she too, becomes ill. Later she and Dad prepare dinner for recovering Mom.

2257. ____. *Jilly's Boat Trip* (Deutsch, 1987) k–3.

2258. Dicks, Terrance. *Ask Oliver: Mystery of the Haunted Hospital* (Pepper, 1982) 2–4.

2259. ____. *Ask Oliver: Vicky's Victory* (Piccadilly, 1985) 2–4. Vicky is the only girl in Pete's gang. Pete is tall and the leader; Oliver is small and young but clever; Gupta is cheerful. But Vicky gets credit for solving the mystery of the missing money.

2260. ____. *Ask Oliver* (Piccadilly, 1985) 2–4. Oliver is a junior detective. He must discover who stole the Christmas Club money from Gupta's father's mini-market.

2261. ____. *Ask Oliver: Gupta's Christmas* (Piccadilly, 1985) 2–4.

2262. ____. *Ask Oliver: Mystery of the Missing Train* (Pepper, 1987) 2–4. The African Belle is a steam en-

gine that takes visitors around Safari Park. Oliver and his friends enjoy the ride but the train goes in a tunnel and doesn't come out. What happened?

2263. Dicks, Terrance. *Enter T.R.* (Piccadilly, 1985) 2–4. Teddy Bear has character and courage. He and Edward Bear and the rag doll frighten away a wild cat from the nursery.

2264. ____. *T.R. Afloat* (Piccadilly, 1986) 2–4. This story describes a holiday on a converted lifeboat in an offshore island bird sanctuary, where the warden is guarding a rare pipit nesting in an old wreck. Jonny scares off two egg poachers by dressing up as a pirate and alarming them.

2265. ____. *T.R.'s Big Game* (Piccadilly, 1987) 2–4.

2266. ____. *T.R.'s Festival* (Piccadilly, 1987) 2–4.

2267. ____. *T.R.'s Halloween* (Barron, 1988) 2–4. Jimmy and his talking teddy bear, T.R. find themselves ensconced in a mystery one Halloween night when Jimmy takes a dare and knocks at the door of a creepy old house.

2268. ____. *T.R.'s Day Out* (Barron, 1988) 2–4. Jimmy takes his Teddy Roosevelt bear and his other talking toys to the American exhibit at the British Museum where they foil the robbery of a portrait of the real Teddy Roosevelt.

2269. ____. *T.R. Goes to Hollywood* (Piccadilly, 1988) 2–4.

2270. ____. *T.R. Down Under* (Piccadilly, 1989) 2–4. An adventure tale with some fantasy about the infringement of the Aboriginal peoples' rights.

2271. ____. *T.R. Goes Skiing* (Piccadilly, 1989) 2–4.

2272. Dicks, Terrance. *Camden Street Kids in the Money* (Piccadilly, 1986) 2–4. Six school kids are involved in raising money for a school extension but their efforts fall apart. They finally do succeed in raising money by getting a cleaning job.

2273. ____. *Camden Street Kids on T.V.* (Piccadilly, 1986) 2–4. Loella is the leader of the six students at Camden Street Primary School. They want to get their amateur pop group into television. They are called Loella and the Love Bugs.

2274. Dicks, Terrance. *Sally Ann Goes to the Hospital* (S & S, 1988) 3–5. Sally Ann, a rag doll, belonging to Lucy needs to get medical care at the hospital. She is prepared for the Children's Hospital visit.

2275. ____. *Sally Ann and the School Show* (S & S, 1992) 3–5. Sally Ann and the other dolls help Mrs. Foster raise enough money to keep the day care center open.

2276. ____. *Sally Ann on Her Own* (S & S, 1992) 3–5. Sally Ann is a doll, one of the toys in a day care center. She is instrumental in saving the building from the clutches of two greedy crooks.

2277. ____. *Nurse Sally Ann* (S & S, 1993) 3–5. When a new girl at Mrs. Foster's day care center has an asthma attack, a doll named Sally Ann accompanies her to the hospital and breaks the rules about coming to life in front of humans.

2278. ____. *Sally Ann and the Mystery Picnic* (S & S, 1993) 3–5. Sally Ann, a rag doll, convinces Lucy to take her along on a nursery school outing with Mrs. Foster's day care center. Lucy is lost and Sally Ann knows how to find her. She helps with a river rescue.

2279. Dicks, Terrance. *Goliath and the Burglar* (Barron, 1987) 2–4. David's small puppy Goliath seems to be growing into a large, noisy problem, until he has the chance to redeem himself by becoming a hero.

2280. ____. *Goliath and the Buried Treasure* (Barron, 1987) 2–4. Canine Goliath's fondness for digging holes gets him into big trouble with the neighbors but also transforms him into the most unlikely hero in town.

2281. ____. *Goliath at the Dog Show* (Barron, 1987) 2–4. When a disappearing dog on the day of the local dog show suggests foul play, David's pet Goliath helps solve the mystery.

2282. ____. *Goliath's Easter Parade* (Barron, 1987) 2–4. The playground used by David and his friends will be closed, unless money to repair it can be raised through an Easter Parade. David and his dog Goliath take matters into their own hands.

2283. ____. *Goliath on Vacation* (Barron, 1987) 2–4. Lovable Goliath disrupts hotel life when David and his parents go on vacation, but the big dog redeems himself by helping solve a mystery of disappearing ponies.

2284. ____. *Goliath Goes to Summer School* (Barron, 1989) 2–4. David's big dog Goliath, follows him to summer school on a farm and helps him to solve a ghostly mystery.

2285. ____. *Goliath at the Seaside* (Barron, 1989) 2–4. David and his big dog, Goliath, solve a mystery involving stinging seaweed and illegal toxic dumping at a seaside resort.

2286. ____. *Goliath and the Cub Scouts* (Barron, 1990) 2–4. Canine Goliath helps David find a most unusual thief who committed an "impossible crime" by removing a valuable trophy from a locked room.

2287. Dicks, Terrance. *Cat Called Max: Magnificent Max* (Barron, 1994) 3–5. One stormy night, Timmy runs outside and stumbles over a big black and white talking cat. Not only is Max able to talk, but he also has exquisite manners.

2288. ____. *Cat Called Max: Max and the Quiz Kids* (Barron, 1994) 3–5. Timmy's school is up against the amazing HiTech team in the finals of the national school's quiz competition. Timmy has one thing going for him: his magical talking pet cat, Max.

2289. ____. *Cat Called Max: Max's Amazing Summer* (Barron, 1994) 3–5. Something sinister is prompting strange happenings around town this summer and Max is the first to see the problem.

2290. Dicks, Terrance. *Meet the MacMagics* (Barron, 1994) 3–5. The hilariously spooky adventures of a hilariously eccentric family. Young Mike MacMagic is the only "normal" person in the whole house.

2291. ____. *MacMagics: My Brother the Vampire* (Barron, 1995) 3–5. Mike's crazy big brother Murdo actually thinks he's a vampire. But things change fast when he falls in love with the clergyman's pretty daughter.

2292. ____. *MacMagics: Spell for My Sister* (Barron, 1995) 3–5. When Mike's sister Meg falls under a powerful spell, the entire family starts behaving even more strangely than usual.

2293. Dicks, Terrance. *Jonathan's Ghost* (Piccadilly, 1991) 4–6. Dave is Jonathan's ghost friend and helper. Sometimes his help is not wanted or understood but Dave stands by his offers.

2294. ____. *Jonathan and the Superstar* (Piccadilly, 1991) 4–6. Jonathan's ghost, Dave, gets Jonathan out of difficulties but now Jonathan resents Dave's warning against the new boy Jason who seems so perfect. The real Jason is a liar, a thief and into drugs. But Dave can unmask him.

2295. Dickson, Gordon. *Secret Under Antarctica* (Holt, 1963) 5–8. It is the year 2013. Robbie and his father are doing research on whale communication. Robbie is held captive by a man who wants to blow up Antarctica.

2296. ____. *Secret Under the Caribbean* (Holt, 1964) 5–8. Robbie is involved with an international art thief who is trying to steal a Spanish galleon of archeological value.

2297. Digby, Anne. *First Term at Trebizon* (Granada, 1980) 2–4. A modern version of a series of stories about the beloved old girls' school stories; it is basically unchanged in the pattern of friendship; misunderstanding, playing fair and unfair, in spite of surfing and parental take-over bids.

2298. ____. *Summer Term at Trebizon* (Barron, 1980) 4–6.

2299. ____. *More Trouble at Trebizon* (Granada, 1981) 2–4. Rebecca's friend Moura's cousin was kidnapped so Moura must have a bodyguard. Rebecca and her friends work at ways to escape fat, bald poppa. Also Lucy, 12, disrupts the peaceful school routine.

2300. ____. *Boy Trouble at Trebizon* (Granada, 1981) 2–4. A modern version of the old girls' school stories. The pattern is basically unchanged: friendship, misunderstanding and playing fair and unfair.

2301. ____. *Summer Camp at Trebizon* (Barron, 1982) 2–4. Rebecca is a helper at the Pegasus Camp for disadvantaged city children. She meets Tommy, an awkward small boy and wins his confidence through the stray dog he has adopted.

2302. ____. *Tennis Term at Trebizon* (Barron, 1982)

4–6. Will Rebecca, even if she is not yet 14, get into the school tennis tournaments? Who planned the hoaxes that twice roused sleepers to an apparent crisis?

2303. ____. *Into the Fourth at Trebizon* (Granada, 1983) 2–4. Rebecca's friendship with Tish's brother Robbie falters when extra tennis coaching prevents her from watching his Saturday tests but there is someone only too ready to take her place—icily, immaculate Ingrid, daughter of a Swedish diplomat, who, ingenious in mischief, manages in a single term to disrupt the new fourth year.

2304. ____. *Fourth Year Triumph at Trebizon* (Granada, 1985) 2–4. Rebecca's prowess on the tennis court is demonstrated in this book. But the focus is in a television documentary which arouses everyone's enthusiasm. But some girls wonder why the emphasis is on sports.

2305. ____. *Ghost Term at Trebizon* (Barron, 1990) 2–4. A story about life in a girl's boarding school: teenage friendships, success games, the girl from the state school finding her feet in a different world; and the worries over coursework.

2306. ____. *Second Term at Trebizon* (Granada, 1991) 4–6.

2307. ____. *Secret Letters at Trebizon* (Barron, 1993) 4–6.

2308. ____. *Unforgettable Fifth at Trebizon* (Barron, 1994) 4–6.

2309. Digby, Anne. *Me, Jill Robinson and the Christmas Pantomime* (Granada, 1983) 4–6. A story about the pantomime put on by a youth club with Jill as Cinderella. A gang of hooligans spoils the dress rehearsal. Harry, their leader, is trying to break up Jill's older sister Sarah's relationship. All ends well.

2310. ____. *Me. Jill Robinson and the Perdou Painting* (Granada, 1985) 4–6. Jill, Sarah and Tony are the Robinson children. Sarah is involved in a mystery when a painting disappears from the home of one of Jill's classmates. Jill and her friend Lindy help solve the mystery. Sarah's suspension from college is lifted. Mr. Perdou recovers.

2311. ____. *Me, Jill Robinson and the Seaside Mystery* (Granada, 1990) 4–6.

2312. ____. *Me, Jill Robinson and the Television Quiz* (Granada, 1990) 4–6.

2313. Dinardo, Jeffrey. *Timothy and the Night Noises* (Prentice, 1986) k–3. Timothy finds a way to deal with the ghosts, monsters and other scary things that make noises in the night and make him afraid of bedtime.

2314. ____. *Timothy and the Big Bully* (S & S, 1988) k–3. Timothy, a frog is bothered by Big Eddie, a bully who steals his lunch every day. Timothy's big brother rescues him.

2315. ____. *Timothy and the Christmas Gift* (S & S, 1989) k–3. As his frog family prepares for Christmas, Timothy worries because he has no money to buy Mama a gift. His inspired solution pleases Mama and involves cooperation from his older brother.

2316. Dinneen, Betty. *Lurk of Leopards* (Walck, 1972) 4–6. In present day Kenya, Karen learns about leopards when she "adopts" two cubs. She later gives them up to a zoo.

2317. ____. *Lion Yellow* (Walck, 1975) 4–8. A family, resident on an African game preserve, enjoy its contact with the wildlife, which sometimes proves dangerous.

2318. ____. *Karen's Leopard* (Walck, 1975) 4–6. Karen, 12, is an animal lover who lives in Kenya and wants a leopard of her own.

2319. Disch, Thomas. *Brave Little Toaster* (Doubleday, 1986) 3–5. Feeling abandoned by their beloved master, a vacuum cleaner, tensor lamp, electric blanket, clock radio and toaster undertake a long and arduous journey to find him in a faraway city.

2320. ____. *Brave Little Toaster Goes to Mars* (Doubleday, 1988) 3–5. A group of angry appliances, having fled to Mars to avoid becoming obsolete, now plan to take over the earth, unless the Brave Little Toaster can stop the invasion.

2321. Dodd, Lynley. *Hairy Maclary from Donaldson's Dairy* (G. Stevens, 1985) k–3. A small black dog and his canine friends are terrorized by the local tomcat.

2322. ____. *Hairy Maclary's Bone* (G. Stevens, 1985) k–3. A small black dog uses a series of slick maneuvers to protect his bone from his canine friends.

2323. ____. *Hairy Maclary Scattercat* (G. Stevens, 1987) k–3. Feeling very frisky, a little black dog enjoys chasing all the cats he meets until he comes across Scarface Claw.

2324. ____. *Hairy Maclary's Rumpus at the Vet* (G. Stevens, 1989) k–3. There is a rumpus at the veterinarian's when all the animals get out of their cages.

2325. ____. *Hairy Maclary Caterwaul Caper* (G. Stevens, 1990) k–3. Hairy Maclary leads all the other dogs in the neighborhood to investigate the terrible caterwauling created when the tough cat Scarface Claw is caught up in a tree.

2326. ____. *Hairy Maclary's Show Business* (G. Stevens, 1992) k–3. A story about a cat show. Disreputable Hairy Maclary breaks into the cat's quarters and completely destroys all their belongings. Hairy Maclary wins a prize for scruffiness.

2327. Donnelly, Liza. *Dinosaur Day* (Scholastic, 1987) k–3. Crazy about dinosaurs, a boy and his dog imagine they see one under every lump of snow until the day they get a big surprise.

2328. ____. *Dinosaurs' Halloween* (Scholastic, 1987) k–3. An encounter with a fellow trick-or-treater whose dinosaur costume is remarkably realistic gives a boy a Halloween full of surprises.

2329. ____. *Dinosaur Beach* (Scholastic, 1989) k–3. Frightened sunbathers flee from a crowded beach when someone yells "Shark," but it is really a friendly elasmasaurus who then takes our boy hero to Dinosaur Beach.

2330. ____. *Dinosaur Garden* (Scholastic, 1990) k–3. When Rex plants a dinosaur garden to attract dinosaurs, an unexpected guest comes to dinner.

2331. ____. *Dinosaurs' Christmas* (Scholastic, 1991) k–3. Rex finds trouble at the North Pole: the elves are making the dinosaurs all wrong and all the reindeer have the flu. Can Rex save Christmas?

2332. ____. *Dinosaur Valentine* (Scholastic, 1994) k–3.

2333. Dowling, Paul. *Meg and Jack Are Moving* (Houghton, 1990) k–3. Meg and Jack experience all the pangs and excitement of selling their old home and moving to a new one.

2334. ____. *Meg and Jack's New Friends* (Houghton, 1990) k–3. Having just moved into a new house, Meg and Jack first shyly, then happily, get to know the children next door.

2335. Dowling, Paul. *Where Are You Going, Jimmy?* (Doubleday, 1993) k–3. Jimmy goes for a walk that takes him to all of his favorite places, gathering animal companions as he goes.

2336. ____. *Jimmy's Sunny Book* (Doubleday, 1994) k–3. Jimmy and his puppy head out-of-doors on a bright, sunny day. They greet a chirping bird, swim in a pool and play with their shadows.

2337. Dragonwagon, Crescent. *I Hate My Brother Harry* (Harper, 1983) k–3. Nobody believes Harry's little sister hates him, and even she is confused by the way he treats her.

2338. ____. *I Hate My Sister Maggie* (Macmillan, 1989) k–3. Harry is fed up with his brat of a younger sister, until his mother tells him a secret that puts things in a totally different perspective.

2339. Du Bois, William Penn. *Otto in Africa* (Viking, 1961) k–3. Prequel. Otto, the giant dog and his master Duke set out alone to save the small city in Africa from an attack from Abou the Fierce and his 170 bandits. This happened many years ago when the otterhound was a puppy.

2340. ____. *Otto at Sea* (Viking, 1958) k–3. After receiving 22 medals for brave adventures in 18 different countries Otto, a giant dog, and his master, Duke, set out on a goodwill tour to America.

2341. ____. *Otto in Texas* (Viking, 1959) k–3. Texas is just the proper size for Otto and he has a wonderful time swimming in his own pool, and digging up bones. He wins fame and a special medal for tracking down a new kind of outlaw—the oil rustler.

2342. ____. *Otto and the Magic Potatoes* (Viking, 1970) k–3. The Baron is sure if he can study closely a dog two and a half stories tall, he can improve the quality of his enormous potatoes and roses.

2343. Du Bois, William Penn. *Bear Party* (Viking, 1951) 3–5. The real teddy bears who lived in Koala Park once became very angry with each other and a wise bear decided to have a masquerade ball with masks and costumes to help the bears get to know each other all over again.

2344. ____. *Bear Circus* (Viking, 1971) 3–5. A story of bears who had their food stolen by grasshoppers and their lives saved by their friends, the kangaroos. To repay the kangaroos for their kindness the bears perform a circus for them.

2345. ____. *Gentleman Bear* (Farrar, 1985) 3–5. Billy Browne-Browne and his bear, Bayard, have a lifelong friendship.

2346. Du Bois, William Penn. *Alligator Case* (Harper, 1965) 3–5. A Dragnet satire. A boy detective solves a mystery about a circus. Neither pork chops and peas nor twisting alligators will keep him from his task.

2347. ____. *Horse in the Camel Suit* (Harper, 1967) 3–5. This time the boy detective meets a magician who is also a horse thief. There are escape artists, karate experts and mind readers.

2348. Dubanevich, Arlene. *Pigs in Hiding* (Four Winds, 1983) k–3. A game of hide-and-seek played by a number of pigs allows the reader to find the animals in their hiding places.

2349. ____. *Pig William* (Bradbury, 1985) k–3. Always a dawdler, Pig William misses his ride to the school picnic but in a sudden turn of events the picnic comes to him.

2350. ____. *Pig at Christmas* (Bradbury, 1986) k–3. As Christmas approaches and panicking pigs prepare for their holiday festivities, one little pig wonders nervously if Santa will really deliver everything as promised.

2351. ____. *Piggest Show on Earth* (Orchard, 1988) k–3. Two young pigs have an exciting time at the circus when one of them loses her balloon in the middle of the circus parade.

2352. Dubois, Claude. *Looking for Ginny* (Viking, 1990) k–3. Bobby and Nicole have a new pet named Ginny.

2353. ____. *He's My Jumbo* (Viking, 1990) k–3. Nicole loves her toy elephant, Jumbo. She can read to him, dress him but can she share him? Bobby loves Jumbo, too. What will they do?

2354. Dubov, Christie. *Aleksandra, Where Is Your Nose?* (St. Martin, 1986) k–3. Aleksandra, clad in diapers, answers where her mouth is, her nose, teeth, etc.

2355. ____. *Aleksandra, Where Are Your Toes?* (St. Martin, 1986) k–3. Aleksandra, clad in diapers, answers where her toes are, her feet, etc.

2356. Duffey, Betsy. *Lucky in Leftfield* (S & S, 1992) 3–5. Lucky, the dog tries to regain his spot as leftfielder on his master's losing baseball team after a new coach arrives and banishes Lucky from the ballpark.

2357. ____. *Lucky on the Loose* (S & S, 1993) 3–5. While George is at camp and his parents are on vacation, his dog Lucky escapes from the kennel where he is being boarded and disappears.

2358. Duffy, James. *Cleaver of the Good Luck Diner* (Macmillan, 1989) 3–5. Clever Cleaver, the big dog at the Good Luck Diner, keeps things stirred up for the family that runs the diner and works at effecting a reconciliation between the estranged parents.

2359. ____. *Cleaver and Company* (Macmillan, 1991) 3–5. The summer she turns 13, Sarah is kept busy working in her family's diner and dealing with their big dog Cleaver.

2360. Duffy, James. *Revolt of the Teddy Bears* (Crown, 1985) 3–5. Teddy bears are running amuck in Paris and Chief Inspector May Gray, a poodle, is determined to find out why.

2361. ____. *Christmas Gang* (Schribner, 1989) 3–5. While celebrating Christmas together, May Gray's family persuade her to tell them again about her first assignment as a police officer when she solved the mystery of the Christmas Gang.

2362. Duke, Kate. *Guinea Pig ABC* (Dutton, 1983) k–3. Each letter of the alphabet is illustrated by a word that applies to pictured guinea pigs.

2363. ____. *Guinea Pigs Far and Near* (Dutton, 1984) k–3. An introduction to words like over, under, far, near, around, behind, between, etc. It is done by showing the ways to circumvent an inconvenient water puddle.

2364. ____. *Playground* (Methuen, 1986) k–3. Dad waits for Junior at the bottom of the slide and contentedly plays ball.

2365. ____. *Clean Up Day* (Methuen, 1986) k–3. A guinea pig helps mom vacuum, launder, and more. Then Mom dozes because of exhaustion.

2366. ____. *Bedtime* (Dutton, 1986) Guinea pig grandmother, father, mother and child romp through this story with glee and mess.

2367. ____. *What Bounces?* (Methuen, 1986) k–3. An inquisitive guinea pig explores the bounceability factor of the items in his refrigerator. Eggs don't have any.

2368. Dumas, Philippe. *Story of Edward* (Parents, 1977) 2–4. Adventures of a clever donkey with a talent for waltzing. He discovers that trying to disguise the fact that he is a donkey is self-defeating.

2369. ____. *Lucie, Edward's Daughter* (Parents, 1977) 2–4. Edward the donkey's daughter, Lucy, wants to see the world. She meets Louis, a small boy and they run away to Paris where they release some captive donkeys. Edward goes to find Lucy. He lets

Louis ride on his back in a race as a reward for taking care of her.

2370. ____. *Lucie, Tale of a Donkey* (Prentice, 1979) 2–4. Lucie and a little boy named Louis see Paris together.

2371. Dumas, Philippe. *Laura on the Road* (Gollancz, 1978) k–3. Laura is a Newfoundland dog whose job is to look after Alice and Emil. Laura is hitched to her dogcart and pulls the children to Paris to deliver a letter.

2372. ____. *Laura, Alice's New Puppy* (Gollancz, 1979) k–3. Laura is a Newfoundland puppy. She is in trouble as she grows large and awkward…with the postman, neighbors and her family. But she became a heroine when Alice and Emil are swept out to sea in a rubber dingy. Laura finds and rescues them.

2373. ____. *Laura and the Bandits* (Gollancz, 1980) k–3. Laura, a large dog, made short work of a gang of fine art thieves. Laura, Alice and Granddad are also involved. Laura is presented with her own key to the new sports center.

2374. ____. *Laura Loses Her Head* (Gollancz, 1982) k–3. Alice, Emil and Laura their dog go to visit grandfather. They take a bath and the tub overflows carrying them to the river. Grandfather rescues but does not punish them.

2375. Dunbar, Joyce. *Five Hungry Mice* (Orchard, 1990) k–3. Five mice want to do something about food and come up with a unique solution.

2376. ____. *Five Hungry Mice and the Moon* (Orchard, 1991) k–3. Five mice use scientific experiments to try to prove that the moon is made of green cheese.

2377. Dunbar, Joyce. *Mouse and Mole* (Doubleday, 1993) k–3. Mouse and Mole deal with the universal problem of waste. They simply move it from room to room.

2378. ____. *Mouse and Mole Have a Party* (Doubleday, 1994) k–3. Mole and his friend Mouse always discuss in advance what to do. But unexpected things happen like a visit from Rat, Rabbit, Hedgehog and Owl. They bring gifts for Mole's birthday.

2379. Dunbar, Joyce. *Software Superslug* (Macmillan, 1995) 2–4. A slug with the brain of a computer is just right for the young reader's passion for minibeasts and computer games. Sprinkled with humor.

2380. ____. *Software Superslug and the Nutty Novelty Knitting* (Macmillan, 1995) 2–4.

2381. ____. *Software Superslug and the Great Computer* (Macmillan, 1995) 2–4.

2382. Duncan, Jane. *Camerons on the Hills* (Macmillan, 1963) 4–6. Shona, Neil and Donald go to visit a shepherd Angus while staying with their aunt. A plane crashes in the snowy mountains and they help with the rescue.

2383. ____. *Camerons on the Train* (St. Martin, 1963) 4–6. Shona, Neil and Donald take a train to visit Scotland. They encounter crooks, thefts and sabotage.

2384. ____. *Camerons at the Castle* (St. Martin, 1964) 4–6. Shona, Neil and Donald and Nink go to Castle Vannish and learn of its history and the mystery of the white hand.

2385. ____. *Camerons Calling* (Macmillan, 1966) 4–6. Shona, Neil and Donald stay at Castle Vannish that is run as a hotel. Evan Cameron is coming as a guest.

2386. Duncan, Jane. *Herself and Janet Reachfar* (Seabury, 1975) k–3. Herself, a matriarchal grandmother, complains that no one listens to her. Even though she talks constantly. Janet goes off to help the sheep caught in a spring snow. She brings home the first spring lamb.

2387. ____. *Brave Janet Reachfar* (Seabury, 1975) k–3. During a sudden snowstorm, Janet ventures out into a forbidden hill to rescue a lost sheep only to wind up needing help herself.

2388. ____. *Janet Reachfar and the Kelpie* (Seabury, 1976) k–3. Janet disobeys and crawls to a deep well. She sees her reflection and scares herself.

2389. ____. *Janet Reachfar and Chickabird* (Seabury, 1978) k–3. Janet is a young farm girl in constant trouble. She accidentally, indirectly breaks the leg of a chicken. She mends it and makes the chicken a pet.

2390. Duncan, Riana. *Emily's Paintbox* (Barron, 1988) k–3. Emily paints her house blue, the flowers purple and the grass red. She paints oak trees orange, the sky yellow and the clouds green.

2391. ____. *When Emily Woke Up Angry* (Barron, 1989) k–3. Waking up in a bad mood, Emily imitates the angry movements of several animals until she meets a frog that jumps for joy.

2392. ____. *Emily's Bed* (Barron, 1992) k–3. Emily, freckle-faced and plain, imagines herself camping in a desert, driving a racing car, drifting on an ice floe, and more.

2393. Dunlop, Eileen. *Finn's Search* (Holiday, 1994) 4–6. Chris, 12, has a learning disability. He is bothered by bully Andrew. Finn is his friend and comes to his rescue. Chris and Finn look for Roman coins in Andrew's father's land. They want to save the land from development.

2394. ____. *Finn's Roman Fort* (Blackie, 1994) 4–6. Chris, who has a learning difficulty, has a good friend Finn. When he goes to senior school without Finn he worries about the bully Andrew. But Andrew needs to make friends so he befriends Finn and Chris is jealous.

2395. Duvoisin, Roger. *Veronica* (Knopf, 1961) k–3. Veronica, the hippopotamus, fulfills her desire to be noticed when she takes an amusing journey into the big city.

2396. ____. *Our Veronica Goes to Petunia's Farm* (Knopf, 1962) k–3. Veronica came to stay with the animals on Mr. Pumpkin's farm. At first she was mocked but when she took sick for a week because nobody talked to her, they worried about her.

2397. ____. *Lonely Veronica* (Knopf, 1963) k–3. Veronica is taken to America where she is bewildered by the skyscrapers, building construction and bustle of city life.

2398. ____. *Veronica's Smile* (Knopf, 1964) k–3. There is so little for Veronica to do on Petunia's farm that yawning is her major activity. But one day, after hours of bored yawning, Veronica finds that a hippo with a big mouth can be very useful.

2399. ____. *Veronica and the Birthday Present* (Knopf, 1971) k–3. The friendship that develops between a kitten and a hippopotamus causes great commotion in two neighboring farms.

2400. Duvoisin, Roger. *Crocus* (Random, 1977) k–3. The barnyard friends of Crocus the crocodile love and admire him for his fierce-looking teeth. When he must have them pulled, life changes for all the animals.

2401. ____. *Importance of Crocus* (Random, 1980) k–3. Crocus, the crocodile discovers his special talents when the Sweetpeas build a pond on their property.

2402. Duvoisin, Roger. *Petunia* (Knopf, 1950) k–3. Petunia was a goose who found a book one day and became the barnyard busybody. After all, a book made her very wise she felt until the day she found out how little she really knew.

2403. ____. *Petunia and the Song* (Knopf, 1951) k–3. Petunia again gets into trouble because she wants to sing but all she can do is honk. She is finally rewarded when her honking leads the farmer to catch a stranger who is stealing his apples.

2404. ____. *Petunia's Christmas* (Knopf, 1952) k–3. Petunia tries to save Charles, the gander, from becoming Christmas dinner.

2405. ____. *Petunia Takes a Trip* (Knopf, 1953) k–3. Petunia, a goose, discovers a huge, exciting world outside the realm of her farm home, but is happy to return to the farm and her friends.

2406. ____. *Petunia, Beware!* (Knopf, 1958) k–3. After nearly a disastrous adventure Petunia, a greedy goose, learns to appreciate the green grass within her own pasture.

2407. ____. *Petunia, I Love You* (Knopf, 1965) k–3. Petunia, a charming goose, manages to outwit the Raccoon who has fallen in love with her—as a full course dinner, of course.

2408. ____. *Petunia's Treasure* (Knopf, 1975) k–3. Petunia finds a treasure chest and thinks she is rich and important. Her barnyard friends are eager to share her fortune.

2409. ____. *Petunia the Silly Goose Stories* (Viking, 1987) k–3. Contains: "Petunia's Christmas"; "Petunia's Treasure"; "Petunia Takes a Trip"; "Petunia Beware."

2410. Dyke, John. *Pigwig* (Methuen, 1978) k–3. Pigwig decides to win the love of pretty Matilda by improving his appearance and begins to make and wear a variety of unusual hats.

2411. ____. *Pigwig and the Pirates* (Methuen, 1979) k–3. Pigwig not only rescues his nephews from pirates, but returns with the pirates' treasure.

2412. Eadington, Joan. *Jonny Briggs and the Ghost* (BBC, 1978) 3–5. Was it a ghost or a thief who snatched the loaf from Jonny's friend while he joined the football game? Jonny's family blames Arnold Jax a local bad boy on the run but Jonny was sure he felt a cold breath at the time.

2413. ____. *Jonny Briggs and the Whitby Weekend* (BBC, 1979) 3–5. Jonny tries to get rid of the stray dog that insists on following him. It causes embarrassment to Jonny with railway officials, his landlady and Jonny's older sister. But then the dog saves Jonny's life when he goes too far in the sea. He is officially adopted.

2414. ____. *Jonny Briggs and the Giant Cave* (BBC, 1982) 3–5. Jonny turns a collection of boxes and rugs into a classroom version of a Stone Age home for his class project. Josie and Jinny cause havoc and Jonny learns a lesson of caution and proper planning.

2415. ____. *Jonny Briggs and the Galloping Wedding* (BBC, 1983) 3–5. Jonny's oldest sister Pat has decided to travel to the church for her wedding in a horse-drawn carriage.

2416. ____. *World of Jonny Briggs* (BBC, 1986) 3–5. Jonny tries to please his teacher at primary school and survive the competition with siblings at home. He wants to look after the school rabbit and win the Great Kite Competition.

2417. ____. *Stand Up for Jonny Briggs* (BBC, 1987) 3–5.

2418. ____. *Jonny Briggs and the Secret Sunflower* (BBC, 1988) 3–5. A story of a boy who joins in the class project to see who can grow the tallest sunflower.

2419. ____. *Jonny Briggs and the Junior Tennis* (BBC, 1991) 3–5.

2420. Earnshaw, Brian. *Dragonfall 5 and the Royal Beast* (Lothrop, 1975) 3–5. Dragonfall 5 is delivering the Royal Beast but it is kidnapped and everyone is searching for the Beast and each other. A funny far-out fantasy.

2421. ____. *Dragonfall 5 and the Space Cowboys* (Lothrop, 1975) 3–5. Tim and Sanchez became involved in a space cattle feud when their ship breaks

down. They are all searching for clues in a treasure hunt where the prize is grazing land.

2422. ____. *Dragonfall 5 and the Hijackers* (Lothrop, 1975) 3–5. A funny, exciting adventure of a starship trapped in a cavern.

2423. ____. *Dragonfall 5 and the Empty Planet* (Lothrop, 1976) 3–5. Tim and Sanchez go on a field trip where half their class disappears. They have been transported to a frozen moon. The class is rescued by the Flying Hound Dog and the Minims.

2424. ____. *Dragonfall 5 and the Super Horse* (Lothrop, 1977) 3–5.

2425. ____. *Dragonfall 5 and the Mastermind* (Lothrop, 1979) 3–5. A vintage starship more than sixty years old, with very complicated machinery, and its inmates help to bring peace to a planet peopled by three races of hares (black, gray and white) and ruled by a Mastermind computer

2426. ____. *Dragonfall 5 and the Haunted World* (Lothrop, 1979) 3–5. A few human inhabitants of Pine Home, refugees from Lost Home, seem less capable than the elephants of conducting themselves in a manner acceptable to the family of Starship Dragonfall 5.

2427. Eaton, Seymour. *Roosevelt Bears Go to Washington* (Dover, 1905) k–3. Teddy B and Teddy G leave Colorado to go to Washington to meet Theodore Roosevelt. On the way they organize a baseball game for poor children. They spend time in Atlantic City and visit a wax museum.

2428. ____. *Roosevelt Bears* (Dover, 1906) k–3. Relates the rhyming adventures of two mischievous bears whose greatest pleasures are eating, playing and playing tricks on grown-ups.

2429. Ecke, Wolfgang. *Face at the Window* (Prentice, 1978) 4–6. A new version of Encyclopedia Brown (Sobol, Donald). Cases to be solved with clues given, some false, some real. The answers are in the back of the book.

2430. ____. *Invisible Witness* (Prentice, 1981) 4–6. Some more short mysteries to be solved by the reader. A bit tougher than Encyclopedia Brown's cases.

2431. ____. *Stolen Paintings* (Prentice, 1981) 4–6. Seventeen more puzzles to solve à la Encyclopedia Brown, some are going to be difficult because of their translation from German.

2432. ____. *Bank Holdup* (Prentice, 1982) 4–6. More bloodless crimes to be solved. Some clues are obvious but some take a little thought.

2433. ____. *Midnight Chess Game* (Prentice, 1985) 4–6. More crimes to be solved with the author giving an indication of the difficulty level of each crime.

2434. Edgar, Marriot. *Lion and Albert* (Methuen, 1979) k–3. Mr. and Mrs. Ramsbottom may have lost their son to Wallace the lion but they have some lovely snapshots. The ghastliness of their visit to Blackpool Zoo is nicely captured in the pictures.

2435. ____. *Albert Comes Back* (Methuen, 1981) k–3. Albert was eaten by Wallace, a lion, in the zoo. Wallace regrets eating Albert. Albert's father is paid by the insurance company and when Albert is regurgitated by the lion, his father sends him back to the zoo to see what the lion will do.

2436. Edmondson, Madeline. *Witch's Egg* (Seabury, 1974) k–3. The creature that hatches from the witch's egg acts like a human but is not the same as a human.

2437. ____. *Anna Witch* (Doubleday, 1982) k–3. A little witch girl makes a discovery about life without mother after a loss of temper clashes with a loss of patience.

2438. Edwards, Dorothy. *My Naughty Little Sister's Friends* (Houghton, 1968) k–3. A series of amusing incidents about a small girl—understanding how little ones think, and what makes them laugh, and how they overcome fears.

2439. ____. *When My Little Sister Was Good* (Methuen, 1973) k–3.

2440. ____. *My Naughty Little Sister and Bad Harry* (Houghton, 1974) k–3.

2441. ____. *My Naughty Little Sister Goes Fishing* (Houghton, 1977) k–3. The vivid and consistent character of the little girl gives a "fellow feeling" for the unfortunate older sister.

2442. ____. *My Naughty Little Sister at the Fair* (Methuen, 1980) k–3. A good story to be read aloud for girls. A revelation of child behavior in everyday life.

2443. ____. *My Naughty Little Sister and Bad Harry's Rabbit* (Prentice, 1981) k–3. A little girl gets the credit she deserves for cleverly fitting a large toy rabbit with a pair of shiny red shoes that make him able to stand. But the rabbit isn't hers and the owner wants the credit.

2444. ____. *More Naughty Little Sister Stories* (Methuen, 1985) k–3. Eleven stories in which the narrator's younger sister turns a quite ordinary event, like helping Mrs. Cocoa Jones do her housework, into an unexpected crisis.

2445. ____. *My Naughty Little Sister and Father Christmas* (Houghton, 1988) k–3.

2446. ____. *My Naughty Little Sister Storybook* (Methuen, 1991) k–3. Features the narrator's rambunctious little sister, her family and her friends.

2447. ____. *My Naughty Little Sister* (Houghton, 1991) k–3. This story, like the others, is told by a mildly scolding, perpetually embarrassed older sister.

2448. ____. *My Naughty Little Sister and Poor Charlie Cocoa* (Methuen) k–3.

2449. ____. *My Naughty Little Sister and the Solid Silver Watch* (Methuen) k–3.

2450. ____. *My Naughty Little Sister Wins a Prize* (Methuen) k–3.

2451. ____. *My Naughty Little Sister and the Baby* (Methuen) k–3.

2452. ____. *My Naughty Little Sister Shows Off* (Methuen) k–3.

2453. ____. *My Naughty Little Sister and the Book-Little-Boy* (Methuen) k–3.

2454. ____. *My Naughty Little Sister and the Big Girl's Bed* (Methuen) k–3.

2455. Edwards, Lynne. *Dead as the Dodo* (Parents, 1973) k–3. Upon reading a book that he is extinct, a dodo bird attempts to set the records straight.

2456. ____. *Dodo is a Solitary Bird* (Parents, 1978) k–3. Dodos are solitary birds who are intruded upon by scientists. Dodo gets rid of the scientists by banding all the birds together in organized activities and persuading the scientists that the birds are not the real thing.

2457. Ehrlich, Amy. *Leo, Zack and Emmie* (Dial, 1981) 3–5. The new girl in Zack and Leo's class affects the boys' friendship.

2458. ____. *Leo, Zack and Emmie Together Again* (Dial, 1987) 3–5. A trio of friends spends the winter of their second grade making snowballs, valentine cards, going to a Christmas party and fighting a bout of chicken pox.

2459. ____. *Tom, Zack and Emmie in Winter* (Dial, 1987) 3–5.

2460. Ehrlich, Amy. *Bunnies and Their Grandma* (Dial, 1985) k–3. Mother Bunny takes her three children for a day of fun and games with their cousins at Grandma's house.

2461. ____. *Bunnies All Day Long* (Dial, 1985) k–3. Mischievous bunny children Harry, Larry and Paulette have a busy day at home and at school.

2462. ____. *Bunnies on Their Own* (Dial, 1986) k–3. When Mother Bunny goes out, Paulette decides that she would rather play her bugle than help her brothers with the cleaning.

2463. ____. *Bunnies at Christmastime* (Dial, 1986) k–3. An invitation to Santa Claus to join the bunnies for a Christmas party brings their Uncle Jack instead, but he comes with toys and Santa whiskers.

2464. Eisenberg, Lisa. *Leave It to Lexie* (Viking, 1989) 4–6. Lexie, nine, is at a loss for ideas for the upcoming Girl Scout talent show until she remembers her father's penchant for riddles at dinnertime.

2465. ____. *Happy Birthday, Lexie* (Viking, 1991) 4–6. Although she had hoped to make her tenth birthday extra special, Lexie reluctantly agrees to have a shared party with an unpopular girl in her class, with surprising results.

2466. ____. *Lexie on Her Own* (Viking, 1992) 4–6. With Christmas around the corner and the world filled with problems, Lexie must draw upon all her resources to overcome some particularly harsh holiday blues.

2467. Elliott, Odette. *Under Sammy's Bed* (Deutsch, 1990) k–3. Sammy is too young to be included in his busy family's activities. He goes under his bed and imagines fantasies that are better than what his family is doing. He even finds an escaped hamster under his bed.

2468. ____. *Sammy Goes Flying* (Deutsch, 1990) k–3. Sammy uses his vivid imagination to enable him to fly, until the day his Gran provides a better way.

2469. ____. *Sammy and the Telly* (Deutsch, 1992) k–3. Sammy draws a birthday cake for the school's 100th anniversary but it is passed over by the T.V. people for grander offerings. An accident ensures that Sammy is filmed and appears on T.V.

2470. ____. *Sammy's Christmas Workshop* (Deutsch, 1992) k–3.

2471. Elmore, Patricia. *Susannah and the Blue House Mystery* (Dutton, 1980) 5–8. Susannah finds clues concerning an old man's missing will. Lucy, Knievel and Susannah discover how Grandpa Withers successfully fulfills a promise to leave his house to his niece, Ivy, and still give Juliet a share of the fortune.

2472. ____. *Susannah and the Poison Green Halloween* (Dutton, 1982) 5–8. In this story poisoned candy in the trick-or-treat bags lands Knievel in the hospital and sends Susannah and Lucy on a search for clues.

2473. ____. *Susannah and the Purple Mongoose Mystery* (Dutton, 1992) 5–8. Susannah and her friends investigate a series of fires in their San Francisco neighborhood.

2474. Elzbieta. *Mimi's Scary Theater* (Hyperion, 1993) k–3. A witch and a skeleton perform against a dramatic black backdrop in this book.

2475. ____. *Mimi and the Witch* (Hyperion, 1994) k–3. A pop-up book with nine scenes and seven characters plus an egg. They all have strange events in the deep, deep forest. There is a hungry wolf, a good little girl, a wicked witch and a slapstick skeleton.

2476. Elzbieta. *Dikou and the Little Troom Who Walks at Night* (Crowell, 1985) k–3. A gardener thinks he found a rabbit in his cabbage patch but he finds a small green creature that is crying and begging not to be eaten. Dikou, a troom, says it's his 283rd birthday and the gardener bakes him a cake. But he lied.

2477. ____. *Dikou and the Mysterious Moon Sheep* (Crowell, 1988) k–3. Little Dikou's father doesn't believe there is a moon sheep in the garden eating the tulips, but when the creature whisks the child off for a moonlight adventure, Papa regrets his disbelief.

2478. ____. *Dikou and the Baby Star* (Crowell, 1988) k–3. Little Dikou tries to take care of a baby star until his parents tell him to return it to the hills where he found it.

2479. Engel, Diana. *Josephina the Great Collector* (Morrow, 1988) k–3. Josephina's passion for collecting anything and everything finally drives her sister out of the room they both share.

2480. ____. *Josephina Hates Her Name* (Morrow, 1989) k–3. After Grandma explains that she named Josephina after her talented, daring older sister, Josephina starts to appreciate her unusual name.

2481. Erickson, John. *Original Adventures of Hank the Cowdog* (Maverick, 1991) 4–6. Hank the Cowdog, head of Ranch Security, is framed for the murder of a chicken and becomes an outlaw with the coyotes.

2482. ____. *Further Adventures of Hank the Cowdog* (Gulf, 1990) 4–6. Hank the Cowdog almost loses his job as head of Ranch Security when he develops a case of Eye-Crosserosis.

2483. ____. *It's a Dog's Life* (Maverick, 1990) 4–6. Duped into thinking the world is coming to an end, Hank the Cowdog winds up in town for some more adventures including getting in and out of a case of "soap hydrophobia."

2484. ____. *Murder in the Middle Pasture* (Gulf, 1991) 4–6. When a calf is murdered, Hank the wily cowdog and head of Ranch Security, pursues a gang of wild dogs and a clan of coyotes to find the killer.

2485. ____. *Hank the Cowdog and Faded Love* (Maverick, 1985) 4–6. Hank the Cowdog quits his job as Head of Ranch Security and travels in search of adventure.

2486. ____. *Hank the Cowdog and Let Sleeping Dogs Lie* (Maverick, 1986) 4–6. Hank the Cowdog, head of Ranch Security, pursues an elusive chicken murderer.

2487. ____. *Curse of the Incredible Priceless Corncob* (Gulf, 1989) 4–6. While trying to outwit his arch enemy Pete the barncat, Hank the Cowdog is duped into believing a worthless corncob will bring him fame and fortune.

2488. ____. *Case of the One-eyed Killer Stud Horse* (Maverick, 1990) 4–6. Hank the Cowdog goes to the rescue as a wild, one-eyed horse creates havoc on the ranch but some of his outrageous stunts get him into more trouble than he bargained for.

2489. ____. *Case of the Halloween Ghost* (Maverick, 1990) 4–6. Hank the Cowdog has one of the scariest adventures of his life when he and his cowardly companion, Drover, find themselves in a strange and spooky place on Halloween night.

2490. ____. *Every Dog Has His Day* (Maverick, 1990) 4–6. Hank the Cowdog gets into more and more trouble before he is able to find a happy solution to his problems.

2491. ____. *Lost in the Dark Uncharted Forest* (Maverick, 1988) 4–6. Fearless Hank the Cowdog, head of Ranch Security, enters the "dark uncharted forest" to rescue his master's son from Sinister the bobcat.

2492. ____. *Case of the Fiddle Playing Fox* (Maverick, 1990) 4–6. While working on a mysterious case involving disappearing eggs and a fiddle-playing fox named Frankie, Hank the Cowdog falls for Miss Beulah, the beautiful collie.

2493. ____. *Wounded Buzzard on Christmas Eve* (Maverick, 1989) 4–6. Accompanying Slim and Little Alfred into town on a Christmas shopping trip, Hank and Drover run up against a gang of toughs so mean and heartless, it's a wonder they ever make it back to the ranch.

2494. ____. *Hank the Cowdog and Monkey Business* (Maverick, 1990) 4–6. Hank the Cowdog, head of Ranch Security, matches wits with an escaped circus monkey.

2495. ____. *Case of the Missing Cat* (Maverick, 1990) 4–6. Pete the barncat swindles the intrepid Cowdog out of his job as head of Ranch's Security.

2496. ____. *Lost in the Blinding Blizzard* (Maverick, 1991) 4–6. While battling a "blinding" blizzard to get cough syrup for Baby Mollie, fearless Hank charms Miss Beulah the collie dog, saves Slim and Drover from freezing, sings a love song about fleas, and outwits Pete the barncat.

2497. ____. *Case of the Car-barkaholic Dog* (Gulf, 1991) 4–6. Hank the Cowdog, head of Ranch Security, finds himself stranded in town and drawn into a dangerous situation involving his sister Maggie and a terrible bully named Rambo.

2498. ____. *Case of the Hooking Bull* (Gulf, 1992) 4–6. Unsupervised for the day, Hank the Cowdog and his human friends, Little Alfred and Slim Chance, mind the ranch with humorous results.

2499. ____. *Case of the Midnight Rustler* (Maverick, 1992) 4–6. Hank the Cowdog investigates the mystery of a cattle rustler who works by night. Hank survives an encounter with fierce coyotes, burps his way through indigestion from too many wieners and detects some marauding rustlers.

2500. ____. *Phantom in the Mirror: Hank the Cowdog* (Maverick, 1993) 4–6. Hank the Cowdog investigates reports of a phantom dog on the ranch.

2501. ____. *Case of the Vampire Cat* (Gulf, 1993) 4–6. Hank the cowdog investigates the mystery of a possible vampire cat.

2502. Erickson, Karen. *Shhh Story* (Methuen, 1985) k–3. A small child settles down to go to sleep.

2503. ____. *Playing Story* (Methuen, 1985) k–3. A small child learns to play all alone in various roles.

2504. ____. *Sharing Story* (Methuen, 1985) k–3. A child wants something that is his alone. "It's mine. No one else may touch it." But he must learn to share. "First you. Then Me. Then you. Then me. Sharing is fun. I can do it."

2505. ____. *Tidy-up Story* (Methuen, 1985) k–3. A small child learns how to tidy his own room.

2506. ____. *Do I Have to Go Home?* (Methuen, 1989) k–3. This story addresses the common problem of a child who is having so much fun that he doesn't want to go home.

2507. ____. *I Like Helping* (Methuen, 1989) k–3. The hero of these stories sets the table, endures pain bravely from a cut leg, enjoys a party and is reproved by Grandma for impatience.

2508. ____. *I'm Brave* (Methuen, 1989) k–3. This story explains bravery in the context of a bruised knee.

2509. ____. *Waiting My Turn* (Methuen, 1989) k–3. A little boy learns what it means to be patient.

2510. Erickson, Russell. *Toad for Tuesday* (Lothrop, 1974) 3–5. Captured by an owl, Warton the toad, becomes his housekeeper to avoid being eaten as birthday dinner.

2511. ____. *Warton and Morton* (Lothrop, 1976) 3–5. Two brother toads, off on a camping trip, are separated during a flash flood and before reuniting have much more adventure than they bargained for.

2512. ____. *Warton's Christmas Eve Adventure* (Lothrop, 1977) 3–5. Lost in a blizzard the day before Christmas, Warton the toad makes two new friends during his attempts to get home in time for his favorite part of Christmas Eve.

2513. ____. *Warton and the King of the Skies* (Lothrop, 1978) 3–5. Two toads take off in a skyborne washtub.

2514. ____. *Warton and the Traders* (Lothrop, 1979) 3–5. Warton Toad turns the wood rats' trading habits to his own advantage by agreeing to help them trap the dreaded wildcat in exchange for their assistance in rescuing a starving fawn.

2515. ____. *Warton and the Castaways* (Lothrop, 1986) 3–5. This takes place in the country with a menacing raccoon and two tree toad ladies Cora and Hester.

2516. ____. *Warton and the Contest* (Lothrop, 1986) 3–5. When a crow steals Grandpa Arbuckle's watch-compass, the two toad brothers, Warton and Morton, try to get it back with the help of an accident prone mouse and a blind blue jay.

2517. Eriksson, Eva. *One Short Week* (Carolrhoda, 1985) k–3. Bored and having no one to play with, Rosalie randomly dials the telephone and reaches Victor who invites her to a birthday party.

2518. ____. *Tooth Trip* (Carolrhoda, 1985) k–3. Rosalie loses a tooth and uses it as bus fare for a trip with her little brother and Victor to visit her grandmother.

2519. ____. *Jealousy* (Carolrhoda, 1985) k–3. While Rosalie has the mumps, her best friend Victor starts playing with another girl, which incites Rosalie's jealousy.

2520. ____. *Hocus-Pocus* (Carolrhoda, 1985) k–3. Victor refuses to go to bed after a game of hide-and-seek with his mother so "hocus pocus" he turns himself into a little witch and continues to have fun with his friend Rosalie.

2521. Ernst, Kathryn F. *ESP McGee and the Mysterious Magician* (Avon, 1983) 5–8. Edward McGee may or may not have ESP but his logical mind is the bane of wrongdoers. He is used by Matt Turell and the local police. The talented popular, ever-smiling new boy at school is seriously suspected by McGee of being responsible for a series of jewel thieves.

(For other books about "ESP McGee," *see* Lawrence, Jino: Packard, Edward; Rodgers, Jesse.

2522. Escott, John. *Alarm Bells* (Hamilton, 1982) 2–4. A story of a youngster trying to persuade an old man to bring his set of handbells into school.
2523. ____. *Bell Rescue* (Hamilton, 1983) 2–4. Suzy Yeung is not doing well in her handbell ringing class. Everything goes wrong. She is shut in the school storeroom at day's end. But this changes her for the better.
2524. ____. *Burglar Bells* (Hamilton, 1984) 2–4. Bernie and Lee are members of the school Handbell Group. They help a man crawl into a window and are appalled to learn that he was a burglar. Is the burglar Mr. Henry? They must find out.
2525. ____. *Bell Puzzle* (Hamilton, 1985) 2–4. Ian, 11, and his brother Tom take pictures of Handbell Group. Emma spots her father in the picture. He should be at work but he lost his job. Emma, her father, Tom and Mr. Bates start a business of their own.

2526. Escott, John. *Wayne's Wedding* (Hamilton, 1989) 2–4. Wayne, left in charge of his sister Gemma, turns a wedding into a succession of minor disasters. This, like the other stories is told from Gemma's point of view.
2527. ____. *Wayne's Luck* (Hamilton, 1990) 2–4. "Wayne is a pain," is the way this story opens. All children with younger siblings will identify with this.

2528. Escott, John. *Radio Alert* (Hamilton, 1984) 2–4. A story of a local radio station.
2529. ____. *Radio Reporters* (Hamilton, 1986) 2–4. Roundbay Radio has a young reporter, Donald, who picks up a toy soldier on his way to the studio. He announces his find over the air and becomes involved in a robbery and the arrest of a petty criminal.
2530. ____. *Radio Detective* (Hamilton, 1987) 2–4. A story of a persistent young investigator from a local radio station. He understands the basic elements of detection and learns to face up to his own mistakes.
2531. ____. *Radio Rescue* (Hamilton, 1989) 2–4. Mia fails to note warning signs while on vacation. She enters a derelict house. The house collapses but Roundbay Radio and "Cruso's Island" come to the rescue.

2532. Estern, Anne. *Picolinis* (Bantam, 1988) 3–5. The Blake family outbids a seedy looking magician for a dollhouse. Peter and Jessica are delighted. There is magic here and at night the dolls come alive.

2533. ____. *Picolinis and the Haunted House* (Bantam, 1989) 3–5. The Picolinis are a family of dolls who come to life when no one is watching. They help Jessica and Peter solve the mystery of the spooky, empty house across the street.

2534. Ethridge, Kenneth. *Viola, Furgy, Bobbi and Me* (Holiday, 1989) 5–8. Steve does yard work for 78-year-old Viola. They become friends because they have baseball in common. They and Steve's friends become a real foursome.
2535. ____. *Viola* (Holiday, 1989) 5–8. Three friends try to protect Viola, a 78-year-old baseball fan. Her daughters want to put her in a nursing home.

2536. Etra, Jonathan. *Aliens for Breakfast* (Random, 1988) 2–4. Finding an intergalactic special agent in his cereal box, Richard joins the extraterrestrial in a fight to save the Earth from the Dranes, one of who is masquerading as a student in Richard's class.
2537. ____. *Aliens for Lunch* (Random, 1991) 2–4. When their bag of microwave popcorn explodes and a space alien emerges, Richard and Henry join him on a top secret interstellar mission to save the deserts of the universe.

2538. Ettinger, Elzbieta. *Little Mops at the Seashore* (Doubleday, 1974) k–3. Little Mops finds a large egg that he intends to grill for a picnic repast. Mother Bird implores Mops to change his mind. He does and gets to be godparent to the new arrival.
2539. ____. *Little Mops and the Moon* (Doubleday, 1974) k–3. Little Mops decides to give his dog a scrubbing and thinks that he has caught the moon in the bath water. He puts a lid on the tub but the moon disappears anyway.
2540. ____. *Little Mops and the Butterfly* (Doubleday, 1974) k–3. Little Mops goes butterfly hunting and finds a tiny shoe. He returns it to its owner, a caterpillar that enters a flower and later emerges a butterfly.

2541. Evans, Shirlee. *Tall Tree and the Whiteskins* (Harald, 1986) 5–8. Tall Tree lives on a reservation in Oregon. He faces prejudice when he ventures into the white man's world.
2542. ____. *Tall Tree and the Horse Race* (Herald, 1986) 5–8. Tall Tree wins a horse in a race. He lives on a reservation in Oregon and is hampered by prejudice and misunderstanding.
2543. ____. *Tall Tree to the Rescue* (Herald, 1987) 5–8. Tall Tree finds God and his life is improved.

2544. Eyles, Heather. *Herbert Saves the Day* (Mondo, 1992) k–3.
2545. ____. *Trouble with Herbert* (Mondo, 1996) k–3. Herbert the guinea pig provides a series of adventures for a class of second graders and their teacher.

2546. Falwell, Cathryn. *Nicky and Alex* (Clarion, 1991) k–3. Nicky makes things—a zoo, a tent, a snack, a parade—with a lot of help from his older brother.

2547. ____. *Nicky and Grandpa* (Clarion, 1991) k–3. Nicky and Grandpa play peekaboo to find his clothes and toys, the sandbox and each other.

2548. ____. *Nicky's Walk* (Clarion, 1991) k–3. On a walk with mommy, Nicky identifies the things he sees, and names the colors.

2549. ____. *Nicky, 1-2-3* (Clarion, 1991) k–3. Nicky counts from one to three as he observes familiar objects in the world around him.

2550. ____. *Where's Nicky* (Clarion, 1991) k–3. Nicky appears and disappears in a playful fashion, hiding in such places as inside his shirt, and within a pile of toys.

2551. ____. *Nicky Loves Daddy* (Clarion, 1992) k–3. Shows Nicky out for a stroll with his father.

2552. Farley, Carol. *Loosen Your Ears* (Atheneum, 1977) 4–6. Josh tells funny stories about himself and his odd farm family.

2553. ____. *Settle Your Fidgets* (Atheneum, 1977) 4–6. Josh tells more stories about his boyhood on the farm and his unusual relatives.

2554. Farris, Stella. *Magic Teddy Bear* (Harper, 1978) k–3. Young Scott looks for his teddy bear before going to bed. The yellow shirt is not teddy bear, the yellow model airplane is not teddy bear, nor is the ocean steamer or the jack-in-the-box. They are all yellow but are not teddy bear.

2555. ____. *Magic Blanket* (Harper, 1979) k–3. Relates Scott's adventures when his favorite blanket takes him and his teddy bear on a trip through the sky.

2556. ____. *Magic Bubble-Pipe* (Harper, 1987) k–3. A story that reveals the strange sights Scott sees when he uses his great-grandmother's pipe in his evening bath.

2557. ____. *Magic Castle* (Harper, 1987) k–3. One night Scott's dreams take him to a castle in a strange land where he meets some extraordinary creatures.

2558. Fatio, Louise. *Happy Lion* (McGraw, 1954) k–3. Happy Lion lived in a zoo of a small French town and was everyone's friend until one day when his cage was left unlocked and he strolled out to return the townspeople's visits.

2559. ____. *Happy Lion in Africa* (McGraw, 1955) k–3. Happy Lion is in Africa where he is scared by the wild animals and longs for his comfortable home in the zoo.

2560. ____. *Happy Lion Roars* (McGraw, 1957) k–3. Happy Lion was unhappy. Francois, who is both his friend and the keeper's son, did not know what was the matter with him. Only the Happy Lion knew as he sighed, "Why am I alone in my house?" The Happy Lion was not alone for long.

2561. ____. *Three Happy Lions* (McGraw, 1959) k–3. Happy Lion, his lioness and son, Baby Francois, are back in the zoo. But Baby Francois grows fast and soon faces the problem of finding a trade so that he can support himself.

2562. ____. *Happy Lion's Quest* (McGraw, 1951) k–3. Dearest of all Happy Lion's friends is Francois, the zookeeper's son. The Happy Lion is sad because Francois is away at the Lycee. So he bids wife and son, Baby Francois, goodbye and starts his quest for his friend Francois.

2563. ____. *Happy Lion and the Bear* (McGraw, 1964) k–3. Happy Lion was eager to meet his new neighbor in the zoo. Everything went well until the bear saw the lion. Then he raised himself up against his bars and let out such fierce growls that the lion jumped back.

2564. ____. *Happy Lion's Vacation* (McGraw, 1967) k–3. Francois and the Happy Lion set out for a vacation. They have trouble because no one wants to sell tickets to a lion. They travel by car, balloon, ocean liner and bus before they end their trip.

2565. ____. *Happy Lion's Treasure* (McGraw, 1970) k–3. Even though he isn't sure what his treasure is, the Happy Lion wants to share it with his friends.

2566. ____. *Happy Lion's Rabbits* (McGraw, 1974) k–3. The Happy Lion and Francois discover that to offer protection from hunters to one rabbit is to be soon overrun by rabbits.

2567. Fatio, Louise. *Hector Penguin* (McGraw, 1973) k–3. Hector Penguin is lost in the forest where none of the animals have seen a penguin before.

2568. ____. *Hector and Christina* (McGraw, 1977) k–3. Hector the penguin is captured and forced to live in a zoo where he falls in love with another penguin named Christina.

2569. Faulkner, Keith. *Sam at the Seaside* (Aladdin, 1988) k–3. Sam surfs on a shark's nose and then reels in a submarine.

2570. ____. *Sam Helps Out* (Aladdin, 1988) k–3. Sam helps his mother with disastrous results. The sink overflows, cans fall at the grocery store and the hose shoots water on the neighbors.

2571. Faulkner, Keith. *Tom's School Day* (Scholastic, 1993) k–3. Tiny Tom is a bright orange cat. He teaches concepts: numbers, shapes, colors, and opposites with great stories and flap lifting.

2572. ____. *Tom's Friends* (Scholastic, 1993) k–3. Tiny Tom is a bright orange cat and these books are about Tiny Tom and his friends. Each one brings a concept. This one is about opposites. The other books are about numbers, shapes and colors.

2573. ____. *Tom's Picnic* (Scholastic, 1993) k–3. Tiny Tom is the bright orange cat who, along with his friends, brings a concept to the readers. This one is about numbers. The other books cover shapes, colors and opposites.

2574. Felix, Monique. *Story of a Little Mouse Trapped in a Book* (Green Tiger, 1980) k–3. A mouse is caught in a book's white pages. He begins to nibble his way through the pages and finally sees a beautiful field of grain.

2575. _____. *Further Adventures of the Little Mouse Trapped in a Book* (Green Tiger, 1984) k–3. A mouse trapped inside the pages of a book chews his way out to an ocean and sails away in a paper boat.

2576. Fife, Dale. *Who's in Charge of Lincoln?* (Coward, 1965) 3–5. When Lincoln, an eight-year-old Black boy, is accidentally left alone by his family in their New York City apartment, he finds a bag of money and a way to go to Washington, D.C.

2577. _____. *What's New, Lincoln?* (Coward, 1970) 3–5. On a dull Saturday, two boys with nothing else to do print a newspaper to the dismay of the neighborhood.

2578. _____. *What's the Prize, Lincoln?* (Coward, 1971) 3–5. By trying to win contest prizes for their clubhouse, Lincoln and his friends end up with a room full of troublesome booby prizes.

2579. _____. *Who Goes There, Lincoln?* (Coward, 1975) 3–5. Lincoln and his friends need a new clubhouse and investigate the possibilities of a building soon to be torn down.

2580. _____. *Who'll Vote for Lincoln?* (Coward, 1977) 3–5. Lincoln, a candidate for class president, makes a campaign promise opposed by a group of criminals.

2581. Fine, Anne. *Sudden Puff of Glittering Smoke* (Piccadilly, 1989) 2–4. A girl summons a genie from a ring she found. He causes her trouble at school, not the prosperity she expected.

2582. _____. *Sudden Swirl of Icy Wind* (Piccadilly, 1990) 2–4. A boy visits his grandmother at Christmas and uses his new toy gun to shoot at animals and people in her manger scene. He is sent to his room where he meets a genie. The genie tells him ancient moral tales.

2583. _____. *Sudden Glow of Gold* (Piccadilly, 1991) 2–4. Tody cannot part with any of his things. He finds a lamp among all his junk and a genie appears. He goes with the genie where he is shown the life of the sultan and his wife. In a fit of temper the wife turns everything to gold.

2584. Fine, Anne. *Goggle-Eyes* (Little, 1989) 5–8. Helen is distraught by her mother bringing home Goggle-Eyes. Kitty's mother had earlier brought home her boyfriend, Gerald. Kitty comforts Helen by telling her tales about herself and Gerald.

2585. _____. *My War with Goggle-Eyes* (Little, 1989) 5–8. Kitty is not pleased with her mother's boyfriend, especially his views on the anti-nuclear issue, until unexpected events prompt her, after all, to help him find his place in the family.

2586. Firmin, Peter. *Pinny Finds A House* (Viking, 1986) k–3. Victor, a tiny wooden sailor, is happy when Pinny comes to the playroom, and he helps her settle into the little china house next to his boat.

2587. _____. *Pinny and the Bird* (Viking, 1986) k–3. Swept outdoors by the wind, Pinny, a tiny wooden doll, finds adventure as she escapes from a bird's nest and rescues her friend Victor when his toy boat becomes stranded in the pond.

2588. _____. *Pinny in the Snow* (Viking, 1986) k–3. Victor and Pinny have an unexpected outdoor adventure and need all their cleverness to get back to the playroom where they belong.

2589. _____. *Pinny and the Floppy Frog* (Viking, 1987) k–3. Two tiny wooden dolls face danger in a gigantic world. Their new seat on a torn soft toy brings a danger when the frog slips and is carried into the garden by the family pup.

2590. _____. *Pinny's Party* (Viking, 1987) k–3. Two tiny wooden dolls face danger in the big world. Pinny and her friend Victor, the sailor doll, are almost thrown out with the rubbish.

2591. Firmin, Peter. *Basil Brush at the Beach* (Prentice, 1976) 3–5. Basil Brush, a fox, gets so mad at his friend Harry the mole for foiling his attempts to win every contest at the beach that he is driven to take action that does result in winning a prize.

2592. _____. *Basil Brush Goes Boating* (Prentice, 1976) 3–5. Basil Brush the fox and his friend Harry the mole go on a camping trip and discover that they have brought along everything—except what they need.

2593. _____. *Basil Brush Builds a House* (Prentice, 1977) 3–5. Basil Brush, the fox, tries to convince his friend Harry the mole to live in another type of dwelling place, rather than his hole in the ground.

2594. _____. *Basil Brush Goes Flying* (Prentice, 1977) 3–5. An intrepid fox tries several methods in his unsuccessful attempts at flying.

2595. _____. *Basil Brush and the Dragon* (Prentice, 1978) 3–5. Basil Brush, a fox, and his friend Harry the mole go on a make-believe dragon hunt.

2596. _____. *Basil Brush Gets a Medal* (Prentice, 1978) 3–5. Basil Brush gets a medal for being a helpful fox, and Harry gets a special gift from the princess for being such a special mole.

2597. _____. *Basil Brush Finds Treasure* (Prentice, 1979) 3–5. Basil and friend Harry, the mole, search a seashore for treasure.

2598. _____. *Basil Brush in the Jungle* (Prentice, 1979) 3–5. Basil the fox and Harry the mole go to India to find an exotic pet to occupy the cage Basil has made.

2599. _____. *Basil Brush on the Trail* (Prentice, 1980) 3–5. When tennis star Nora Nett's trophies begin disappearing, her house sitters, Basil Brush and Harry, the mole, turn into super sleuths.

2600. _____. *Basil Brush and the Windmills* (Prentice, 1980) 3–5. With only one penny left with which to pay the electricity, water and gas bills, Basil Brush and his friend Harry, the mole, decide to live as people did in the old days and build windmills for power.

2601. Fisher, Lois. *Wretched Robert* (Dodd, 1982) 4–6. Eleven-year-old Robert, tired of being considered nice, starts on a campaign to become "wretched" with some unintentional results.

2602. _____. *Radio Robert* (Dodd, 1985) 4–6. When a sixth grader begins regularly appearing on his divorced father's radio show, his ad libs about his life affect his relationship with a number of friends.

2603. Fisher, Paul. *Ash Staff* (Atheneum, 1979) 5–8. Mole and five other orphans have adventures with goblins and Ammar. Mole must kill Ammar with his magic sword.

2604. _____. *Princess and the Thorn* (Atheneum, 1980) 5–8. Mole goes to an island kingdom and uncovers a plot against the high king and destroys the sorcerer with the sword.

2605. _____. *Hawks of Fellheath* (Atheneum, 1980) 5–8. Orne runs off after Llan dies. The rest of the orphan band travel to Vivrandon where they go through many adversities.

2606. Fisk, Nicholas. *Starstormers* (Hodder, 1980) 4–6. Vawn, Spex, Makenzi and Tsui (white, Indian and Chinese) build a spaceship from junk. They look for their parents on a newly colonized planet. They meet the dreaded Octopus Emperor and avoid being brainwashed.

2607. _____. *Sunburst* (Hodder, 1980) 4–6. Vawn, Ispex, Tsui and Makenzi are in outer space. They meet a deserted spaceship with a cargo of nuclear waste. With the help of the computer, Shambles, they devise a means of escape.

2608. _____. *Evil Eye* (Knight, 1982) 4–6. Another Space Stormer space fiction story.

2609. Flack, Marjorie. *Angus and the Ducks* (Doubleday, 1930) k–3. Describes the amusing experiences of Angus, a Scotch terrier puppy, when curiosity led him to slip under the hedge.

2610. _____. *Angus and the Cat* (Doubleday, 1931) k–3. The story of Angus the Scotch terrier. It has an element of both surprise and humor.

2611. _____. *Angus Lost* (Doubleday, 1989) k–3. A little Scottish terrier leaves his home to see what the outside world is like.

2612. Fleischman, Sid. *McBroom Tells the Truth* (Norton, 1966) 3–5. Mr. McBroom, his dear wife Melissa and his 11 children live on his incredible farm where everything grows so fast that life on the farm becomes downright dangerous.

2613. _____. *McBroom Tells a Lie* (Little, 1976) 3–5. A farmer and his family save their farm by using a popcorn machine, frozen sunlight and jumping beans.

2614. _____. *McBroom and the Beanstalk* (Little, 1978) 3–5. McBroom gets ready to tell one of his many preposterous stories in the World Champion Liar's contest only to be disqualified for telling the truth.

2615. _____. *McBroom* (Little, 1979) 3–5. Jose McBroom buys an 80-acre property from a friend. Later he discovers that each of the 80 acres is placed directly on top of the other.

2616. _____. *McBroom and the Great Race* (Little, 1980) With his one-acre farm as the prize, Josh McBroom, riding a giant chicken, races Heck Jones, who is on a Wyoming jackalope.

2617. _____. *McBroom's Ghost* (Little, 1981) 3–5. The McBroom family is plagued by a mysterious ghost that visits their farm after every prolonged freezing spell.

2618. _____. *McBroom, the Rain Maker* (Little, 1982) 3–5. When a great drought on the prairie causes the cows to give powered milk and mosquitoes to grow almost as large as small cowsheds, McBroom comes up with a novel idea for producing rain.

2619. _____. *McBroom's Zoo* (Little, 1982) 3–5. The McBrooms start a zoo with the Desert Vamooser, Silver-Tailed Teakettler, Sidehill Gouger and other rare animals dropped from the path of the passing tornado.

2620. _____. *McBroom's Ear* (Little, 1982) 3–5. The war is on when the grasshoppers attack Josh McBroom's fabulous one-acre farm and prize ear of corn.

2621. _____. *McBroom and the Big Wind* (Little, 1982) 3–5. Josh McBroom relates how he and his family harness the rambunctious prairie wind.

2622. _____. *McBroom's Almanac* (Little, 1984) 3–5. Entries in McBroom's almanac include farm tips, how-to's, McProverbs, nature lore, cartoons and McBroom's calendar of important dates.

2623. Fleischman, Sid. *Bloodhound Gang in the case of the Secret Message* (Random, 1981) 3–5. The Bloodhound Gang is made up of three youngsters who use their deductive skills to solve this mystery.

2624. _____. *Bloodhound Gang in the Case of Princess Tomorrow* (Random, 1981) 3–5. The Bloodhound Gang solves a mystery involving a fortune-teller who predicts horse races.

2625. _____. *Bloodhound Gang in the Case of the Crackling Ghost* (Random, 1981) 3–5. Mrs. Fairbanks, seemingly cursed by the Darjeeling Necklace as were its previous owners, hires the Bloodhound Gang to sort out the nightmare.

2626. _____. *Bloodhound Gang in the Case of the Flying Clock* (Random, 1981) 3–5. Members of the Bloodhound Detective Agency are called in to investigate the theft of a valuable clock.

2627. _____. *Bloodhound Gang in the Case of the Veiled Thief* (Western, 1981) 3–5.

2628. _____. *Bloodhound Gang in the Case of the Girl from Outer Space* (Western, 1981) 3–5.

2629. _____. *Bloodhound Gang in the Case of the*

264-pound Burglar (Random, 1982) 3–5. The Bloodhound Gang is called in to find out who stole Mrs. Tolliver's life savings.

2630. Fleming, Susan. *Pig at 37 Pinecrest Drive* (Westminster, 1982) 4–6. His mother's latest "educational experience" gives Terry the notoriety he thought he wanted, in addition to a quick lesson in politics and handy knowledge about pigs.

2631. ____. *Countdown at 37 Pinecrest Drive* (Westminster, 1982) 4–6. A middle child who has a hard time measuring up to his older brother and staying out of mischief uncovers a plot to rob the **Vista** restaurant.

2632. Fletcher, Susan. *Flight of the Dragon Kyn* (Macmillan, 1993) 5–8. Prequel. Kara, 15, is summoned by King Orrik, who believes she has the power to call down the dragons that have been plundering his realm and she is caught up in the fierce rivalry between Orrik and his jealous brother Rog.

2633. ____. *Sign of the Dove* (Atheneum, 1995) 5–8). Kaeldrae is now seven years older. Her sister Lyf is the heroine of this book. It is her turn to be the dravling (baby dragon) keeper. As the last of the dragon eggs, laid long ago, begin to hatch, Lyf becomes a reluctant friend who tries to save both the dragon mothers and their newly born children from their enemies.

2634. ____. *Dragon's Milk* (Macmillan, 1992) 5–8. Kaeldrae, 15, babysits for Flora, a mother dragon, in exchange for dragon's milk needed for her ill sister. Flora gets killed and Kaeldrae becomes surrogate mother to the baby dragons.

2635. Flora, James. *Grandpa's Farm* (Harcourt, 1965) k–3. Grandfather tells his grandson tall tales about his farm: a hurricane that set up a barn on the farm; a salve that healed and grew anything to enormous size; and words that froze in the air.

2636. ____. *Grandpa's Ghost Stories* (Atheneum, 1978) k–3. Three grisly short stories told by an old man to his grandson.

2637. ____. *Grandpa's Witched-up Christmas* (Harcourt, 1982) k–3. Grandpa tells a ghoulish tale of Christmas. This is more a ghost story than a Christmas one.

2638. Flournoy, Valerie. *Patchwork Quilt* (Dial, 1985) k–3. The story of the completion of a yearlong project that brings a family together in a new way with a fresh understanding and appreciation of each other.

2639. ____. *Tanya's Reunion* (Dial, 1995) k–3. Grandma has recovered from her illness and goes to the family reunion. Tanya finds the farm strange but when Grandma tells her about the quilt she cheers up.

2640. Foreman, Michael. *Panda's Puzzle and His Voyage Discovery* (Hamilton, 1977) k–3. A panda sees his own reflection in the lid of a tin can. He tries to find out if he's black with white spots or white with black spots. After traveling everywhere and asking everyone, he decides it doesn't matter.

2641. ____. *Panda and the Odd Lion* (Hamilton, 1981) k–3. A lion is rejected by his family and goes off into the world and meets a wise panda. The panda tells the lion that his humpity back is really a pair of wings and to have wings is special. He goes home happy and confident.

2642. ____. *Panda and the Bunnyips* (Schocken, 1984) k–3. Panda and his friend the winged lion journey to Australia, where they encounter the legendary bunnyips and continue their adventures of exploration.

2643. ____. *Panda and the Bushfire* (Prentice, 1986) k–3. With the help of Flying Lion, Panda and his animal friends escape a fire in the Australian bush and aid the firefighters in battling the blaze.

2644. Foreman, Michael. *Ben's Box* (Bradbury, 1978) k–3. An empty box serves as a castle to be defended against dragons; a boat swamped by an octopus, a submarine attacked by sharks and a spaceship defying hostile enemies.

2645. ____. *Ben's Baby* (Harper, 1987) k–3. Ben asks his parents for a baby for his next birthday and by the time of his next birthday he has a baby brother.

2646. Forest, Antonia. *Autumn Term* (Faber, 1948/199) 5–8. An introduction to the six Marlow girls at Kingscote School. The twins, Nicole and Lawrie are the youngest of the six. They are all determined to uphold the family tradition of sporting and academic achievement.

2647. ____. *Marlows and the Traitor* (Faber, 1953) 5–8. The twins spend Easter on the coast with Ginty, their next youngest sister and Peter, on holiday from Dartmouth. This is a spy thriller.

2648. ____. *Falconer's Lure* (Faber, 1957) 5–8. The Marlows inherit Trennels, the eleventh century Dorset farm where the next holiday books are set. Rowan leaves school to manage the farm so Captain Marlow can stay in the Navy, and Nicola discovers falconry with Patrick Merrick from neighboring Mariot Chase.

2649. ____. *End of Term* (Faber, 1959/1991) 5–8. Karen is now at Oxford and Rowen is at home on the farm. All the other girls are still at Kingscote School. Nicola is dropped from the netball team "to develop her character." Lawrie wants to play the Shepherd Boy in the Christmas play but is frustrated.

2650. ____. *Peter's Room* (Faber, 1962) 5–8. The Marlows are spending their first winter at Trennels. Lawrie revels in acting, Peter secretly identifies with his Civil War ancestor; Ginty has a romantic passion for Bronte (and Patrick); Nicola does not believe in make-believe.

2651. ____. *Thuggery Affair* (Faber, 1964) 5–8. A thriller in which drug smuggling by carrier pigeon is discovered by Peter, Lawrie and Patrick when Patrick's falcon kills a pigeon.

2652. ____. *Ready Made Family* (Faber, 1967) 8. *Ready-Made Family* is a family story crossed with social realism. Karen, 19, leaves Oxford to marry a 41-year-old widower with three young children, whom she brings home to Trennels until they can find a house.

2653. ____. *Player's Boy* (Faber, 1970) 5–8. Nicholas finally becomes an actor after spending some time with Christopher Marlowe. He meets Shakespeare and enjoys the Elizabethan theater.

2654. ____. *Players and the Rebels* (Faber, 1971) 5–8. Nicholas, the player's boy, plays in the Shrove Tuesday Revels at Whitehall. The players rely on gossip to learn about happenings at Court. They get mixed up with current politics.

2655. ____. *Cricket Term* (Faber, 1974/1991) 5–8. Karen's archivist husband begins deciphering a 16th century farm log discovered in Trennels' old shippen in *Peter's Room*. Nicola is overjoyed to find a kindred spirit in Nicholas, whose experiences are told more fully in *Player's Boy* and *Players and the Rebels*.

2656. ____. *Attic Term* (Faber, 1976) 5–8. Ginty is lovesick for Patrick but telephones him once to often. She is grieving for the loss of her best friend due to an accident. Nicky and Lawrie play for the school, deflate the Head and are just girls at a boarding school.

2657. ____. *Run Away Home* (Faber, 1982) 5–8. Mrs. Marlowe leaves Paris to tend to an ailing grandmother and the children are left with a depressing Christmas without their mother. They get involved in a kidnapping plot and help young Edward return to his father in Switzerland. Ginty spends Christmas with a friend; Nicola spends it with Patrick.

2658. Forrester, John. *Forbidden Beast* (Bradbury, 1988) 5–8. The Round Beast challenges the Forbidden Beast to a fight on Earth. A decisive battle between Old Earth and Luna.

2659. ____. *Secret of the Round Beast* (Bradbury, 1986) 5–8. Tamara and Drewyn battle the geneticists Lave and Pyland—the power hungry against altruists. The Round Beast is revealed some more in this second book.

2660. Forsyth, Anne. *Baxter, the Travelling Cat* (Hodder, 1981) 2–4.

2661. ____. *Baxter and the Golden Pavements* (Hodder, 1986) 2–4. Baxter, a young cat, goes to visit London. There he finds the Tower where he is warned by another cat not to catch the ravens. He leaves pawprints in fresh cement and has many other adventures with Mouse, Gog and Magog and Lord Mayor.

2662. ____. *Baxter by the Sea* (Hodder, 1987) 2–4. Baxter, the traveling cat journeys to the seaside on a school outing.

2663. Foster, Marian. *Miss Flora McFlimsey's Christmas Eve* (Lothrop, 1949) 3–5. A story about an old, forgotten doll who is restored to love in the arms of a child. From a toy cupboard in the attic with only Timothy Mouse for a friend, Miss Flora McFlimsey moves downstairs on Christmas Eve.

2664. ____. *Miss Flora McFlimsey and the Baby New Year* (Lothrop, 1951) 3–5. Flora, the doll, is feeling unhappy because everyone has gone to a New Year's Eve party and left her alone with Pookoo the cat. When the baby New Year stops by and lets Flora rock him for a while, she feels better.

2665. ____. *Miss Flora McFlimsey's Birthday* (Lothrop, 1952) 3–5. Miss Flora McFlimsey ran away from the Doll House when she decided that everyone had forgotten her birthday. She has adventures on Puffin Island but soon returns to Dolls House and a wonderful surprise.

2666. ____. *Miss Flora McFlimsey and Little Laughing Water* (Lothrop, 1954) 3–5. Miss Flora goes for a walk in the forest where she meets a new friend, a little Indian girl.

2667. ____. *Miss Flora McFlimsey's Valentine* (Lothrop, 1962) 3–5. Miss Flora McFlimsey celebrates St. Valentine's Day. The tokens of affection she makes for all her friends are packed in a little basket and ready to be delivered by Pookoo Cat.

2668. ____. *Miss Flora McFlimsey's Halloween* (Lothrop, 1972) 3–5. A doll's Halloween adventures are interrupted by the news that her house is invaded by goblins.

2669. ____. *Miss Flora McFlimsey's May Day* (Lothrop, 1987) 3–5. Although Miss McFlimsey knows she isn't beautiful, she discovers she has the potential for another queenly attribute.

2670. ____. *Miss Flora McFlimsey's Easter Bonnet* (Lothrop, 1987) 3–5. Miss Flora McFlimsey remembers the day when Peterkins the rabbit brought her first Easter bonnet.

2671. Fowler, Richard. *Cat's Story* (Grosset, 1985) k–3. A cat causes chaos through the house while chasing a mouse.

2672. ____. *Cat's Car* (Barron, 1988) k–3. Cat's automobile trip to the beach is interrupted when his animal friends ask for a lift.

2673. ____. *Cat's Cake* (Barron, 1988) k–3. Cat's animal friends all like his cake, but each wishes it was flavored with just a little more of his own favorite thing.

2674. Fowler, Richard. *Mr. Little's Noisy Boat* (Grosset, 1986) k–3. All the animals are making strange noises in various parts of Mr. Little's boat.

2675. ____. *Mr. Little's Noisy Car* (Grosset, 1986) k–3. Mr. Little inspects his car and finds various animals making noises in it.

2676. ____. *Mr. Little's Noisy Train* (Grosset, 1987) k–3. All the animals are making strange noises in various parts of Mr. Little's freight train.

2677. ____. *Mr. Little's Noisy ABC* (Grosset, 1987) k–3. Mr. Little leads a noisy active but alphabetical existence, yelling "Ahhh" as he falls from the apple tree and zipping zoomingly to the moon.

2678. ____. *Mr. Little's Noisy 1 2 3* (Grosset, 1987) k–3. Mr. Little dreams of "one owl hooting, two donkeys braying, three trains tooting…fifteen builders banging" up to 100 bees buzzing. Then the alarm shatters his peace.

2679. ____. *Mr. Little's Noisy Plane* (Grosset, 1988) k–3. Mr. Little flies his plane at the local air show. He hears strange noises. As he looks for the trouble he names parts of the plane. What he finds is an assortment of animals.

2680. ____. *Mr. Little's Noisy Truck* (Grosset, 1989) k–3. Mr. Little's truck, full of boxes, is making noises. A pig is being chased by a wolf; a frog is at the piano keyboard; a grasshopper is in the clock. No wonder there is noise.

2681. ____. *Mr. Little's Noisy Fire Engine* (Grosset, 1990) k–3. A peek-a-boo book naming objects on each page.

2682. Frascino, Edward. *Eddie Spaghetti* (Harper, 1978) 4–6. Eddie goes to the zoo, takes piano lessons and fights with his brother. He has a dog that bites the mailman, wears corduroy knickers and goes to $.25 movies.

2683. ____. *Eddie Spaghetti on the Home Front* (Harper, 1983) 4–6. Eddie does as much as a boy can for the war effort during World War II.

2684. Frascino, Edward. *Nanny Noony and the Magic Spell* (Pippin, 1988) k–3. When a magic spell is cast on a farm causing everyone to act contrary, the cat decides to find out who did it.

2685. ____. *Nanny Noony and the Dust Queen* (Pippin, 1990) k–3. Nanny Noony and the cat must try to undo the Dust Queen's evil spell, which has brought a drought to the farm and suffering to the animals.

2686. Freeman, Don. *Corduroy* (Viking, 1968/1976) k–3. A toy bear in a department store wants a number of things, but when a little girl finally buys him he finds what he has always wanted most of all.

2687. ____. *Pocket for Corduroy* (Puffin, 1978/1980) k–3. A toy bear who wants a pocket for himself searches for one in a laundromat.

2688. ____. *Corduroy's Day* (Viking, 1985) k–3. Follows a teddy bear through his daily activities and introduces the numbers from one to ten. "Good Morning. Here is 1 bear called Corduroy." "In his bath Corduroy counts 10 bubbles."

2689. ____. *Corduroy's Toys* (Viking, 1985) k–3. Each illustration is captioned with the name of the toy illustrated. Labeled pictures introduce the many toys of a young bear.

2690. ____. *Corduroy's Party* (Viking, 1985) k–3. Corduroy makes and sends birthday party invitations and decorates his house. His friends, a rag doll, a pink bunny, a gray mouse and a brown dog arrive. They eat cake and play games.

2691. ____. *Corduroy Goes to the Doctor* (Viking, 1987) k–3. Corduroy's going to see the doctor. He likes everyone in the doctor's office, and they know he is a very brave bear.

2692. ____. *Corduroy's Busy Street* (Viking, 1987) k–3. Corduroy the bear observes the world around him: he watches a fire, watches a garbage truck and then sees an ice cream truck.

2693. ____. *Corduroy's Christmas* (Viking, 1992) k–3. Corduroy trims the tree, bakes cookies, wraps gifts and enjoys Christmas with his friends.

2694. Frere, Maud. *My Name Is Nicole* (Random, 1965) k–3. Nicole and her dog Boniface have a good time together.

2695. ____. *Nicole: A Little French Schoolgirl* (Random, 1966) k–3. Nicole tells of her family, pets, teachers and friends. Measles, annoying cousins and playground games are also covered.

2696. ____. *Nicole's Birthday* (Random, 1967) k–3. Nicole and Arlette, looking like mannequins, flirt and fight with their cousins and make sly comments about the adults.

2697. Freschet, Berniece. *Bernard Sees the World* (Scribner, 1976) k–3. Bernard, a mouse, decides to see the world, about which he has read so much, and he even makes a trip to the moon, returning home in time for Christmas with a tiny moon rock to add to the holiday decorations.

2698. ____. *Bernard of Scotland Yard* (Scribner, 1978) k–3. Bernard, the mouse, is on the trail of some English jewel thieves.

2699. ____. *Bernard and the Catnip Caper* (Scribner, 1981) k–3. When the quietest, sleepiest, most timid cat in Boston is catnapped, a ransom note is sent to Bernard, the mouse.

2700. Freschet, Berniece. *Little Black Bear Goes for a Walk* (Scribner, 1977) k–3. While Mother Bear sleeps, Little Black Bear steals away for his first solo adventure.

2701. ____. *Black Bear Baby* (Putnam, 1981) k–3. Describes the first months of life of Bear Baby and his sister.

2702. Friskey, Margaret. *Indian Two Feet and His Horse* (Children's, 1959) k–3. Indian Two Feet wanted a horse. He searched all the likely places without success, but he did get his wish.

2703. ____. *Indian Two Feet and His Eagle Feather* (Children's, 1967) k–3. A young Indian boy tries several ways to earn an eagle feather.

2704. ____. *Indian Two Feet and the Wolf Cubs* (Children's, 1971) k–3. Indian Two Feet tries to adopt a baby wolf cub. He watches the wolves so closely that they make him one of their family.

2705. ____. *Indian Two Feet and the Grizzly Bear* (Children's, 1974) k–3. Indian Two Feet is looking for a bearskin to keep him warm. He can't lure the bear from its den. But he does get a warm cover.

2706. ____. *Indian Two Feet and the ABC Moose Hunt* (Children's, 1977) k–3. Indian Two Feet goes out to hunt a moose with his bow and arrow and is dumped in the river.

2707. ____. *Indian Two Feet Rides Alone* (Children's, 1980) k–3. Because he cannot tolerate being bested by a "mere girl" Indian Two Feet loses his salt when he can't find the animals' salt lick.

2708. Fry, Rosalie. *Matelot, Little Sailor of Brittany* (Dutton, 1958) 4–6. Lucinda and Robin try to find a home for a sea-going kitten, Matelot, who is set on going to sea.

2709. ____. *Fly Home, Columbia* (Dutton, 1960) 4–6. Lucinda meets an Italian boy, Fran, and his homing pigeon Columbia, who end up carrying a wonderful message to Fran's crippled sister, Clare.

2710. Fujikawa, Gyo. *Jenny Learns a Lesson* (Grosset, 1980) k–3. Jenny learns how to play with her friends without being too bossy.

2711. ____. *Jenny and Jupie to the Rescue* (Putnam, 1982) k–3. Jenny joins her friends Jupie, Orrie and Zorrie on an outer space search for their lost dog.

2712. Fujikawa, Gyo. *Shags Has a Dream* (Grosset, 1981) k–3. After chasing a small rabbit, Shag, the dog, has a dream that he is small in a terrifyingly big world.

2713. ____. *Shag Finds a Kitten* (Grosset, 1983) k–3. A dog suffers from neglect when a cute, tiny kitten enters his life.

2714. Fulton, Mary. *Detective Arthur on the Scent* (Golden, 1971) 3–5. By scratching and sniffing treated strips in the illustrations, the reader and Arthur, the bloodhound, follow the same scents in trying to track down the missing birthday cake.

2715. ____. *Detective Arthur, Master Sleuth* (Golden, 1974) 3–5. Scrappy challenges Arthur to solve two out of three mysteries in order to prove he is a master sleuth.

2716. ____. *Detective Arthur in the Case of the Mysterious Stranger* (Western, 1982). 3–5. Arthur follows a mysterious-looking stranger around town until the mystery is solved.

2717. Furlong, Monica. *Juniper* (Random, 1992) 4–6. Prequel. Juniper is a young girl, raised as a medieval princess. She slowly comes to accept her special powers. Her Godmother Euny helps her understand to use her powers for good, not for her own selfish benefits.

2718. ____. *Wise Child* (Knopf, 1987) 4–6. Wise Child, nine, is a young girl abandoned by her parents and adopted by Juniper, a local wise woman (sorceress/witch). Wise Child learns reading, herb craft, Latin and the beginning of magic.

2719. Gackenbach, Dick. *Hound and Bear* (Seabury, 1976) k–3. Hound and Bear are very good friends until Hound plays one practical joke too many.

2720. ____. *More from Hound and Bear* (Houghton, 1979) k–3. A continuation of the humorous adventures started in Hound and Bear.

2721. ____. *Pepper and All the Legs* (Seabury, 1978) k–3. A dachshund explores his legs' eye view of people.

2722. Gackenbach, Dick. *Hattie Rabbit* (Harper, 1976) k–3. Two stories about Hattie Rabbit who has a tendency to overlook possible consequences of her actions.

2723. ____. *Hattie Be Quiet, Hattie Be Good* (Harper, 1977) k–3. Hattie Rabbit valiantly tries to be quiet for an hour; she also visits a sick friend.

2724. ____. *Mother Rabbit's Son, Tom* (Harper, 1977) k–3. Tom keeps Mother and Father Rabbit busy by asking for hamburgers and pets.

2725. ____. *Hattie, Tom and the Chicken Witch* (Harper, 1980) k–3. A book that proves both chickens and rabbits are important to Easter.

2726. ____. *Hurray for Hattie Rabbit* (Harper, 1986) k–3. Hattie Rabbit finds that mothers are sometimes difficult and sometimes helpful.

2727. Gackenbach, Dick. *Claude the Dog: A Christmas Story* (Seabury, 1974) k–3. Claude, the dog, gives away all his Christmas presents to his down-and-out friend but receives an even better present from his younger owner.

2728. ____. *Claude and Pepper* (Seabury, 1976) k–3. Pepper, a feisty dachshund, involves Claude in his attempt to run away from home.

2729. ____. *What's Claude Doing?* (Clarion, 1984) k–3. A dog refuses all the neighborhood pets' invitations to come out to play, not admitting that he's generously keeping his sick master company.

2730. ____. *Claude Has a Picnic* (Clarion, 1993) k–3. After resolving his neighbors' problems, Claude the dog joins them in a picnic.

2731. Gaeddert, Lou Ann. *Noisy Nancy Norris* (Doubleday, 1965) 2–4. The landlady threatens to evict the Norris family from their apartment unless Nancy stops making noise. Nancy clomps, bangs, clatters, shouts and thumps. Nancy must learn about proper noise.

2732. ____. *Noisy Nancy and Nick* (Doubleday, 1970) 2–4. Noisy Nancy shows her new neighbor from the country the delights of city living.

2733. Gage, Wilson. *Mrs. Gaddy and the Ghost* (Greenwillow, 1979) 3–5. Mrs. Gaddy finds a ghost in the kitchen can be good company.

2734. ____. *Crow and Mrs. Gaddy* (Greenwillow, 1984) 3–5. A crow and a farmer spend all their time playing tricks on each other and get nothing else done.

2735. ____. *Mrs. Gaddy and the Fast-Growing Vine* (Greenwillow, 1985) 3–5. Mrs. Gaddy buys a fast-growing vine that begins to take over her house, her animals and herself.

2736. ____. *My Stars, It's Mrs. Gaddy* (Greenwillow, 1991) 3–5. Life on Mrs. Gaddy's farm is made exciting by a ghost in her kitchen, a war with a pesky crow, and a vine that will not stop growing.

2737. Gallico, Paul. *Day Jean-Pierre Was Pignapped* (Watts, 1965) 3–5. Story of an Abyssinian guinea pig and Cecile, age nine. They follow fingerprints to solve a mystery.

2738. ____. *Day Jean-Pierre Went Around the World* (Doubleday,) 1965. 3–5

2739. ____. *Day Jean-Pierre Joined the Circus* (Watts, 1969) 3–5. When Cecile gave her guinea pig to a poor old clown who needed to improve his act, she had no idea that the clown would repay her kindness with everything he owned.

2740. Galloway, Priscilla. *Good Times, Bad Times, Mummy and Me* (Women's) Press, 1981. k–3

2741. ____. *Good Times, Bad Times* (Women's Press, 1982) k–3. A single mother goes to work; a daughter goes to school. Each learns to share, support and accept each other.

2742. Gantos, Jack. *Rotten Ralph* (Houghton, 1976) k–3. A book about a very naughty cat named Ralph. Sarah, his owner, never seems to believe how badly he behaves, but the reader can.

2743. ____. *Worse Than Rotten, Ralph* (Houghton, 1978) k–3. Rotten Ralph makes an earnest attempt at good behavior but is enticed, not too reluctantly, into a series of misadventures by some ruffian alley cats.

2744. ____. *Rotten Ralph's Rotten Christmas* (Houghton, 1984) k–3. Rotten Ralph, the cat, is not at all nice to the Christmas visitor.

2745. ____. *Rotten Ralph's Trick or Treat* (Houghton, 1986) k–3. Sarah's rotten cat Ralph goes to a Halloween costume party dressed as her and creates horrible mischief under the protection of his disguise.

2746. ____. *Rotten Ralph's Show and Tell* (Houghton, 1989) k–3. Susan takes her rotten cat Ralph to school for Show and Tell and he behaves terribly, as usual by spoiling everyone's show.

2747. ____. *Happy Birthday, Rotten Ralph* (Houghton, 1990) k–3. Rotten Ralph the cat is up to his rotten behavior as Sarah prepares for his birthday party.

2748. ____. *Not So Rotten Ralph* (Houghton, 1994) k–3. Sarah's mischievous cat, Rotten Ralph, is sent to feline finishing school, but Sarah finds she likes him better the way he was.

2749. Gantz, David. *Captain Swifty Counts to Fifty* (Doubleday, 1982) k–3. Captain Swifty and his animal friends count to 50.

2750. ____. *Captain Swifty's Book of Opposites* (Doubleday, 1984) k–3. A book about opposites— lots and lots of opposites.

2751. ____. *Captain Swifty and His Happy Heart's Band* (Doubleday, 1984) k–3. A book about sounds explained through the use of musical instruments.

2752. Gardam, J. *Kit in Books* (Macrae, 1983) 3–5. Kit, nine, is the daughter of a farmer who is dedicated to work. Lonesome Jones, a traveling camper stays on the farm for three consecutive summers. Lonesome Jones is getting married and wants Kit as a bridesmaid. She has her moment of glory and goes home with a gift of paper and paints. Kit draws and draws and draws.

2753. ____. *Kit* (Macrae, 1986) 3–5. A story about a small girl growing up on an isolated farm.

2754. Garden, Nancy. *Mystery of the Night Raiders* (Farrar, 1988) 5–8. Brian, Darcy and Numbles are the Monster Hunters in this series of books about mysteries.

2755. ____. *Mystery of the Midnight Menace* (Farrar, 1988) 5–8. Pigeons, rats and cats have been found mangled in the park. The "Monster Hunters" investigate, especially the two new boys in town.

2756. ____. *Mystery of the Secret Marks* (Farrar, 1989) 5–8. Darcy is in a private school where strange events are happening to her roommate, Ro. Darcy, Brian and Numbles solve the mystery by using the code.

2757. ____. *Mystery of the Kidnapped Kidnapper* (Farrar, 1989) 5–8. Where's Casey? She's the prisoner of a living dinosaur-like creature. This is a case for the Monster Hunters. "Numbles" calls in his monster-hunting friends to help him find Casey, six, lost during a sleepover at the museum.

2758. Garland, Sarah. *Tex and Bad Hank* (Collins, 1983) k–3. A rodeo, a sinister bandit, a ferocious bull—scenes in the life of a gangling cowboy whose disasters become triumphs.

2759. ____. *Tex and Gloria* (Collins, 1983) k–3. Relates the adventures of Tex the cowboy and his remarkable horse Gloria.

2760. ____. *Tex the Cowboy* (Dutton, 1983) Tex may know more. about cornflakes than rodeo-riding but with Gloria's help, he can rope a bull in 30 seconds flat and Tex can also catch a bad man and even find gold…sort of.

2761. ____. *Tex the Champion* (Collins, 1983) k–3.

2762. Garland, Sarah. *Sam's the Name* (Walker, 1987) k–3. Sam is called Sausage or Pudding by his two older sisters but when he goes to school he is called Sam.

2763. ____. *Sam's Cat* (Walker, 1987) k–3. Sam is concerned about the expectant cat and makes a maternity bed, only to find the cat and her newborn kittens in the bottom drawer of his clothes closet.

2764. ____. *Sam and Joe* (Walker, 1987) k–3.

2765. Garland, Sarah. *Rose and Her Bath* (Faber, 1976) k–3. A dream-like tale of Rosie and her flying bath.

2766. ____. *Rose, the Bath and the Merboy* (Faber, 1972) k–3. At a whisper down the drainpipe, Rosie's bath spreads pink wings and takes flight to cooperate with her in receiving a captive merboy from the circus and restoring him to his home at the Bay of Biscay.

2767. Gascoigne, Bamber. *Fearless Freddy's Sunken Treasure* (Methuen, 1983) k–3. Freddy Frog dives into his pond and finds a sunken damaged toy steamer. He raises it with help from friends and repairs it and then takes his friends for a ride.

2768. ____. *Fearless Freddy's Magic Wish* (Methuen, 1983) k–3. Freddy was happy in his peaceful pond. His adventures saddle him with a domineering princess who criticizes the plain bowlegged man he became. The princess wishes him to be a handsome prince but Freddy has other ideas.

2769. Gates, Doris. *Morgan for Melinda* (Viking, 1980) 5–8. Melinda was afraid of horses but with the help of her father and Missy she overcomes her fear and rides, wins shows and loves horses.

2770. ____. *Horse for Melinda* (Viking, 1981) 5–8. A story about a girl who actually doesn't like horses until she gets the responsibility for one.

2771. ____. *Filly for Melinda* (Viking, 1984) 5–8. Melinda, 12, faces the difficult choice between keeping her beloved filly, Little Missy, or helping her parents through a family crisis.

2772. Gathorne-Hardy, Jonathon. *Terrible Kidnapping of Cyril Bonhamy* (Lippincott, 1979) 3–5. Cyril is mistaken for the great O'Noonagan by his Arab kidnappers who want his knowledge of bombs. His bomb fails to explode and he escapes back to England aided by his own folly.

2773. ____. *Cyril Bonhamy v. Madame Big* (Lippincott, 1981) 3–5. Cyril tries to fail as Father Christmas in a department store by attacking children, giving away too many presents and dozing. But he stumbles on a plot to infiltrate stores with hundreds of burglars dressed alike. Madame Big is the criminal behind the affair.

2774. ____. *Cyril Bonhamy and the Great Drain Robbery* (Lippincott, 1983) 3–5. An English tourist vacationing in France becomes mixed up with a notorious gang of jewel thieves.

2775. ____. *Cyril Bonhamy and Operation Ping* (Cape, 1985) 3–5. Cyril Bonhamy is a small fat scholarly writer. His antagonist is R.S.M. Rude, a bully. A spoof on the SAS and all things military.

2776. ____. *Cyril of the Apes* (Lippincott, 1987) 3–5. Cyril is employed as a scriptwriter for the filming of *Tarzan of the Apes.* He has hair-raising experiences with heat, insects and disease. The chief actor doesn't like the script. After many outrageous adventures he returns from South America to England.

2777. Gathorne-Hardy, Jonathon. *Jane's Adventures on the Island of Peeg* (Overlook, 1969) 4–6. Jarred loose from the ocean floor by a tremendous explosion, an island occupied by a young girl and her two companions floats out to sea under the command of two British sailors who believe that World War II is still in progress.

2778. ____. *Jane's Adventures in and out of the Book* (Overlook, 1972/1981) 4–6. Lady Jane is bored in the castle when her parents go away. She learns how to enter into other worlds through the pages of a mysterious book.

2779. ____. *Jane's Adventures in a Balloon* (Overlook, 1975) 4–6. Jane floats away with Mrs. Deal, the housekeeper, in the airship her father just constructed. There is a crash and more adventures.

2780. ____. *Airship Ladyship Adventure* (Lippincott, 1977) 4–6. Jane and Mrs. Deal are aboard an airship named *Ladyship.* It crash lands in the Alps. They are aided and then stranded in Africa.

2781. Gauch, Patricia. *Christina Katerina and the Box* (Coward, 1971) k–3. Christina finds many uses for the large box that housed the new refrigerator.

2782. ____. *Christina Katerina and the First Annual Grand Ballet* (Coward, 1973) k–3. Christina Katerina's debut as prima ballerina in her family's newly finished basement is marred by disaster but nonetheless successful.

2783. ____. *Christina Katerina and the Time She Quit the Family* (Putnam, 1987) k–3. When Christina quits her family so she can do whatever she pleases, ignoring her brother and her parents, she finds total self-reliance can sometimes be lonely.

2784. ____. *Christina Katerina and the Great Bear Train* (Putnam, 1990) k–3. Not happy that a new baby sister is coming home from the hospital, Christina Katerina takes her toy bears on a faraway train journey all over the neighborhood.

2785. Gauch, Patricia. *Dance, Tanya* (Philomel, 1989) k–3. Tanya loves ballet dancing, repeating the moves she sees her older sister using when practicing for class or a recital, and soon Tanya is big enough to go to ballet class herself.

2786. ____. *Tanya Loved to Dance* (Philomel, 1989) k–3. Tanya copies her older sister's dance steps. Elise is in a special dancing display and all the family is gathered to see this. Tanya starts to dance to "Swan Lake." Later that Christmas she receives ballet slippers and leotards and goes to ballet school, too. "She is not too little anymore."

2787. ____. *Bravo, Tanya* (Philomel, 1992) k–3. Tanya loves to dance but has trouble integrating her steps with the clapping and counting of her ballet teacher, until she tries moving to the music and the sounds inside her head.

2788. ____. *Tanya and Emily in a Dance for Two* (Philomel, 1994) k–3. When Tanya, the smallest and wiggliest girl in her ballet class, makes friends with a talented newcomer, they both learn something.

2789. Gault, Clare. *Norman Plays Ice Hockey* (Scholastic, 1975) k–3. Using his turtle shell and some unorthodox tactics Norman brings his team to victory.
2790. ____. *Norman Plays Soccer* (Scholastic, 1978) k–3. Norman the turtle comes off the bench to save the day. And they win the tournament for his soccer-playing buddies.
2791. ____. *Norman Plays Basketball* (Scholastic, 1978) k–3. Norman, the turtle, becomes a hero when he is called on to substitute for Hound Dog on his basketball team. His passing strategy enables the team to win.

2792. Gault, William. *Big Stick* (Dutton, 1975) 5–8. Rusty played hockey in high school and college. He is now a pro with the National Hockey League.
2793. ____. *Thin Ice* (Dutton, 1978) 5–8. Rusty and Sven play together as a team after Sven's skills increase and his use of violence decreased. Lots of hockey action.

2794. Gault, Michael. *Brim's Boat* (Coward, 1966) 4–6. Brim, a terrier and his friend Twill, a sheepdog, find an old barge that they rebuild. Brim is now captain of a boat.
2795. ____. *Brim Sails Out* (Coward, 1957) 4–6. Brim is a terrier who sails on a barge and helps other animals. He built the boat with some help and some hindrances from others. One day he and Twill, a sheepdog, are caught in a storm.

2796. Gauthier, Bertrand. *Zachary in the Present* (G. Stevens, 1993) k–3. Zachary's excitement grows as he searches for the present his father has hidden.
2797. ____. *Zachary in the Wawabongbong* (G. Stevens, 1993) k–3. Four days before Christmas, Zachary becomes lost when he and his father try to visit the department store's Land of Wawabongbong.
2798. ____. *Zachary in the Winner* (G. Stevens, 1993) k–3. Zachary doesn't understand why his dad lets Zachary's friend Andrea Abbott have her way.
2799. ____. *Zachary in Camping Out* (G. Stevens, 1993) k–3. Zachary and his dad camp at the seashore with friends at the time of the full moon.
2800. ____. *Zachary in I'm Zachary* (G. Stevens, 1993) k–3. Zachary goes to kindergarten, watches television, eats pancakes, and sometimes gets mad at his father, but not for long.
2801. ____. *Zachary in the Championship* (G. Stevens, 1993) k–3. "To the one and only 'Zachary Jacques Plante.'" Zachary's dad lets him down on a very important hockey game.

2802. Gavin, Jamila. *Kamla and Kate* (Mammoth,

1992) k–3. Kamla and Kate are six years old and are next door neighbors. They learn much from each other, Kamla learns about life in England where she now lives and Kate hears about India from where glorious presents and glamorous visitors come.
2803. ____. *Kamla and Kate Again* (Methuen, 1992) k–3. Kamla is Indian, Kate is white. Each chapter tells of different incidents in their lives. They are best friends and learn about how each other lives. Their lives are changed by this knowledge.

2804. Gay, Michel. *Bibi Birthday Surprise* (Morrow, 1987) k–3. Bibi, the penguin, celebrates his birthday with a party. He gets a yellow and white boat, a replica of the King's own craft. His boat sails out of sight and he asks for help in finding it.
2805. ____. *Bibi Takes Flight* (Morrow, 1988) k–3. A young penguin resolves to learn how to fly rather than swim in the cold ocean.

2806. Gee, Maurice. *Halfmen of O* (Oxford, 1982) k–3. Susan and Mick find themselves in the world of O. Susan learns that because of the strange mark on her arm only she can recapture the Motherstone from Claw and reinstate goodness for the Halfmen of O.
2807. ____. *Priests of Ferris* (Oxford, 1985) 5–8. The priests of O rule in Susan's name but are Nazi-like in the destruction of "alien" life. Susan tries to stop this by logic and truth but only force will end this reign.
2808. ____. *Motherstone* (Oxford, 1986) 5–8. Susan and Nicholas have freed the world of O and are trying to return to Earth. Orso is still planning to destroy O. Susan and Nick save O again, just in time.

2809. Geisert, Arthur. *Pa's Balloon and Other Pig Tales* (Houghton, 1984) 3–5. A pig family takes their new balloon for a ride, race it, and eventually fly it over the North Pole.
2810. ____. *Pigs from A to Z* (Houghton, 1986) 3–5. Seven piglets cavort through a landscape of hidden letters as they build a tree house.
2811. ____. *Oink* (Houghton, 1991) k–3. When their mother falls asleep, the baby pigs sneak away, get into big trouble, and must be rescued.
2812. ____. *Pigs from One to Ten* (Houghton, 1992) k–3. Ten pigs go on an adventurous quest. The reader is asked to find all ten of them, and the numerals from one to nine in each picture.
2813. ____. *Oink, Oink* (Houghton, 1993) k–3. Eight piglets wander off while their mother is still sleeping and enjoy a feast in a cornfield before she brings them home again.

2814. George, David. *Freddie Freightliner to the Rescue* (Children's, 1983) 2–4. Freddie the truck talks to other vehicles and their drivers. The rescue is of traffic that is buried in a sudden blizzard.
2815. ____. *Freddie Freightliner Learns to Talk* (Children's, 1983) 2–4. Freddie the truck is a super

truck hero. Foreigners try to hijack a shuttle component.

2816. ____. *Freddie Freightliner Goes to Kennedy Space Center* (Children's, 1983) 2–4. Freddie the super truck hero is involved with a mysterious professor who animates a truck using robots and computers.

2817. George, Jean. *Julie of the Wolves* (Harper, 1972) 5–8. Julie, an Eskimo, tries to find her deserted father. She gets lost and learns survival skills from the wolves. Her father has accepted modern ways but she still clings to the traditional.

2818. ____. *Julie* (Harper, 1991) 5–8. When Julie returns to her father's Eskimo village, with the help of a young Siberian man, she struggles to find a way to save her beloved wolves in a changing Arctic world.

2819. German, Tony. *Tom Penny* (P. Martin, 1977) 5–8.

2820. ____. *Tom Penny and the Grand Canal* (McClelland, 1982) 5–8. During the 1830s Tom Penny, 16 and his family plan to construct a canal in Canada between Montreal and Lake Superior, but when a company employee is killed, Tom finds his own life in danger as he uncovers a plot to swindle money from canal investors.

2821. Gerrard, Roy. *Sir Cedric* (Farrar, 1984) k–3. Tiny Sir Cedric, bored with castle life, rides out on his faithful steed Walter, rescues a princess called Fat Matilda and defeats the nasty villain Black Ned.

2822. ____. *Sir Cedric Rides Again* (Farrar, 1986) k–3. This continues the story of Sir Cedric and Fat Matilda and introduces their daughter, Edwina the Pest.

2823. Gerson, Corinne. *Son for a Day* (Atheneum, 1980) 4–6. Danny goes to the zoo often because he can easily be "adopted" by families there.

2824. ____. *Oh, Brother!* (Atheneum, 1982) 4–6. Danny establishes himself as the favorite adopted kid brother for four Chicago teenage boys who in turn inspire him to become a Renaissance Man.

2825. Getz, Arthur. *Hamilton Duck* (Golden, 1972) k–3. When Duck realizes the hard stuff on the pond is ice, he knows winter has come.

2826. ____. *Hamilton Duck's Springtime Story* (Golden, 1974) k–3. Hamilton Duck falls asleep under an apple tree and wakes up to a pink snowstorm.

2827. Gibson, Gloria. *Mouse in the Attic* (Methuen, 1980) 4–6. New Zealand outback in the 1920s: Family life, swimming, rabbit shooting, riding and surviving a rising river flood. The girl wants to be a writer and tries to tie these experiences into a story.

2828. ____. *Mouse in School* (Methuen, 1983) 4–6. Mouse, 12, enters high school in New Zealand. Her

brother Matthew makes a dangerous error of mistaking a bull for his old tramp's donkey.

2829. Giff, Patricia. *Beast in Ms. Rooney's Room* (Dell, 1984) 3–5. Held back for a year in second grade, Richard can't seem to help getting in trouble, until he gets really interested in reading and helps his class in a special way.

2830. ____. *Fish Face* (Delacorte, 1986) 3–5. Making friends with the new girl in Ms. Rooney's room, is hard for Emily after she replaces Emily as the fastest runner and steals her lucky unicorn.

2831. ____. *Candy Corn Contest* (Delacorte, 1986) 3–5. Richard determines to win the Thanksgiving Candy Corn Contest by guessing the right number of candies in the jar but before he realizes what he's done he eats three big pieces. What will the teacher do when she finds out?

2832. ____. *December Secrets* (Delacorte, 1986) 3–5. Each student in Ms. Rooney's room celebrates the December holidays by being a secret pal to a classmate.

2833. ____. *In the Dinosaur's Paw* (Delacorte, 1986) 3–5. When the kids in Ms. Rooney's class return to school after Christmas, one of them suspects he has found a magic ruler that makes wishes come true.

2834. ____. *Valentine Star* (Delacorte, 1986) 3–5. As Valentine's Day approaches and her class becomes busy making cards, Emily is worried about her fight with Sherri, who tells her, "You'll be sorry."

2835. ____. *Lazy Lions, Lucky Lambs* (Delacorte, 1986) 3–5. March is the worst month for Richard Best, it's report card time and if he doesn't get good grades he might be left back again.

2836. ____. *Snaggle Doodles* (Delacorte, 1985) 3–5. Emily Arrow has two problems, trying to work in her invention group with bossy Linda Lorca in charge and thinking of a wedding present for Mr. Vincent, the student teacher.

2837. ____. *Purple Climbing Days* (Delacorte, 1986) 3–5. With the help of the meanest substitute teacher in the whole school, Richard "Beast" Best learns a lesson about fear.

2838. ____. *Say "Cheese"* (Delacorte, 1985) 3–5. At the close of the school year, Emily thinks about the fun she had with her classmates.

2839. ____. *Sunny Side Up* (Delacorte, 1985) 3–5. Summer for Richard Best, nicknamed "Beast," means facing the two ordeals of summer school and losing his best friend, who is moving to a distant state.

2840. ____. *Pickle Puss* (Delacorte, 1986) 3–5. Emily Arrow determines to get the most fish in the library's Fish for a Good Book Contest but she doesn't take into account the equal determination of Dawn Bosco.

2841. ____. *Case of the Cool-itch Kid* (Dell, 1989) 3–5. Dawn is happy to be at summer camp until her shell mirror and favorite pin disappear. She's forgotten her detective kit but she decides to investigate anyway. She receives a surprising offer of help, and discovers a new friend.

2842. ____. *Pet Parade* (Yearling, 1996) 3–5. The whole Polk Street Gang wants to have the best pet. Richard's dog is fat and almost toothless. But a surprise is in store and the kids learn a lot about pet care.

2843. ____. *Look Out, Washington, D.C.* (Doubleday, 1995) 2–4. Ms. Rooney's entire class from the Polk Street School is going on a two-day class trip to Washington, D.C.

2844. Giff, Patricia. *Meet the Lincoln Lions Band* (Dell, 1992) 2–4. Crissie, a third grader, can hardly wait to join the band at Lincoln school. She is so sure she will be great that she tells her friend she has already made it. Then it is announced that students must be fourth graders to join!

2845. ____. *Yankee Doodle Drumsticks* (Dell, 1992) 2–4. The Lincoln Lions are going to march in their first football game on Thanksgiving. Willie's father probably won't be there to hear him play his drums. Will the uniforms get there on time? Will the day be saved?

2846. ____. *Jingle Bells Jam* (Dell, 1992) 2–4. It's Christmastime and the Lincoln Lions Band is getting ready to play carols at the Sunrise Mall. But Crissie is dreading the concert. On her fife "Jingle Bells" sounds like nothing more than squeaks and squeals.

2847. ____. *Great Shamrock Disaster* (Dell, 1993) 3–5. When the uniforms borrowed for the St. Patrick's Day Parade turn out to be too old and too big, Michelle Swoop tries to find a way to save the day for the Lincoln Lions Band.

2848. Giff, Patricia. *Watch Out, Ronald Morgan* (Viking, 1985) k–3. Ronald has many humorous mishaps until he gets a pair of eyeglasses.

2849. ____. *Happy Birthday, Ronald Morgan* (Viking, 1986) k–3. Ronald, worried about losing his best friend, thinks his birthday is going to come too late for a class party, but he may be in for a surprise.

2850. ____. *Ronald Morgan Goes to Bat* (Viking, 1988) k–3. Although he can't hit or catch, Ronald Morgan loves to play baseball and his enthusiastic spirit helps the team.

2851. ____. *Morgan Goes to Camp* (Viking, 1995) 3–5. Ronald Morgan is afraid he won't get a medal at camp because he is not especially good at swimming, running or singing, but on Medal Day he discovers what he is really good at.

2852. ____. *Good Luck, Ronald Morgan* (Viking, 1996) k–3. Ronald has a new puppy and a new neighbor. The neighbor is a girl with a cat. Ronald tries to train Lucky (who'd rather play with Tiger and dig in the yard) and become friends with Kelly.

2853. Giff, Patricia. *Today Was a Terrible Day* (Viking, 1980) k–3. Follows the humorous mishaps of a second grader who is learning to read.

2854. ____. *Almost Awful Play* (Viking, 1984) k–3. Second grader Ronald Morgan inadvertently turns a failing class play into a success. Winky the Cat is the change agent that makes this possible.

2855. Giffard, Hannah. *Red Fox* (Dial, 1991) k–3. Red Fox searches all night long for food for himself and his wife returns to find a happy surprise in his den.

2856. ____. *Red Fox on the Move* (Dial, 1992) k–3. When they are moved out of their cozy den by an invading bulldozer, Red Fox and his family find a new home in an unexpected place.

2857. Gikow, Louise. *What's a Fraggle?* (Holt, 1984) k–3. Describes in rhyme the Fraggles and where they live.

2858. ____. *Sprocket's Christmas Tale* (Holt, 1984) k–3. Gobo Fraggle and Sprocket the dog each have a special wish for Christmas and on Christmas morning both wishes come true.

2859. ____. *Legend of the Doozer Who Didn't* (Holt, 1984) k–3. This "old legend" explains what happened to one Doozer who violated Doozer traditions by stopping working and going to school.

2860. ____. *Boober Fraggle's Celery Souffle* (Holt, 1984) k–3. Boober Fraggle shares his favorite recipe for celery souffle.

2861. ____. *Boober Fraggle's Ghosts* (Holt, 1985) k–3. Boober is sure he is seeing ghosts, but none of the other Fraggles will believe him.

2862. ____. *Last Days of Fraggle Rock* (Holt, 1985) k–3. The inhabitants of Fraggle Rock rejoice when Gorgs leave the Garden for a vacation but soon discover the Garden needs care in order to survive.

2863. ____. *Follow That Fraggle* (Holt, 1985) k–3. Sprocket the dog has an exciting day when he follows Uncle Traveling Matt Fraggle, the famous Fraggle explorer.

2864. ____. *Wembley and the Soggy Map* (Holt, 1986) k–3. When Wembley accidentally ruins Gobo's map, he learns that being very angry doesn't mean you stop caring about someone.

2865. ____. *Wembley Fraggle and the Magic Stone* (Muppet, 1986) k–3. Wembley wishes on a "magic stone" that he be able to make decisions more easily, and his belief in the witch changes his life dramatically.

(For additional books on the Fraggles, Boober, Gobo, Mokey, Red or Wembley, ***see*** Brennan, Joseph; Calder, Lyn; Calmenson, Stephanie; Gilmour, H.B.; Grand, Rebecca; Muntean, Michaela; Perlberg, Deborah; Stevenson, Jocelyn; Teitelbaum, Michael; Weiss, Ellen; Young, David.

2866. Gilge, Jeanette. *City-Kid Farmer* (Cook, 1975) 4–6. A city boy, Mark Cooper, tried to adjust to country life when his family moves to a Wisconsin farm.

2867. ____. *Growing Up Summer* (Cook, 1976) 4–6.

Adjusted to farm life, but still an outsider in his new community, Mark Cooper finds that growing up is not an easy task.

2868. Gilmour, H.B. *Why Wembley Fraggle Couldn't Sleep* (Holt, 1985) k–3. When Wembley can't fall asleep he bothers all the other inhabitants of Fraggle Rock by keeping them awake with him.

(For additional books on the Fraggles, Boober, Gobo, Mokey, Red or Wembley, *see* Brennan, Joseph; Calder, Lyn; Calmenson, Stephanie; Gilkow, Louise; Grand, Rebecca; Muntean, Michaela; Perlberg, Deborah; Stevenson, Jocelyn; Teitelbaum, Michael; Weiss, Ellen; Young, David.)

2869. Gilson, Jamie. *Harvey, the Beer Can King* (Lothrop, 1978) 4–6. Harvey is a collector, he is going to have the largest collection of beer cans in town. He knows he will win the contest but he doesn't count on some misadventurous trading.

2870. ____. *Hello, My Name Is Scrambled Eggs* (Lothrop, 1984) 4–6. Harvey, the school's best known student (for a number of different reasons) meets Tuyan from Vietnam. His job? Make an American out of him.

2871. Gilson, Jamie. *Thirteen Ways to Sink a Sub* (Lothrop, 1982) 4–6. Hobie and his friends think of a contest that will make the substitute teacher cry. Girls team up against the boys to see who can make her leave. They try everything imaginable.

2872. ____. *Four B. Goes Wild* (Lothrop, 1983) 4–6. The class is at Camp Trotter and faces a lot of new experiences. How does one handle a skunk who is sharp and determined? How do you face a midnight meeting in a cemetery?

2873. ____. *Hobie Hanson, You're Weird* (Lothrop, 1987) 4–6. Hobie Hanson is looking forward to the summer. Instead of going away he is going to stay at home. He teams up with his schoolmate Molly Bosco and has a hilarious time.

2874. ____. *Double Dog Dare* (Lothrop, 1988) 3–5. Because he wants to be "someone" Hobie feels he must make a name for himself. Nick was at Computer Camp, Molly is talented and Lisa was popular. But what is Harvey? Could he outwit Molly?

2875. ____. *Hobie Hanson, Greatest Hero of the Mall* (Lothrop, 1989) 4–6. When his town is devastated by a flood, Hobie's fifth grade class is forced to meet every day in the shopping mall.

2876. Gilson, Jamie. *Dial Leroi Rupert* (Lothrop, 1979) 4–6. Mitch's imitation of a local disk jockey gets him into trouble.

2877. ____. *Can't Catch Me, I'm the Gingerbread Man* (Lothrop, 1981) 4–6. When the family health food store burns down, 12-year-old Mitch is even more determined to win first prize in a Bake-a-thon with his special gingerbread.

2878. Gleeson, Libby. *Mum Goes to Work* (Omnibus, 1992) k–3. A story of the impact on children when the mother goes to work.

2879. ____. *Where's Mum?* (Omnibus, 1993) k–3. Amusing speculation on the whereabouts of a missing mother.

2880. Gleitzman, Morris. *Blabber Mouth* (Harcourt, 1995) 4–6. Rowena Batts is a resilient preteen who was born mute. She talks with her hands. She refuses to be looked upon as someone who needs to be somebody's community service project. Ro has an eccentric, loving father.

2881. ____. *Sticky Beak* (Harcourt, 1995) 4–6. Rowena is upset about the birth of a new sibling. When Rowena throws a sticky pink dessert into a fan during a school party, the descriptions of pineapple dripping off the principal's head are of much more interest than the family dynamics. The title refers to a foulmouthed, destructive cockatoo that Rowena rescues from a classmate.

2882. Glen, Maggie. *Ruby* (Putnam, 1991) k–3. Ruby, a teddy bear accidentally made out of the wrong material, leads other rejected toy bears in an escape from the toy factory and seeks a place where she will be appreciated.

2883. ____. *Ruby to the Rescue* (Putnam, 1992) k–3. Ruby, the teddy bear, is taken to school by her owner and carries out a plan to save two unwanted teddies in the playhouse there.

2884. Glendinning, Sally. *Jimmy and Joe Find a Ghost* (Garrard, 1969) k–3. Jimmy and Joe set out to find a ghost and finally think they have found a very wet one in the bathtub of a new house, which turns out to be a seal who has escaped from the zoo.

2885. ____. *Jimmy and Joe Catch an Elephant* (Garrard, 1969) k–3. Jimmy and Joe help capture an elephant which escapes from the circus and is upsetting the town.

2886. ____. *Jimmy and Joe Look for a Bear* (Garrard, 1970) k–3. Jimmy and Joe are on a Cub Scout picnic and hope to see a bear. They see their bear—and lost a birthday cake.

2887. ____. *Jimmy and Joe Get a Hen's Surprise* (Garrard, 1970) k–3. Jimmy and Joe are given two unusual gray hens. They are promised an unusual happening from them. They wonder what the surprise will be. The Arucana hens lay blue and green eggs.

2888. ____. *Jimmy and Joe Fly a Kite* (Garrard, 1970) k–3. Jimmy and Joe fly a kite and end up in City Hall with a strange bird they have found.

2889. ____. *Jimmy and Joe Meet a Halloween Witch* (Garrard, 1971) k–3. Jimmy and Joe, trick-or-treating at a spooky house, get a scare and a surprise.

2890. ____. *Jimmy and Joe Go to the Fair* (Garrard, 1971) k–3. A monkey and Rags the dog join Jimmy and Joe at the Fair.

2891. ___. *Jimmy and Joe Save a Christmas Deer* (Garrard, 1973) k–3. Jimmy and Joe are on their way to pick up a Christmas tree at Mr. Jones' dairy. They come upon a weak, undersized white-tailed deer. Joe bundles him up in his jacket and takes him on their sled to Mr. Jones' dairy. He is given milk and returned to the state park. The boys get a reward.

2892. Glenn, Mel. *Play-by-Play* (Clarion, 1986) 4–6. Fourth graders Jeremy and Lloyd are best friends until an interest in soccer makes Lloyd wildly competitive and changes their relationship.
2893. ___. *Squeeze Play* (Clarion, 1989) 4–6. With the support of gentle Mr. Janowicz, a Holocaust survivor, Jeremy speaks out against the bullying sixth grade teacher and his mandatory after-school baseball teams.

2894. Glydal, Monica. *When Olly Had a Little Brother* (Hodder, 1976) k–3. A story to help children cope with the stress caused by a new baby in the family.
2895. ___. *When Olly Went to the Hospital* (Hodder, 1976) k–3. A story to help children cope with the stress of a hospital visit.
2896. ___. *When Olly's Granddad Died* (Hodder, 1976) k–3. A story to help children cope with the stress of the death of a loved one.
2897. ___. *When Olly Saw an Accident* (Hodder, 1977) k–3. Olly has to learn not only a healthy measure of fear for traffic but that not all anger felt by others is directed at him.
2898. ___. *When Olly Moved House* (Hodder, 1977) k–3. Olly has to accept a new home, new friends and eventually a new school. He must transfer allegiance from old friends to new.

2899. Goble, Paul. *Iktomi and the Boulder* (Orchard, 1988) k–3. Iktomi, a Plains Indian trickster, attempts to defeat a boulder with the assistance of some bats, this story explains why the Great Plains are covered with small stones.
2900. ___. *Iktomi and the Berries* (Orchard, 1989) k–3. Relates Iktomi's fruitless efforts to pick some buffalo berries.
2901. ___. *Iktomi and the Ducks* (Orchard, 1990) k–3. After outwitting some ducks, Iktomi, the Indian trickster, is outwitted by Coyote.
2902. ___. *Iktomi and the Buffalo Skull* (Orchard, 1992) k–3. Mischievous Iktomi gets his comeuppance when he shows off for the girls.
2903. ___. *Iktomi and the Buzzard* (Orchard, 1994) k–3. Iktomi, the trickster, tries to fool a buzzard into carrying him across the river on the buzzard's back.

2904. Goldsmith, John. *Mrs. Babcary Goes to Town* (Pelham, 1980) k–3. Mrs. Babcary lives in a large cello, has a pet spider named Sophocles and wears a colander on her head secured with a hat pin.
2905. ___. *Mrs. Babcary Goes to Sea* (Pelham,

1980) k–3. Mrs. Babcary is an eccentric character who lives in a cello in the country. She insists on joining her sea-faring husband on a voyage in his gravy-boat. But she is glad to be back home after they are shipwrecked in a violent storm.
2906. ___. *Mrs. Babcary Goes West* (Pelham, 1980) k–3. Mrs. Babcary lives in a large cello, has a pet spider named Sophocles and wears a colander on her head secured with a hat pin. She goes on several adventures with her husband and by herself. This is an account of her western trip.

2907. Goodall, John S. *Adventures of Paddy Pork* (Harcourt, 1968) 3–5. A story of what befalls a young pig after he runs away to join a traveling circus.
2908. ___. *Ballooning Adventures of Paddy Pork* (Harcourt, 1969) 3–5. The further adventures of Paddy Pork as he sets out on a journey that takes him to many strange places.
2909. ___. *Paddy's Evening Out* (Atheneum, 1973) 3–5. When his companion drops her fan into the orchestra pit, Paddy's attempts to retrieve it inadvertently make him the star of the show.
2910. ___. *Paddy Pork's Holiday* (Altheneum, 1976) 3–5. A summer camping expedition turns into a series of unexpectedly dramatic adventures for young Paddy.
2911. ___. *Paddy's New Hat* (Atheneum, 1980) 3–5. The purchase of an elegant straw hat leads Paddy Pork into a series of wild adventures.
2912. ___. *Paddy Finds a Job* (McElderry, 1981) 3–5. Paddy goes to work as a waiter in an elegant restaurant, where he quickly becomes entangled in a lady poodle's feather boa.
2913. ___. *Paddy Goes Traveling* (Atheneum, 1982) 3–5. Paddy's vacation trip to the Riveria is not without incident, from the moment his umbrella trips the waiter in the dining car to his surprise trip down a snow-capped mountain.
2914. ___. *Paddy Pork, Odd Jobs* (Atheneum, 1983) 3–5. Several odd jobs lead Paddy Pork into a series of wild adventures.
2915. ___. *Paddy Under Water* (Atheneum, 1984) 3–5. Paddy's underwater adventures include rescuing a small sea monster from an octopus, meeting King Neptune and following a pack of mermaids to find a treasure chest.
2916. ___. *Paddy to the Rescue* (Atheneum, 1985) 3–5. Paddy Pig pursues a jewel thief over land and water and has the pleasure of returning the stolen goods to their very charming (???) owner.

2917. Goodall, John S. *Midnight Adventures of Kelly, Dot, and Esmeraldo* (Atheneum, 1972) k–3. A koala bear, a rag doll and a mouse journey together into a magic land.
2918. ___. *Kelly, Dot, and Esmeraldo* (Macmillan, 1972) k–3. A koala bear, a doll and a mouse are involved in a kidnapping, a rescue and a furious chase.

2919. Goodall, John S. *Shrewbettina's Birthday* (Harcourt, 1980) 2–4. The gallant gentleman who rescues Shrewbettina from a purse snatcher goes on to help her plan and give a grand birthday party.
2920. ____. *Shrewbettina Goes to Work* (Atheneum, 1981) 2–4. While employed as an assistant in a hat shop, Shrewbettina pursues and captures a purse snatcher.

2921. Goodall, John S. *Naughty Nancy* (Atheneum, 1975) 2–4. Nancy, a venturesome small mouse, creates a series of crises at her sister's wedding and reception.
2922. ____. *Naughty Nancy Goes to School* (Atheneum, 1985) 2–4. A story of Nancy's day at school. She is being dragged to school by her mother, she imitates the teacher behind her back, she falls off the roof and buries her teacher in sand on a field trip.

2923. Gordon, Margaret. *Wilberforce Goes on a Picnic* (Morrow, 1982) k–3. A depiction of the activities from sunrise to sunset the day Wilberforce and his family go on a picnic.
2924. ____. *Wilberforce Goes to a Party* (Viking, 1985) k–3. Wilberforce, a rambunctious young bear, goes to his first party where he makes plenty of mischief and has a good time.
2925. ____. *Wilberforce Goes Shopping* (Viking, 1985) k–3. A young bear gets into mischief when his grandparents take him on a shopping trip.
2926. ____. *Wilberforce Goes to the Playgroup* (Viking, 1987) k–3. Wilberforce is a naughty little bear who creates mayhem and gets what he wants. Miss Fudge, the playgroup leader, is the target for Wilberforce in this book.

2927. Gordon, Shirley. *Crystal is the New Girl* (Harper, 1976) k–3. Although Susan is determined not to be friends with the new girl in her class, her friendship with Crystal grows along with their ability to get into trouble.
2928. ____. *Crystal Is My Friend* (Harper, 1978) k–3. When Susan invites Crystal to spend the night, both learn the meaning of friendship.
2929. ____. *Happy Birthday, Crystal* (Harper, 1981) k–3. Susan copes with jealousy when she meets Crystal's other friend at Crystal's birthday party.
2930. ____. *Crystal's Christmas Carol* (Harper, 1989) k–3. Vivacious Crystal shows a reluctant Susan how to spread her Christmas spirit around when the two entertain customers in a shopping mall with a medley of carols.

2931. Gormley, Beatrice. *Fifth Grade Magic* (Dutton, 1982) 4–6. Devastated at not getting a part in the fifth grade play, Gretchen is surprised when her desperation conjures up a well-meaning but not very efficient fairy godmother.
2932. ____. *More Fifth Grade Magic* (Dutton, 1989) 4–6. Wishing she could be more assertive with her domineering mother, fifth grader and professional model Amy Sacher finds a magic calendar that can change her life.

2933. Goscinny, Rene. *Nicholas and the Gang Again* (Abelard, 1977) 4–6. When Nicholas visits the Art Gallery he is more interested in the highly polished floor on which he can slide than in the pictures. His teacher is not happy. Nicholas thinks it's because she doesn't like the pictures she sees.
2934. ____. *Nicholas and the Gang at School* (Abelard, 1977) 4–6. The school and home life of Nicholas and his friends. He is a pest to his teachers. Nicholas refers to Cuthberts as "teachers' pet" (but he wears glasses so you can't thump him) and Alec as "my fat friend who is always eating."
2935. ____. *Nicholas and the Gang* (Abelard, 1978) 4–6. Nicholas is incorrigible. He and his gang rampage through life, fighting and yelling and turning somersaults, etc. He means well but all his ideas turn to disasters.
2936. ____. *Nicholas on Holiday* (Abelard, 1978) 4–6. Nicholas and his friends savage hotels, render beaches uninhabitable and ruin teachers.
2937. ____. *Nicholas at Large* (Abelard, 1979) 4–6. Nicholas and his friends set up the most ridiculous pranks at school; at home his behavior is not much better. At the first sign of trouble Nicholas starts to cry and his parents quarrel among themselves about discipline.
2938. ____. *Chronicles of Little Nicholas* (Farrar, 1993) 4–6. A little French boy recounts the many escapades that he and his classmates indulge in as they make their way through a year at primary school.

2939. Gould, Marilyn. *Golden Daffodils* (Addison, 1982) 4–6. Wishing for a miracle to make her perfect and normal, a fifth grader with cerebral palsy transfers from a special school to a regular classroom.
2940. ____. *Twelfth of June* (Lippincott, 1986) 4–6. Janis, 12, copes with her cerebral palsy and her changing feelings for her good friend Barney as he approaches his bar mitzvah.

2941. Gowans, Elizabeth. *Shepherd's Warning* (Hamilton, 1985) 4–6. The Blair children's home is to be sold. They discover deliberate devilment. At Morlie Bay lighthouse they discover a clue that saves their home and the estate from the hands of developers.
2942. ____. *Shepherd's Flock* (Hamilton, 1987) 4–6. A positive story of the life of a shepherd's impoverished but not deprived family.

2943. Gower, Mick. *Billy and the Man-Eating Plant* (Macmillan, 1989) 4–6. Billy's sculpture of a man-eating plant wins a prize after many trials and tribulations.
2944. ____. *Billy and the Ghastly Ghost* (Macmillan, 1990) 4–6. Billy and Keith see a figure rising

from a grave in the churchyard and are convinced it is a ghost. But Christine won't believe it. They visit the churchyard at night with a camera but are stopped by the police. They go again in the daylight.

2945. Goyder, Alice. *Holiday in Catland* (Crowell, 1978) k–3. Four cats take a holiday at the seashore.
2946. ____. *Party in Catland* (Crowell, 1979) k–3. Two cats, Minnie and Tilly, decide to give a party for all of their friends.
2947. ____. *Christmas in Catland* (Crowell, 1979) k–3. Tilly and Minnie help the family get ready for Christmas and make secret wishes for the presents they want.

2948. Graham, Amanda. *Who Wants Arthur?* (G. Stevens, 1987) k–3. Arthur, a dog in a pet store waiting to be adopted, takes on the identity of other animals he thinks might be more appealing, until discovering that he can be a success as himself.
2949. ____. *Educating Arthur* (G. Stevens, 1988) 2–4. Rambunctious adopted dog Arthur wreaks havoc with his attempts to "help" the James family, until they start training him with a rewards system.
2950. ____. *Always Arthur* (G. Stevens, 1990) 2–4. Good-natured Arthur is happy when another dog comes to live in his household but he soon begins to feel ignored and left out as the new dog seems to claim all the family's attention.

2951. Graham, Bob. *Here Comes Theo* (Little, 1983) k–3. A small bouncy dog likes to give the children he lives with the "licking treatment."
2952. ____. *Here Comes John* (Little, 1983) k–3. A snail must tolerate the threats of pesticides, a dog, a little girl and, more importantly, one small boy.
2953. ____. *Bathtime for John* (Little, 1985) k–3. While John bathes, his dog Theo steals his plastic frog out of the tub.

2954. Graham, Brenda. *Patterson at Turkey Hill House* (Broadman, 1980) 4–6. Frank, 12, and Rita, 10, spend the summer in their country home. They befriend a 17-year-old recluse living in the woods. He is a runaway. All ends well with Frank and Rita's family and also the runaway's.
2955. ____. *Patterson and the Mysterious Airplane* (Broadman, 1981) 4–6. Children try to start a worm farm to raise money. An airplane crashes on their property. The children rescue the pilot. The publicity helps the children's father save his land.

2956. Graham, Harriet. *Ring of Zoraya* (Atheneum, 1982) 5–8. In the late 19th century while traveling on the Orient Express to St. Petersburg, William, Flora and their guardian meet the Crown Prince of Slovidia and find themselves unexpectedly caught up in an adventure.
2957. ____. *Chinese Puzzle* (Houghton, 19088) 5–8. In London of the 1890s, William and Flora set out to find their guardian a magician, who has disappeared, and find themselves captive in an opium den.

2958. Graham, Margaret. *Benjy and the Barking Bird* (Harper, 1971) k–3. When Aunt Sarah brings her barking parrot for a visit, Benjy the dog feels terribly unwanted.
2959. ____. *Benjy's Dog House* (Harper, 1973) k–3. Unwilling to sleep in his new doghouse, Benjy looks elsewhere for a nighttime home.
2960. ____. *Benjy's Boat Trip* (Harper, 1977) k–3. A small dog takes a surprise boat trip and meets the ship's angry cat.
2961. ____. *Benjy and His Friend Fifi* (Harper, 1988) k–3. Lovable mutt Benjy accompanies his shy nervous poodle friend Fifi to her first dog show where chaotic adventures ensue.

2962. Graham, Thomas. *Mr. Bear's Chair* (Dutton, 1987) k–3. When Mrs. Bear's chair breaks, Mr. Bear spends all day making her a new one that's just right.
2963. ____. *Mr. Bear's Boat* (Dutton, 1988) k–3. Mr. Bear builds a sailboat and takes Mrs. Bear for what they hope will be a peaceful ride—but is not.

2964. Gramatky, Hardie. *Little Toot* (Putnam, 1939) 3–5. Little Toot is a saucy little tugboat too pleased with himself to do any real work until one day when he finds himself out in the ocean in a storm. Then Little Toot earns the right to be called a hero.
2965. ____. *Little Toot on the Thames* (Putnam, 1964) 3–5. Little Toot, the little tugboat, becomes involved in many adventures with the inhabitants along the Thames river when he gets lost and finds himself in London.
2966. ____. *Little Toot on the Grand Canal* (Putnam, 1968) 3–5. Little Toot visits the beautiful palaces of Venice, travels its secluded waterways and learns to blow Venetian glass bubbles which helps him to save the city from a ship of thieving pirates.
2967. ____. *Little Toot on the Mississippi* (Putnam, 1973) 3–5. Little Toot finally finds the old steamboats just in time to urge them out of retirement to save the bayou animals from the flooding Mississippi.
2968. ____. *Little Toot Through the Golden Gate* (Putnam, 1975) 3–5. Little Toot has fun in San Francisco Bay until he gets lost in the fog.
2969. ____. *Little Toot and the Loch Ness Monster* (Putnam, 1989) 3–5. Little Toot travels to Scotland where he befriends the Loch Ness Monster.

2970. Grambling, Lois. *Elephant and Mouse Get Ready for Christmas* (Barron, 1990) k–3. Elephant and Mouse are hanging their stockings for Santa Claus, but Mouse's stocking is so small, Elephant tries to think of a way to rectify this but his solution mystifies Santa.
2971. ____. *Elephant and Mouse Get Ready for Easter* (Barron, 1991) k–3. Tomorrow is Easter, and

Elephant and Mouse are excited. They plan to leave a gift for Easter Rabbit.

2972. ____. *Elephant and Mouse Celebrate Halloween* (Barron, 1991) k–3. Elephant and Mouse give a Halloween party for a strange assortment of guests. This story has a comical, spooky ending.

2973. Grand, Rebecca. *Case of the Missing Socks* (Holt, 1986) k–3. Wembley and Boober, two Fraggle friends, set out to catch the mysterious thief who is stealing Boober's socks.

(For additional books on the Fraggles, Boober, Gobo, Mokey, Red or Wembley, *see* Brennan, Joseph; Calder, Lyn, Calmenson, Stephanie; Gilkow, Louise; Gilmour, M.B; Muntean, Michaela; Perlberg, Deborah; Stevenson, Jocelyn; Teitelbaum, Michael; Weiss, Ellen; Young, David.)

2974. Grant, John. *Littlenose, the Hero* (Hodder, 1971) 3–5.
2975. ____. *Littlenose the Fisherman* (Hodder, 1972) 3–5. Littlenose, his family and his pet mammoth, Two-Eyes, live in Neanderthal times.
2976. ____. *More Adventures of Littlenose* (Hodder, 1976) 3–5.
2977. ____. *Littlenose Goes South* (Hodder, 1976) 3–5. Littlenose and his pet mammoth, Two-Eyes, live in the Ice Age. He goes to the warm South for the winter with his Uncle Redhead. They cross the Alps, go down the Nile and avoid a cannibal tribe. They witness a volcano eruption and have an exciting time.
2978. ____. *Littlenose* (Hodder, 1983) 3–5. Littlenose can get into mischief with his pet mammoth, Two-Eyes.
2979. ____. *Littlenose and Two-Eyes* (Hodder, 1986) 3–5.

2980. Grant, Myrna. *Ivan and the Star of David* (Tyndale, 1977) 4–6. Ivan and his family use all their ingenuity and courage to help a Jewish girl leave Russia.
2981. ____. *Ivan and the Secret in the Suitcase* (Stang, 1988) 4–6. Ivan, 13, wants to help a needy family who have members in prison. They smuggle in clothes and books from Hungary.
2982. ____. *Ivan and the Hidden Bible* (Stang, 1988) 4–6.
2983. ____. *Ivan and the American Journey* (Stang, 1988) 4–6.
2984. ____. *Ivan and the Informer* (Stang, 1989) 4–6.
2985. ____. *Ivan and the Daring Escape* (Stang, 1989) 4–6. A young Russian Christian uses his ingenuity and faith to rescue his friend held by the secret police.

2986. Gray, Patricia. *Star Lost* (Norton, 1965) 4–6. Deb and Maureen want to prove that Deb is responsible enough to care for a horse. But Star Bright runs away and Maureen's horse, Patches, and the two girls look for him.

2987. ____. *Star Bright* (Norton, 1964) 4–6. Deb's colt, Star Bright, is mischievous and causes trouble because of Deb's lack of training. She must get rid of him. She does but finds that miracles do happen.
2988. ____. *Star, the Sea Horse* (Nelson, 1968) 4–6. Deb and her cousin Kathy have Star Bright on their vacation. They get jobs in a local stable and learn more about horses and riding.

2989. Greaves, Margaret. *Charlie, Emma and Alberic* (Methuen, 1980) 3–5. Charlie found what he thought was a lizard but turned out to be a talking dragon. This cheerful little dragon settles down to life on Mill Street as Charlie's pet. He remains invisible most of the time to everyone except Charlie and Emma.
2990. ____. *Charlie, Emma and the Dragon Family* (Methuen, 1982) 3–5. In this story two adults can now see the baby dragon, Aunt Sophie gets Alberic and family to stop Mr. Pott from turning a vacant lot into a parking lot but instead make it a children's playground.
2991. ____. *Charlie, Emma and the School Dragon* (Methuen, 1984) 3–5. The dragons have decided that their youngest son Ashley should attend school with Charlie and Emma. Ashley has a tendency to get carried away and does not always remember to stay invisible.
2992. ____. *Charlie, Emma and Dragon to the Rescue* (Methuen, 1986) 3–5. Ashley, Godric, and Lu San are dragons who come to spend a vacation on Earth. They help Charlie and Emma raise money for an Animal Sanctuary and rescue an old donkey. But no one believes they see dragons because they don't exist.

2993. Greene, Carol. *Robin Hill* (Harper, 1986) 3–5. Despite the loving support of her parents and little brother, Robin finds life unfair because she must deal with a crabby landlord and the impossibility of getting everything she wants.
2994. ____. *Jenny Summer* (Harper, 1988) 3–5. When a new family with a girl her own age moves in next door, Robin discovers the pleasure of having a best friend and the pain of losing her.

2995. Greenleaf, Ann. *Max and Molly's Fall* (Outlet, 1994) k–3. A family of moles participate in activities associated with autumn.
2996. ____. *Max and Molly's Winter* (Outlet, 1994) k–3. A family of moles participate in activities associated with winter.
2997. ____. *Max and Molly's Summer* (Outlet, 1994) k–3. A family of moles participate in activities associated with summer.

2998. Greenwald, Sheila. *Give Us a Great Big Smile, Rosy Cole* (Little, 1981) 4–6. Uncle Ralph is to do a pictorial on Rose but all she can do is play violin and not very good. The book *A Very Young Fiddler* is all a lie but it works out well in the end.

2999. _____. *Valentine Rosy* (Little, 1984) 4–6. When Rosy's friend Hermione announces that Rosy is having a Valentine party, a dismayed Rosy finds herself in unwilling competition with the sophisticated Christi who is planning an exclusive party on the same day.

3000. _____. *Rosy Cole's Great American Guilt Club* (Atlantic, 1985) 4–6. Convinced that she doesn't have any of the things that matter (trendy clothes and a house in the country), Rosy Cole decides to form a club which will allow her rich friends to give her their surplus things.

3001. _____. *Write on, Rosy* (Little, 1988) 4–6. Young Author's Day sets Rosy on her way to becoming a writer. She writes about the school principal and draws all the wrong conclusions.

3002. _____. *Rosy's Romance* (Little, 1989) 4–6. Rosy and her friend Hermione attempt to help Rosy's teenage sisters live out the romantic fantasies they have been reading about in paperback books.

3003. _____. *Here's Hermione* (Little, 1991) 4–6. Rosy becomes the manager of her best friend's unusual rock band.

3004. _____. *Rosy Cole Discovers America* (Joy Street, 1992) Disappointed in the poor European immigrant ancestors she discovers during a class project to research family roots, Rosy cooks up a clan of royal relatives.

3005. _____. *Rosy Cole: She Walks in Beauty* (Little, 1994) 4–6. Rosy finds out how difficult it is to become one of the beautiful people.

3006. Greenwald, Sheila. *Mariah Delany's Lending Library Disaster* (Houghton, 1977) 4–6. Mariah, 11, sets up her own lending library in competition with the New York Public Library and finds herself involved in more than she bargained for.

3007. _____. *Mariah Delany's Author of the Month Club* (Joy Street, 1990) 4–6. Mariah invites authors to speak at her Author of the Month Club with near disastrous results.

3008. Greer, Gery. *Max and Me and the Time Machine* (Harcourt, 1983) 4–6. Steve buys a time machine at a garage sale and takes his friend Max to the year 1250, where they land in the middle of a jousting match, with the fierce Sir Bevis as an enemy.

3009. _____. *Max and Me and the Wild West* (Harcourt, 1988) 4–6. Steve and his friend Max use their time machine to return to the richest, roughest boom town in the old Wild West.

3010. Greer, Gery. *Jason and the Aliens Down the Street* (Harper, 1991) 2–4. Jason meets Cooper Vor and Lootna, aliens from space now living on Earth, and travels with them to a distant planet in an attempt to retrieve a stolen energy crystal.

3011. _____. *Jason and the Lizard Pirates* (Harper, 1992) 2–4. Jason, Cooper Vor, and Lootna kick a band of Lizard Pirates off the planet Lumaloon in the further adventures of the Intergalactic Troubleshooting Team.

3012. _____. *Jason and the Escape from the Bat Planet* (Harper, 1993) 2–4. Jason, Cooper Vor and Lootna grapple with General Batso and his evil Demon Bats in more adventures of the Intergalactic Troubleshooting Team.

3013. Gregory, Philippa. *Princess Florizella* (Candlewick, 1990) 3–5. Princess is not interested in getting married. She wants to help the people of her country. She saves a prince from a dragon and earns his respect for her independence.

3014. _____. *Florizella and the Wolves* (Candlewick, 1993) 3–5. While riding in the Purple Forest, a young princess finds four wolf cubs that cause quite a commotion when she brings them back to the castle and tries to hide them from the king and queen.

3015. Gregory, Valiska. *Terribly Wonderful* (Macmillan, 1986) k–3. When Scamp loses his voice, Mr. Poggle prescribes plenty of sunlight, books and warm blankets to make him feel better.

3016. _____. *Sunny Side Up* (Four Winds, 1986) k–3. Scamp helps Mr. Poggle make breakfast and learns that even broken eggs and burnt toast have a sunny side.

3017. Gretz, Susanna. *Teddy Bears 1 to 10* (Four Winds, 1969/1987) k–3. As teddy bears are washed, dried, take the bus, and have tea they introduce the numbers one to ten.

3018. _____. *Teddy Bears Stay Indoors* (Four Winds, 1971/1989) k–3. The five teddy bears amuse themselves on a rainy day playing that they go into space, but mostly they eat.

3019. _____. *Teddy Bears at the Seaside* (Four Winds, 1973/1989) k–3. Five teddy bears and their dog enjoy a variety of activities at the seashore.

3020. _____. *Teddy Bears ABC* (Four Winds, 1975/1986) k–3. The letters of the alphabet describe the various activities of five teddy bears, from arriving in an airplane to zipping off to the zoo.

3021. _____. *Teddy Bears Go Shopping* (Four Winds, 1982) k–3. The teddy bears cause a commotion in the supermarket when they go grocery shopping.

3022. _____. *Teddy Bears Cure a Cold* (Four Winds, 1984) k–3. When William's cold seems to be lingering too long and his demands for attention increase, the other teddy bears work a miraculous cure.

3023. _____. *I'm Not Sleepy* (Four Winds, 1986) k–3. While all the other teddy bears are sleepily going off to bed, John feels wide awake and wants to play.

3024. _____. *Ready for Bed* (Four Winds, 1986) k–3. Teddy Bear Andrew has trouble getting ready for bed.

3025. _____. *Too Dark* (Four Winds, 1986) k–3. Even familiar objects can look scary for a teddy bear trying to fall asleep in a dark room.

3026. _____. *Hide-and-Seek* (Four Winds, 1986) k–3.

Louise finds the perfect place to hide in the teddy bears' game of hide-and-seek.

3027. ____. *Teddy Bears Take the Train* (Four Winds, 1987) k–3. The teddy bears' train trip to see Uncle Jerome is filled with songs, games and surprises.

3028. ____. *Teddy Bears Moving Day* (Four Winds, 1988) k–3. Five teddy bears move to a new house on Green Street.

3029. Gretz, Susanna. *It's Your Turn, Roger* (Dutton, 1985) k–3. After Roger, the pig, visits the other families in his apartment building to find out who has to help with dinner, he realizes the value of taking his turn to set the dinner table.

3030. ____. *Roger Takes Charge* (Dial, 1987) k–3. Roger, the pig, and his neighbor's bossy daughter vie for the honor of being in charge when a parental absence frees them for rambunctious activities.

3031. ____. *Roger Loses His Marbles* (Dial, 1988) k–3. When Aunt Lulu pays a visit, she stays in Roger's room and tidies it up which makes him mad until she finds something that Roger lost.

3032. ____. *Roger Mucks In* (Dial, 1991) k–3. Roger learns the meaning of sharing. He makes the family's (of pigs) journey to the beach as difficult as possible. When he gets there he doesn't want to share anything. But Uncle Tim and Auntie Lulu soon put him in his place. He is almost cured by the time its time to go home.

3033. Gretz, Susanna. *Frog in the Middle* (Four Winds, 1991) k–3. Both Frog and Rabbit can hop, both Frog and Duck can swim. This can lead to hurt feelings, especially when Duck and Rabbit start whispering secrets which turn out to be about a party for Frog.

3034. ____. *Duck Takes Off* (Four Winds, 1991) k–3. Bossy Duck insists that the others learn to dive, fly, quack and waddle. Disgusted, the others leave but loneliness reunites them under Rabbit's more accommodating tutelage.

3035. ____. *Rabbit Rambles On* (Four Winds, 1992) k–3. Rabbit boasts to his friends Duck and Frog that he can do juggling and balancing tricks. But when they ask for proof, Rabbit rambles on. Fed up with his stories, Duck and Frog decide to teach Rabbit a lesson.

3036. ____. *Frog, Duck and Rabbit* (Four Winds, 1992) Frog, Duck and Rabbit are making a costume for a parade and can't agree on what it should look like. What begins as a fun project ends up in a battle. But they put their differences aside and make the best costume.

3037. Grifalconi, Ann. *Darkness and the Butterfly* (Little, 1987) k–3. Small Osa is fearless during the day, climbing trees or exploring the African valley where she lives, but at night she becomes afraid of the strange and terrifying things that might lie in the dark.

3038. ____. *Osa's Pride* (Little, 1989) k–3. Osa's grandmother tells her a tale about the sins of pride and helps Osa gain a better perspective on what things are important.

3039. Griffith, Helen. *Alex and the Cat* (Greenwillow, 1982) 3–5. Three stories about Alex, who wants to be treated like the family cat, or live wild like a wolf, and who tries to restore a baby bird to a robin's nest.

3040. ____. *Alex Remembers* (Greenwillow, 1983) 3–5. A dog and a cat are restless and troubled in the autumn moonlight as primordial fears stir in them, but their young owner is there to comfort them.

3041. ____. *More Alex and the Cat* (Greenwillow, 1983) 3–5. The cat teaches Alex the dog a few more lessons, and vice versa.

3042. Griffith, Helen. *Georgia Music* (Greenwillow, 1986) 3–5. A little girl and her grandfather share two different kinds of music; that of his mouth organ and that of the birds and insects around his cabin.

3043. ____. *Granddaddy's Place* (Greenwillow, 1987) 3–5. At first Janetta does not like Granddaddy, his farm or his animals—but they like her, and as she gets use to them, she likes them too.

3044. ____. *Granddaddy and Janetta* (Greenwillow, 1993) 3–5. Janetta enjoys her visit to her grandfather, including such highlights as listening to the night insects make music and admiring his cat's new kittens.

3045. Griffith, John. *Griff and Tommy* (Dent, 1956/1967) 3–5. Two brothers, aged 8 and 11, get in and out of trouble and have fun in a South Wales mining village where they live.

3046. ____. *Griff and Tommy and the Golden Image* (Dent, 1977) 3–5.

3047. Grimshaw, Nigel. *Wildkeepers' Guest* (Faber, 1976) 5–8. Three beings from outer space and time come into Earth's world and become involved in a supernatural conflict. Joan, a girl with unusual powers, and the Wildkeepers, an ancient race who live in secret, help to successfully resolve the conflict.

3048. ____. *Blunkstone and the Wildkeepers* (Faber, 1978) 5–8. When the Wildkeepers are threatened by a builder named Bluntstone and his "yellow soil eating monsters," the little people call on dark magic to save themselves.

3049. Grisae, Jeannette. *Robert Benjamin and the Great Blue Dog Joke* (Westminster, 1978) 4–6. Fond of playing practical jokes, a fifth grader finally realizes that it is more fun to make people laugh at you than to embarrass and humiliate them.

3050. ____. *Robert Benjamin and the Disappearing Act* (Westminster, 1980) 4–6. While checking out tourist attractions in the Philadelphia area for a teacher-guidebook, writer Robert becomes involved with a girl who keeps disappearing into other time periods.

3051. Grogaard, John. *Jeg, Wilhelm, 11 ar 1889* (Tilden, 1981) 5–8. Set in Oslo 100 years ago this is a story of everyday blue-collar life. It describes labor strikes and hard times along with class solidarity and helpfulness among families.
3052. ____. *Jeg, Wilhelm, 12 ar 1890* (Tilden, 1986) 5–8. A young boy living in Oslo 100 years ago tells what it is like to grow up in that time and place.
3053. ____. *Jeg, Wilhelm, 13 ar 1891* (Tilden, 1986) 5–8. The further descriptions of growing up in Oslo 100 years ago. Wilhelm is now older and we learned about three years of his life.

3054. Groman, Gal. *Gertie McMichaels Finds Blood and Gore and Much More* (McGraw, 1971) 5–8. Gertie becomes a teenage detective when the local stable burns and the owner and Gertie's horse disappear.
3055. ____. *Gertie McMichaels and the Odd Body Mystery* (McGraw) 5–8. Continues the adventures of Gertie as she manages to create an international incident and get herself and her family kidnapped to a primitive island.

3056. Guy, Rosa. *Paris, Pee Wee and Big Dog* (Delacorte, 1984) 4–6. When his mother goes off to work one Saturday, ten-year-old Paris and two friends spend the day on the streets of New York having fun and some hair-raising adventures, too.
3057. ____. *Pee Wee and Big Dog* (Delacorte, 1985) 4–6. Paris and his friend Pee Wee go skating and are joined by Big Dog who is only nine. They get into one misadventure after another.

3058. Haas, Dorothy. *Burton's Zoom Zoom Va-Room Machine* (Bradbury, 1990) 4–6. Evil Professor Savvy tries to steal Burton's newest invention, a rocket-powered skateboard.
3059. ____. *Burton and the Giggle Machine* (Bradbury, 1992) 4–6. When Burton invents a machine to make people laugh, it arouses curiosity and greed in the evil Professor Savvy.

3060. Haas, Dorothy. *Dorothy and the Seven-Leaf Clover* (Random, 1985) 3–5. When Toto disappears while they are visiting their friends in Oz, Dorothy finds him caught by an unusual Golden Boy who is under the spell of the Wicked Witch of the West.
3061. ____. *Dorothy and Old King Crow* (Random, 1986) 3–5. Luckily for Dorothy, Spelling Bee helps her spell a hard word so she can break King Crow's spell over Scarecrow.

3062. Haas, Jessie. *Keeping Barney* (Greenwillow, 1982) 4–6. Actually having a horse and taking care of it, instead of just dreaming about it, turns out to be more than Sarah bargained for.

3063. ____. *Horse Like Barney* (Greenwillow, 1993) 4–6. Finally given permission to have a horse of her own, Sarah looks at a series of Morgans and finds herself being scared, being bored and falling in love with too many horses.

3064. Haddon, Mark. *Baby Dinosaurs in the Garden* (Western, 1994) k–3. Baby Dinosaur observes all the activities that can be done in the garden.
3065. ____. *Baby Dinosaurs on Vacation* (Western, 1994) k–3. Baby Dinosaur goes on vacation and learns about new activities.
3066. ____. *Baby Dinosaurs at Home* (Western, 1994) k–3. Baby Dinosaur shows the many activities that take place in his home.
3067. ____. *Baby Dinosaurs at Playground* (Western, 1994) k–3. Baby Dinosaur demonstrates all the activities of the playground.

3068. Haigh, Sheila. *Watch for the Ghost* (Methuen, 1975) 4–6. Resentful, backward, 11-year-old Dan is redeemed by an old woman's encouragement.
3069. ____. *Watch for Smoke* (Methuen, 1978) 4–6. Dan has a phobia about swimming; he is scorned by his schoolmates. What is the dilemma that comes from a good cause but flouts rules?
3070. ____. *Watch for the Champion* (Methuen, 1980) 4–6. Dan Rivers, amateur detective, wonders why Smoke disappears after school. He follows her and finds she's training as a gymnast at the local Sports Center.
3071. ____. *Watch for Danger* (Methuen, 1983) 4–6. Dan wants to go to camp but he has to share a tent with Archie with whom he never got along. Archie dares Dan to go on a cave expedition, all ends well.
3072. ____. *Watch for the Tide* (Methuen, 1988) 4–6.

3073. Halacy, D.S. *Rocket Rescue* (Nelson, 1968) 5–8. Lee is in Space Squadron and Grant is in Space Rescue. Little does he realize that his training is going to be used to rescue Lee.
3074. ____. *Sky Trap* (Nelson, 1975) 5–8. Grant is involved with a gang of smugglers bringing heroin across the border. He makes best use of his glider plane.

3075. Halam, Ann. *Daymaker* (Watts, 1987) 5–8. Zanne uses her PSI talents to resurrect the machines that sapped Earth's vitality; animals and plants die. She must decide between magic and science.
3076. ____. *Transformations* (Watts, 1988) 5–8. Zanne is asked to shut down a destructive energy source, a machine. She runs into resistance before she completes her task.

3077. Hale, Kathleen. *Orlando, the Marmalade Cat* (Warne, 1990) 4–6. It is easy to believe in cats who keep a poodle for a pet, walk on stilts and drive a car that covers its headlights with thick eyelashes at night because it can see better in the dark.

3078. ____. *Orlando's Camping Holiday* (Warne, 1950/1990) 4–6. A republished edition in its original large format. Orlando entertains the kittens with a demonstration of cat's cradle.

3079. ____. *Orlando Goes to the Moon* (Warne, 1968/1984) 4–6. Catmint Mewing-gum and glow worms are packed in Orlando's moon rocket; the cats are comforted after a rough landing by a hospitable Man in the Moon and summer visitors provide added interest.

3080. ____. *Orlando Buys a Cottage* (Warne, 1971) 4–6.

3081. ____. *Orlando and the Water Cats* Describes a family visit to France to visit the Water cats. The water cats turn out to be reflections of themselves in the water.

3082. ____. *Orlando and the Frisky Housewife* (Warne, 1972) 4–6. Orlando opens a shop, The Frisky Housewife, which will not sell what consumers do not need. He is helped by cats, zoo animals, a poor artist and a magic carpet. The shop is a success.

3083. ____. *Orlando and the Three Graces* (Warne, 1984) 4–6. Orlando and his family are transported to the baroque world of Santa Claws.

3084. ____. *Orlando the Judge* (Warne, 1984) 4–6.

3085. ____. *Orlando Buys a Farm* (Warne, 1990) 4–6. Orlando and his family purchase a run-down farm and make it into a profitable enterprise.

3086. ____. *Orlando Keeps a Dog* (Warne, 1990) k–3. Orlando, the Marmalade cat, keeps a poodle for a pet.

3087. ____. *Orlando's Home Life* (Warne, 1992) 4–6. Things don't turn out as Orlando and his wife, Grace, planned for their three children. Despite his ambitions his children prove highly resistant to education.

3088. ____. *Orlando Has a Silver Wedding* (Warne, 1994) 4–6.

3089. Hall, Lynn. *Mystery of Plum Park Pony* (Garrard, 1980) 3–5. Searching the amusement park for a pony only Susan has seen, Susan and Kent track it into the Tunnel of Terror. Just as they realize the pony is trapped inside, the train begins its test run.

3090. ____. *Mystery of Pony Hollow* (Gerrard, 1983) 3–5. Sarah must put to rest the ghost of a horse.

3091. ____. *Mystery of the Pony Hollow Panda* (Garrard, 1983) 3–5. A bewildering mystery told in a humorous way.

3092. Hall, Lynn. *In Trouble Again, Zelda Hammersmith?* (Harcourt, 1987) 3–5. Zelda, a fourth grader, deals with a bad report card, a boy who does not want to be her boyfriend, the loss of her best friend and other tribulations.

3093. ____. *Zelda Strikes Again* (Harcourt, 1988) 3–5. Zelda crashes a stranger's funeral, sneaks on board an airplane, causes her substitute teacher to collapse and gets into all kinds of trouble.

3094. ____. *Here Comes Zelda Claus* (Harcourt, 1989) 3–5. Relates the amusing holiday misadventures of Zelda Hammersmith, whose good intentions only lead to trouble.

3095. Hall, Lynn. *Horse Called Dragon* (Follett, 1971) 3–5. Dragon was the leader of a herd of wild mustangs. He was captured, tamed and sires a new breed of horse: The Pony of the Americas (POA) pony. This new breed is intelligent, courageous and proud.

3096. ____. *New Day for Dragon* (Follett, 1975) 3–5. The story gives more background about Dragon, the Mexican mustang. His development was due in large part to the love and devotion shown him by his owners.

3097. ____. *Dragon Defiant* (Follett, 1977) 3–5. Dragon, prized as one of the foundation sires of the Pony of the Americas breed, is sold as a stud for a small breeding farm in Michigan.

3098. ____. *Dragon's Delight* (Follett, 1981) 3–5. With their horse breeding operation threatened, Wilda and Abby experience mixed feelings about the discovery that before he dies, their stallion Dragon had mated with the yearling filly Delight. As a yearling, is Delight too young to have a foal?

3099. Hall, Lynn. *Secret Life of Dagmar Schultz* (Scribner, 1988) 4–6. Living in a small Iowa community with few boys her age, Dagmar, 12, invents a fantasy boyfriend, who causes trouble when he argues with her and makes her talk back to him.

3100. ____. *Dagmar Schultz and the Angel Edna* (Scribner, 1989) 4–6. Boy-crazy Dagmar, 13, finally locates potential romance in her quiet Iowa community, only to find herself the special project of a guardian angel with very old-fashioned morals.

3101. ____. *Dagmar Schultz and the Power of Darkness* (Scribner, 1989) 4–6. Dagmar makes a deal with Edgar, New Berlin, Iowa's only warlock; he'll use his powers to make James Mann fall in love with her if Dagmar can convince Aunt Gretchen to go out on a date with Edgar.

3102. ____. *Dagmar Schultz and the Green Eyed Monster* (Scribner, 1991) 4–6. Jealous of a pretty and popular new student, Dagmar, 13, decides to get even with humorous results.

3103. Hall, Terry. *Kevin's Dirty Shirt* (Hart-Davis, 1977) k–3.

3104. ____. *Kevin at the Launderette* (Hart-Davis, 1977) k–3.

3105. ____. *Kevin Plays Leapfrog* (Hart-Davis, 1977) k–3.

3106. Hall, Willis. *Antelope Company Ashore* (Bodley, 1986) 4–6. The perils and narrow escapes suffered by Spelbush, Brelia and Fistram when they were established in Mr. Garstanton's house. Gerald and Philipa store the refugees in a dolls' house.

3107. ____. *Antelope Company at Large* (Bodley, 1988) 4–6. Harwell tries to capture the Liliputians (Spelbush, Fistram and Brelia) for public exhibition. Ernest, a boot-black and Emily, an escaped orphan, try to protect them.

3108. ____. *Return of the Antelope* (Bodley, 1990) 4–6. Gerald and Philipa find the wreckage of a tiny ship and three small survivors who prove to be Liliputians. It is no easy task for them to conceal and protect their little guests.

3109. Hamilton, Virginia. *House of Dies Drear* (Macmillan, 1968) 5–8. The brooding house, former station on the Underground Railroad and reputedly the last stop for runaway slaves, holds secrets unlocked by Thomas Small, whose family is threatened by dangers from attitudes as old as their home.

3110. ____. *Mystery of Drear House* (Greenwillow, 1987) 5–8. A black family living in the house of the long-dead abolitionist Dies Drear must decide what to do with his stupendous treasure, hidden for one hundred years in a cavern near their home.

3111. Hamilton, Virginia. *Time-Age Tales of Jahdu* (Macmillan, 1969) k–3. Mama Luka, baby-sitter, tells these tales to Lee Edward. They are the adventures of Jahdu, who is both mischievous and benevolent.

3112. ____. *Time-Ago Lost More Tales of Jahdu* (Macmillan, 1973) k–3. Mama Luka's building is to be demolished and she must move away. Lee Edward will miss her stories of Jahdu but knows he will see her again.

3113. Hammond, Ray. *Bobby Meets a Pirate* (Century, 1984) 2–4. Bytes as polymorphous people shaping themselves to the requirements of the users, and getting caught up with the topics of the programs that are being executed, is the basis of this story.

3114. ____. *Bobby Catches a Bug* (Century, 1984) 2–4. The eponymous blob (fat, green and yellow and made up of eight bits) has exciting adventures participating in computer programs.

3115. Hanford, Martin. *Where's Waldo?* (Walker, 1987) k–3. Waldo is going to go hiking; he has his walking stick, his sleeping bag, binoculars and other gear. He goes through town, by the seaside, on ski slopes, and on and on.

3116. ____. *Find Waldo Now* (Walker, 1988) k–3. The reader searches for Waldo from the Stone Age to the Space Age. He sees all the activities of the people: fighting, beheading and other unsavory things.

3117. ____. *Great Waldo Search* (Little, 1989) k–3. Waldo embarks on a fantastic journey among the Gobbling Gluttons, the Battling Monks, the Deep-sea Divers, the Underground Hunters, and the Land of Waldos in search of a special scroll.

3118. ____. *Where's Waldo? In Hollywood* (Can-

dlewick, 1993) k–3. The reader is invited to find Waldo in the detailed illustrations of several crowded Hollywood movie sets.

3119. Hannan, Peter. *Sillyville or Bust* (Knopf, 1990) k–3. Ruby and her brother's boring car trip with Aunt Ida and Uncle Guss turns exciting when they make an unscheduled stop in Sillyville.

3120. ____. *Battle of Sillyville* (Knopf, 1991) k–3. Lemuel B. Nutty comes to the aid of the residents of Sillyville when Delbert S. Dullard threatens to turn the town into Drabville II.

3121. Hansen, Carla. *Barnaby Bear Builds a Boat* (Random, 1979) k–3. A bear and his animal friends build a boat.

3122. ____. *Barnaby Bear Visits the Farm* (Random, 1970) k–3. Even though Barnaby Bear and his friends know nothing about farming they decide to help Gregory Goat with his spring planting anyway.

3123. Hansen, Joyce. *Which Way Freedom?* (Walker, 1987) 5–8. Obi escapes from slavery during the Civil War, joins a Black Union regiment, and soon becomes involved in the bloody fighting at Fort Pillow, Tennessee.

3124. ____. *Out from This Place* (Walker, 1988) 5–8. A 14-year-old black girl tries to find a fellow ex-slave, who had joined the Union Army during the Civil War, during the confusing times after the emancipation of the slaves.

3125. Hansen, Joyce. *Gift-Giver* (Houghton, 1980) 4–6. Doris is friends with Amir, a foster boy. He helps her understand her own family and its rules and love.

3126. ____. *Yellow Bird and Me* (Clarion, 1986) 4–6. Doris becomes friends with Yellow Bird as she helps him with his studies and his part in the school play and discovers that he has a problem known as dyslexia.

3127. Hanson, June. *Summer of the Stallion* (Macmillan, 1979) 4–6. Janey, 12, spends the summer on a ranch. She takes part in a stallion round-up.

3128. ____. *Winter of the Owl* (Macmillan, 1980) 4–6. Janey wants to break a colt on Christmas vacation but doesn't have the time. The colt is trapped in ice and an owl alerts Janey. She saves the horse's life.

3129. Hardcastle, Michael. *Roar to Victory* (Methuen, 1982) 4–5. Lee and his brother look like twins but are different in character. Joanne encourages Lee to race, he does so and wins and the cheaters get their comeuppance.

3130. ____. *Fast from the Gate* (Methuen, 1984) 4–6. Lee excels in Motocross racing. His rival is his older brother, Darren. His bike is stolen and he might miss an important race.

3131. Hargreaves, Roger. *Mr. Tickle* (Price, 1974) k–3. Mr. Tickle stretches his long, long arms till he finds tickle, tickle, tickle...you!

3132. ____. *Mr. Funny* (Price 1981) k–3. Mr. Funny lived in a teapot and drove a shoe to the zoo where he cheered up all the animals.

3133. ____. *Mr. Mischief* (Price, 1981) k–3. Mr. Mischief is always getting into trouble. Where will he strike next?

3134. ____. *Mr. Quiet* (Price, 1982) k–3. Mr. Quiet can't stand loud noises but Mr. Happy makes him find a nice quiet job.

3135. Hargreaves, Roger. *Little Miss Late* (Price, 1981) k–3. Little Miss Late, who arrives for everything after it's over, has trouble keeping an employer until she meets Mr. Lazy.

3136. ____. *Little Miss Contrary* (Price, 1984) k–3. Little Miss Contrary always says and does the opposite of what she really means, to the confusion of those around her.

3137. ____. *Little Miss Giggles* (Price, 1984) k–3. Little Miss Giggles is distressed when she loses her giggle.

3138. ____. *Little Miss Naughty* (Price, 1988) k–3. Little Miss Naughty was naughty all the time, but Mr. Impossible cured her in just one tweak.

3139. ____. *Little Miss Scatterbrain* (Price, 1988) k–3. Little Miss Scatterbrain couldn't remember anything, but most people liked her anyhow.

3140. ____. *Little Miss Trouble* (Price, 1988) k–3. Little Miss Trouble got everyone in trouble by telling fibs about them until Dr. Makeyouwell gets Mr. Tickle and Mr. Bump to give her a taste of her own medicine.

3141. ____. *Little Miss Shy* (Price, 1991) k–3. Miss Shy is terrified of leaving her house and meeting people until Mr. Funny whisks her off to his party.

3142. Hargreaves, Roger. *John Mouse Raises the Alarm* (Fabbri, 1973) k–3. John Mouse is apprehensive of a full-sized human burglar.

3143. ____. *John Mouse in the News* (Fabbri, 1973) k–3. John Mouse visits the television center where he plays havoc with the nine o'clock news.

3144. ____. *John Mouse Goes to Wormland* (Fabbri, 1973) k–3. John Mouse goes on an expedition underground to visit the town of Wormingham.

3145. ____. *John Mouse Goes to Work* (Fabbri, 1973) k–3.

3146. ____. *John Mouse* (Fabbri, 1973) k–3.

3147. ____. *John Mouse and the Apple Adventure* (Fabbri, 1973) k–3.

3148. ____. *John Mouse Down on the Farm* (Fabbri, 1973) k–3.

3149. Harnett, Cynthia. *Caxton's Challenge* (World, 1960) 5–8. Bendy is apprenticed to William Caxton, the publisher, who wants to print books instead of handcopying them.

3150. ____. *Cargo of the Madelena* (Lerner, 1984) 5–8. Bendy solves the mystery when William Caxton fails to receive the paper shipped to him on the *Madelena*.

3151. Harper, Anita. *It's Not Fair* (Putnam, 1986) k–3. A girl kangaroo, resenting the preferential treatment enjoyed by her new baby brother, finds that she does get to do some things he cannot.

3152. ____. *Just a Minute* (Putnam, 1987) k–3.

3153. ____. *What Feels Best?* (Putnam, 1988) k–3. A young kangaroo discovers the benefits of sharing such things as gifts, ideas and feelings with others.

3154. Harris, Christie. *Mouse Woman and the Vanished Princesses* (Atheneum, 1976) 5–8. Six legends of vanishing princesses and the tiny character sometimes mouse, sometimes woman, who helps young people in many Northwest Coast Indian stories.

3155. ____. *Mouse Woman and the Mischief-Makers* (Atheneum, 1977) 5–8. Mouse Woman, a tiny creature, part mouse, part grandmother helps young people and restores the proper balance to life for the Indians and the supernatural beings on the Northwest Coast.

3156. ____. *Mouse Woman and the Muddleheads* (Atheneum, 1979) 5–8. More exploits of Mouse Woman, the tiny supernatural being of the Northwest Coast Indian legends.

3157. Harris, Dorothy. *House Mouse* (Warne, 1973) k–3. Four-year-old Jonathan's new friend Mouse takes up residence in his sister's dollhouse—but only in the winter months.

3158. ____. *School Mouse* (Warne, 1977) k–3. Knowing that his mouse is now living at school makes first grade more appealing to a six-year-old.

3159. ____. *School Mouse and the Hamster* (Warne, 1979) k–3. When his friend Toby gets the mumps, Jonathan finds that after-school blackboard duty isn't much fun until he meets an enterprising mouse with interesting ideas.

3160. Harris, Robie. *Rosie's Double Dare* (Knopf, 1980) 4–6. When she accepts two dares from the Willard Street Gang in order to play baseball with them, eight-year-old Rosie finds herself on television on the field of a Red Sox baseball game.

3161. ____. *Rosie's Razzle Dazzle Deal* (Knopf, 1982) 4–6. Rosie is the culprit but because she is so likeable, mischievous pranks played by her are blamed on her brother.

3162. ____. *Rosie's Secret Spell* (Knopf, 1991) 4–6. Rosie, nine, doesn't like spelling but wants to win the All-American Spelling Bee. She visualizes words and also gains access to the list intended for the finals.

3163. Harvey, Brett. *My Prairie Year* (Holiday, 1986) k–3. Elenore, nine, describes her experiences living with her family in the Dakota Territory in the late nineteenth century.

3164. ____. *My Prairie Christmas* (Holiday, 1990) k–3. On the first Christmas after Elenore's family moves to a house on the prairie, everyone becomes worried when Papa goes out to cut down a Christmas tree and does not come back.

3165. Hass, E.A. *Incognito Mosquito, Private Insective* (Lothrop, 1982) 3–5. The mosquito detective tells a cub reporter of his exploits and encounters with such notables as Mickey Mantis, Flea Bailey and the Warden of Sting Sting prison.

3166. ____. *Incognito Mosquito Flies Again* (Random, 1985) 3–5. The Mosquito detective tells a class of FBI agents of his exploits and encounters with such insect offenders and notables as Russian Caget Bees, Goldfungus, Mikhail Baryshnimoth and Gnat King Cole.

3167. ____. *Incognito Mosquito Takes to the Air* (Lothrop, 1986) 3–5. While appearing on a TV talk show, the famous insect detective describes his adventures outwitting malefactors and solves a mystery on the air.

3168. Haswell, Peter. *Pog* (Orchard, 1989) k–3. Relates, in simple text and illustrations, the adventures of an inquisitive pig named Pog.

3169. ____. *Pog Climbs Mount Everest* (Orchard, 1990) k–3. Getting a cup of tea inspires Pog to climb Mount Everest.

3170. Hatfield, John. *Quintilian and the Curious Weather Shop* (Cape, 1969) 3–5. A story of Oliver's escape into the world of his father's toy museum. Quintilian, the toy china dog, has the key and shares Oliver's adventures. They solve mysteries and confront strange creatures.

3171. ____. *Quintilian Meets Mr. Punch* (Cape, 1970) 3–5. Toys come alive in their own self-contained toy museum world, which Oliver can only enter at night, led by a little china dog, Quintilian. Mr. Punch scares off the birds at Winter Fayre.

3172. ____. *Quintilian* (Cape, 1981) 3–5. Oliver and his guide the China Dog are involved in the search for the Black Swans crown, stolen by a clockwork soldier from the Castle whose machinery soon surrenders to the tin army's superior strength and strategies.

3173. Hautzig, Deborah. *Grover's Lucky Jacket* (Random, 1989) k–3. Grover is worried that he won't remember his lines in the class play without his lucky jacket.

3174. ____. *Grover's Bad Dream* (Random, 1990) k–3. Grover feels neglected at Big Bird's birthday party when Big Bird gets everything his way.

3175. Havill, Juanita. *Jamaica's Find* (Houghton, 1986) k–3. A little girl finds a stuffed dog in the park and decides to take it home.

3176. ____. *Jamaica Tag-along* (Houghton, 1989) k–3. When her older brother refuses to let her tag along with him, Jamaica goes off by herself and allows a younger child to play with her.

3177. ____. *Jamaica and Brianna* (Houghton, 1993) k–3. Jamaica hates wearing hand-me-down boots when her friend Brianna has pink fuzzy ones.

3178. ____. *Jamaica's Blue Marker* (Houghton, 1996) k–3. Jamaica is bothered by a classmate she terms "a mean brat." Russell not only borrows her markers, he uses them to ruin a picture she worked so hard on. She hears that Russell is moving. Happy that she doesn't need to leave the school and home she loves, Jamaica reacts in a way that surprises both Russell and herself.

3179. Havill, Juanita. *It Always Happens to Leona* (Crown, 1989) 4–6. Feeling left out between her older sister and younger brother, Leona decides to run away with Uncle Rosco, a motorcycle racer.

3180. ____. *Leona and Ike* (Crown, 1991) 4–6. Leona discovers the ups and downs of friendship with her new neighbor Ike.

3181. Hawes, Louise. *Nelson Malone Meets the Man from Mush-Nut* (Lodestar, 1986) 5–8. Six episodes in the life of Nelson. His piano teacher is a witch, his pink sneakers do amazing things, and on and on.

3182. ____. *Nelson Malone Saves Flight 942* (Dutton, 1988) 5–8. Follows the exciting adventures of Nelson Malone as he meets his sixth grade teacher, Terrible Tuckman, makes a video with his favorite rock group, and becomes a hero during a plane trip to Phoenix.

3183. Hawkins, Colin. *What Time Is it, Mr. Wolf?* (Putnam, 1983) k–3. Mr. Wolf's busy schedule helps the reader tell the time.

3184. ____. *Mr. Wolf's Week* (Heinermann, 1986) k–3. Mr. Wolf wears different clothes every day of the week. The names of the days of the week, the items of clothing and the weather conditions are introduced.

3185. ____. *Mr. Wolf's Birthday Surprise* (Heinemann, 1989) k–3.

3186. Hayes, Geoffrey. *Patrick Comes to Puttyville* (Harper, 1978) k–3. Mama and Patrick Bear leave their home in the seafaring town of Catfish Bay and start a new life in the country.

3187. ____. *Secret Inside* (Harper, 1980) k–3. Patrick, a small bear, meets a mysterious innkeeper who shows him the secret of his innermost thoughts.

3188. ____. *Patrick and Ted* (Four Winds, 1984) k–3. Best friends, Patrick and Ted, find their relationship strained when Ted goes away for the summer and Patrick finds other activities and friends to occupy his time.

3189. ____. *Patrick Goes to Bed* (Knopf, 1985) k–3. Patrick finds many excuses to delay going to bed.

3190. ____. *Patrick Buys a Coat* (Knopf, 1985) k–3. Patrick goes shopping with his mother and finds just the right coat for himself.

3191. ____. *Patrick Takes a Bath* (Knopf, 1985) k–3. Patrick has a wonderful time taking a bath.

3192. ____. *Patrick Eats His Dinner* (Random, 1985) k–3. Patrick finds a way to eat his hated peas.

3193. ____. *Patrick and His Grandpa* (Random, 1986) k–3. A bear spends a pleasant day with his grandfather.

3194. ____. *Patrick and Ted at the Beach* (Random, 1987) k–3. Patrick and his best friend Ted spend a fun-filled day at the beach.

3195. ____. *Patrick and Ted Ride the Train* (Random, 1988) k–3. When they travel by train to see Uncle Poopdeck, Patrick and Ted take along their squirt guns to protect the train from bandits.

3196. Hayes, Geoffrey. *Alligator and His Uncle Tooth* (Harper, 1977) 3–5. Corduroy is an alligator to whom his Uncle Tooth tells old sea yarns.

3197. ____. *Secret of Foghorn Island* (Random, 1988) 3–5. Otto and Uncle Tooth, detectives, investigate a series of shipwrecks, which brings them in touch with the dangerous Sid Rat.

3198. Hayes, Sarah. *Happy Christmas, Gemma* (Lothrop, 1986) k–3. Little Gemma and her family prepare for Christmas all week and have a happy celebration on the day.

3199. ____. *Eat Up, Gemma* (Lothrop, 1988) k–3. Baby Gemma refuses to eat, throwing her breakfast on the floor and squashing her grapes, until her brother gets an inspired idea.

3200. Hayes, Sarah. *This Is the Bear* (Lippincott, 1986) k–3. A toy bear is accidentally taken to the dump, but is rescued by a boy and a dog.

3201. ____. *This Is the Bear and the Picnic Lunch* (Little, 1989) k–3. What happens when a boy leaves his sleepy bear to guard their picnic lunch and a hungry dog comes along?

3202. ____. *This Is the Bear and the Scary Night* (Little, 1992) k–3. The lovable toy bear is mistakenly left in the park overnight, where he must face the darkness and its many challenges.

3203. Hayes, Sheila. *Carousel Horse* (Nelson, 1978) 5–6. Fran spends the summer out of town and meets Andrea whom she is sure she won't like because she is a rich girl. However, they do become friends and Fran understands that money isn't everything.

3204. ____. *You've Been Away All Summer* (Nelson, 1986) 5–8. Fran comes back to the city after a summer away and wants to see her best friend, Sarah. But Sarah has a new friend, Marcie. Fran continues her friendship with Andrea, finds that change is normal.

3205. Haynes, Betsy. *Against Taffy Sinclair Club* (Bantam, 1984) 4–6. A group of school girls victimize a classmate.

3206. ____. *Taffy Sinclair, Queen of the Soaps* (Bantam, 1985) 4–6. When gorgeous, conceited Taffy Sinclair wins a part on a television soap opera, 11-year-old Jana's jealousy skyrockets until she begins to mix television fantasy with real life.

3207. ____. *Down With Taffy Sinclair* (Bantam, 1987) 4–6. Jana and her friends have just reached the stage of being jealous of the first girl to develop breasts.

3208. ____. *Taffy Sinclair, Baby Ashley and Me.* (Bantam, 1988) 4–6. Jana and Taffy hear a baby cry on the front steps of their school. Taffy's parents offer to adopt the baby, but Jana wants to find the real mother.

3209. ____. *Truth About Taffy Sinclair* (Bantam, 1988) 4–6. Taffy is vain and cloying. Her diary is stolen and eventually returned. It reveals her lack of friends and some of her ugly thoughts. She gains friends in the process of getting her diary back.

3210. ____. *Taffy Sinclair and the Melanie Makeover* (Bantam, 1988) 4–6.

3211. ____. *Taffy Sinclair and the Secret Admirer Epidemic* (Bantam, 1988) 4–6.

3212. ____. *Taffy Sinclair Goes to Hollywood* (Bantam, 1990) 4–6. Taffy is in Hollywood to make a movie. She makes an enemy of Paige Taylor, a former child star, who wants Taffy's role to resurrect her own career.

3213. ____. *Taffy Sinclair Strikes Again* (Bantam, 1991) 4–6. Jana is now a sixth-grader and is driven to the beautiful Taffy's side because of a falling out of her four former friends. Jana used Taffy to try to get even, and what she learns is to have friends one must be one.

3214. ____. *Nobody Likes Taffy Sinclair* (Bantam, 1991) 4–6.

3215. Hays, Wilma P. *Little Yellow Fur* (Coward, 1973) 3–5. Story of a white, blonde girl who lives with her pioneering family in Sioux territory.

3216. ____. *Yellow Fur and Little Hawk* (Coward, 1980) 3–5. A young girl living near a Sioux reservation in South Dakota tries to find out why the Indians won't move into the new houses built by her father.

3217. Haywood, Carolyn. *"B" Is for Betsy* (Harcourt, 1939/1986) 4–6. Betsy experiences an interesting first year in school and looks forward to summer vacation at her grandfather's farm.

3218. ____. *Betsy and Billy* (Harcourt, 1941) 4–6. This is the story of Betsy's second year in school.

3219. ____. *Back to School with Betsy* (Harcourt, 1943) 4–6. Betsy and Billy in the third grade continue to have good times in school and out.

3220. ____. *Betsy and the Boys* (Harcourt, 1945/1976) 4–6. Betsy and Billy are in the fourth grade and have many lively adventures.

3221. ____. *Betsy's Little Star* (Morrow, 1950) 4–6. Star, four, looked forward to the day when she would be old enough to go to kindergarten, in the meantime, however, she had a way of making interesting things happen.

3222. ____. *Betsy and the Circus* (Morrow, 1954) 4–6. Betsy, 10, has lots of tickling adventures. With her friends Billy and Ellen and her younger sister Star, Betsy drinks cambric tea, survives a rotten egg in the classroom, thrills to the circus in town, and more.

3223. ____. *Betsy's Busy Summer* (Morrow, 1956) 4–6. Whether Betsy and her friends were trying to fry eggs on the sidewalk or reveling in a watermelon party there wasn't a dull moment. The summer house in Betsy's big yard was the favorite place to play until....

3224. ____. *Betsy's Winterhouse* (Morrow, 1958) 4–6. Betsy, Ellen and Billy have a New Year's party in the winter house in the basement. One day they found a stray cat and two kittens in the washing machine. They participated in a musical puppet show complete with chorus.

3225. ____. *Snowbound with Betsy* (Morrow, 1962) 4–6. When a snowstorm closed the schools Betsy enjoyed being snowbound. Her father brought home Miss Byrd and the two Byrd children whose car was stalled in the snow. Mr. Byrd came for them just before Christmas.

3226. ____. *Betsy and Mr. Kilpatrick* (Morrow, 1967) 4–6. When their favorite school crossing policeman is to be transferred, Betsy and all her friends form a club to give him a present.

3227. ____. *Merry Christmas from Betsy* (Morrow, 1970) 4–6. These are excerpts from other Betsy books that deal with Christmas.

3228. ____. *Betsy's Play School* (Morrow, 1977) 4–6. Betsy manages a summer play school for neighborhood children.

3229. Haywood, Carolyn. *Here's a Penny* (Harcourt, 1944) 4–6. Penny, an adopted son, his kitten, his friends, Patsy and Peter and a Halloween party, a picnic, a baseball game and a summer of sailing make up this story of adopted children.

3230. ____. *Penny and Peter* (Harcourt, 1946) 4–6. Penny now has a brother, age eight, also adopted. The story is one of everyday fun and happy family relationships.

3231. ____. *Penny Goes to Camp* (Morrow, 1948) 4–6. Penny and Peter have never been to camp and don't want to go, but when they learn that a real Indian chief teaches archery, they change their mind. There is rivalry between two camps, secrets, campfires and more.

3232. Haywood, Carolyn. *Little Eddie* (Morrow, 1947) 4–6. Seven-year-old Eddie Wilson is a little boy who knows what he wants and goes after it. His projects, which sometimes inconvenience his parents, are graphically told.

3233. ____. *Eddie and the Fire Engine* (Morrow, 1949) 4–6. Eddie's father buys him an old fire engine as a birthday gift at an auction. Unusual situations then follow in which his classmate, Anne Patricia and his goat Gardenia, share.

3234. ____. *Eddie and Gardenia* (Morrow, 1951) 4–6. Eddie's pet goat Gardenia was banished to Uncle Ed's ranch in Texas, while Eddie was permitted to stay for a visit. Both Gardenia's abnormal appetite and the ranch offered many exciting adventures.

3235. ____. *Eddie's Pay Dirt* (Morrow, 1953) 4–6. Enterprising Eddie comes home from his uncle's ranch complete with sombrero, parrot, snake and an old souvenir bucket of Texas soil given him by a ranch friend, Manuel.

3236. ____. *Eddie and His Big Deals* (Morrow, 1955) 4–6. In his efforts to collect valuable property Eddie faces one harrowing situation after another. In the course of trying to make a deal for the printing press many objects change hands: a wig, feathers and a baby doll.

3237. ____. *Eddie Makes Music* (Morrow, 1957) 4–6. Eddie took no interest in music but he tried to become a vocalist in the school band when he decided he was a good baritone. Someone else is chosen.

3238. ____. *Eddie and Louella* (Morrow, 1959) 4–6. Eddie was always bringing home stray animals but his favorite was Louella, a parrot. He loaned Louella to a charity ball and was given back the wrong parrot. The error was finally corrected.

3239. ____. *Annie Pat and Eddie* (Morrow, 1960) 4–6. When Annie Pat announces that she is going to be an actress, Eddie is skeptical. He shows no interest at all. But when he is invited to join Annie Pat at the seashore he is delighted.

3240. ____. *Eddie's Green Thumb* (Morrow, 1964) 4–6. Eddie and Annie Pat work on their Green Thumb Project for school. They decide to raise the baby rabbits they find in their garden-to-be. They give Boodle a birthday present from his own garden.

3241. ____. *Eddie, the Dog Holder* (Morrow, 1966) 4–6. Eddie starts a dog holding business. He persuades owner to have Annie Pat paint their dogs and he holds them for a price. But the dogcatcher, Boodle and others discourage Eddie from earning enough money for a puppy.

3242. ____. *Ever-Ready Eddie* (Morrow, 1968) 4–6. Too late to be a candidate for class president, Eddie decides to be campaign manager for his friend.

3243. ____. *Eddie's Happenings* (Morrow, 1971) 4–6. Eddie finds a list of special days to celebrate and adventures escalate from there.

3244. ____. *Eddie's Valuable Property* (Morrow, 1975) 4–6. Eddie collects junk but when they are going to move Eddie must get rid of some of his treasures. He has a garage sale and acquires a dog. When he moves he makes a new friend and has new adventures.

3245. ____. *Eddie's Menagerie* (Morrow, 1978) 4–6. Eddie Wilson becomes a volunteer detective for a pet store.

3246. ____. *Merry Christmas from Eddie* (Morrow, 1986) 4–6. Nine stories about Eddie and the Christmas season.

3247. ____. *Eddie's Friend Boodle* (Morrow, 1991) 4–6. A visit to the circus inspires Boodle to experiment with clown make-up and try to teach his dog Poochie to do tricks.

3248. Haywood, Carolyn. *Christmas Fantasy* (Morrow, 1972) 4–6. Relates the boyhood of Santa Claus and how he got into the "present business."

3249. ____. *How the Reindeer Saved Santa* (Morrow, 1986) 4–6. Deciding that his sleigh is too old to use for delivering presents, Santa Claus tries a helicopter.

3250. ____. *Santa Claus Forever* (Morrow, 1983) k–3. After a particularly difficult Christmas Eve, Santa decides to retire, but when he sees his replacement, he changes his mind.

3251. Hazen, Barbara. *Fang* (Atheneum, 1987) k–3. Although he is so big and looks fierce, Fang the dog is afraid of so many things that he is even afraid of himself.

3252. ____. *Stay Fang* (Atheneum, 1990) k–3. A dog who likes to follow his master everywhere finally learns to "stay."

3253. Hazen, Barbara. *Gorilla Did It* (Atheneum, 1974) k–3. A gorilla not only wakes up a little boy, but it messes up his room and makes his mother angry.

3254. ____. *Gorilla Wants to Be the Baby* (Atheneum, 1978) k–3. A youngster has a comforting talk with his gorilla who understands the problems of living with a new baby.

3255. Hearn, Emily. *Good Morning, Franny; Good Night Franny* (Woman's Press, 1984) k–3. Franny, a wheelchair child, and Ting, a Chinese child who speaks no English, meet and become friends. Franny teaches Ting to say "Good Morning, Franny" which is used when Ting must move away.

3256. ____. *Race You, Franny* (Woman's Press, 1986) k–3. Franny and her friend Danny and his dog, Lena, have their friendship tested when Franny wants to let Lena run free.

3257. ____. *Franny and the Music Girl* (Woman's Press, 1990) k–3. Franny is a spunky little kid who doesn't let her wheelchair dampen her spirits. She has a small irritating apartment mystery to solve— and a musician friend to give her life a whole new dimension.

3258. Hedderwick, Mairi. *Katie Morag Delivers the Mail* (Bodley, 1984) k–3. Little Katie is charged with delivering the mail, but a fall in the water obliterates the addresses.

3259. ____. *Katie Morag and the Two Grandmothers* (Little, 1986) k–3. Katie's two different grandmothers, plain Grannie Island and sophisticated Granma Mainland, don't seem to like each other until Granma's secret beauty formula saves the day for Grannie's prize sheep.

3260. ____. *Katie Morag and the Tiresome Ted* (Little, 1986) k–3. Katie's bad mood at the birth of a baby sister ends in her throwing her teddy bear into the sea, fortunately he comes back, and in restoring him she becomes her old self.

3261. ____. *Katie Morag and the Big Boy Cousins* (Little, 1987) k–3. Katie Morag's visit to her grandmother is disrupted by her wild and unruly Big Boy Cousins. They tempt her into a naughty game in the village when they should be doing chores.

3262. ____. *Katie and the New Pier* (Little, 1993) k–3. Katie's father welcomes the idea of a new pier and a boat coming three times a week to the isle of Struay. Lady Artist is also in favor of the plan. But the ferryman will become redundant and Granny believes the old ways will be forgotten.

3263. ____. *Katie Morag and the Wedding* (Little) k–3.

3264. Heide, Florence. *Banana Twist* (Holiday, 1978) 4–6. Jonah arrives at school. He likes junk food but his roommate is a health nut. He enters a TV contest to get money for junk food.

3265. ____. *Banana Blitz* (Holiday, 1983) 4–6. Television and candy bar addict Jonah thinks his problems will be over if he can just win the prize offered by the American Banana Institute for watching its commercials.

3266. Heide, Florence. *Maximilian* (Funk & Wagnall, 1967) k–3. This is the story of the difficulties of a baby mouse who lives in a bird's nest, eats worms, and tries to fly. He is finally reconciled to the ways of mice.

3267. ____. *Maximilian Becomes Famous* (Funk & Wagnall) k–3. A young mouse who thinks mice must be famous for something hopes a visit to well-known animals at the zoo might bring some answers.

3268. Heine, Helme. *Three Little Friends* (Atheneum, 1982) k–3. "Good friends always stick together." That is what Charlie Rooster, Johnny Mouse and fat Percy the pig, always said—and that was what they did all day long. They find that being together all the time is just not possible.

3269. ____. *Three Little Friends: Alarm Clock* (Atheneum, 1985) k–3. Fat Percy (pig), Charlie Rooster and Johnny Mouse borrow a clock so Charlie won't oversleep after a night of revelry. They stay up after midnight and play pranks on the sleeping animals. The clock doesn't go off but Charlie's friends awaken him in time to usher in the dawn.

3270. ____. *Three Little Friends: Visitor* (Atheneum, 1985) k–3. Johnny and Charlie become jealous when Percy pays a lot of attention to the Visitor, a lamb. But they get to know her and decide she is their friend, too.

3271. ____. *Three Little Friends: Racing Cart* (Atheneum, 1985) k–3. Johnny Mouse finds an old cart and insists on trying it out first. The cart crashes and he realizes that everything is better when friends do things together.

3272. ____. *Three Little Friends: Friends Have a Visitor* (Atheneum, 1986) k–3.

3273. Henderson, Kathy. *Sam and the Big Machines* (Deutsch, 1985) k–3. Sam trespasses into a building site and gets himself buried in a sand mountain. He is picked up and dumped by cranes, mixed and whirled in a cement mixer.

3274. ____. *Sam and the Box* (Deutsch, 1987) k–3. Sam and his friends use a cardboard box as a monster, a van, a boat, a hospital and a house. But rain destroyed the cardboard house and the children use the remains as an umbrella and hurry home.

3275. ____. *Sam, Lizzie and the Bonfire* (Deutsch, 1989) k–3. Sam and Lizzie pretend being hunters, stalk shadows and play with sheets of old newspapers in their back yard. A smoke monster blows over and engulfs Sam. Lizzie comes to the rescue, with a wooden sword and a bucket of dirty water.

3276. Henri, Adrain. *Eric, the Punk Cat* (Magnet, 1983) k–3. A satire about the punk rock business and a sorrowful and exploited hero, told with humor and sympathy.

3277. ____. *Eric and Frankie in Las Vegas* (Magnet, 1988) k–3. An odd tale of show business cats.

3278. Henry, Marie. *Bunnies All Day Long* (Dial, 1985) k–3. Mischievous bunny children Harry, Larry and Paulette have a busy day at home and at school.

3279. ____. *Bunnies and Their Grandma* (Dial, 1985) k–3. Mother Bunny takes her three children for a day of fun and games with their cousins at grandma's house.

3280. ____. *Bunnies at Christmastime* (Dial, 1986) k–3. An invitation to Santa Claus to join the bunnies for a Christmas party brings their Uncle Jack instead, but he comes with toys and Santa whiskers.

3281. Herman, Charlotte. *Max Malone and the Great Cereal Ripoff* (Holt, 1990) 2–4. Tired of being cheated by the cereal companies, Max decides to fight back after not receiving a free glow-in-the-dark sticker in his box of Choco-fish.

3282. ____. *Max Malone Makes a Million* (Holt, 1991) 2–4. Max Malone, along with his best friend Gordy, is continually frustrated in his attempts to get

rich, while his neighbor, little Austin Healy, makes money at every turn.

3283. ____. *Max Malone Superstar* (Holt, 1992) 2–4. After losing a part of an audition for a Peppy Peanut Butter commercial, Max decides his true role in show business is to manage the career of his friend Austin Healy.

3284. ____. *Max Malone the Magnificent* (Holt, 1993) 2–4. After seeing Great Butoni perform at the local public library, Max decides he wants to become a magician.

3285. Herman, Charlotte. *Millie Cooper, 3B* (Dutton, 1985) 3–5. As she tries to cope with school and other problems, third grader Millie discovers some special things about herself.

3286. ____. *Millie Cooper, Take a Chance* (Dutton, 1988) 3–5. In 1947, Millie recognizes the importance of taking chances to make her life more interesting and satisfying.

3287. Herrmann, Frank. *Giant Alexander* (McGraw, 1965) k–3. Giant Alexander pushes a ship off a sandbank, walks to London, spring cleans Nelson' Column, and has tea with Lord Mayor. He then invites hundreds of children to a special "Giant's Treat"—a very large breakfast.

3288. ____. *Giant Alexander and the Circus* (McGraw, 1966) k–3. Alex is both gallantly fighting a barn fire and crawling into the big top to watch a circus.

3289. ____. *Giant Alexander in America* (McGraw, 1968) k–3. The unique adventures of Giant Alexander, who, at the president's request, traveled from London to America to help scientists at Cape Kennedy with their space program.

3290. ____. *Giant Alexander and Hannibal the Elephant* (McGraw, 1972) k–3. A giant's chase on motor skates along a superhighway to rescue a stolen elephant, climaxes months of work laying underground electric cables.

3291. ____. *All About Giant Alexander* (McGraw, 1975) k–3. Alexander is two telegraph poles tall but he uses his strength for the benefit of all.

3292. Hertz, Ole. *Tobias Goes Seal Hunting* (Carolrhoda, 1984) k–3. In Greenland, a boy and his father hunt seals in their kayaks.

3293. ____. *Tobias Catches Trout* (Carolrhoda, 1984) k–3. Tobias, a young Greenlander, goes on a trout fishing expedition with his family in their motor boat.

3294. ____. *Tobias Has a Birthday* (Carolrhoda, 1984) k–3. Tobias, who lives on a Greenland settlement with his family, celebrates his twelfth birthday in the traditional manner.

3295. ____. *Tobias Goes Ice Fishing* (Carolrhoda, 1984) k–3. In Greenland, a boy and his father fish through the ice that covers a fjord.

3296. Heuck, Sigrid. *Pony, the Bear and the Stolen*

Apples (Hart, 1978/198) k–3. Relates the adventures of a horse and a bear as they try to discover who stole the apples from the tree that grows in a forest clearing.

3297. ____. *Pony, the Bear and the Parrot* (Hart, 1985) k–3. When winter comes, pony and bear decide to leave their apple orchard and travel south for warmth. A rescued parrot offers to be their guide.

3298. ____. *Pony and Bear Are Friends* (Knopf, 1990) k–3. Relates, in rebus format, the further adventures of two good friends.

3299. Hildick, E.W. *Calling Questers Four* (Hawthorn, 1967) 4–6. Pete directs the activities of his gang from his sick bed with the aid of a walkie-talkie set. Remotely controlled by Peter, they run into a little mob of boys who are putting objects on the railway line. A mix-up occurs but with impunity they escape.

3300. ____. *Questers* (Hawthorn, 1970) 4–6. Bedridden Peter and his friends work out a master plan to win several contests.

3301. Hildick, E.W. *Birdy Jones* (Stackpole, 1969) 5–8. The ambition of an English teenager when he leaves school is to be the first with the New Sound—pop whistler.

3302. ____. *Birdy and the Group* (Stackpole, 1969) 5–8. Birdy Jones, English pop whistler, needs a back-up group but finding the right one becomes a major problem.

3303. ____. *Birdy Swings North* (Stackpole, 1971) 5–8. To further extend his career, pop whistler Birdy Jones and his manager travel to the clubs of northern England.

3304. ____. *Birdy in Amsterdam* (Stackpole, 1971) 5–8. On the way to Amsterdam for his first foreign appearance, pop whistler Birdy Jones becomes the unknowing accomplice of a gang of smugglers and counterfeiters.

3305. ____. *Birdy Jones and the New York Heads* (Doubleday, 1974) 5–8. While trying to further their careers in New York, Birdy, the pop whistler, and his manager have a variety of misadventures including involvement with rival dope-pushing rings.

3306. Hildick, E.W. *Meet Lemon Kelly* (Cape, 1963) 4–6.

3307. ____. *Lemon Kelley* (Doubleday, 1968) 4–6. When a junior school gang is suspected in a rash of vandalism in the neighborhood, they set up a patrol to try and catch the older vandals and clear themselves, but they find their own group even more suspect.

3308. ____. *Lemon Kelly Digs Deep* (Doubleday, 1977) 4–6. Lemon Kelly's gang has a tough guy leader, an irritating little brother, a tough girl and a brainy kid. The rival gang has about the same make-up.

3309. Hildick, E.W. *Secret Winners* (Crown, 1970) 4–6. Tim and his uncle have a lottery ticket and win half a million dollars but must keep it a secret from Aunt Bridget. They spend it secretly and she never finds out.

3310. ____. *Secret Spenders* (Crown, 1971) 4–6. Tim and his uncle spend their $500,000 on luxury living. A girl sleuth in the same building and a phony kidnapping that turns out to be real, adds to the humor.

3311. Hildick, E.W. *Louie's Lot* (White, 1968) 5–8. Louie is a milkman who has a lot of boys working for him. They meet savage dogs, milk money thieves and would-be competitors.

3312. ____. *Louie's S.O.S.* (Doubleday, 1978) 5–8. Louie's Lot are his handpicked boys who work the milk route. Someone is sabotaging his milk. Is it a rival milkman? Louie and his lot must find out.

3313. ____. *Louie's Snowstorm* (Doubleday, 1974) 5–8. Louie tries to beat a snowstorm and give his customers their milk. He has a girl on the truck for the first time. They capture a would-be burglar, rescue an injured man and assist in delivering a baby.

3314. ____. *Louie's Ransom* (Knopf, 1978) 5–8. Louie and his lot travel to New England and get captured by kidnappers.

3315. Hill, Eric. *Where's Spot?* (Putnam, 2980) k–3. A mother dog finds eight other animals hiding around the house before finding her lost puppy.

3316. ____. *Spot's First Walk* (Putnam, 1981) k–3. A puppy finds many animals and surprises when his mother sends him out on his first walk.

3317. ____. *Puppy Love* (Putnam, 1982) k–3. Spot shows he needs a kiss and a cuddle from his mom; whether he's alone or in a crowd, happy or sad, naughty or good, Spot needs puppy love.

3318. ____. *Spot's Birthday Party* (Putnam, 1982) k–3. Spot and his animal friends play hide-and-seek at his birthday party.

3319. ____. *Spot's First Christmas* (Putnam, 1983) k–3. A puppy's first Christmas is a time of many delights.

3320. ____. *Sweet Dreams, Spot* (Putnam, 1984) k–3. Spot is an inquisitive and alert puppy. In this story he puts away his toys, listens to a bedtime story and curls up for the night.

3321. ____. *Spot's Toys* (Putnam, 1984) k–3. A bathtime book allows Spot to join in bathtime routines and tells all about Spot's favorite playthings and the games he enjoys.

3322. ____. *Spot's Alphabet* (Putnam, 1984) k–3. Fun and learning can be integrated with bumbly Spot frolicking among the letters of the alphabet.

3323. ____. *Spot Learns to Count* (Putnam, 1984) k–3. Fun and learning can be integrated with bumbly Spot frolicking among the numbers.

3324. ____. *Spot Tells the Time* (Putnam, 1984) k–3. Fun and learning can be integrated with bumbly Spot frolicking among time-telling symbols.

3325. ____. *Spot Goes to School* (Putnam, 1984) k–3. Spot the dog, has an eventful first day at school.

3326. ____. *Spot Goes on Holiday* (Putnam) k–3. Spot the puppy spends a fun-filled day on the beach with his parents.

3327. ____. *Spot's Busy Year* (Putnam, 1984) k–3.

3328. ____. *Spot's Friends* (Putnam, 1985) k–3.

3329. ____. *Spot Goes Splash* (Putnam, 1985) k–3.

3330. ____. *Spot on the Farm* (Putnam, 1985) k–3. Spot visits a farm and is a big help to all the animals.

3331. ____. *Spot at Play* (Putnam, 1985) k–3. Spot and his friends enjoy swimming, jumping rope, and many other activities together.

3332. ____. *Spot at the Fair* (Putnam, 1985) k–3. Spot and his animal friends have an enjoyable day riding the rides of the amusement park. .

3333. ____. *Spot Goes to the Beach* (Putnam, 1985) k–3. Spot is escorted by Mom and Pop to the beach. He buries his father in the sand, almost catches a fish, falls out of a rowboat but stays afloat in his rubber tube. He meets a girl puppy and shares adventures.

3334. ____. *Spot Goes to the Circus* (Putnam, 1986) k–3. Spot goes behind the scenes at the circus to find his ball and learns a clever trick.

3335. ____. *Spot's First Words* (Putnam, 1986) k–3. Spot introduces a variety of words and uses them in sentences as he goes about his daily activities.

3336. ____. *Spot Looks at Colors* (Putnam, 1986) k–3. Dog Spot introduces the colors and presents an item for each one.

3337. ____. *Spot Looks at Shapes* (Putnam, 1986) k–3. Dog Spot introduces shapes that are round, square, diamond, star, oblong, triangle and oval.

3338. ____. *Spot Visits the Hospital* (Putnam, 1987) k–3. Spot the dog visits his friend Steve in the hospital and gets to explore its many aspects.

3339. ____. *Spot's First Picnic* (Putnam, 1987) k–3. Spot and his friends have a very eventful picnic.

3340. ____. *Spot Goes to the Farm* (Putnam, 1987) k–3. Spot searches for new babies among the farm animals, each of which greets him with its own distinctive noise.

3341. ____. *Spot's Big Book of Words* (Putnam, 1988) k–3. Spot the dog introduces words, such as soap, tractor, suitcase and birthday cake, while he goes on with his daily activities.

3342. ____. *Spot's First Easter* (Putnam, 1988) k–3. Spot the puppy joins Helen the hippopotamus in a search for six hidden Easter eggs.

3343. ____. *Spot Looks at Opposites* (Putnam, 1989) k–3. Spot discovers the difference between such opposites as full and empty, soft and hard and fast and slow.

3344. ____. *Spot Looks at the Weather* (Putnam, 1989) k–3. Spot gets out and enjoys whatever the weather has to offer.

3345. ____. *Spot Counts from 1 to 10* (Putnam, 1989) k–3. Spot the dog counts animals on the farm, from one cow munching to ten bees buzzing.

3346. ____. *Spot's Baby Sister* (Putnam, 1989) k–3. Spot the dog enjoys romping with his new baby sister and discovers what it is like to be a big brother.

3347. ____. *Spot Sleeps Over* (Putnam, 1990) k–3. Spot packs his toys for his first sleep over at his friend's house next door, forgetting one essential item—his beloved teddy bear.

3348. ____. *Spot at Home* (Putnam, 1991) k–3. Describes Spot the dog's rainy day spent at home.

3349. ____. *Spot Goes to the Park* (Putnam, 1991) k–3. Spot the puppy, his mother, and his animal friends have a fun-filled day playing in the park.

3350. ____. *Spot's Toy Box* (Putnam, 1991) k–3. Describes some of the toys found in Spot the dog's toy box.

3351. ____. *Spot in the Garden* (Putnam, 1991) k–3. Describes Spot the dog's daily activities in his family's garden.

3352. ____. *Spot Goes to a Party* (Putnam, 1992) k–3. Spot the dog gets an invitation to a costume party.

3353. ____. *Spot's Walk in the Woods* (:Putnam, 1993) k–3. Join Spot and his friends on their first class trip to the woods and see what they find.

3354. ____. *Spot Stays Overnight* (Putnam, 1993) k–3.

3355. ____. *Spot Bakes a Cake* (Putnam, 1994) k–3. Dad's birthday is just around the corner and who better to bake his cake than Spot? From the visit to the supermarket to the closing birthday celebration readers will find a surprise.

3356. Hill, Eric. *At Home* (Random, 1983) k–3. Baby Bear, a toy, watches television; he sees a chair, a table, a vase of flowers, a clock, a telephone, a curtained window, a mirror, a lamp, and other household items.

3357. ____. *My Pets* (Random, 1983) k–3. Baby Bear sees a great variety of pets.

3358. ____. *Park* (Random, 1983) k–3. Baby Bear looks at a bench, flowers, trees, a pond, playground equipment and other things in the park.

3359. ____. *Up There* (Random, 1983) k–3. Baby Bear points to the sky. He sees a bird, a kite, a balloon, a squirrel in a tree, clouds, sun and a rainbow.

3360. ____. *Good Morning, Baby Bear* (Random, 1984) k–3. Baby Bear wakes up, washes, has his breakfast, and is ready to begin his day.

3361. ____. *Baby Bear's Bedtime* (Random, 1984) k–3. After a hard day playing, Baby Bear gets ready for bed with a bath and a story.

3362. Hiller, B.B. *Karate Kid* (Scholastic, 1984) 5–8. Daniel, 15, just moved to California and makes new friends including Ali who becomes his girlfriend. He makes an enemy of Johnny a black belt in karate. Dan learns karate and faces Johnny in the All Valley Championship.

3363. ____. *Karate Kid Pt. 2* (Scholastic, 1984) 5–8. Karate student Daniel LaRusso accompanies his teacher, Miyagi, to Miyagi's ancestral home in Okinawa and becomes involved in a collision of cultures and combat.

3364. ____. *Karate Kid III* (Scholastic, 1989) 5–8. Dan is fighting for his honor against the Cobra Kais whom he defeated earlier. Cobra Kais wants revenge and reclaim his title.

3365. Hillert, Margaret. *Happy Birthday, Dear Dragon* (Follett, 1977) k–3. A youngster is delighted with his birthday present, especially when it helps him do things such as toast marshmallows.

3366. ____. *Merry Christmas, Dear Dragon* (Follett, 1980) k–3. A boy and his pet dragon share many winter activities and celebrate Christmas by chopping down and decorating a tree, making cookies, and sitting by a fire.

3367. ____. *Let's Go, Dear Dragon* (Follett, 1981) k–3. A boy and his pet dragon celebrate the Fourth of July by going to the beach, having a picnic, and watching the fireworks.

3368. ____. *It's Halloween, Dear Dragon* (Follett, 1981) k–3. A boy and his pet dragon play in the autumn leaves, make a jack o' lantern, eat pumpkin pie, dress in costumes, go trick-or-treating, enter a costume contest and fly together.

3369. ____. *Happy Easter, Dear Dragon* (Follett, 1981) k–3. A boy and his pet dragon celebrate Easter by enjoying the spring flowers and baby animals, coloring eggs, making an egg tree, hunting Easter eggs, marching in the Easter parade, and going to church.

3370. ____. *Come to School, Dear Dragon* (Mod Curr, 1985) k–3. A boy's pet dragon visits him at school and joins in the classroom activities.

3371. ____. *Go to Sleep, Dear Dragon* (Mod Curr, 1985) k–3. After reading a book about medieval times, a boy falls asleep and dreams that he is in a medieval setting where he finds a large egg out of which a baby dragon hatches.

3372. ____. *I Need You, Dear Dragon* (Mod Curr, 1985) k–3. Dear Dragon feels somewhat rejected when his master's new baby sister comes home from the hospital, but love and reassurance put things right.

3373. ____. *It's Circus Time, Dear Dragon* (Mod Curr, 1985) k–3. A boy and his dragon go to the circus where the dragon performs some unexpected tricks on a high wire.

3374. ____. *Help for Dear Dragon* (Mid Curr, 1985) k–3. When Dear Dragon feels sick, he receives help from a friendly veterinarian.

3375. ____. *Friend for Dear Dragon* (Mod Curr, 1985) k–3. A boy and his pet dragon make friends with their new neighbors, a girl and her unicorn.

3376. ____. *I Love You, Dear Dragon* (Mod Curr, 1981) k–3. A boy and his pet dragon celebrate Valentine's Day by noticing all the red things they see, making Valentines, and eating Valentine cake.

3377. Himmelman, John. *Amanda and the Witch Switch* (Viking, 1985) k–3. A friendly witch named Amanda gives a toad three wishes, but her good intentions backfire when he uses one of the wishes to become a witch.

3378. ____. *Amanda and the Magic Garden* (Viking, 1987) k–3. Amanda's garden, grown from magic seeds, is a great success until its vegetables cause the animals who eat them to grow to giant size.

3379. Hinds, Bill. *Buss Beamer's Radical Sports* (Little, 1990) 4–6. Buss, the hip, quick, sports-type dude reinvents today's major sports.

3380. ____. *Buzz Beamer's Out of the World Series* (Little, 1991) 4–6. When a crew of intergalactic all-stars drops by, Buzz and his pals are up against the wildest team of aliens ever to sing "Take Me Out to the Ball Game."

3381. ____. *Buzz Beamer's Radical Olympics* (Little, 1992) 4–6. Buzz is back with his wacky imagination and some radical suggestions for reinventing Olympic sports. Wouldn't the hurdles be more fun if the runners wore clown shoes?

3382. Hines, Anna. *Cassie Bowen Takes Witch Lessons* (Dutton, 1985) 4–6. Cassie, a fourth grader, learns a great deal about herself and friendship when a school assignment pairs her with an unpopular new girl instead of her best friend.

3383. ____. *Boys Are Yucko* (Dutton, 1988) 4–6. While hoping her divorced father will come from California to help celebrate her tenth birthday with her mother and brother, Cassie agrees to Stacy's suggestion to have a party including boys and dancing.

3384. Hines, Anna. *They Really Like Me* (Greenwillow, 1989) k–3. Unenthusiastic about babysitting their brother Joshua, Abby and Penny play a trick on him, but they are dismayed when the trick backfired.

3385. ____. *Secret Keeper* (Greenwillow, 1990) k–3. Unhappy to be the only one in his house without Christmas secrets, Joshua is relieved when Grandma comes and helps him have some secrets of his own.

3386. Hissey, Jane. *Little Bear's Trousers* (Philomel, 1987) k–3. While looking for his missing trousers, Little Bear discovers that other animals have found many different uses for them.

3387. ____. *Little Bear Lost* (Philomel, 1989) k–3. Old Bear and the other toys play hide-and-seek but no one can find Little Bear.

3388. ____. *Little Bear's Bedtime* (Random, 1993) k–3. The antics of Little Bear on his way to bed.

3389. ____. *Little Bear's Day* (Random, 1993) k–3. The delights of Little Bear as he gets up and about.

3390. Hissey, Jane. *Old Bear* (Philomel, 1986) k–3. A group of toy animals try various ways of rescuing Old Bear from the attic.

3391. ____. *Old Bear Tales* (Philomel, 1988) k–3.

Adventures of the playroom toys as they have parties, enjoy the seasons and go on a holiday.

3392. Hoban, Julia. *Amy Loves the Wind* (Harper, 1988) k–3. While walking in the park on a windy day, Amy and her mother see what the wind can do.

3393. ____. *Amy Loves the Sun* (Harper, 1988) k–3. Amy picks some flowers on a sunny day and gives them to her mother.

3394. ____. *Amy Loves the Rain* (Harper, 1989) k–3. Amy and her mother drive through the rain to pick up Daddy.

3395. ____. *Amy Loves the Snow* (Harper, 1989) k–3. Amy builds a snowman with her parents.

3396. Hoban, Lillian. *Arthur's Christmas Cookies* (Harper, 1972) 3–5. Arthur finds a way to enjoy his Christmas cookies even after he discovers they can't be eaten.

3397. ____. *Arthur's Honey Bear* (Harper, 1974) 3–5. Arthur decides to sell his old toys but is reluctant to part with his old bear.

3398. ____. *Arthur's Pen Pal* (Harper, 1976) 3–5. Arthur views his little sister in a different light after receiving a revealing letter from a pen pal.

3399. ____. *Arthur's Prize Reader* (Harper, 1978) 3–5. Although Arthur loses the Super Chimp Club contest, his pupil, sister Violet, wins the first grade reading competition and a prize for them both.

3400. ____. *Arthur's New Power* (Crowell, 1978) k–3. The lovable chimp faces a situation when father states there is to be no more electricity in the house.

3401. ____. *Arthur's Funny Money* (Harper, 1981) 3–5. When Violet has a numbers problem and Arthur is penniless, they go into business and solve both problems.

3402. ____. *Arthur's Halloween Costume* (Harper, 1984) 3–5. Arthur the chimpanzee, after worrying that his Halloween costume won't be scary enough, wins a prize for the most unusual costume in the school.

3403. ____. *Arthur's Loose Tooth* (Harper, 1985) 3–5. Arthur the chimp is a little worried about losing his loose tooth, until his sister and their babysitter show him the real meaning of bravery.

3404. ____. *Arthur's Great Big Valentine* (Harper, 1989) 3–5. After they have a falling out, Arthur and his best friend Norman make up with very special valentines.

3405. ____. *Arthur's Camp Out* (Harper, 1993) 3–5. Bored with spring vacation, Arthur decides to go alone on an overnight field trip in the woods behind his house.

3406. ____. *Arthur's Back to School Day* (Harper, 1995) 3–5. For Arthur the adventures begin before he even gets to school.

3407. Hoban, Lillian. *Ready...Set...Robot* (Harper, 1982) 3–5. When robots all over Zone One gather to race in the Digi-Maze, a power pack mix-up almost causes disaster for Sol-1.

3408. ____. *Laziest Robot in Zone One* (Harper, 1983) 3–5. Sol-1 helps all his friends with their work in the process of avoiding his own.

3409. Hoban, Lillian. *Mr. Pig and Sonny, Too* (Harper, 1977) 3–5. Sonny Pig and his father have adventures skating, exercising, finding greens for supper and going to a wedding.

3410. ____. *Mr. Pig and Family* (Harper, 1980) 3–5. When Mr. Pig marries Selma Pig, there are many adventures in store for the new family.

3411. Hoban, Lillian. *Silly Tilly and the Easter Bunny* (Harper, 1987) 3–5. Silly Tilly Mole is so forgetful and silly on Easter morning that she cannot find her bonnet and fails to let the Easter Bunny into the house.

3412. ____. *Silly Tilly's Thanksgiving Dinner* (Harper, 1990) 3–5. Forgetful Silly Tilly Mole nearly succeeds in ruining her Thanksgiving dinner, but her animal friends come to the rescue with tasty treats.

3413. Hoban, Russell. *Bedtime for Frances* (Harper, 1960) k–3. Frances is a very human–like badger, who had trouble falling asleep at night because she saw so many things—real and imaginary.

3414. ____. *Baby Sister for Frances* (Harper, 1964) k–3. What can you do when you have a baby sister who seems to get all the attention? Frances, the little badger, solves the problem.

3415. ____. *Bread and Jam for Frances* (Harper, 1964) k–3. Frances, a little badger, thought she could eat bread and jam at every meal. Her wise parents let her try it, until Frances finally sees the wisdom of a variety of food.

3416. ____. *Birthday for Frances* (Harper, 1968) k–3. Jealous of her sister's birthday, Frances becomes mean and selfish, until a rare generosity and birthday spirit move her to reluctantly give her coveted gift.

3417. ____. *Best Friends for Frances* (Harper, 1969) k–3. When friend Albert decides that he must exclude girls from his "wondering day" and baseball game, Frances chooses younger sister Gloria as a companion.

3418. ____. *Bargain for Frances* (Harper, 1992) k–3. Frances foils Thelma's plot to trick her out of a new china set.

3419. Hoban, Russell. *Jim Hedgehog and the Lonesome Tower* (Clarion, 1992) k–3. Jim Hedgehog, who likes heavy metal music, buys a cassette tape and a musical instrument from Mr. Strange, which lead him to a haunted castle.

3420. ____. *Jim Hedgehog's Supernatural Christmas* (Clarion, 1992) k–3. Jim Hedgehog is converted to a healthy diet and life style by confronting a frightening image of his future self in his favorite film the Revolting Blob.

3421. Hoban, Russell. *Charlie the Tramp* (Four Winds, 1967) k–3. A boy beaver decides he wants to be a tramp who sleeps in open fields and does odd jobs for food, but his beaver instincts eventually get the best of him.

3422. ____. *Charlie Meadows* (Holt, 1984) k–3. While delivering the news to the other field mice, Charlie Meadows, who loves dancing with his shadow in the moonlight, narrowly escapes being eaten by the owl.

3423. Hoban, Russell. *Little Brute Family* (Macmillan, 1969) k–3. The Brute family and their equally disagreeable home are transformed by the actions of Baby Brute.

3424. ____. *Stone Doll of Sister Brute* (Macmillan, 1968) k–3. Sister Brute has no one to love until she makes a stone doll and finds an ugly dog.

3425. Hoban, Russell. *How Tom Beat Captain Najork and His Hired Sportsmen* (Atheneum, 1974) k–3. Impish fun in this story of Tom, who triumphs over those intent on punishing him for his constant fooling around.

3426. ____. *Near Thing for Captain Najork* (Atheneum, 1976) k–3. Tom builds a jam-powered frog vehicle and is pursued by his enemy.

3427. Hodges, Margaret. *What's for Lunch Charley?* (Dial, 1961) 3–5. Some days were good ones for Charley Rivers, some were bad. One rainy morning Charley had not finished his homework, he was late for school, and he had forgotten his lunch box.

3428. ____. *Sing Out, Charley* (Farrar, 1968) 3–5. Charley's choice of a Christmas gift helps him find the true spirit of the holiday season.

3429. Hoff, Syd. *Henrietta Lays Some Eggs* (Garrard, 1978) 3–5. Henrietta runs away from the farm and has several adventures that culminate in a special egg hunt she creates for city children.

3430. ____. *Henrietta, the Early Bird* (Garrard, 1978) 3–5. Henrietta the hen decides to wake everyone up herself.

3431. ____. *Henrietta, Circus Star* (Garrard, 1978) 3–5. Henrietta the chicken sneaks in to see the circus for the first time and unexpectedly becomes one of the performers.

3432. ____. *Henrietta Goes to the Fair* (Garrard, 1979) 3–5. Farmer Gray chooses Winston the pig to represent his farm at the fair, but it is Henrietta the hen who wins the blue ribbon.

3433. ____. *Merry Christmas, Henrietta* (Garrard, 1980) 3–5. When Henrietta the chicken looks for a Christmas present for Farmer Gray, she becomes Santa's special helper.

3434. ____. *Henrietta's Halloween* (Garrard, 1980) 3–5. Despite Mr. Gray's warnings about Halloween night and the eerie tricks her imagination plays on her, Henrietta dons a costume and attempts to trick Mr. Gray.

3435. ____. *Henrietta's Fourth of July* (Garrard, 1981) 3–5. Farmer Gray and the barnyard friends, including Henrietta, join in the annual Fourth of July festivities.

3436. ____. *Happy Birthday, Henrietta* (Garrard, 1983) 3–5. When Henrietta the chicken has a birthday, her friends plan a big surprise party in the barn.

3437. Hol, Coby. *Tippy Bear Goes to a Party* (North-South, 1991) k–3. Tippy Bear and his mother make a clown costume for him to wear to his class party.

3438. ____. *Tippy Bear Hunts for Honey* (North-South, 1991) k–3. Hungry Tippy Bear sets off to buy a jar of honey and meets some bees that are glad to give him their best honey in exchange for his help repairing their hive.

3439. ____. *Tippy Bear Visits Little Sam* (North-South, 1992) k–3. Tippy Bear visits his new baby cousin Sam and helps take care of him.

3440. ____. *Tippy Bear's Christmas* (North-South, 1992) k–3. Tippy Bear makes two new animal friends who help him celebrate Christmas.

3441. Holabird, Katherine. *Angelina Ballerina* (Crown, 1983) k–3. A pretty little mouse wants to become a ballerina more than anything else in the world.

3442. ____. *Angelina and the Princess* (Crown, 1984) k–3. Angelina is too sick to dance well during the tryouts for the lead in the "Princess of Mouseland" ballet, but when the leading ballerina sprains her foot, Angelina is ready to prove she is the best dancer.

3443. ____. *Angelina at the Fair* (Crown, 1985) k–3. Angelina's annoyance at having to take her little cousin Henry to the fair turns into a friendship after a day filled with adventure and surprises.

3444. ____. *Angelina's Christmas* (Crown, 1985) k–3. Angelina and her cousin Henry bring Christmas to a lonely old postman.

3445. ____. *Angelina on Stage* (Crown, 1986) k–3. When cousin Henry gets all the attention in the grown-up musical in which they have roles, Angelina becomes jealous, but she demonstrates her fondness for him when a crisis occurs on opening night.

3446. ____. *Angelina and Alice* (Crown, 1987) k–3. Angelina and her best friend Alice discover the importance of teamwork when their acrobatics are the hit of the gymnastics show at the village fair.

3447. ____. *Angelina's Birthday Surprise* (Crown, 1989) k–3. Angelina the dancing mouse discovers what a special day a birthday can be.

3448. ____. *Angelina' Baby Sister* (Crown, 1991) k–3. Polly is Angelina's baby sister. She is always in the spotlight, upstaging everyone. Angelina breaks her toys in anger including her favorite statue she won at ballet school. But she settles down and promises to teach Polly to dance.

3449. ____. *Angelina Dances* (Random, 1992)

3450. ____. *Angelina Ice Skates* (Crown, 1993) k–3. Angelina organizes a New Year's Eve figure skating show. She has some obstacles to overcome: pesky hockey players and a snowball fight.

3451. Holiday, Jane. *Gruesome and Bloodsocks Move House* (Collins, 1987) 3–5.
3452. ____. *Gruesome and Bloodsocks on Wheels* (Collins, 1988) 3–5. A story about the motoring experiences of a young vampire and her cat.

3453. Holl, Alelaide. *Small Bear's Busy Day* (Garrard, 1977) 2–4. Small Bear goes looking for adventure. He meets several friends including Owl who gives him advice.
3454. ____. *Wake-up, Small Bear* (Garrard, 1977) 2–4. Small Bear wakes up from his winter nap in the springtime and finds a new playmate.
3455. ____. *Small Bear's Birthday Party* (Garrard, 1977) 2–4. Small Bear is very literal-minded; he constantly seeks advice from his wise friend Owl. He plays games with Frog and cuddles up with his mother.
3456. ____. *Small Bear Builds a Playhouse* (Garrard, 1978) 2–4. Small Bear's friends prefer their own kind of houses to the playhouse he constructs.
3457. ____. *Small Bear's Name Hunt* (Garrard, 1978) 2–4. Small Bear thinks he needs a prettier moniker so he asks other animals what they are called. He finally realizes that Small Bear is the best name he can have.
3458. ____. *Small Bear and the Secret Surprise* (Garrard, 1978) 2–4. Two bear cubs frantically search for the "secret surprise" that has wandered off into the forest.
3459. ____. *Small Bear Solves a Mystery* (Garrard, 1979) 2–4. In search of an apple thief, Small Bear and his friends find a hungry old bear whom they decide to adopt.

3460. Holl, Kristi. *Just Like a Real Family* (Atheneum, 1983) 4–6. June's foster grandparent turns out to be a crabby old man who doesn't like children in general and June in particular.
3461. ____. *No Strings Attached* (Atheneum, 1988) 4–6. June finds sharing a house with her mother and her foster grandfather requires a difficult adjustment to his forgetfulness and his crabby remarks to her school friends, but she also loves him as family.

3462. Holleyman, Sonia. *Mona the Vampire* (Delacorte, 1991) k–3. Mona disrupts her school and ballet classes when she pretends to be a vampire.
3463. ____. *Mona the Hairdresser* (Doubleday, 1993) k–3. To earn money for a new bike, Mona opens up a hairdressing salon with disastrous results.
3464. ____. *Mona the Champion* (Doubleday, 1994) k–3.

3465. Holm, Jens K. *Kim and the Burried Treasure* (Barker, 1975) 3–5. The treasure is there—then stolen and recovered. Some mystery and tension.
3466. ____. *Kim the Detective* (Barker, 1975) 3–5. The adventures of a small gang in Zealand, the biggest of the Danish Islands.

3467. Honeycutt, Natalie. *All New Jonah Twist* (Bradbury, 1986) 4–6. Jonah has trouble being on time, trouble trying to live up to his older brother, Todd, and trouble with Granville, a fellow student who is a bully. But Jonah is going to change.
3468. ____. *Best Laid Plans of Jonah Twist* (Bradbury, 1988) 4–6. Jonah and Granville become friends. Jonah wants a kitten and wants to find his brother's missing hamster. And he wants to keep Juliet out of his science project plans. He won't be stopped.

3469. Hoobler, Thomas. *Dr. Chill's Project* (Putnam, 1987) 5–8. Allie, 15, joins a group of young people living in a group house run by the jolly Dr. Chill, who is experimenting with ways to help them develop their various psychic powers.
3470. ____. *Dr. Chill* (Putnam, 1990) 5–8.

3471. Hooker, Ruth. *Gertrude Kloppenberg (Private)* (Abingdon, 1970) 3–5. Tells in a first person diary style, day by day, of her reactions to school, the apartment house gang of boys, her lack of friends. She saves some flowers grown in a backyard, gets pneumonia and goes to the hospital.
3472. ____. *Gertrude Kloppenberg II* (Abingdon, 1974) 3–5. Trudy records in her diary her search for a true blue friend, her daily skirmishes with the Murphy boys and gardening at Mrs. Blonski's. She also writes of her camping trip with her new friend Sandra and her family.

3473. Hooks, William. *Mystery on Bleeker Street* (Knopf, 1980) 4–6. Chase is a friend of 78-year-old Babette and her dog. One day she disappears and Chase look for her. The counterfeiters that Babette had seen have kidnapped her dog, so that she will help them.
3474. ____. *Mystery on Liberty Street* (Knopf, 1982) 4–6. Two friends become involved with a police operation investigating the suspicious activities taking place in an abandoned warehouse.

3475. Hope, Laura. *Blue Poodle Mystery* (Wanderer, 1980) 4–6. The Bobbsey twins search for a poodle that interrupted a ballet performance and was then stolen.
3476. ____. *Secret in Pirates Cave* (S & S, 1980) 4–6. A missing teenager, sinister men, kidnapped boys and a threatening note are the clues in solving this mystery.
3477. ____. *Dune Buggy Mystery* (Wanderer, 1981) 4–6. The mystery surrounding a dune buggy bought at the town dump deepens when the vehicle is stolen.
3478. ____. *Missing Pony Mystery* (Wanderer, 1981)

4–6. The Bobbsey twins try to track down a missing pony and saddlebag.

3479. ____. *Rose Parade Mystery* (Wanderer, 1981) 4–6. The Bobbsey twins search to find the culprit who is sabotaging the floats for the famous Rose Parade in Pasedena, California.

3480. ____. *Camp Fire Mystery* (Wanderer, 1982) 4–6. The Bobbsey twins help the members of the Camp Fire club catch the culprits who stole their bicycles.

3481. ____. *Mystery of the Laughing Dinosaur* (Wanderer, 1983) 4–6. When a valuable stamp is stolen from a museum, the four Bobbsey twins try to help find the thieves.

3482. ____. *Music Box Mystery* (Wanderer, 1983) 4–6. When Flossie receives a music box that may have been intended as a gift for someone else, the twins quickly realize that a mystery is involved.

3483. ____. *Scarecrow Mystery* (Wanderer, 1984) 4–6. A scarecrow who disappears and reappears at other locations and an odd shaped key lead the Bobbsey twins into another mystery.

3484. ____. *Haunted House Mystery* (Wanderer, 1985) 4–6. The Bobbsey twins suspect that odd events at the historic Oklahoma mansion and the theft of a duplicate dollhouse may be connected with rare animals being stolen from the zoo.

3485. ____. *Mystery of the Hindu Temple* (Wanderer, 1985) 4–6. The Bobbsey twins travel to Nepal, where they become involved in investigating the theft of valuable Hindu temple treasures.

3486. ____. *Grinning Gargoyle Mystery* (Wanderer, 1986) 4–6. The Bobbsey twins are drawn into a mystery involving the manufacturing of perfume while on a family vacation in Paris.

3487. ____. *Weird Science Mystery* (Pocket, 1990) 4–6. A mystery surrounding a science project.

3488. ____. *Freedom Bell Mystery* (Grosset, 1970) 4–6. The Bobbsey twins hope to expose some rather suspicious activities at the Silver Town Mint Center.

3489. ____. *Smoky Mountain Mystery* (Grosset, 1977) 4–6. The four twin detectives investigate the mysterious thefts and vandalism that threaten to close a Smoky Mountain crafts market.

3490. ____. *T.V. Mystery Show* (Grosset, 1978) 4–6. While in California appearing in a television show, the Bobbsey twins stumble upon a mystery involving a key, a missing dog and some photographs.

3491. ____. *Coral Turtle Mystery* (Grosset, 1979) 4–6. While staying with their cousins on Grand Cayman Island, the Bobbsey twins and their friends search for an exquisite art object and the thief that stole it.

3492. Horvath, Betty. *Hooray for Jasper* (Watts, 1966) k–3. Jasper was too little. He tried to grow bigger but nothing ever happened. Grandpa told him "You get bigger when you do something wonderful." He climbs a tree to rescue a kitten and sure enough that is what happened.

3493. ____. *Jasper Makes Music* (Watts, 1967) k–3. Jasper, eight, yearns for a guitar. He finds a snow shovel which he hopes to put to good use over the winter earning the money to buy what he wants and needs.

3494. ____. *Jasper and the Hero Business* (Watts, 1977) k–3. A young boy plans to become a hero, and he does—in an unexpected way.

3495. Hough, Richard. *Four-wheel Drift* (Harper, 1959) 5–8. Nick and Sam work on their car and make it perfect for the race at Monte Carlo. Nick drives the highly efficient car to victory.

3496. ____. *Fast Circuit* (Harper, 1961) 5–8. Nick is driving for a team that is being sabotaged by a rival team. An accident is caused and a fuel injector is stolen. A team member is the traitor but Nick still wins the race.

3497. Houston, James. *Frozen Fire* (Atheneum, 1977) 5–8. Matthew's father is lost in an Arctic storm. Matthew and Kayak, his friend, go to look for him. The trip is dangerous and they run out of gas for their snowmobile before they reach home.

3498. ____. *Black Diamonds* (Atheneum, 1982) 5–8. While returning home they find gold nuggets. When Matthew's father does reach home they all set out to find the mother lode of these nuggets. Is it "black diamonds" as oil is known up there?

3499. ____. *Ice Sword* (Atheneum, 1985) 5–8. Matthew, Kayak, and Jill, along with Dr. Luman spend the summer in the Arctic. There are shark attacks and a night spent on the ice. There are also strong friendships and mutual dependency.

3500. Houston, James. *White Archer* (Harcourt, 1967) 5–8. Kungo lost his parents in a massacre. He wants revenge. But when the time comes to inflict it, he has doubts.

3501. ____. *Falcon Bow* (McElderry, 1986) 5–8. Kungo finds the Inuit people starving because of the loss of the caribou. Something must be done about the ecological chain.

3502. Howard, Elizabeth. *Train to Lulu's* (Bradbury, 1988) k–3. A story about the experiences of two young sisters alone on the train to their grandmother's house.

3503. ____. *Mac and Marie and the Train Toss Surprise* (Four Winds, 1993) k–3. One summer evening a brother and sister eagerly await the train that runs by their house, wondering about the surprise their uncle has promised them.

3504. Howe, James. *Bunnicula* (Atheneum, 1979) 3–5. Bunnicula is a vampire bunny. He was found in a shoe box at the movies. Harold, the dog, and Chester, the cat, know he's no ordinary rabbit.

3505. ____. *Howliday Inn* (Atheneum, 1982) 4–6.

Harold and Chester, a dog and a cat, are in the crime detection business.

3506. ____. *Celery Stalks at Midnight* (Atheneum, 1983) 4–6. Chester the cat is now more than ever convinced that Bunnicula is a vampire when more white vegetables show up.

3507. ____. *Nighty-Nightmare* (Atheneum, 1987) 4–6. When scary strangers appear at the Monroes' overnight campsite, Chester the cat tries to convince the family's two dogs that foul play is intended.

3508. ____. *Harold and Chester in the Fright Before Christmas* (Morrow, 1988) 4–6. Harold the dog and Chester the cat try to figure out why Howie the puppy dreads the arrival of Santa Claus.

3509. ____. *Harold and Chester in Scared Silly* (Morrow, 1989) 4–6. The Monroes leave their cat and two dogs alone on Halloween night, unaware that their pets are about to be visited by a strange figure who might be a wicked witch.

3510. ____. *Hot Fudge* (Morrow, 1990) 4–6. The Monroe family tests Harold the dog's willpower when they leave him alone with a pan of fudge.

3511. ____. *Return to Howliday Inn* (Atheneum, 1992) 4–6. The Monroe family pets are again boarded at Chateau Bow-Wow, where some spooky goings-on serve as a distraction from the kennel's poor food.

3512. ____. *Rabbit-cadabra* (Morrow, 1993) 4–6. When the animals in the Monroe household see a picture of Bunnicula the rabbit on a poster for a magician, they jump to an alarming conclusion about vampire rabbits.

3513. ____. *Bunnicula Escapes* (Atheneum, 1994) 4–6. Bunnicula is at the county fair, complete with fun house and roller coaster.

3514. Howe, James. *What Eric Knew* (Atheneum, 1986) 3–5. After Eric moves away he sends cryptic notes to his friends David and Sebastian who investigate a mysterious death. A Sebastian Barth mystery.

3515. ____. *Stage Fright* (Atheneum, 1986) 3–5. Sebastian Barth is involved in a theater mystery. There are warnings and some strange accidents as a famous actress comes to visit his home town. "House of Cards" seems jinxed.

3516. ____. *Eat Your Poison, Dear* (Atheneum, 1986) 4–6. Young sleuth Sebastian and three friends probe the mystery of a poisoning in their school cafeteria.

3517. ____. *Dew Drop Dead* (Atheneum, 1990) 4–6. While setting up a homeless shelter at the church, Sebastian and his friends, Corrie and David, solve the mystery of a dead man found in an abandoned inn.

3518. Howe, James. *Pinky and Rex* (Atheneum, 1990) k–3. Rex and her best friend, Pinky, each the proud possessor of 27 stuffed animals of dinosaurs, find their visit to the museum and its gift shop complicated by Pinky's little sister Amanda.

3519. ____. *Pinky and Rex Get Married* (Atheneum, 1990) k–3. Rex and her best friend Pinky decide they like each other enough to get married, and all their stuffed toys and dinosaurs appear as guests at the wedding.

3520. ____. *Pinky and Rex and the Spelling Bee* (Atheneum, 1991) k–3. Excited about holding onto his position as the best speller in the second grade, Pinky has an embarrassing accident but is cheered up by his best friend, Rex.

3521. ____. *Pinky and Rex and the Mean Old Witch* (Atheneum, 1991) k–3. Pinky, Rex and Amanda plot revenge on the bad-tempered old woman who lives across the street, until Pinky realizes that she is lonely and needs new friends.

3522. ____. *Pinky and Rex Go to Camp* (Atheneum, 1992) k–3. Although his best friend Rex is excited about going to camp, Pinky is afraid of leaving home.

3523. ____. *Pinky and Rex and the New Baby* (Atheneum, 1993) k–3. Determined to be a good big sister, Rex starts spending all her time with the baby her family has adopted, making her neighbor Pinky, fear that he has lost her friendship.

3524. ____. *Pinky and Rex and the Bully* (Atheneum, 1996) k–3. Pinky learns the importance of identity as he defends his favorite color, pink, and his friendship with a girl, Rex, from the neighborhood bully.

3525. ____. *Pinky and Rex and the Double-Dad Weekend* (Atheneum, 1995) k–3. Pinky and Rex share a weekend with their fathers camping indoors due to rain.

3526. Howe, Raymond. *Hannibal on the Farm* (1977) k–3.

3527. ____. *Hannibal Runs Away* (1977) k–3.

3528. ____. *Hannibal on Holiday* (1977) k–3.

3529. ____. *Hannibal Goes to School* (1979) k–3. At school Hannibal the hamster discusses with a mouse and a swallow their respective homes.

3530. ____. *Hannibal on the Nature Trail* (1979) k–3. Hannibal and his friends talk to sundry birds, mammals and insects while going through Country Park.

3531. ____. *Hannibal and the Pet Show* (1979) k–3.

3532. Hubner, Carol. *Tattered Tallis* (Judaica, 1980) 4–6. There are several strange mysteries solved: a museum robbery and a spy from East Germany.

3533. ____. *Whispering Mezuzah* (Judaica, 1980) 4–6. There are several strange mysteries solved: the strange disappearance of mezuzahs and a counterfeiting ring.

3534. Huddy, Delia. *Sandwich Street Blue* (Hamilton, 1974) 3–5. There is a new school being built on the waste ground next to the old school and the students watch the progress. Then the school is broken into and Miss Woodford's class is going to find out who did it.

3535. ____. *Sandwich Street Safari* (Hamilton, 1977) 3–5. A class of school children have an outing to a safari park. There is drama, a suspense and humor between the children.

3536. Hughes, Dean. *Nothing But Net* (Bullseye, 1992) 4–6. A black boy from Los Angeles has some trouble fitting in with the twelve-and-under basketball team, in his new, mostly white neighborhood in Angel Park.

3537. ____. *Point Guard* (Bullseye, 1992) 4–6. Jackie Willis hopes to convince the coach of the basketball team in Angel Park that she can play as well as the boys.

3538. ____. *Go to the Hoop* (Bullseye, 1993) 4–6. Assigned to play center in the starting lineup of his basketball team because he is a tall, fifth grader Harlan feels pressure to perform well and tries to develop some self-confidence.

3539. ____. *On the Line* (Bullseye, 1993) 4–6. Unless star guard Miles "Tip" Harris can keep his cool under pressure from opposing players, the Angel Park Lakers could have a short season.

3540. Hughes, Dean. *Making the Team* (Bullseye, 1990) 4–6. Three third grade rookies who make the Little League team aren't immediately accepted by the older players.

3541. ____. *Big Base Hit* (Knopf, 1990) 4–6. Harlan Sloan, a rookie on the Little League baseball team, gets his first big base hit.

3542. ____. *Winning Streak* (Knopf, 1990) 4–6. Kenny, a rookie star of Angel Park's Little League baseball team, finds himself in a major slump because he is trying too hard.

3543. ____. *What a Catch* (Bullseye, 1990) 4–6. Brian Waters is so nervous that he can't seem to do anything right on his little league team, the Angel Park Dodgers, but a pep talk from a big league star psyches him up to make a winning catch.

3544. ____. *Rookie Star* (Bullseye, 1990) 4–6. A talented first baseman for the Angel Park Dodgers, is determined to prove that the name has not gone to his head.

3545. ____. *Pressure Play* (Random, 1990) 4–6. When the Angel Park Dodgers get so rattled by the Red that they can hardly play baseball, rookie Jacob attempts to relax them with meditation exercises he finds in a sports psychology book.

3546. ____. *Line Drive* (Bullseye, 1990) 4–6. When Jeff Reinhold breaks his arm, a small Asian boy named Kian Jie becomes the new second baseman.

3547. ____. *Championship* (Bullseye, 1990) 4–6. Members of the Angel Park community wonder where Coach Wilken's loyalties lie when he helps players on rival teams before the championship baseball game.

3548. Hughes, Richard. *Gertrude's Child* (Harlin Quist, 1966) k–3. Gertrude, a wooden doll, eager to be free from the little girl who owns her, runs away. She meets with a strange old man whose store is filled with peculiar merchandise—children for sale.

3549. ____. *Gertrude and the Mermaid* (Harlin Quist, 1971) k–3. In this triangle story of a doll, her little owner and an intruding mermaid-child, the loves and jealousies of wooden-headed, wooden-hearted Gertrude (the unsinkable unbruisable, much ill-used doll) typifies every child's first necessary struggles toward independence as a "person."

3550. Ichikawa, Satomi. *Nora's Castle* (Philomel, 1986) k–3. Accompanied by her doll Maggie, Teddy the stuffed bear, and Kiki the dog, a little girl set out to explore the mysterious castle on the hill.

3551. ____. *Nora's Stars* (Philomel, 1988) k–3. While visiting her grandmother, Nora joins with the animated toys from an old chest to bring the star down from the night sky, but their loss might make the night sky look black and sad.

3552. ____. *Nora's Surprise* (Philomel, 1991) k–3. Nora, Maggie, Teddy and Kiki receive an invitation to a tea party to be given by the geese. It soon becomes a picnic when Benjy the sheep can't get through the house door. Benjy turned the picnic into chaos but later apologizes and sends Nora a knitted wool sweater.

3553. ____. *Nora's Duck* (Philomel, 1991) k–3. Nora finds a duckling in the woods and takes it to Doctor John, who provides love and care for many wild and domestic animals who have come to grief.

3554. ____. *Nora's Roses* (Putnam, 1993) k–3. Nora has a head cold and must stay in her room while others walk by and pluck roses from a bush near her window. She is determined to keep the last rose—and she does by drawing its picture.

3555. Ichikawa, Satomi. *Suzanne and Nicholas in the Garden* (Watts, 1976) k–3. Two children talk about their garden and other gardens that they have seen. A light ecology lesson for children.

3556. ____. *Suzanne and Nicholas at the Market* (Watts, 1977) k–3. A visit to a French countryside market causes two children to discuss where the things for sale come from and they reflect about them.

3557. ____. *Suzanne and Nicholas and the Four Seasons* (Watts, 1979) k–3.

3558. Impey, Rose. *Desperate for a Dog* (Dutton, 1989) 3–5. Two sisters, who are desperate to get a dog, meet with firm opposition from their father, until their family is asked to take care of a sick neighbor's dog for several weeks.

3559. ____. *No-Name Dog* (Dutton, 1990) 3–5. A family tries to find just the right name for a new dog.

3560. ____. *Houdini Dog* (Dutton, 1989) 3–5. Dad is portrayed as the villain in this story told by "me and my sister."

3561. Impey, Rose. *Rabbit's Story* (Dutton, 1990) 3–5.

3562. ____. *Revenge of the Rabbit* (Orchard, 1990) 3–5. Pooh (Philippa) is fat and awkward. Piglet (Meena) is small and timid. They are good friends, ready to do good deeds and are in constant trouble. Snuggles is a mean-tempered rabbit that Pooh and Piglet want to free.

3563. Inkiow, Dimiter. *Me and My Sister Clara* (Pantheon, 1979) 3–5. A story of a small boy and his sister.
3564. ____. *Me and Clara and Casimir the Cat* (Pantheon, 1979) 3–5. The adventures of a brother and sister with each other, their parents and their pets.
3565. ____. *Me and Clara and Snuffy the Dog* (Pantheon, 1980) 3–5. Clara's five-year-old brother tells of domestic mischief, a robber protection devise, outsmarting a vacuum cleaner salesman, and others.
3566. ____. *Me and Clara and the Baldwin Pony* (Pantheon, 1980) 3–5. A five-year-old boy relates the adventures he shares with his sister.

3567. Inkpen, Mick. *Kipper* (Little, 1992) k–3. Kipper the dog is tired of his smelly old blanket and his chewed up basket. He looks for a better place to sleep. He tries the flowerpot, the grass, the lily pond. Will he ever find a bed as good as his old one?
3568. ____. *Kipper's Toybox* (Harcourt, 1992) k–3. Kipper the dog's life changes when he discovers why there is a hole in his toy box.
3569. ____. *Kipper's Birthday* (Harcourt, 1993) k–3. Kipper's busy with preparations for his own birthday party. The cake looked flat but came out fine. The invitations, delivered the day after they were written say "tomoro." He spends a lonely day but has a surprise party the day after his birthday.
3570. ____. *Kipper's Book of Colors* (Harcourt, 1995) k–3. Kipper, a brown and white dog, flies a blue kite and eats red strawberries.
3571. ____. *Kipper's Book of Counting* (Harcourt, 1995) k–3. Kipper, a dog, feeds four hens and digs holes with four moles.
3572. ____. *Kipper's Book of Weather* (Harcourt, 1995) k–3. Kipper the dog experiences rain, sun, snow, ice, fog, wind, hail and finally, a rainbow.
3573. ____. *Kipper's Book of Opposites* (Harcourt, 1995) k–3. Kipper, a dog, has a happy face and a big balloon but he has a sad face when it pops.
3574. ____. *Where, Oh Where, Is Kipper's Bear?* (Harcourt, 1995) k–3. The reader helps Kipper search through the pages for his lost Teddy Bear.

3575. Isenberg, Barbara. *Adventures of Albert, the Running Bear* (Clarion, 1982) k–3. Following his escape from the zoo, Albert Bear encounters a series of mishaps and finally finds himself running in a marathon.
3576. ____. *Albert the Running Bear Gets the Jitters* (Clarion, 1987) k–3. Albert the Running Bear is challenged to a race by a new bully bear at the zoo and has to deal with all sorts of stress symptoms.

3577. Isherwood, Shirley. *Is That You, Mrs. Pinkerton-Trunks* (Hutchinson, 1984) k–3. The adventures of Billie and all her toys: Mr. Mulford-Haven the lion, Monkey and Mrs. Pinkerton-Trunks, an elephant.
3578. ____. *Surprise for Mrs. Pinkerton-Trunks* (Hutchinson, 1986) k–3. A little girl, her dog, her father and three special stuffed animals who behave like people. Short stories about picnics, wallpaper, nightmares, etc.

3579. Iwamura, Kazuo. *Fourteen Forest Mice and the Harvest Moon Watch* (G. Stevens, 1991) k–3. Members of the Forest Mouse family encounter tree frogs, dragonflies, inchworms, and birds as they climb a tree to enjoy the beauty of the setting sun and the rising moon.
3580. ____. *Fourteen Forest Mice and the Winter Sledding Day* (G. Stevens, 1991) k–3. Members of the Forest Mouse family wait out a winter blizzard with indoor games and then go outside to enjoy sledding.
3581. ____. *Fourteen Forest Mice and the Spring Meadow Picnic* (G. Stevens, 1991) k–3. Members of the Forest Mouse family enjoy the delights of nature as they go on an invigorating spring picnic.
3582. ____. *Fourteen Forest Mice and the Summer Laundry Day* (G. Stevens, 1991) k–3.

3583. Iwamura, Kazuo. *Tan Tan's Hat* (Bradbury, 1983) k–3. Tan Tan's hat is for tossing up into the sky, rolling and catching things. But, Tan Tan is no ordinary monkey!
3584. ____. *Tan Tan's Suspenders* (Bradbury, 1983) k–3. A pair of ordinary suspenders becomes a hammock, a slingshot, and other sources of fun for a happy-go-lucky monkey.

3585. Iwamura, Kazuo. *Ton and Pon, Big and Little* (Bradbury, 1984) 3–5. Two young dogs, one tall and large and the other short and small, disagree about which is better—big or little.
3586. ____. *Ton and Pon, Two Good Friends* (Bradbury, 1984) 3–5. Sharing the carrying of a heavy basket to a friend inspires Ton and Pon, two young dogs, to find a way to lighten it.

3587. Iwasaki, Chihiro. *Momoko's Lovely Day* (Follett, 1969) k–3. A child's eye view of a single day as she looks out of the window at flowers blurred by rain, hides behind the curtain when the telephone rings, and plays with her kitten.
3588. ____. *Brother For Momoko* (Follett, 1970) k–3. Momoko waits for the new baby to be brought home: she looks at the pram, wonders about a present, and shows the cradle to her teddy bear. Her anticipation is both fearful and happy.
3589. ____. *Momoko and the Pretty Bird* (Follett, 1972) k–3. Longing for a singing bird, a little girl catches one but realizes he is unhappy in a cage.
3590. ____. *Momoko's Birthday* (Follett, 1973) k–3.

Tomorrow she is five but today she shares in her friend's all too brief birthday. When her own fifth birthday arrives, the countryside is covered with snow in celebration, and her Mummy's present of a wooly hat and mittens is put to instant use.

3591. Jacob, Helen. *Secret of the Strawbridge Place* (Atheneum, 1976) 5–8. Two friends look for a place rumored as a former underground railway station. One of them disappears.

3592. ____. *Diary of the Strawbridge Place* (Atheneum, 1978) 5–8. Quakers operate an Underground Railroad from Ohio across the Erie to Pennsylvania.

3593. Jacques, Brian. *Mossflower* (Philomel, 1988) 5–8. Prequel. Martin the warrior mouse and Gonff the mouse thief set out to find the missing ruler of Mossflower, while the other inhabitants of the woodland prepare to rebel against the evil wildcat who has seized power.

3594. ____. *Redwall* (Philomel, 1986) 5–8. When the peaceful life of Redwall Abby is shattered by the arrival of the evil rat Cluny and his villainous hordes, Matthias, a young mouse determines to find the sword of Martin the Warrior to destroy this enemy.

3595. ____. *Mattimeo* (Philomel, 1990) 5–8. Mattimeo, the son of the warrior mouse Matthias, learns to take up the sword and joins the other animal inhabitants of Redwall Abby in resisting Slagar the fox and his band of marauders.

3596. ____. *Mariel of Redwall* (Philomel, 1992) 5–8. The mousemaid Mariel achieves victory at sea for the animals of Redwall Abbey, fighting the savage pirate rat Gabool the Wild, warlord of rodent corsairs.

3597. ____. *Salamandastron* (Philomel, 1992) 5–8. In the woods and mountains of Redwall the badgers and mice and moles live in peace. That was until one day when a weasel assassin came to change their world forever.

3598. ____. *Martin the Warrior* (Philomel, 1994) 5–8. The story revolves around a community of mice in an abbey. Their arch rivals are rats. There is one mouse who is the epitome of innocence with high ideals. There is one rat, the leader, who is "evil" personified.

3599. ____. *Bellmaker* (Philomel, 1995) 5–8. The story has four different settings: Castle Gloret, where a fox rules as the Urgan Naguru, chief of the Horderats; Mossflower Abbey, where two infants befriend Blaggut, a gentle Searat; Southward, where river otters and moles fight to protect Serena and Truffen; and at sea where Joseph the Bellmaker join forces with Finnbar to search for Joseph's daughter, Mariel.

3600. Jacques, Faith. *Tilly's House* (Atheneum, 1979) k–3. Tilly leaves the dollhouse where she works as a kitchen maid to find a home of her own.

3601. ____. *Tilly's Rescue* (Atheneum, 1981) k–3.

When her friend does not return from a Christmas shopping trip, Tilly a tiny wooden doll, sets out to find him.

3602. James, Simon. *Day Jake Vacuumed* (Bantam, 1989) k–3. Jake, who does not like helping people or have others tell him what to do, signals his displeasure at being asked to vacuum by sucking his entire family into the vacuum cleaner.

3603. ____. *Jake and the Babysitter* (Bantam, 1992) k–3.

3604. Janosch. *Trip to Panama* (Andersen, 1978) k–3. Little Bear and Little Tiger are living together happily. Bear goes fishing and Tiger collects mushrooms. One day they discover bananas and set off for Panama where they come from. They stay with Hare and Hedgehog.

3605. ____. *Treasure Hunting Trip* (Andersen, 1980) k–3. Little Bear and Little Tiger go on an unsuccessful quest for treasure but get unexpected rewards when they get home.

3606. Jaman, Julia. *When Poppy Ran Away* (Andersen, 1987) 4–6.

3607. ____. *Poppy and the Vicarage Ghost* (Andersen, 1988) 4–6. Poppy finds a boy hiding in an old vicarage when she goes to feed a cat there. With the help of Alice, a ghost, they find a tunnel and the boy escapes from his divorced father. They also find Alice's bones which will be properly buried.

3608. Jenkin-Pearce, Suzie. *Bad Boris and the New Kitten* (Children's, 1987) k–3. Boris the elephant gets into many humorous predicaments when a kitten comes to live in his house.

3609. ____. *Bad Boris's Big Ache* (Dial, 1988) k–3. Boris knows he will not like school. But once there he comforts a new-found friend (a crocodile) and realizes he is not alone. Boris joins in all the activities and his teacher praises him.

3610. ____. *Bad Boris Goes to School* (Macmillan, 1989) k–3. Boris the elephant knows he's going to hate school, but his first day turns out quite differently from what he expected.

3611. ____. *Bad Boris Moves House* (Macmillan, 1993) k–3.

3612. Jennings, Michael. *Mattie Fritts and the Flying Mushrooms* (Macmillan, 1973) 4–6. When an old lady buys a giant mushroom a wind carries them off on an adventurous trip.

3613. ____. *Mattie Fritts and the Cuckoo Caper* (Macmillan, 1976) 4–6. Two children and their resourceful baby-sitter, Mattie Fritts, set out to rescue Gretel, the cuckoo bird kidnapped by an evil toy soldier.

3614. Jennings, Sharon. *Jeremiah and Mrs. Ming*

(Firefly, 1990) k–3. An account of Jeremiah's reasons for not settling down for the night. A series of nighttime antics, each gently dealt with by Mrs. Ming.

3615. ____. *When Jeremiah Found Mrs. Ming* (Annick, 1992) k–3.

3616. ____. *Sleep Tight, Mrs. Ming* (Annick, 1993) k–3. Mrs. Ming assures Jeremiah about his fears and in turn is assured by Jeremiah when she becomes afraid of a thunderstorm.

3617. Jezard, Alison. *Albert in Scotland* (Gollancz, 1969) 2-4. Albert is a good humored bear. He visits Scotland and takes in most things (except the monster) that any sassenach has heard of.

3618. ____. *Albert and Henry* (Gollancz, 1970) 2–4. Albert is a bear and Henry is a horse. They are friends. They set out on a caravan trip to see the hop fields, the morris dancers, Dover and the hovercraft, Ramsgate and Canterbury.

3619. ____. *Albert* (Schroeder, 1971) 2–4. Albert lives by himself in London. He shops, rides a horse, goes on a cruise and goes to tea. He also goes to a football game and is asked to make the kick-off.

3620. ____. *Albert Goes to Sea* (Gollancz, 1973) 2–4. The adventures and misadventures of a trip down the Thames by motor cruiser. They visit a nuclear submarine, go aboard a pirate ship and investigate a sunken Spanish galleon.

3621. ____. *Albert, Police Bear* (Gollancz, 1975) 2–4. Albert and his friends, Henry, Jason and Loopy meet the Queen. Albert becomes a police bear, Henry is a police horse and Loopy a tracker police dog.

3622. ____. *Albert Goes Trekking* (Gollancz, 1976) 2–4. Albert goes trekking along Hadrian's Wall. Here again are Henry the horse. Digger the Koala bear and Tum Tum the panda.

3623. ____. *Albert's Circus* (Gollancz, 1977) 2–4. The animals drive red cars and eat Chinese food. They raise money for good causes. Tum Tum juggles, Digger walks a tightrope, Angus rides Dobie the elephant while Albert is the clown.

3624. ____. *Albert Goes Treasure Hunting* (Gollancz, 1978) 2–4. Albert discovers a metal detector in the junk yard and goes hunting for treasure. He gets four tin cans, an electrical light fitting, a carriage wheel, a 1934 penny and a toy top. But he meets an archaeologist who invites Albert to a digging.

3625. ____. *Albert's Christmas.* (Gollancz, 1978) 2–4. A fresh look at turkey, mistletoe, pantomime and a decorated tree, with Albert standing in as Father Christmas.

3626. ____. *Albert on the Farm* (Puffin, 1981) 2–4. A story of chunky Albert, the bear who is learning how to cope on a farm. This is a list of only 16 of 90 stories by W.E. Johns.

3627. Johns, W.E. *Biggles Flies West* (Hodder, 1916) 4–6. The plot of this story depends on a cursed dou-

bloon that brings bad luck to anyone who possesses it.

3628. ____. *Biggles and Company* (Hodder, 1932/1992) 4–6.

3629. ____. *Another Job for Biggles* (Hodder, 1951/1991) 4–6. Biggles is a fatalistic young flier in realistic war time.

3630. ____. *Biggles, Secret Agent* (Hodder, 1940/1991) 4–6. Biggles gives an old Central European Jew the money that will help him escape to Switzerland. He is a friend of the Jews.

3631. ____. *Biggles Buries the Hatchet* (Hodder, 1969) 4–6.

3632. ____. *Biggles and the Golden Bird* (Hodder, 1978) 4–6. This story involves lotions that made the wearer invisible (worn by villainous Chinese) death rays and lost worlds.

3633. ____. *Biggles, Foreign Legionnaire* (Armada, 1972) 4–6. Biggles, encouraged by a colleague in the French Surete enlists incognito in the Foreign Legion in order to track down an international gang skilled in the timely provocation of incidents designed to boost the demand for arms supplies.

3634. ____. *Biggles and the Saragasso Triangle* (Hodder, 1978) 4–6. A battle between Biggles and Erich von Stalheim. German Fokkers and British Camels are hurtling through the skies. A large oceanic oil rig is capable of surfacing and submerging at high speed, it has a laser gun that can bring down anything.

3635. ____. *Biggles and the Plot That Failed* (Hodder, 1969) 4–6. With World War II Biggles was back in the world of realism, in charge of his own squadron. Then after the war, he became a cold warrior, even joining up with his old antagonist, von Stalheim, against the real enemy in the east. Finally he became a policeman.

3636. ____. *Biggles and the Tiger* (Knight, 1981) 4–6. A story set in never-never land where jet fighters and de Havilland Leopard Moths share the sky.

3637. ____. *Biggles Defies the Swastika* (Hodder, 1992) 4–6.

3638. ____. *Biggles in the Orient* (Hodder, 1992) 4–6.

3639. ____. *Biggles Learns to Fly* (Hodder, 1992) 4–6.

3640. ____. *Biggles Flies East* (Hodder, 1992) 4–6.

3641. ____. *Biggles in Spain* (Hodder, 1992) 4–6.

3642. ____. *Rescue Flight* (Hodder, 1992) 4–6.

3643. Johnson, Angela. *Joshua by the Sea* (Orchard, 1994) k–3. Joshua goes to the shore with his family.

3644. ____. *Joshua's Night Whispers* (Orchard, 1994) k–3. Joshua and his father listen to the night sounds.

3645. Johnson, Crockett. *Harold and the Purple Crayon* (Harper, 1955) 2–4. Harold's purple crayon helps him to create wonderful adventures as he walks in the moonlight.

3646. ____. *Harold's Fairy Tale* (Harper, 1956) 2–4.

3647. ____. *Harold's Trip to the Sky* (Harper, 1957) 2–4. Harold travels to the sky with the help of his purple crayon.

3648. ____. *Harold at the North Pole* (Harper, 1957) 2–4. Harold sets off with his purple crayon to find a Christmas tree. He draws his way to Santa's workshop. Santa is snowed in but Harold's crayon sends him off on his annual journey.

3649. ____. *Harold's Circus* (Harper, 1959/1981) 2–4. Harold and his purple crayon are in command of a large laughter-filled circus.

3650. ____. *Picture for Harold's Room* (Harper, 1960) 2–4. Harold wades through an ocean, escapes being bumped by a jet and sees a large daisy, all with the help of his magic purple crayon. He then discovers that he is smaller than some objects and larger than others.

3651. ____. *Harold's ABC* (Harper, 1963) 2–4. Harold takes a trip to the moon and comes home again simply by drawing his way through the letters of the alphabet with a purple crayon.

3652. Johnston, Joanna. *Sugarplum* (Knopf, 1955) k–3. A tiny little doll named Sugarplum was always getting lost and accused by the larger dolls of being no more than a trinket. But when she falls into a jar of newly made jelly and is lost for months, Sugarplum gets her chance to prove she is a little girl's real doll.

3653. ____. *Sugarplum and Snowball* (Knopf, 1968) k–3. After she gets a new dress, a little doll is almost forgotten because she looks too nice to be played with—too nice, that is, for everybody but a mischievous kitten.

3654. Johnston, Joanna. *Edie Changes Her Mind* (Putnam, 1964) k–3.

3655. ____. *That's Right Edie* (Putnam, 1967) k–3. Edie preferred to scribble instead of learning how to write properly. But one day she was required to sign her name to receive her new birthday bicycle.

3656. ____. *Speak Up, Edie* (Putnam, 1974) k–3. Edie is a talkative little girl. She gets to be narrator of the class Thanksgiving pageant. Then Edie gets a sudden attack of stage fright. But the red-haired, bigmouth makes a spirited comeback.

3657. Johnston, Tony. *Odd Jobs* (Putnam, 1977) 3–5. Three episodes in which Odd Jobs does all sorts of jobs, the odder the better.

3658. ____. *Odd Jobs and Friends* (Putnam, 1982) 3–5. Presents the further adventures of Odd Jobs, the boy who would tackle any job, including teaching someone to blow bubbles.

3659. Johnston, Tony. *Adventures of Mole and Troll* (Putnam, 1972) 3–5. Two very good friends plan for

Mother's Day, go to the beach, experiment with new shoes and dig tunnels.

3660. ____. *Mole and Troll Trim the Tree* (Putnam, 1974) 3–5. Mole and Troll agree to trim a tree for Christmas but disagree on the ornaments as each dislikes the other's choices.

3661. ____. *Night Noises* (Putnam, 1977) 3–5. Episodes in which Mole makes four wishes; Troll visits Mole; Troll loses a tooth; and night noises scare the pair of friends.

3662. ____. *Happy Birthday, Mole and Troll* (Putnam, 1979) 3–5. Mole and Troll learn several lessons about friendship in these stories.

3663. Jones, Diana. *Lives of Christopher Chant* (Greenwillow, 1988) 5–8. Prequel. Christopher (Chrestomanci) is the famous magician of Caprona. He has nine lives. Uncle Ralph is an evil enchanter who is using Christopher to increase his own power. Set earlier than *Charmed Life.*

3664. ____. *Charmed Life* (Macmillan, 1978) 5–8. A story of a parallel world of the magician Chrestomanci. Gwendole wants supernatural powers from her mysterious guardian.

3665. ____. *Magicians of Caprona* (Macmillan, 1987) 5–8. The two houses of magicians in Caprona: Montanas and Petrocchis are so engrossed in their rivalry that they fail to notice an outside threat to their power. Tonino Montana and Angelica Petrocchi are captured but in the end save the day.

3666. ____. *Witch Week* (Greenwillow, 1982) 5–8. When a teacher at an English boarding school finds a note on his desk accusing someone in the class of being a witch, magical things begin to happen and an inquisitor is summoned.

3667. Jones, Rebecca. *Germy Blew It* (Dutton, 1987) 4–6. Dying to get on television and become famous, Jeremy Bluett tries all sorts of schemes.

3668. ____. *Germy Blew It—Again* (Holt, 1988) 4–6. In order to pay off a school debt, Germy goes into the gerbil breeding business.

3669. ____. *Germy Blew the Bugle* (Arcade, 1990) 4–6. Jeremy Bluett starts a school newspaper with dreams of making a fortune; but as usual, his grand plans backfire.

3670. ____. *Germy in Charge* (Dutton, 1993) 4–6. Sixth grader Jeremy is elected as student representative on the school board, but he finds that the job brings certain complications and not as much power as he had expected.

3671. Joosee, Barbara. *Anna and the Cat Lady* (Harper, 1992) 4–6. When Anna, nine, rescues a stray kitten, it leads her into friendship with Mrs. Darafiny, an eccentric old woman with many cats and a paranoid conviction that the Martians are after her.

3672. ____. *Anna, the One and Only* (Lippincott, 1988) 4–6. Anna Skogge, a third grader, struggles to express her true personality, and finally finds a way to be herself and become friends with her older sister, Kimberly.

3673. Joy, Margaret. *Tales from Allotment Lane School* (Faber, 1983) 4–6. A collection of stories about the activities of students at Allotment Lane School.

3674. ____. *Allotment Lane School Again* (Faber, 1985) 4–6. More stories of Miss Moe's class and their adventures at Allotment Lane School.

3675. ____. *Hild at Allotment Lane School* (Faber, 1987) 4–6. Hild is a scamp; she jokes and lies. Miss Moe is her teacher and is on her side even though she disrupts the swimming class and lunch period.

3676. ____. *Allotment Lane in London* (Faber, 1990) 4–6. The children go on a tour and experience the zoo, Tower of London, Buckingham Palace, and the Thames in four days. Hild eats too much, the twins get lost, Stevie gets a cold, Gary meets an uncle on the Underground, and more.

3677. Jungman, Ann. *Lucy and the Big Bad Wolf* (Grafton, 1986) 4–6. A series of episodes in which the wolf is gradually weaned away from his traditional role after Lucy has persuaded him to masquerade as a dog. He calls himself 2:15, he plays football, does odd jobs and baby-sits.

3678. ____. *Lucy Keeps the Wolf from the Door* (Young Lions, 1989) 4–6. In this story we see 2:15, the well-read mannerly wolf from the land of fairy tales and his cynical wife 3:45. He has decided to become environmentally aware and a vegetarian. He lands in the hospital from playing cricket and later fathers three cubs.

3679. ____. *Lucy and the Wolf in Sheep's Clothing* (Young Lions, 1992) 4–6. Lucy renews her acquaintance with wolf, 2:15 and his mate, 3:45. She is dismayed when he wants to leave his London flat and return to his old home ground.

3680. Jungman, Ann. *Day Teddy Didn't Clean Up* (Barron, 1989) k–3. Teddy and the little boy who is his friend are very naughty and make a terrible mess in the little boy's room.

3681. ____. *Day Teddy Got Very Worried* (Barron, 1989) k–3. Teddy worries that his friend, the little boy, will go on vacation without him.

3682. ____. *Day Teddy Made New Friends* (Barron, 1989) k–3. Teddy and his friend, the little boy, go to play school and learn to make new friends.

3683. ____. *Day Teddy Wanted Granddad to Notice Him* (Barron, 1989) k–3. Teddy and his friend, the little boy, try all sorts of antics to get Grandpa to notice them.

3684. Kahl, Virginia. *Gunhilde's Christmas Booke* (Scribner, 1972) k–3. Although her family is imprisoned in a strange land on Christmas, Gunhilde still has her book containing all the ingredients for a happy holiday.

3685. ____. *Gunhilde and the Halloween Spell* (Scribner, 1975) k–3. On Halloween Gunhilde and her 12 sisters are led astray by a wicked old witch who turns them into small brown toads.

3686. Kahn, Peggy. *Ten Little Care Bears Counting Book* (Random, 1983) k–3. Verses describe how the Care Bears float away one by one, thus counting from one to ten.

3687. ____. *Care Bears and the New Baby* (Random, 1983) k–3. The Care Bears help Jill get over her disappointment when she gets a new baby brother instead of a sister.

3688. ____. *Care Bears' Book of ABC's* (Random, 1983) k–3. The Care Bears introduce the letters from A to Z.

3689. ____. *Care Bears Help Santa* (Random, 1984) k–3. The Care Bears help Santa Claus when he gets lost in a fog on Christmas Eve.

3690. ____. *Care Bears' Up and Down* (Random, 1984) k–3. A book of opposites with basic child appeal.

3691. ____. *Care Bears' Circus of Shapes* (Random, 1984) k–3. The reader is asked to find a variety of shapes in the circus parade.

3692. ____. *Care Bears' Night Before Christmas* (Random, 1985) k–3. An adaptation of "The Night Before Christmas" in which Santa visits the Care Bears, who are nestled on Puffy Cloud beds.

3693. ____. *Care Bears: Try, Try Again!* (Random, 1985) k–3. Tommy thinks he can't play baseball, until the Care Bears lend a hand.

3694. ____. *Care Bears and the Whale Tale* (Random, 1992) k–3. The Care Bears and their human friends rescue Emma the humpback whale when she becomes entangled in a fishing net.

3695. Kahn, Peggy. *Popple Opposites* (Random, 1986) k–3. The Popples explore the world of opposites, experiencing such contrasts as little/big and push/pull.

3696. ____. *Popples and King Most* (Random, 1986) k–3. King Most tries to think of a way in which his kingdom can be the very most.

3697. ____. *Popples' Vacation* (Random, 1987) k–3.

3698. Kalman, Maira. *Max Makes a Million* (Viking, 1990) k–3. When Max the dog finally sells his book of poetry, he is able to fulfill his life-long dream of traveling to Paris.

3699. ____. *Ooh-La-La* (Viking, 1991) k–3. As he experiences Paris, the city of love, Max the millionaire poet dog knows he is missing something.

3700. ____. *Max in Hollywood, Baby* (Viking, 1995) k–3. Max the millionaire poet dog and his Parisian poodle friend Crepes Suzette leave Paris for the lure of glittering Hollywood. Can movie stardom be far behind?

3701. ____. *Swami on Rye: Max in India* (Viking, 1995) k–3. Max, the famous dog poet and Hollywood director, faces fatherhood and searches for meaning of life in exotic India.

3702. Kalman, Maira. *Hey Willy, See the Pyramids* (Viking, 1989) k–3. When Alexander has trouble falling to sleep late at night, he wakes up his sister Lulu and asks her to tell him stories.
3703. ____. *Sayonora, Mrs. Kackelman* (Viking, 1989) k–3. Alexander and his older sister Lulu visit Japan and discover many fascinating things including fish markets, outdoor baths, futons, and a frog who writes haiku.

3704. Karp, Naomi. *Nothing Rhymes with April* (Harcourt, 1974) 5–8. An 11-year-old learns about dignity while being raised during the Depression.
3705. ____. *Turning Point* (Harcourt, 1976) 5–8. Hannah moves from the city to the suburbs in the late 1930s where she faces a lot of anti–Semitic prejudice among neighbors and schoolmates.

3706. Katz, Bobbie. *Manifesto and Me—Meg* (Watts, 1974) 5–8. Meg forms a women's liberation consciousness-raising group. Abigail appoints herself as adult advisor and leads the action.
3707. ____. *1,001 Words* (Watts, 1975) 5–8. Meg finds a pornographic book. She and her best friend, Suzy, decide it's a coded message about Meg's brother and their unpopular teacher. They investigate and find out differently.

3708. Kavanagh, Ed. *Amanda Greenleaf Visits a Distant Star* (Moonstone, 1987) 3–5.
3709. ____. *Amanda Greenleaf and the Boy Magician* (Moonstone, 1991) 3–5. Through the magical waterfall she guards on her distant, galactic home, Amanda hears a call from her friends, Frances and Trina, whose mother was imprisoned on the troubled Blue Star where global war is impending. But, deciding that people who can make beautiful music, can't be all bad, Amanda, aided by Nollekens, the boy magician, gets permission form Queen Cressida to do what she can to restore harmony to its citizens.
3710. ____. *Amanda Greenleaf and the Spell of the Water* (Moonstone, 1990) 3–5.

3711. Kaye, Geraldine. *Summer in Small Street* (Methuen, 1992) 4–6. A multicultural story, especially for inner-city children and children in all-white schools who have little chance to know about the lives of children from Asian or Traveller backgrounds. Ben's rabbit escapes and is found in Mrs. Ali's shop, Leroy wears his Anansi costume to the Carnival; Tong brings a lizard to school and Poppy learns to like a fierce looking lady.
3712. ____. *Winter in Small Street* (Methuen, 1990) 4–6. Mrs. Robinson's class co-exist in multiethnic harmony. The story tells of the pleasures of autumn term beginning with Diwali and ending with Christmas.

3713. Kaye, Geraldine. *Comfort Herself* (Deutsch, 1985) 5–8. Comfort, a child of an interracial marriage, goes to Ghana to live with her father, but she is more at ease with her mother in England.
3714. ____. *Great Comfort* (Deutsch, 1990) 5–8. Comfort is part English (her mother) and part Ghanaian (her father). She goes to spend the summer in Ghana. There she is considered a woman; in England she is a schoolgirl. In England she is black and in Ghana she is not black enough.

3715. Kaye, Marilyn. *Max on Earth* (Archway, 1986) 5–8. Randi befriends Max, an alien girl who has come from another planet to learn about Earth people. Max's embarrassingly literal view of teenage social rituals and language is upsetting.
3716. ____. *Max in Love* (Archway, 1986) 5–8. Max decides she wants to experience love and sets her sights on Chad the leader of a local rock band.
3717. ____. *Max on Fire* (Archway, 1986) 5–8. Max starts a new school year and has to deal with not being "preppy."
3718. ____. *Max All Over* (Archway, 1990) 5–8.

3719. Keats, Ezra. *Louie* (Greenwillow, 1975) k–3. A shy, withdrawn boy loses his heart to a puppet.
3720. ____. *Trip* (Greenwillow, 1978) k–3. Lonely in a new neighborhood, Louis creates a magic boat from a shoebox and sees his old friends trick-or-treating
3721. ____. *Louie's Search* (Four Winds, 1980) k–3. Louis goes out looking for a new father and instead finds a music box which he is accused of stealing. Or is that all he finds?

3722. Keef, C. *Melanie Mall and the Pie in the Sky* (Warne, 1978) k–3. Melanie Mall goes for a ride to imaginary lands on the back of a horse. She arranges for her granny to marry a lonely king.
3723. ____. *Melanie Mall and the Circus Animals* (Warne, 1980) k–3. Melanie Mall visits the circus and wonders if the animals really enjoy themselves. She has a plan to have her uncle, who drives a bus to Delhi, take them all home. She and the ringmaster come to a solution.

3724. Keeping, Charles. *Alfie and the Ferryboat* (Watts, 1968) k–3. A tale about an East End boy who gets lost in the fog, wanders into dockland and boards a ferryboat which takes him across the Thames where he finds a different world.
3725. ____. *Alfie Finds "The Other Side of the World"* (Watts, 1968) k–3. Relates how Alfie went to the other side of the world looking for a friend.

3726. Keller, Beverly. *No Beasts! No Children!* (Lothrop, 1983) 5–8. After her mother goes away to find herself, Desdemona, her father, the twins, and the three dogs learn to cope by themselves with a strict housekeeper, a heartless landlord and an old aunt.

3727. ____. *Desdemona, Twelve Going on Desperate* (Lothrop, 1986) 5–8. Calamity stalks a seventh grader in the form of social disasters, and throughout it all, to her great embarrassment, she keeps running into the most attractive boy in school.
3728. ____. *Fowl Play Desdemona* (Lothrop, 1989) 5–8. While speculating on the merits of her father's new girlfriend, Dez teams up with Sherman, a vegetarian and animal rights activist, to design posters for the school play with humorous results.
3729. ____. *Desdemona Moves On* (Bradbury, 1992) 5–8. Chronicles the comic mishaps of 12-year-old Desdemona and her family after they move into a luxurious new house.

3730. Keller, Beverly. *Fiona's Bee* (Coward, 1975) 3–5. A lonely little girl rescues a bee from drowning and suddenly finds herself with lots of new friends.
3731. ____. *Fiona's Flea* (Coward, 1981) 3–5. Fiona befriends a flea and helps get it started in show business.
3732. ____. *Only Fiona* (Harper, 1988) 3–5. Despite several comic mishaps, eight-year-old Fiona's campaign to convince those around her to the importance of being humane to animals brings her respect and new friends.

3733. Keller, Holly. *Geraldine's Blanket* (Greenwillow, 1984) k–3. When her mother and father insist that Geraldine get rid of her baby blanket, she finds a new way to keep it with her all the time.
3734. ____. *Geraldine's Big Snow* (Greenwillow, 1988) k–3. Geraldine can't wait for the snow to come so that she can coast down the hill on her sled.
3735. ____. *Geraldine's Baby Brother* (Greenwillow, 1994) k–3. Geraldine resents all the attention her baby brother gets, until she spends some time with him.

3736. Keller, Holly. *Henry's Fourth of July* (Greenwillow, 1985) k–3. Henry has a fun-filled day celebrating the Fourth of July with his family and friends.
3737. ____. *Henry's Picnic* (Greenwillow, 1987) k–3.
3738. ____. *Henry's Happy Birthday* (Greenwillow, 1990) k–3. Relates the disappointments and joys of Henry's birthday party.

3739. Kelley, Anne. *Daisy and the Dog Show* (Barron, 1985) k–3. Daisy's owners carefully groom her for a dog show, but she has other ideas.
3740. ____. *Daisy's Discovery* (Barron, 1985) k–3. Daisy the dog is not having a good day. She hasn't been fed, tracks mud over the carpet, and chews up wrapping paper. Mom lost her diamond ring and Daisy finds it in the birthday cake.

3741. Kelley, True. *Mouse's Terrible Christmas* (Lothrop, 1978) k–3. The mouse's chimney collapses; the cardboard replacement burns and Santa gets tarred with Mum's sticky Christmas candy.

3742. ____. *Mouse's Terrible Halloween* (Lothrop, 1980) k–3. Halloween brings further misadventures to the Mouse family.

3743. Kellogg, Steven. *Pinkerton, Behave* (Dial, 1979) k–3. His behavior may be rather unconventional, but Pinkerton the dog proves it doesn't really matter.
3744. ____. *Rose for Pinkerton* (Dial, 1981) k–3. Pinkerton's family decides he needs a friend, but is a cat named Rose really suitable?
3745. ____. *Tallyho, Pinkerton* (Dial, 1982) k–3. While accompanying their owners on a field trip, a dog and a cat disrupt a hunting class.
3746. ____. *Prehistoric Pinkerton* (Dial, 1987) k–3. Pinkerton's natural canine urge to chew on things while teething coincides with the chaotic visit to the museum's collection of dinosaur bones.

3747. Kemp, Gene. *Prime of Tamworth Pig* (Faber, 1972) 3–5. A mixture of humans, talking animals and talking toys. A funny story.
3748. ____. *Tamworth Pig and the Litter* (Faber, 1975) 3–5. A world of talking animals. Tamworth follows up his crusade for growing more food and saving trees with a "keep tidy" campaign.
3749. ____. *Christmas with Tamworth Pig* (Faber, 1977) 3–5. This cultivated porker swears off causes for Christmas, but invites the down-and-outer to Pig House. Chaos ensues when everyone comes. Pigs and showoffs are the bad ones.
3750. ____. *Tamworth Pig Saves the Trees* (Faber, 1981) 3–5. Tamworth, president of the Animals Union, crusades to save a forest. He has a romance with a pretty pig named Melanie. The forest is spared and Tamworth and Melanie have some piglets.
3751. ____. *Tamworth Pig Stories* (Faber, 1987) 3–5. Tamworth is a huge golden pig. He and Thomas are best friends and Thomas needs a friend because he is always in trouble. Tamworth rescues him from his worst predicaments and Thomas saves him from the butcher.
3752. ____. *Tamworth Pig Rides Again* (Faber, 1992) 3–5. Tamworth Pig is visited by eccentric Great Aunt Hattie and her bad tempered cat. Her cat teases the soft toys.

3753. Kemp, Gene. *Turbulent Term of Tyke Tiler* (Faber, 1980) 5–8. Tyke and Danny are friends. Danny stole money, Tyke tries to return it. Tyke steals a test to coach Danny so he can stay in class. The surprise comes at the end when Tyke is "Theodora."
3754. ____. *Gowie Corby Plays Chicken* (Faber, 1980) 5–8. Gowie is mean and nasty because his father and brother are in jail and his mother is unreliable. Then he meets Rosie and his life improves. In Tyke's belltower they discover three skeletons.
3755. ____. *Just Ferret* (Faber, 1990) 5–8. A first person account of the struggles of an outsider to fit in at a new school. Ferret, 12, is a new boy at Crick-

lepit Combined School. He must come to terms with his dyslexia, make new friends and deal with a bully.

3756. Kennedy, Pamela. *A, B, C Bunny* (Word, 1990) k–3. A bunny recites the alphabet.

3757. ____. *1, 2, 3 Bunny* (Word, 1990) k–3. A story of a bunny who counts.

3758. ____. *All Mine, Bunny* (Word, 1990) k–3. Bunny has a greedy fit.

3759. ____. *Night, Night, Bunny* (Focus, 1990) k–3. A young rabbit who is afraid at bedtime learns that God is with us when we're afraid.

3760. ____. *Oh, Oh, Bunny* (Focus, 1990) k–3. Little Bunny learns that, according to the Bible, telling the truth is the best choice.

3761. ____. *Red, Yellow, Blue Bunny* (Word, 1990) k–3. Bunny learns about colors.

3762. ____. *No. No, Bunny* (Word, 1992) k–3. After stealing pennies, a toy and some candy, Bunny is very sad but he finds a way to make things right again.

3763. ____. *Big Brother Bunny* (Word, 1992) k–3. When a new baby arrives in the family, it takes Little Bunny a while to learn that both he and the new baby are special.

3764. ____. *So, Mad Bunny* (Word, 1992) k–3. A young rabbit who has trouble controlling his anger asked Jesus to help him not to push or scream or throw things.

3765. Kent, Jack. *Clotilda* (Random, 1978) k–3. Tommy doesn't believe in a fairy godmother's magic so he gets a donkey's head while his sister gets the fairy godmother and three wishes.

3766. ____. *Clotilda's Magic* (Random, 1969) k–3.

3767. Kent, Jack. *Joey* (Prentice, 1984) k–3. Joey, a young kangaroo, becomes bored with playing alone in his mother's pouch and invites some friends over to play with him.

3768. ____. *Joey Runs Away* (Prentice, 1985) k–3. After Joey, a young kangaroo, runs away in search of a better place to live, other animals try out his mother's empty pouch while she is looking for him.

3769. Kent, Lorna. *Seasonal Norm* (Hamilton, 1990) 4–6. A story about a boy who develops special powers when he is hit on the head by a meteorology book. He can now predict the weather. After saving America from a hurricane, he goes back to being a register monitor.

3770. ____. *Norman Thorman and the Mysterious Mutant Marrows* (Hamilton, 1992) 4–6. A book about strange marrows from outer space which make Norman glow a bright green.

3771. Kepes, Juliet. *Five Little Monkeys* (Houghton, 1952) k–3. About five little monkeys, the tricks they played on all the animals in the jungle, what the animals did to them in retaliation, and how the monkeys reformed and later become heroes.

3772. ____. *Five Little Monkey Business* (Houghton, 1964) k–3. The mischievous capers of Buzzo, Binki, Bibi, and Bali have the entire jungle in an uproar until the lion finds a way to make them behave.

3773. ____. *Run, Little Monkeys! Run, Run, Run* (Pantheon, 1974) k–3. Three jolly monkeys begin a wild humorous chase through the jungle.

3774. Kerr, Judith. *Mog, the Forgetful Cat* (Parents, 1972) k–3. A cat's forgetfulness gets her into continual trouble.

3775. ____. *Mog's Christmas* (Collins, 1976) k–3. Mog's Christmas is spent exposed to the elements since, distrustful of the tree and of company, the family feline high-tailed it to the roof.

3776. ____. *Mog and the Baby* (Collins, 1960) k–3. Mog the cat helps Nicky mind the baby…indeed saves the life of that somewhat meddlesome infant when he wanders onto the road.

3777. ____. *Mog in the Dark* (Collins, 1964) k–3. Mog is afraid of the dark. He fears huge birds and big mice; dogs chase him. But he wakes up with his own people, his basket and his supper.

3778. ____. *Mog and Bunny* (Knopf, 1988) k–3. The family threatens to throw away their cat's favorite toy bunny until they discover the extent of Mog's love and loyalty toward Bunny.

3779. ____. *Look Out, Mog* (Random, 1991) k–3. Mog the cat has an unexpected guest, a yappy puppy, and must behave himself with his energetic and overly friendly visitor.

3780. ____. *Mog's Amazing Birthday Caper* (Collins, 1989) k–3. An alphabetical sequence begins when Mog bursts an alligator shaped balloon at Emily's birthday party. Disgraced he slinks under the table and enjoys a prolonged dream of floating frogs, a monster mouse and a purple palace, which ends when the party moves to the zoo.

3781. ____. *Mog on a Fox Night* (Collins, 1994) k–3. Mog upsets Mrs. Thomas by refusing two suppers in the hopes of having a change of diet. But no more food will be given until Mog eats both suppers. Mog sulks in the cold where she meets a fox and two hungry cubs. They gobble up Mog's supper.

3782. Kerr, Sue. *Here Comes Weezie* (Whitman, 1967) k–3. Weezie, four, entertains herself while her big sister is at school. First she helps her mother do household chores. Then she plays with her sister's dollhouse. She breaks some furniture but she and her mother mend it and Weezie is forgiven

3783. ____. *Weezie Goes to School* (Whitman, 1969) k–3. A little girl beginning school waits for the day she can surprise her family with something important she has learned.

3784. Kessler, Ethel. *Pig's New Hat* (Garrard, 1981) k–3. Pig's new hat is the cause of much admiration and excitement during an outing in the park.

3785. ____. *Pig's Orange House* (Garrard, 1981)

k–3. Pig sets out to paint her house orange but finds her plans upset by help from too many well-meaning friends.

3786. ____. *Baby-Sitter, Duck* (Garrard, 1981) k–3. Duck discovers how exhausting baby-sitting Pinky Pig can be.

3787. ____. *Big Fight* (Garrard, 1981) k–3. A friendship is tested when Pig accidentally breaks Duck's new chair.

3788. Kessler, Leonard. *Kick, Pass and Run* (Harper, 1978) 3–5. A group of animals imitate the big boys' football game with their own—a mock game.

3789. ____. *On Your Mark, Get Set, Go* (Harper, 1972) 3–5. Everyone gets to participate in the first All-Animal Olympics except Worm, but he keeps training anyway.

3790. ____. *Super Bowl* (Greenwillow, 1980) 3–5. The Animal Olympics play the Super Birds in the football Super Bowl, and the losers console themselves that there is another year coming.

3791. ____. *Big Mile Race* (Greenwillow, 1983) 3–5. The animals prepare for and participate in the Big Mile Race.

3792. Kessler, Leonard. *Forgetful Pirate* (Garrard, 1974) k–3. Forgetful Ben, a pirate captain starts out with his crew and pet parrot in search of the treasure he hid, in spite of the fact that he can't remember where he hid it.

3793. ____. *Pirates Adventure on Spooky Island* (Garrard, 1978) k–3. Cowardly Captain Ben and his sidekick, a parrot, lead their pirate crew on an adventure to Spooky Island.

3794. Kessler, Leonard. *Mr. Pine's Purple House* (Grosset, 1965) k–3. Mr. Pine decides to set his house apart from the others on the block. He plants a tree and then so does everyone else. Everything he does the others do also. So he paints his house purple.

3795. ____. *Mrs. Pine Takes a Trip* (Grosset, 1966) k–3. When Mrs. Pine decides to take a trip, she leaves a long list of household chores for Mr. Pine. Mr. Pine loses the list, forgets what has to be done and pretty soon finds himself in the middle of a big mess.

3796. ____. *Paint Me a Picture, Mr. Pine* (Ginn, 1972) k–3. A sign painter decides to take the day off to paint pictures.

3797. ____. *Mr. Pine's Storybook* (Grosset, 1982) k–3. Mr. Pine tells how the town now called Pineville was called Town until a man named Pine came and improved it; he tells of a dancing monkey disappearing from the zoo and Mr. Pine's signs soon follow, he tells how Mrs. Pine wins a gold ribbon for her paintings, and Mr. Pine a blue one for an old paint cloth.

3798. Kessler, Leonard. *Old Turtle's Baseball Stories* (Greenwillow, 1982) 3–5. While gathering around the wood stove in winter, Old Turtle tells his friends unbelievable baseball stories of Cleo Octopus, Melvin Moose, Clara Kangaroo and Randy Squirrel.

3799. ____. *Old Turtle's Winter Games* (Greenwillow, 1983) 3–5. A group of animals organize winter games, and compete in events such as sled races, skating, skiing and ice hockey.

3800. ____. *Old Turtle's Soccer Team* (Greenwillow, 1988) 3-5. Under Old Turtle's guidance, the animals learn how to play soccer and the meaning of good sportsmanship.

3801. Key, Alex. *Sprockets—a Little Robot* (Westminster, 1963) 3–5. Sprockets accidently got the wrong brain. It was only to go to a specialized group of robots. He used it to get into and out of trouble.

3802. ____. *Rivets and Sprockets* (Westminster, 1964) 3–5. Rivets, Sprockets and Jimmy explore Mars to find out who is sending messages back to the Earth.

3803. Khalsa, Dayal. *I Want a Dog* (Crown, 1987) k–3. When her parents refuse to get her a dog, May creates an imaginary dog out of a roller skate.

3804. ____. *My Family Vacation* (Crown, 1988) k–3. May takes her first vacation with her family to Florida. She and her older brother have adventures in Miami which bring them to a better understanding of each other.

3805. Kherdian, David. *It Started with Old Man Bean* (Greenwillow, 1980) 5–8. Ted and Joe go camping along a river. It rains and the river floods and Ted is swept downstream.

3806. ____. *Beyond Two Rivers* (Greenwillow, 1981) 5–8. Ted and Joe return from their camping trip. They think they see a Japanese prisoner. But Mr. Matsu is a nature lover like themselves.

3807. Kiesel, Stanley. *War Between the Pitiful Teachers and the Splendid Kids* (Dutton, 1980) 4–6. Mr. Foreclosure declares war on the students and Big Alice declares war on the teachers. The principal's weapon is Status Quo Solidifier. It turns rowdy kids into conformers.

3808. ____. *Skinny Malinky Leads the War for Kidness* (Dutton, 1984) 4–6. Mr. Forecloser is looking for the kids that escaped his Status Quo Solidification Program, especially Skinny Malinky.

3809. Killien, Christie. *Putting on an Act* (Houghton, 1986) 5–8. Skeeter lied to her pen pal and when she comes to town Skeeter must examine her attitude toward her brother, her best friend and boyfriend.

3810. ____. *Fickle Fever* (Houghton, 1988) 5–8. Skeeter is dating different boys looking for the right one. She "adopts" different interests for each guy. Then decides that "honesty is the best policy."

3811. Killingback, Julia. *Catch the Red Bus* (Morrow, 1985) k–3. The Busy Bears learn all about colors as they travel on differently colored vehicles.

3812. ____. *One, Two, Three, Go* (Morrow, 1985) k–3. While the reader may count them, Mrs. Bear has a time convincing ten busy bears to go to bed.

3813. ____. *What Time Is It, Mrs. Bear?* (Morrow, 1985) k–3. Bears arise at 8 a.m. and have to fit all the day's activities before their 6 p.m. bedtime. Mrs. Bear shops, cooks, cleans and plays with the children.

3814. ____. *Monday is Washing Day* (Morrow, 1985) k–3. Monday may be washing day but taking care of laundry is a week long affair for the Bear family. Mrs. Bear and eight children wash, dry, mend, iron and put away clothes before relaxing on a Sunday outing with Mr. Bear.

3815. ____. *Follow That Bear* (Oxford, 1987) k–3. Baby Bear leads the way through a fun park with prepositions: Climb Up, Slide Down, etc.

3816. ____. *Wake Up, Busy Bears* (Oxford, 1987) k–3. Baby Bear learns about opposites: sleeping vs. awake; sad (Mrs. Bear goes to work) vs. happy (having fun with dad).

3817. ____. *Busy Bear at the Fire Station* (Methuen, 1988) k–3. Small bears act out various scenes where fire threatens the young—at home, in a shop, in the country. Smaller bears are led on a tour of the fire station.

3818. ____. *Watch Out, Busy Bear* (Methuen, 1988) k–3.

3819. ____. *Busy Bear's Picnic* (Methuen, 1988) k–3.

3820. ____. *Busy Bear to the Rescue* (Methuen, 1988) k–3.

3821. Kilroy, Sally. *Twins in France* (Orchard, 1989) k–3. Katie, one of the twins, tells her story of their visit to Paris. She tells of their journey there, their stay at a campsite and one or two visits.

3822. ____. *Twins in Greece* (Orchard, 1989) k–3. The twins, brother and sister, in journal form, tell of the food, weather, sights, money exchange and local interest when they visit Greece on vacation.

3823. Kimmel, Eric. *Hershel and the Hanukkah Goblins* (Holiday, 1989) k–3. Relates how Hershel outwits the goblins that haunt the old synagogue and prevent the village people from celebrating Hanukkah.

3824. ____. *Adventures of Hershel of Ostropol* (Holiday, 1995) k–3. Stories about a clever man who lived by his wits as his pockets were always empty.

3825. Kimura, Yasuko. *Fergus* (McGraw, 1976) k–3. A selfish puppy's friends help him hunt for his hidden treasure, but he doesn't tell them it's a bone.

3826. ____. *Fergus and the Sea Monster* (McGraw, 1977) k–3. Fergus doesn't know what to do with the funny blue monster who is growing bigger and bigger and following him everywhere.

3827. ____. *Fergus and the Snow Deer* (McGraw, 1979) k–3. Fergus is taken on a snowy nighttime adventure by the snow deer.

3828. King, B. Anthony. *Best Christmas Tree Ever* (Godine, 1984) k–3. Mr. Bones prefers a very large Christmas tree and Mrs. Bones prefers a very small one, but together they pick out the best Christmas tree ever.

3829. ____. *Christmas Junk Box* (Godine, 1987) k–3. One Christmas Mr. Bones decided to give his family a junk box, filled with odds and ends. Instead of the shiny, store bought presents.

3830. King-Smith, Dick. *Mouse Butcher* (Gollancz, 1989) 4–6. A story of a group of cats living on an island abandoned by humans. Tom Plug lives in the old butcher shop. He falls in love with Diana, the delicate Persian in the Big House. They prey on the mice of the island.

3831. ____. *Magnus Powerhouse* (Puffin, 1988) 4–6. In this book the mice are not treated so harshly. A baby mouse who won't stop growing is carried off by a rat catcher and begins a series of adventures.

3832. King-Smith, Dick. *Sophie's Snail* (Delacorte, 1989) 2–4. Follows the humorous adventures of four-year-old Sophie as she pursues her dreams of becoming a farmer.

3833. ____. *Sophie's Tom* (Candlewick, 1991) 2–4. Befriending a stray cat helps a very determined five-year-old adjust to school, learn about friends and pursue her dream of one day becoming a farmer.

3834. ____. *Sophie in the Saddle* (Candlewick, 1991) 2–4. Having added the puppy Puddle to her growing menagerie of cat and rabbit, animal-mad Sophie makes friends with a Vietnamese pot-bellied pig and a gray pony named Bumblebee.

3835. ____. *Sophie Hits Six* (Candlewick, 1993) 2–4. The year that Sophie turns six, she sees a cat give birth to kittens, gets a pet rabbit from her Aunt Al, and pursues her dream of acquiring a dog.

3836. ____. *Sophie Is Seven* (Candlewick, 1995) 2–4. Sophie, a young girl who takes a no-nonsense approach to life's problems, pursues her dream of becoming a "lady farmer."

3837. ____. *Sophie's Lucky* (Candlewick, 1996) 2–4. A visit to Great Aunt Al in the Scottish Highlands leads to an exciting change in Sophie's life.

3838. Kingman, Lee. *Saturday Gang* (Doubleday, 1961) 4–6. A TV company wants to film in Teddy's town and the Saturday Gang win over the town to go along with the idea. They solve some mysterious robberies in a humorous manner.

3839. ____. *Private Eyes; Adventures of the Saturday Gang* (Doubleday, 1964) 4–6. Teddy and his friends find detective work dangerous.

3840. Kirk, David. *Miss Spider's Tea Party* (Scholastic, 1994) k–3. When lonely Miss Spider tries to host a tea party, the other bugs refuse to come for fear of being eaten.
3841. ____. *Miss Spider's Wedding* (Scholastic, 1995) k–3. Miss Spider proves her heart knows best when it comes to choosing a husband.

3842. Klass, Sheila. *To See My Mother Dance* (Scribner, 1981) 5–8. Jessica, 13, was abandoned as a baby and fantasizes having a perfect mother. She resents her father's new wife. Martha looks for Jessica's missing mother and arranges for her to see her (spaced out in a commune).
3843. ____. *Alive and Starting Over* (Scribner, 1983) 5–8. Jessica no longer resents her stepmother. Grandmother has a heart attack; she meets a new boy, Peter, but is still loyal to Jason.

3844. Kleberger, Ilse. *Grandmother Oma* (Atheneum, 1967) 4–6. Grandmother Oma could roller skate and ice skate. She could hatch eggs and rescue her grandson from a bull. She was not your ordinary grandmother.
3845. ____. *Traveling with Oma* (Atheneum, 1970) 4–6. When an injured burglar leaves his horse and caravan in her care, Grandmother Oma uses it to take the children on a vacation.
3846. ____. *Stories of Grandmother Oma* (Atheneum, 1975) 4–6. Contains: Grandma Oma; Grandma Oma and the Green Caravan.

3847. Klein, Norma. *Confessions of an Only Child* (Pantheon, 1974) 4–6. A story of Antonia's life between the birth of her baby brothers. The first died and she adjusts to her new baby brother.
3848. ____. *Tomboy* (Four Winds, 1978) 4–6. Antonia, 10, has many changes as she grows up. It's hard to leave your past for the unknown future.

3849. Klein, Robin. *Penny Pollard in Print* (Oxford, 1986) 4–6. Penny keeps a diary of all the events leading to her friend's sister's wedding where she will be a flowergirl.
3850. ____. *Penny Pollard's Diary* (Oxford, 1987) 4–6. Penny records in her diary her hatred of Annette and all elderly people. Her attitudes change through some satisfying experiences.
3851. ____. *Penny Pollard's Letters* (Oxford, 1987) 4–6. Penny stays with Great-Aunt Winifred while her mother is in the hospital. She writes to everyone she knows. She tells about the removal of a rat by Dad from her wardrobe. Alistan turns from a despised egghead into a friend.
3852. ____. *Penny Pollard's Passport* (Oxford, 1990) 4–6. Penny, 12, copes with awful hotels and misprinted tour schedules when she takes a cut-rate bus tour. She fights with a snobbish rich girl and tries to be matchmaker for two single people on the tour.

3853. Kelvin, Jill. *Turtle Street Trading Co.* (Delacorte, 1982) 4–6. The Turtles of Turtle Street plot a way to make enough money to go to Disneyland by establishing a trading company, which turns out to be an enormous success.
3854. ____. *Turtles Together Forever* (Delacorte, 1982) 4–6. Fergy carries on the Turtle Street Trading Company tradition by establishing an ice cream business in San Francisco where he now lives with his divorced mother.

3855. Kline, Suzy. *Horrible Harry in Room 2B* (Viking, 1988) 3–5. Doug discovers that though being Harry's best friend in Miss Mackle's second grade class isn't always easy, as Harry likes to do horrible things, it is often a lot of fun.
3856. ____. *Horrible Harry and the Green Slime* (Viking, 1989) 3–5. Follows the school activities of second graders, Harry and Doug.
3857. ____. *Horrible Harry and the Ant Invasion* (Viking, 1989) 3–5. Horrible Harry of classroom 2B cuts back on his mischievous pranks after falling for Song Lee.
3858. ____. *Horrible Harry's Secret* (Viking, 1990) 3–5. Horrible Harry falls in love with Song Lee and Harry's best friend, Doug, can't stand all the mush.
3859. ____. *Horrible Harry and the Christmas Surprise* (Viking, 1991) 3–5. Horrible Harry and the rest of Miss Mackie's class at South School guarantee fun for the holidays. It all starts when Miss Mackie's reading chair collapses while she is in it.
3860. ____. *Horrible Harry and the Kickball Wedding* (Viking, 1992) 3-5. As Valentine's Day approaches, the students in room 2B are preoccupied with kickball and a possible wedding between Horrible Harry and Song Lee.
3861. ____. *Song Lee in Room 2B* (Viking, 1993) 3–5. Spring becomes a memorable time for Miss Mackle's second-grade because of the antics of Horrible Harry and the special insights of shy Song Lee.
3862. ____. *Song Lee and the Hamster Hunt* (Viking, 1994) 3–5. When Song Lee's hamster escapes from its cage in room 2B the class members and other students in South School become involved in the search for him.
3863. ____. *Song Lee and the Leech Man* (Viking, 1995) 3–5. Harry plots revenge against Sidney, the class tattletale, when Miss Mackle's second graders go on a field trip to the pond.

3864. Kline, Suzy. *Mary Marony and the Snake* (Putnam, 1992) 3–5. With support of her mother and new classmates, Mary sees a speech therapist about her stuttering problem.
3865. ____. *Mary Marony Hides Out* (Putnam, 1993) 3–5. A second grader is so embarrassed about her stuttering that she almost misses a chance to have lunch with her favorite author who has come to speak at school.
3866. ____. *Mary Marony, Mummy Girl* (Putnam,

1994) 3–5. Mary Marony, second grader, needs the perfect Halloween costume to scare mean teasing Marvin. She tears a sheet into strips and creates a scary costume, a mummy girl. After she wins the Halloween painting contest she pays her parents for the torn sheet.

3867. _____. *Mary Marony and the Chocolate Surprise* (Putnam, 1995) 3–5. Mary decides it's all right to cheat to make sure she wins a special lunch with her favorite teacher but the results of her dishonesty end up surprising the whole second grade class.

3868. Kline, Suzy. *Herbie Jones* (Putnam, 1985) 3–5. Herbie's experience in the third grade includes finding bones in the boy's bathroom, wandering away from his class on their field trip, and being promoted to a higher reading group.

3869. _____. *What's the Matter with Herbie Jones?* (Putnam, 1986) 3–5. When Herbie gets the dreaded girl disease and becomes lovesick for Annabelle Hodgekiss, it threatens to break up his friendship with his good pal Raymond.

3870. _____. *Herbie Jones and the Class Gift* (Putnam, 1987) 3–5. Disaster strikes when Annabelle trusts Herbie Jones and Raymond with the job of picking up the class's gift to their teacher.

3871. _____. *Herbie Jones and the Monster Ball* (Putnam, 1988) 3–5. Strike-out king, Herbie Jones, feels that the summer is ruined when his uncle arrives to coach a baseball team and asks Herbie to join up.

3872. _____. *Herbie Jones and Hamburger Head* (Putnam, 1989) 3–5. After Herbie and Ray foil a robbery attempt at the local bank, they try to find a good home for the robber's dog.

3873. _____. *Herbie Jones and the Dark Attic* (Putnam, 1992) 3–5. Herbie's friend Ray and some classmates in his fourth grade reading group help him adjust when he moves into a new bedroom in the attic.

3874. _____. *Herbie Jones and the Birthday Showdown* (Putnam, 1993) 3–5. When Ray decides to throw a party for his ninth birthday, in competition with another boy with the same birthday and more money, he asks his best friend Herbie to help him find an idea that is new, exciting and free.

3875. Kline, Suzy. *ORP* (Putnam, 1989) 3–5. Orville Rudmeyer Pygenski, Jr.'s decision to form an "I Hate My Name Club" has some surprising results.

3876. _____. *ORP and the Chop Suey Burgers* (Putnam, 1990) 3–5. Eleven-year-old Orville enters a cooking contest, which he has high hopes of winning with his recipe for chop suey burgers.

3877. _____. *ORP Goes to the Hoop* (Putnam, 1991) 3–5. All-star baseball pitcher Orp goes out for basketball in the seventh grade and finds that the skills he was developed in his old sport can be effectively transferred to his new one.

3878. _____. *Who Is ORP's Girlfriend?* (Putnam, 1993) 3–5. Orp's life becomes very complicated when he realizes that he likes two girls at the same time.

3879. _____. *Orp and the FBI* (Putnam, 1995) 3–5. Orp, his movie-buff best friend, Derrick, and his annoying but clever sister, Chloe, determine to find out what a mysterious letter, an escaped madman and a lurking shadow have in common.

3880. Knowles, Anthony. *Mice Next Door* (Hodder, 1986) k–3. Dad does not like the Hardy mice who live next door. But they have their uses: unblocking a drain and fun to play with. Dad relents when Mr. Hardy brings home-brew and they are asked to Sunday lunch.

3881. _____. *Christmas with the Mice Next Door* (Macmillan, 1990) k–3. Mr. and Mrs. Hardy are mice. Nan lives next door and is afraid of "rats." But the Hardys are so polite and so well behaved that she can't really criticise them.

3882. Knuppel, Helga. *Adventures of Christabel Crocodile* (Interlink, 1991) k–3. After pulling the plug out of the pool at the zoo, a young crocodile finds herself lost in an underground sewer until Reni Rat comes to her rescue.

3883. _____. *Christabel Crocodile's Birthday Egg* (Crocodile Books, 1992) k–3. When Reni Rat gives Christabel Crocodile a penguin egg for her birthday and they try to hatch it together, an exciting zoo adventure ensues.

3884. _____. *Christabel Crocodile's Egg-citing Present* (Interlink, 1993) k–3.

3885. Koller, Jackie. *Mole and Shrew* (Atheneum, 1991) k–3. When his relatives crowd Mole out of his house, Shrew tries to find him another dwelling.

3886. _____. *Mole and Shrew Step Out* (Atheneum, 1992) k–3. Mole commits a comic blunder regarding a fancy ball, but his good friend Shrew sticks by him.

3887. Korchunow, Irina. *Small Fur* (Harper, 1988) 2–4. After losing his best friend, Small Fur meets an elf and has an incredible adventure before he finds a new best friend.

3888. _____. *Small Fur is Getting Bigger* (Harper, 1990) 2–4. Small Fur has trouble standing up to his gruff uncle and relating to his friend Curly Fur, until an incident in the swamp convinces him of his self-reliance.

3889. Kozikowski, Renate. *Titus Bear Goes to the Beach* (Harper, 1984) k–3. A series of events all related to Titus Bear's time at the beach.

3890. _____. *Titus Bear Goes to Town* (Harper, 1984) k–3. Titus Bear fills his day with many activities during his visit to town.

3891. _____. *Titus Bear Goes to Bed* (Harper, 1984) k–3. This is the main character who demonstrates all the independence desired by babies struggling to accomplish growth tasks.

3892. ____. *Titus Bear Goes to School* (Harper, 1984) k–3. Titus Bear goes to school, plays with his friends, paints a picture, hears his teacher read a story and experiences other enjoyable school activities.

3893. ____. *Titus Bear's Summer* (Harper, 1986) k–3. Titus Bear, the chubby dark brown bear goes camping in summer.

3894. ____. *Titus Bear's Winter* (Harper, 1986) k–3. On a beautiful winter day, Titus Bear plays outdoors in the snow.

3895. ____. *Titus Bear's Spring* (Harper, 1986) k–3. The adventures of Titus Bear, a chubby dark brown bear. He lives by himself, does his own shopping and home repairs.

3896. ____. *Titus Bear's Fall* (Harper, 1986) k–3. Young Titus Bear experiences an autumn day: raking leaves, eating apple pie, and more.

3897. Krahn, Fernando. *Here Comes Alex Pumpernickel* (Little, 1981) k–3. Follows Little Alex Pumpernickel through a series of misadventures from dawn to dusk.

3898. ____. *Sleep Tight, Alex Pumpernickel* (Little, 1982) k–3. Presents the further nocturnal adventures of Alex Pumpernickel.

3899. Kramon, Florence. *Eugene and the New Baby* (Follett, 1967) k–3. Eugene is not happy about the new baby and wants to put him someplace out of the way. But when the baby comes home Eugene changes his mind and wants the baby in his room. They will share a room when the baby gets bigger.

3900. ____. *Eugene and the Policeman* (Follett, 1967) k–3. Eugene's parents threaten to call the police whenever Eugene misbehaves. So he is afraid of the police. The wind blows away his cap and Officer B. comes along and helps him. He now thinks police are really nice.

3901. ____. *Wallpaper for Eugene's Room* (Follett, 1967) k–3. Eugene gets a new wallpaper with giraffes and kangaroos, cats, cuckoos and owls. They fight over their different sizes and shapes and colors, until owl tells them to live together happily.

3902. ____. *Nobody Looks at Eugene* (Follett, 1968) k–3. Eugene thinks no one really notices him. He goes through a day doing outrageous things. Parents and teachers ignore his antics. He discovers he is noticed when he is just himself.

3903. Kraus, Robert. *Adventures of Wise Old Owl* (Troll, 1993) k–3. Wise Old Owl, beloved author, takes time out from his work to visit a class of aspiring young writers in Miss Bear's class.

3904. ____. *Wise Old Owl's Halloween Adventure* (Troll, 1993) k–3. Wise Old Owl, who plans to spend Halloween writing his mystery story, finds himself involved in a real mystery when his typewriter disappears.

3905. ____. *Wise Old Owl's Canoe Trip Adventure* (Troll, 1993) k–3. With Slow Turtle as his guide, Wise Old Owl has a memorable canoe trip over a waterfall.

3906. ____. *Wise Old Owl's Christmas Adventure* (Troll, 1994) k–3. Wise Old Owl almost misses Amanda Bear's Christmas party at which he is supposed to play Santa Claus.

3907. Kraus, Robert. *How Spider Saved Christmas* (Windmill, 1970/1988) k–3. Spider thought his Christmas presents to Fly and Ladybug were unappreciated until they were used to prevent a disaster.

3908. ____. *How Spider Saved Halloween* (S & S, 1973/1988) k–3. Fly and Ladybug's squashed jack o' lantern helps Spider think of a costume that saves Halloween from disaster.

3909. ____. *How Spider Saved Turkey* (S & S, 1981) k–3. Spider and his friends share their meager Thanksgiving meal with an unexpected guest.

3910. ____. *How Spider Saved Valentine's Day* (Scholastic, 1986) k–3. On Valentine's Day Spider buys candy and cards for his friends Fly and Ladybug, but he forgot about the two caterpillars who sleep through class. But then spider solves the problem.

3911. ____. *How Spider Saved Easter* (Scholastic, 1988) k–3. Although he doesn't usually celebrate Easter, Spider has some pleasant adventures with Ladybug and Fly.

3912. ____. *How Spider Saved the Flea Circus* (Scholastic, 1991) k–3. Spider and his friends save the day by performing for the already assembled audience when the fleas desert the flea circus.

3913. ____. *How Spider Stopped the Litterbugs* (Scholastic, 1991) k–3.

3914. ____. *How Spider Saved Thanksgiving* (Scholastic, 1991) k–3.

3915. Kraus, Robert. *My Son the Mouse* (Harper, 1966) k–3. A mother mouse's image of her son who is, she believes, brave as a lion, sharp as a tack, and who swims like a fish.

3916. ____. *Whose Mouse Are You?* (Macmillan, 1970) k–3. An accounting of the determined heroics of nobody's mouse, who alters his solo status by intrepidly rescuing mother, father and sister from cat trap, and mountaintop.

3917. ____. *Pinchpenny Mouse* (Windmill, 1974) k–3. Of all the mice employed by the Ajax Mousetrap Company, only Pinchpenny saves his money. When the company folds, can he help his fellow mice? Will he?

3918. ____. *Good Mousekeeper* (Windmill, 1977) k–3. A mousekeeper relates how she takes care of her mice.

3919. ____. *I, Mouse* (Windmill, 1978) k–3. A lovely hero mouse is both humorous and delightful. A story of how a mouse changes from a house mouse to a house hero.

3920. Kraus, Robert. *Another Mouse to Feed* (S & S, 1980) k–3. When Mr. and Mrs. Mouse become exhausted from overwork, caring for their many children, the little mice decide to take over.

3921. ____. *Where Are You Going, Little Mouse?* (Greenwillow, 1986) k–3. Having decided that no one loves him, there's nothing left for Little Mouse to do but run away from home. He gets to the nearest phone booth, and his parents come to the rescue.

3922. ____. *Come Out and Play, Little Mouse* (Greenwillow, 1987) k–3. Little Mouse is busy helping his family five days of the week, but he gets to play with them on weekends.

3923. Kraus, Robert. *Daddy Long Ears* (Windmill, 1970) k–3. When the poor, harassed father rabbit decorates some eggs for his 31 children, he becomes known as the Easter Rabbit.

3924. ____. *Daddy Long Ears' Christmas Surprise* (S & S, 1989) k–3. Worn out from caring for his 32 children, Daddy Long Ears doesn't know how he is going to cope with Christmas; but his children take things in hand and surprise him instead.

3925. ____. *Daddy Long Ears' Halloween* (Little Simon, 1990) k–3. Daddy Long Ears loves Halloween but this year he cannot go trick-or-treating because Bunny Parker is ill and yet they have the best Halloween ever.

3926. Kraus, Robert. *Springfellow* (Windmill, 1978) k–3. Springfellow's one desire is to run and play with his fellow colts. But it seems he will never stop falling down on his wobbly young legs.

3927. ____. *Springfellow's Parade* (Windmill, 1982) k–3. Mr. Rabbit won't let Springfellow in the parade because he is too young. Also, Raymond the Rabbit is too silly and Abigail the chick is too fuzzy. So Springfellow, Raymond and Abigail make a parade of their own.

3928. Kraus, Robert. *Mummy Knows Best* (Warner, 1988) k–3. The disappearance of Mr. Milkghost's sheets, prompts detective Mummy to investigate the festivities at the Creepy Hollow costume ball.

3929. ____. *Private Eyes Don't Blink* (Warner, 1988) k–3. Relates how Mummy Dearest receives first prize for creative cooking despite the plotting of the Ol' Professor.

3930. ____. *Phantom of Creepy Hollow* (Warner, 1988) k–3. Mummy succeeds in cornering the Phantom of the Opry and revealing his secret identify

3931. ____. *Noah Count, Vampire Detective in Mummy Vanishes* (Warner, 1988) k–3. Noah Count, the vampire detective, rescues Mummy from the high priest of the mummy worshipers, Three Eyes Mazurkski.

3932. ____. *Mummy Vanishes* (Warner, 1989) k–3. Noah, the vampire detective, rescues Mummy Dearest and her big ape fiancé and returns them to the Bronx.

3933. Kraus, Robert. *Pip Squeak, Mouse in Shining Armor* (Windmill, 1971) k–3. By accomplishing what seven knights failed to do, a mouse becomes Sir Pip Squeak, a small knight with rather large ears.

3934. ____. *Pip Squeak's Through* (Dutton, 1973) k–3. Pip and his steed, a large frog, set out to capture the great Gorgonzola cheese to feed the starving mice of the kingdom. He duels with Sir Prise and escapes from a giant cat and captures the cheese.

3935. Kraus, Robert. *Good Morning, Miss Gator* (Silver, 1989) k–3. We meet Miss Gator, Buggy Bear, who learns about cleanliness, Tardy Toad who is always late, Punky Skunky, Blade the Snake and Ella, the bad speller. Miss Gator teaches them many things in her one room schoolhouse.

3936. ____. *Squirmy's Big Secret* (Silver, 1990) k–3. The worm in the apple on Miss Gator's desk joins in the learning activities of the other animal students in her schoolroom, but they do not know his name until a good deed draws more attention to him.

3937. ____. *Here Comes Tardy Toad* (Silver, 1989) 2–4. All the animal students in Miss Gator's school try to help Tardy Toad break his habit of always being late to school.

3938. ____. *Ella the Bad Speller* (Silver, 1989) 2–4. Ella, the elephant, the worse speller in Miss Gator's schoolhouse works very hard with the help of the other animals to improve her spelling.

3939. Kraus, Robert. *Trouble with Spider* (Harper, 1962) k–3. A humorous parable telling of the ways in which a fly, a ladybug and a spider solve the problem of getting along together.

3940. ____. *Spider's First Day at School* (Scholastic, 1987) k–3. Spider is sure he won't like school and he is scared. He doesn't know anybody and doesn't make friends easily. He goes along with bedbugs, flies and a ladybug to Miss Quito's class.

3941. ____. *Dance, Spider, Dance* (Western, 1993) k–3. Spider longs to go to the big dance and enter the dancing contest, but, alas, spiders can't dance. Undaunted, he heads to the event anyway, prepared to be a wallflower, but he saves the day with his remarkable talent for jumping.

3942. Krensky, Stephen. *Dragon Circle* (Atheneum, 1977) 4–6. Five dragons awake from hibernation. Peter's fake sword picks up the presence of dragons. One by one the dragons are vanquished.

3943. ____. *Witching Hour* (Atheneum, 1981) 4–6. The Wynd family pit their forces against a coven of witches who want to turn the chicken into monsters. The witches capture Old Magic and the children must save him. A funny, scary story.

3944. ____. *Ghostly Business* (Atheneum, 1984) 4–6. The five Wynd children are determined to foil the army of ghosts intent on helping an unscrupulous developer acquire some of the best land in the city.

3945. Krensky, Stephen. *Wilder Plot* (Atheneum, 1982) 5–8. Charlie would do anything to get out of taking a part in the class play.

3946. ____. *Wilder Summer* (Atheneum, 1983) 5–8. Charlie Wilder is unenthusiastic about summer camp until he sets eyes on Lydia Travers, but getting to know Lydia turns out to be far more complicated than he had ever anticipated.

3947. Krensky, Stephen. *Lionel at Large* (Dial, 1986) 3–5. Lionel faces such ordeals as having to eat green beans, going to the doctor, and looking for the snake his sister lost in his room.

3948. ____. *Lionel in the Fall* (Dial, 1987) 3–5. For Lionel, fall means starting a new school year, raking leaves, and getting to dress up as a knight and chase a dragon from house to house on Halloween.

3949. ____. *Lionel in the Spring* (Dial, 1990) 3–5. Lionel's spring activities include plans to plant a vegetable garden, helping celebrate his parent's anniversary, playing with his friend, and participating in spring cleaning.

3950. ____. *Lionel and Louise* (Dial, 1992) 2–4. Four stories about Lionel and his big sister Louise at the beach, cleaning up a mess, fighting a "dragon" and camping out in the backyard.

3951. ____. *Lionel in the Winter* (Dial, 1994) 2–4. Lionel's winter adventures include pretending to be an Arctic explorer, building a snowman and making some New Year's resolutions.

3952. ____. *Lionel and His Friends* (Dial, 1996) 2–4. Friends who outdo you in politeness to adults. Parents who mess up your school lunch by putting the jelly on the bread before the peanut butter. These familiar situations are in Lionel's latest book.

3953. Krings, Antoon. *Oliver's Pool* (Hyperion, 1992) k–3. Oliver is a koala bear who wears red overalls. It takes him so long to inflate his pool that it is dark when he finishes.

3954. ____. *Oliver's Bicycle* (Hyperion, 1992) k–3. While trying to amuse himself on a rainy day, Oliver breaks his bicycle by riding it down the stairs.

3955. ____. *Oliver's Strawberry Patch* (Hyperion, 1992) k–3. Someone is eating strawberries from Oliver's beloved patch.

3956. Kroll, Steven. *Big Bunny and the Easter Eggs* (Holiday, 1982) k–3. Poor Wilbur, the Easter Bunny, gets so sick that he almost misses his Easter deliveries.

3957. ____. *Big Bunny and the Magic Show* (Holiday, 1986) k–3. Tired of being the Easter Bunny, Wilbur decides to get a new job as assistant to Morgan the Magician.

3958. Krull, Kathleen. *Alex Fitzgerald's Cure for Nightmares* (Little, 1990) 2–4. When nine-year-old Alex moves to weird California to live with her father for a year, she is plagued by disturbing nightmares and fears her new friends will learn her babyish secret.

3959. ____. *Alex Fitzgerald, TV Star* (Little, 1991) 2–4. Fourth grader Alex's new friendships in California are endangered when her chance to appear in a rock video brings her glamour and an inflated ego.

3960. Krumpet, Susie. *Messie Bessie of Krumpetville* (Character Imprints, 1978) k–3. Because Messie Bessie never hangs up her clothes or puts her toys away, she soon can't find anything and must call upon her friend Neat Pete for help.

3961. ____. *Itzi Bitzi Mitzi of Krumpetville* (Character Imprints, 1979) k–3. A tiny girl is unhappy with her size until she is able to experience what it would be like to be bigger.

3962. ____. *Happy Zappy of Krumpetville* (Character Imprints, 1979) k–3. After 50 days of rain Happy Zappy is called upon by the mayor of Krumpetville to restore the smiles of its very unhappy citizens.

3963. ____. *Dreamie Jeannie of Krumpetville* (Character Imprints, 1979) k–3. Dreamie Jeannie spends so much time daydreaming that she nearly misses out on the one thing she wants most.

3964. Kunhardt, Edith. *Danny's Birthday* (Greenwillow, 1986) k–3. After his father videotapes the party for his fifth birthday, Danny the alligator wants to watch the tape over and over again.

3965. ____. *Danny's Mystery Valentine* (Greenwillow, 1987) k–3. Danny and his mother go in search of the person who left Danny an unsigned valentine.

3966. ____. *Trick or Treat, Danny* (Greenwillow, 1988) k–3. Danny's parents and friends make sure he has a happy Halloween even though a cold prevents him from going trick-or-treating.

3967. ____. *Danny's Christmas Star* (Greenwillow, 1989) k–3. After Danny accidentally drops the star for the Christmas tree, he makes a replacement.

3968. ____. *Danny and the Easter Egg* (Greenwillow, 1989) k–3. Danny colors Easter eggs with his friends, then hunts for them after they are hidden by the Easter Bunny, and gives a special one to his grandmother.

3969. Kunnas, Mauri. *Ricky, Rocky and Ringo Count on Pizza* (Crown, 1986) k–3. Ricky the Rhino plans a pizza party for nine cousins and tries to add something for everyone.

3970. ____. *Ricky, Rocky and Ringo's Colorful Day* (Crown, 1986) k–3. Ricky, Rocky and Ringo help a multitude of animals chase a mysterious chameleon as he uses his color-changing ability to hide from them.

3971. ____. *Ricky, Rocky and Ringo Go to the Moon* (Crown, 1986) k–3. The misadventures of Ricky, Rocky and Ringo as they fly their rocket ship to the moon and find out why Zack the robot isn't working.

3972. ____. *Ricky, Rocky and Ringo on T.V.* (Crown, 1986) k–3. Ricky, Rocky and Ringo make a television appearance to sing a pirate song, but Ricky experiences stage fright and can't remember the words.

3973. Kuratomi, Chizuko. *Helpful Mr. Bear* (Parents, 1968) k–3. Mr. Bear visits Rabbit Town where he is out of place because of his size. He wants to be helpful but brings only disaster. He finds he is better suited to mountain life.

3974. ____. *Mr. Bear Goes to Sea* (Macdonald, 1968) k–3. Mr. Bear goes to sea with Captain Rabbit and his rabbit crew but Bear's enormous size makes him an awkward passenger. When a storm blows up Mr. Bear holds on to the cargo until the wind abates.

3975. ____. *Remember Mr. Bear* (Macdonald, 1968) k–3. A huge, lonely bear journeys into Rabbit Town to make some friends. He means well but causes chaos and trudges home leaving sacks of presents for the rabbits but goes home without friends.

3976. ____. *Mr. Bear and the Robbers* (Dial, 1970) k–3. Mr. Bear offers to help three rabbits move furniture out of a cottage not realizing, until it is almost too late, that they were robbers.

3977. ____. *Mr. Bear's Trumpet* (Judson, 1971) k–3. Mr. Bear goes to a Rabbit Circus but he has no ticket so he listens from outside. He is invited in at night and dreams of playing a trumpet. The next day he is allowed to play the trumpet at a performance. He keeps the trumpet and practices.

3978. ____. *Mr. Bear in the Air* (Judson, 1971) k–3. Mr. Bear wants to water all the flowers in the world. He builds an airplane like a grasshopper. The remodeled plane goes up but Mr. Bear comes down. But a rain cloud opens and the flowers are watered.

3979. ____. *Mr. Bear, Station Master* (Macdonald, 1972) k–3. Mr. Bear, amid flying bunting and the music of the band, welcomes the first train to arrive at his very own railroad station.

3980. ____. *Mr. Bear and Apple Jam* (Dial, 1973) k–3. Mr. Bear's mistakes and misunderstandings lands him in trouble. He almost deprives Mrs. Rabbit of her means of livelihood. But kind friends and neighbors help out.

3981. ____. *Mr. Bear's Drawings* (Macdonald, 1975) k–3. The students of Rabbit Art School ask Mr. Bear to pose for them. He in turn asks an ant to pose for him. He then produces his own wax crayon drawing and his ant picture wins acclaim.

3982. ____. *Mr. Bear, Babyminder* (Macdonald, 1976) k–3. Mr. Bear looks after a lost rabbit child he has stumbled across.

3983. ____. *Mr. Bear's Meal* (Macdonald, 1978) k–3.

3984. ____. *Mr. Bear the Postman* (Macdonald, 1980) k–3. When Mr. Bear discovers that an elderly rabbit never has any mail, he writes a letter to him each day, pretending to be an unknown granddaughter, but it is doomed to failure because he has no stamps.

3985. ____. *Mr. Bear, Baker* (Macdonald, 1981) k–3.

Mr. Bear is a brown bear. He takes over a bakery for a day. He and the rabbits get carried away and make bread in the shape of bears and rabbits, then cars, crabs and even spectacles. The real baker is upset but he likes the window display.

3986. ____. *Mr. Bear's Winter Sleep* (Macdonald, 19083) k–3. Mr. Bear takes in a family of rabbits from the snow before he goes to sleep for the winter. They tend to his bruised leg and bring in provisions before the winter really sets in.

3987. ____. *Mr. Bear's Journey* (Macdonald, 1984) k–3. Mr. Bear goes to visit Rabbit who lives in a lighthouse. He decides to go by river so he builds a raft and drifts toward Rabbit's home. The river becomes wild and he is tossed about. He drifts out to sea but the lighthouse keeper rescues him.

3988. ____. *Mr. Bear Shipwrecked* (Macdonald, 1987) k–3. Mr. Bear is feared by adult rabbits and loved and trusted by the children. He protected them from a hurricane.

3989. Kurelek, William. *Prairie Boy's Winter* (Houghton, 1973) k–3. A prairie farm in winter during the 1930s is vividly recalled.

3990. ____. *Prairie Boy's Summer* (Houghton, 1975) k–3. Describes a young boy's summer on the Canadian prairie during the 1930s.

3991. Kwitz, Mary. *Shadow Over Mousehaven Manor* (Scholastic, 1989) 4–6. Minabell Mouse's animal friends come to her rescue when she becomes ensnarled with the Prairie Pirates. A gang of vicious rats determined to take over the mouse family's ancestral home, Mousehaven Manor.

3992. ____. *Bell Tolls at Mousehaven Manor* (Scholastic, 1990) 4–6. Count Van Flittermouse, a body-changing vampire bat, kidnaps Violet Mae Mouse in hopes of gaining a bottle of fluid from the Fountain of Youth.

3993. Kwitz, Mary. *Little Chick's Story* (Harper, 1978) k–3. Broody Hen lays an egg, hatches Little Chick and explains how Little Chick will grow up to lay eggs of her own.

3994. ____. *Little Chick's Big Day* (Harper, 1981) k–3. Little Chick ventures away from her mother and discovers the wonders of the world beyond home.

3995. ____. *Little Chick's Breakfast* (Harper, 1983) k–3. Little Chick becomes hungrier and hungrier and more and more impatient as she watches all the other barnyard animals getting their breakfast before she gets hers.

3996. ____. *Little Chick's Friend Duckling* (Harper, 1992) k–3. While wondering if they will remain best friends after Broody Hen's six eggs hatch, Little Chick and Duckling investigate several big, scary things on the farm.

3997. Kyte, Dennis. *Puppy Gets Around* (Little,

1985) k–3. A rabbit named puppy, who likes to roam, must remember his key for when he comes home.

3998. ____. *Puppy in the Garden* (S & S, 1985) k–3. Puppy is a gentleman rabbit and the constant companion to Abiner Smoothie, "The Last Elegant Bear."

3999. ____. *Puppy Plays a Song* (S & S, 1985) k–3. On a trip to the market to sell his produce, a rabbit named Puppy entertains his animal friends with music.

4000. ____. *Puppy Tidies Up* (S & S, 1985) k–3. A rabbit named Puppy needs a rest after cleaning his house.

4001. Laird, Elizabeth. *Day Sidney Ran Off* (Morrow, 1991) k–3. Duncan the tractor helps Stan the farmer look for a missing piglet.

4002. ____. *Day Sidney Was Lost* (Collins, 1991) k–3. Little Red Tractor helps Stan care for his farm and animals. Sidney, a piglet, wanders away. Stan and Tractor trace his steps and bring him back.

4003. Lakin, Pat. *Don't Touch My Room* (Little, 1985) k–3. "Don't touch my room" becomes "Don't touch my baby" when a child's antipathy turns into protective feelings towards his new baby brother, Benji.

4004. ____. *Oh, Brother!* (Little, 1987) k–3. Eight-year-old Aaron's arguments and playful battles with his three-year-old brother Benji lead him to an appreciation of the special benefits of being a big brother.

4005. ____. *Just Like Me* (Little, 1989) k–3. Big brother Aaron, on the verge of leaving home for a class field trip, gives young Benji firm instructions to leave his things alone while he is gone, but then finds himself missing his little brother on the trip.

4006. Lambert, Thelma. *No Photos for Sam* (Hamilton, 1992) k–3. Sam wants to win a competition for the best wildlife photograph. He is unsuccessful but receives a prize for his imaginative use of a stuffed swan.

4007. ____. *No Swimming for Sam* (Hamilton, 1992) k–3. The clumsiest person in class saves a child's life.

4008. Landa, Norbert. *Rabbit and Chicken Count Eggs* (Tambourine, 1992) k–3. Rabbit and Chicken have fun counting such objects as one egg, three buckets and four apples.

4009. ____. *Rabbit and Chicken Find a Box* (Tambourine, 1992) k–3. Rabbit looks for a nesting spot for Chicken but has trouble locating one the right size.

4010. ____. *Rabbit and Chicken Play Hide-and-Seek* (Tambourine, 1992) k–3. Rabbit finds a cozy place to hide during a game of hide-and-seek with Chicken.

4011. ____. *Rabbit and Chicken Play with Colors* (Tambourine, 1992) k–3. Rabbit and Chicken paint their Easter eggs a variety of colors.

4012. Landon, Lucinda. *Meg Mackintosh and the Case of the Missing Babe Ruth* (Atlantic, 1986) 2–4. Meg follows a series of notes hidden in her grandfather's house to solve an old mystery of a missing baseball signed by Babe Ruth.

4013. ____. *Meg Mackintosh and the Case of the Curious Whale Watch* (Joy Street, 1987) 2–4. On a whale watch, Meg tries to solve a puzzling case involving a stolen treasure map.

4014. ____. *Meg Mackintosh and the Mystery at the Medieval Castle* (Joy Street, 1989) 2–4. Meg and her classmates visit a medieval castle and become eyewitnesses to the theft of a priceless chalice.

4015. ____. *Meg Mackintosh and the Mystery at Camp Creepy* (Little, 1990) 2–4. While attending summer camp for the first time, Meg tries to solve the mystery of the camp's legendary ghost.

4016. ____. *Meg Mackintosh and the Mystery of the Locked Library* (Joy Street) 1993 2–4. Meg investigates the theft of a rare book from a locked library.

4017. Landshoff, Ursula. *Daisy and Doodle* (Bradbury, 1969) k–3. When Daisy is separated from Doodle, her poodle, she gets into trouble and needs his help.

4018. ____. *Daisy and the Stormy Night* (Bradbury, 1971) k–3. Daisy and her dog, Doodle, stay alone in the apartment while Daisy's parents visit down the hall. A storm sends Doodle into the closet. First Daisy tries to coax him out, then she joins him. Her parents come home and try to find them.

4019. Landstrom, Olof. *Will's New Cap* (R & S, 1992) k–3. Will is thrilled with his new red and green baseball cap, especially the sun visor. A rain storm drenches the cap, making its visor droop. Will's mother tries to make repairs.

4020. ____. *Will Gets a Haircut* (R & S, 1993) k–3. Will doesn't want to get a haircut but, while waiting his turn at the barber's he sees exactly what he wants in a magazine.

4021. Lastrego, Christina. *Dragon at the Gates* (Blackie, 1978) k–3.

4022. ____. *Dragon in the Woods* (Blackie, 1980) k–3. A small girl, Julia, dreams that she and a dragon friend are being persecuted by a bad baron.

4023. Latimer, Jim. *Going the Moose Way Home* (Scribner, 1988) k–3. A year in the life of a very unusual moose, who shares his root beer with hungry cows, helps smaller animals across a troll bridge, and mistakes a train for a lady moose.

4024. ____. *When Moose Was Young* (Scribner, 1990) k–3. Follows the adventures of Moose and his animal friends as they venture into the Crab Apple Woods, make Elm Syrup Mousse, befriend the pilgrim turkeys and discover a carousel.

4025. ____. *Moose and Friends* (Scribner, 1992)

k–3. Moose and his animal friends have four adventures in Moosewood.

4026. Lattimore, Eleanor. *Little Pear* (Harcourt, 1931/1991) *3–5*. A classic story of Little Pear's life in China in the early 1900s. This is the same Little Pear that was so popular in the 1930s. The book is still read and enjoyed by children.

4027. _____. *Little Pear and His Friends* (Harcourt, 1934/1991) 3–5. A story about a little Chinese boy whose curiosity and activity lead him into mischief. There are scenes of village and family life, games and festivals are described.

4028. _____. *Little Pear and His Rabbits* (Morrow, 1956) 3–5. Little Pear is a Chinese boy living on a farm. At a nearby fair he buys a pair of rabbits that are soft and pretty.

4029. _____. *More About Little Pear* (Morrow, 1971) 3–5. Little Pear is now seven years old (40 years after he was introduced as a young child). He gets into more mischief now that he is older.

4030. Lauber, Patricia. *Clarence, the TV Dog* (Coward, 1955) 2–4. A dog who never growls at strangers meets a burglar in his house.

4031. _____. *Clarence Goes to Town* (Coward, 1957) 2–4. Clarence goes to New York City with Brian and Sis and their mother to keep shop for a sick aunt. Clarence was thought to be in the way at first, but he was a means of entertainment for Brian and Sis, not to mention lots of other people.

4032. _____. *Clarence and the Cat* (Coward, 1977) 2–4. Clarence, a very friendly dog, finally finds a novel way of teaching the visiting Cat to be a perfect guest.

4033. Lavelle, Sheila. *Ursula Exploring* (Hamilton, 1980) k–3. A fantasy about a little girl who can turn herself into a bear.

4034. _____. *Ursula Dancing* (Hamilton, 1980) k–3. A magic spell turns Ursula into a small brown bear. She uses the spell to get her into the visiting circus. She ends up as a performer.

4035. _____. *Ursula Sailing* (Hamilton, 1984) k–3. Ursula is a bear and can both climb well enough to rescue her glide when it lands in a tree and swims well enough to survive when the branch snaps and lands her in the river.

4036. _____. *Ursula Climbing* (Collins, 1984) k–3. Ursula's magic trick enables her to turn into a bear. She climbs down the gorge to the buzzard's nest and rescues poor Fredbear.

4037. _____. *Ursula by the Sea* (Hamilton, 1986) k–3.

4038. _____. *Ursula Camping* (Hamilton, 1986) k–3.

4039. _____. *Ursula at the Zoo* (Hamilton, 1986) k–3.

4040. _____. *Ursula Flying* (Corgi, 1989) k–3. Ursula can turn herself into a bear and do what she wants.

4041. _____. *Ursula on the Farm* (Hamilton, 1988) k–3.

4042. Lavelle, Sheila. *Fiend Next Door* (Hamilton, 1982) 2–4. A story of Angela and her next door friend Charlie, a girl. Angela involves Charlie in wrong doings and Charlie gets the blame. One of her tricks backfires and reveals her to be mean and spiteful.

4043. _____. *Trouble with the Fiend* (Hamilton, 1984) 2–4. Angela involves Charlie in tricks and then leaves her to take the blame. One time Angela admits her share in the mischief and the tables turn on Angela.

4044. _____. *Holiday with the Fiend* (Hamilton, 1986) 2–4. Charlie and her so called friend, Angela, go on vacation to the sea. Angela pulls outrageous pranks at Guest House and Charlie must turn the tables.

4045. _____. *Disaster with the Fiend* (Hamilton, 1991) 2–4. Charlie and her next door neighbor, Angela, are friends but Angela always plays tricks on Charlie. But finally Charlie stands up for her rights.

4046. Lavelle, Sheila. *Harry's Aunt* (Hamilton, 1985) 2–4. The aunt, a secret witch, upsets the town bus when she becomes an elephant and disturbs a shop as a chimpanzee. So Harry needs to watch her closely. When a cat interrupts a dog show, Harry carries it home and waits for it to change back to his aunt. Instead Aunt turns up as an Old English sheepdog and wins a cup. She is willing to keep the cat.

4047. _____. *Harry's Horse* (Hamilton, 1987) 2–4.

4048. _____. *Harry's Dog* (Hamilton, 1988) 2–4.

4049. _____. *Harry's Cat* (Hamilton, 1993) 2–4. Aunt Winnie sprinkles magic powder over the cat and Harry and Ali find themselves face to face with a roaming tiger. They barely capture the tiger and then find their cat, unchanged and unmagical.

4050. Lavelle, Sheila. *Maisy in the Mud* (Macmillan, 1994) k–3. Getting in a mess is Maisy's misfortune but also her strength. This story of messy Maisy concerns a competition for a fancy dress.

4051. _____. *Maisy's Masterpiece* (Macmillan, 1994) k–3. A story of Maisy, her family and her cats (who make humorous comments throughout). This story concerns a competition for a painting.

4052. _____. *Messy Maisy* (Macmillan, 1994) k–3. Maisy is the messiest girl in class. She is from a large supportive family which includes two wonderful cats.

4053. _____. *Maisy Measles* (Macmillan, 1994) k–3.

4054. Lawlor, Laurie. *Addie Across the Prairie* (Whitman, 1986) 4–6. Unhappy to leave her home and friends. Addie reluctantly accompanies her family to the Dakota Territory and slowly begins to adjust to life on the prairie.

4055. _____. *Addie's Dakota Winter* (Whitman, 1989) 4–6. In her new pioneer home of Dakota, ten-year-old Addie finds an unlikely friend and, stranded alone during a blizzard, learns about courage.

4056. Lawrence, Ann. *Travels of Oggy* (Gollancz, 1973) 4–6. When Oggy's benevolent humans leave on vacation, he sets off to find them, meeting Otter, Badger, Rat, Crow and others.
4057. _____. *Oggy at Home* (Gollancz, 1977) 4–6. Oggy the hedgehog was wakened from his winter sleep by a small kitten, Tiggy. He is delighted because here is a creature that knows less than he does. He teaches her to climb trees and hunt. But Tiggy still gets into trouble.
4058. _____. *Oggy and the Holiday* (Gollancz, 1980) 4–6. When Tiggy the kitten is taken on vacation by her people, her friend Oggy, the hedgehog, stows away in the car. Oggy and Tiggy are at the seaside where they again meet Barge Rat.

4059. Lawrence, James. *Binky Brothers, Detectives* (Harper, 1968) 3–5. When the Binky brothers investigate a case involving a missing catcher's mitt, the younger brother proves the better detective and establishes his right to be a full partner in the agency.
4060. _____. *Binky Brothers and the Fearless Four* (Harper, 1970) 3–5. When the snow fort is threatened and then wrecked, the obvious suspect is the new boy in the neighborhood.

4061. Lawrence, Jim. *ESP McGee and the Haunted Mansion* (Avon, 1983) 5–8. Convinced that something spooky is going to happen at the old Frome mansion, Edward "ESP" McGee and his best friend Matt Terrell, decide to test McGee's ESP and explore the supposedly empty house.
(For other books about the "ESP McGee," **see** Packard, Edward.)

4062. Lebrun, Claude. *Little Brown Bear's Story* (Methuen, 1982) k–3.
4063. _____. *Little Brown Bear is Cross* (Methuen, 1982) k–3. A simple story of Little Bear whose disappointments, temper and disagreements are very important.
4064. _____. *Little Brown Bear Is Big* (Methuen, 1984) k–3. Little Brown Bear can lace his shoes, climb a ladder and ride a tricycle as he grows up.
4065. _____. *Little Brown Bear's Bad Day* (Methuen, 1984) k–3. Father Bear goes away to his son's dismay. Little Brown Bear gets cross, bored and frightened and finally goes to sleep in front of the television, clutching teddy.
4066. _____. *Little Brown Bear Can Cook* (Methuen, 1984) k–3. Little Brown Bear wears an apron and helps Mother with the cooking.
4067. _____. *Little Brown Bear Goes Exploring* (Children's, 1995) k–3. While walking, Little Brown Bear fills his basket with a round pebble, three white daisies, a buttercup, a striped snail, and a stick to dip in the water.

4068. _____. *Little Brown Bear is Afraid of the Dark* (Children's, 1995) k–3. Little Brown Bear is sure there are monsters in his bedroom when Papa turns out the light, but Papa Bear reassured his Little Brown Bear that they are only shadows on the wall.
4069. _____. *Little Brown Bear Dresses Himself* (Children's, 1995) k–3. Little Brown Bear feels proud because he can get dressed by himself.
4070. _____. *Little Brown Bear Does Not Want to Eat* (Children's, 1995) k–3. Little Brown Bear resists all the efforts to get him to eat his soup.
4071. _____. *Little Brown Bear Helps His Mama* (Children's, 1995) k–3. Little Brown Bear helps Mama Bear with her purse and coat, helps put the groceries away and brings her slippers.
4072. _____. *Little Brown Bear and His Chair* (Children's, 1995) k–3. Little Brown Bear uses his chair for a little bed, for brushing his teeth, for being tall and for sitting as well.
4073. _____. *Little Brown Bear Has Fun in the Park* (Children's, 1995) k–3. Little Brown Bear is afraid to go down the big slide at the park, so he and Mama Bear go down the slide together, and then he is not afraid anymore.
4074. _____. *Good Morning, Little Brown Bear* (Children's, 1995) k–3. Little Brown Bear feels cranky when he gets up in the morning, but a hug from Mama Bear makes everything better.
4075. _____. *Little Brown Bear Takes a Bath* (Children's, 1995) k–3. Little Brown Bear enjoys bathtime.
4076. _____. *Little Brown Bear is Sick* (Children's, 1995) k–3. Poor Little Brown Bear has a cold but with Mama Bear's tender loving care, Little Brown Bear feels much better by the next morning.
4077. _____. *Little Brown Bear Loves Mama and Papa* (Children's, 1995) k–3. Mama Bear reminds Little Brown Bear that she loves her baby bear and she also loves Daddy Bear.
4078. _____. *Little Brown Bear Wants to Go to School* (Children's, 1995) k–3. Even though he is too young to go to school Mama Bear shows her Little Brown Bear all the fun things he will get to do once he's there.
4079. _____. *Little Brown Bear Goes on a Trip* (Children's, 1995) k–3. Little Brown Bear packs for a sleepover.
4080. _____. *Little Brown Bear Plays with Shoes* (Children's, 1995) k–3. Little Brown Bear tries on the various shoes which he finds in the closet including a pair of house slippers, Mama's high heels and Papa's big boots.
4081. _____. *Little Brown Bear Plays in the Snow* (Children's, 1995) k–3. Little Brown Bear makes snowballs and does other fun things in the snow.
4082. _____. *Little Brown Bear Says "No" to Everything* (Children's, 1995) k–3. Little Brown Bear's response to everything is negative.
4083. _____. *Little Brown Bear Learns the Value of Money* (Children's, 1995) k–3. When Little Brown

Bear spends his coin at the bakery he is pleased to receive two coins in exchange because before he had only one.

4084. _____. *Little Brown Bear Wants to Be Read To* (Children's, 1995) k–3. Little Brown Bear is impatient for Mama or Daddy to read a book to him.

4085. _____. *Little Brown Bear Is Growing Up* (Children's, 1995) k–3. Little Brown Bear takes pride in the things he can do all by himself including getting down from his bed in the morning and peeling a banana.

4086. _____. *Little Brown Bear's Breakfast Egg* (Methuen, 1996) k–3.

4087. _____. *Little Brown Bear's Snowball* (Methuen, 1996) k–3.

4088. _____. *Little Brown Bear's Playtime* (Methuen, 1996) k–3.

4089. Lee, Robert. *Iron Arm of Michael Glenn* (Little, 1965) 5–8. Mike, 12, was invited to help Professor Von Heiner with an experiment. When he put his arm in the experiment box it came out the strongest arm in the world. In Little League he could throw fastballs but in time it wore off.

4090. _____. *Day It Rained Forever* (Little, 1968) 5–8. Mike visits his professor friend in the hospital and learns of the machine that is causing the rain. It must be stopped. Mike also plays basketball and runs for student body president.

4091. Leedy, Loreen. *Number of Dragons* (Holiday, 1985) k–3. Introduces the numbers one through ten as a group of young dragons play together and alone.

4092. _____. *Dragon ABC Hunt* (Holiday, 1986) k–3. Ten little dragons try to find an object for each letter of the alphabet.

4093. _____. *Dragon Halloween Party* (Holiday, 1986) k–3. The dragons prepare a Halloween party complete with costumes, decorations, and appropriate food and activities.

4094. Leeson, Robert. *Grange Hill Rules—OK?* (BBC, 1980) 5–8. A pudding eating contest to raise funds pits Grange Hill against Brookdale. Doyle vs. Tucker, Penny vs. Templeton and Cathy vs. Madelin. Grange Hall won, of course.

4095. _____. *Grange Hill Goes Wild* (BBC, 1981) 5–8. Teachers Baxter and Peterson hope that Tucker and Doyle will learn something from camp. But they secretly smoke and threaten a farmer's crop, but they do learn something: the ghostly prowler, an airman living in a hut, gives them a brief insight into his war.

4096. _____. *Grange Hill for Sale* (BBC, 1981) 5–8. Tucker and her friends are tying to clear up the confusion centered around the concept of closing Grange Hill because of declining enrollment.

4097. _____. *Grange Hill After Hours* (BBC, 1982) 5–8. Julia and Laura plan to go to an all-night party and are caught; Ziggy stows away on a plane for Lon-don; Gonch and Hollo invade school at night to return a borrowed transistor.

4098. Leeson, Robert. *Third Class Genie* (Hamilton, 1981) 5–8. Alec acquired a beer can inhabited by a genie, Abu Salem. Their association provoked a series of zany escapades.

4099. _____. *Genie on the Loose* (Hamilton, 1984) 5–8. Alec totes up the day's events on a mental scoreboard: Disasters 2, Triumphs 1. He meets Abu's unruly son, Abdul. Alec falls for Abdul's claim that he is uneducated and inexperienced. Meanwhile he wreaks havoc in the community and woos Alex's schoolmate.

4100. Le Guin, Ursula. *Catwings* (Orchard, 1988) 2–4. Four young cats with wings leave the city slums in search of a safe place to live, finally meeting two children with kind hands.

4101. _____. *Catwings Return* (Orchard, 1988) 2–4. Wishing to visit their mother, two winged cats leave their new country home to return to the city, where they discover a winged kitten in a building about to be demolished.

4102. _____. *Wonderful Alexander and the Catwings* (Orchard, 1994) k–3. A story of a self-important kitten from nearby who discovers that his true worth is not what he has supposed. Alexander never noticed that his sisters are quite tired of him, but when he sets out to explore the world he soon learns that his cocky preconceptions don't serve him well.

4103. Lehmann, Linda. *Better Than a Princess* (Nelson, 1978) 4–6. Tilli is at last reunited with her mother in America but needs to adjust to this plain-looking, plain-living woman. A gift of a beautiful doll does this.

4104. _____. *Tilli's New World* (Nelson, 1981) 4–6. Tilli wants to go to school to learn to read but she is needed to help her poor family. She hires herself out as a housemaid and gets to go to school sometimes.

4105. Lenski, Lois. *Little Family* (Doubleday, 1932) k–3. Mr. and Mrs. Little and their two children live in a little house with a cat, a dog, a garden, chickens and a motorcar that takes them on picnics.

4106. _____. *Little Auto* (Walck, 1934/1965) k–3. Mr. Small has a little red auto. He takes very good care of his favorite auto.

4107. _____. *Little Sailboat* (Walck, 1937/1965) k–3. Captain Small goes sailing, fishes from his boat, goes for an unexpected swim and braves a storm on his way home.

4108. _____. *Little Airplane* (Walck, 1938/1959) k–3. Pilot Small flies his airplane over the countryside, does a loopy-loop, makes an emergency landing and finally returns safely to the hanger.

4109. _____. *Little Train* (Walck, 1940/1960) k–3.

Engineer Small at the throttle takes the little train on its run from Tiny Town to the big city.

4110. _____. *Little Farm* (Walck, 1942/1959) k–3. Throughout the year Farmer Small does many chores from morning until night.

4111. _____. *Little Fire Engine* (Walck, 1946/1960) k–3. Fireman Small and his little fire engine answer a call, rescue a little girl and save a house from burning down.

4112. Lenski, Lois. *Cowboy Small* (Walck, 1949/1980) k–3. Cowboy Small takes good care of his horse, rides the range, helps in the roundup and rides a bucking bronco.

4113. _____. *Papa Small* (Walck, 1951/1966) k–3. Papa shaves and the small Smalls come in to watch. Mama cleans and fixes dinner, Paul and Polly help. Mama does laundry and Papa hangs the clothes on the line. A together family.

4114. _____. *Policeman Small* (Walck, 1962) k–3. Describes the many daily duties of a corner traffic cop.

4115. _____. *Songs of Mr. Small* (Walck, 1966) k–3. Twenty-one songs about Mr. Small in his many roles as Farmer, Cowboy, etc.

4116. _____. *More Mr. Small* (Walck, 1979) k–3. Contains: "Little Auto"; "Little Sailboat"; "Little Airplane."

4117. _____. *Lois Lenski's Big Book of Mr. Small* (Walck, 1978) k–3. Contains: "Policeman Small"; "Cowboy Small"; "Little Farm."

4118. Lenski, Lois. *Debbie and Her Grandma* (Walck, 1967) k–3. A story of the small events of three-year-old Debbie's 24-hour visit to her grandmother's.

4119. _____. *Debbie Herself* (Walck, 1969) k–3. Shows games and other activities enjoyed by three-year-old Debbie.

4120. _____. *Debbie and Her Family* (Walck, 1969) k–3. Debbie, three, tells of her daily life and family.

4121. _____. *Debbie Goes to Nursery School* (Walck, 1970) k–3. Debbie tells a little about nursery school treatment and Debbie's solution.

4122. _____. *Debbie and Her Dolls* (Walck, 1970) k–3. Debbie plays with her dolls. Her brother and sister hide the dolls; she finds them in a laundry pail.

4123. _____. *Debbie and Her Pets* (Walck, 1971) k–3. A story of a pet show that concludes with the moral that tame pets are best, after all, rather than worms, insects, spiders or frogs.

4124. Le Saux, Alain. *King Daddy* (Holt, 1992) k–3. Daddy's ordinary daily activities amuse his young son in these following stories.

4125. _____. *Daddy Shaves* (Holt, 1992) k–3.

4126. _____. *Daddy Sleeps* (Holt, 1990) k–3.

4127. _____. *Daddy Scratches* (Holt, 1990) k–3.

4128. Leverich, Kathleen. *Best Enemies* (Greenwillow, 1989) 3–5. After Felicity trades her nasty tricks for friendship, Priscilla decides she'd rather have Felicity as an enemy.

4129. _____. *Best Enemies Again* (Greenwillow, 1991) 3–5. Wealthy Felicity continues to complicate Priscilla's life both in school and out.

4130. Levin, Betty. *Sword of Culann* (Macmillan, 1973) 5–8. Claudia and Evan find an ancient sword hilt and disappear from Maine, to reappear in Iron Age Ireland where they become involved in magical battles.

4131. _____. *Griffon's Nest* (Macmillan, 1975) 5–8. Claudia and Evan with the help of their ancient sword become enmeshed with the intrigue of the Irish courts of the seventh century.

4132. _____. *Forespoken* (Macmillan, 1976) 5–8. Claudia is with the shepherd Thomas, who believes himself to be bewitched. She has concern for him and also feels the need to return the crow to Mr. Colman who is dying.

4133. Levitin, Sonia. *Journey to America* (Atheneum, 1970) 4–6. Papa goes to America from Germany. The rest of the family goes to Switzerland until Papa can send for them. It is a time of hardship and terror of being caught and sent back.

4134. *Return* (Atheneum, 1987) 5–8. Desta and her family go from Ethiopia to Israel. Her brother dies during their escape, but courage, physical and mental horrors end in relief as they reach their destination.

4135. _____. *Silver Days* (Aladdin, 1992) 4–6. The Platt family, reunited, works hard at settling into America, but the specter of the war in Europe continues to affect their lives.

4136. Levy, Elizabeth. *Something Queer Is Going On* (Delacorte, 1973) 3–5. The mysterious kidnapping of Fletcher, the inert Basset hound, leads Jill and Gwen on a frantic search that ends up in front of a TV camera shooting a dog food commercial.

4137. _____. *Something Queer at the Ballpark* (Delacorte, 1975) 3–5. Gwen, an amateur sleuth, sets out to discover who took her best friend's lucky baseball cap.

4138. _____. *Something Queer at the Library* (Delacorte, 1977) 3–5. Gwen and Jill's discovery of some mutilated library books strangely links up with a dog show in which they have entered their dog.

4139. _____. *Something Queer on Vacation* (Delacorte, 1980) 3–5. Gwen and Jill determine to win the weekly sandcastle contest on the beach but something always seems to go wrong.

4140. _____. *Something Queer at the Haunted School* (Delacorte, 1982) 3–5. Two amateur detectives investigate a haunting of their school that starts around Halloween.

4141. _____. *Something Queer at the Lemonade*

Stand (Delacorte, 1982) 3–5. When Gwen and Jill open a lemonade stand, something strange happens to their lemonade every time their dog Fletcher disappears.

4142. _____. *Something Queer in Rock 'n' Roll* (Delacorte, 1987) 3-5. Preparing for a rock and roll contest in which they need a dog's howl over a pizza, the gang becomes desperate when their dog loses all interest in pizza.

4143. _____. *Something Queer at the Birthday Party* (Delacorte, 1990) 3–5. Jill makes up a fiendish plan to surprise Gwen on her birthday but is surprised herself by an unexpected turn of events.

4144. _____. *Something Queer in Outer Space* (Hyperion, 1993) 3–5. It's Gwen and Jill to the rescue when somebody tries to sabotage Fletcher the Basset hound's mission in space.

4145. _____. *Something Queer in the Cafeteria* (Hyperion, 1994) 3–5. Jill and Gwen have never gotten in trouble before, but suddenly every time they are in the cafeteria, something goes terribly wrong.

4146. Levy, Elizabeth. *Case of the Wild River Ride* (S & S, 1978) 5–8. Jody, 15, and Jake join three others on a trip down the Colorado River. They rescue a man who turns out to be an escaped killer. They leave Jody and Jake stranded. The others rescue their friends and solve the mystery.

4147. _____. *Case of the Frightened Rock Star* (S & S, 1980) 5–8. Jody asks rock star Michael Markson to sing at a fund-raiser. Jody becomes the target of jokes aimed at sabotaging the concert, forcing Jody and Jake, her brother, to solve the mystery and for the concert to succeed.

4148. _____. *Case of the Counterfeit Race Horse* (S & S, 1981) 5–8. Jake and Jody have jobs at the racetrack for the summer. Jody becomes a victim of an arranged accident. She, Jake and her boyfriend Pete prove that the horse who wins the Gold Cup is a substitute.

4149. _____. *Cast of the Fired Up Gang* (S & S, 1981) 5–8. Jake, the witty 14-year-old gourmet, is likable. His sister Jody, hardworking straight–A student, is solemn and humorless. A mysterious fire starts in an old house and a young man is accused of starting it.

4150. Levy, Elizabeth. *Case of the Gobbling Squash* (S & S, 1988) 5–8. A young detective and her partner, an amateur magician, solve a case involving missing bunnies, a pink sock ghost, and a remote-control squash that gobbles like a Thanksgiving turkey.

4151. _____. *Case of the Mind Reading Mommies* (S & S, 1989) 5–8. A young detective and her partner, an amateur magician solve a case involving disappearing presents, a talking doorknob and a magical Mother's Day show.

4152. _____. *Case of the Tattletale Heart* (S & S, 1990) 5–8. A young detective and her partner, an amateur magician solve a Valentine's Day mystery involving a mummy's finger, a mind-reading act and a mysterious laughing heart.

4153. _____. *Case of the Dummy with Cold Eyes* (S & S, 1991) 5–8. When a young detective and her partner, an amateur magician, add a ventriloquist's dummy to their magic act, they find themselves involved in a case with mysterious voices, disappearing cases, and stolen jewels.

4154. Levy, Elizabeth. *Running Out of Time* (Knopf, 1980) 4–6. Through the fog the three children go back to the time of Spartacus and the gladiators.

4155. _____. *Running Out of Magic with Houdini* (Knopf, 1981) 4–6. The three children are working out for the marathon when they are transported back to 1912 and Houdini's East River escape trick.

4156. Levy, Elizabeth. *Rude Rowdy Rumors* (Harper, 1994) 3–5. Seven-year-old Brian enlists the help of his little sister Penny to discover which of his soccer teammates is spreading rude rumors about him.

4157. _____. *School Spirit Sabotage* (Harper, 1994) 3–5. Brian and his younger sister Penny try to catch the culprit who has been sabotaging School Spirit Week.

4158. Lewin, Hugh. *Jafta's Father* (Carolrhoda, 1981) k–3. While his father works in the city over the winter, a young boy thinks of some good times they've shared and looks forward to his return to their South African home in the spring.

4159. _____. *Jafta and the Wedding* (Carolrhoda, 1983) k–3. A South African boy describes the week-long village festival in celebration of his sister's wedding.

4160. _____. *Jafta* (Carolrhoda, 1983) k–3. Jafta describes some of his everyday feelings by comparing his actions to those of various African animals.

4161. _____. *Jafta's Mother* (Carolrhoda, 1983) k–3. A little boy living in a South African village describes his mother and the love he feels for her.

4162. _____. *Jafta—The Town* (Carolrhoda, 1984) k–3. Jafta gets his first exposure to the hustle and bustle of the city.

4163. _____. *Jafta—The Journey* (Carolrhoda, 1984) k–3. Jafta, a South African boy, travels with his mother to the city where his father works.

4164. _____. *Jafta—The Homecoming* (Knopf, 1994) k–3. A young black South African boy describes his feelings about his father's return from working in the city.

4165. Lewis, Thomas. *Call for Mr. Sniff* (Harper, 1981) 3–5. A detective hound is lured with a mystery to a birthday party in his honor.

4166. _____. *Mr. Sniff and the Motel Mystery* (Harper, 1984) 3–5. The famous detective hound discovers why guests are being frightened away from a beach hotel.

4167. Lewiton, Mina. *Especially Humphrey* (Delacorte, 1987) 2–4. No one spoke to their neighbors on Little Street until the arrival of Humphrey, who, being a sheep dog, knows little about remaining aloof.

4168. ____. *Humphrey on the Town* (Delacorte, 1971) 2–4. Humphrey, a large sheep dog, sees to it that many residents of New York City will always remember the winter he and his mistress spend there.

4169. Lexau, Joan. *Benjie* (Dial, 1964) k–3. Benjie just had to overcome his shyness before he could make any progress in his search for Granny's lost earring which was a wedding present from Granddaddy.

4170. ____. *Benjie on His Own* (Dial, 1970) k–3. When his grandmother becomes quite ill, young Benjie discovers that the people in his big city neighborhood can be friendly and helpful after all.

4171. Lindbergh, Anne. *People in Pineapple Place* (Morrow, 1982) 4–6. Ten-year-old August Brown adjusts to his new home in Washington, D.C., with the help of the seven children of Pineapple Place, invisible to everyone but him.

4172. ____. *Prisoner of Pineapple Place* (Harcourt, 1988) 4–6. Pineapple Place, an invisible street that moves from city to city and keeps its inhabitants the same age forever, is threatened with change when Jeremiah becomes bored and makes contact with the outside world.

4173. Lindgren, Astrid. *Happy Days at Bullerby* (Methuen, 1965) k–3. Christmas and New Year is celebrated with games and sleigh rides, taking a hamper of goodies to old Kristina who lives all alone in her red cottage and carrying presents to friends and relations.

4174. ____. *All About the Bullerby Children* (Methuen, 1970) k–3. A children's tea party includes five candles in their candlesticks and a jug of ginger beer for the New Year Celebration.

4175. ____. *Springtime in Bullerby* (Methuen, 1981) k–3. Spring in Bullerby, where seven children live on three farms, is exciting. There they have a tea party, play hide-and-seek, walk along the fence, and jump off the woodshed. Little Kerstin pats a hedgehog, falls in a stream and tugs a cat by its "handle."

4176. Lindgren, Astrid. *Emil in the Soup Tureen* (Follett, 1970) 4–6. Emil lived with his parents and a sister, Ida. He was constantly in trouble. In this book he gets his head caught in a soup bowl and can't get it out. It took a lot of different events to do so.

4177. ____. *Emil's Pranks* (Follett, 1971) 4–6. Emil's pranks include locking himself in the tool chest three times in one day, trying to catch a rat (but he caught his father's toe instead), and accidentally spilling pudding on his father's head.

4178. ____. *Emil and the Piggy Beast* (Follett, 1973)

4–6. Emil buys his sister a velvet-lined box at an auction. The box contains a letter with a valuable stamp. He has adventures with his pet pig.

4179. ____. *That Emil* (Follett, 1973) k–3. Emil is accident-prone. He seems to produce unique catastrophes. He helps his sister up the flagpole, sets fire to the minister's wife's hat and rides a horse into the middle of a party.

4180. ____. *Emil and His Clever Pig* (Follett, 1975) k–3. Emil is always in trouble and his mother records all of his dreadful deeds in a blue exercise cook.

4181. ____. *Emil and the Bad Tooth* (Hodder, 1976) k–3. Emil's pranks, although well-intentioned, exasperate adults but amuse the children.

4182. ____. *Emil's Sticky Problem* (Follett, 1986) k–3. A story of how Emil fails to solve his mother's troubles with the flies.

4183. ____. *Emil's Little Sister* (Follett, 1986) k–3. Emil's sister is well-behaved for her young age and size. She cracks every egg in the hidden nest to see if it is good enough to make pancakes.

4184. Lindgren, Astrid. *Karlsson-on-the-Roof* (Viking, 1971) 4–6. Eric had a friend, Karlsson, who could fly with a machine on his back. Together they put on a magic show, foil some thieves and take dangerous walks along the rooftops.

4185. ____. *Karlsson Flies Again* (Viking, 1977) 4–6. Karlsson is a fat little man with a propeller on his back who lives on the roof of Midge's house. He makes Midge's life more interesting.

4186. ____. *World's Best Karlsson* (Methuen, 1980) 4–6. Karlsson and Midge, a newspaper owner's daughter, get into awkward situations. Uncle Julius comes for his annual visit when Midge's family is away. Miss Black looks after the house, Karlsson plays tricks on Uncle Julius and Miss Black.

4187. Lindgren, Astrid. *Lotta Leaves Home* (Macmillan, 1969) 2–4. Lotta, five, thinks she is misunderstood so she sets up house in Mrs. Berg's garden shed. Mrs. Berg helps her with what she needs. How does she now go home without losing dignity?

4188. ____. *Lotta's Christmas Surprise* (Macmillan, 1979) 2–4. Because of deep snow no Christmas trees are in Lotta's village. While in the village Lotta meets a truck driver with a load of trees for the city. He will not sell Lotta a tree but as he pulls out a tree falls off the truck and Lotta takes it home.

4189. ____. *Lotta on Troublemaker Street* (Macmillan, 1984) 2–4. Angry because everyone at home is so mean, five-year-old Lotta takes her favorite toy and goes to live in a neighbor's attic.

4190. ____. *Lotta's Bike* (Farrar, 1989) 2–4. Lotta, five, wants a bicycle more than anything else. She secretly takes a neighbor's bicycle, which is so large she is unable to stop it. But before the day is over her father finds a used bicycle; it's her size.

4191. ____. *Lotta's Easter Surprise* (Farrar, 1991) 2–4. While Lotta waits to be dressed up as an Easter witch, she wanders into a candy store to see the chocolate eggs. The store is going out of business and the owner gives her some Christmas candy. She surprises her family with Christmas gifts on Easter morning.

4192. ____. *Children on Troublemaker Street* (Macmillan, 1991) k–3. Jonas, Maria and Lotta have exciting times wherever they go.

4193. Lindgren, Astrid. *Tomten* (Sandcastle, 1961/ 1990) k–3. A book of winter scenes and of barnyard animals who heard many fascinating secrets from the trolls who wandered through the farmhouse talking to them in their own special language, Tomten.

4194. ____. *Tomten and the Fox* (Coward, 1965/ 1979) k–3. Tomten, a little troll, saves the chickens by feeding the poor hungry fox who comes to the farm in search of food.

4195. Lindgren, Astrid. *Pippi Longstocking* (Viking, 1950/1981) 4–6. Pippi, a tomboy, lives with her horse and her monkey (but no grown-ups) next door to Tommy and Annika. Her strength is prodigious. She can lift her horse and place him anywhere. She also has great powers of invention.

4196. ____. *Pippi Goes on Board* (Viking, 1957/ 1981) 4–6. Pippi's neighbors, Tommy and Annika, find Pippi's adventures—like getting shipwrecked—so fascinating that when her father suddenly appears to take her off to sea they are miserable. But Pippi makes an unexpected decision.

4197. ____. *Pippi in the South Seas* (Viking, 1959/ 1977) 4–6. Pippi decides to take her two measles-stricken friends, Tommy and Annika, to Kurrekurre-dutt Island where her father is busy being king.

4198. ____. *Pippi on the Run* (Viking, 1976) 4–6. When her friends Tommy and Annika decide to run away from home, Pippi Longstocking goes along to keep an eye on them.

4199. ____. *New Adventures of Pippi Longstocking* (Viking, 1988) 4–6. Pippi, while sailing with her father, is washed overboard and is lost in a fierce storm. But holding onto a raft and with her optimistic spirit, Pippi eventually drifts ashore to a small coastal town where she sets up a house in an ancient, vacated mansion. Villa Villekulla. There, with her horse Alphonso and monkey Mr. Neilson, Pippi begins a new life without any adult supervision.

4200. Lindgren, Astrid. *Mardie* (Methuen, 1979) 4–6. Mardie is a tomboy. Her sister Lisbet thinks she is crazy. Mardie blames all her mishaps on her fictional friend Richard. They are two sisters in constant trouble.

4201. ____. *Mardie to the Rescue* (Methuen, 1981) 4–6. Mardie and her five-year-old sister live with their parents in Sweden in the 1920s. There is a May Fire celebration that marks the return of. Spring. There is a picnic; a visit of an airplane; the Autumn Ball and the birth of baby sister Katie.

4202. Lindgren, Astrid. *Of Course Polly Can Ride a Bike* (Follett, 1972) k–3. On her fifth birthday Polly determines to prove she can ride a bicycle like her older brother and sister.

4203. ____. *Of Course Polly Can Do Almost Everything* (Follett, 1978) k–3. Polly, five, finds a Christmas tree for her family after all the trees in their town have been sold.

4204. Lindgren, Barbro. *Wild Baby* (Greenwillow, 1981) k–3. Baby Ben gets into one difficulty after another, from which Mama rescues him—but not for long.

4205. ____. *Wild Baby Goes to Sea* (Greenwillow, 1983) k–3. When his mother cleans house, rambunctious baby Ben sets sail in a wooden box and has many adventures.

4206. ____. *Wild Baby's Boat Trip* (Greenwillow, 1983) k–3. A story that combines a domestic setting with a child's wild fantasies.

4207. ____. *Wild Baby's Dog* (Greenwillow, 1987) k–3. Bodger is a naughty boy who wants a dog. He gets a stuffed one and it comes alive and takes Bodger on exciting adventures.

4208. ____. *Wild Baby Gets a Puppy* (Greenwillow, 1988) k–3. Anxious to have a real puppy, baby Ben is disappointed when he gets a rag puppy for his birthday until he discovers that "Rags" has some special qualities of his own.

4209. Lindgren, Barbro. *Sam's Teddy Bear* (Morrow, 1982) k–3. Doggie rescues Sam's beloved Teddy Bear.

4210. ____. *Sam's Cookie* (Morrow, 1982) k–3. Sam and Doggie have a disagreement about Sam's cookie.

4211. ____. *Sam's Car* (Morrow, 1982) k–3. Sam and Lisa fight over a car until Mother intervenes.

4212. ____. *Sam's Ball* (Morrow, 1983) k–3. A toddler and his cat clash over who gets to play with the ball.

4213. ____. *Sam's Bath* (Morrow, 1983) k–3. A toddler tries to give his dog a bath in a tub which is already full of his possessions.

4214. ____. *Sam's Lamp* (Morrow, 1983) k–3. A toddler tries to reach a lamp he likes but instead falls down and hurts himself.

4215. ____. *Bad Sam* (Methuen, 1983) k–3. A small boy's equally small misdemeanors reflect his moods of rage, pain, joy and curiosity.

4216. ____. *Sam's Potty* (Morrow, 1986) k–3. In demonstrating that his potty is intended for him rather than Doggie, Sam overcomes his dislike for it.

4217. ____. *Sam's Wagon* (Morrow, 1986) k–3. Doggie helps Sam try to keep his cookie and all his toys in his wagon and gets a tasty reward.

4218. Lindman, Maj. *Snipp, Snapp, Snurr and the Red Shoes* (Whitman, 1932/1994) 2–4. Each of three young brothers works hard to earn his share of the money needed to buy a special birthday present for their mother.

4219. ____. *Snipp, Snapp, Snurr and the Buttered Bread* (Whitman 1934/1995) 2–4. Three little Swedish brothers want some butter for their bread, but the cow will give no milk because she has no fresh green grass, and there is no grass because the sun has not been shining.

4220. ____. *Snipp, Snapp, Snurr and the Magic Horse* (Whitman, 1935) k–3.

4221. ____. *Snipp, Snapp, Snurr and the Gingerbread* (Whitman, 1936/1994) 2–4. Three brothers, who cannot agree on anything, fall into a batch of gingerbread batter, and then astonish everyone as they run through town looking like three gingerbread boys.

4222. ____. *Snipp, Snapp, Snurr and the Yellow Sled* (Whitman, 1936/1995) 2–4. Three little Swedish brothers help their mother with all the chores at home to earn two bright yellow sleds, one for themselves and one for a poor, unhappy little boy.

4223. ____. *Snipp, Snapp, Snurr and the Reindeer* (Whitman, 1957/1995) 2–4. Three little Swedish brothers spend their vacation in Lapland where they ski, visit a village of Laplanders and almost get lost in the snow.

4224. ____. *Snipp, Snapp, Snurr and the Seven Dogs* (Whitman, 1959) k–3.

4225. ____. *Snipp, Snapp, Snurr Learn to Swim* (Whitman, 1995) 2–4. On a summer vacation at the seashore, three little Swedish brothers almost float away in a washtub before they learn to swim well enough to place first, second or third in the boy's race.

4226. ____. *Snipp, Snapp, Snurr, and the Big Surprise* (Whitman, 1996) 2–4. While mother is on a trip three brothers plan a surprise for her homecoming.

4227. Lindman, Maj. *Flicka, Ricka, Dicka and the New Dotted Dresses* (Whitman, 1939/1994) k–3. Three little girls get their new red dresses all dirty while helping an old woman with her chores.

4228. ____. *Flicka, Ricka, Dicka and the Three Kittens* (Whitman, 1941/1994) k–3. When their aunt and uncle's cat disappears while they are supposed to be taking care of it, three young sisters frantically look for it and get quite a surprise.

4229. ____. *Flicka, Ricka, Dicka and Their New Friend* (Whitman, 1942/1995) k–3. A big snowball helps the girls make a new friend of the sometimes cross Mr. Fogel.

4230. ____. *Flicka, Ricka, Dicka and the Strawberries* (Whitman, 1996) k–3. Three little girls go off on a picnic to pick wild strawberries, and with the money they earn buy gifts for a poor family they met in the woods.

4231. ____. *Flicka, Ricka, Dicka and the Little Dog* (Whitman, 1946/1995) k–3. Three little Swedish sisters find a wet and unhappy dog on a rainy day, care for him, return him to his owner, and find him outside again the next day.

4232. ____. *Flicka, Ricka, Dicka Bake a Cake* (Whitman, 1955/1995) k–3. Three little Swedish sisters bake two cakes for their mother's birthday surprise; one a burned catastrophe, but the second a golden success.

4233. ____. *Flicka, Ricka, Dicka Go to Market* (Whitman, 1958) k–3. Three little Swedish girls cultivate a big vegetable garden, sell their crops each Saturday at the market, and earn money for bicycles.

4234. ____. *Flicka, Ricka, Dicka and the Big Red Hen* (Whitman, 1960/1995) k–3. While caring for their aunt's chickens, three little Swedish sisters are upset when the big red hen disappears.

4235. Lippman, Peter. *Know-It-Alls Go to Sea* (Doubleday, 1982) k–3. A family of alligators experience misadventures when they take their uncle's boat for a sail.

4236. ____. *Know-It-Alls Help Out* (Doubleday, 1982) k–3. A family of accident-prone alligators try to help a neighbor with her household chores.

4237. ____. *Know-It-Alls Mind the Store* (Doubleday, 1982) k–3. An inattentive but well-meaning alligator family minds cousin Angus' store in his absence, and chaos results.

4238. ____. *Know-It-Alls Take a Winter Vacation* (Doubleday, 1982) k–3. The know-it-alls pursue their favorite winter sport while misadventure pursues them.

4239. Littler, Angela. *Jim and Jam Have a Party* (Hodder, 1985) k–3. Jim is a little boy and Jam his mouse. Together they teach children basic reading, counting, and identifying skills.

4240. ____. *Jim and Jam At the Beach* (Hodder, 1985) k–3. A small boy, Jim and his white mouse, Jam experiences sights at the beach and are impressed with the sand castles.

4241. ____. *Jim and Jam and the Band* (Hodder, 1985) k–3. Jim is again looking for his pet white mouse Jam and while searching observes many musical instruments.

4242. ____. *Jim and Jam and the Builders* (Hodder, 1985) k–3. Jim, a small boy, observes big planks of wood near a new building while looking for his pet white mouse, Jam.

4243. Lively, Penelope. *Wild Hunt of Hagworthy* (Dutton, 1971) 4–6. Lucy, 12, goes back to Hagworthy but the children she knew are grown up and gone away. Kester became a community maverick. He teases the other boys. Later the boys don masks for the Horn Dance of Hagworthy and hunt for Kester over Exmoor.

4244. ____. *Wild Hunt of the Ghost Hounds* (Dutton, 1972) 4–6. An ancient dance is revived for a village fair. After Lucy discovers that the dance had its origins in a vicious hunt, she fears for her friend who has been chosen to play the victim.

4245. Lively, Penelope. *Fanny's Sister* (Dutton, 1980) 2–4. Fanny is hopeful that one day soon, her sister will just go away.

4246. ____. *Fanny and the Battle of Potter's Piece* (Dutton, 1980) 2–4. Fanny's favorite place, Potter's Piece, is threatened. New neighbors claim Potter's Piece as their own territory. Fanny and the neighbor children fight over it and then settle for a Treaty.

4247. ____. *Fanny and the Monsters* (Dutton, 1980) 2–4. Fanny, ten, is taken to the Crystal Palace for her birthday. She visits the dinosaur models and meets Dr. Halliday and learns about Darwin and his ideas. When she tells her father he is upset but Fanny explains her ideas.

4248. Livingstone, Malcolm. *Eric, the Wild Car* (Bobbs, 1978) k–3. When city inhabitants find the introduction of cars into their lives is destructive to their environment and makes them unhappy, Eric, a wild car solves the problem.

4249. ____. *Eric and the Mad Inventor* (Bobbs, 1979) k–3. Eric, a wild car, and Mr. Flywheel, an inventor, clean up a polluting oil spill and remind a misguided scientist that he can't improve on nature.

4250. ____. *Eric and the Lost Planes* (Bobbs, 1979) k–3. An accident lands Eric, Granny Flywheel, and Mr. Flywheel in a cave, where they discover some very hungry little lost planes which they attempt to rescue.

4251. Lloyd, Errol. *Nini at Carnival* (Crowell, 1979) k–3. A little Jamaican girl enjoys Carnival. She has no costume but her friend, Betti, drapes her in strips of cloth. She is so outstanding she becomes queen of the carnival.

4252. ____. *Nini On Time* (Crowell, 1981) k–3. A picture of life in the hustle and bustle of a mixed multiracial society with all the variety of dress and shops.

4253. Lobel, Arnold. *Frog and Toad Are Friends* (Harper, 1970) k–3. Five tales recounting the adventures of two best friends, Frog and Toad.

4254. ____. *Frog and Toad Together* (Harper, 1971) k–3. Five further adventures of two best friends as they share cookies, plant a garden and test their bravery.

4255. ____. *Frog and Toad All Year* (Harper, 1976) k–3. Five tales recounting the adventures of two best friends, Frog and Toad.

4256. ____. *Days with Frog and Toad* (Harper, 1979/1985) k–3. Frog and Toad spend their days together, but find sometimes it's nice to be alone.

4257. Lofgren, Ulf. *Alvin Lends a Hand* (Carolrhoda, 1973) k–3. Alvin is really not very helpful but can be in his imaginative way. He helps the dustman, the fireman and the doctor.

4258. ____. *Alvin and His Friend Ala Baba* (Carolrhoda, 1984) k–3.

4259. ____. *Alvin and the Magic Wand* (Carolrhoda, 1984) k–3.

4260. ____. *Alvin and the Parrot* (Carolrhoda, 1984) k–3.

4261. ____. *Alvin and the Rainbow* (Carolrhoda, 1984) k–3.

4262. ____. *Alvin the Pirate* (Carolrhoda, 1990) k–3. Young Alvin sails off with a band of pirates, who seem to think that he is their captain, and they all engage in a food fight with the crew of another pirate ship.

4263. ____. *Alvin the Zookeeper* (Carolrhoda, 1991) k–3. Young Alvin lets the animals out of the zoo for a lovely picnic, and no one eats anyone else or runs away.

4264. ____. *Alvin the Knight* (Carolrhoda, 1992) k–3. When Alvin visits the museum and sees an exhibit of medieval costumes, he is suddenly drawn into an imaginary adventure where he gets the opportunity to prove his skill as a knight in a medieval land of kings and castles.

4265. ____. *Alvin and the Unruly Elves* (Carolrhoda, 1992) k–3. When Santa finds it impossible to control his mischievous elves and stop them from ruining his workshop, he brings Alvin to the North Pole to solve the problem.

Logan, Richard. Ten stories of a good natured brontosaurus and his friends, a group of ordinary kids, experiencing everyday events with a twist.

4266. ____. *Thunder* (Creative, 1987) 3–5.

4267. ____. *Thunder and the Dinosaur Puppet* (Creative, 1987) 3–5.

4268. ____. *Thunder Makes a Sand Castle* (Creative, 1987) 3–5.

4269. ____. *Thunder Gets a House* (Creative, 1987) 3–5.

4270. ____. *Thunder Goes for a Walk* (Creative, 1987) 3–5.

4271. ____. *Thunder Goes to a Party* (Creative, 1987) 3–5.

4272. ____. *Thunder Comes to the Rescue* (Creative, 1987) 3–5.

4273. ____. *Thunder Eats a Haystack* (Creative, 1987) 3–5.

4274. ____. *Thunder Disappeared* (Creative, 1987) 3–5.

4275. ____. *Thunder and the Circus* (Creative, 1987) 3–5.

4276. Lord, Athena. *Today's Special Z.A.P. and Zoe* (Macmillan, 1984) 4–6. Zach, an 11-year-old Greek-American boy, contends with the varied problems and pleasures of growing up and with his little sister Zoe.

4277. ____. *Luck of Z.A.P. and Zoe* (Macmillan, 1987) 4–6. Zach and Zoe are from Greece. Zach's initials are Z.A.P. and form the basis for the Z.A.P. club in his rich life.

4278. ____. *Z.A.P., Zoe, and the Musketeers* (Macmillan, 1992) 4–6. Zach, 12, begins to think about his future, he copes with his family's luncheonette business, watches his pesky six-year-old sister, Zoe and plays with neighborhood friends.

4279. Lord, Berman. *Day the Spaceship Landed* (Walck, 1967) 2–4. Mike saw a spaceship land and met the friendly spacemen. He helped them gather information. When they left, Mike and his parents went to Washington but everyone there was dubious. The spacemen were to come back in two years and the strange stone they gave Mike made his story more believable.
4280. ____. *Spaceship Returns* (Walck, 1970) 2–4. Mike has to move away so he instructs Charlie to meet the spacemen when they return. The spacemen want to contact the U.S. government. Charlie tries to convince the men in Washington that the men from Barko are real.

4281. Lynam, Terence. *Sally and Tom and the Road Roller* (G. Stevens, 1984) 2–4. Sally and Tom are introduced to the whirling of a big road roller.
4282. ____. *Sally and Tom and the Helicopter* (Macdonald, 1988) 2–4. Uncle Jack takes Sally and Tom to the helicopter port where he works. They learn about how helicopters work and also get a ride. They spot the escaped kangaroo from the zoo.
4283. ____. *Sally and Tom and the Tractor* (G. Stevens, 1988) 2–4. Sally and Tom spend a year on a farm behind a tractor.

4284. Lynam, Terence. *BMX Gang Turns Detective* (G. Stevens, 1988) 2–4. Members of the BMX bunch take a break from practicing on their bikes to investigate a suspicious character in the park.
4285. ____. *Andy Joins the BMX Bunch* (G. Stevens, 1988) 2–4. Andy handles disappointment and joy as he tries to earn entry into the BMX bunch.
4286. ____. *BMX Bunch on Vacation* (G. Stevens, 1988) 2–4. Practicing bicycle tricks at their campsite, the members of the BMX bunch stumble into a hidden cave and into the life of a homeless man.
4287. ____. *Greg's First Race* (G. Stevens, 1988) 2–4. Greg enters his first BMX race and meets a rider who seems very confident.
4288. ____. *Andy Joins the Gang* (G. Stevens, 1986) 2–4.

4289. Lynch, Patricia. *Brogeen and the Bronze Lizard* (Macmillan, 1970) 4–6. Brogeen, the leprechaun, is sent by the queen of the fairies to track down a monster rumored to be ravaging the countryside.
4290. ____. *Brogeen and the Green Shoes* (Macmillan, 1983) 4–6. Brogeen the Kerry leprechaun uses leftover leather from shoes ordered by a tinker to make a pair for himself. But they run away and lure him into strange adventures.
4291. ____. *Brogeen Follows the Magic Tune* (Mac-

millan, 1988) 4–6. Brogeen the leprechaun sets out to get back the Fairies' magic tune from the human fiddler who stole it.

4292. McBratney, Sam. *Uncle Charlie Weasel and the Cuckoo Bird* (Magnet, 1988) k–3. A story about a disreputable and vicious beast.
4293. ____. *Uncle Charlie Weasel's Winter* (Magnet, 1988) k–3.

4294. McBratney, Sam. *Jimmy Zest* (Hamilton, 1982) 4–6. Jimmy Zest has the most outrageous ideas of all his friends. He makes a corner in egg boxes to produce the largest ever model of a dinosaur. He discovers an alien being in Mrs. Cricketwood-Holmsy's garden (the lady herself in beekeeping garb). His aunt who lives in the country is a witch.
4295. ____. *Jimmy Zest All-Stars* (Hamilton, 1983) 4–6. Loyal friends help Jimmy in his dotty schemes in school and out.
4296. ____. *Zesty* (Hamilton, 1984) 4–6. Zesty conceives a scheme for insuring his classmate's belongings for a small fee each week. His efforts to reimburse himself for his losses involve the whole class.

4297. McBrier, Michael. *Oliver and the Lucky Duck* (Troll, 1986) 3–5. Oliver takes in a wild duck with a broken wing and hopes to keep it as a pet after it has been healed.
4298. ____. *Oliver's Lucky Day* (Troll, 1986) 3–5. When Oliver and his mother acquire a Pekinese, hardly Oliver's idea of a "buddy," Oliver starts a pet care service so he can have a pet people respect.
4299. ____. *Oliver's High Flying Adventure* (Troll, 1987) 3–5. When Oliver reluctantly takes on a pet-sitting job with a menagerie of birds during Christmas vacation in which he had planned to compete in a snow sculpture contest, a naughty parrot escapes to further complicate his life.
4300. ____. *Oliver and the Runaway Alligator* (Troll, 1987) 3–5. Despite his mother's protests, Oliver determines to care for a homeless baby alligator until he can find its owner.
4301. ____. *Oliver's Back-Yard Circus* A visit to the circus with his classmates gives Oliver an idea about how to raise money for a much needed animal shelter.
4302. ____. *Oliver Smells Trouble* (Troll, 1988) 3–5. Anxious to earn some money to buy his friend Sam a birthday present, Oliver agrees to take care of a pet skunk.
4303. ____. *Oliver and the Amazing Spy* (Troll, 1988) 3–5. Oliver enlists the help of his friend's pet ferret to pull a prank on a blackmailing bully.
4304. ____. *Oliver's Barnyard Blues* (Troll, 1988) 3–5. Information about cows and their habits is the main theme of this story.
4305. ____. *Getting Oliver's Goat* (Troll, 1988) 3–5.

Information about goats is the main value of this story.

4306. McCabe, Bernard. *Bottle Rabbit* (Faber, 1988) 2–4. Bottle Rabbit was given the bottle as a kindness prize and must "pongle" it to produce results. It doesn't change rabbit's size but it does bring him useful gifts. Among other things he visits the bottom of Grumble Lake and meets a goat who writes poetry.

4307. ____. *Bottle Rabbit and Friends* (Faber, 1989) 2–4. A story of life-like characters featuring rabbit and his magic bottle and assorted friends and enemies.

4308. McCarthy, Ruth. *Three Little Rabbits' Christmas* (Heinemann, 1986) k–3. The rabbits are instructed to invite old Mr. Nicholas to their party but he is away and they invite Father Christmas. Mr. Nicholas turns up later; a completely changed person.

4309. ____. *Three Little Rabbits Go Visiting* (Heinemann, 1985) k–3. Three little rabbits go to visit their cousins, go to school, eat meals, have minor accidents and play games.

4310. ____. *Day with Three Little Rabbits* (Heinemann, 1985) k–3.

4311. ____. *Three Naughty Little Rabbits* (Heinemann) k–3.

4312. McCaughren, Tom. *Run with the Wind* (Dufour, 1983) 3–5. Tired of being hunted by humans, several foxes in Ireland band together to outwit their captors.

4313. ____. *Run to Earth* (Dufour, 1984) 3–5. To protect their new cubs, the foxes band together to stop the construction of a dam which would flood their homeland, the Irish valley of Glensinna.

4314. ____. *Run Swift, Run Free* (Wolfhound, 1984) 3–5. A story of real-life foxes and their struggle against a dull-witted and brutal enemy—humans.

4315. ____. *Run to the Ark* (Wolfhound, 1991) 3–5. A group of foxes are joined by other animals as they set out on a perilous journey to the Edge of the World in search of a home safe from human predators.

4316. McCay, William. *Young Indiana Jones and the Tomb of Terror* (Random, 1990) 5–8. In 1913 in Luxor, Egypt, an ancient ring leads Indy to a hidden tomb and into terrifying adventures with a German archaeologist.

4317. ____. *Young Indiana Jones and the Circle of Death* (Random, 1990) 5–8. While investigating some strange incidents at an archaeological dig at Stonehenge in 1913, the young Indiana Jones and his pal Herman encounter a mysterious band of Drak Druids with a connection to German espionage activities.

4318. ____. *Young Indiana Jones and the Secret City.* (Random, 1990) 5–8. Visiting Turkey in 1914, young Indiana Jones and his pal Herman stumble onto an evil cult that lives in a secret underground city.

4319. ____. *Young Indiana Jones and the Princess of Peril* (Random, 1991) 5–8. In 1913 in Russia, Indy befriends a young Georgian princess involved in the Georgian independence movement and is pursued by secret police and agents of an evil religious Fanatic.

4320. ____. *Young Indiana Jones and the Gypsy Revenge* (Random, 1991) 5–8. In France, in 1914, young Indiana Jones and his father's assistant Thornton pursue a rare manuscript that may reveal secrets of history involving a medieval king, mysterious gypsies and a legendary treasure.

4321. ____. *Young Indiana Jones and the Plantation Treasure* (Random, 1991) 5–8. In the spring of 1913, 14-year-old Indiana Jones traces the route of the Underground Railroad to help a young woman find her family fortune lost before the Civil War.

4322. ____. *Young Indiana Jones and the Curse of the Ruby Cross* (Random, 1991) 5–8. While visiting New York City in 1914, teenaged Indy runs across his old friend Lizzie Ravenall and becomes involved in retrieving a stolen family heirloom for an immigrant Italian labor-organizer.

4323. ____. *Young Indiana Jones and the Titanic Adventure* (Random, 1993) 5–8. In 1912, Indy has hair-raising adventures with German saboteurs, Irish revolutionaries, and a fortune hunter aboard the ill-fated Titanic.

4324. ____. *Young Indiana Jones and the Ghostly Riders* (Random, 1991) 5–8. In 1913 young Indiana Jones finds an ancient silver ring that may have belonged to King Arthur, investigates sabotage of a Welsh friend's coal mines, and travels back in time to solve a crisis in the present.

4325. ____. *Young Indiana Jones and the Face of the Dragon* (Random, 1994) 5–8. In November 1914 Indy and his father are in China, where a valuable gold and jeweled dragon leads them into a series of terrifying adventures as they try to find someone worthy of the dragon's powers.

4326. ____. *Young Indiana Jones and the Mountain of Fire* (Bullseye, 1994) 5–8. While visiting Hawaii in the early days of World War I Indy and his friend Lizzie Ravenall uncover a plot to sabotage British shipping in the Pacific.

(For other books about "Young Indiana Jones," *see* Stine, Megan; Martin, Les.)

4327. McCrum, Robert. *Brontosaurus Birthday Cake* (S & S, 1984) k–3. When Bobby's brontosaurus birthday cake turns into a real creature and begins to grow, both problems and joys begin.

4328. ____. *Brontosaurus, Superstar* (Hamilton, 1985) k–3. Brontosaurus is in America breaking records with his own musical "Bones!" His parents take him to Hollywood to see his old friend. The friend is overweight, miserable. He goes back to England and lives among the flowers.

4329. ____. *Dream Boat Brontosaurus* (Methuen, 1989) k–3.

4330. McCully, Emily. *First Snow* (Harper, 1985) k–3. A timid little mouse discovers the thrill of sledding in the first snow of the winter.
4331. ____. *School* (Harper, 1987) k–3. A curious little mouse decides to find out what school is all about.
4332. ____. *New Baby* (Harper, 1988) k–3. The youngest mouse in a large family discovers excitement and frustration when a new baby arrives.
4333. ____. *Christmas Gift* (Harper, 1988) k–3. When a little mouse's treasured Christmas gift is broken, Grandpa consoles her with a toy train from his own childhood.
4334. ____. *Picnic* (Harper, 1984) k–3. A large mouse family goes on a picnic. The youngest mouse is bounced out of the car and was left behind. He finds a raspberry bush and stuffs himself. The family finally misses him and everyone looks for him. He was found by the side of the road on their way home.

4335. McCully, Emily. *Grandma Mix-up* (Harper, 1988) 3–5. Young Pip doesn't know what to do when two different grandmothers come to baby-sit, each with her own way of doing things.
4336. ____. *Grandmas at the Lake* (Harper, 1990) 3–5. Pip and Ski have a hard time enjoying themselves at the lake with Pip's two grandmothers, who cannot agree on anything.
4337. ____. *Grandma at Bat* (Harper, 1993) 3–5. Pip's two grandmothers, who cannot agree on anything, take over coaching her baseball team and create chaos.

4338. McDaniel, Becky. *Katie Did It* (Children's, 1983) k–3. Katie, the youngest of three children, who gets the blame for everything bad, does something good for a change.
4339. ____. *Katie Couldn't* (Children's, 1985) k–3. Too little to ride a two-wheel bike or walk to the park like her older brother and sister, Katie finds there is something she can do that they cannot.
4340. ____. *Katie Can* (Children's, 1987) k–3. Although she is too small to roller skate backwards or ride a bike with no hands, Katie surprises her older brother and sister when she teaches their dog a new trick.

4341. MacDonald, Betty. *Mrs. Piggle-Wiggle* (Lippincott, 1947) 4–6. Mrs. Piggle-Wiggle has magical cures for all children's ailments, including the won't pick-up-toys cure, the answer-backer cure and the selfishness cure.
4342. ____. *Mrs. Piggle-Wiggle's Farm* (Lippincott, 1954) 4–6. Mrs. Piggle-Wiggle's Farm is a home for the bad. Each of the chapters tells of a different child who is sent there by distraught parents to take the cure.

4343. ____. *Hello, Mrs. Piggle-Wiggle* (Lippincott, 1957) 4–6. Mrs. Piggle-Wiggle loves children and she loves them equally whether good or bad.
4344. ____. *Mrs. Piggle-Wiggle's Magic* (Harper, 1992) 4–6. Seven families are helped out by Mrs. Piggle-Wiggle's cure when they are faced with thought-you-saider, tattletales, bad table manners, interrupters, heedless breakers, never-want-to-go-to-schoolers and waddle doers.

4345. Macdonald, Maryann. *Little Hippo Starts School* (Dial, 1988) k–3. Little Hippo discovers that the first day at school is hard on the teacher as well as the pupils.
4346. ____. *Little Hippo Gets Glasses* (Dial, 1992) k–3. Little Hippo is upset when he has to get glasses until he makes a surprising new friend who helps him accept his new look.

4347. Macdonald, Maryann. *Rosie Runs Away* (Atheneum, 1990) k–3. When her mother chastises her for taking her little brother out on a blueberry-picking adventure, Rosie decides to run away.
4348. ____. *Rosie's Baby Tooth* (Atheneum, 1991) k–3. Rosie loses a tooth and has to be convinced to leave it for the Tooth Fairy.
4349. ____. *Rosie and the Poor Rabbits* (Atheneum, 1994) k–3. Rosie's reluctance to give some of her clothes and toys to other rabbits who are not as well off as she, changes after a revealing dream.

4350. McDonnell, Christine. *Don't Be Mad, Ivy* (Dial, 1981) 3–5. Ivy's world of fun, frustration and excitement is revealed in six episodes.
4351. ____. *Lucky Charms and Birthday Wishes* (Viking, 1984) 3–5. Emily Mott enjoys the new school year with a new group of friends.
4352. ____. *Just for the Summer* (Viking, 1987) 3–5. Reunited for the summer, friends Emily, Ivy and Lydia keep busy at day camp, creating a toddler day care center, and pursuing other projects.

4353. McGowen, Tom. *Magician's Apprentice* (Lodestar, 1987) 4–6.
4354. ____. *Magician's Company* (Lodestar, 1988) 4–6. Armindor and Tigg return from the Wild Lands to warn the rest of the world that intelligent ratlike creatures lurk in the cities, ready to destroy all humans.
4355. ____. *Magician's Challenge* (Dutton, 1989) 4–6. Armindor and his young apprentice Tigg travel to their home city of Ingarron to continue humanity's battle against the ratlike creatures, reen, who lurk in many cities and plan a bloody takeover.

4356. McGowen, Tom. *Magical Fellowship* (Dutton, 1991) 4–6. In 3000 B.C. Lithin, an apprentice magician, and his father set out to unite the warring races of wizards, humans, Little People and the dragons in an effort to save the Earth from being destroyed by creatures from beyond the sky.

4357. ____. *Trial of Magic* (Lodestar, 1992) 4–6. Having secured the aid of the wizards of the Dragons, and the Little People in an effort to prevent the prophesied Earthdoom. Milng and his son Lithim and the other magicians of Atlan Domain must face the fearsome opposition of a very powerful Alfar Master image.

4358. ____. *Question of Magic* (Dutton, 1993) 4–6. When creatures from beyond the sky threaten to destroy the five intelligent races of ancient Earth and the mages of the land cannot agree on a plan, Lithin, 12, and his father come up with their own solution.

4359. MacGregor, Ellen. *Miss Pickerell Goes to Mars* (McGraw, 1951) 4–6. Miss Pickerell is accidentally stowed away on a ship bound for Mars. She is not welcome by the crew.

4360. ____. *Miss Pickerell Goes Underseas* (McGraw, 1953) 4–6. Miss Pickerell puts on a diver's suit and goes underwater to recover her famous red rock collection from Mars.

4361. ____. *Miss Pickerell and the Geiger Counter* (McGraw, 1953) 4–6. Miss Pickerell takes her pet cow to the veterinarian. She finds herself substituting for the sheriff and somehow discovers uranium.

4362. ____. *Miss Pickerell Goes to the Arctic* (McGraw, 1954) 4–6. Miss Pickerell flies to the Arctic to rescue a downed plane. She is downed herself and must be rescued along with the other plane survivors.

4363. ____. *Miss Pickerell on the Moon* (McGraw, 1965) 4–6. Miss Pickerell's cow (and her cat) have fallen ill from an epidemic of unknown germs. There is no treatment so she goes to the moon to look for some molds that are needed.

4364. ____. *Miss Pickerell Goes on a Dig* (McGraw, 1966) 4–6. Miss Pickerell goes on an archaeological excavation to unearth some history before the road department comes along and digs everything up as they widen the road.

4365. ____. *Miss Pickerell Harvests the Sea* (McGraw, 1968) 4–6. Miss Pickerell helps a friend who has an ocean farm. She doesn't understand at first but learns a great deal about oceanography.

4366. ____. *Miss Pickerell and the Weather Satellite* (McGraw, 1971) 4–6. Miss Pickerell learns a lot about modern technology at the weather station. She prevents a flood by using laser beams and space stations.

4367. ____. *Miss Pickerell Meets H.U.M.* (McGraw, 1974) 4–6. While trying to think of a name for her cow, the telephone rings and a chain of events starts. It was all very upsetting. H.U.M. is a computer that's going to take over the world.

4368. ____. *Miss Pickerell Takes the Bull by the Horns* (McGraw, 1976) 4–6. Miss Pickerell is dead set against cloning. There is a bill in Congress and she does her civic duty with letters and a protest march.

4369. ____. *Miss Pickerell to the Earthquake Rescue* (McGraw, 1977) 4–6. Earthquakes in a nearby county and the disappearance of earthquake prevention scientists bring Miss Pickerell on the run to tackle the crisis.

4370. ____. *Miss Pickerell and the Supertanker* (McGraw, 1978) 4–6. Miss Pickerell plugs a leak in a tanker and feeds oil-eating microbes.

4371. ____. *Miss Pickerell Tackles the Energy Crisis* (McGraw, 1980) 4–6. Miss Pickerell's trip to the long awaited fair is canceled. There is a fuel shortage because of an earthquake and the fair must be postponed. She gets a formula for ethanol.

4372. ____. *Miss Pickerell on the Trail* (McGraw, 1982) 4–6. Miss Pickerell is joined by her nephew and a team of his classmates as she tries to discover what is causing the mysterious attack on the western side of Square Toe Mountain.

4373. ____. *Miss Pickerell and the Blue Whales* (McGraw, 1983) 4–6. Miss Pickerell organizes a boycott to save the blue whales from harpoonists.

4374. ____. *Miss Pickerell and the War of the Computers* (Watts, 1985) 4–6. Miss Pickerell goes to the governor for help in fixing a computer system that is crippling the economy. They and Euphus go where the programs are written and find a substitute program. Miss Pickerell is kidnapped by the programmer.

(For other books about "Miss Pickerell," *see* Doral Pantell.)

4375. Mackay, Claire. *Mini-Bike Rescue* (Scholastic, 1992) 4–6. Steve's friend, Julie, another mini-biker, meets and matches wits with a con artist.

4376. ____. *Mini-Bike Hero* (Scholastic, 1992) 4–6. Steve, 12, an aspiring mini-biker in spite of his parent's protests, is befriended by a local bike shop owner who teaches him riding tricks which he later uses in a daring rescue effort.

4377. ____. *Mini-Bike Racer* (Scholastic, 1992) 4–6. Based on a championship race, with a sub-plot about a dangerous escaped criminal.

4378. MacKay, Hilary. *Exiles* (McElderry, 1992) 4–6. The four Conroy sisters spend a wild summer at the seaside with Big Grandma, who tries to break them of their reading habit by substituting fresh air and hard work for books and gets unexpected results.

4379. ____. *Exiles at Home* (McElderry, 1994) 4–6. The four Conroy sisters' efforts to raise money in order to sponsor a ten-year-old boy in Africa get them into one difficult situation after another.

4380. McKean, Thomas. *Vampire Vacation* (Methuen, 1985) 4–6. Beth, Leo and Teasdale investigate a mystery at Hidden Valley Hotel. Screams in the night are scaring guests away. Is it a vampire or something else?

4381. ____. *Moroccan Mystery* (Avon, 1985) 4–6. Beth, Leo and Teasdale fly to Morocco with their dad and Granny Bea. Beth tells of Teasdale's abduction and how they slip past Dad and Granny to search for Teasdale. They narrowly escape from the crooks. Their baby monkey, rescued from an abusive owner, helps solve the case and unmask the kidnap gang.

4382. ____. *Anti-Peggy Plot* (Methuen, 1985) 4–6. Three children, Beth, Leo and Teasdale, do not want their father to marry Peggy. They form an Anti-Peggy Plot. They plan to stop the marriage and they do. Peggy marries someone else.

4383. McKee, David. *King Rollo and the New Shoes* (Little, 1979) k–3. King Rollo's new shoes have laces and he is very proud when he learns to tie them himself.

4384. ____. *King Rollo and the Birthday* (Little, 1979) k–3. King Rollo attempts to make a special card for Queen Gwen's birthday.

4385. ____. *King Rollo and the Bread* (Little, 1979) k–3. King Rollo insists that his magician change a farmer's noontime bread into anything he wants to eat, but the farmer prefers his homemade bread.

4386. ____. *King Rollo and the Balloons* (Creative, 1982) k–3. Rollo plays a mild trick on the magician with balloons and feathers.

4387. ____. *King Rollo and the Tree* (Creative, 1982) k–3. King Rollo climbs a tree despite adult warnings of dirt and mess.

4388. ____. *King Rollo and the Dishes* (Creative, 1982) k–3. Rollo persuaded the magician to wash dishes by magic.

4389. ____. *King Rollo and the Bath* (Creative, 1982) k–3. Rollo is tricked into taking a bath by the arrival of a toy boat.

4390. ____. *King Rollo and King Frank* (Creative, 1982) k–3. King Rollo finds that once you get to know a person you probably won't dislike him.

4391. ____. *King Rollo and the Search* (Creative, 1982) k–3. Rollo helps the magician find the remembering spell so he can remember where he put his book of spells.

4392. ____. *King Rollo's Playroom* (Andersen, 1983) k–3. Rollo is, of course, not so much a king as a child playing at king. Cook, Magician and Cat make characteristic appearances.

4393. ____. *King Rollo's Summer* (Viking, 1987) k–3. King Rollo finds a familiar way to cool off in the summer.

4394. ____. *King Rollo's Autumn* (Viking, 1987) k–3. King Rollo is astonished that the leaves fall from the trees. After the court magician assures him that magic is not needed, the queen shows him how to enjoy this.

4395. ____. *King Rollo's Winter* (Viking, 1987) k–3.

4396. ____. *King Rollo's Spring* (Viking, 1987) k–3.

4397. ____. *King Rollo and the Letter* (Andersen, 1988) k–3.

4398. ____. *King Rollo and Santa's Beard* (Creative, 1990) k–3. Santa's stolen whiskers are restored by magic which wearies the royal cook.

4399. McKee, David. *Mr. Benn: Red Knight* (McGraw, 1968) k–3. When Mr. Benn enters the fitting room to try on a suit of armor for a costume party, he suddenly finds himself in a strange land helping restore a kind dragon's good reputation.

4400. ____. *123456789 Benn* (McGraw, 1970) k–3. When Mr. Benn steps into a fitting room to try on a convict uniform, he finds he is a prisoner in a very drab correctional institution.

4401. ____. *Big Game Benn* (Dobson, 1980) 2–4. Mr. Benn goes through a magic door into a jungle. He tries to keep hunters from shooting the animals. He wants them to change their guns for cameras.

4402. ____. *Big Top Benn* (Dobson, 1981) 2–4. Mr. Benn visits a magic costume shop. He is given a clown's suit. His friend, Smasher Lagra clears the road for the circus; then a bridge must be built with Smasher's help. Finally a show is given with Smasher as strong man.

4403. ____. *Extraordinary Adventures of Mr. Benn* (Lothrop) k–3.

4404. McKee, David. *Elmer* (Lothrop, 1968/1989) k–3. All the elephants of the jungle were gray except Elmer, who was a patchwork of brilliant colors until the day he got tired of being different and making the other elephants laugh.

4405. ____. *Elmer Again* (Lothrop, 1992) k–3. Elmer, the patchwork elephant, plays an amusing trick on his gray elephant friends.

4406. ____. *Elmer Again and Again* (Lothrop, 1992) k–3. More and more of Elmer, the patchwork elephant.

4407. ____. *Elmer on Stilts* (Lothrop, 1993) k–3. Elmer, the patchwork elephant, must learn to evade hunters. But hunters look down, not up; so elephants merely have to walk on stilts and they will be invisible.

4408. ____. *Elmer in the Snow* (Lothrop, 1995) k–3. Elmer, the patchwork elephant, finds out about hot and cold. Both feelings are relative and both can be fun.

4409. ____. *Elmer and Wilbur* (Lothrop, 1995) k–3. Elmer searches for his cousin Wilbur. Wilbur is stuck in a tree, Elmer and the herd help Wilbur from his perch.

4410. McKee, David. *Magician Who Lost His Magic* (Abelard, 1970) k–3. The king's magician has done everyone's work with magic for so long that the kingdom appears helpless when his power disappears.

4411. ____. *Magician and the Sorcerer* (Parents, 1974) k–3. With the help of his sister the witch, a bird, and a wise man, a magician confronts the evil sorcerer who tries to gain favor with the king.

4412. ____. *Magician and the Petnapping* (Houghton, 1976) k–3. The king's magician must find all the petnapped animals of the realm or lose the favor of the king.

4413. ____. *Magician and Double Trouble* (Abelard, 1982) k–3. King's magician Melric is accused of making mischief. His sister and his cousin with the help of Kra the Wise Man, they find that the Sorcerer Sandrak has stolen Melric's Magic and takes on his appearance to cause havoc.

4414. ____. *Magician and the Balloon* (Blackie, 1986) k–3. When his view from the royal magician's balloon inspires the king to make a map of his kingdom, the magician fears unnecessary changes to the countryside and launches a counterplot using his balloon.

4415. ____. *Magician and the Dragon* (Harper, 1986) k–3. When the king sends out his army to hunt dragons in the eastern part of the kingdom, his magician decides to take a look at them himself.

4416. ____. *Magician and the Crown* (Blackie, 1986) k–3. A comic fantasy about Melric the Magician saving his native king from a wicked rival's attempted coup.

4417. McKenna, Colleen. *Good Grief, Third Grade* (Scholastic, 1993) 4–6. Marsha Cessano, Collette Murphy's neighbor, is determined to be good in third grade—no messy desk, no temper, no tricks—but Roger Friday is making it difficult.

4418. ____. *Fourth Grade Is a Jinx* (Scholastic, 1990) 4–6. When fourth grader Collette sees her own mother taking over the job of teaching her class, life becomes more embarrassing and chaotic than she can stand.

4419. ____. *Merry Christmas, Miss McConnell* (Scholastic, 1990) 4–6. A fifth grade girl with a tough new teacher and problems at home expects a terrible Christmas, only to have it turn out to be one of the best.

4420. ____. *Fifth Grade, Here Comes Trouble* (Scholastic, 1992) 4–6. Unlike the other girls in her class, Collette Murphy becomes worried and embarrassed when she is invited to her first boy/girl party

4421. ____. *Live from Fifth Grade* (Scholastic, 1994) 4–6. Roger Friday loves to play tricks on Marsha Cessano, but when he investigates a robbery at school, he finds the best man for the job is Marsha.

4422. ____. *Truth About Sixth Grade* (Scholastic, 1991) 4–6. Collette finds herself unexpectedly popular when her fellow students find out her family knows the world's most gorgeous teacher personally.

4423. McKenna, Colleen. *Too Many Murphy's* (Scholastic, 1988) 5–8. The first of three novels featuring Collette Murphy, her family and friends.

4424. ____. *Einie Meanie Murphy, No* (Scholastic, 1990) 5–8. Collette is at summer camp dealing with rivalries and friendships. She and her friends are learning to grow up and cope with social skills.

4425. ____. *Murphy's Island* (Scholastic, 1990) 5–8. Collette Murphy has to go with her large, often trying family to a small island and start sixth grade there as the new girl in school.

4426. ____. *Mother Murphy* (Scholastic, 1992) 5–8. When Mrs. Murphy has to get off her feet because she's expecting a baby, Collette takes over with surprising results.

4427. ____. *Camp Murphy* (Scholastic, 1993) 5–8. When Collette and two sixth grade classmates try to run a neighborhood day camp, they face a series of problems, including arguments over who is in charge and the disappearance of Collette's brother.

4428. McLerran, Alice. *Roxaboxen* (Viking, 1995) 3–5. Roxaboxen is an imaginary place made up by Emily and her sisters.

4429. ____. *Year of the Ranch* (Viking, 1996) 3–5. Mom, Dad, Emily and three sisters live in Yuma, Arizona, in 1919. They learn to cope with sandstorms, tarantulas and rattlesnakes, but they do enjoy tea parties and tennis.

4430. McMahan, Ian. *Fox's Lair* (Macmillan, 1983) 4–6. With the help of ALEC, a personality brought into being by some freak accident in the circuits of giant computers, Ricky Foster clears his friend's father of charges of computer fraud.

4431. ____. *Lost Forest* (Macmillan, 1985) 4–6. ALEC, a disembodied personality inside the circuits of a giant computer system, helps Ricky Foster investigate his mother's mysterious disappearance in a forest wilderness.

4432. ____. *ESP McGee and the Ghost Ship* (Avon, 1984) 5–8. McGee uncovers illegal chemical dumping and salvage operations.

4433. ____. *Lake Fear* (Macmillan, 1985) 4–6. While investigating the source of a strange disease, Ricky and his computer friend ALEC uncover a case of computer fraud, chemical pollution, and the illegal production of explosives.

4434. McMullan, Kate. *Great Ideas of Lila Fenwick* (Dial, 1986) 4–6. Fifth grader Lila has some truly amazing "Great Ideas" that get her out of and into all kinds of trouble.

4435. ____. *Great Advice from Lila Fenwick* (Dial, 1988) 4–6. Lila and a friend spend two weeks of the summer between fifth and sixth grade at a Boy Scout camp, where Lila's father is camp doctor, having a wonderful time learning about nature and boys.

4436. ____. *Great Eggspectations of Lila Fenwick* (Farrar, 1991) 4–6. When faced with challenges of sixth grade, Lila sees her "Great Ideas" backfire and soon discovers that good things can happen when they're least "eggspected."

4437. McNaughton, Colin. *Rat Race* (Doubleday, 1978) k–3. Anton B. Stanton wanders into a rat hole and is captured as a spy. He hears of the "Grand Annual Rat Race" and convinces the king to let him run. He wins the obstacle race against the rat champion, in spite of his cheating.

4438. ____. *Anton B. Stanton and the Pirates* (Candlewick, 1979) k–3. Anton, six inches high, is discovered hiding in a pirate ship and is forced to walk the plank. But he is saved by friendly Water Rats. He helps them save their kidnapped princess.

4439. ____. *Pirates* (Benn, 1980) k–3. A Tom Thumb of a little boy gets involved in a feud between the Pirates and the Water Rats.

4440. ____. *Abdul's Pirate School* (Candlewick, 1994) k–3. Sent to pirate school against her will, Maisy Pickles organizes a mutiny among the students.

4441. McPhail, David. *Bear's Toothache* (Little, 1973) k–3. A small boy gets a night visit from a bear with a sore tooth. He can't pull the tooth, eating doesn't loosen it and a pillow breaks a lamp instead. A cowboy rope is tied to the tooth and the bear jumps out of the window and the tooth pops out. The bear gives it to the boy to put under his pillow.

4442. ____. *Lost* (Joy Street, 1991) k–3. A city boy helps a lost brown bear get back home. The bear returns the favor when the boy becomes lost in the forest.

4443. McPhail, David. *Pig Pig Grows Up* (Dutton, 1980) k–3. Only when faced with a dire emergency does Pig Pig finally react like a grown-up and admit he is not a baby any more.

4444. ____. *Pig Pig Rides* (Dutton, 1982) k–3. Over breakfast, Pig Pig informs his mother about all the wonderful feats he intends to accomplish that day, such as jumping 500 elephants on his motorcycle and driving a rocket to the moon.

4445. ____. *Pig Pig Goes to Camp* (Dutton, 1983) k–3. Pig Pig finally agrees to go to camp for the summer and has a wonderful time.

4446. ____. *Pig Pig and the Magic Photo Album* (Dutton, 1986) k–3. While waiting to have his picture taken, Pig Pig practices saying "Cheese" as he looks through a photo album and is amazed at the outcome.

4447. ____. *Pig Pig Gets a Job* (Dutton, 1990) k–3. Pig Pig thinks of all the jobs he could get, from cook to auto mechanic, and is enthusiastic about performing similar tasks for his family at home.

4448. ____. *Pigs Aplenty, Pigs Galore* (Dutton, 1993) k–3. Pigs galore invade a house and have a wonderful party.

4449. McPhail, David. *Emma's Pet* (Dutton, 1985) k–3. Emma's search for a soft, cuddly pet has a surprising ending.

4450. ____. *Emma's Vacation* (Dutton, 1987) k–3. Emma's idea about a good vacation is quite different from that of her parents.

4451. McPhail, David. *Henry Bear's Park* (Little, 1976) 2–4. During the long wait for his balloonist father's return, Henry the Bear devotes himself to beautifying their park.

4452. ____. *Stanley, Henry Bear's Friend* (Little, 1979) 2–4. Stanley Raccoon's life story.

4453. Maddox, Tony. *Fergus, the Farmyard Dog* (Barron, 1993) k-3. The farmyard is the perfect place for Fergus to take a nap. But whenever he closes his eyes he hears noises—ducks, hens, pigs. Then came a squeak! What is it?

4454. ____. *Fergus's Upside-Down Day* (Barron, 1995) k–3. Fergus finds a place for a nap but Farmer Bob goes away and leaves him in charge. All the animals get into mischief and Fergus must make them behave.

4455. Maestro, Betsy. *Harriet Goes to the Circus* (Crown, 1977) k–3. Harriet the elephant, is determined to be first in line for the circus.

4456. ____. *Harriet Reads Signs and More Signs* (Crown, 1981) k–3. While walking to her grandmother's house, Harriet reads all the signs she sees on the way.

4457. ____. *Around the Clock with Harriet* (Crown, 1984) k–3. Depicts Harriet and her activities at each hour of the day.

4458. ____. *Harriet at Home* (Crown, 1984) k–3. Harriet the elephant is shown doing the things she does at home. She moves from room to room around the house.

4459. ____. *Harriet at Work* (Crown, 1985) k–3. Harriet, an elephant, rakes leaves, washes windows, bakes a cake and does other household chores.

4460. ____. *Harriet at School* (Crown, 1984) k–3. Harriet the elephant enjoys many activities at her nursery school.

4461. ____. *Harriet at Play* (Crown, 1984) k–3. Harriet the elephant likes to play with her many toys.

4462. ____. *Through the Year with Harriet* (Crown, 1985) k–3. Follows Harriet the elephant through the 12 months of the year as she engages in many activities in all kinds of weather.

4463. ____. *Dollars and Cents for Harriet* (Crown, 1988) k–3. As Harriet attempts to earn $5 for a new kite; the reader learns about the coins that add up to a dollar.

4464. Mahood, Kenneth. *Losing Willy* (Prentice, 1977) k–3. A child who loses everything from his toothbrush to his parents eventually becomes a finder.

4465. ____. *Looking for Willy* (Prentice, 1982) k–3.

4466. Mahy, Margaret. *Good Fortunes Gang* (Delacorte, 1993) 4–6. After living like a gypsy in Australia all his life, Pete tries to adjust to living in a permanent place—his father's New Zealand hometown where Pete must pass a test to belong to his cousin's exclusive gang.

4467. ____. *Fortunate Name* (Delacorte, 1993) 4–6. As the only Bancroft in a family of Fortunes, Lolly has always felt left out of her Fortune cousin's exclusive gang but when her parents separate Lolly discovers a new inner strength and aspects of kinship that go beyond names.

4468. ____. *Fortune Branches Out* (Delacorte, 1994) 4–6. Tessa Fortune and her cousins want to raise $100 for the New Zealand National Telethon, but when their plans begin to go awry, Tessa learns a valuable lesson about her goal of becoming a rich executive.

4469. ____. *Tangled Fortunes* (Delacorte, 1994) 4–6. The relationship between Tracey Fortune and her brother Jackson is temporarily strained by Tracey's desire to be a bridesmaid in her cousin's wedding and by the mysterious messages that Jackson begins to receive.

4470. Mahy, Margaret. *Pirate Uncle* (Overlook, 1977/1994) 4–6. Well behaved Nicholas and Caroline try to reform their pirate uncle when they spend a holiday at his New Zealand beach home.

4471. ____. *Pirate's Mixed-Up Voyage* (Dial, 1993) 4–6. Captain Water and the crew of the *Sinful Sausage* set sail for the Thousand Islands with a plot to kidnap a famous inventor, only to be thwarted by a witch, a firedrake, and the dastardly Dr. Silkweed.

4472. Manes, Stephen. *Hooples on the Highway* (Coward, 1978) 3–5. Alvin is headed for Philadelphia but car problems and travel setbacks keep him short of his destination. This is a humorous tale of the "joys of motoring."

4473. ____. *Hooples' Haunted House* (Delacorte, 1981) 3–5. Alvin offers his garage as a substitute haunted house. He fusses about his Halloween costume, the garage cleaning crew and his pesty sister. But the evening of spooks and scares come off all right.

4474. Mann, Peggy. *Street of the Flower Boxes* (Coward, 1966) 3–5. A story with a run down New York City setting, in which Carlos, a Puerto Rican boy and a group of youngsters from West 94th Street set about beautifying their part of the block by selling window boxes.

4475. ____. *When Carlos Closed the Street* (Coward, 1969) 3–5. Carlos's gang and Jimmy's gang had territorial lines that nobody crossed. One day Carlos crossed it and was challenged to a game of stickball. They closed off the street and caused a traffic tie-up.

4476. Manning, Rosemary. *Green Smoke* (Doubleday, 1958) 4–6. Susan makes friends with a dragon. He takes her for rides and tells her stories of King Arthur's day. He also teaches her dragon-charming songs.

4477. ____. *Dragon in Danger* (Doubleday, 1960) 4–6. R. Dragon visits Susan in her hometown and charms the people there.

4478. ____. *Dragon's Quest* (Doubleday, 1962) 4–6. R. Dragon wins his knighthood in the court of King Arthur. He is tested for patience and control; he overcame a witch and made good friends.

4479. ____. *Dragon in the Harbour* (Doubleday, 1980) 4–6. R. Dragon is accepted into the yachting around of Weymouth. He can cause a tidal wave or merely gently rock the harbor with his rhythmic snoring. Adam and John plague him with jokes and riddles and soon get into a smuggling plot.

4480. Mantle, Winifred. *Jonnesty in Winter* (Chatto, 1975) 2–4. Jonnesty, who resides in a jam jar called Nasturtium Villa, is a non-human hero, a symbol of human frailty and courage.

4481. ____. *Jonnesty* (Chatto, 1983) 2–4. Jonnesty, a little green man who is made out of an honesty plant, stresses his exploits in a manner of the tailor who slew seven flies, yet remains humble throughout. He talks to Arabella, the paper doll with whom he sets up house in a stone jar.

4482. Mantle, Winifred. *Penderel House* (Gollancz, 1966) 5–8. Henry, Nan and James Penderel take French leave of their grandmother with whom they are staying and go off to investigate the house they believe once belonged to their family. They meet the Holt family and solve a mystery.

4483. ____. *Penderel Puzzle* (Holt, 1966) 5–8. Nan, Henry and James move into an old house. But Robin and Aldick say they live there and they have a houseguest, Lik, a Thai princess. Lik is kidnapped and the adventure begins.

4484. Manushkin, Fran. *Little Rabbit's Baby Brother* (Crown, 1986) k–3. Little Rabbit finds her own way of coming to terms with her new baby brother.

4485. ____. *Be Brave, Baby Rabbit* (Crown, 1990) k–3. While playing follow the leader, Baby Rabbit can't jump over a bushel basket, but after he stands up to a Halloween Monster he has the confidence to make the leap.

4486. Marel, Nadja. *Me, Molly Midnight, the Artist's Cat* (Stemmer, 1977) 3–5. Nadja allows Molly Midnight, her cat, to tell the story of her adoption. Molly wants to win over Herman, the head of the house who doesn't like cats. He is a painter and immortalizes Molly in his drawings and paintings.

4487. ____. *Runaway Molly Midnight, the Artist's Cat* (Stemmer, 1986) 3–5. Molly Midnight tells of the time she ran away for ten days. She goes hungry, is chased by a broom and is locked in a cage. She is glad to be home but felt she had to do it, to see the world.

4488. Margolis, Richard. *Wish Again, Big Bear* (Macmillan, 1972) k–3. The crafty fish Big Bear catches avoids being eaten by granting his captor three wishes.

4489. ____. *Big Bear to the Rescue* (Greenwillow, 1975) k–3. A cumulative series of trades results when Big Bear tries to borrow a rope to rescue Mr. Mole.

4490. ____. *Big Bear Spare That Tree* (Greenwillow, 1980) k–3. Big Bear wants to chop down his tree but Blue Jay is frantic because her eggs are due to hatch in a nest in that very tree.

4491. Marino, Dorothy. *Buzzy Bear Goes South* (Watts, 1961) k–3. Buzzy, a bear cub, decides that going south with the birds is better than hibernating. His parents allow him to try it. His try against nature doesn't work.

4492. ____. *Buzzy Bear and the Rainbow* (Watts, 1961) k–3. As Buzzy searched for the end of the rainbow he was told that the pot of gold was only a fable. Buzzy ignored their advice and found some special gold, to the delight of his friends and family.

4493. ____. *Buzzy Bear in the Garden* (Watts, 1963) k–3. The story of Buzzy Bear's confused attempts to help his father with the gardening.

4494. ____. *Buzzy Bear Goes Camping* (Watts, 1964) k–3. On an overnight camping trip with his cousin Alec, Buzzy Bear learns that bear ways are best for bears, even though they differ from those of other creatures.

4495. ____. *Buzzy Bear's Busy Day* (Watts, 1965) k–3. Buzzy, bored with watching Mother Bear do the household chores, finds simple enjoyments to while away the morning.

4496. ____. *Buzzy Bear's First Day at School* (Watts, 1970) k–3. Buzzy Bear feels insecure going to his first day at school. Buzzy learns the sounds of the first letter of his name and is delighted how well he does in school. He decides he likes it.

4497. Maris, Ron. *Are You There, Bear?* (Greenwillow, 1984) k–3. In a darkened bedroom, several toys search for a bear, finally find him reading a book behind a chair.

4498. ____. *Hold Tight, Bear* (Delacorte, 1989) k–3. A teddy bear wanders away from his toy companions on an outing in the woods and has a mishap.

4499. Mark, Michael. *Toba* (Bradbury, 1984) 4–6. Toba, ten, tells about herself and her Jewish family as they lived in Poland around 1910.

4500. ____. *Toba at the Hands of a Thief* (Bradbury, 1985) 4–6. The life of a Polish teenager as she prepares to leave her Jewish family for a new life in America during the early 1900s.

4501. Markham, Marion. *Halloween Candy Mystery* (Houghton, 1982) 2–4. Twins Mickey and Kate use their powers of deduction and scientific expertise to catch a burglar on Halloween night.

4502. ____. *Christmas Present Mystery* (Houghton, 1984) 2–4. Twin sisters Mickey and Kate combine their skills to discover the explanation for a mysterious face that has appeared in a family photograph.

4503. ____. *Thanksgiving Day Parade Mystery* (Houghton, 1986) 2–4. Twin detectives Katie and Mickey suspect that the disappearance of a marching band before a parade is linked to an attempted robbery at the local bank.

4504. ____. *Birthday Party Mystery* (Houghton, 1986) 2–4. Attending Debbie's birthday party at the zoo, twin sleuths Kate and Mickey investigate the mysterious disappearance of her presents.

4505. ____. *April Fool's Day Mystery* (Houghton, 1991) 2–4. The Dixon twins try to discover who put the snake in the school cafeteria flour bin on April Fool's Day, clearing an unjustly suspected classmate in the process.

4506. ____. *Valentine's Day Mystery* (Houghton, 1992) 2–4. Kate wants to be a famous scientist and Mickey wants to be a detective like Sherlock Holmes. They attend a Valentine's Day party where a garnet pin belonging to one of the guests disappears. They solve the mystery.

4507. Marks, James. *Hijacked!* (Nelson, 1973) 5–8. On his return to school in Thailand, Jason' plane is hijacked by a Japanese terrorist group working for Arab interests.

4508. ____. *Border Kidnap* (Nelson, 1977) 5–8. Jason, Angus, Meg and Peter are kidnapped by rebels who are running uncut heroin through the Golden Triangle. They escape and chase the smugglers through Thailand.

4509. Marray, Denis. *Duck Street Gang* (Houghton, 1984) 4–6. Episodes of Class 2D at Duck School give an account of a nativity play in which Nellie and her friends upstage the rest of the cast.

4510. ____. *Duck Street Gang Returns* (Hamilton, 1987) 4–6. Duck Street teachers are firm with a sense of humor; the policeman who helps Ant land a large pike is friendly. A television filming of a school play and the capture of a jewel thief moves this good story along.

4511. Marshall, Edward. *Fox and His Friends* (Dial, 1982) 4–6. Fox wants to play with his friends, but duty in one form or another interferes.

4512. ____. *Fox in Love* (Dial, 1982) 2–4. Fox falls in love with several girls and then enters a dance contest with his sister.

4513. ____. *Fox at School* (Dial, 1983) 2–4. Contains: Fox on Stage; Fox Escapes; Fox in Charge.

4514. ____. *Fox on Wheels* (Dial, 1983) 2–4. Fox baby-sits for his sister Louise, learns to climb a tree for some grapes, and wins a shopping cart race.

4515. ____. *Fox All Week* (Dial, 1984) 2–4. Fox and his friends have a different adventure every day of the week.

4516. ____. *Fox on the Job* (Dial, 1988) 2–4. Fox tries to earn the money for a new bicycle in several different jobs.

4517. ____. *Fox Be Nimble* (Dial, 1990) 2–4. Fox

baby-sits for the miserable Ling children, makes a big scene when he slips on a skate and hurts himself, and gets to lead the band in the big parade.

4518. ____. *Fox Outfoxed* (Dial, 1992) 2–4. Fox competes in a big race, gives away his comic books and goes trick-or-treating on Halloween with his friends.

4519. ____. *Fox on Stage* (Dial, 1993) 2–4. Fox makes a film for Grannie, takes part in a magic show and puts on a play.

4520. Marshall, James. *Cut-Ups* (Viking, 1984) k–3. Practical jokers Spud and Joe get away with every trick in the book until the day they meet a little girl named Mary Frances Hooley.

4521. ____. *Cut-Ups Cut Loose* (Viking, 1987) k–3. At the end of the summer Spud and Joe eagerly return to school for more practical jokes, unaware that Principal Lamar J. Spurgle is out of retirement and awaiting them.

4522. ____. *Cut-Ups at Camp Custer* (Viking, 1989) k–3. Spud and Joe are determined to catch the mysterious prankster who keeps getting them into trouble when they spend their summer at Camp Custer with Mary Frances Hooley and Lamar J. Spurgle.

4523. ____. *Cut-Ups Carry On* (Viking, 1990) k–3. Spud and Joe are forced by their mothers to take ballroom dancing lessons and scheme to win a contest on television.

4524. ____. *Cut-Ups Crack Up* (Viking, 1992) k–3. When Spud and Joe get behind the wheel of Principal Lamar J. Spurgle's prized sports car, things soon get out of control.

4525. Marshall, James. *George and Martha* (Houghton, 1972) k–3. The friendship of two hippos leads to some very humorous situations.

4526. ____. *George and Martha Encore* (Houghton, 1973) k–3. In five brief episodes two hippopotamuses reinforce their friendship.

4527. ____. *George and Martha One Fine Day* (Houghton, 1978) k–3. Five funny stories involving the hippo friends.

4528. ____. *George and Martha Rise and Shine* (Houghton, 1979) k–3. Five brief episodes about two friends, George and Martha, who happen to be hippopotamuses.

4529. ____. *George and Martha, Tons of Fun* (Houghton, 1980) k–3. George wants to tell the truth without offending Martha. Martha wants to reform George's sweet tooth.

4530. ____. *George and Martha Back in Town* (Houghton, 1984) k–3. Though their friendship is often tested, George and Martha survive with a sense of humor.

4531. ____. *George and Martha Round and Round* (Houghton, 1988) k–3. Five episodes chronicle the ups and downs of a special friendship.

4532. Marshall, James. *Yummers!* (Houghton, 1973)

k–3. Emily Pig is worried about her weight, so she walks for exercise. Unfortunately, the walk is interrupted for several snacks, (and a bellyache), which, Emily Pig suggests, is due to the exercise not the food.

4533. ____. *Yummers, Too* (Houghton, 1986) k–3. Emily Pig tries to earn money to pay off debts created by her love of food, but her large appetite keeps getting in the way.

4534. Marshall, James. *What's the Matter with Carruthers?* (Houghton, 1972) 4–6. Carruthers, a very large bear, gets grumpy because it's time for his sleep.

4535. ____. *Taking Care of Carruthers* (Houghton, 1981) 4–6. When Carruthers is miserable with a cold, Eugene and Emily cheer him up with a story about a wonderful adventure shared by three friends one summer afternoon on the river.

4536. Marshall, James. *Space Case* (Dial, 1980) 2–4. When the thing from outer space visits earth, it is taken first for a trick-or-treater and then for a robot.

4537. ____. *Merry Christmas, Space Case* (Dial, 1986) 2–4. Buddy McGee eagerly awaits a promised Christmas visit from his friend, the thing from outer space.

4538. Marshall, James. *Three by Sea* (Dial, 1981) k–3. Lolly, Spider and Sam tell each other stories. Lolly and Spider tell about the cat and rat they find in their uninteresting school reader. Spider tells a story about a monster.

4539. ____. *Three Up a Tree* (Dutton, 1986) k–3. Spider and Sam decide to build a tree house. They ban Lolly because she didn't help build it. But she got in by telling a story. Then each one tells a story about a monster and a doll., about a fox and a chicken and about a monster and bank robbers.

4540. ____. *Four on the Shore* (Dial, 1985) k–3. Spider, Sam and Lolly are doing their homework but Willie, Spider's little brother, is being a pest. They leave but he follows. To get rid of him they begin telling scary stories. They have no effect on Willie. But when Willie tells his story he scares everyone.

4541. Martin, Ann. *Kristy's Great Idea* (Scholastic, 1986/1991) 4–6. Kristy, a seventh grader, organizes her friends into a baby-sitting club. She comes to terms with her mother's engagement. Her friends Stacey, Claudia and Mary Anne help each other cope with problems.

4542. ____. *Claudia and the Phantom Phone Calls* (Scholastic, 1986) 4–6. Claudia decides to investigate when she and the other members of the baby-sitters club receive mysterious phone calls while out on assignments.

4543. ____. *Truth About Stacey* (Scholastic, 1986) 4–6. Describes how Stacey, a diabetic, must take control of her own life when her parents insist on dragging her from one doctor to another.

4544. ____. *Mary Anne Saves the Day* (Scholastic, 1987) 4–6. When a fight breaks out among members of the baby-sitting club, timid Mary Anne finds herself becoming more assertive as a baby-sitter and in her relationships with her father and friends.

4545. ____. *Dawn and the Impossible Three* (Scholastic, 1987) 4–6. As a new member of the baby-sitters club, Dawn tries to win the acceptance of the club's president by tackling a tough baby-sitting job.

4546. ____. *Kristy's Big Day* (Scholastic, 1987) 4–6. Kristy and her friends decide to organize a baby-sitters club. They have fun and make money but they also run into several problems.

4547. ____. *Claudia and Mean Janine* (Scholastic, 1987) 4–6. Claudia's anticipation in the baby-sitters club is curtailed when Grandmother Mimi suffers a stroke and Claudia finds herself Mimi-sitting and fighting more frequently with her sister.

4548. ____. *Boy-Crazy Stacy* (Scholastic, 1987) 4–6. While spending two weeks at the New Jersey shore as mother's helpers, Mary Anne objects when Stacey neglects her baby-sitting duties after falling in love with Scott the lifeguard.

4549. ____. *Ghost at Dawn's House* (Scholastic, 1988) 4-6. Members of the baby-sitters club split their time between baby-sitting and investigating the spooky noises behind Dawn's bedroom wall.

4550. ____. *Logan Likes Mary Anne* (Scholastic, 1988) 4–6. The girls in the baby-sitters club face new complications when Logan tries to become the club's first male member and shows an interest in Mary Anne.

4551. ____. *Kristy and the Snobs* (Scholastic, 1990) 4–6. The kids in Kristy's new neighborhood are S.N.O.B.S.

4552. ____. *Claudia and the New Girl* (Scholastic, 1988) 4–6. Claudia's friendship with a new student who shares her interest in art threatens Claudia's membership in the baby-sitters club.

4553. ____. *Good-bye Stacey, Good-bye* (Scholastic, 1988) 4–6. Stacey's friends are crushed when they hear she is moving back to New York City. How will the baby-sitters club cope without her?

4554. ____. *Hello, Mallory* (Scholastic, 1988) 4–6. Mallory, 11, is excited when it looks like the eighth grade girls will invite her to join their baby-sitters club and she might become best friends with the new African American girl in the neighborhood, but the club members have to learn some lessons in fairness first.

4555. ____. *Little Miss Stoneybrook...and Dawn* (Scholastic, 1988) 4–6. Each member of the baby-sitters club sponsors a different girl in the Little Miss Stoneybrook competition. Dawn tries to cope with the break-up of her family after her parents are divorced.

4556. ____. *Jessi's Secret Language* (Scholastic,

1988) 4–6. Introduces sign language and shows how Matt and Jessi—and then a widening circle of children—learn to use it.

4557. ____. *Mary Anne's Bad Luck Mystery* (Scholastic, 1988) 4–6. When Mary Anne suffers from a run of bad luck after throwing away a chain letter, her baby-sitters club friends try to help.

4558. ____. *Stacey's Mistake* (Scholastic, 1988) 4–6. Stacey invites her baby-sitters club friends to New York City for a long weekend full of activities but, much to her dismay, nothing turns out exactly as planned.

4559. ____. *Claudia and the Bad Joke* (Scholastic, 1988) 4–6. The members of the baby-sitters club think they can handle a young practical joker, but when one of her tricks causes Claudia to break her leg, the girls know they must teach their new charge a lesson.

4560. ____. *Kristy and the Walking Disaster* (Scholastic, 1989) 4–6. Can Kristy's Krushers beat Bart's Bashers?

4561. ____. *Mallory and the Trouble with Twins* (Scholastic, 1989) 4–6. Mallory, 11, finds a real challenge in baby-sitting for the troublesome Arnold twins.

4562. ____. *Jessi Ramsey, Pet Sitter* (Scholastic, 1989) 4–6. With snakes on the loose and sick hamsters, Jessi's got plenty of pet-sitting troubles.

4563. ____. *Dawn on the Coast* (Scholastic, 1989) 4–6. Since her parents' divorce, Dawn lives with her mother while her brother lives with her father. Dawn visits her father in sunny California and isn't sure she wants to go back to the East coast.

4564. ____. *Kristy and the Mother's Day Surprise* (Scholastic, 1989) 4–6. Emily Michelle is the big surprise.

4565. ____. *Mary Anne and the Search for Tigger* (Scholastic, 1994) 4–6. While trying to find her missing kitten with the help of other members of the baby-sitters club, Mary Anne almost loses her good friend Logan.

4566. ____. *Claudia and the Sad Good-bye* (Scholastic, 1989) 4–6. Claudia has always been close to her grandmother, Mimi, so she needs the help of her friends in the baby-sitters club to deal with Mimi's death.

4567. ____. *Jessi and the Superbrat* (Scholastic, 1994) 4–6. Jessi counts on her friends in the baby-sitters club as she prepares for ballet auditions and tries to help a young television star adjust to being the new boy in school.

4568. ____. *Welcome Back Stacey* (Scholastic, 1989) 4–6. A story of Stacey's difficult choice when her parents divorce and she could live in New York with her father or in Stoneybrook with her mother.

4569. ____. *Mallory and the Mystery Diary* (Scholastic, 1994) 4–6. While helping Stacey move back into her house in Stoneybrook, Mallory and Claudia find an old trunk containing the diary of a girl who lived in Stacey's house in the 1890s.

4570. ____. *Mary Anne and the Great Romance* (Scholastic, 1994) 4–6. Best friends Mary Anne and Dawn are ecstatic to discover that Dawn's mother and Mary Anne's father are planning to get married.

4571. ____. *Dawn's Wicked Stepsister* (Scholastic, 1990) 4–6. After Dawn's mom marries Mary Anne's dad, the two friends, suddenly sisters, find their home turned into a battlefield, until Dawn realizes that her new stepsister only needs some room in which to breathe.

4572. ____. *Kristy and the Secret of Susan* (Scholastic, 1990) 4–6. A look at autism and the difficulties of deciding whether or not a special school is the wisest course. Even Kristy can't learn all of Susan's secrets.

4573. ____. *Claudia and the Great Search* (Scholastic, 1990) 4–6. Claudia, 13, concludes she is adopted since she sees no resemblance between herself and her brainy older sister whom she rivals.

4574. ____. *Mary Anne and Too Many Boys* (Scholastic, 1995) 4–6. While baby-sitting during a vacation at the beach, Mary Anne, 13, realizes that boys can really make life complicated for her and her girlfriends.

4575. ____. *Stacey and the Mystery of Stoneybrook* (Scholastic, 1990) 4–6. Kristy and the other kids of Stoneybrook suspect that the old, deserted house slated to be demolished soon sits over a graveyard and that restless spirits lurk underneath its foundation.

4576. ____. *Jessi's Baby-Sitter* (Scholastic, 1990) 4–6. Jessi, who feels she is old enough to take care of herself, is humiliated when strict and bossy Aunt Cecelia moves in to control her life and interfere with the baby-sitters club.

4577. ____. *Dawn and the Older Boy* (Scholastic, 1990) 4–6. The baby-sitters club members are uncertain about Dawn's new older boyfriend Travis, especially when he continually tells her what to do.

4578. ____. *Kristy's Mystery Admirer* (Scholastic, 1990) 4–6. When Baby-sitter Kristy begins receiving letters from a secret admirer, the other girls are convinced that they know who it is and they set out to smoke him out.

4579. ____. *Poor Mallory* (Scholastic, 1990) 4–6. Mallory, whose family is suddenly short of money, takes a baby-sitting job and needs the help of the baby-sitters club in adjusting to her new employer's wealth.

4580. ____. *Claudia and the Middle School Mystery* (Scholastic, 1991) 4–6. Claudia is surprised when her math teacher accuses her of cheating on a test and enlists the rest of the baby-sitters club to help her clear her name.

4581. ____. *Mary Anne vs. Logan* (Scholastic, 1996) 4–6. Shy Mary Anne must decide whether she has to break up with her handsome boyfriend to regain her independence.

4582. ____. *Jessi and the Dance School Phantom* (Scholastic, 1991) 4–6. Jessi is thrilled when she earns the lead in her dance school's latest ballet, but someone in Jessi's class wants her out of the show.

4583. ____. *Stacey's Emergency* (Scholastic, 1991) 4–6. Stacey hasn't been feeling well, her schoolwork and baby-sitting jobs are almost out of control. And Stacy's tired of being in the middle of her parents' fights.

4584. ____. *Dawn and the Big Sleepover* (Scholastic, 1996) 4–6. When a group of children learn that fire destroyed their pen pals' school, Dawn, 13, organizes a fundraiser and then rewards the contributors with a sleepover.

4585. ____. *Kristy and the Baby Parade* (Scholastic, 1991) 4–6. Kristy gets the great idea of entering a float in the Stoneybrook Baby Parade. It sounded easy, but the float looks like a big orange blob, the costumes are hideous, and the babies won't stop crying.

4586. ____. *Mary Anne Misses Logan* (Scholastic, 1996) 4–6. Mary Anne begins to have second thoughts about having told Logan to cool their relationship.

4587. ____. *Mallory on Strike* (Scholastic, 1996) 4–6. Mallory needs peace and quiet if she's going to win the Young Author's Day Award for Best Overall Fiction in the sixth grade, but the only way to get it is to stop baby-sitting.

4588. ____. *Jessi's Wish* (Scholastic, 1991) 4–6.

4589. ____. *Claudia and the Genius of Elm Street* (Scholastic, 1991) 4–6. Claudia gets stuck baby-sitting for Rosie, an obnoxious little girl who is also a genius.

4590. ____. *Dawn's Big Date* (Scholastic, 1992) 4–6.

4591. ____. *Stacey's Ex-Best Friend* (Scholastic, 1992) 4–6. Stacey is very excited to learn that Laine, her best friend from New York, is coming to visit Stoneybrook. But the minute Laine arrives, things don't go as planned. Laine is used to hanging out at high school parties and thinks Stacey and her friends are childish.

4592. ____. *Mary Anne + 2 Many Babies* (Scholastic, 1992) 4–6.

4593. ____. *Kristy for President* (Scholastic, 1992) 4–6. Kristy is not too happy with some things at Stoneybrook Middle School, so she decides to run for class president. But can Kristy coach a softball team, get straight A's, baby-sit, run the BSC and be president?

4594. ____. *Mallory and the Dream Horse* (Scholastic, 1992) 4–6.

4595. ____. *Jessi's Gold Medal* (Scholastic, 1992) 4–6.

4596. ____. *Keep Out, Claudia* (Scholastic, 1992) 4–6.

4597. ____. *Dawn Saves the Planet* (Scholastic, 1992) 4–6. Dawn thinks studying ecology is cool. She wants to start a recycling center at Stoneybrook Middle School, but she is so busy lecturing people she doesn't have the time.

4598. ____. *Stacey's Choice* (Scholastic, 1992) 4–6. Stacey's parents are divorced, but they both depend on her. But how can she choose between them, when her mother is home sick, and her father wants her to go with him to the dinner celebrating his promotion to vice-president.

4599. ____. *Mallory Hates Boys (and Gym)* (Scholastic, 1992) 4–6.

4600. ____. *Mary Anne's Makeover* (Scholastic, 1993) 4–6.

4601. ____. *Jessi and the Awful Secret* (Scholastic, 1993) 4–6.

4602. ____. *Kristy and the Worst Kid Ever* (Scholastic, 1993) 4–6. Need a baby-sitter for Lou? Don't call the Baby-Sitter's Club!

4603. ____. *Claudia's Friend* (Scholastic, 1993) 4–6.

4604. ____. *Dawn's Family Feud* (Scholastic, 1993) 4–6. Dawn's little brother is visiting the new Schafer-Spier family. He is miserable because all his old friends have changed, and Mary Anne's dad is trying too hard to be Jeff's best friend. Dawn hopes that the family trip to Boston will bring everyone together, but now the Schafers and the Spiers aren't talking at all. Could this mean divorce for the family?

4605. ____. *Stacey's Big Crush* (Scholastic, 1993) 4–6.

4606. ____. *Maid Mary Anne* (Scholastic, 1993) 4–6.

4607. ____. *Dawn's Big Move* (Scholastic, 1993) 4–6.

4608. ____. *Jessi and the Bad Baby-sitter* (Scholastic, 1993) 4–6.

4609. ____. *Get Well Soon, Mallory* (Scholastic, 1993) 4–6.

4610. ____. *Stacey and the Cheerleaders* (Scholastic, 1993) 4–6.

4611. ____. *Claudia and the Perfect Boy* (Scholastic, 1993) 4–6.

4612. ____. *Dawn and the We Love Kids Club* (Scholastic, 1994) 4–6.

4613. ____. *Mary Ann and Miss Priss* (Scholastic, 1994) 4–6.

4614. ____. *Kristy and the Copycat* (Scholastic, 1994) 4–6. Kristy's done something bad—something she'd never want Karen to copy.

4615. ____. *Jessi's Horrible Prank* (Scholastic, 1994) 4–6.

4616. ____. *Stacey's Life* (Scholastic, 1994) 4–6.

4617. ____. *Dawn and Whitney, Friends Forever* (Scholastic, 1994) 4–6.

4618. ____. *Claudia and the Crazy Peaches* (Scholastic, 1994) 4–6.

4619. ____. *Mary Anne Breaks the Rules* (Scholastic, 1994) 4–6.

4620. ____. *Mallory Pike, #1 Fan* (Scholastic, 1994) 4–6.

4621. ____. *Kristy and Mr. Mom* (Scholastic, 1994) 4–6. Kristy's stepfather Watson has a new job.

4622. ____. *Jessi and the Troublemaker* (Scholastic, 1995) 4–6.

4623. ____. *Stacey vs. BSC* (Scholastic, 1995) 4–6.

4624. ____. *Dawn and the School Spirit War* (Scholastic, 1995) 4–6.

4625. ____. *Claudia Kishi. Live from WSTO!* (Scholastic, 1995) 4–6.

4626. ____. *Mary Anne and Camp BSC* (Scholastic, 1995) 4–6.

4627. ____. *Stacey and the Bad Girls* (Scholastic, 1995) 4–6.

4628. ____. *Farewell, Dawn* (Scholastic, 1995) 4–6.

4629. ____. *Kristy and the Dirty Diapers* (Scholastic, 1995) 4–6. Will Kristy lose the Krushers when they change their name to the Diapers.

4630. ____. *Welcome to BSC, Abby* (Scholastic, 1995) 4–6.

4631. ____. *Claudia and the First Thanksgiving* (Scholastic, 1995) 4–6.

4632. ____. *Mallory's Christmas Wish* (Scholastic, 1995) 4–6.

4633. ____. *Mary Anne and the Memory Garden* (Scholastic, 1996) 4–6.

4634. ____. *Stacey McGill, Super Sitter* (Scholastic, 1996) 4–6.

4635. ____. *Kristy + Bart = ?* (Scholastic, 1996) 4–6.

4636. ____. *Abby's Lucky Thirteen* (Scholastic, 1996) 4–6. Abby is worried about Bath Mitzvah, her entry into adulthood with responsibilities.

4637. ____. *Claudia and the World's Cutest Baby* (Scholastic, 1996) 4–6.

4638. ____. *Dawn and Too Many Sitters* (Scholastic, 1996) 4–6.

4639. ____. *Kristy's Worst Idea* (Scholastic, 1996) 4–6.

4640. Martin, Ann. *Stacey and the Missing Ring* (Scholastic, 1991) 4–6.

4641. ____. *Beware, Dawn* (Scholastic, 1991) 4–6.

4642. ____. *Mallory and the Ghost Cat* (Scholastic, 1992) 4–6. While Mallory is baby-sitting she finds a cat in the Craine's attic and names him Ghost Cat.

4643. ____. *Kristy and the Missing Child* (Scholastic, 1992) 4–6. Kristy is determined to find Jake, a member of her softball team who has been missing for over two days.

4644. ____. *Mary Anne's Secret in the Attic* (Scholastic, 1992) 4–6.

4645. ____. *Mystery at Claudia's House* (Scholastic, 1992) 4–6. Claudia's room has been ransacked and her sister, Janine, is acting strange. It is up to the baby-sitters to solve the mystery.

4646. ____. *Dawn and the Disappearing Dogs* (Scholastic, 1993) 4–6. With the help of her friends in the baby-sitters club, Dawn is able to find out what happened to several dogs that have mysteriously disappeared.

4647. ____. *Jessi and the Jewel Thieves* (Scholastic, 1993) 4–6. Jessi can't wait to get to New York City to see her friend Quint dance in his first big ballet.

4648. ____. *Kristy and the Haunted Mansion*

(Scholastic, 1993) 4–6. Kristy and the Krushers are spending the night in a spooky old house.

4649. ____. *Stacey and the Mystery Money* (Scholastic, 1993) 4–6.

4650. ____. *Claudia and the Mystery at the Museum* (Scholastic, 1993) 4–6.

4651. ____. *Dawn and the Surfer Ghost* (Scholastic, 1994) 4–6.

4652. ____. *Mary Anne and the Library Mystery* (Scholastic, 1994) 4-6.

4653. ____. *Stacey and the Mystery at the Mall* (Scholastic, 1994) 4–6.

4654. ____. *Kristy and the Vampires* (Scholastic, 1994) 4–6. A vampire movie is being shot in Stoneybrook. Can Kristy and the BSC find out who's out to get the star?

4655. ____. *Claudia and the Clue in the Photograph* (Scholastic, 1994) 4–6.

4656. ____. *Dawn and the Halloween Mystery* (Scholastic, 1994) 4–6.

4657. ____. *Stacey and the Mystery at the Empty House* (Scholastic, 1995) 4–6.

4658. ____. *Kristy and the Missing Fortune* (Scholastic, 1995) 4–6. The fortune could all be Kristy's—if she and the BSC crack the case.

4659. ____. *Mary Ann and the Zoo Mystery* (Scholastic, 1995) 4–6.

4660. ____. *Claudia and the Recipe for Danger* (Scholastic, 1995) 4–6.

4661. ____. *Stacey and the Haunted Masquerade* (Scholastic, 1995) 4–6.

4662. ____. *Abby and the Secret Society* (Scholastic, 1995) 4–6.

4663. ____. *Mary Anne and the Silent Witness* (Scholastic, 1995) 4–6.

4664. ____. *Kristy and the Middle School Vandal* (Scholastic, 1996) 4–6.

4665. Martin, Charles. *Island Winter* (Greenwillow, 1984) k–3. Staying behind on an island after the summer people have left, Heather wonders what there will be to do.

4666. ____. *Summer Business* (Greenwillow, 1984) k–3. By running small businesses catering to the summer visitors to their island home, Heather and her friends earn enough money for a trip to the Harvest Fair on the mainland.

4667. ____. *Island Rescue* (Greenwillow, 1985) k–3. When Mae breaks her leg she is taken by boat off the island where she lives, to the mainland hospital.

4668. Martin, David. *K9 and the Roving Planet* (Rourke, 1981) k–3. Technically a robot dog capable of independent missions in situations classed as too dangerous for Time Lord intervention, more familiarly called a mechanical bloodhound, K9 performs daring rescues in distant star-worlds, observes alternate evolutions and averts galactic destruction.

4669. ____. *K9 and the Beasts of Vega* (Rourke, 1982) k–3. K9, the robot dog, destroys a horde of space monsters.

4670. ____. *K9 and the Missing Planet* (Rourke, 1982) k–3. K9, the robot dog, sent to locate a missing planet, enters a universe where early life forms still thrive.

4671. ____. *K9 and the Time Trap* (Rourke, 1982) k–3. Searching for the vanished Rigelian Seventh Fleet, K9, a robot dog, encounters a deposed Time Lord who seeks revenge for his betrayal.

4672. ____. *K9 and the Zeta Rescue* (Rourke, 1983) k–3. K9, the robot dog, rescues survivors of an interplanetary war.

4673. Martin, David. *Lizzie and Her Kitty* (Candlewick, 1993) k–3. Lizzie cuddles with her kitty and ends up with pudding in her hair.

4674. ____. *Lizzie and Her Puppy* (Candlewick, 1993) k–3. Lizzie and her puppy have fun playing together in a box.

4675. ____. *Lizzie and Her Dolly* (Candlewick, 1993) k–3. Lizzie and her doll transform the living room with their games.

4676. ____. *Lizzie and Her Friend* (Candlewick, 1993) k–3. Lizzie and Penny have fun playing with water.

4677. Martin, Graham. *Giftwish* (Houghton, 1978) 5–8. A fantasy fraught with wizards, magical beasts and Ewan. Caperstaff, the sword Giftwish and Catchfire, a witch, are the good elements that help Feydom out of evil.

4678. ____. *Catchfire* (Houghton, 1982) 5–8. Hoodwill has lost his shadow. The shadow becomes the monster Erebor. The Earth Dragon swallows Erebor. Catchfire is united with her twin and she and King Ewan are betrothed.

4679. Martin, J.P. *Uncle* (Coward, 1966) 2–4. Uncle, an elephant, and his friends battle the Hateman. There is Mallet Crackbone, Isadore Hitmouse, Fulljug Hateman and Firton Hootman.

4680. ____. *Uncle and His Detective* (Cape, 1966) 2–4. Uncle, the hero, is an affluent elephant. The detective is a fox. When secret paneling in Uncle's house slides back it reveals a notice saying "TO MALLEY'S TEA ROOM" and a row of parrots screaming "Malley's for good grub."

4681. ____. *Uncle and the Treacle Trouble* (Cape, 1967) 2–4. Old Dr. Lyre and Anna the Respectable Horse is back but there are new characters and inventions: Brashbag the Antique dealer, the Monkey-and-Engine Room Wood and the Snowstorm volcano.

4682. ____. *Uncle Cleans Up* (Coward, 1967) 2–4. The riotous escapades of Uncle, the elephant, as he defends his castle against the onslaught of the scruffy crew from the dingy fortress across the way.

4683. ____. *Uncle and Claudius the Camel* (Cape, 1969) 2–4. A story of Uncle's efforts to have a seaside holiday, efforts that are persistently thwarted by the machinations of his enemy, Beaver Hateman, Claudius the camel and his friends join the other characters.

4684. ____. *Uncle and the Battle for Badgertown* (Cape, 1973) 2–4. Describes the adventures of a rich and eccentric elephant and his friends and foes, animal and human.

4685. Martin, Jacqueline. *Bizzy Bones and Uncle Ezra* (Lothrop, 1984) k–3. A young mouse named Bizzy Bones is afraid the wind will blow away the old shoe that is his home, but his Uncle Ezra helps him overcome his fear.

4686. ____. *Bizzy Bones and Moosemouse* (Lothrop, 1986) k–3. Shy Bizzy does not look forward to his stay with big, loud Moosemouse when Uncle Ezra goes away but the visit does not turn out as expected.

4687. ____. *Bizzy Bones and the Lost Quilt* (Lothrop, 1988) k–3. When Bizzy loses the quilt he needs to go to sleep, Uncle Ezra and the orchard mice try to make him a new one.

4688. Martin, Janet. *Ten Little Babies Play* (St. Martin, 1986) k–3. As ten toddlers play with balloons, the reader may count from one to ten.

4689. ____. *Ten Little Babies Eat* (St. Martin, 1986) k–3. In Ten Little Indians fashion, babies eat their food.

4690. ____. *Ten Little Babies Dress* (St. Martin, 1986) k–3. Ten toddlers in various stages of dressing lead the reader to count from one to ten.

4691. ____. *Ten Little Babies Count* (St. Martin, 1986) k–3. The counting is done by babies appearing one by one in the style of the "Ten Little Indians."

4692. Martin, Les. *Indiana Jones and the Temple of Doom* (Random, 1984) 5–8. While trying to recover a sacred stone belonging to an Indian village, Indiana Jones and his two companions become prisoners of a ruthless sect dedicated to the worship of the evil goddess Kali.

4693. ____. *Indiana Jones and the Last Crusade* (Random, 1989) 5–8. Indiana Jones tries to save his father from the Nazis as they all search for the Holy Grail.

(For other books about "Indiana Jones," *see* Stine, Megan.)

4694. Martyn, Harriet. *Jenny and the Syndicate* (Deutsch, 1984) 4–6. Jenny's first term at boarding school brings unexpected problems when a new friend keeps getting Jenny into increasingly serious trouble.

4695. ____. *Jenny and the New Headmistress* (Deutsch, 1984) 4–6. Jenny takes a puppy to Babcombe Hall School where pets are not allowed. She has trouble caring for it but the house mistress helps.

Also Sylvia goes to the fair without permission and Ariel is kidnapped.

4696. ____. *Jenny and the New Girls* (Deutsch, 1986) 4–6. Maggie is unpopular at White House school. She is supported by an aunt who won the money to put her in this school. She is out of place and terrified. She made friends with trouble-making twins.

4697. Marzollo, Jean. *Jed's Junior Space Patrol* (Dial, 1982) 3–5. Jed, his teddy bear robot, and two creatures called cogs save planet X-5.

4698. ____. *Jed and the Space Bandits* (Dial, 1987) 3–5. Jed's Junior Space Patrol helps Molly, a girl who can turn invisible, to rescue her parents from bandits.

4699. Maschler, Fay. *T.G. and Moonie Move Out of Town* (Doubleday, 1977) k–3. Finding city life disagreeable, two cats leave their apartment and seek a home in the country.

4700. ____. *T.G. and Moonie Go Shopping* (Doubleday, 1978) k–3. T.G. and Moonie Adkins go on a shopping spree to buy things for their new house.

4701. ____. *T.G. and Moonie Have a Baby* (Doubleday, 1979) k–3. The arrival of a cat couple's first baby coincides with a visit from helpful cousin Fraser.

4702. Masefield, John. *Midnight Folk* (Heinemann, 1984) 4–6. Kay is eight, talking paintings and cats are his companions in the search for his great-grandfather's buried treasure, entrusted to and lost by an ancestor. His governess Sylvia Pouncer is both a bullying teacher and a secret witch, while her ally, the infamous Abner Brown, is both thief and wizard.

4703. ____. *Box of Delights* (Heinemann, 1984) 4–6. Now a 12-year-old schoolboy, Kay opposes his old enemies in search for a box of strange powers, lost and found many times since the Middle Ages; there was danger of floods, kidnapping, treachery…and potent magic.

4704. Massie, Diane. *Baby Beebee Bird* (Harper, 1963) k–3. The zoo is very quiet and all the animals are asleep, then the beebee bird begins to sing: Beebeebobbibobbi. The animals are frantic and their keeper is desperate by the time the lion has a bright idea and saves the night.

4705. ____. *Birthday for Bird* (Parents, 1966) k–3. A bird announces his birthday and gifts are given to him by Quail, Wren, Grouse, Mole and Duck.

4706. Massie, Diane. *Chameleon Was a Spy* (Crowell, 1979) 3–5. Chameleon becomes a spy in order to recover the formula for the world's best pickles.

4707. ____. *Chameleon the Spy and the Terrible Toaster Trap* (Crowell, 1982) 3–5. A spy encounters strange events in Beantown as the entire population appears to be asleep amid a rash of robberies.

4708. ____. *Chameleon the Spy and the Case of the Vanishing Jewels* (Crowell, 1984) 3–5. Chameleon the Spy outwits a phony prince and princess who have robbed Beantown residents of their jewels.

4709. Matas, Carol. *Lisa* (Lester, 1988) 5–8. Lisa, 12, is a Jewish girl living in Copenhagen under Nazi rule. She joins the Danish resistance and moves from passing out leaflets to blowing up factories. She fears she is becoming as violent as the Nazis but she knows she will move on to better things.

4710. ____. *Lisa's War* (Scribner, 1989) 5–8. Lisa, 12, joins the resistance movement in Denmark. She escapes to Sweden. A World War II Jewish story.

4711. Matsuno, Masako. *Taro and Tofu* (World, 1962) k–3. Taro was given too much money in change. He is tempted to keep it but them makes the right decision.

4712. ____. *Taro and the Bamboo Shoot* (Pantheon, 1964) k–3. Taro enters the bamboo grove looking for his dinner and comes away with much more than he expected.

4713. Matthews, Andrew. *Mallory Cox and His Magic Socks* (Dent, 1990) 3–5. Aunt Enid, a mildly mischievous witch, bestows upon Mallory the power to wreak humorous discomfiture at home, at school and in the neighborhood.

4714. ____. *Mallory Cox and His Viking Box* (Dent, 1991) 3–5. Mallory is carried back to Viking times by means of some magic socks. The story gives a good description of a Viking settlement.

4715. ____. *Mallory Cox and His Interstellar Socks* (Dent, 1993) 3–5.

4716. Matthews, Liz. *Teeny Witch and the Terrible Twins* (Troll, 1990) k–3. Teeny Witch's attempt to watch her aunts' house and baby-sit some terrible twins at the same time results in horrible chaos, but her aunts have a surprising reaction.

4717. ____. *Teeny Witch Goes to the Library* (Troll, 1990) k–3. On a rainy day Teeny Witch visits the library, where she sees a pet exhibit, enjoys a puppet show, and reads an exciting horse story.

4718. ____. *Teeny Witch and Christmas Magic* (Troll, 1990) k–3. When Santa Claus gets injured in her house on Christmas Eve, Teeny Witch gets to take his place on the sleigh and deliver presents.

4719. ____. *Teeny Witch and the Tricky Easter Bunny* (Troll, 1990) k–3. On Easter Teeny Witch chases the Easter Bunny all over town and gets a surprise at the end of her search.

4720. ____. *Teeny Witch and the Great Halloween Ride* (Troll, 1990) k–3. Teeny Witch and her three witch aunts find an unusual way of fulfilling witch rule Number 13, which states that they must ride on Halloween night.

4721. ____. *Teeny Witch Goes to School* (Troll, 1990) k–3. Teeny Witch does not want to leave her aunts and spend a day in school, but after the first day of school she finds it to be a place of fun.

4722. ____. *Teeny Witch Goes on Vacation* (Troll, 1990) k–3. When Teeny Witch and her three witch aunts cannot decide where to spend their vacation, she satisfies them all by taking three vacations in three different places.

4723. ____. *Teeny Witch and the Perfect Valentine* (Troll, 1990) k–3. Teeny saves money to buy a box of candy for her aunts, only to find the store sold out. (Her aunts have bought them all for her.)

4724. Mattingley, Christobel. *Surprise Mouse* (Hodder, 1974) k–3. Nicky gave the Surprise Mouse to his mother for her birthday.

4725. ____. *Budgerigar Blue* (Hodder, 1978) k–3. The locale is an Australian fair: stallholders, weather, the movement and color of the crowds. The story is of a boy's search for a present for his mother.

4726. Mattson, Olle. *Mickel and the Lost Ship* (Watts, 1960) 5–8. Mickel lived in Sweden with his grandmother and a dog. They are poor and waiting for Mickel's father to return.

4727. ____. *Mickel Seafarer* (Watts, 1962) 5–8. After strange happenings in his village, disappearances and thefts, Mickel goes to sea in his own boat, a surprise from his father.

4728. Maury, Inex. *My Mother the Mail Carrier* (Feminist, 1976) k–3. Lupita and her working mother share love and respect in a one-parent home.

4729. ____. *My Mother and I Are Growing Strong* (New Seed, 1979) k–3. Emilita's father is in jail. Emilita and her mom are taking his place at the flower garden. Her mother does men's chores but also gains strength and courage.

4730. May, Kara. *Knickerless Nicola* (Macmillan, 1989) k–3. The new uses for her knickers (undies) devised by a small girl, including garments for the cat and a hat for the park, lead Mother to leave her knickerless but the tickly surface of Gran's sofa and the cold wood of a swing force Nicola to beg for another pair which she then wears with pride.

4731. ____. *Grumpy Nicola* (Macmillan, 1990) k–3.

4732. May, Robert. *Rudolph the Red-Nosed Reindeer* (Follett, 1980) 3–5. Although the other reindeers laugh at him because of his bright red nose, Rudolph proves his worth when he is chosen to lead Santa Claus's sleigh on a foggy night.

4733. ____. *Rudolph Shines Again* (Follett, 1981) 3–5. Devastated when his nose loses its shine, Rudolph spends all his time feeling sorry for himself until he becomes involved in the search for two abby rabbits.

4734. Mayer, Mercer. *Professor Wormbog in Search*

for the Zipperump-A-Zoo (Golden, 1977) k–3. Professor Wormbog's zoo won't be complete until he finds a zipperump-a-zoo but he seems to be looking in the wrong places.

4735. ____. *Professor Wormbog's Gloomy Kerploppus* (Golden, 1977) k–3. Professor Wormbog tries to cheer up his gloomy pet.

4736. Mayer, Mercer. *Little Monster at Work* (Golden, 1970) k–3. Traveling with his grandfather, a little monster discovers the variety of occupations in his community.

4737. ____. *Little Monster at School* (Golden, 1978) k–3. Little Monster describes his day at school.

4738. ____. *Little Monster's Counting Book* (Golden, 1978) k–3. The little monsters introduce the numbers from 1 to 21.

4739. ____. *Little Monster at Home* (Golden, 1978) k–3. A little monster describes his house and some of his family's activities.

4740. ____. *Little Monster's Bedtime* (S & S, 1979) k–3. Contains rhymes about Coonis the Peevish and the Typhoonigator the Useless.

4741. ____. *Little Monster's Alphabet Book* (Western, 1979) k–3. A is apple, D is a dragon and J is a jester. Monster and Kerploppus explain the alphabet.

4742. ____. *Little Monster's Mother Goose* (Golden, 1979) k–3. A story of the success of a road company Mother Goose tour with the grand dame electing Little Monster as a star player.

4743. ____. *Little Monster's Neighborhood* (S & S, 1979) k–3. Little Monster goes through sections of his town, visiting his secret clubhouse, the gas station, a church and the park.

4744. ____. *Little Monster's Scratch and Sniff* (Golden, 1981) k–3. Little Monster in his trench coat plays sleuth. Someone is switching scents and spreading confusion all over town, oranges smell like peanut butter, for instance. Who is doing this?

4745. ____. *Little Monster's Mystery* (Western, 1979) k–3.

4746. Mayer, Mercer. *Fireman Critter* (S & S, 1986) k–3. A young critter stands behind a chair waiting while his father lights his pipe. Fire extinguisher in hand (shaving cream) he says "A fireman's work is never done."

4747. ____. *Astronaut Critter* (S & S, 1986) k–3. A young critter is riding his lunar land rover (his tricycle attached to the vacuum cleaner) over the frame of his sister's sandbox; he reports that "the moon is very bumpy."

4748. ____. *Cowboy Critter* (S & S, 1986) k–3.

4749. ____. *Police Critter* (S & S, 1986) k–3.

4750. ____. *Construction Critter* (S & S, 1987) k–3. Pretending to be a construction worker, a young critter annoys his sister when he tries to build a skyscraper in the playground where she is playing.

4751. ____. *Doctor Critter* (S & S, 1987) k–3. A young critter plays doctor and tries to give medical care to unsuspecting family members.

4752. Mayer, Mercer. *Little Critter's Holiday Fun* (Western, 1984) k–3.

4753. ____. *Just Me and My Babysitter* (Western, 1986) k–3. Little Critter does his enthusiastic best to help his baby-sitter, although his efforts frequently make a bad situation worse.

4754. ____. *Little Critter's Bedtime Storybook* (Western, 1987) k–3. Little sister acting selfish, fussy, and grumpy and refusing to go to sleep, Little Critter tells her four bedtime stories in which the characters reflect her bad behavior.

4755. ____. *Little Critter's Little Sister's Birthday* (Western, 1988) k–3. Little Critter helps Mom and Dad prepare a surprise birthday party for his little sister.

4756. ____. *Little Critter's Staying Overnight* (Golden, 1988) k–3. Little Critter causes quite a commotion when he spends the night at his friend's mansion.

4757. ____. *Little Critter's the Trip* (Golden, 1988) k–3. During the car trip to Lake Wakalookee, the Critter family introduces the letters from A to Z.

4758. ____. *Little Critter's the Picnic* (Golden, 1988) k–3. Chased by cows, disturbed by bulldozers and surprised by bears, the Critter family finally finds the perfect spot for a picnic.

4759. ____. *Little Critters: These Are My Pets* (Golden, 1988) k–3. Little Critter describes his pets which include a frog, fish, turtle, dog, kitten, bug and snake.

4760. ____. *Little Critters: This Is My House* (Golden, 1988) k–3. Little Critter introduces us to his house and family as the illustrations depict misbehavior, fun and lots of love.

4761. ____. *Happy Easter, Little Critter* (Western, 1988) k–3.

4762. ____. *Little Critters: This Is My Friend* (Golden, 1989) k–3. Two friends experience the vicissitudes of friendship.

4763. ____. *Little Critter's Christmas Book* (Western, 1989) k–3. Little Critter and his family celebrate the Christmas season as fully as possible.

4764. ____. *Just a Daydream* (Western, 1989) k–3. Little Critter daydreams about what he would do to the local bully if he were Super Critter.

4765. ____. *Little Critter's the Fussy Princess* (Western, 1989) k–3. A fussy princess learns the hard way it isn't always important that everything be just right.

4766. ____. *Just Going to the Dentist* (Western, 1990) k–3. Little Critter goes to the dentist for a checkup, and finds that going to the dentist isn't so bad.

4767. ____. *Just Me and My Mom* (Western, 1990) k–3. Little Critter and his mother take a trip to the city exploring the department stores and museums.

4768. ____. *Little Critters: This Is My School* (Western, 1990) k–3. Describes Little Critter's first day at school.

4769. ____. *Little Critter at Scout Camp* (Western, 1991) k–3.

4770. ____. *Just Too Little* (Western, 1993) k–3. Little Critter's younger sister always wants to do what he does, and even though most of the time he thinks that she is too little, sometimes he is surprised.

4771. ____. *Trick or Treat, Little Critter* (Western, 1993) k–3.

4772. ____. *Little Critter Book Club* (Western, 1993) k–3.

4773. ____. *Just Me and My Bicycle* (Western, 1993) k–3. Little Critter enjoys riding around town on his shiny red bicycle, especially when his mother, father, and sister join him.

4774. ____. *Very Special Critter* (Western, 1993) k–3. Little Critter discovers that the new boy in class is really not so different from anyone else, even though he is in a wheelchair.

4775. Mayer, Mercer. *Appelard and Liverwurst* (Four Winds, 1978) k–3. Aided by a wayward rhinoceros, Appelard and his motley farm animals finally have a successful harvest.

4776. ____. *Liverwurst Is Missing* (Four Winds, 1981) k–3. When Liverwurst, the rhinosterwurst disappears, Wackatoo Indians, survivors of the 49th Cavalry, and children from the Koala Scouts join the circus company in rescuing him from a burger tycoon.

4777. Mayer, Mercer. *Boy, a Dog and a Frog* (Dial, 1967) k–3. A boy's discoveries and amusing adventures.

4778. ____. *Frog, Where Are You?* (Dial, 1969) k–3. A boy and his dog suffer through several adventures while searching for a pet frog that escaped during the night.

4779. ____. *Boy, a Dog, a Frog and a Friend* (Dial, 1971/1985) k–3. A quiet fishing party is interrupted when something unexpected bites on the line.

4780. ____. *Frog on His Own* (Dial, 1973/1980) k–3. On a walk in the park with his friends, Frog decides to do some exploring on his own.

4781. ____. *Frog Goes to Dinner* (Dial, 1974) k–3. Having stowed away in a pocket, Frog wreaks havoc and creates disgrace for the family at the posh restaurant where they are having dinner.

4782. ____. *One Frog Too Many* (Dial, 1975) k–3. A boy's pet frog thinks that the new little frog the boy gets for his birthday is one frog too many.

4783. Mayer, Mercer. *There's a Nightmare in My Closet* (Dial, 1968) k–3. A small boy conquers his fear of the dark by letting his nightmare out of the closet and shooting it with his popgun. (The nightmare is a big, ugly monster.) Poor monster is really a big baby who cries at being lost.

4784. ____. *There's an Alligator Under My Bed* (Dial, 1987) k–3. The alligator under his bed makes a boy's bedtime hazardous operation, until he lures it out of the house and into the garage.

4785. Mayer, Mercer. *Tinka Bakes a Cake* (Bantam, 1984) k–3. Tinka bakes a cake for her friend Tink, with a little help from other friends and after many mishaps and several trips to the grocery store.

4786. ____. *Tuk Takes a Trip* (Bantam, 1984) k–3. Tuk packs his toothpaste, pajamas, pillows and his favorite toys to go on a trip—to his friend's house next door.

4787. ____. *Tink Goes Fishing* (Bantam, 1984) k–3. Tink has a long hard day. When he finally does catch a fish, he realizes how hungry he is. They all (including the fish) rush home and have pizza for supper.

4788. ____. *Teep and Beep Go to Sleep* (Bantam, 1984) k–3. Two characters can't sleep, so they read and play games. They locate tinkybear who was missing and was the cause of their sleeplessness.

4789. Mayhew, James. *Katie's Picture Show* (Bantam, 1989) k–3. Katie visits the Art Gallery. She steps inside the pictures to meet the people portrayed. She has tea with Madame Moitesseur and plays with a girl in Les Parapluies. She explores Tropical Storm with a tiger.

4790. ____. *Katie and the Dinosaurs* (Bantam, 1992) k–3. Katie's visit to the natural history museum turns into an adventure when she steps through a door and finds herself in a land of real live dinosaurs, one of whom is lost and needs her help to find his way home.

4791. Mayle, Peter. *Amazing Adventures of Chilly Billy* (Magnet, 1981) k–3. Chilly Billy lives in the refrigerator and tidies it up.

4792. ____. *Chilly Billy* (Crown, 1983) k–3. Billy's unique job is to place needed contents of the refrigerator near the front before each meal. Billy's friends are a caterpillar in the lettuce, and a beautiful nurse who arrives via an egg carton to cure his "warm" and remains as a live-in in their freezer compartment home.

4793. Mayne, William. *Red Book of Hob Stories* (Philomel, 1984) k–3. A story of Hob, a goblin, and the family he lives with and protects. Only the children can see him.

4794. ____. *Green Book of Hob Stories* (Philomel, 1984) k–3. More adventures of Hob, the goblin who lives under the stairs, and only visible to children and whose job is to chase away trouble and keep the house in order.

4795. ____. *Blue Book of Hob Stories* (Philomel, 1984) k–3. Hob, the friendly household spirit, continues to make life better for his human family.

4796. ____. *Yellow Book of Hob Stories* (Philomel,

1984) k–3. Hob protects his human family and solves problems dealing with Eggy Palmer, Sootkin, Hinky Punk, Sleepyhead, and the Tooth Fairy.

4797. ____. *Hob and the Goblins* (Kindersley, 1994) k–3. Hob, the friendly spirit who lives under the stairs and protects the house, must do battle with a variety of evil beings trying to take control of his family's home.

4798. Mayne, William. *Skiffy* (Hamilton, 1972) 4–6. A colonizing mission has arrived on a distant planet. Among the team members are two children, chosen because they have a higher telepathic gift than adults. It is a cold planet with strange flowers and trees.

4799. ____. *Skiffy and the Twin Planets* (Hamilton, 1982) 4–6. Three children are on a space mission with Margaret, the Mission Mother.

4800. Mazer, Harry. *War on Villa Street* (Delacorte, 1978) 5–8. Willis is a loner because of his alcoholic father. He runs away from bullies and from girls. He is training a mentally handicapped boy to run, this makes him more sociable.

4801. ____. *Girl of His Dreams* (Harper, 1987) 5–8. Willis meets Sophie, a country girl who just moved to the city. She helps him train for a track race. They have a fight, she moves back to the country and he comes in second in the race. But there is a happy ending.

4802. Mazzola, Toni. *Wally Koala and Friends* (Little, 1993) k–3. Describes the adventures of Wally, Sadie Kangaroo and Timmy Kookaburra as they travel to America by plane. Timmy is a stowaway under Sadie's hat but they are caught.

4803. ____. *Wally Koala and the Little Green Peach* (Little, 1993) k–3. A talking peach cries because it is not ready to be picked with its peers. Wally reassures the peach that it will one day be a fruit-producing tree.

4804. Mendoza, George. *Need A House? Call Ms. Mouse* (Grosset, 1981) k–3. Henrietta Mouse designs houses to fit the special needs of her animal friends.

4805. ____. *House by Mouse* (Deutsch, 1982) k–3. A story of Henrietta, an architect mouse. She has problems in meeting the individual needs of her clients. She designs settings for the needs of a sea trout and a bear.

4806. Mendoza, George. *Henri Mouse* (Viking, 1985) k–3. Henri Mouse goes to Paris to become an artist, but causes much confusion when everything he paints disappears onto his canvas.

4807. ____. *Henri Mouse, the Juggler* (Viking, 1986) k–3. Henri Mouse becomes a world-famous juggler with magical powers when he chances upon a special juggler's ball.

4808. Meyer, Franklyn. *Me and Caleb* (Follett, 1962) 5–8. Who put the bacon grease on Mrs. Filgerson's doorknob? Who was Sir Chief Assassin and who put the elf in the snow fort? It was either Bud, his brother Caleb or both of them.

4809. ____. *Me and Caleb Again* (Follett, 1969) 5–8. Bud and Caleb tease the town grouch, torment girls, aggravate their sister and annoy their teacher. Dad gets sick and they help out with whatever needs to be done.

4810. Meyers, Susan. *P.J. Clover, Private Eye—Case of the Stolen Laundry* (S & S, 1981) 4–6. P.J. Clover and Stacy Jones try to find mysteriously missing laundry from Mrs. Baxter's back yard. Will they unravel the seemingly endless trail of false clues in time to save their clubhouse and give Mrs. Baxter a chance to enter the flower contest?

4811. ____. *P.J. Clover, Private Eye—Case of the Missing Mouse* (Dutton, 1985) 4–6. P.J. and Stacy are on the trail of a missing mouse bank that belongs to their archenemy.

4812. ____. *P.J. Clover, Private Eye—Case of the Borrowed Baby* (Dutton, 1988) 4–6. P.J. and Stacy investigate a jewelry store heist and a mystery involving a missing doll.

4813. ____. *P.J. Clover, Private Eye—Case of the Halloween Hoot* (Dutton, 1990) 4–6. While designing the perfect costumes for a Halloween contest, P.J. and Stacy try to clear their school custodian's name by tracking down the thief who entered the school after hours and stole an antique samovar.

4814. Meynell, Laurence. *Smoky Joe* (Goodchild, 1985) 3–5. By day Smoky Joe is a docile, pettable little cat; at night he is a different animal: independent, wild and confrontational. He challenges Gru the Growler, Lord of the Council. Fu the Ferocious, who is Smoky Joe's mother, deserves her name when she is outside but her name is Fluffy at the farm.

4815. ____. *Smoky Joe in Trouble* (Goodchild, 1985) 3–5. Smoky Joe tells of his successful campaign as a candidate for the Lord of the Council and the terrible dilemma he faces when the farm family goes on holiday and he is carried off in a basket by Aunt Emma when he should be presiding over his first council meeting.

4816. ____. *Smoky Joe Goes to School* (Goodchild, 1986) 3–5. Smoky Joe, the young cat, suffers when he is taken to boarding school with Ann while her parents are abroad. He escapes from the kitchen and finds Ann's dormitory. He later meets a friendly tortoise shell and a hostile ginger.

4817. Mian, Mary. *Take Three Witches* (Houghton, 1971) 4–6. Sammy and Lynn meet Miss Hartigan and Curly (invisible). Together they stop the mayor from taking land illegally and spraying insecticide that kills birds.

4818. ____. *Net to Catch War* (Houghton, 1975) 4–6. Lynn and Sammy are transported back in time to get a Navajo net that catches and stops war. They are aided by Miss Hartigan and Curly.

4819. Miller, Edna. *Mousekin's Golden House* (Prentice, 1964) k–3. Frightened at first when his path is blocked by a jack o' lantern Mousekin finds the pumpkin a safe retreat from danger, converts it into a house perfect for a mouse, and spends the winter in it.

4820. ____. *Mousekin's Christmas Eve* (Prentice, 1965) k–3. From the soft, white world of December, Mousekin ventures into a house and there beholds a tree unlike any in the forest shimmering with icicles and hung with glowing balls and with a crèche below it.

4821. ____. *Mousekin Finds a Friend* (Prentice, 1967) k–3. The twilight search of a little mouse for a friend of his own kind.

4822. ____. *Mousekin's Family* (Prentice, 1969) k–3. Complications occur when a little whitefoot mouse mistakenly believes she has found a relative.

4823. ____. *Mousekin's ABC* (Prentice, 1972) k–3. As a mouse journeys through the forest he investigates something for each letter of the alphabet— acorns, bats, cottontails, etc.

4824. ____. *Mousekin's Woodland Birthday* (Prentice, 1974) k–3. Introduces the early life of a mouse, from birth to weaning.

4825. ____. *Mousekin Takes a Trip* (Prentice, 1976) k–3. While searching for food in a house on wheels, a white-footed mouse takes an unexpected trip to the desert and sees some unusual sights.

4826. ____. *Mousekin's Woodland Sleepers* (Prentice, 1977) k–3. As he searches for a new home, Mousekin, the white-footed mouse learns how many of the forest creatures spend the winter.

4827. ____. *Mousekin's Close Call* (Prentice, 1978) k–3. Mousekin observes an opossum playing dead to escape a hungry fox. But Mousekin is caught by a weasel even though he was frozen with fear (not playing) but he was saved by a sparrow.

4828. ____. *Mousekin's Fables* (Prentice, 1982) k–3. A retelling of Aesop's fables including Mousekin and his woodland friends.

4829. ____. *Mousekin's Mystery* (Prentice, 1983) k–3. After his house is burned by lightning during a summer storm, Mousekin is frightened by a strange pale light in the dark forest which he eventually learns to be foxfire, a glow caused by fungi in decaying wood.

4830. ____. *Mousekin's Thanksgiving* (Prentice, 1985) k–3. Mousekin and his forest friends struggle to survive the winter together with a wild turkey.

4831. ____. *Mousekin's Easter Basket* (Prentice, 1986) k–3. After a harsh winter, Mousekin's springtime search for food brings him in contact with brightly colored eggs, a white rabbit, and other symbols of Easter.

4832. ____. *Mousekin's Frosty Friend* (S & S, 1990) k–3. Among many other animal tracks in the snow,

Mousekin finds a set of unfamiliar and puzzling tracks, the origin of which is eventually revealed.

4833. ____. *Mousekin's Lost Woodland* (S & S, 1992) k–3. A white-footed mouse finds himself all alone as the woodland he lives in is destroyed.

4834. Miller, Elizabeth. *Cat and Dog Raise the Roof* (Watts, 1980) 3–5. When the rain makes the roof on Pig's house fall in, Cat and Dog get all their friends to help raise the roof and make the house whole again.

4835. ____. *Cat and Dog Have a Contest* (Watts, 1980) 3–5. As the animal's friends participate in a painting contest, the reader learns about mixing the primary colors to make others.

4836. ____. *Cat and Dog Take a Trip* (Watts, 1980) 3–5. Despite the directions they've been given, Cat, Dog and Squirrel have become lost on the way to visit Rabbit in the city.

4837. ____. *Cat and Dog Give a Party* (Watts, 1980) 3–5. When Cat and Dog give a party, the guests arrive one by one until there are ten.

4838. ____. *Cat and Dog and the Mixed-up Week* (Watts, 1980) 3–5. When Cat enters the hospital to have her tonsils removed, Dog must wait a whole week for her return.

4839. ____. *Cat and Dog and the ABC's* (Watts, 1981) 3–5. While he is trying to learn the letters of the alphabet, Dog dreams of an around the world alphabet adventure.

4840. ____. *Cat and Dog Have a Parade* (Watts, 1981) 3–5. Dog can't tell left from right and the animals' parade is jeopardized, until Cat comes up with a grand idea.

4841. Miller, J.P. *Learn About Colors with Little Rabbit* (Random, 1984) k–3.

4842. ____. *Learn to Count with Little Rabbit* (Random, 1984) k–3.

4843. ____. *What Time Is It, Little Rabbit?* (Random, 1985) k–3. Little Rabbit learns how to tell time.

4844. ____. *Good Night, Little Rabbit* (Random, 1986) k–3. Little Rabbit gets ready for bed, though he tries to put off that final moment.

4845. ____. *Little Rabbit Goes to the Doctor* (Random, 1987) k–3. Little Rabbit is apprehensive when an earache necessitates a visit to the doctor's office, but kindly Dr. O'Hare relieves him of his worries.

4846. Miller, Judi. *Ghost in My Soup* (Bantam, 1985) 4–6. Scottie moves and is without friends until he meets the ghost that lives in his new house.

4847. ____. *Ghost a la Mode* (Bantam, 1990) 4–6. Scott is in a new school and is lonely, his only friends are nerdy Howard and Malcolm the mischievous ghost.

4848. Miller, Moira. *Oh, Abigail* (Methuen, 1981) 3–5. Abigail is noisy and inquisitive, bad tempered and angelic, imaginative and enthusiastic and a bit greedy. On her bad days she blames the monster she invented.

4849. ____. *Just Like Abigail* (Magent, 1983) 3–5. Abigail often finds life boring and does a lot of giggling, whether she's looking after a little baby, finding difficulty falling asleep, is scared of gurgling noises in the loft or making too frank observations about a fat shopper in the supermarket.

4850. Miller, Moira. *What Size Is Andy?* (Methuen, 1984) 2–4. Andy is child three among five. They live next door to Mrs. Anderson. When Andy complains about dragons under his bed Mrs. Anderson invites him to see hers.

4851. ____. *What Does Andy Do?* (Methuen, 1990) 2–4. Andy is the middle child of five. He has an identity problem. Dave plans a dog walking service; Tivoy is designing costumes for a play and even Uncle Billy gets into the act. But the Parent Committee gives Andy a prize for his skill as a "middle man."

4852. ____. *Where Does Andy Go?* (Methuen, 1990) 2–4.

4853. Mills, Claudia. *Dynamite Dinah* (Macmillan, 1990) 4–6. Mischievous Dinah struggles to remain the center of attention when her baby brother comes home from the hospital and her best friend gets a lead role in the class play.

4854. ____. *Dinah for President* (Macmillan, 1992) 4–6. Dinah, now in her first year of middle school, struggles to become a big fish in what seems like an ocean. In the process she discovers the value of recycling and of friendship with the elderly.

4855. ____. *Dinah in Love* (Macmillan, 1993) 4–6. Dynamite Dinah finds her feelings about sixth grade classmate Nick changing when they share involvement in a school play, a debate and a sock hop. She wonders about the importance of the seventh grade elections, the school play and even her relationship with Nick.

4856. ____. *Dinah Forever* (Farrar, 1995) 4–6. Dinah tries to cope with her thoughts about death by writing poems and talking to her elderly friend Mrs. Briscoe.

4857. Minarik, Else. *Little Bear* (Harper, 1957) 2–4. How Mother Bear copes with her Little Bear as he decides what to wear, as he makes birthday vegetable soup for fear she'd forget to bake him a cake, and as he makes a brief excursion to the moon.

4858. ____. *Father Bear Comes Home* (Harper, 1959) 2–4. Little Bear and his Friends tell of their fishing trip with Owl, and of Father Bear's homecoming. Father Bear gives his method for curing hiccups and his views on mermaids.

4859. ____. *Kiss for Little Bear* (Harper, 1959/1968) 2–4. Little Bear's thank you kiss from grandmother gets passed on to clear mountain air, and to other animals and greatly aids the skunk's romance.

4860. ____. *Little Bear's Friend* (Harper, 1960) 2–4.

Little Bear makes friends with a child named Emily. With their friends, a duck, a cat, an owl, and a hen, they play all through the happy summer. Only the departure of Emily brings tears to Little Bear.

4861. ____. *Little Bear's Visit* (Harper, 1961) 2–4. Little Bear loved to visit his grandparents. There was always so much to do , so much to see and so much to eat. His grandfather was never too tired to play and his grandmother told him stories about Mother Bear.

4862. Mirsky, Rita. *Thirty-one Brothers and Sisters* (Follett, 1952) 4–6. Nomusa's father is a Zula chief. After Nomusa's encounter with a wild boar, her father rewards her bravery. Maybe being a girl is not too bad.

4863. ____. *Seven Grandmothers* (Follett, 1955) 4–6. Nomusa wants to become a nurse and help the sick and needy. The line between witch doctor and registered nurse is a fine one.

4864. Mitchell, Adrian. *Baron Rides Out* (Philomel, 1985) k–3. Retells Baron Munchausen's boastful account of his amazing adventures as he travels around the world.

4865. ____. *Baron on the Island of Cheese* (Philomel, 1986) k–3. Retells Baron Munchausen's boastful account of some of his incredible adventures around the world, including his descent into an erupting volcano and his discovery of an island made entirely of cheese.

4866. ____. *Baron All at Sea* (Philomel, 1987) k–3. Baron Munchausen undertakes a perilous journey to aid a choir of 1,000 Africans in returning home from a European concert.

4867. Mitchell, Adrian. *Our Mammoth* (Harcourt, 1987) k–3. The Grumble twins discover a mammoth frozen inside an iceberg at the beach and take it home for a pet.

4868. ____. *Our Mammoth Goes to School* (Harcourt, 1988) k–3. The Grumble twins take their pet mammoth to school, causing quite a spectacle both there and on the class trip to the animal's park.

4869. Mitchell, Elyne. *Silver Brumbles of the South* (Hutchinson, 1965) 4–6.

4870. ____. *Silver Brumby Kingdom* (Hutchinson, 1966) 4–6. In the world of wild horses of Australia a tale of the rise of power of Silver Brumby's grandson. It is a story of storms, floods and stallion battles and their love and care of their mares.

4871. ____. *Jinki, Dingo of the Snows* (Hutchinson, 1970) 4–6. Jinki, a dingo born in a cave on Mt. Jagungal in the Snowy Mountain, is found while his parents are away hunting, by a young Aborigine boy, Koonda who caresses and talks to him but does not take him away because the pup is too young to leave his mother.

4872. ____. *Silver Brumby Whirlwind* (Hutchinson,

1973) 4–6. Last of the Brumby horse stories with stallion Thowra in a cave-in adventure.

4873. ____. *Colt from Snowy River* (Hutchinson, 1980) 4–6. A horse jumps a fence to pursue a beautiful brumby filly. They go up the Snowy River to a remote valley. They romp, fend off stallions and the filly gives birth to a foal.

4874. ____. *Snowy River Brumby* (Hutchinson, 1980) 4–6. Buzz and Yarrawa brought their stallion Nooroo to adulthood but a storm stampedes him to disaster. Nooroo is rescued and nursed back to health. He is later successful at the race track.

4875. ____. *Silver Brumby, Silver Dingo* (Hutchinson, 1960) 4–6. A life story of Thowra, a wild palomino of the Australian bush country; how he outwitted the men and stallions who hunted him, how he carried off a domesticated mare and why he eventually became a legend.

4876. Mogensen, Jan. *Teddy and the Chinese Princess* (Hamilton, 1985) k–3. Mary and Jack take Ted, a bear, for a walk. He is frightened by a hedgehog and jumps in the lake. He is rescued by a duck and has tea with a Chinese princess.

4877. ____. *Teddy's Seaside Adventure* (Hamilton, 1985) k–3. Ted, riding a fish with a bucket on his head and a net in his hand, sets off to rescue a shell princess from the claws of a cruel crab. Then he wakes up and his dream is gone.

4878. ____. *When Teddy Woke Early* (G. Stevens, 1985) k–3. When he falls from the bedroom window while Max his owner is still asleep, Teddy finds a way to get back home with the help of friends he meets along the way.

4879. ____. *Teddy's Christmas Gift* (G. Stevens, 1985) k–3. When he befriends a wounded bird, Teddy is rewarded with a flying adventure to the North Country where he finds the perfect gift for his friend Norah.

4880. ____. *Teddy in the Undersea Kingdom* (G. Stevens, 1985) k–3. While visiting the undersea kingdom of the royal clam family, Teddy daringly rescues the little clam princess from the wicked King Crab.

4881. ____. *Teddy Runs Away from Home* (Hamilton, 1986) k–3. Ted the pale-eyed bear feels he is being ignored by Jack and Mary. He takes to his heels and clambers around the house until in the attic he meets a very nice couple (a soldier and a doll) living with their friend the clockwork mouse. They all troop back to the nursery world and get lots of attention and love.

4882. Mohr, Nicholasa. *Felita* (Dial, 1979) 4–6. Felita is Puerto Rican and has difficulty making friends in her new neighborhood. The Maldonado family move back to their old neighborhood.

4883. ____. *Going Home* (Dial, 1986) 4–6. Felita is going to spend the summer in Puerto Rico. There are restrictions for young girls both at home and in Puerto Rico but Felicia finds friends in both places.

4884. Molarsky, Osmond. *Song of the Empty Bottles* (Walck, 1968) 2–4. A young boy finds collecting bottles a slow way to earn money for the guitar he wants, but his search for bottles pays off when it inspires a song which he sells.

4885. ____. *Song of the Smoggy Stars* (Walck, 1972) 3–5. After experiencing clear mountain air, a fourth grade boy is inspired to write a song to aid in the fight against air pollution.

4886. Moncure, Jane. *Magic Monsters Count to Ten* (Child's World, 1979) k–3. A counting book of monsters from one to nine. The reader makes monster ten.

4887. ____. *Magic Monsters Look for Shapes* (Child's World, 1979) k–3. Magic Monsters introduce the basic shapes and find representative examples.

4888. ____. *Magic Monsters Look for Colors* (Child's World, 1979) k–3. The magic monsters search for different colors around town.

4889. ____. *Magic Monsters Learn About Manners* (Child's World, 1980) k–3. Magic Monsters demonstrate good manners and how they apply to everyday situations.

4890. ____. *Magic Monsters Learn About Health* (Child's World, 1980) k–3. Magic Monsters demonstrate the results of following a few basic health rules.

4891. ____. *Magic Monsters Learn About Space* (Child's World, 1980) k–3. The Magic Monsters visit and study about the planets.

4892. ____. *Magic Monsters Act the Alphabet* (Child's World, 1980) k–3. Magic Monsters act out the letters of the alphabet.

4893. Moncure, Jane. *Word Bird's Circus Surprise* (Children's, 1981) k–3. Uses a very simple vocabulary to describe Word Bird's trip to the circus.

4894. ____. *No! No! Word Bird* (Children's, 1981) k–3. Word Bird's mother presents such cautions as a stove being hot, snow being cold and keeping warm and dry on a winter day.

4895. ____. *Stop! Go! Word Bird* (Children's, 1981) k–3. Uses a very simple vocabulary to follow Word Bird and his family's trip by car to their mountaintop retreat.

4896. ____. *Hi, Word Bird* (Children's, 1981) k–3. Uses a very simple vocabulary to follow Word Bird as he hatches and learns to hop, jump, swim and fly.

4897. ____. *What Does Word Bird See?* (Children's, 1982) k–3. Word Bird sees the homes of a number of different animals.

4898. ____. *Hide-and-Seek Word Bird* (Children's, 1982) k–3. Uses simple vocabulary to depict Word Bird's game with Papa.

4899. ____. *Word Bird's Hats* (Children's, 1982) k–3. Describes the hats from different occupations that Word Bird tries on during the week.

4900. ____. *Watch Out! Word Bird* (Children's, 1982) k–3. When Word Bird doesn't stay in the yard as his mother told him to, he learns the hard way that she was right.

4901. ____. *Happy Birthday, Word Bird* (Children's, 1983) k–3. Word Bird learns about the 12 months of the year as he tries to figure out when his birthday will be.

4902. ____. *Word Bird Builds a City* (Children's, 1983) k–3. Word Bird uses his blocks to build a city complete with an airport, zoo, roads, and neighborhoods.

4903. ____. *Word Bird Asks What? What?* (Children's, 1983) k–3. Word Bird goes for a walk in the country with his father and asks a lot of questions about what he sees.

4904. ____. *Word Bird's Shapes* (Children's, 1983) k–3. Word Bird uses his blocks to build various shapes.

4905. ____. *Word Bird's Spring Words* (Children's, 1985) k–3. Word Bird puts words about spring in his word house—mud puddles, shamrocks, seeds, kites and others.

4906. ____. *Word Bird's Winter Words* (Children's, 1985) k–3. Word Bird puts words about winter in his word house—snow, mittens, sled, icicles, Santa Claus and others.

4907. ____. *Word Bird's Summer Words* (Children's, 1985) k–3. Word Bird puts words about summer in his new word house—swimming pool, seashells, boat, fireworks, lemonade, parade and others.

4908. ____. *Word Bird's Fall Words* (Children's, 1985) k–3. Word Bird puts words about fall in his word house—leaves, playground, football, Pilgrims, monsters and others.

4909. ____. *Word Bird's Rainy-Day Dance* (Child's World, 1990) k–3. Animal students in school use a story dance to show how seeds, sun, and rain combine to produce growing plants.

4910. ____. *Word Bird's Magic Wand* (Child's World, 1990) k–3. Word Bird and his friends use their magic wands to make signs, stories and a variety of words.

4911. ____. *Word Bird's Dinosaur Days* (Child's World, 1990) k–3. Word Bird becomes acquainted with dinosaurs on a class trip to the museum.

4912. Moncure, Jane. *If a Dinosaur Came to Dinner* (Children's, 1978) k–3. A child imagines having a pet dinosaur.

4913. ____. *Wish-for Dinosaur* (Children's, 1988) k–3. Darrin's wish comes true when he receives a pet dinosaur for a day.

4914. Montgomery, John. *Foxy* (Watts, 1959) 4–6. David, an orphan, goes to live in the country with new foster parents. He finds a fox cub in the forest and takes it home and cares for it. He almost loses it in a fox hunt.

4915. ____. *My Friend Foxy* (Watts, 1962) 4–6. Stories about David and Foxy. Some humorous, some mysterious but all warm and satisfying. The ones about the gypsies and of the teacher are funny.

4916. ____. *Foxy and the Badgers* (Watts, 1970) 4–6. David has a pet fox. But a compulsive hunter stalks them. David and his friends outwit the hunter and save the badgers he is after.

4917. Montgomery, Robert. *Show* (Troll, 1989) 5–8. To help pay off his father's medical bills, a talented young catcher leaves college to play baseball in the minor leagues.

4918. ____. *Home Run* (Troll, 1991) 5–8. Yearning to show what he can do as a pitcher for his high school baseball team, Robbie, 15, is dismayed when the coach decides to make him a catcher instead.

4919. ____. *Grand Slam* (Troll, 1991) 5–8. Riverton High School's talented catcher, Robbie Belmont, struggles to overcome injuries and to hide his pitching aspirations.

4920. ____. *MVP* (Troll, 1991) 5–8. Freshman catcher Robbie Belmont sees the spirit of Redstone University's baseball team threatened by a serious feud between him and star pitcher Eagle Wilson.

4921. Montgomery, Rutherford. *Golden Stallion to the Rescue* (Little, 1954) 4–6. After a hard winter on Bar L Ranch Charlie and his father are visited by Mr. Wharton and Rodney. Mr. Wharton wants the Bar L for digging oil and Rodney wants Golden Boy, Charlie's horse.

4922. ____. *Golden Stallion's Victory* (Little, 1956) 4–6. Charlie and his horse, Golden Boy, are in the high country where Golden Boy watches his mares. The new owner of the ranch next to Bar L is usurping Bar L's water rights.

4923. ____. *Golden Stallion and the Mysterious Feud* (Little, 1967) 4–6. A bitter feud erupts when a family of dirt farmers purchase a piece of land near the property of a long established cattle ranching outfit.

4924. Moore, Elaine. *Grandma's House* (Lothrop, 1985) k–3. A little girl spends the summer at her grandmother's house in the country, a time which they both thoroughly enjoy.

4925. ____. *Grandma's Promise* (Lothrop, 1988) k–3. Kim spends the week after Christmas with her grandmother and enjoys every minute.

4926. ____. *Grandma's Garden* (Lothrop, 1994) k–3. Kim visits her grandmother in the spring to help her plant her garden.

4927. Moore, Inga. *Aktil's Bicycle Ride* (Oxford, 1981) k–3. Aktil, a rat, goes on a bicycle ride with his cousin Arnie. He loses control and lands in a wizard's garden. The wizard fixes his bike; then the unexpected happens but they make it home safe and sound.

4928. ____. *Aktil's Big Swim* (Oxford, 1981) k–3. Aktil is a young mouse who attempts to swim the English Channel and who, with the help of a mackerel and seagulls gets to France and back.

4929. ____. *Aktil's Rescue* (Oxford, 1983) k–3. Aktil, a rat with musical talent, rescues the Rat Racers Reggae Band from the clutches of a gang of kidnappers. Having freed the band Aktil joins them on the stage.

4930. Moore, Lilian. *I'll Meet You at the Cucumbers* (Atheneum, 1988) 2–4. Adam Mouse agrees to leave his farm for a day to visit Amanda Mouse in the city.
4931. ____. *Don't Be Afraid Amanda* (Atheneum, 1992) 2–4. Amanda Mouse repays the visit of her pen-friend Adam Mouse. Adam shows Amanda his favorite things on the farm; they have a picnic, watch baby wrens and explore a creek.

4932. Moore, Lilian. *Little Raccoon and the Thing in the Pool* (McGraw, 1963) 2–4. Little raccoon overcomes his fears of the pool and catches crayfish for dinner.
4933. ____. *Little Raccoon and the Outside World* (Whittlesey, 1965) 2–4. An inquiring raccoon ventures into the world outside the woods to explore the exciting possibilities of clotheslines, garbage cans and showers.
4934. ____. *Little Raccoon and No Trouble at All* (McGraw, 1972) 2–4. Little Raccoon has never babysat before and it's some time before he gets two baby chipmunks under control.
4935. ____. *Little Raccoon Takes Charge* (McGraw, 1972) 2–4.

4936. Moore, Ruth. *Mystery of the Lost Treasure* (Herald, 1978) 4–6. Sam and Sarah are spending the summer with a horse to ride, new friends and a mystery of lost gold coins hidden in the attic when the farm was used as an underground railroad.
4937. ____. *Mystery of the Missing Stallions* (Herald, 1984) 4–6. Sarah and Sam investigate a young Vietnamese refugee hiding in an abandoned cabin and the mysterious disappearance of thoroughbred stallions from a neighbor's horse farm.
4938. ____. *Mystery of the Secret Code* (Herald, 1985) 4–6. Teenagers searching for a treasure hidden at an old farm find a secret message written in code.
4939. ____. *Mystery of the Lost Heirloom* (Herald, 1986) 4–6. While accompanying their father to Wyalosing, Pennsylvania, to do research on a French refugee settlement of 200 years ago, twins Sam and Sarah become involved in a search for the stolen pendant of an Indian Princess.
4940. ____. *Mystery at Camp Ichthus* (Herald, 1986) 4–6. While working as counselors at a summer camp, twins Sara and Sam investigate the double mystery of food disappearing from a locked storeroom and strange occurrences in the wood.
4941. ____. *Ghost Town Mystery* (Herald, 1987) 4–6. Accompanying their father on a project that takes them to a ghost town in Nevada, teenage twins Sara and Sam discover peculiar nocturnal activities and clues to a hidden treasure of gold nuggets.

4942. ____. *Mystery at the Spanish Castle* (Herald, 1990) 4–6. While visiting relatives in Florida, teenage twins Sara and Sam investigate a mystery on a nearby key, where strange incidents are occurring in a villa left abandoned by the death of a stage magician.
4943. ____. *Mystery at Captain's Cove* (Herald, 1992) 4–6. While visiting Aunt Kay in Hawaii, twins Sara and Sam are involved in a mystery concerning a lost idol, a phantom figure and an ancient curse.

4944. Mooser, Stephen. *Funnyman's First Case* (Watts, 1981) k–3. A wise-cracking waiter uses some of his best jokes to foil a robbery.
4945. ____. *Funnyman and the Penny Dodo* (Watts, 1984) k–3. Funnyman, a detective who can't stop making jokes and puns, tried to catch the thief of the world's rarest stamp at the Royal Stamp Show.
4946. ____. *Funnyman Meets the Monster from Outer Space* (Scholastic, 1987) k–3.

4947. Mooser, Stephen. *Babe Ruth and the Home Run Derby* (Dell, 1992) 4–6. Homer stumbles into his new classroom and finds Molly and her invisible dog, Godzilla and Darryl who wears his clothes inside-out and backwards. Even the teacher is peculiar.
4948. ____. *Scary Scraped-up Skaters* (Dell, 1992) 4–6. Everything is riding on how Homer does in the Halloween costume contest—if he wins he can buy the Meatballs their own clubhouse. If he loses the Jokers will make the Meatballs disband.
4949. ____. *Headless Snowman* (Dell, 1992) 4–6. It is winter break and the Meatballs are on a school trip to the mountains for five days of skiing, sledding and snowball fights. Molly loses her plastic bear. Could be a bad omen!

4950. Mooser, Stephen. *Case of the Slippery Shark* (Troll, 1987) 3–5. A story about three children, the Hounds of Snorkeling, who search for sunken treasure. They are aided by their friend Captain Jib.
4951. ____. *Case of the Mummy Secret* (Troll, 1986) 3–5. Some hieroglyphics found on an old locket are a clue to a lost treasure for the Hounds to find.
4952. ____. *Secret of the Gold Mine* (Troll, 1987) 3–5. The Hounds go in search of cantankerous Hermit John who is rumored to know the whereabouts of a fortune in gold.
4953. ____. *Secret of the Old Mansion* (Troll, 1987) 3–5. The Hounds are hired by feuding siblings to find their aunt's lost treasure.

4954. Morey, Kathleen. *Otto Shares a Hug and Kiss* (Kid-love, 1983) k–3. Whether one is feeling fine, or something is amiss, there is joy to be found in a hug and a kiss.
4955. ____. *Otto Shares a Giggle* (Kid-love, 1984) k–3. Recounts in rhyme the travels of a giggle all through the body.

4956. ____. *Otto Shares a Tear* (Kid-love, 1986) k–3. Otto is a little guy who believes in sharing in this one he shares tears with Mom (but not with Dad). A little out-of-date in today's world.

4957. Morgan, Allen. *Christopher and the Elevator Closet* (Kids Can, 1981) k–3. Christopher's closet becomes an elevator which takes him to the clouds where he meets the giants responsible for our rain and thunder.

4958. ____. *Christopher and the Dream Dragon* (Kids Can, 1985) k–3. Christopher transports himself to the land of the Giants. He is taken to see the Dream Dragon who eats the moon, thus changing its shape.

4959. Morgan, Allen. *Matthew and the Midnight Tow Truck* (Firefly, 1987) k–3. At suppertime Matthew can't have licorice and he loses his toy van. At midnight he goes on an adventure with a truck driver. They snack on licorice, they get into a car wash that shrinks cars to matchbox size—just like the one Matthew lost.

4960. ____. *Matthew and the Midnight Turkeys* (Firefly, 1985) k–3. Matthew is being very silly and his mother calls him a turkey. He traps the midnight turkeys and together they eat pizza and then Matthew eats them.

4961. ____. *Matthew and the Midnight Money* (Firefly, 1984) k–3. Matthew needs a Mother's Day gift. The midnight money van man causes it to "rain pennies" and will split the proceeds with Matthew if he will help him clean up. They go to Midnight Mall and meet characters from the two previous books.

4962. Morgan, Helen. *Mary Kate and the Jumble Bear* (Faber, 1967) k–3. Mary Kate, five, has a happy ordinary home. The story gives a very detailed description of familiar things that appeal to little girls.

4963. ____. *Mary Kate and the School Bus* (Faber, 1970) k–3.

4964. ____. *Mary Kate* (Nelson, 1972) k–3. Recounts the special experiences of a five-year-old girl at home and at school.

4965. Morgan, Michaela. *Visitors for Edward* (Dutton, 1987) k–3. Edward imagines all sorts of interesting possibilities when he overhears his parents discussing the arrival of some mysterious visitors.

4966. ____. *Edward Gets a Pet* (Dutton, 1987) k–3. When his mother takes him to the pet shop to make a selection, Edward imagines what it would be like to own a tiger, eagle, gorilla, and whale.

4967. ____. *Edward Hurts His Knee* (Dutton, 1988) k–3. Edward's vivid imaginings on the way to Grandma's energize him but enervate his mother.

4968. ____. *Edward Loses His Teddy Bear* (Dutton, 1988) k–3. Edward's teddy bear seems to have disappeared while his mother was cleaning up his room, but his fate is revealed at the end of the laundry cycle.

4969. Morgan, Michaela. *Helpful Betty Solves a Mystery* (Carolrhoda, 1994) k–3. Helpful Betty hippopotamus finds a magnifying glass while tidying up the jungle and goes looking for a mystery to solve.

4970. ____. *Helpful Betty to the Rescue* (Carolrhoda, 1994) k–3. Helpful Betty the hippopotamus hears a cry and sets off to rescue a monkey she assumes is stuck up in a tree.

4971. Morgan, Patricia. *River Adventure* (Troll, 1987) 4–6. This story follows a group of canoeist as they explore and enjoy 92 miles of waterway along the Allagash River in northern Maine.

4972. ____. *Mountain Adventure* (Troll, 1988) 4–6. Follows a group of hikers as they climb Mount Katahdin, highest peak in Maine, observing the flora, fauna and sights of interest along the way.

4973. Morressy, John. *Humans on Ziax II* (Walker, 1974) 4–6. Toren is a prisoner on a foreign planet. After falling from an aircraft, he is nursed back to health by the Imbur creatures who are similar to Earthlings but are pacifists. Toren learns their peaceful ways.

4974. ____. *Drought on Ziax II* (Walker, 1978) 4–6. Life on Ziax II is threatened by a severe drought, the Earth Pioneers and the Imbur search for a probable cause for the problem. In their search they discover that the slaying of the Sork has upset the ecology.

4975. Morris, Ann. *Eleanora Mousie Catches a Cold* (Collier, 1987) k–3. Eleanora Mousie learns how to take care of her cold and how to have fun while she rests and recovers.

4976. ____. *Eleanora Mousie's Gray Day* (Collier, 1987) k–3. On a gray, rainy day, everything seems to go wrong for Eleanora, but her friend Fiona helps her through.

4977. ____. *Eleanora Mousie Makes a Mess* (Collier, 1987) k–3. Everything Eleanora Mousie does creates a mess, but she enjoys herself and makes others happy.

4978. ____. *Eleanora Mousie in the Dark* (Collier, 1987) k–3. Fear of the dark hinders Eleanora's going to sleep, but Mama helps to soothe her.

4979. Moss, Elaine. *Peter Piper's Birthday Party* (Deutsch, 1984) k–3. Everyday life of eight small children. In turn they go to birthday parties. The book ends with a question and the answer is found on the facing page.

4980. ____. *Peter Pipers at the Fair* (Deutsch, 1984) k–3. The everyday life of eight small children. In turn they visit a fair. The book ends with a question and the answer to be found on the facing page.

4981. ____. *Peter Pipers at the Wildlife Park* (Deutsch, 1984) k–3. Eight children in turn visit the

Wildlife Park. The book ends with a question and the answer is found on the facing page.

4982. ____. *Peter Pipers in the Garden* (Deutsch, 1984) k–3. Eight children in turn visit the garden. Each book ends with a question and the answer is found on the facing page.

4983. Mueller, Virginia. *Playhouse for Monster* (Whitman, 1985) k–3. Sitting in his playhouse alone with one cookie and one glass of milk, Monster realizes it is more fun to share than to keep everything for himself.

4984. ____. *Monster and the Baby* (Whitman, 1985) k–3. Trying to entertain his baby brother by building a tower out of blocks, Monster finds there is only one way to stop him from crying.

4985. ____. *Halloween Mask for Monster* (Whitman, 1986) k–3. Monster tries on girl, boy, cat, and dog masks at Halloween but since they are all too scary he decides to go as himself.

4986. ____. *Monster Can't Sleep* (Whitman, 1986) k–3. Monster can't fall asleep no matter what his parents do until he tries to put his pet spider to sleep.

4987. ____. *Monster Goes to School* (Whitman, 1991) k–3. At school Monster learns about time, drawing a clock with pictures that represent his day.

4988. ____. *Monster's Birthday Hiccups* (Whitman, 1991) k–3. At his birthday party, nothing helps Monster get rid of his hiccups until he has a wonderful idea.

4989. Muir, Frank. *What-a-Mess* (Doubleday, 1977) k–3. A puppy uses the painful process of trial and error to find what kind of animal he is or isn't.

4990. ____. *What-a-Mess, the Good* (Doubleday, 1978) k–3. A well-meaning puppy decides to show everyone how good he can be by ridding his owners' home of ants.

4991. ____. *Prince What-a-Mess* (Benn, 1980) k–3. An Afghan hound wants to be called "Prince" not "What-a-Mess." He tries to improve his appearance by rolling in varnish, then sand and then in a rose bed. He then runs away in disgrace and is attacked by a snake, bitten by a tiger and wants to return home.

4992. ____. *Super What-a-Mess* (Benn, 1980) k–3. What-a-Mess is a dog. He watches television, imagines himself as Superman and jumps off the roof.

4993. ____. *What-a-Mess and the Cat Next Door* (Benn, 1982) k–3. Without realizing it was a Christmas tree What-a-Mess takes it out and burns it. He does this as a good deed to earn him a sister which he wants because he feels he can boss her around.

4994. ____. *What-a-Mess in Summer* (Blackie, 1982) k–3. What-a-Mess tries to tunnel through to Australia and in so doing breaks the main water pipe and everyone gets a refreshing bath. The next three books feature What-a-Mess in the three other seasons.

4995. ____. *What-a-Mess in Winter* (Blackie, 1982) k–3.

4996. ____. *What-a-Mess in Autumn* (Blackie, 1982) k–3.

4997. ____. *What-a-Mess in Spring* (Blackie, 1982) k–3.

4998. ____. *What-a-Mess at the Beach* (Benn, 1984) k–3.

4999. ____. *What-a-Mess Goes to School* (Blackie, 1985) k–3. What-a-Mess, an Afghan hound, wants to escape being sent to a training school. He saves the life of a hedgehog and names her Cynthia. He is the worst pupil at school but enjoys the social life. He is helped to pass his test by Cynthia.

5000. ____. *What-a-Mess Has Breakfast* (Blackie, 1987) k–3. Left alone in the house as punishment for a whole day, What-a-Mess empties all four bowls of food at once and spends the remaining hours looking for food, getting involved with the next-door cat, a passing mongrel and a hedgehog, all of which help in his depredations. The next three books feature What-a-Mess and further meals.

5001. ____. *What-a-Mess Has Tea* (Benn, 1987) k–3.

5002. ____. *What-a-Mess Has Lunch* (Benn, 1987) k–3.

5003. ____. *What-a-Mess Has Supper* (Benn, 1987) k–3.

5004. ____. *What-a-Mess and the Hairy Monster* (Benn, 1991) k–3.

5005. Muntean, Michaela. *Bicycle Bear* (Parents, 1983) k–3. Items are never too big or too small—Bicycle Bear delivers them all.

5006. ____. *Bicycle Bear Rides Again* (Parents, 1989) k–3. When his uncle, Bicycle Bear, takes a vacation, Trike Bear attempts to take over his delivery job and finds it more difficult than he had thought.

5007. Muntean, Michaela. *They Call Me Boober Fraggle* (Holt, 1983) k–3. Unlike the other Fraggles (Furry, fuzzy creatures the size of monkeys) living in Fraggle Rock, Boober is a worrier and he really worries when he realizes that his fellow Fraggles thinks he is a wet blanket.

5008. ____. *Tale of Traveling Matt* (Holt, 1984) k–3. A Fraggle ponders on the adventures of his Uncle Matt in the outside world as he meets for the first time cows, garbage trucks, and people.

5009. ____. *What Do Doozers Do?* (Holt, 1984) k–3. The Fraggles can't understand why the Doozers love to work and build.

5010. ____. *Doozer Disaster* (Holt, 1984) k–3. Wembley Fraggle, longing for something exciting to happen to him, picks a giant radish in the garden of the Gorgs, then falls down the hole it has left behind.

5011. ____. *Fraggle Countdown* (Holt, 1985) k–3. Fifteen Fraggles set off on a day of adventures at the end of which Wembley finds he has been left all alone.

5012. ____. *Monkey and the Festival of the Bells* (Holt, 1985) k–3. On the eve of the Festival of the

Bells, Mokey is busy giving presents to the other Fraggles, but it takes one of the wise Minstrels to make her realize the holiday's true meaning.

5013. ____. *Meet the Fraggles* (Holt, 1985) k–3. Introduces Doozer, Fraggles, and Grogs and offers advice on how to handle them as houseguests. It would be best NOT to let a Gorg in your house.

(For additional books on the Fraggles, Boober, Gobo, Mokey, Red or Wembley, *see* Brennan, Joseph; Calder, Lyn; Calmenson, Stephanie; Gilkow, Louise; Gilmour, H.B.; Grand, Rebecca; Perlberg, Deborah; Stevenson, Jocelyn; Teitelbaum, Michael; Weiss, Ellen; Young, David.)

5014. Murphy, Elspeth. *Mystery of the Candy Box* (Bethany House, 1989) 2–4. Sarah-Jane and her cousins investigate the mystery of a box full of odd items, the legacy of an elderly man she befriended before his recent death.

5015. ____. *Mystery of the White Elephant* (Bethany House, 1994) 2–4. When Timothy and his cousins go to the church swap meet, they discover a thief who has stolen the white elephant they plan to buy, and it's up to them to find the culprit.

5016. ____. *Mystery of the Silent Nightingale* (Bethany House, 1994) 2–4. Sarah-Jane and her two cousins solve a mystery involving an antique locket they plan to give their favorite baby-sitter.

5017. ____. *Mystery of the Wrong Dog* (Bethany House, 1994) 2–4. Titus and his cousins are taking care of their neighbors' crabby Yorkshire terrier when the dog suddenly becomes sweet-tempered and the cousins have a mystery on their hands.

5018. ____. *Mystery of the Dancing Angels* (Bethany, 1995) 2–4. Cousins Sarah-Jane, Timothy and Titus have a distant four-year-old, precocious cousin who comes to visit. There is a mystery of great-great-grandmother Patience's missing necklace.

5019. ____. *Mystery of the Hobo's Message* (Bethany, 1995) 2–4. Sarah-Jane, Timothy and Titus visit their grandparents. They and two new friends find a secret code carved in a tree and learn that the carvings are old hobo symbols. They use the code to warn their grandfather of a developer's scam.

5020. ____. *Mystery of the Haunted Lighthouse* (Bethany, 1995) 2–4. Titus, Timothy and Sarah-Jane go to look at a lighthouse with the intent to buy. It shows signs of vandalism and is "haunted" by a boy to whom the lighthouse was a special place and who doesn't want anyone to buy it.

5021. ____. *Mystery of the Dolphin Detective* (Bethany House, 1995) 2–4. Ten-year-old cousins Titus, Timothy, and Sarah-Jane go on vacation together and set out to discover why dolphins they are visiting don't seem to want to eat.

5022. ____. *Mystery of the Eagle Feathers* (Bethany, 1995) 2–4. Sarah-Jane, Timothy and Titus go to a powwow. Tim meets his pen pal Anthony Two Trees. Feathers are disappearing from the Indian outfits. They are stolen to be sold on the black market.

5023. ____. *Mystery of the Silly Goose* (Bethany House, 1996) 2–4. Ten-year-old Timothy and his cousins Sarah-Jane and Titus, who make up the Three Cousins Detective Club investigate when all the lawn ornaments in the neighborhood disappear and then are put back in the wrong places.

5024. ____. *Mystery of the Copycat Clown* (Bethany House, 1996) 2–4. Titus, Timothy and Sarah-Jane help to solve the related mysteries surrounding a missing photograph and the appearance of a copycat clown at a hospital fundraiser.

5025. ____. *Mystery of the Honeybee's Secret* (Bethany House, 1996) 2–4. While watching over her neighbor's beehives, Sarah-Jane, Titus and Timothy find an important clue to the location of a missing strongbox, which contains a valuable recipe.

5026. Murphy, Elspeth. *Mystery of the Empty School* (Chariot, 1989) 2–4. With the help of a teacher, three cousins investigate strange happenings at a school.

5027. ____. *Mystery of the Disappearing Papers* (Bethany House, 1989) 2–4. Three cousins investigate the disappearance of a college student's research paper.

5028. ____. *Mystery of the Secret Snowman* (Bethany House, 1989) 2–4. Three cousins explore the mysterious circumstances around a snowman and a quarreling brother and sister.

5029. ____. *Mystery of the Golden Pelican* (Bethany House, 1990) 2–4. Three cousin detectives figure out the meaning of a sick man's cryptic words about a pelican.

5030. ____. *Mystery of the Princess Doll* (Bethany House, 1990) 2–4. The three cousins investigate the disappearance of an old doll from an antique show.

5031. ____. *Mystery of the Hidden Egg* (Bethany House, 1991) 2–4. Timothy and his two cousins try to solve the mystery of a key hidden inside an Easter egg.

5032. ____. *Mystery of the Clumsy Juggler* (Bethany House, 1991) 2–4. Three cousins helping Professor McKay at a medieval fair are able to collect enough information to trap the thief of a valuable old Gospel.

5033. Murphy, Elspeth. *Mystery of the Silent Idol* (Chariot, 1988) 2–4. Three cousins uncover a drug dealing operation.

5034. ____. *Mystery of the Tattletale Parrot* (Chariot, 1988) 2–4. Three cousins solve the mystery of who owns the parrot that has been taught to misuse God's name in swearing; they uncover a burglary ring.

5035. ____. *Mystery of the Vanishing Present* (Chariot, 1988) 2–4. Three cousins endeavor to find out who gave a painting entitled Sabbath Day to their grandfather for a birthday present.

5036. ____. *Mystery of the Double Trouble* (Chariot, 1988) 2–4. Tim and two cousins set out to find a boy who seems to be his double.

5037. ____. *Mystery of the Second Map* (Chariot,

1988) 2–4. The suspicions of three cousins about a possible theft at a building site lead them to prevent a crime.

5038. ____. *Mystery of the Silver Dolphin* (Chariot, 1988) 2–4. Titus and his two cousins set out to prove his innocence in the disappearance of a small silver dolphin.

5039. Murphy, Elspeth. *Barney Wigglesworth and the Church Flood* (Bethany House, 1988) k–3. When Barney the mouse's family takes in a family of flood victims, Barney resents having to play and share his toys with little Christopher.

5040. ____. *Barney Wigglesworth and the Birthday Surprise* (Bethany House, 1988) k–3. When the Mouse friends encounter difficulties in making a surprise birthday cake for Nana, they consider giving up until Nana offers some good advise.

5041. ____. *Barney Wigglesworth and the Party That Almost Wasn't* (Bethany House, 1988) k–3. The party plans of Barney and his mouse friends are threatened until they decide to cooperate.

5042. ____. *Barney Wigglesworth and the Smallest Christmas Pageant* (Bethany House, 1988) k–3. Barney and his mouse friends cheer up and help Gwendolyn, the Christmas pageant director, during a crisis.

5043. Murphy, Jill. *Five Minutes Peace* (Putnam, 1986) k–3. Mrs. Large's elephant children follow her everywhere. She finally retreats to the bathtub. They follow her. She slips away, leaving them to play in the tub while she catches a cup of coffee in peace.

5044. ____. *All in One Piece* (Putnam, 1987) k–3. Four young elephants help their parents get ready to go to a dinner dance.

5045. ____. *Piece of Cake* (Putnam, 1989) k–3. When Mama Elephant puts her family on a diet, their willpower remains strong until Granny sends a cake.

5046. Murphy, Jill. *Peace at Last* (Dial, 1980) k–3. Mr. Bear spends the night searching for enough peace and quiet to go to sleep.

5047. ____. *What Next, Baby Bear* (Dial, 1984) k–3. Baby Bear wants to go to the moon. He finds a cardboard box for a rocket, a colander for a space helmet and off he goes. He has a picnic on the moon. On the way back he gets dirty and makes it home in time for a bath.

5048. Murphy, Jill. *Worst Witch* (Viking, 1988) 3–5. Mildred goes to Miss Cackle's Academy for witches and has a disastrous time.

5049. ____. *Worst Witch Strikes Again* (Viking, 1988) 3–5. At Miss Cackle's Academy the witch girls learn broomstick riding, cat training, spells, potions and chants.

5050. ____. *Bad Spell for the Worst Witch* (Viking, 1982) 3–5. The story of Mildred Hubble's misadventures at Miss Cackle's Academy for Witches.

5051. ____. *Worst Witch at Sea* (Candlewick, 1995) 3–5. Young Mildred, an apprentice witch with a reputation for being the worst student at Miss Cackle's Academy for Witches, smuggles her cat Tabby on a class trip to Gloomy Cove with unexpected results.

5052. Musgrave, Florence. *Oh, Sarah* (Ariel, 1953) 5–8. Sarah is an unusual child. She steals money from the Missionary Fund for candy and then regrets it. But she helps when disaster comes and gets the bicycle she has worked for.

5053. ____. *Sarah Hastings* (Hastings, 1960) 5–8. Sarah is now 15 and befriends a German family at the start of World War II. She gets her first boyfriend, takes piano lessons, and is in a singing contest and, most alarming is in a mine cave-in.

5054. Myers, Bernice. *Herman and the Bears Again* (Four Winds, 1976) 2–4. Herman is happily visiting his bear friends in the woods when a scout leader and his troop discover him and insist on "rescuing" him.

5055. ____. *Herman and the Bears and the Giants* (Four Winds, 1979) 2–4. The adventures of a boy who rides his bicycle with three bears on his shoulders. He also performs in the circus.

5056. Myers, Bernice. *Not at Home?* (Lothrop, 1981) 2–4. A misunderstanding causes a rift in Sally and Lorraine's very strong friendship.

5057. ____. *Extraordinary Invention* (Macmillan, 1984) 2–4. Sally and her father, who love to invent things together, make a time machine as a present for Sally's mother—only something goes terribly wrong.

5058. Myers, Walter. *Me, Mop and the Moondance Kid* (Delacorte, 1988) 4–6. Adoption has taken T.J., 11, and his brother Moondance out of the institution where they grew up, but they stay in touch with their friend Mop's attempts to become adopted herself.

5059. ____. *Mop, Moondance and the Nagasaki Knights* (Delacorte, 1992) 4–6. After T.J. and his younger brother are adopted the biggest problems they face are winning an international baseball tournament, held in their hometown, and helping a homeless teammate.

5060. Nabb, Magdalen. *Josie Smith* (McElderry, 1989) 3–5. Follows the amusing misadventures of a little girl as she shops for the perfect birthday gift for her mother, blackens a blackboard, and cares for a lost cat.

5061. ____. *Josie Smith at the Seashore* (McElderry, 1990) 3–5. Josie, six, spends a day at the beach with Mum and Gran. The day is highlighted by a donkey ride, making a dog friend, and getting lost.

5062. ____. *Josie Smith at School* (McElderry, 1991) 3–5. A story of Josie's adventures in school told from the point of view of Josie. The tribulations and triumphs of a child whose best intentions often land her in trouble.

5063. ____. *Josie Smith and Eileen* (McElderry, 1992) 3–5. Josie gets into a fight with her best friend, Eileen, but they make up. Josie spends the night with Eileen and they pretend to be bride and bridesmaid.

5064. Namioka, Lensey. *Yang the Youngest and His Terrible Ear* (Little, 1992) 3–5. Recently arrived in Seattle from China, musically untalented Yingtao is faced with giving a violin performance to attract new students for his father; he would rather be working on friendships and playing baseball.

5065. ____. *Yang the Third and Her Impossible Family* (Yearling, 1996) 3–5. Yingmel changed her name to Mary to be American; but her family is still Chinese. Mary adopts her friend Holly's kitten but she must keep it a secret because of family objections.

5066. Naylor, Phyllis. *Boys Start the War* (Delacorte, 1993) 4–6. Disgusted that a family with three girls moves into the house across the river, nine-year-old Wally and his three brothers declare a practical joke war on the girls.

5067. ____. *Girls Get Even* (Delacorte, 1993) 4–6. As Halloween approaches, the three Malloy sisters find themselves continually trying to get even with the four Hatford brothers, who have been playing tricks on them since the Malloys moved from Ohio to West Virginia.

5068. ____. *Boys Against Girls* (Delacorte, 1994) 4–6. The Hatford brothers cannot imagine spending Thanksgiving dinner with the Malloy sisters as the practical jokes and rivalries between the two families continue.

5069. Naylor, Phyllis. *Witch's Sister* (Atheneum, 1975) 4–6. Lynn thinks her sister is learning witchcraft from a neighbor and is convinced on the weekend she and her sister are left in the neighbor's care.

5070. ____. *Witch Water* (Atheneum, 1977) 4–6. Lynn knows that Mrs. Tuggle is involved in witchcraft but can't convince anyone of her evil.

5071. ____. *Witch Herself* (Atheneum, 1978) 4–6. Lynn and Mouse look into Mrs. Tuggle's past to see if they can prove she is a witch.

5072. ____. *Witch's Eye* (Delacorte, 1990) 4–6. Though suspected witch-neighbor Mrs. Tuggle has died, her glass eye resurfaces, bringing new dangers and terrors to Lynn's family.

5073. ____. *Witch Weed* (Delacorte, 1991) 4–6. A series of mysterious events and the strange behavior of a group of their schoolmates convince Lynn and her best friend, Mouse, that the destructive power of a witch recently killed in a fire is still very much alive.

5074. ____. *Witch Returns* (Delacorte, 1992) 4–6. Convinced that the old woman who recently moved into the neighborhood is really the "dead" Mrs. Tuggle, Lynn and Mouse try to find help in withstanding her witchcraft.

5075. Naylor, Phyllis. *Agony of Alice* (Atheneum, 1985) 4–6. Alice is a motherless teenager. Her friends are Pamela and Elizabeth. She wants Miss Cole for a teacher but gets Mrs. Plotkin. At the end she realizes this was for the best.

5076. ____. *Alice in Rapture, Sort Of* (Atheneum, 1989) 4–6. Alice and Patrick are dating and in love. She wonders about the effects of kissing and decides they should be friends. Alice, Elizabeth and Pamela have a secret pact to find a boyfriend.

5077. ____. *Reluctantly Alice* (Delacorte, 1992) 5–8. Alice experiences the joys and embarrassments of seventh grade while advising her father and older brother on their love lives.

5078. ____. *All But Alice* (Atheneum, 1992) 5–8. Alice is now in seventh grade. She faces questions about sisterhood, her brother's three girlfriends, her father dating one of her teachers, sex education, in-crowds and the opposite sex.

5079. ____. *Alice in April* (Macmillan, 1993) 5–8. While trying to survive seventh grade, Alice discovers that turning 13 will make her the woman of the house at home, so she starts a campaign to get more appreciation for taking care of her father and older brother.

5080. ____. *Alice In-Between* (Atheneum, 1994) 5–8. When motherless Alice turns 13 she feels in-between, no longer a child but not yet a woman, and discovers that growing up can be both frustrating and wonderful.

5081. ____. *Alice the Brave* (Atheneum, 1995) 5–8. The summer before eighth grade, Alice tries to confront her fears, not the least of which is her fear of deep water.

5082. ____. *Alice in Lace* (Atheneum, 1996) 5–8. While planning a wedding as part of an assignment for her eighth grade health class, Alice thinks about her father and older brother's love lives and learns that you cannot prepare for all of life's decisions.

5083. Naylor, Phyllis. *Mad Gasser of Bessledorf Street* (Atheneum, 1983) 4–6. Sam suspects the culprit who is gassing assembly line workers in the parachute factory lives in the hotel his family manages.

5084. ____. *Bodies in the Bessledorf Hotel* (Atheneum, 1986) 4–6. Dead bodies which appear and disappear mysteriously are threatening to lose Sam's father his job as manager of the Bessledorf Hotel. What can be done? How do you find a ghost?

5085. ____. *Bernie and the Bessledorf Ghost* (Atheneum, 1990) 4–6. Living at the Bessledorf Hotel where his father works as the manager, Bernie tries to solve the mystery of the troubled young ghost who wanders the halls of the hotel at night.

5086. ____. *Face in the Bessledorf Parlor* (Atheneum, 1993) 4–6. Convinced that the strange things happening at the funeral parlor next door to his family's hotel are somehow connected to a recent robbery, Bernie determines to become famous by proving his theory and catching the thief.

5087. Newman, Robert. *Case of the Baker Street Irregulars* (Atheneum, 1978) 4–6. Andrew and his tutor come to London. Mr. Dickinson is kidnapped and Andrew is taken in by a Baker Street family.

5088. ____. *Case of the Vanishing Corpse* (Atheneum, 1980) 4–6. Andrew and Sara are involved in a series of jewel robberies, Andrew's mother being one of the victims. They suspect an Egyptian priest who lives on the estate next door.

5089. ____. *Case of the Somerville Secret* (Atheneum, 1981) 4–6. Andrew and Sara help an inspector from Scotland Yard uncover the identity of a murderer and a monster associated with Lord Somerville, an Assyriologist.

5090. ____. *Case of the Threatened King* (Atheneum, 1982) 4–6. Sara is missing and Andrew must find out why she was abducted, why Maria was also taken and where they are. The visit of the king of Serbia is somehow at the bottom of all this.

5091. ____. *Case of the Etruscan Treasure* (Atheneum, 1983) 4–6. Already in New York with Andrew's actress mother, Sara and Edward join inspector Wyatt on a mysterious case when he arrives from London. They recover jewels that are hidden in an Etruscan statuary.

5092. ____. *Case of the Frightened Friend* (Atheneum, 1984) 4–6. Andrew and inspector Wyatt help a friend whose father has mysteriously died, whose grandfather is a complete invalid, and whose stepmother is behaving suspiciously with the doctor.

5093. ____. *Case of the Murdered Players* (Atheneum, 1985) 4–6. When two actresses of the London stage in the 1890s die under circumstances suspiciously like those that killed three actresses ten years before, Andrew and inspector Peter Wyatt fear for Andrew's actress mother.

5094. ____. *Case of the Indian Curse* (Atheneum, 1986) 4–6. While inspector Wyatt and Andrew's mother are on their honeymoon, Andrew and Sara investigate a mysterious statue that produces light and sound.

5095. ____. *Case of the Watching Boy* (Atheneum, 1987) 4–6. Two English schoolboys inadvertently become involved in a kidnapping which strangely connects with the succession to the throne of Rumania.

5096. Newman, Robert. *Merlin's Mistake* (Atheneum, 1970) 5–8. Tertius was endowed with knowledge of the future instead of the past. He and David set out on a quest to find a dragon and save King Galleron's kingdom from the Black Knight.

5097. ____. *Testing of Tertius* (Atheneum, 1973) 5–8. Tertius and Brian, with Lianor, set out to undo the spell put on Merlin by an evil sorcerer.

5098. Newton, Suzanne. *End to Perfect* (Viking, 1984) 5–8. Arden and Dorjo have perfect attendance records. Then Dorjo doesn't show up at school; her sister doesn't show up at work; and their mother doesn't seem to care.

5099. ____. *Place Between* (Viking, 1986) 5–8. Arden's family must move to a new city and she is determined not to like it, but when she visits her hometown it is not as she remembered it. She learns that everything changes, even herself.

5100. Nicoll, Helen. *Meg and Mog* (Atheneum, 1973) k–3. Meg the witch meets her friends for a Halloween party but something goes wrong with the spell they cast.

5101. ____. *Meg's Eggs* (Atheneum, 1973) k–3. Meg's spells go wrong and the super eggs hatch dinosaurs.

5102. ____. *Meg on the Moon* (Heinemann, 1973) k–3. Meg takes a trip through outer space.

5103. ____. *Meg at Sea* (Harvey, 1974) k–3. Meg, Mog (her cat) and Owl are stranded on a desert island.

5104. ____. *Mog at the Zoo* (Puffin, 1984) k–3. Meg and Mog go to the zoo, where Mog is captured and caged until Meg thinks of a spell to free him.

5105. ____. *Mog in the Fog* (Puffin, 1986) k–3. Climbing up a mountain, Meg the witch and Mog the cat run into thick fog and bump into something very strange.

5106. ____. *Mog's Box* (Heinemann, 1987) k–3. Meg the witch mixes a magic potion to make a lunch box for her cat, Mog. Inside is a caterpillar. It then becomes a butterfly.

5107. Nielsen, Shelly. *Just Victoria* (Chariot, 1986) 5–8. The summer after sixth grade, Vic tries to prepare for seventh grade so she won't be a nerd; she has problems with her best friend and worries about her grandmother's health.

5108. ____. *More Victoria* (Cook, 1986) 5–8. Vic's first semester at junior high brings her worries: a rowdy but popular guy has a crush on her; she gets sent to the principal's office for misbehaving; and her parents begin arguing.

5109. ____. *Take a Bow, Victoria* (Cook, 1986) 5–8. Besides the embarrassment of her pregnant mother coming to school and her grandmother working on a school production, Victoria must deal with her own mixed desires of being a star or remaining safely backstage.

5110. ____. *Only Kidding, Victoria* (Cook, 1986) 5–8. Victoria's summer at a resort in Minnesota, far from her Minneapolis friends, forces her to rely on her own resources and results in a new appreciation for her family.

5111. ____. *Maybe It's Love, Victoria* (Chariot, 1987) 5–8. As Vic enters eighth grade, she has a number of things to think about: her friend Chel's feelings about becoming a Christian, and the mysteries of falling in love.

5112. ____. *Autograph, Please, Victoria* (Chariot, 1987) 5–8. Junior high student Victoria learns to deal with a young brother's learning disability, wins a writing contest and remembers that God loves people just the way they are.

5113. ____. *Who's Your Hero, Victoria?* (Chariot, 1989) 5–8. Feeling left out when her friends fall madly in love with a young television star, Vic, 13, turns to God during a difficult time.

5114. ____. *Then and Now, Victoria* (Chariot, 1990) 5–8. Victoria's thirteenth year is highlighted by her family's impending adoption of a new baby and a school report on her great-grandfather.

5115. Nightingale, Sandy. *Hamnet and the Pig Afloat* (Dent, 1983) k–3. Hamnet finds his Uncle Nugent's treasure, loses it at cards to a pirate captain and then regains it and escapes with the help of a friendly whale.

5116. ____. *One Pink Pig* (Andersen, 1992) k–3. A counting book. Acrobatic pigs perform tricks. There is a pig pyramid, a pillow fight and a picnic.

5117. ____. *Pink Pigs Aplenty* (Harcourt, 1992) k–3. Just how many pink pigs are there in the piggies circus and what are those pastel porcine performers doing?

5118. Nilsson, Ulf. *Little Sister Rabbit* (Atlantic, 1983) k–3. While their parents are out gathering carrots, a young rabbit baby-sits his little sister for the first time.

5119. ____. *Little Bunny Gets Lost* (Chronicle, 1988) k–3. Little Bunny is happy to be off on an adventure without her annoying older brother until she gets lost.

5120. ____. *Little Bunny and Her Friends* (Chronicle, 1988) k–3. Six animal friends have a problem finding a recreational activity that they will all be able to complete and enjoy.

5121. ____. *Little Bunny and the Hungry Fox* (Chronicle, 1989) k–3. Little Bunny's relaxing walk is interrupted by a hungry fox.

5122. ____. *Little Bunny at the Beach* (Chronicle, 1989) k–3. At the beach Little Bunny's big brother comes to the rescue when her playful antics cause her to drift out to sea.

5123. Nixon, Joan. *Family Apart* (Bantam, 1987) 5–8. When their mother can no longer support them, six siblings are sent by the Children's Aid Society of New York City to live with farm families in Missouri in 1860.

5124. ____. *Caught in the Act* (Bantam, 1988) 5–8. Michael, 11, from New York City is sent to a foster home, a Missouri farm with a sadistic owner, a bullying son, and a number of secrets, one of which may be murder.

5125. ____. *In the Face of Danger* (Bantam, 1988) 5–8. This is another episode in the lives of the six Kelly children. Each book covers one orphan's touching story of the people who adopted them and their adjustment to it.

5126. ____. *Place to Belong* (Bantam, 1989) 5–8. In

1856, having traveled with his sister from New York to a foster home on a farm in Missouri, Danny, 10, plans to get his foster father to send for and marry his mother.

5127. ____. *Dangerous Promise* (Delacorte, 1994) 5–8. After being taken in by Captain Taylor and his wife in Kansas, Mike Kelly, 12, and his friend Todd Blakely join the Union army as musicians and see the horrors of war firsthand in Missouri.

5128. Nixon, Joan. *High Trail to Danger* (Bantam, 1991) 5–8. Sarah sets out alone in 1879 to find her father. Her mother just died and she thinks her aunt and uncle are trying to take their boardinghouse away from her. She has many adventures and close calls.

5129. ____. *Deadly Promise* (Delacorte, 1992) 5–8. Sarah risks her life to clear her murdered father's name and expose big time criminal activity in the lawless mining town of Leadville.

5130. Nixon, Joan. *If You Say So, Claude* (Warne, 1980) k–3. Shirley and Claude move across Texas in their covered wagon, looking for a peaceful place to settle down.

5131. ____. *Beats Me, Claude* (Viking, 1986) k–3. Exciting escapades follow Shirley's attempts to make an apple pie for Claude until one day an orphan boy makes a pie that wins him Claude's favor.

5132. ____. *Fat Chance, Claude* (Viking, 1987) k–3. A zany Texas couple, Shirley and Claude, grow up and meet in the gold mining hills of Colorado.

5133. ____. *You Bet Your Britches, Claude* (Viking, 1989) k–3. Shirley and Claude lead a settled life with their adopted son, Tom, until Shirley goes to town to retrieve Tom's sister, Bessie, and the two run into more than their share of trouble with criminals.

5134. ____. *That's the Spirit, Claude* (Viking, 1992) k–3. When Shirley convinces her husband Claude to help fulfill their adopted daughter's dream of a visit from Santa, she doesn't reckon on the real Santa Claus showing up at their place in Texas.

5135. Noble, Trinka. *Day Jimmy's Boa Ate the Wash* (Dial, 1984) k–3. Jimmy's boa constrictor wreaks havoc on the class trip to a farm.

5136. ____. *Jimmy's Boa Bounces Back* (Dial, 1984) k–3. Jimmy's boa constrictor creates some difficulties at a garden club meeting. There are hilarious, madcap adventures.

5137. ____. *Jimmy's Boa and the Big Splash* (Dial, 1989) k–3. Jimmy's birthday party at Sealand turns out to be a big splash when everyone ends up in the big tank.

5138. Norby, Lisa. *Holly Hudnut Admiration Society* (Bullseye, 1989) 4–6. Rejected by Holly Hudnut and the other popular girls in the fifth grade's in crowd, Jan and her friends from their own club S.T.A.R.'s (Sugar Tree Acres Route) and discover that there are more valuable things than popularity.

5139. ____. *Rent-a-Star* (Knopf, 1989) 4–6. The Clovers start bragging about their new clubhouse. The jealous S.T.A.R.s hire themselves out for odd jobs to earn money to fix up their clubhouse, an old stone building, but discover that it is in danger of being torn down by developers.

5140. ____. *Crazy Campout* (Knopf, 1989) 4–6. The Fifth Grade S.T.A.R.s are excited about a weekend campout, until they discover a rival clique at the next campsite.

5141. ____. *Twin Trouble* (Knopf, 1989) 4–6. A new baby in the family compounds Sara's already shaky problem of identity as a twin in a growing family. Her town's 150th anniversary celebration further complicates things as her fifth grade club competes with a rival club to win the most prizes.

5142. ____. *Star Reporter* (Knopf, 1989) 4–6. Competing with a rival club for the best school project, Karen and the other members of the S.T.A.R.s learn about reporting when they start a newspaper.

5143. Nordqvist, Sven. *Pancake Pie* (Morrow, 1985) k–3. Despite many difficulties, a farmer named Festus is determined to celebrate his cat Mercury's birthday by baking a pancake pie.

5144. ____. *Fox Hunt* (Morrow, 1986) k–3. Farmer Festus and his cat Mercury find a way of getting rid of a troublesome fox by using their brains instead of a gun.

5145. ____. *Merry Christmas, Festus and Mercury* (Carolrhoda, 1989) k–3. Unable to continue with Christmas preparations because of his injured foot, old man Festus and his cat Mercury face a bleak Christmas until the neighbors come to the rescue.

5146. ____. *Festus and Mercury: Ruckus in the Garden* (Carolrhoda, 1991) k–3. Festus and his cat Mercury come up with elaborate methods to protect their garden from chickens, pigs and cows.

5147. ____. *Festus and Mercury Wishing to Go Fishing* (Carolrhoda, 1991) k–3. Mercury the cat tries to cheer up his grouchy old master through elaborate plans to get him to go fishing.

5148. ____. *Festus and Mercury Go Camping* (Carolrhoda, 1993) k–3. Festus and his cat, Mercury, change their plans for a camping trip when the chickens insist on going along.

5149. Norton, Andre. *Elvenbane* (1991). The world was run by the Elvenlards; they had dominion over humans and halfbreeds. They built cities and kept slaves. Serina, a human, was driven to the desert when she becomes pregnant. She dies as she gives birth to Shana. This halfbreed is that most dangerous and treasured person, the fulfillment of the Prophesy, whose magic and fortune will remake the world.

5150. ____. *Elvenblood* (1995). Lord Tylar decides to marry off his daughter, Rina, to an aristocratic dolt. His son, Larry, is a halfblooded human. He and Rina plan to escape to the iron People and help LaShana and Diric overthrow Jamal.

5151. Nygren, Tord. *Fiddler and His Brothers* (Morrow, 1987) k–3. Three brothers go off to seek their fortunes, but the one who plays the fiddle, having the most wit and courage, comes off best.

5152. ____. *Fiddler and the Witches* (Morrow, 1987) k–3. Teddy is strong. Neddy is swift. Fiddler likes music. Fiddler saves his brother from two witches who have stolen a waistcoat, a goat with a golden horn and a magic lantern. Fiddler steals them back for the King and wins a pretty princess.

5153. O'Connor, Jane. *Lulu and the Witch Baby* (Harper, 1986) 3–5. Lulu Witch begins to change her mind about her pesky baby sister when she thinks one of her magic spells has made the baby disappear.

5154. ____. *Lulu Goes to Witch School* (Harper, 1986) 3–5. Lulu starts witch school and meets a classmate who is best at everything.

5155. Oakden, David. *Buttercup Willie* (Methuen, 1981) 3–5. Whenever Buttercup Willie gets caught in some inadvertent pranks he protests: "But, but…"

5156. ____. *Buttercup Willie Rides Again* (Methuen, 1985) 3–5. Buttercup Willie is silly. A story full of puns and funny antics.

5157. ____. *Buttercup Willie is a Great Help* (Methuen, 1987) 3–5.

5158. Oakley, Graham. *Church Mouse* (Atheneum, 1972) k–3. The humorous escapades of Arthur, the church mouse and Sampson, the church cat. All goes well, until one Sunday when Sampson, who is dreaming, chases some mice and disrupts the service.

5159. ____. *Church Cat Abroad* (Atheneum, 1973) k–3. Sampson, the tomcat, sails to the South Seas to appear in a cat food advertisement.

5160. ____. *Church Mice and the Moon* (Atheneum, 1974) k–3. Two of the church mice are captured by scientists and are being readied for a space flight when they are rescued by Sampson, the church cat.

5161. ____. *Church Mice Spread Their Wings* (Atheneum, 1976) k–3. With Sampson the church cat as a reluctant protector, the church mice set out on a country outing that is almost disastrous.

5162. ____. *Church Mice Adrift* (Atheneum, 1977) k–3. The church cat and the church mice use brains instead of brawn to rout a scurvy gang of displaced rats who have taken over the church.

5163. ____. *Church Mice at Bay* (Atheneum, 1978) k–3. Mice inhabit a church in Wortlethorpe. The arrival of a new curate, long-haired and in jeans, threatens traditional ways, and the mice rise in arms.

5164. ____. *Church Mice at Christmas* (Atheneum, 1980) k–3. When Arthur and Humphrey decide to rally the church mice into having a Christmas party, the result is a series of disasters.

5165. ____. *Church Mice in Action* (Atheneum, 1983) k–3. The church mice enter Sampson in a cat show to win money to fix the church roof, but in doing so, they unknowingly put him in danger.

5166. ____. *Diary of a Church Mouse* (Atheneum, 1987) k–3. Humphrey, the church mouse, decides to keep a diary. The reader follows a year's adventures of the mice and their cat friend, Sampson.

5167. ____. *Church Mice and the Ring* (Macmillan, 1992) k–3. The church mice carry out a convoluted plan to find a home for their new friend Percy, a stray dog.

5168. Oana, Kay. *Timmy Tiger and the Butterfly Net* (Oddo, 1981) k–3. Tommy has a terrifying experience with angry bees, but his brother Timmy comes to the rescue with a butterfly net.

5169. ____. *Timmy Tiger and the Masked Bandit* (Oddo, 1981) k–3. Tommy and Timmy go camping deep in the jungle where they are frightened in the middle of the night by a masked bandit.

5170. Older, Effin. *Best Ice Show Ever* (Skylark, 1996) 2–4. Randi's friend Woody is the class clown. Randi passes a note to her friend Kate and Woody is being blamed. She doesn't say anything and because of detention Woody misses skating practice and Randi misses him.

5171. ____. *Bossy Anna* (Skylark, 1996) 2–4. Randi's friend Anna is a good skater but always has to be in charge. Everyone is fed up with her bossiness and tells her. Anna stops coming to practice and they find she is missed.

5172. Older, Jules. *Hank Prank in Love* (Heinemann, 1987) 3–5. Linh Tran, a Vietnamese girl is in Hank's class and he likes her. They become good friends but Linh must move and she and Hank say good-byes.

5173. ____. *Hot Henrietta and the Nailbiters United* (Heinemann,) 1987. 3–5

5174. ____. *Hank Prank and Hot Henrietta* (Scholastic, 1992) 3–5. Presents the lively escapades of mischievous Hank Prank and his hot-tempered sister, Henrietta.

5175. Oldfield, Pamela. *Gumby Gang Again* (Blackie, 1979) 3–5. A story of four children and their dog Buster. Buster decides to chase a group of heifers and upsets the farmer and all their plans. Good intentions go awry.

5176. ____. *Gumby Gang on Strike Again* (Blackie, 1981) 3–5. The concert for parents with its tragic drama of orphans and their fate; the parrot borrowed for a Cage Bird contest who tactlessly imitates a catarrhal judge; the accident that befalls their large headquarters in a flood, are all part of the Gumby Gang adventures.

5177. ____. *Gumby Gang on Holiday* (Blackie, 1983) 3–5. The adventures complicated by the innocent awfulness of the youngest member, Bet.

5178. ____. *More About the Gumby Gang* (Hall, 1990) 3–5. A story of the Gumby Gang's money-making schemes and detective work.

5179. Oldfield, Pamela. *Melanie Brown and the Jar of Sweets* (Faber, 1975) 2–4. Melanie Brown, six, is allowed to take charge of a "guess the number of sweets in a jar" competition at school. She argues with Michael, five, and the answer is revealed, but she solves the problem by eating one sweet. This is one of several stories.

5180. ____. *Melanie Brown Goes to School* (Faber, 1979) 2–4. Melanie, five, like the title character in the Ramona series (Cleary) is a mischievous but likable girl who is in constant trouble. A British version of Cleary's heroine.

5181. ____. *Melanie Brown Climbs a Tree* (Faber, 1980) 2–4. Melanie gets in trouble by following her own plans instead of the directions given to her by adults.

5182. Oldfield, Pamela. *Willerbys and the Burglar* (Blackie, 1981) 3–5. Claire's great-aunt is suspicious of the Willerby family because she thinks their shop is taking trade away from the old-fashioned little sweet shop. The children work hard to become friendly with her and succeed.

5183. ____. *Willerbys and the Haunted Mill* (Blackie, 1981) 3–5. Story of the Willerby family and their new friend Claire.

5184. ____. *Willerbys and the Sad Clown* (Blackie, 1982) 3–5. Three more stories about the Willerby children and their activities in the village.

5185. ____. *Willerbys and the Mystery Man* (Blackie, 1984) 3–5. A pantomime is to be put on in the village and the Willerby children are involved in suspicion and intrigue.

5186. Oleksy, Walter. *If I'm Lost, How Come I Found You?* (McGraw, 1981) 5–8. Quacky, 12, escapes from an orphanage and goes to Aunt Maggie's home, but she is in jail for shoplifting. Maggie reforms and she and Quacky get reward money for finding two robbers.

5187. ____. *Quacky and the Crazy Ball* (McGraw, 1981) 5–8. When faced with two challenges, making a baseball team for 13-year-olds and trapping the "Hungry Burglar" a 12-year-old orphan proves his resourcefulness.

5188. ____. *Quacky and the Haunted Amusement Park* (McGraw, 1982) 5–8. Quacky and his dog, Puddles, find a dognapping ring when Puddles disappears.

5189. Olsen, Violet. *Growing Season* (Atheneum, 1982) 5–8. Marie is growing up during the Great Depression with little money. She learns of the plight of the farmers, sees poverty worse than her own and learns that trust in people is sometimes shaken.

5190. ____. *View from the Pighouse Roof* (Atheneum, 1987) 5–8. Marie, 12, living on an Iowa farm during the Great Depression, tries to cope with the difficulties of growing up.

5191. Oppenheim, Joanne. *Mrs. Peloki's Snake*

(Dodd, 1980) k–3. A report of a snake in the boys' bathroom causes quite a stir in Mrs. Peloki's classroom.

5192. ____. *Mrs. Peloki's Class Play* (Dodd, 1984) k–3. After a disastrous dress rehearsal, the second-grade play is a great success but has an unexpected ending.

5193. ____. *Mrs. Peloki's Substitute* (Dodd, 1987) k–3. Mrs. Peloki's substitute experiences the second grade class at its most difficult.

5194. Orgel, Doris. *Cindy's Snowdrips* (Knopf, 1966) k–3. Cindy gets some bulbs that are called snowdrops. She plants them and on her birthday in March she is rewarded with blossoms of snowdrops.

5195. ____. *Cindy's Sand and Happy Tree* (Knopf, 1967) k–3. Cindy chooses a weeping cherry tree to replace the old elm tree that died. She loved the old tree and a weeping cherry is both sad (because of the old elm) and happy (because it makes her cheerful).

5196. Orgel, Doris. *My War with Mrs. Galloway* (Viking, 1985) 3–5. Rebecca, eight, has an ongoing war with her baby-sitter, Mrs. Galloway, until one day the two reach an unexpected truce. Rebecca's divorced mother is a doctor.

5197. ____. *Whiskers Once and Always* (Viking, 1986) 3–5. When her beloved cat Whiskers dies, Rebecca finds it difficult to vent her anger and accept her mother's comfort.

5198. ____. *Midnight Soup and a Witch's Hat* (Viking, 1987) 3–5. Having anticipated a whole week with her father in Oregon, Becky arrives to find that she has to share her dad with his friend Rosellen and her spoiled six-year-old daughter.

5199. ____. *Starring Becky Suslow* (Viking, 1989) 3–5. Becky and her two best friends have to make room for a worldly newcomer in their lives.

5200. Orlev, Uri. *Island on Bird Street* (Houghton, 1984) 5–8. During World War II a Jewish boy is left on his own for months in a ruined house in the Warsaw Ghetto, where he must learn all the tricks of survival under constantly life-threatening conditions.

5201. ____. *Man from the Other Side* (Houghton, 1991) 5–8. Living on the outskirts of the Warsaw Ghetto during World War II, Marek, 14, and his grandparents shelter a Jewish man in the days before the Jewish uprising.

5202. Ormondroyd, Edward. *Theodore* (Parnassus, 1966) k–3. Lucy loves her teddy bear Theodore, rumpled and scruffy. One day someone decides to wash poor Theodore and he becomes a stranger to himself. How he returns to his old rumpled self shows how resourceful he can be.

5203. ____. *Theodore's Rival* (Parnassus, 1971) k–3. Theodore is jealous of the new "bear" in the house until he finds out it's really a panda.

5204. Osborne, Mary. *Spider Kane and the Mystery Under the Mayapple* (Random, 1991) 4–6. With the help of a spider, a moth and two ladybug friends, a young butterfly tries to uncover a mystery involving a gossamer-winged butterfly with whom he has fallen in love.

5205. ____. *Spider Kane and the Mystery at Jumbo Nightcrawler's* (Knopf, 1993) 4–6. Lieutenant Leon Leafwing and Detective Spider Kane investigate the mysterious disappearance of Leon's mother and members of the Order of the North.

5206. Osborne, Mary P. *Mo to the Rescue* (Dial, 1985) 3–5. Mo, a good-natured sheriff, does his best to protect the members of his rural community, who are also his friends.

5207. ____. *Mo and His Friends* (Dial, 1988) 3–5. Brief stories feature Sheriff Mo and his animal friends.

5208. Osborne, Maureen. *Here Comes the Horrorbilly* (Heinemann, 1979) k–3. Horrorbilly is like a huge melon with a funny face and very fuzzy hair. He gets into many scrapes.

5209. ____. *Horrorbilly Goes to School* (Heinemann, 1979) k–3. Horrorbilly gets into trouble at school and his teacher—who is also Hairy Mary, in whose home the Horrorbilly lives, is furious.

5210. Ostheeren, Ingrid. *Jonathan Mouse* (Holt, 1986) k–3. A group of farmland animals comes to a mouse's aid when a spell dooms him to turn the same color as everything he eats.

5211. ____. *Jonathan Mouse at the Circus* (North-South, 1988) k–3. A mischievous mouse visits a circus and has exciting adventures with his friends.

5212. ____. *Jonathan Mouse and the Magic Box* (Holt, 1990) k–3. Jonathan Mouse finds magic dust and pigs fly, cows dance, the dog conducts music, goats perform handstands, ponies juggle cabbages and ducks turn to hippos. Cat chases Jonathan into the pond and the magic is washed off and things go back to normal.

5213. ____. *Jonathan Mouse and the Baby Bird* (North-South, 1991) k–3. Jonathan Mouse enlists the help of all the farm animals to care for a lost baby bird and teach it how to fly back to its family.

5214. ____. *Jonathan Mouse, Detective* (Holt, 1993) k–3. Although a mouse detective visiting from the city claims he will help the farm animals find a missing locket, it is Jonathan Mouse who solves the mystery.

5215. Oterdahl, Jeanna. *April Adventure* (Harcourt, 1962) 4–6. Tina went to Sun Village to visit her great-aunt. Her adventure started on the train and continued at the house with its attic and nearby woods.

5216. ____. *Island Summer* (Harcourt, 1964) 4–6. Tina and Annika look for seashells, build a playhouse and make a new friend, Sten, who is lame.

5217. Oxenbury, Helen. *Tom and Pippo Read a Story* (Aladdin, 1988) k–3. Tom likes his father to read to him and his toy monkey, Pippo, but when his father gets tired Tom "reads" to Pippo himself.
5218. ____. *Tom and Pippo Make a Mess* (Aladdin, 1988) k–3. Tom is not very successful when he tries to help his father paint a room and blames his toy monkey, Pippo, for the mess.
5219. ____. *Tom and Pippo Go for a Walk* (Aladdin, 1988) k–3. Tom and his toy monkey, Pippo, go out for a walk and fall into a mud puddle.
5220. ____. *Tom and Pippo and the Washing Machine* (Aladdin, 1988) k–3. Pippo the toy monkey gets washed in the washing machine after playing in the mud with Tom.
5221. ____. *Tom and Pippo's Day* (Aladdin, 1989) k–3. Tom spends the day indoors with his toy monkey.
5222. ____. *Tom and Pippo Go Shopping* (Aladdin, 1989) k–3. Mommy takes Tom and his toy monkey, Pippo, on a shopping trip.
5223. ____. *Pippo Gets Lost* (Aladdin, 1989) k–3. Tom is very worried when he searches the house and can't find Pippo.
5224. ____. *Tom and Pippo and the Dog* (Aladdin, 1989) k–3. While out for a walk with Mommy, Tom and Pippo have an adventure with a dog.
5225. ____. *Tom and Pippo in the Garden* (Aladdin, 1989) k–3. Tom has fun playing in the garden with his toy monkey, Pippo, and a wheelbarrow.
5226. ____. *Tom and Pippo See the Moon* (Aladdin, 1989) k–3. Tom asks his father questions about the moon and imagines flying there with his toy monkey.
5227. ____. *Tom and Pippo in the Snow* (Aladdin, 1989) k–3. After a few tries, Tom and Pippo decide that they can go sledding without Daddy's help.
5228. ____. *Tom and Pippo Make a Friend* (Aladdin, 1989) k–3. Tom and Pippo go to play in a sandbox and end up making a new friend.
5229. ____. *Tom and Pippo on the Beach* (Candlewick, 1993) k–3. Tom and his stuffed monkey Pippo trade sun hats when they go to the beach with Daddy. Daddy puts a hat on Tom, Tom puts it on Pippo. Daddy makes a paper hat for Pippo and Tom puts it on his head.
5230. ____. *Tom and Pippo and the Bicycle* (Candlewick, 1994) k–3. Because his toy monkey Pippo keeps falling off the back of his bike, Tom envies Stephanie for having a big new bike with a passenger seat in the back.

5231. Oxenbury, Helen. *Dressing* (S & S, 1981) k–3. In this series of five books, Baby is seen enthralled by a real book (held upside down), and fast asleep on a long suffering marmalade cat, bemused on the pot, and tucking fistfully into a bowl of green sludge.
5232. ____. *Family* (S & S, 1981) k–3. Introduces words that represent familiar subjects. Here baby learns about mother, father, sister, brother, grandmother, grandfather and baby.
5233. ____. *Friends* (S & S, 1981) k–3. Introduces words that represent pets: dog, rabbit, guinea pig, sparrow and hen.
5234. ____. *Playing* (Wanderer, 1981) k–3. In this book the words introduced are representing toys: box, block, etc.
5235. ____. *Working* (Walker, 1981) k–3. Introduces household items: bowl, using the potty, highchair, bathtub, carriage, bottle, crib.
5236. ____. *Playschool* (Walker, 1984) k–3. A depiction of a sniffling but gallant heroine shows the vulnerability and resilience of childhood.

5237. Oxenbury, Helen. *Birthday Party* (Walker, 1983) k–3. A small girl is a guest at a birthday party. She is more interested in the birthday present than John, the birthday boy. She goes home with a balloon.
5238. ____. *Dancing Class* (Walker, 1983) k–3. A shaggy-haired little girl with her hair in clips and wearing too large wrinkled tights, trips over the laces of her dancing shoes.
5239. ____. *Eating Out* (Dial, 1983) k–3. A shaggy-haired small girl fidgets in the restaurant. She plays with her rolls, needs to go to the bathroom, trips the waiter and spills her food.

5240. Oxenbury, Helen. *Car Trip* (Dial, 1983) k–3. "We've just had a really great time" the hero tells his friends after having spent hours on the highway and vomiting in the car.
5241. ____. *Check-up* (Dial, 1983) k–3. Townspeople are whispering about the antics of the naughty little boy.
5242. ____. *First Day of School* (Dial, 1983) k–3. Nora and the heroine find they are wearing the same kind of new shoes and become friends. They play, sing, listen to a story and share raisins.

5243. Packard, Edward. *ESP McGee* (Avon, 1983) 5–8. Introducing a new mystery solver and his sidekick, Matt Terrell. When Matt Terrell, new to the neighborhood, makes friends with ESP McGee, a supposed genius with extrasensory perception, they become involved with terrorists interested in sabotaging a nuclear plant.
　　(For other books about "ESP McGee," **see** Lawrence, Jim.)

5244. Palmer, C. Everard. *Dog Called Houdini* (Deutsch, 1979) 3–5. Houdini is a stray dog who is disliked but admired for his cunning. He can't be captured. He is finally tranquilized by drugged food and hit by a car. Red, the dog catcher's son, finds, rescues and keeps him.
5245. ____. *Houdini, Come Home* (Deutsch, 1981) 3–5. Red O'Malley, searching for his dog, Houdini, in the woods north of Lake Superior, finds himself trapped by a raging forest fire.

5246. Palmer, C. Everard. *Wooing of Beppo Tate* (Deutsch, 1972) 4–6. A portrait of West Indian villages. Beppo, 11, has adventures and meets entertaining people.

5247. ____. *Beppo Tate and Roy Penner* (Deutsch, 1981) 4–6. Beppo Tate and Roy Penner run away from home, Huckleberry fashion, in an attempt to jolt their families into appreciating them more than they do. But in the escape they find an abandoned baby.

5248. ____. *Runaway Marriage Brokers* (Deutsch, 1983) 4–6. Roy spots a budding romance in the big house where he works and turns Beppo's literary ability and his own self-confidence to good account. They write the love letters, for a small consideration and deliver them, for another consideration. The elopement of the parties brings their career as marriage brokers to a swift end.

5249. Panek, Dennis. *Catastrophe Cat* (Bradbury, 1978) k–3. A cat named Catastrophe demonstrates how he got his name and why it is appropriate.

5250. ____. *Catastrophe Cat at the Zoo* (Bradbury, 1979) k–3. Catastrophe Cat gets off a city bus hoping to snooze under a tree, but starts a romp through the zoo instead.

5251. Pantell, Dora E. MacGregor. *Miss Pickerell and the Lost World* (Watts, 1986) 4–6. When a flood in Square Toe Country washes in a strange creature, Miss Pickerell goes on a perilous journey to return it to its native habitat.

(For other books about "Miss Pickerell," *see* MacGregor, Ellen.)

5252. Parish, Peggy. *Amelia Bedelia* (Harper, 1963) 3–5. Amelia Bedelia, the new maid, is left alone on her first day of work with only a written list of instructions to follow. That is exactly what she did: "draw the drapes, dress the chicken," and more.

5253. ____. *Thank You, Amelia Bedelia* (Harper, 1964) 3–5. Preparing for the arrival of an important visitor, Amelia, a wacky housekeeper follows her employer's instructions with humorous results.

5254. ____. *Amelia Bedelia and the Surprise Shower* (Harper, 1966) 3–5. Amelia Bedelia and her cousin, helping to prepare a surprise shower, make some arrangements that are not quite what the guests expected.

5255. ____. *Come Back, Amelia Bedelia* (Harper, 1971) 3–5. Because she does exactly as she is told, Amelia Bedelia is fired from one job after another.

5256. ____. *Play Ball, Amelia Bedelia* (Harper, 1972) 3–5. Amelia Bedelia, who knows very little about baseball, stands in for a sick player during the game.

5257. ____. *Good Work, Amelia Bedelia* (Greenwillow, 1976) 3–5. Literal-minded Amelia Bedelia does household chores and gets dinner ready.

5258. ____. *Teach Us, Amelia Bedelia* (Greenwillow, 1977) 3–5. A very literal-minded Amelia Bedelia becomes a substitute teacher for a day.

5259. ____. *Amelia Bedelia Helps Out* (Greenwillow, 1979) 3–5. Amelia Bedelia shows her niece Effie Lou how to follow instructions to the letter as they dust the potato bugs and sew seeds.

5260. ____. *Amelia Bedelia and the Baby* (Greenwillow, 1981) 3–5. Amelia Bedelia follows to the letter the list of instructions for looking after the Lanes' baby.

5261. ____. *Amelia Bedelia Goes Camping* (Greenwillow, 1985) 3–5. As always, Amelia Bedelia follows exactly the instructions given to her on a camping trip, including pitching a tent and rowing boats.

5262. ____. *Merry Christmas, Amelia Bedelia* (Greenwillow, 1986) 3–5. As Amelia Bedelia helps Mrs. Rogers prepare for Christmas, she bakes a date cake with a calendar in it and stuffs the children's stockings with turkey stuffing.

5263. ____. *Amelia Bedelia's Family Album* (Greenwillow, 1988) 3–5. Amelia Bedelia entertains Mr. and Mrs. Rogers by showing them her family album and describing what her relatives do.

5264. Parish, Peggy. *Granny and the Indians* (Macmillan, 1969) k–3. Granny Guntry proves such a menace to the Indians that they promise to bring her food everyday if she will only stay out of their forest.

5265. ____. *Granny and the Desperadoes* (Macmillan, 1970) k–3. Granny catches two desperadoes with an apple pie.

5266. ____. *Granny, the Baby and the Big Gray Thing* (Macmillan, 1972) k–3. Granny Guntry causes consternation among the Indians when she leaves her new "dog" to baby-sit with a papoose.

5267. Park, Barbara. *Maxie, Rosie, and Earl...Partners in Grime* (Knopf, 1990) 4–6. Maxie, Rosie and Earl are to be disciplined by the principal but he postpones it and they skip school.

5268. ____. *Rosie Swanson, Fourth Grade Geek for President* (Knopf, 1991) 4–6. Average, unpopular Rosie runs for class president against two of the most popular kids in the fourth grade.

5269. Park, Barbara. *Junie B. Jones and the Stupid Smelly Bus* (Random, 1992) 3–5. In her own words, a young girl describes her feelings about starting kindergarten and what she does when she decides not to ride the bus home.

5270. ____. *Junie B. Jones and Her Big Fat Mouth* (Random, 1993) 3–5. When her kindergarten class has Job Day, Junie B. goes through much confusion and excitement before deciding on the "bestest" job of all.

5271. ____. *Junie B. Jones and a Little Monkey Business* (Random, 1993) 3–5. Through a misunderstanding, Junie B. thinks that her new baby brother is really a baby monkey, and her report of this news creates excitement and trouble in her kindergarten class.

5272. ____. *Junie B. Jones and Some Sneaky Peeky*

Spying (Random, 1994) 3–5. Junie B., six, has a penchant for spying on people and her curiosity about the private lives of her teacher gets her in trouble at kindergarten.

5273. ____. *Junie B. and the Yucky Blucky Fruitcake* (Random, 1995) 3–5. Junie B., a spunky, sometimes exasperating kindergartner, looks forward to winning lots of prizes at the school carnival, but a fruitcake was not exactly what she had in mind.

5274. ____. *Junie B. and the Meanie Jim's Birthday* (Random, 1996) 3–5. Junie B. is very upset when a boy in her class plans to invite everyone except her to his birthday party. Her grandfather helps her deal with the situation.

5275. Park, Barbara. *Skinnybones* (Random, 1982) 4–6. Alex's active sense of humor helps him to get along with the school braggart, to make the most of his athletic talents, and to simply get by in a hectic world.

5276. ____. *Almost Starring Skinnybones* (Knopf, 1988) 4–6. Irrepressible Alex, 12, is convinced that he will be a star and impress his schoolmates when, as a winner of a cat food essay contest, he is asked to make a commercial for national television.

5277. Park, Ruth. *Callie's Castle* (Angus, 1975) 3–5. Callie, 10, is the one child of the four who was her mother's first husband's child. She quarrels with her best friend, she has trouble with her stepbrother and wants to reject her new stepfather. She goes to her grandfather who helps her find space where she can be alone and cope.

5278. ____. *Callie's Family* (Angus, 1989) 3–5. Callie, 12, tells about herself, her siblings and her parents, all of whom live in Australia.

5279. Park, Ruth. *Muddle-Headed Wombat on a Rainy Day* (Angus, 1970) 3–5. Wombat muddles his way endearingly through various rainy adventures. He made a "terribabble" wombat cake, which includes tomatoes and eggshells.

5280. ____. *Muddle-Headed Wombat in the Springtime* (Angus, 1971) 3–5. Wombats need a hat to be seen. They sit on the grass as an audience to play. Bandicoot is sick in bed and Mouse uses a match to scare away a magpie but is aware of smoke and fire as a hazard.

5281. ____. *Muddle-Headed Wombat on Holiday* (Angus, 1975) 3–5.

5282. ____. *Muddle-Headed Wombat and the Invention* (Angus, 1976) 3–5.

5283. Parker, Nancy. *Love from Uncle Clyde* (Dodd, 1977) k–3. A little boy receives a hippopotamus from his Uncle Clyde in Africa for his birthday with instructions on how to take care of it.

5284. ____. *Love from Aunt Betty* (Dodd, 1983) k–3. Aunt Betty sends Charlie an old Transylvanian gypsy recipe for chocolate fudge cake, which calls for cobwebs and dried Carpathian tree toad flakes.

5285. ____. *Christmas Camel* (Dodd, 1983) k–3. For Christmas Charlie receives a camel from the Holy Lands that possesses an enchanting mysterious quality.

5286. Parks, Van Dyke. *Jump!* (Harcourt, 1986) 3–5. A retelling of five folktales in which crafty Brer Rabbit tries to outsmart all the other creatures in the animal community.

5287. ____. *Jump Again!* (Harcourt, 1987) 3–5. Contains: "Brer Rabbit"; "He's a Good Fisherman"; "Wonderful Tar Baby Story"; "How Brer Weasel Was Caught"; "Brer Rabbit and the Mosquitoes"; "Brer Rabbit's Courtship."

5288. ____. *Jump on Over!* (Harcourt, 1989) 3–5. A collection of five tales in which Brer Rabbit outwits Brer Fox, Brer Wold, and Brer Bear in order to ensure his family's survival during a drought.

5289. Parsons, Virginia. *Pinocchio and Geppetto* (McGraw, 1977) k–3. From a log of wood, Geppetto carves a little puppet who runs away and becomes lost in the woods.

5290. ____. *Pinocchio Goes on Stage* (McGraw, 1979) k–3. Pinocchio sells his new spelling book to buy a seat at a visiting puppet show.

5291. ____. *Pinocchio Plays Truant* (McGraw, 1979) k–3. On his first day of school Pinocchio plays hooky, joins a group of big boys, and robs a vineyard of its ripe grapes.

5292. ____. *Pinocchio and the Money Tree* (McGraw, 1979) k–3. Another episode taken from the story of Pinocchio by Collode.

5293. Patchett, Mary. *Tam the Untamed* (Bobbs, 1955) 4–6. Only Mary could handle the silver horse, Tam; and only Ajax, the golden dog, could be friends with him.

5294. ____. *Golden Wolf* (Bobbs, 1962) 4–6. Ajax has disappeared and Mary sees a sign "Golden Wolf of the Steppes" and fears it is Ajax. The dog is closely guarded but it is Ajax and she must rescue him.

5295. ____. *Ajax and the Haunted Mountain* (Bobbs, 1966) 4–6. Ajax, half-wild dog, and his mistress, Mary, travel through Australia and meet adventure and mystery.

5296. Paterson, Bettina. *Bun and Mrs. Tubby* (Orchard, 1987) k–3. Baby elephant Bun and sitter Mrs. Tubby play hide-and-seek, she gives him dinner and a bath and then tells him a bedtime story. Bun had a very nice time.

5297. ____. *Bun's Birthday* (Orchard, 1988) k–3. Mother and Father Elephant plan a wonderful party to celebrate their son's third birthday.

5298. Paterson, Cynthia. *Foxwood Treasure* (Barron, 1985) 8–3. Three friends trying to help raise funds for a village hall have an amazing adventure.

5299. ____. *Robbery at Foxwood* (Barron, 1985) k–3. When Mr. McGruffey's grocery store is robbed, Willy Hedgehog, Harvey Mouse and Rue Rabbit devise an ingenious plan to capture the robbers.

5300. ____. *Foxwood Regatta* (Barron, 1986) k–3. With the help of Captain Otter, three animal friends build a paddle steamer and foil the schemes of the rascally rats to win the big regatta dishonestly.

5301. ____. *Foxwood Kidnap* (Garron, 1986) k–3. When Uncle Henry is kidnapped by a band of nasty rats, three animal friends go to his rescue and discover that he has rebuilt the town's old railroad train.

5302. ____. *Foxwood Smugglers* (Barron, 1989) k–3. On holiday at the seaside with Mr. McGruffey, Willy, Harvey and Rue manage to do some good works and have fun, too.

5303. ____. *Foxwood Surprise* (Barron, 1989) k–3. Willy, Rue and Harvey's Christmas adventure starts badly when they are snubbed by Squire Fox's butler at the manor.

5304. Patron, Susan. *Burgoo Stew* (Orchard, 1991) k–3. A crown of five rowdy bad boys accost a mellow, wise old man who sends them home for a carrot to make a stew.

5305. ____. *Five Bad Boys, Billy Que and the Dustdobbin* (Orchard, 1992) k–3. Two of the five rowdy bad boys, Billy Que and Dustdobbin, have a falling out when the man carelessly steps on the little fellow and fails to show any remorse.

5306. Patterson, Francine. *Koko's Kitten* (Scholastic, 1987) 5–8. The real life experience of Koko, a gorilla in California who uses sign language, and a young kitten whom she loved and the grief she felt when it died.

5307. ____. *Koko's Story* (Scholastic, 1988) 5–8. Koko, a gorilla spends 14 years learning to communicate with humans through sign language.

5308. Paulsen, Gary. *Case of the Dirty Bird* (Dell, 1922) 4–6. Dunc and his best pal Amos aren't impressed when they meet a smelly, scruffy parrot until they learn it speaks four languages and seems to know something about buried treasure.

5309. ____. *Dunc's Doll* (Dell, 1992) 4–6. Dunc and Amos are hot on the trail of a band of doll thieves. Will a vicious watchdog stop them from retrieving a valuable missing doll? And why is Amos wearing a dress?

5310. ____. *Culpepper's Cannon* (Dell, 1992) 4–6. Amos and Dunc are researching the town's Civil War cannon when they find a note inside it telling them about a time portal. The boys find themselves in downtown Culpepper on March 8, 1862, and are being held as spies.

5311. ____. *Dunc Gets Tweaked* (Dell, 1992) 4–6. Dunc and Amos continue their sleuthing habits as they back down a stolen prototype skateboard in this funny adventure.

5312. ____. *Dunc's Halloween* (Dell, 1992) 4–6. Dunc and Amos almost give up their plans to hit all the good candy houses on Halloween when Amos is attacked by a werewolf. It is only a little bite and he becomes a werepuppy. He sleeps curled up on the rug.

5313. ____. *Dunc Breaks the Record* (Dell, 1992) 4–6. Dunc and Amos are trapped in a cave that is the lair of a mad Vietnam veteran. The two friends must outwit and save the vet while surviving in the wilderness. Luckily, Amos has read *Hatchet*.

5314. ____. *Dunc and Amos and the Red Tattoos* (Dell, 1993) 4–6. Dunc and Amos head for camp and face two weeks of fresh air—along with the regulations, demerits, KP and inedible food. They overhear a threat and discover that funds have been stolen. Is there a tie-in with these crimes and the red tattoo some of the camp staff have on their arms?

5315. ____. *Dunc and the Scam Artist* (Dell, 1993) 4–6. Dunc and Amos are best friends. Some older residents of their town have been bilked by con artists and the two boys went to look into these crimes.

5316. ____. *Dunc and the Greased Sticks of Doom* (Dell, 1994) 4–6. Someone is out to stop Olympic superstar Francesco Bartoli from clinching the world slalom speed record, and Dunc thinks he can save the day.

5317. ____. *Amos Goes Bananas* (Yearling, 1995) 4–6.

5318. ____. *Dunc and Amos Go to the Dogs* (Yearling, 1996) 4–6. Amos is not liked by even his own dog. He doesn't like Scruff very much, either. But Scruff gets dognapped so Amos and his friend Dunc team up to rescue him.

5319. ____. *Dunc and Amos Hit the Big Top* (Dell, 1995) 4–6. More Culpepper adventures with "best friends for life" Dunc and Amos.

5320. Paulsen, Gary. *Hatchet* (Bradbury, 1987) 5–8. The hatchet was a going away present from his mother. When the pilot of the private plane he was on died, Brian was obliged to land the plane and survive 54 days in the Canadian woods—with a secret.

5321. ____. *River* (Delacorte, 1991) 5–8. Brian survived 54 days in the wilderness after a plane crash. Now the government wants him to show Derek how he did it so they can train others in survival skills. But this trip has hazards, too.

5322. ____. *Brian's Winter* (Delacorte, 1996) 5–8. Brian's Winter begins where Hatchet might have ended: Brian is not rescued, but must build on his survival skills to face his deadliest enemy—a northern winter.

5323. Pearce, Philippa. *Picnic for Bunnykins* (Viking, 1984) k–3. After young Bunting falls into the stream during a family picnic, he and his brothers and sisters engage in a very daring activity.

5324. ____. *Two Bunnykins Out to Tea* (Viking, 1984) k–3. Brother and sister bunnies quarrel over sharing a dollybunny their grandmother made them until that wise lady finds a very satisfactory solution.

5325. Peck, Richard. *Lost in Cyberspace* (Dial, 1995) 4–6. While dealing with changes at home, sixth grader Josh and his friend Aaron use the computer at their New York prep school to travel through time learning some secrets from the school's past and improving Josh's home situations.
5326. ____. *Great Interactive Dream Machine* (Dial, 1996) 4–6. Josh Lewis is unwillingly drawn into the computer experiments of Aaron, his friend and fellow classmate at an exclusive New York private school and the two find themselves uncontrollably transported through space and time.

5327. Peck, Robert. *Little Soup's Hayride* (Dell, 1991) 3–5. Young Soup and Rob go for a wild hayride after salvaging a wagon from the garbage dump, fitting it with boards and loading it with hay.
5328. ____. *Little Soup's Birthday* (Dell, 1991) 3–5. Soup, nine, and Rob have plans for a big birthday party. They want to play Hog Pile and Rat Race. A horse and sleigh pick up the guests when a snowstorm hampers transportation to the party.

5329. Peck, Robert. *Arly* (Walker, 1989) 4–6. Although in 1927 Arly seems bound to follow in his father's footsteps as a field worker in Jailtown, Florida, where his family lives in the shadow of a cruel boss, his world suddenly is larger when a teacher comes to town.
5330. ____. *Arly's Run* (Walker, 1991) 4–6. Arly, an orphan in search of a home and a family, escapes from a brutal migrant labor camp, joins a traveling religious show, and battles a devastating Florida hurricane.

5331. Pelham, David. *Sam's Sandwich* (Dutton, 1991) k–3. Sam adds a fly, a worm, a slug, a caterpillar and some ants to the sandwich made for his sister.
5332. ____. *Sam's Surprise* (Dutton, 1992) k–3. Samantha, Sam's sister, gave him a box of chocolates for his birthday, each containing none-too-toothsome surprises.

5333. Pellowski, Michael. *Puppy Who Wanted a Playmate* (Willowisp, 1987) k–3. A Basset hound can't keep up with the other bigger dogs and feels lonely, until he finds a little girl to play with who likes him exactly as he is.
5334. ____. *Puppy Nobody Wanted* (Willowisp, 1988) k–3.

5335. Peppe, Rodney. *Henry's Exercise* (Methuen, 1975) k–3.

5336. ____. *Henry's Garden* (Methuen, 1975) k–3.
5337. ____. *Henry's Present* (Methuen, 1975) k–3.
5338. ____. *Henry's Sunbath* (Methuen, 1975) k–3.
5339. ____. *Henry's Toy Cupboard* (Methuen, 1978) k–3. Henry, a toy elephant, tidies up his toy cupboard looking for his toy tractor.
5340. ____. *Henry's Airplane* (Methuen, 1978) k–3. Henry the elephant has small adventures. Here he tries to climb into the cockpit of a plane.
5341. ____. *Henry Eats Out* (Methuen, 1978) k–3. Henry, a toy elephant, goes to eat in a restaurant. He has trouble because of his size. The dinner is a disaster.

5342. Peppe, Rodney. *Mice Who Live in a Shoe* (Lothrop, 1981) k–3. A mouse family living in mortal dread of a cat decides to build a safe and secure house through cooperative effort.
5343. ____. *Kettleship Pirates* (Lothrop, 1983) k–3. Finding that a familiar kettle has been turned into a pirate ship, Pip Mouse sets out on a wild adventure on his birthday.
5344. ____. *Mice and the Flying Basket* (Lothrop, 1985) k–3. A family of mice decide to make an airplane out of a big basket and learn to fly.
5345. ____. *Mice and the Clockwork Bus* (Lothrop, 1987) k–3. To avoid riding in D. Rat's rattletrap bicycle bus, a family of mice decide to build its own clockwork bus.
5346. ____. *Mice on the Moon* (Lothrop, 1993) k–3. The Mouse family builds a spaceship out of an egg carton and sets off for the moon, little realizing that they have an unwelcome passenger along on the trip.

5347. Peppe, Rodney. *Huxley Pig's Airplane* (Doubleday, 1990, k–3). Huxley Pig has a dangerous but exciting flight in his new airplane and never quite makes it to his granny's house.
5348. ____. *Huxley Pig the Clown* (Delacorte, 1990) k–3. Huxley Pig's imagination takes him to a circus where his exploits please the crowd, though nearly causing disaster to himself.
5349. ____. *Here Comes Huxley Pig* (Delacorte, 1990) k–3. In the first of many possible adventures involving dressing up in colorful old clothes, Huxley Pig dons a sailor suit and takes an imaginative sea voyage from his bedroom.
5350. ____. *Huxley Pig's Model Car* (Doubleday, 1990) k–3. Huxley Pig takes an imaginative car ride in his own mind.

5351. Percy, Graham. *Meg and Her Circus Tricks* (Child's World, 1991) k–3. The tricks Meg learns at Uncle Zeb's circus stand her in good stead during a lull in her brother's birthday party.
5352. ____. *Max and the Very Rare Bird* (Child's World, 1991) k–3. Although he forgets to stay with his grandparents and his sister Meg on their trip to see a rare bird, Max the elephant remembers why they came.

5353. ____. *Max and the Orange Door* (Child's World, 1994) k–3. An accident with orange paint helps Max, Meg, Grandma and Grandpa to have a vacation.

5354. ____. *Meg and the Great Race* (Child's World, 1994) k–3. An elephant asks her brother to help her train for a swimming contest.

5355. Perkins, Al. *Tubby and the Lantern* (Beginner, 1971) 2–4. Ah Mee has a special friend: Tubby the elephant. They have a great adventure when carried away by Ah Mee's father's lantern.

5356. ____. *Tubby and the Poo-Bah* (Random, 1972) 2–4. A story of an elephant who steals and smashes a Chinese dignitary's boat.

5357. Perlberg, Deborah. *Wembley Fraggle Gets the Story* (Holt, 1984) k–3. Wembley and his friends decide to write and publish the first-ever Fraggle Rock newspaper.

(For additional books on the Fraggles, Boober, Gobo, Mokey, Red or Wembley, *see* Brennan, Joseph; Calder, Lyn; Calmenson, Stephanie; Gilkow, Louise; Gilmour, L.B.; Grand, Rebecca; Muntean, Michaela; Stevenson, Jocelyn; Teitelbaum, Michael, Weiss, Ellen; Young, David.)

5358. Perry, Ritchie. *George H. Ghastly* (Hutchinson, 1981) 3–5. George H. Ghastly is a ghost but can't frighten anyone. Wizard Yuck gives him a fearsome yell. But the sounds scare George more than his victims. He becomes friends with a lonely human boy.

5359. ____. *George Ghastly to the Rescue* (Hutchinson, 1983) 3–5. George lives with Mr. Merryfellow. He still can't frighten anyone but has learned to move things (which seem to move by themselves). This did not please Mr. Merryfellow, but George redeems himself when a burglar comes in.

5360. Perry, Ritchie. *Fenella Fang* (Hutchinson, 1986) 4–6. Fenella, a vampire, lives in a coffin. Her peaceful existence is ruined when a little girl seeks shelter in her crypt. She is running away from Fred and looking for her dog Spot. Fenella names her Heinz Beans. They both fly away and teach Fred a lesson.

5361. ____. *Fenella Fang and the Great Escape* (Hutchinson, 1987) 4–6. Vampires from the past and present behave like people and often exhibit the less likable characteristics of humans. This story features a time track machine.

5362. ____. *Fenella Fang and the Wicked Witch* (Hutchinson, 1989) 4–6. Fenella and her Uncle Sam are vampires. A magician turns his wife into a toad for 700 years and she is resentful. There is a Red Indian ghost, a wicked witch, a wizard and, of course, friend "Heinz Beans." Anything can happen.

5363. Peterson, Hans. *Magnus and the Squirrel* (Farrar, 1959) 4–6. When lonely Magnus, seven, meets an older boy, who in turn gives him a squirrel, he devotes himself ardently to both. But seasons turn and Magnus' pet must leave his shelter and return to his own life.

5364. ____. *Magnus in the Harbor* (Pantheon, 1966) 4–6. Magnus, seven, searches the harbor and the city looking for his friend, Matthew.

5365. ____. *Magnus and the Wagon Horse* (Pantheon, 1966) 4–6. Magnus, seven, lives in an apartment on a busy street where there are no other children his age. He makes friends with Matthew, 14.

5366. ____. *Magnus in Danger* (Pantheon, 1967) 4–6. A story of Magnus' day near the port of his Swedish hometown. He meets friends, gets a dog, and helps round up some smugglers.

5367. ____. *Magnus and the Ship's Mascot* (Pantheon, 1967) 4–6.

5368. ____. *Magnus and the Christmas Horse* (Lothrop, 1970) 4–6. Magnus feels sorry for the delivery man and his horse; he invites them to Christmas dinner. But Mr. Lindberg has a nice home for himself and his horse. Mr. Lindberg gives Magnus a present of a wooden horse.

5369. Peterson, Hans. *Pelle Jansson* (Burke, 1973) 4–6. Pelle is trying to settle in his new house in town. His parents quarrel so he retreats into himself. But he gets to understand his father.

5370. ____. *Pelle in the Big City* (Burke, 1975) 4–6. Pelle and his parents just moved to the city. Dad is homesick but Mom is delighted. Pelle is mixed up. Dad goes back to the country but Mom stays in the city and Pelle chases back and forth trying to bring Dad back.

5371. ____. *Pelle in Trouble* (Burke, 1977) 4–6. Pelle moves from a lonely hut to Gottenburg, a crowded city. His mother loves it and his father hates it. Pelle is mocked at school and no one has time for him. His mother tries to bring the family together.

5372. Peterson, Hans. *Peter Comes Back* (Coward, 1966) k–3. Peter's father is out of work and his family live in a one room tenement. Peter introduces his country cousin to city gang life and they get into mischief. Peter's father later gets a job in the country.

5373. ____. *Peter Makes His Way* (Coward, 1968) k–3. Peter goes to live in the country and soon finds his city wits put to test. Peter makes friends with Anna and Anders.

5374. ____. *When Peter Was Lost in the Forest* (Coward, 1971) k–3. Peter, seven, follows rabbit tracks into the forest. He gets lost when it snows and covers the tracks. He finds a deserted house where he spends the night. He is found by two men who take him home.

5375. Peterson, Hans. *Lisa Settles In* (Burke, 1987) 2–4. Lisa, her mother and young sister move to a village. Her foot deformity sets her apart and she makes few friends. She gets into trouble and then rescues a boy from drowning.

5376. ____. *Just Lisa* (Burke, 1969) 2–4. The emotional problems of an imaginative little girl about her feelings, her friends, family and the world.

5377. Peterson, Hans. *Sara and Her Brother* (Burke, 1972) k–3.
5378. ____. *Sara in Summertime* (Burke, 1973) k–3. Depicts the small adventures of childhood.

5379. Peterson, John. *Littles and the Trash Tinies* (Scholastic, 1977) 2–4.
5380. ____. *Littles Go Exploring* (Scholastic, 1978) 2–4.
5381. ____. *Littles and the Big Storm* (Scholastic, 1979) 2–4. The Littles live secretly inside the walls of the Biggs' home. A storm, while the Biggs are away on vacation, damages the roof and floods the basement. The Littles repair the damage. They meet the House Tinies as welcomed guests.
5382. ____. *Littles and Their Friends* (Scholastic, 1981) 2–4. A description of the Littles' cozy quarters; the lifestyle of Little kin. There are Tree Tinies, Trash Tinies and Brook Tinies.
5383. ____. *Littles to the Rescue* (Scholastic, 1981) 2–4. A family of tiny people experience a crisis when a baby is born during a snowstorm.
5384. ____. *Littles' Scrapbook* (Scholastic, 1984) 2–4. Mr. Little's scrapbook highlights the daily life, recreation and history of a group of tiny people.
5385. ____. *Tom Little's Great Halloween Scare* (Scholastic, 1986) 2–4. The Littles are miniature human beings. As Halloween approaches Tom and Lucy plan a trick that will scare their elders. Tom fakes a radio broadcast warning of the Littles' presence and urging an all out war. But Lucy's quick thinking saves the day.
5386. ____. *Littles Go to School* (Scholastic, 1985) 2–4.
5387. ____. *Littles* (Scholastic, 1986) 2–4. The Littles are a family of miniature quasi-humans with tails. They live by using what they can find in the home of the Briggs family. The Briggs rent their home to summer people who allow mice in and Tom Little must devise a plan to deal with this danger.
5388. ____. *Littles Take a Trip* (Scholastic, 1986) 2–4.
5389. ____. *Littles Have a Wedding* (Scholastic, 1986) 2–4.
5390. ____. *Littles and the Terrible Tiny Kid* (Scholastic, 1993) 2–4. The Littles are in for big trouble when many messes around the house suggest that they have a terrible tiny kid on their hands.
5391. ____. *Littles and the Lost Children* (Scholastic, 1991) 2–4.

5392. Peterson, John. *Secret Hide-out* (Four Winds, 1966) 2–4. While on a visit to their grandfather's farm two brothers find a secret book that tells about a secret club. All its rules and requirements. It turns out it was their father's book when he was young.

5393. ____. *Enemies of Secret Hide-out* (Four Winds, 1966) 2–4. The members of the Viking Club outwit the enemy to protect their secret hideout.

5394. Pfanner, Louise. *Louise Builds a House* (Orchard, 1989) k–3. Louise's dream house grows to elaborate proportions with each new imaginary addition.
5395. ____. *Louise Builds a Boat* (Orchard, 1990) k–3. Louise is a visionary who wants to design her dream house. She includes a moat, a life-sized chess board, and lots of beehives. Louise gives it to her sister and looks forward to designing a boat.

5396. Pfeffer, Susan. *Kid Power* (Watts, 1977) 4–6. Janie is trying to earn money for a new bike. In spite of some setbacks she builds a business of odd jobs called Kid Power. It snowballs and she hires other kids to help.
5397. ____. *Kid Power Strikes Back* (Watts, 1984) 4–6. Kid Power hits a slump when school begins but the coming of winter gives Janie new ideas on how to revive business.

5398. Pfeffer, Susan. *April Upstairs* (Holt, 1990) 5–8. April, 12, has trouble making friends at her new middle school, until her father's friendship with a missing rock star catapults her into the news and suddenly makes her popular.
5399. ____. *Darcy Downstairs* (Holt, 1990) 4–8. When 12-year-old Darcy's cousin April moves into the upstairs apartment and they become inseparable, Darcy has trouble with her former best friend and her schoolwork.

5400. Pfeffer, Susan. *Just Between Us* (Delacorte, 1980) 4–6. Cass talks too much. Her mother promises her a dollar if she can keep a secret. She works hard at it with some success but new problems arise with her friends.
5401. ____. *What Do You Do When Your Mouth Won't Open?* (Delacorte, 1981) 4–6. Ressa is a classmate of Cass and is afraid to read out loud. She won an essay contest and must represent the school in front of 500 people.

5402. Pfeffer, Susan. *Rewind to Yesterday* (Delacorte, 1988) 4–6. After Kelly discovers how to set her family's new VCR so that it sends her back in time, she and Scott argue over how the secret should be used.
5403. ____. *Future Forward* (Delacorte, 1989) 4–6. Having kept the secret that the family VCR can send people back in time, Scott and Kelly continue to search for the best way to use that power and make an amazing new discovery.

5404. Pfister, Marcus. *Penguin Pete* (Holt, 1987) k–3. Pete the penguin has a good time playing on land with his fellow birds and learning how to swim in the sea.

5405. ____. *Penguin Pete's New Friends* (North-South, 1988) k–3. Pete is angry because he can't go fishing with the bigger penguins. He goes alone and falls asleep atop a whale who takes him to play with an Eskimo boy, an elephant seal and some sea lions, and then brings him home.

5406. ____. *Penguin Pete and Pat* (Holt, 1989) k–3. Upon returning from his travels, Penguin Pete is captivated by a girl penguin with a blue beak, cultivates her friendship, and wins her flipper in marriage.

5407. ____. *Penguin Pete, Ahoy* (North-South, 1993) k–3. Penguin Pete befriends Horatio, a mouse dwelling on a shipwreck, and finds that he has a lot to learn about life on board a ship.

5408. ____. *Penguin Pete and Tiny Tim* (North-South, 1994) k–3. While taking a walk with his father, a little penguin throws snowballs, rides a dogsled, slides down a slippery slope, gets lost in the snow, swims with seals, gets carried home and asks to do it all again tomorrow.

5409. Pfister, Marcus. *Hopper* (North-South, 1991) k–3. Even though he doesn't like the cold snow, Hopper, a little hare, enjoys playing with a friend and the adventure of searching for food with his mother.

5410. ____. *Hopper Hunts for Spring* (North-South, 1992) k–3. In looking for spring, Hopper meets some new animal friends.

5411. Philpot, Lorna. *Amazing Anthony Ant* (Random, 1993) k–3. The book incorporates song, rhyme and the element of surprise as Anthony Ant winds his way through anthill mazes. Anthony takes the reader on a fun-filled adventure.

5412. ____. *Amazing Ant's Creepy Crawly Party* (Random, 1993) k–3.

5413. Phipson, Joan. *Family Conspiracy* (Harcourt, 1964) 5–8. Mrs. Barker's children try to raise money for her needed operation. Each member tries secretly to do their project.

5414. ____. *Threat to the Barkers* (Harcourt, 1963) 5–8. Jack bought a flock of stud sheep. Edward hears of a plan to steal the sheep and makes plans to catch them at it.

5415. Pierce, Tamara. *Wild Magic* (Atheneum, 1992) 5–8. Daine, a common girl, lives in a land inhabited by great mages. She has been gifted with a rare form of magic known as wild magic, which allows her to commune with animals. Daine's magic is discovered by Numair the greatest magician in the land. He teaches her how to control her special magic.

5416. ____. *Wolf Speaker* (Random, 1997) 5–8. With the help of her animal friends, Daine fights to save the kingdom of Tortall from the ambitious mortals and dangerous immortals.

5417. ____. *Emperor's Mage* (Random, 1997) 5–8. When she is sent as part of a delegation from Tortall to negotiate a peace treaty with Carthak, Daine, 15, uses her powers to communicate with animals for more than healing the Carthak emperor's dying birds.

5418. ____. *Realms of the Gods* (Atheneum, 1996) 5–8. This conclusion to the previous three books about Daine and her wild magic solves many of her problems and hints at the love that lies in her future.

5419. Pilkey, Dav. *Friend for Dragon* (Orchard, 1991) 2–4. Dragon becomes such close friends with an apple that he deeply mourns its loss and is overjoyed when more grow to take its place.

5420. ____. *Dragon Gets By* (Orchard, 1991) 2–4. Dragon wakes up groggy and does everything wrong all day long.

5421. ____. *Dragon's Merry Christmas* (Orchard, 1991) 2–4. Dragon has a merry time in the Christmas season, decorating a tree outdoors, making a chocolate candy wreath, and sharing his Christmas gifts with needy animals.

5422. ____. *Dragon's Fat Cat* (Orchard, 1992) 2–4. Dragon finds a fat cat in the snow outside his house, brings it inside and soon has a family.

5423. ____. *Dragon's Halloween* (Orchard, 1993) 2–4. Dragon has a busy and fun-filled Halloween, turning six small pumpkins into one big jack o' lantern, going to a costume party, and taking a spooky walk in the woods.

5424. Pinkwater, D.M. *Magic Moscow* (Four Winds, 1980) 4–6. A humorous story of an ice cream parlor in Hoboken, New Jersey.

5425. ____. *Attila the Pun: A Magic Moscow Story* (Four Winds, 1981) 4–6. A seven foot self-styled guru conjures up the brother of Attila the Hun and Norman and Steve find a ghost on their hands.

5426. ____. *Slaves of Spiegel: A Magic Moscow Story* (Four Winds, 1982) 4–6. Norman and Steve are captured and transported to the planet Spiegel. They are forced to compete in a junk food cooking contest. They lose and their punishment is to be returned to Earth.

5427. Pinkwater, D.M. *Blue Moose* (Dodd, 1975) 3–5. The maitre d' of Mr. Breton's gourmet restaurant in the wild is a talking blue moose.

5428. ____. *Return of the Moose* (Dodd, 1979) 3–5. The blue moose who helps Mr. Breton run his restaurant writes what he is sure is the greatest book written by man or moose.

5429. Pittman, Helena. *Dinosaur for Gerald* (Carolrhoda, 1990) k–3. Mom and Dad find a way to satisfy Gerald, who wants a real dinosaur for his birthday.

5430. ____. *Gerald-Not-Practical* (Carolrhoda, 1990) k–3. Despite his family's opinion that his love of drawing is impractical, Gerald insists that his art is important because it makes him feel good.

5431. Pizer, Abigail. *Nosey Gilbert* (Dial, 1987) k–3. When Gilbert the dog mischievously chases the bees around his garden he gets a nasty sting on the nose that requires a dreaded trip to the veterinarian.
5432. ____. *Harry's Night Out* (Dial, 1987) k–3. Harry the cat makes a nocturnal foray in search of food and encounters a number of other creatures of the night.
5433. ____. *Percy the Duck* (Macmillan, 1988) k–3. Mr. and Mrs. Potter and their daughter Amy are happy with life on their immaculate, old-fashioned farm, but their animals have unsuitable ambitions. The young duck longs to fly and falls off several jumping places, watched with smug satisfaction by the ginger cat Billingsgate.
5434. ____. *Hattie the Goat* (Macmillan, 1988) k–3. The tale of a very hungry goat's unorthodox gastronomic tastes.
5435. ____. *Penelope the Pig* (Macmillan, 1988) k–3. Mr. and Mrs. Potter and their daughter Amy are happy with life on their immaculate, old-fashioned farm, but their animals have unsuitable ambitions. Penelope, seeing herself as a lady of leisure, is found sitting on the sofa in the parlor.
5436. ____. *Charlie the Puppy* (Carolrhoda, 1989) k–3. Winsome hound Charlie is lonely for his mistress, Amy, while she is at school. He tried to engage the other animals in play.

5437. Platt, Kin. *Big Max* (Harper, 1965) 2–4. The king of Pooka Pooka called upon Big Max, the world's greatest detective, for help in finding his stolen elephant. A story of how Big Max looked and what he thought, and where Jumbo was finally found.
5438. ____. *Big Max in the Mystery of the Missing Moose* (Harper, 1977) 2–4. Big Max, the world's greatest detective, helps the zoo keeper find a missing moose.

5439. Polisar, Barry. *Snake Who Was Afraid of People* (Rainbow, 1988) 2–4. Tells the story of a snake whose fears of people are confirmed when a young child holds him captive in a jar.
5440. ____. *Snakes and the Boy Who Was Afraid of Them* (Rainbow, 1988) 2–4. A book about fears. Everybody has them and there's really nothing wrong with having them. Lenny thinks for himself against a popularly held belief and is not necessarily wrong about what he thinks.

5441. Polushkin, Maria. *Kitten in Trouble* (Bradbury, 1986) k–3. A kitten wakes up early and decides to explore the house.
5442. ____. *Here's That Kitten* (Bradbury, 1989) k–3. A kitten causes havoc in the house knocking over things, climbing onto the roof and hiding in the

chimney and then spreading soot everywhere before charming the family with its cuteness.

5443. Pope, Ray. *Telford and the American Visitor* (Macdonald, 1970) 3–5. Mark has to protect Telford and his family from the prying eyes and cine-film of an American visitor.
5444. ____. *Telford and the Festiniog Railway* (Macdonald, 1973) 3–5. Telford and his family live in Mark's 00 gauge railway. Mark makes friends with Peter, who takes Telford to search for his son, Drummond on the Festiniog Railway.
5445. ____. *Telford Saves the Line* (Macdonald, 1974) 3–5. The attempt to save a rural branch line from closure. This small family lives in Mark's model railroad system.
5446. ____. *Telford Goes Dutch* (Macdonald, 1976) 3–5. Telford goes to Holland and meets a Dutch model-railroad family. He almost drowns when there is a flood and he also goes hungry. He is rescued by Mark, Jan and Vincent, Dutch boys who are from the Dutch model family.
5447. ____. *Telford Tells the Truth* (Macdonald, 1977) 3–5. In Mark's attic is a railway layout where Telford lives. Telford makes his first contact with the outside world. He is looking for a steam roller in an old graveyard of abandoned locomotives.
5448. ____. *Telford and the Prairie Battle* (Macdonald, 1979) 3–5. Telford, 70, Brindly, 80, Drummond, Telford's son and Stanier Telford's grandson work on a 00 gauge railway. They are tiny railway men who live in Mark's railway system. They are stolen from a cab, sold to a dealer and then bought by a model railway. They are finally returned to their rightful owners.

5449. Poploff, Michelle. *Busy O'Brien and the Great Bubble Gum Blowout* (Walker, 1991) 4–6. Busy O'Brien, ten, tries to raise funds for the town's Meal Mobile by organizing the Great Bubblegum Blowout.
5450. ____. *Busy O'Brien and the Caterpillar Punch Bunch* (Walker, 1992) 4–6. Busy O'Brien works hard campaigning for her friend Mr. Ficken to win the town's Good Neighbor of the Year Contest, aware that her rival Jolly Van Pelt has entered her aunt in the contest.

5451. Porte, Barbara. *Harry's Visit* (Greenwillow, 1983) 2–4. Expecting he won't have a good time, Harry visits his parents' friends.
5452. ____. *Harry's Dog* (Greenwillow, 1984) 2–4. Harry wants very much to keep Girl, his new dog, even though his father is allergic to dogs.
5453. ____. *Harry's Mom* (Greenwillow, 1985) 2–4. Even though Harry's mother died when he was one, he still has loving family members who can tell him how brave and wonderful she was.
5454. ____. *Harry in Trouble* (Greenwillow, 1989) 2–4. Harry is upset about losing his library card three times in a row, but feels better when he learns that

his father and his friend Dorcas sometimes lose things.

5455. ____. *Harry Gets an Uncle* (Greenwillow, 1991) 2–4. Harry is worried about being the ring boy at his Aunt Rose's wedding. After he hears his friend Dorcas tell horror stories about what went wrong at her Uncle Fred's wedding.

5456. ____. *Harry's Birthday* (Greenwillow, 1994) 2–4. Harry, who is hoping to get a cowboy hat for his birthday, is quite surprised when he opens all the presents at his party.

5457. Porter, Connie. *Meet Addy* (Pleasant, 1993) 2–4. Nine-year-old Addy Walker escapes from a cruel life of slavery to freedom during the Civil War.

5458. ____. *Addy Learns a Lesson* (Pleasant, 1993) 4–6. After escaping from a plantation in North Carolina, Addy and her mother arrive in Philadelphia, where Addy goes to school and learns a lesson in true friendship.

5459. ____. *Happy Birthday Addy* (Pleasant, 1993) 4–6. Trying to shape a new life of freedom in Philadelphia after having been a slave, Addy finds inspiration from a new friend.

5460. ____. *Addy's Surprise* (Pleasant, 1993) 4–6. Addy and her mother forgo their Christmas plans to help the newly freed slaves arriving in Philadelphia during the Civil War.

5461. ____. *Addy Saves the Day* (Pleasant, 1994) 4–6. Addy and Harriet feud over everything, including fund-raising plans to help the families of freed slaves, but tragedy finally forces them to stop fighting and work together.

5462. ____. *Changes for Addy* (Pleasant, 1994) 4–6. After the Civil War ends, Addy desperately hopes that her family will be reunited in freedom in Philadelphia, but the future may hold both happiness and heartache.

5463. Postgate, Oliver. *King of the Nogs* (Holiday, 1968) 2–4. Noggin leaves the fjords to voyage to the Land of the Midnight Sun. There he finds Niika of the Nooks and returns with her as his bride. He fights his Uncle Nogbad the Bad who flies to Finland.

5464. ____. *Ice Dragon* (Holiday, 1968) 2–4. Noggin the Nog takes an expedition to fight a fearsome ice dragon in the hot-water valley of Nog. Instead of fighting, Nog helps the dragon recover the treasure of the Dragons' Friendly Society, stolen by Nogbad the Bad.

5465. ____. *Nogmania* (Kaye, 1977) 2–4. Noggin the Nog shows life in the Far Northland with whimsical illustrations.

5466. Postgate, Oliver. *Noggin, the King* (White, 1966) 2–4. King Noggin is a good king, loved by his people; but he wants to become king of the birds, too. The story tells how he achieves this.

5467. ____. *Noggin and the Whale* (White, 1967)

2–4. The villagers on the Land of Nog try to get a whale out of the harbor.

5468. ____. *Nogbad and the Elephants* (White, 1967) 2–4. A story of the efforts of King Noggin's son to cheer up his baby elephant and of Nogbad the Bad's attempts to steal the elephant.

5469. ____. *Noggin and the Moon Mouse* (White, 1967) 2–4. A spaceship that operates on oil, vinegar and soapflakes and carries a moon mouse lands in the village horse-trough.

5470. ____. *Noggin and the Flowers* (White, 1980) 2–4. A reprint of an episode in the life of the Nogs, in which Nogbad's evil plans with a fast-growing plant are turned against him. A cheerful warning of how man can invent forces beyond his control.

5471. Postgate, Oliver. *Ivor's Outing* (Abelard, 1967) k–3. Jones the Steam Engine and Dai conspire to include Ivor in the Choral Society's annual seaside outing.

5472. ____. *Ivor's Birthday* (Collins, 1984) k–3. Ivor the machine eats a birthday cake of coal dust and cement mixed with gunpowder and chopped Roman candles. He has knitted a large pullover and gives it to a cold elephant.

5473. ____. *Ivor the Engine* (Collins) k–3.

5474. Potter, Bronson. *Isfendiar and the Wild Donkeys* (Atheneum, 1967) 3–5. Isfendiar goes across the desert looking for wild donkeys. The daily life of a village just outside the desert is detailed.

5475. ____. *Isfendiar and the Bears of Mazandaran* (Atheneum, 1969) 3–5. Isfendiar leaves his desert village to seek his fortune in the mountains of Iran. There he outwits a fabled killer bear in combat and is then content to return home.

5476. Poulet, Virginia. *Blue Bug and the Bullies* (Children's 1971) k–3. One word on each page describes a blue bug's reaction to the bullies that threaten him.

5477. ____. *Blue Bug's Safety Book* (Children's, 1973) k–3. By observing the safety signs, Blue Bug arrives home unharmed.

5478. ____. *Blue Bug's Vegetable Garden* (Children's, 1973) k–3. Blue Bug encounters many vegetables while searching for his favorite one.

5479. ____. *Blue Bug's Beach Party* (Children's, 1973) k–3. Before they can have their beach party, Blue Bug and his friends have to clean the litter off the beach.

5480. ____. *Blue Bug to the Rescue* (Children's, 1976) k–3. Blue Bug warns the other bugs never to taste or to eat the common poisonous plants such as holly, azaleas, and buttercups.

5481. ____. *Blue Bug's Surprise* (Children's, 1977) k–3. Blue Bug surprises his friend by giving her many kinds of flowers. Then she surprises him.

5482. ____. *Blue Bug Finds a Friend* (Children's, 1977) k–3. Blue Bug looks in many kinds of trees before he finds Peebee's hiding place.

5483. ____. *Blue Bug's Circus* (Children's, 1977) k–3. Blue Bug unsuccessfully tries many different acts in the circus before becoming the clown.

5484. ____. *Blue Bug Visits Mexico* (Children's, 1978) k–3. In Mexico, Blue Bug enjoys looking at the toys and crafts, watching people before the fiesta, and dancing with the jumping beans.

5485. ____. *Blue Bug Goes to the Library* (Children's, 1979) k–3. Brief text and illustrations outline the activities and materials at the library.

5486. ____. *Blue Bug's Book of Colors* (Children's, 1981) k–3. Blue Bug discovers through trial and error how colors mix to make different colors.

5487. ____. *Blue Bug Goes to School* (Children's, 1985) k–3. Blue Bug enjoys many school activities, such as printing his name, cutting out snowflakes, learning new games, and making a special surprise for the teacher.

5488. ____. *Blue Bug goes to Paris* (Children's, 1986) k–3. Blue Bug goes to Paris, where he sees the sights and buys postcards and souvenirs.

5489. ____. *Blue Bug's Christmas* (Children's, 1987) k–3. Blue Bug and his friends choose and decorate a tree for Christmas.

5490. Poulin, Stephane. *Have You Seen Josephine?* (Tundra, 1986) k–3. Daniel trails his cat through the streets of Montreal to find out where she goes each Saturday.

5491. ____. *Can You Catch Josephine?* (Tundra, 1987) k–3. When Daniel's cat sneaks into school with him he spends a long time trying to capture her from various areas of the school building.

5492. ____. *Could You Stop Josephine?* (Tundra, 1988) k–3. Josephine the cat leads her master Daniel on a merry chase all over his cousin's farm.

5493. Powling, Chris. *Hiccup Harry* (Dutton, 1988) 2–4. Harry disrupts the school when he tries to get rid of a bad case of the hiccups.

5494. ____. *Harry's Party* (Dutton, 1989) 2–4

5495. ____. *Harry with Spots On* (Dutton, 1992) 2–4.

5496. ____. *Harry Moves House* (Dutton, 1993) 2–4.

5497. Pressense, de Domitille. *Emily and Arthur* (Tundra, 1977) k–3. Emily loves Arthur and looks for him everywhere. During her search she finds her green and white necklace, a missing earring, a storybook and a lost stocking. But not Arthur. She and her friend Stephen finally find him munching lettuce in the garden.

5498. ____. *Emily* (Checkerboard, 1978) k–3. Emily's family and her pet hedgehog, Arthur, are introduced. When Emily goes for a walk and can't find her way home, Arthur leads her back.

5499. ____. *Emily Won't Take a Bath* (Checkerboard,) 1992. k–3

5500. ____. *Emily and the Snails* (Checkerboard, 1992) k–3.

5501. ____. *Emily Won't Eat* (Checkerboard, 1992) k–3.

5502. ____. *Emily Wet the Bed* (Checkerboard, 1992) k–3.

5503. Preussler, Otfried. *Robber Hotzenplotz* (Abelard, 1965) 4–6. Kasperl and Seppel found themselves in quite a fix in trying to retrieve Grandmother's musical coffee mill from the wicked robber Hotzenplotz.

5504. ____. *Further Adventures of Robber Hotzenplotz* (Abelard, 1971) 4–6. Robber Hotzenplotz escapes from the firehouse and holds up Grandma and eats all the sausages. He also kidnaps her. The hero uses a crystal ball and a dog to track them down.

5505. ____. *Final Adventures of Robber Hotzenplotz* (Abelard, 1975) 4–6. A bicycle is missing and Hotzenplotz is caught returning it to its owner. He is caught blowing up his own stock of gunpowder. His reputation is hard to live down. Kasperl and Seppel try to help..and so does Fido.

5506. Price, Willard. *Amazon Adventures* (Day, 1949) 4–6. An account of a trip down the Amazon River on an animal-collecting tour led by Hal and Roger and their Indian guide.

5507. ____. *South Sea Adventure* (Day, 1952) 4–6. Hal and Roger are collecting deep sea specimens and looking for a secret pearl lagoon. They encounter sea monsters, hurricanes and escape from a desert island on a raft.

5508. ____. *Volcano Adventure* (Day, 1956) 4–6. Hal and Roger explore a volcano in a diving bell and are trapped in a volcano ring.

5509. ____. *Whale Adventure* (Day, 1960) 4–6. Hal and Roger sign up on an old square rigger and go whaling. The captain is cruel but the crew reaches shore and the captain is disgraced.

5510. ____. *African Adventure* (Day, 1949/1962) 4–6. Hal and Roger go to Africa on an animal collecting tour for American zoos. (A reissue of the 1949 version.)

5511. ____. *Elephant Adventure* (Day, 1964) 4–6. Hal and Roger are to trap young African elephants for the zoo. They encounter native superstitions and slave trading.

5512. ____. *Safari Adventure* (Day, 1966) 4–6. Hal and Roger are helping an African game warden catch animal poachers.

5513. ____. *Lion Adventure* (Day, 1967) 4–6. Hal and Roger are after two man-eating lions. They must be careful not to kill any innocent lions.

5514. ____. *Gorilla Adventure* (Day, 1969) 4–6. Hal and Roger search for and capture a giant gorilla. They see a rare white python and a black panther.

5515. ____. *Diving Adventure* (Day, 1970) 4–6. Hal and Roger make friends with dolphins as they collect fish specimens for their father. Another adventure with sea snakes, man-eating sharks and their old murderous friend Merlin Kaggs.

5516. Provost, Gary. *Good If It Goes* (Bradbury, 1984) 5–8. David has a few problems: Bar Mitzvah practice, his dying grandfather, a girl he just met and a younger brother. He survives it all.

5517. ____. *David and Max* (Bradbury, 1988) 5–8. David learns from his grandfather the horrors of the Holocaust and uses this knowledge to be stronger.

5518. Proysen, Alf. *Mrs. Pepperpot's Busy Day* (Astor, 1970) 3–5. Mrs. Pepperpot can shrink to any size, sometimes at inconvenient moments.

5519. ____. *Mrs. Pepperpot's Outing* (Pantheon, 1971) 3–5. Each time Mrs. Pepperpot shrinks she encounters an animal that becomes a pet when she returns to normal size.

5520. ____. *Mrs. Pepperpot's Christmas* (Astor, 1972) 3–5. Mrs. Pepperpot can shrink to the size of a pepperpot. She hides her husband's knapsack when he goes to the Christmas market. She can get him to buy everything she needs even though he thinks it's a waste of money.

5521. ____. *Mrs. Pepperpot's Year* (Astor, 1973) 3–5. Mrs. Pepperpot is shrewd, benevolent and fun. She can shrink in size to protect and help people and animals in need. There is a story for each month of the year.

5522. ____. *Mrs. Pepperpot to the Rescue* (Dell, 1981) 3–5. Seven more short stories about this Norwegian housewife who can shrink in size upon demand.

5523. ____. *Mrs. Pepperpot Again* (Astor, 1986) 3–5. In these stories Mrs. Pepperpot copes with a sly fox, a wolf, and a bear, she gains the friendship of mice and cats; and outwits a mouse.

5524. ____. *Mrs. Pepperpot in the Magic Wood* (Puffin, 1988) 3–5. Mrs. Pepperpot is a fiery lady who shrinks in size at different times. She attempts to learn how to swim with a frog as a teacher, she befriends a misused parakeet and participates in a puppet show.

5525. ____. *Little Old Mrs. Pepperpot* (Astor, 1989) 3–5. Stories about a woman who can shrink to the size of a pepper shaker.

5526. ____. *Mrs. Pepperpot and the Bilberries* (Puffin, 1960/1990) 3–5. Mrs. Pepperpot was collecting bilberries. As she was putting the last batch into her basket, her quick wits tricked greedy animals, whose intentions were clear.

5527. ____. *Mrs. Pepperpot and the Moose* (Farrar, 1991) 3–5. How Mrs. Pepperpot manages to frighten away a moose from her yard, even though she has shrunk to the size of a teaspoon.

5528. ____. *Mrs. Pepperpot's Omnibus* (Hutchinson, 1966) 3–5. Contains: "Little Miss Pepperpot"; "Mrs. Pepperpot Again"; "Mrs. Pepperpot to the Rescue."

5529. Pryor, Anslie. *Baby Blue Cat and the Dirty Dog Brothers* (Viking, 1987) k–3. Baby Blue Cat has a romp of a good time playing with the Dirty Dog Brothers in the sooty ashes and the very big mud puddle.

5530. ____. *Baby Blue Cat Who Said No* (Viking, 1988) k–3. The Baby Blue Cat loves to say "no" to everything from Mama Cat's delicious supper to a bedtime story.

5531. ____. *Baby Blue Cat and the Whole Batch of Cookies* (Viking, 1989) k–3. When Mama cat decides to make a special snack of milk and cookies, Baby Blue Cat can't resist sneaking into the kitchen and eating the whole bunch.

5532. ____. *Baby Blue Cat and the Smiley Worm Doll* (Viking, 1990) k–3. Baby Blue Cat is sad when he misplaces his favorite stuffed toy, a smiley worm doll, while gathering leaves for Mr. Gray Rabbit. Other cats offer their toys and Grandma Dog tries to make another one like it but he is only happy when Mr. Gray Rabbit returns the tattered doll.

5533. Pryor, Bonnie. *Rats, Spiders and Love* (Morrow, 1986) 5–8. Samantha's mother remarries and is going to move to Ohio with her new husband. Samantha does all she knows to keep from going along.

5534. ____. *Horses in the Garage* (Morrow, 1992) 5–8. Sixth grader Samantha finds a way to cope with her difficulties in adjusting to a new stepfather, a new home and a new school when she makes friends with the unconventional Jasmine and learns to ride a horse.

5535. Pryor, Bonnie. *Amanda and April* (Morrow, 1986) k–3. Amanda has many misadventures on the way to Violet's party and discovers how really helpful her little sister April can be.

5536. ____. *Merry Christmas, Amanda and April* (Morrow, 1990) k–3. Trying her best to be good before Christmas, Amanda Pig does an errand for her mother and is helped by her little sister April.

5537. Pryor, Bonnie. *Grandpa Bear* (Morrow, 1985) k–3. Relates the imaginative games Grandpa Bear plays with Samantha and the affection between them.

5538. ____. *Grandpa Bear's Christmas* (Morrow, 1986) k–3. The Bear family's winter adventures prepare them for Christmas.

5539. Pryor, Bonnie. *Mr. Munday and the Rustlers* (Prentice, 1987) k–3. Mr. Munday, a bumbling mailman, outwits ornery rustlers when he and his cat take care of the farm.

5540. ____. *Mr. Munday and the Space Creatures* (S & S, 1989) k–3. When bumbling mailman Mr. Munday trades places with a space creature, everyone gets unexpectedly wonderful surprises.

5541. Pulver, Robin. *Mrs. Toggle's Zipper* (Four Winds, 1990) k–3. A teacher is pulled out of her zipped-up coat by students, the school nurse and the principal by pulling her arms, legs and head.

5542. ____. *Mrs. Toggle and the Dinosaur* (Macmillan, 1991) k–3. Mrs. Toggle and her class prepare for the arrival of a new student whom they expect to be a dinosaur.

5543. ____. *Mrs. Toggle's Beautiful Blue Shoe* (Four Winds, 1994) k–3. Mrs. Toggle joins the children in a game of kickball and loses her beautiful blue shoe.

5544. Quackenbush, Robert. *Henry's Awful Mistake* (Parents, 1980) 2–4. Henry the duck tries all sorts of methods to rid his kitchen of an ant before his guest comes to dinner.

5545. ____. *Henry's Important Date* (Parents, 1981) 2–4. Due to circumstances beyond his control, Henry arrives at Clara's birthday party just before he thinks it will end.

5546. ____. *Henry Goes West* (Parents, 1982) 2–4. Lonely without his friend Clara who is vacationing out West, Henry the duck decides to pay her a surprise visit.

5547. ____. *Henry Babysits* (Parents, 1982) 2–4. Henry the duck has his hands full when all the neighbors bring their babies for him to watch one day.

5548. ____. *Henry's World Tour* (Doubleday, 1992) 2–4. Henry the duck goes to visit his far-flung cousins. He wants to know from whom he inherited a speckled feather. He gets covered with chocolate mousse, yodels in Switzerland and is squashed by a camel in Egypt. He is kidnapped by a kangaroo in Australia and dances in Brazil. But he doesn't find out the mystery of the speckled feather…yet.

5549. Quackenbush, Robert. *Funny Bunnies* (Clarion, 19084) k–3. While little Lucy is out for a swim, various bunnies from the staff crowd into her family's hotel room.

5550. ____. *Funny Bunnies on the Run* (Clarion, 1989) k–3. When the lights go out at home, the Bunny family flips every switch with no success until the power returns and the bunnies find themselves in trouble when all the appliances go on at once.

5551. Quackenbush, Robert. *Chuck Lends a Paw* (Clarion, 1986) k–3. Chuck Mouse helps his friend, Maxine, move a tall chest of drawers with disastrous results.

5552. ____. *Mouse Feathers* (Clarion, 1988) k–3. While Maxine Mouse baby-sits her two nephews, a pillow fight gets out of control and the nephews come down with bad cases of "Mouse Feathers."

5553. Quackenbush, Robert. *Piet Potter's First Case* (McGraw, 1980) 2–4. A boy detective uses a blank sheet of paper, a key and a subway map to help a neighbor solve a puzzling message in a will.

5554. ____. *Piet Potter Returns* (McGraw, 1980) 2–4. Amazing boy detective Piet and his friend Amy track down clues that lead to the solution of elevator tie-ups and crime.

5555. ____. *Piet Potter Strikes Again* (McGraw, 1981) 2–4. Piet Potter, the amazing boy private eye, sets out to discover who is trying to sabotage a neighbor's birthday party.

5556. ____. *Piet Potter to the Rescue* (McGraw, 1981) 2–4. Amazing boy detective Piet Potter races against time to save a public event from ruin, although he has only a series of mysterious phone calls as clues.

5557. ____. *Piet Potter's Hot Clue* (McGraw, 1982) 2–4. While attending an Off Off Broadway opening, amazing boy detective Piet Potter is called upon to investigate the mysterious disappearance of one of the show's leading players.

5558. ____. *Piet Potter on the Run* (McGraw, 1982) 2–4. A mysterious envelope, mistakenly placed in his motel pool locker, launches amazing boy detective Piet Potter on a chase across Manhattan which ends at the United Nations.

5559. Quackenbush, Robert. *Pete Pack Rat* (Lothrop, 1976) 3–5. When the vallainous Gizzard Coyote comes to Pebble Junction he strikes terror in the hearts of the animal inhabitants—but Pete Pack Rat works out a plan.

5560. ____. *Pete Pack Rat and the Gila Monster Gang* (Lothrop, 1978) 3–5. The Gila Monster Gang robs the Pebble Junction bank and kidnaps Sheriff Sally Gopher, but Pete Pack Rat's ingenuity saves the day.

5561. ____. *Pete Pack Rat's Christmas Eve Surprise* (Lothrop, 1981) 3–5. Pete Pack Rat saves Christmas for Pebble Junction by substituting a fake piñata for the real thing when the Gila Monster Gang escapes from jail. The gang steals the fake, which contains chocolate-covered soap. Pete produces the real piñata and all goes well.

5562. Quackenbush, Robert. *Detective Mole* (Lothrop, 1976) 2–4. Detective Mole finds solutions to other animals' mysteries.

5563. ____. *Detective Mole and the Secret Clues* (Lothrop, 1977) 2–4. Detective Mole helps the Chicken family decipher the secret clues that will permit them to inherit their rich uncle's mansion.

5564. ____. *Detective Mole and the Tip Top Mystery* (Lothrop, 1978) 2–4. When mysterious mishaps drive guests away from the Tip Top Inn, Detective Mole investigates.

5565. ____. *Detective Mole and the Seashore Mystery* (Lothrop, 1979) 2–4. With cool-headed logic, Detective Mole tracks down the robber of Captain Bills' valuable pearl.

5566. ____. *Detective Mole and the Circus Mystery* (Lothrop, 1980) 2–4. When Melba the amazing tattooed cow disappears from the circus on her wedding day, Detective Mole is called to solve the mystery.

5567. ____. *Detective Mole and the Halloween Mystery* (Lothrop, 1981) 2–4. When the jack o' lanterns from every porch in town are stolen Detective Mole investigates.

5568. ____. *Detective Mole and the Haunted Castle Mystery* (Lothrop, 1985) 2–4. Detective Mole investigates the mystery of hidden treasure, strange noises, and the disappearing guests at the castle of the Rabbit family.

5569. Quackenbush, Robert. *Express Train to Trouble* (Prentice, 1981) 2–4. When troublesome George Ruddy Duck disappears on the express train to Cairo, Miss Mallard applies her detective genius to find out what happened and save the reputation of the train.

5570. ____. *Dig to Disaster* (Prentice, 1982) 2–4. When the terrifying headless demon of Kimbu Tacka threatens an archaeological expedition in the South American jungle, Miss Mallard uses her detective skills to unravel the clues and uncover the true villain.

5571. ____. *Cable Car to Catastrophe* (Prentice, 1982) 2–4. While riding a cable car in the Alps, Miss Mallard witnesses a robbery at the retreat of the famed Madame Merganzer.

5572. ____. *Gondola to Danger* (Prentice, 1983) 2–4. While attending an opera festival in Venice, Miss Mallard investigates the theft of a masterpiece from Doges Palace.

5573. ____. *Stairway to Doom* (Prentice, 1983) 2–4. As one of 13 guests invited to historic Duckinbill Castle to hear the will of her late great-aunt, Miss Mallard finds the other guests have disappeared overnight and it is up to her to solve the mystery.

5574. ____. *Rickshaw to Horror* (Prentice, 1984) 2–4. Miss Mallard, the world famous ducktective, visits Hong King, where she encounters a retired English military duck who seems to have the power to predict disasters.

5575. ____. *Taxi to Intrigue* (Prentice, 1984) 2–4. On the seat of a London taxi Miss Mallard, the ducktective, finds a knitting bag containing secret plans for a high-powered missile.

5576. ____. *Bicycle to Treachery* (Prentice, 1985) 2–4. While on a bicycle trip across Holland, Miss Mallard runs into danger when she unwittingly uncovers a smuggling operation.

5577. ____. *Stage Door to Terror* (Prentice, 1985) 2–4. In Paris to visit an old friend, Miss Mallard becomes involved in one of the most terrifying cases of her career centering around the disappearance of her friend's granddaughter and the long-ago theft of a jewel.

5578. ____. *Surfboard to Peril* (Prentice, 1986) 2–4. While surfing in Hawaii, world-famous Miss Mallard launches into one of the most dangerous cases, which involves the ownership of sacred lands. There are kidnappings, bribery, blackmail and mistaken identities.

5579. ____. *Texas Trail to Calamity* (Prentice, 1986) 2–4. When her horse runs away with her across the desert, Miss Mallard, the famous ducktective, finds

herself at a forbidding ranch where she must spend the night despite mysterious warnings about her safety.

5580. ____. *Dogsled to Dread* (Prentice, 1987) 2–4. When Miss Mallard, the famous ducktective, is invited to Alaska to see the start of the famous dog-sled race, her skills are challenged by the dognapping of a prize husky.

5581. ____. *Danger in Tibet* (Pippin, 1989) 2–4. The world-famous ducktective investigates the disappearance of her nephew Inspector Willard Widgeon, during a secret mission in the Himalayas, and uncovers a dastardly plot that could destroy Mt. Everest.

5582. ____. *Lost in the Amazon* (Pippin, 1990) 2–4. When a brilliant scientist is abducted from a hotel in Rio de Janeiro, Miss Mallard, the famous ducktective, embarks on a dangerous search that takes her deep into the Amazon jungle.

5583. ____. *Evil Under the Sea* (Pippin, 1992) 2–4. Jacques Canard, noted undersea explorer, asks Miss Mallard to help discover who is destroying the coral in Australia's Great Barrier Reef.

5584. Radford, Derek. *Harry Builds a House* (Aladdin, 1990) k–3. Harry Hippo and his friends build a house, step by step from digging a ditch for the pipes to putting in the last joints and plugs.

5585. ____. *Harry at the Airport* (Aladdin, 1991) k–3. As a hippopotamus family goes to the airport to take a flight, the reader can observe activities behind the scenes and see the things travelers do both at the airport and on the plane.

5586. ____. *Harry at the Garage* (Candlewick, 1995) k–3. Harry Hippo and his family take the car to the garage for servicing and learn how cars work and are repaired.

5587. Radin, Ruth. *Tac's Island* (Macmillan, 1986) 2–4. Steve is vacationing off the Virginia coast. He meets Tac, a year-round resident. Their friendship builds as they share adventures exploring the island.

5588. ____. *Tac's Turn* (Macmillan, 1987) 2–4. Now Tac is visiting Steve in Philadelphia. They test each other's friendship through personality clashes and action.

5589. Radlauer, Ruth. *Molly* (Prentice, 1987) k–3. Molly, a rambunctious four-year-old, has a busy day at the nursery school painting, playing, pasting, and tricycle riding.

5590. ____. *Molly Goes Hiking* (Prentice, 1987) k–3. Adventurous Molly, four, goes hiking in the "mountains" of her backyard.

5591. ____. *Breakfast by Molly* (S & S, 1988) k–3. For Mom's birthday Molly makes her a breakfast of orange juice, milk, a peanut butter sandwich, cereal with chocolate sauce and a pickle.

5592. ____. *Molly at the Library* (S & S, 1988) k–3. Molly, four, goes to the library with her father and is thrilled to discover that she can take home ten books for fourteen days.

5593. Rae, Gwyneed. *Mary Plain on Holiday* (Routledge, 1976) k–3. Four stories about a mischievous bear cub. Contains: "Mostly Mary"; "All Mary"; "Mary Plain in Town"; "Mary Plain on Holiday."

5594. ____. *Mostly Mary* (Routledge, 1976) k–3. Mary is a little orphan girl bear living with her grandmother, Big Wool. She fights for attention with her cousins, Marionetta and Little Wool.

5595. ____. *All Mary* (Routledge, 1976) k–3.

5596. ____. *Mary Plain in Town* (Routledge, 1976) k–3.

5597. Rana, Indi. *Devil on Auntie's Shoulder* (Hodder, 1986) 4–6. Ravi's Indian aunt comes to England to visit. Ravi has difficulty accepting his Indian heritage. But he must come to terms with Usha Auntie and her "devils."

5598. ____. *Devil in the Dustbin* (Hamilton, 1990) 4–6. The devil is a tree-devil from Madras but got accidentally transported to England. He is befriended by Ranjana. He and Ranjana and her friends have many adventures.

5599. Rand, Gloria. *Salty Dog* (Holt, 1989) k–3. Salty the dog helps his master Zack build a sailboat.

5600. ____. *Salty Sails North* (Holt, 1990) k–3. Salty the dog and his master Zack sail north to Alaska, encountering other ships, a storm, wild animals on the shore, and an iceberg.

5601. ____. *Salty Takes Off* (Holt, 1991) k–3. While wintering in Alaska, Salty the dog falls from an airplane and must survive until his master Zack finds him.

5602. Ransom, Candice. *Who Needs Third Grade?* (Troll, 1993) 4–6. Amber, eight, still adjusting to her parents' divorce, starts third grade and finds herself torn with jealousy over the new girl Delight, who seems to be stealing away Amber's best friend Mindy.

5603. ____. *Third Grade Stars* (Troll, 1994) 4–6. Third grader Amber experiences the jealousy of her friend Delight, a longing to recapture her lost popularity and a new passion for gymnastics.

5604. ____. *Third Grade Detective* (Troll, 1994) 4–6. Amber is looking forward to a fun-filled summer vacation, but when her beloved stuffed raccoon disappears and her two best friends start acting funny, she discovers that things don't always turn out the way you want.

5605. ____. *Today 5th Grade, Tomorrow the World* (Willowisp, 1989) 4–6. Amber, ten, tries to join the "in group" by presenting her mother as an actress and her father as a football star. One lie needs to be covered by another lie in this attempt to belong.

5606. Ransom, Candice. *My Sister, the Meanie* (Scholastic, 1988) 5–8. Seeking to become a "seventh grade somebody," Jackie goes too far in copying her older sister which precipitates war between them.

5607. ____. *My Sister, the Traitor* (Scholastic, 1989) 5–8. Jackie lives in the shadow of her older sister. She meets Russ and likes him but it's Shaun she dates in spite of the fact that she has a boyfriend.

5608. ____. *My Sister the Creep* (Scholastic, 1989) 5–8. Jackie comes to terms with her older sister Sharon and herself when Sharon leaves home to attend cosmetology school.

5609. Raphael, Elaine. *Donkey and Carlo* (Harper, 1978) k–3. Carlo becomes so involved at the market that he forgets his promise to Donkey.

5610. ____. *Donkey, It's Snowing* (Harper, 1981) k–3. A farmer and his donkey enjoy the first snowfall of the winter.

5611. Rayner, Mary. *Mr. and Mrs. Pig's Evening Out* (Atheneum, 1976) k–3. When Mr. and Mrs. Pig go out for the evening, Mrs. Wolf is sent to baby-sit for the ten piglets, with almost disastrous results. But ten piglets to one wolf is overwhelming.

5612. ____. *Mrs. Pig's Bulk Buy* (Atheneum, 1981) k–3. The piglets are delighted when Mrs. Pig stocks up on ketchup, their favorite food, until they realize it's all they will be eating.

5613. ____. *Mrs. Pig gets Cross and Other Stories* (Dutton, 1987) k–3. Life in the busy Pig household is always eventful, as Father, Mother and ten children have a big party, struggle against bad moods, and all end up in the same bed one night.

5614. Rayner, Mary. *Garth Pig and the Ice Cream Lady* (Macmillan, 1977) k–3. A wolf disguised as an ice cream vendor almost succeeds in making a piglet dinner out of Garth.

5615. ____. *Bathtime for Garth Pig* (Macmillan, 1991) k–3. Benjamin Pig is having a disagreeable day of sulks and rotten behavior, so big sister Sarah asks him to do all the things she intends him to refuse. Naturally he obliges.

5616. ____. *Garth Pig Steals the Show* (Dutton, 1993) k–3. During a musical concert for the mayor, the family Pig Players discover that their newest member, a lady sousaphonist, likes pig just a little too much.

5617. Razzi, Jim. *Sherluck Bones Mystery #1* (Troll, 1982) 4–6. Sherluck Bones solves five mysteries. His amiable scottie assistant, Scotson helps this dog detective. Very much like "Encyclopedia Brown."

5618. ____. *Sherluck Bones Mystery #2* (Troll, 1982) 4–6. Sherluck Bones and Scotson solve five more mysteries, following clues that the reader also shares.

5619. ____. *Sherluck Bones Mystery #3* (Troll, 1983) 4–6. Six cases for Sherluck Bones one about robots and electricity. Some are obvious, some are clever and some are so-so.

5620. ____. *Sherluck Bones Mystery #4* (Troll, 1984) 4–6. Sherluck Bones and Scotson are in Kennelwood where dogs dress and act like humans. There are several mysteries and crimes for Bones and Scotson to solve.

5621. ____. *Sherluck Bones Mystery #5* (Troll, 1984) 4–6. Six new mysteries to be solved by Sherluck Bones and Scotson.

5622. Reed, Giles. *Banana Bunch* (Rourke, 1981) k–3. Despite the nasty tricks Billy, Peanut and Scruff play on them, the Banana Bunch thrills its audience with lively songs and dances.

5623. ____. *Learn the Alphabet with the Munch Bunch* (Rourke, 1981) k–3. The Munch Bunch engage in various activities using objects with names beginning with each letter of the alphabet.

5624. ____. *Learn to Count with the Munch Bunch* (Rourke, 1981) k–3. The members of the Munch Bunch visit a fair and enjoy games and rides using the numbers from one to twenty.

5625. Reese, Bob. *Scary Larry the Very Very Hairy Tarantula* (Children's, 1981) k–3. Papa Grasshopper attempts to protect the other grasshoppers from a scary hairy tarantula.

5626. ____. *Scary Larry* (Children's, 1981) k–3. Scary Larry is one of Rapid Robert's critter pals. This story includes the telling of grasshoppers that eventually scare Larry off.

5627. ____. *Scary Larry Meets Big Willie* (Children's, 1983) k–3. Tired of being terrorized by Scary Larry, the tarantula, the grasshoppers "create" Big Willie in their defense.

5628. ____. *Calico Jack and the Desert Critters* (Children's, 1983) k–3. Calico Jack tells two lost children about the time Scarry Larry got lost playing hide-and-seek with the desert critters.

5629. Reese, Bob. *Rapid Robert Roadrunner* (Children's, 1983) k–3. Rapid Robert explains why he loves to run through the desert.

5630. ____. *Rapid Robert and Hiss the Snake* (Children's, 1983) k–3. Rapid Robert finds a way to get Hiss the snake off his special rock.

5631. Reese, Bob. *Huzzard Buzzard* (Children's, 1981) k–3. The desert animals and plants try to help Huzzard Buzzard fly.

5632. ____. *Critter Race* (Children's, 1981) k–3. The desert animals have a race for fun.

5633. Reid, Norman. *Zoe's Windy Day* (Scholastic, 1991) k–3. A wordless book depicting scenes of what it's like on a windy day, from the child's point of view.

5634. ____. *Zoe's Snowy Day* (Scholastic, 1991) k–3. A wordless book of different typical winter scenes with a child's perspective.

5635. ____. *Zoe's Rainy Day* (Scholastic, 1991) k–3. This wordless book depicts scenes of a child enjoying a rainy day.

5636. ____. *Zoe's Sunny Day* (Scholastic, 1991) k–3. A wordless book of typical scenes of a child's activities on a sunny day.

5637. Remkiewicz, Frank. *Last Time I Saw Harris* (Lothrop, 1991) k–3. When a fierce windstorm blows away his clever parrot Harris, Edmond is inconsolable and goes with the family chauffeur on a long search through town and country.

5638. ____. *There's Only One Harris* (Lothrop, 1993) k–3. On a week's visit at Waterfall Lodge, Edmond, Harris and Higgins almost meet with disaster.

5639. Remy, Georges. *Tintin in the Land of the Soviets* (Little, 1929/1989) 4–6.

5640. ____. *Tintin in the Congo* (Methuen, 1931) 4–6.

5641. ____. *Tintin in America* (Little, 1980) 4–6. Tintin, the boy reporter and his faithful dog, Snowy, are called to Chicago to clean up the Capone Mob there. They battle some real baddies.

5642. ____. *Cigars of the Pharaoh* (Little, 1975) 4–6. Tintin's activities are improbable but he goes through each terrifying episode unruffled.

5643. ____. *Blue Lotus* (Little, 1936/1984) 4–6. The underlying story concerns drug trafficking and the Japanese aggression in China from 1934 onward.

5644. ____. *Broken Ear* (Little, 1978/1994) 4–6. Determined to recover an Indian fetish stolen from the Museum of Ethnography, Tintin and Snowy follow a curious trail that leads to South America, revolution and hostile jungle Indians.

5645. ____. *Black Island* (Little, 1947/1975) 4–6. Tintin, with Thompson and Thomson, pursue a gang with aircraft and fast cars. They find them in a ruined castle where they keep a gorilla to scare everyone away.

5646. ____. *King Ottokar's Scepter* (Little, 1974) 4–6. Tintin becomes involved in political plotting, he ventures into Europe to try to keep King Ottokar from losing his throne to Syldavia.

5647. ____. *Crab with Golden Claws* (Little, 1974) 4–6. Tintin is in the Sahara desert on the hunt for opium smugglers. Two detectives in black bowlers and Captain Haddock along with Snowy are in on the chase.

5648. ____. *Shooting Star* (Little, 1942/1978) 4–6.

5649. ____. *Secret of the Unicorns* (Little, 1974) 4–6. Tintin is a roving boy reporter with his talking terrier, Snowy, and his cohort Captain Haddock and some other scoundrels. They go back in history to recall the voyages of his pirate ancestor Red Radham on the ship *Unicorn*.

5650. ____. *Red Radham's Treasure* (Little, 1945/1974) 4–6. Tintin and his friend Captain Haddock and his dog, Snowy, go to the bottom of the Caribbean in a shark-like submarine after Red Radham's treasure.

5651. ____. *Seven Crystal Balls* (Little, 1948) 4–6. The setting is in Peru.

5652. ____. *Prisoners in the Sun* (Methuen, 1949)

4–6. The professor falls under the curse of the Incas of Peru.

5653. ____. *Land of Black Gold* (Methuen, 1950/1972) 4–6. Prince Abdullah is a dreadful credible royal delinquent.

5654. ____. *Destination Moon* (Little, 1953) 4–6. Tintin goes to the moon.

5655. ____. *Explorers on the Moon* (Little, 1954/1992) 4–6. The adventures of Tintin and his friends on the first manned flight to the moon.

5656. ____. *Calculus Affair* (Methuen, 1960) 4–6. The professor's inventions take him to the Balkan Syldavia.

5657. ____. *Red Sea Sharks.* (Methuen, 1958) 4–6. Deals with the obnoxious black slave traffic in Arab countries.

5658. ____. *Tintin in Tibet* (Little, 1960) 4–6. Tintin searches the mountains of Nepal and Tibet for his friend, victim of an airplane crash.

5659. ____. *Castafiore Emerald* (Methuen, 1963) 4–6. The author adds a woman as a star to his characters: an opera singer Bianca Castafiore. She appeared briefly in other books driving Captain Haddock mad with her signature tune, "The Jewel Song" from Faust.

5660. ____. *Flight 714* (Methuen, 1968/1975) 4–6. Millionaire Carreidas, who has developed a truth serum, is hijacked in his supersonic jet. Tintin, Haddock and Snowy rescue him. They then find a cave from which a flying saucer saves them.

5661. ____. *Tintin and the Picaros* (Little, 1974) 4–6. Tintin returns again to San Theodoros, engineers the ouster of the guerrilla General Tapioca, and triumphantly reinstates his friend General Alcazar as president.

5662. ____. *Adventures of Tintin* (Methuen, 1974) 4–6. A boy in britches with a tuft of hair. His sidekick is Captain Haddock, bearded, and Milou (Snowy), a small white dog. Together they have exciting adventures.

5663. Remy, Georges. *Adventures of Tintin Volume 1* (Little, 1993) 4–6. Contains: "Tintin in America"; "Cigar for the Pharaoh"; "Blue Lotus."

5664. ____. *Adventures of Tintin Volume 2* (Little, 1993) 4–6. Contains: "Black Island"; "King Ottokar's Sceptre"; "Broken Ear."

5665. ____. *Adventures of Tintin Volume 3* (Little, 1993) 4–6. Contains: "Crab with Golden Claws"; "Shooting Stars"; "Secret of the Unicorn."

5666. ____. *Adventures of Tintin Volume 4* (Little, 1991) 4–6. Contains: "Red Radham's Treasure"; "Seven Crystal Balls"; "Prison in the Sun."

5667. ____. *Adventures of Tintin Volume 5* (Little, 1992) 4–6. Contains: "Land of Black Gold"; "Destination"; "Explorers of the Moon."

5668. Ressner, Philip. *Dudley Pippin* (Harper, 1965) 2–4. Twelve stories about the world of Dudley Pippin in which extraordinary things happen

with bewitching regularity: an elephant can't remember, a policeman gets lost and a principal plays a blue flute.

5669. ____. *Dudley Pippin's Summer* (Harper, 1979) 2–4. Eleven short stories recount Dudley Pippin's discoveries and adventures during a summer holiday.

5670. Rettino, Ernie. *Psalty in the Soviet Circus* (Word, 1991) k–3. Separated from his family on a visit to the Soviet Union and taken to jail for minor violations, Psalty finds comfort in a remembered Bible verse.

5671. ____. *Psalty in Alaska* (Word, 1991) k–3. Rhythm's experience in a dog-sled race in Alaska shows him that God does not expect you to win every time, as long as you do your best.

5672. ____. *Psalty in Egypt* (Word, 1991) k–3. When Psalty and his family, visiting Egypt, are kidnapped by jewel thieves, they are able to prove that prayer and God's love can change the lives of our enemies.

5673. ____. *Psalty on Safari* (Word, 1991) k–3. After she wins $10,000 and an African safari on a game show, Melody sees firsthand the extreme need in Africa and decides to donate her cash to the missionary work being done there.

5674. ____. *Psalty in Australia* (Word, 1991) k–3. Psalty and his family go to Australia to see where God's creativity worked overtime in creating an underground opal field and such animals as the kangaroo and platypus.

5675. ____. *Psalty in the South Pacific* (Word, 1991) k–3. Psalty and his family grow spiritually when they take a cruise in the South Pacific and are stranded on an island.

5676. Reuter, Bjarne. *Buster's World* (Dutton, 1989) 4–6. A would-be musician copes with teasing classmates and an alcoholic father. Buster gets revenge on his tormentors, sometimes with humor, sometimes not.

5677. ____. *Buster the Sheik of Hope Street* (Dutton, 1991) 4–6. The adventures and misadventures of Buster, a highly imaginative Danish schoolboy, comes to a climax when he must take over the lead role in the school play on the night of the performance.

5678. Rey, Hans. *Curious George* (Houghton, 1941) k–3. Describes the adventures of a curious small monkey, and the difficulties he had in getting used to city life, before he went to live in the zoo.

5679. ____. *Curious George and the Dinosaur* (Houghton, 1941) k–3. Curious George visits a museum with a class of school children and causes much excitement by climbing up onto a dinosaur skeleton.

5680. ____. *Curious George Takes a Job* (Houghton, 1947) k–3. This time Curious George escapes from the zoo and follows his curious impulses all over town.

5681. ____. *Curious George Rides a Bike* (Houghton, 1952) k–3. George sets off on his new bicycle to deliver newspapers. He builds a whole navy of paper boats, lands in a traveling circus as a daring bicycle rider, gets an ostrich in trouble, and rescues a runaway bear.

5682. ____. *Curious George Gets a Medal* (Houghton, 1957) k–3. Curious George's adventure starts when he tries to write a letter: the ink spills all over. Mountains of soap bubbles submerge the room. George rides a cow in to the museum and finally he flies into space.

5683. ____. *Curious George Flies a Kite* (Houghton, 1958) k–3. Besides playing games with a rabbit, Curious George, the monkey, tries to fly a kite and ends up following along after it with a firm grasp on the kite string.

5684. ____. *Curious George Learns the Alphabet* (Houghton, 1963) k–3. The letters really become the creatures and objects they represent in the alphabet that Curious George learns.

5685. ____. *Curious George Goes to the Hospital* (Houghton, 1966) k–3. Curious George swallows a piece of jigsaw puzzle. Then he has to go to the hospital for an operation. He is the favorite of the children's ward and his curiosity leads him into an hilarious train of events.

5686. Rey, Margaret. *Curious George Goes to the Dentist* (Houghton, 1984) k–3. Curious George accompanies his friend to the dentist's office and helps alleviate a girl's fear of the chair.

5687. ____. *Curious George Goes to the Circus* (Houghton, 1984) k–3. Curious George becomes the star of the circus after he inadvertently gets in the way of the acrobats' performance.

5688. ____. *Curious George Goes to the Aquarium* (Houghton, 1984) k–3. Curious George jumps in with the seals during his visit to the aquarium and becomes the star attraction.

5689. ____. *Curious George Goes Sledding* (Houghton, 1984) k–3. George is in and out of trouble in this new version of the old Curious George.

5690. ____. *Curious George Goes Hiking* (Houghton, 1985) k–3. Curious George distresses his companions when he loses the picnic food but makes them happy again when he finds their way back to civilization.

5691. ____. *Curious George and the Pizza* (Houghton, 1985) k–3. Curious George creates havoc in a pizza shop but redeems himself by making an unusual delivery.

5692. ____. *Curious George at the Fire Station* (Houghton, 1985) k–3. Curious George sets off a false alarm while visiting the fire station but redeems himself by rescuing a Dalmatian puppy.

5693. ____. *Curious George and the Dump Truck* (Houghton, 1985) k–3. An updated edition of old Curious George. A black policeman is added. And

George is shown watching his own heroics on the six o'clock news.

5694. ____. *Curious George Visits the Zoo* (Houghton, 1985) k–3. Curious George visits the zoo and manages to both cause trouble and make up for it in his inimitable fashion.

5695. ____. *Curious George at the Ballet* (Houghton, 1986) k–3. George goes to the ballet but his curiosity interferes with the performance.

5696. ____. *Curious George Goes to a Costume Party* (Houghton, 1986) k–3. While trying to find a costume for a party, George looks through Aunt Harriet's attic and makes a huge mess.

5697. ____. *Curious George Walks the Pets* (Houghton, 1986) k–3. George the curious monkey creates chaos when he tries to take all four of his neighbor's pets for a walk, especially since they are a dog, cat, canary and goldfish.

5698. ____. *Curious George Goes Fishing* (Houghton, 1987) k–3. Curious George's interest in helping a fisherman catch more fish ends in disaster, but he is able to redeem himself later.

5699. ____. *Curious George Visits a Police Station* (Houghton, 1987) k–3. Curious George creates havoc at the new police station when he accidentally locks the mayor and the police chief in one of the cells.

5700. ____. *Curious George Plays Baseball* (Houghton, 1989) k–3. Curious George's natural inclination to find out more about everything leads him to interfere with a baseball game.

5701. ____. *Curious George Goes to School* (Houghton, 1989) k–3. Curious George makes a mistake in the art room of his school but finds a missing painting in time for an open house for parents of the students.

5702. ____. *Curious George Goes to an Ice Cream Shop* (Houghton, 1989) k–3. Curious George makes a messy mistake while visiting a new ice cream shop, but he redeems himself by attracting attention when he puts together a big sundae in the window.

5703. ____. *Curious George Goes Camping* (Houghton, 1990) k–3.

5704. ____. *Curious George Goes to an Air Show* (Houghton, 1990) k–3.

5705. ____. *Curious George Bakes a Cake* (Houghton, 1990) k–3.

5706. ____. *Curious George Goes to a Toy Store* (Houghton, 1990) k–3.

5707. Rey, Margaret. *Pretzel* (Harper, 1941/1984) k–3. Pretzel wins a blue ribbon but it fails to impress Greta, the dachshund he yearns to marry. Greta doesn't like long dogs. In the end his persistence and bravery (he saves her from danger) wins out and they marry.

5708. ____. *Pretzel and the Puppies* (Harper, 1946) k–3. Pretzel, the longest dachshund in the world, and his wife, Greta, now have five puppies.

5709. Richards, Frank. *Billy Bunter, Sportsman*

(Armada, 1965) 4–6. Stories about Bunter at school with pompous but easily gullible masters, lashings of practical jokes, scoldings, sports, schoolboy slang—Bunter always missing the point but coming through all right in the end.

5710. ____. *Bunter's Last Fling* (Cassell, 1965) 4–6. The plot is similar to *Treasure Island* with Bunter in the box playing the role of Jim Hawkins in the apple barrel. A good, clean school story.

5711. ____. *Billy Bunter's Postal Order* (Armada, 1969) 4–6.

5712. ____. *Billy Bunter and the Bank Robber* (Armada, 1968) 4–6.

5713. Richardson, Dorothy. *Brownie Explorers* (Hodder, 1983) 3–5. Elizabeth finds life in a wheelchair greatly improved when she becomes a Brownie; then there are badges to be worn and challenges to meet. Finally the pack has to find a new meeting place and are soon fully occupied in cleaning and fitting out a barn damaged by a fire.

5714. ____. *Brownie Ventures* (Hodder, 1983) 3–5.

5715. ____. *Brownie Elephant Hunters* (Hodder, 1986) 3–5. Ita, a Brownie of Ferndale Pack, finds a pin in the shape of a dragon and wants to keep it. But she must find the rightful owner. It belongs to Heromi, a Japanese Brownie, and Ita is resentful. But when they have a White Elephant sale, friendship wins out.

5716. Richardson, Jean. *First Step* (Hodder, 1979) 4–6. Moth wants to learn ballet. She stays with Great-Aunt Marian and goes to dance school. She sees Anthony Dowell dance at Convent Garden. She also visits a toy museum.

5717. ____. *Dancer in the Wings* (Hodder, 1985) 4–6. Moth is a student at the Fortune School of Dancing. Her parents don't understand her love of ballet. Moth's friend, Ruth, gives up dancing for acting and Moth feels abandoned. But in the end her family is brought closer together.

5718. ____. *One Foot on the Ground* (Knight, 1983) 4–6. Moth, 16, has reached the point of auditioning for a place at the Royal Ballet School. She finds an outlet in modern dance and choreography. She is supported by her great-aunt and her cousin from Australia.

5719. Richler, Mordecai. *Jacob Two-Two Meets the Hooded Fang* (Knopf, 1975) 3–5. Jacob Two-Two is teased for his habit of saying everything twice, but he proves his courage after he is captured by the Slimers and their chief, the Hooded Fang.

5720. ____. *Jacob Two-Two and the Dinosaur* (Random, 1987) 3–5. When Jacob Two-Two's father brings him back a small lizard from Kenya, it grows to enormous proportions, and to protect his now identifiable Diplodocus, Jacob runs away with him to British Columbia.

5721. ____. *Jacob Two-Two's First Spy Case* (Farrar, 1996) 3–5. Jacob Two-Two, three, enlists the aid of his new neighbor, master spy X. Barney Dinglebat, when I.M. Greedyguts, the new headmaster at his school, makes the lives of the students miserable.

5722. Riddell, Chris. *Ben and the Bear* (Lippincott, 1986) k–3. Ben invites a bear home for tea, and the two have a fun-filled afternoon.

5723. ____. *Bear Dance* (S & S, 1990) k–3. When Jack Frost brings gray winter to a forest where it has always been summer, a young girl brings sunlight back by engaging Mr. Frost in a vigorous Bear Dance.

5724. Rikys, Bodel. *Red Bear* (Dial, 1992) k–3. Red Bear dresses, feeds the cat, and heads outside for a day of fun. The names of the colors are given on each page.

5725. ____. *Red Bear's Fun with Shapes* (Dial, 1993) k–3. Red Bear explores the shapes in his world, both inside and outdoors.

5726. Riley, Jocelyn. *Only My Mouth Is Smiling* (Morrow, 1982) 5–8. Merle, Ron and Diane's mother is mentally unstable. Merle tells how they lived before she became aware that her mother needed help and called her grandmother. It ends on a hopeful note.

5727. ____. *Crazy Quilt* (Morrow, 1984) 5–8. Merle, Ron and Diane live with their grandmother while their mother recovers her health. Her mother wants to get out of the hospital but Merle is aware that she is not yet ready.

5728. Ringner-Lundgren, Ester. *Little Trulsa* (Methuen, 1965) k–3. Little Trulsa is the youngest of a troll family. She finds pleasure in sunlight, flowers, a stray cat and a ball of wool.

5729. ____. *Little Trulsa's Secret* (Methuen, 1967) k–3. The secret is a kettle holder Trulsa is knitting for her mother's birthday.

5730. Roberts, Bethany. *Waiting-for-Spring Stories* (Harper, 1985) k–3. As the family passes the winter in their cozy home. Papa Rabbit tells them stories about other rabbits.

5731. ____. *Waiting-for-Papa Stories* (Harper, 1990) k–3. As Papa Rabbit's family anxiously awaits his return home, Mama Rabbit eases their fears by telling funny stories about Papa.

5732. ____. *Waiting-for-Christmas Stories* (Clarion, 1994) k–3. Papa Rabbit tells his children seven bedtime stories on Christmas Eve.

Robins, Eleanor. In this series Meg and her friend Kate help Uncle Bob, the town police chief, solve mysteries. Kate and Meg spend a lot of time driving around in Meg's car and eating ice cream at a shop where their boyfriends work.

5733. ____. *Look Alike Mystery* (High Noon, 1985) 4–6.

5734. ____. *Hub Cap Mystery* (High Noon, 1985) 4–6. Meg and her best friend Kate help Uncle Bob, the town police chief, solve a mystery. They drive around in Meg's car and eat ice cream at a shop where their boyfriends are employed.

5735. ____. *Bank Robbers Map* (High Noon, 1985) 4–6. Meg and her best friend Kate help Uncle bob, the town police chief, solve a mystery.

5736. ____. *Mystery of the Old Book* (High Noon, 1985) 4–6.

5737. ____. *Lost Dog Mystery* (High Noon, 1985) 4–6.

5738. Robins, Joan. *Addie Meets Max* (Harper, 1985) k–3. Addie discovers that the new boy next door, Max, and his dog are not so terrible when she helps Max bury his newly lost tooth.

5739. ____. *Addie Runs Away* (Harper, 1989) k–3. Not wishing to be sent away to Camp Putt, Addie is determined to run away, unless her friend Max can convince her to change her mind.

5740. ____. *Addie's Bad Day* (Harper, 1993) k–3. When Addie gets a haircut she hates, she is too embarrassed to come to her friend Max's birthday party.

5741. Robinson, Barbara. *Best Christmas Pageant Ever* (Harper, 1988) 3–5. The six mean Herdman kids lie, steal, smoke cigars (even the girls) and then become involved in the community Christmas pageant.

5742. ____. *Best School Year Ever* (Harper, 1994) 3–5. The Herdman children, the worst kids in the history of the world are back. They become part of the school's fire safety team after most of the team comes down with chicken pox.

5743. Robinson, Catherine. *Lizzie Oliver* (Scholastic, 1987) 5–8. Lizzie, 13, is angry when her father remarries. Her mother was killed two years ago. Miss Bullock will never replace mother. She also has to move now. But eventually she comes to terms with her situation.

5744. ____. *Lizzie's Worst Year* (Scholastic, 1990) 5–8.

5745. ____. *Lizzie's Luck* (Scholastic, 1990) 5–8.

5746. Robinson, Nancy. *Oh, Honestly Angela* (Scholastic, 1985) 3–5. Tina is unhappy about being "poor" until she witnesses some real poverty. She and her brother and sister are more aware of helping those in real need. She wants to adopt an orphan.

5747. ____. *Angela, Private Citizen* (Scholastic, 1989) 3–5. Angela, six, has faith in order and fairness but it is frequently shaken as she tries to cope with all the mysteries of life that keep turning up in her busy family.

5748. ____. *Angela and the Broken Heart* (Scholastic, 1991) 3–5. Angela, now in second grade, tries to ease the broken heart of her brother Nathaniel as he enters high school and worries about being popular.

5749. Robinson, Nancy. *Veronica, the Show-off* (Four Winds, 1982) 4–6. Although lonely and desperately in need of friends, Veronica overwhelms her new classmates with her outrageous behavior in a bid for attention.

5750. ____. *Veronica Knows Best* (Scholastic, 1986) 4–6. No longer a show-off, Veronica decides the best way to make friends is to take an interest in people.

5751. ____. *Veronica Meets Her Match* (Scholastic, 1990) 4–6. Veronica's fervent attempts to gain peer acceptance continue as she claims the new girl as her own special friend.

5752. ____. *Countess Veronica* (Scholastic, 1994) 4–6. When an overseas telephone conversation traps Veronica into agreeing to play a renowned chess champion, she decides that she needs to learn how to play the game.

5753. Roche, P.K. *Good-bye, Arnold* (Dial, 1979) k–3. Webster's big brother goes away for a week, and Webster realizes how much he misses him.

5754. ____. *Webster and Arnold and the Giant Box* (Dial, 1980) k–3. Webster and Arnold are brother mice. They turn a packing box into a cave, a rocketship and other things. Webster gives the orders and Arnold does the work. Arnold pesters him till Webster quits and goes away.

5755. ____. *Webster and Arnold Go Camping* (Viking, 1988) k–3. The mouse brothers go on a backyard camping trip. The tent is lonely and frightening. They scare themselves with stories about a giant chicken and about an alien spaceship. They are happy to be back home but agreed it was a great time.

5756. Rock, Gail. *House Without a Christmas Tree* (Knopf, 1974) 3–5. Addie lives with her father and grandmother. They spend the holidays the best they can.

5757. ____. *Thanksgiving Treasure* (Knopf, 1974) 3–5. Addie is still with her father and grandmother. She wants a horse and one day takes some food to a recluse her father has been feuding with. They become friends and when he dies he leaves her his horse.

5758. ____. *Addie and the King of Hearts* (Knopf, 1975) 3–5. Addie has a crush on her teacher and her boyfriend asks someone else to the dance; she goes with her father.

5759. ____. *Dream for Addie* (Knopf, 1976) 3–5. Addie makes friends with Constance and asks her father if she can stay with them awhile.

5760. Rockwell, Anne. *First Comes Spring* (Crowell, 1985) k–3. Bear Child notices that the clothes he wears, the things everyone does at work and play, and the other parts of his world all change with the seasons.

5761. ____. *In Our House* (Crowell, 1985) k–3. A member of the Bear family explores the rooms in their house, relating all the activities that take place there to make their house a happy home.

5762. ____. *Bear Child's Book of Hours* (Crowell, 1987) k–3. For each hour of the day Bear Child participates in a new activity, and as he does the reader sees the time on the clock.

5763. ____. *Bear Child's Book of Special Days* (Dutton, 1989) k–3. Bear Child explains how he celebrates holidays and other special occasions for each month of the year.

5764. Rockwell, Anne. *Hugo at the Window* (Macmillan, 1988) k–3. Hugo the dog waits and waits at the window for his friend who is gone for a long time, but there is a surprise for Hugo when his friend returns.

5765. ____. *Hugo at the Park* (Macmillan, 1990) k–3. Hugo the Labrador puppy goes for a walk in the park with his human friend and sees many interesting things.

5766. ____. *When Hugo Went to School* (Macmillan, 1991) k–3. Following his new friends to school lands Hugo the dog in jail.

5767. Rockwell, Anne. *Willy Runs Away* (Dutton, 1978) k–3. An adventurous dog runs away from home only to find the world isn't as pleasant and attractive as he imagined.

5768. ____. *Willy Can Count* (Arcade, 1989) k–3. While outdoors, Willy and his mother observe and count a number of colorful objects, encompassing everything from shirt buttons and hay stacks to birds and bugs.

5769. Rockwell, Anne. *Gogo's Car Breaks Down* (Doubleday, 1978) k–3. Gogo's car breaks down on his way to visit his mother. He is rescued by a black policeman who gets a tow truck operated by Molly and Joe.

5770. ____. *Gogo's Pay Day* (Doubleday, 1978) k–3. The generosity of Gogo the circus clown leads him to learn the value of money.

5771. Rockwell, Thomas. *How to Eat Fried Worms* (Watts, 1973) 4–6. To win a bet Billy must eat 15 worms in 15 days. How he manages to win makes a fun story.

5772. ____. *How to Fight a Girl* (Watts, 1987) 4–6. Joe and Alan's plan to get revenge on Billy backfires when their secret weapon, the prettiest girl in their fifth grade class becomes Billy's friend instead.

5773. ____. *How to Get Fabulously Rich* (Watts, 1990) 4–6. After Billy wins $410,000 in the lottery his friends claim that he owes them a share for helping him play, creating a tangle of lies, memory and money.

5774. Rodgers, Jesse. *ESP McGee and the Dolphin's Message* (Avon, 1984) 5–8. McGee's house with its sophisticated computer system is the target of a thief.

(For other books about "ESP McGee," *see* Ernst, Kathryn F.; Lawrence, Jim; and Packard, Edward.)

5775. Rodgers, Raboo. *Magnum Fault* (Houghton, 1984) 5–8. Jill's father disappears after a crash and she escapes from a "hospital." She gets to an airport the same time as Cody and his dog, Riley. Together they solve the mystery of her father's accident.

5776. ____. *Rainbow Factor* (Houghton, 1985) 5–8. Cody is hijacked by Audry, an orphan who has recently inherited a small estate and is now being followed by a sinister, mysterious man. Cody and she attempt to discover why she is being followed.

5777. Roland, Betty. *Forbidden Bridge* (McGraw, 1965) 3–5. Jamie, seven, is lonely so he crosses the railway bridge to visit his friends. Upon his return a train is coming across the bridge, only quick action by his cousin saves his life.

5778. ____. *Jamie's Summer Visitor* (McGraw, 1967) 3–5. Jamie is not looking forward to the visit of a friend's daughter at Christmas. Nola is disdainful and a show-off. But Nola is only trying to hide her feeling of rejection.

5779. Rooke, Anne. *When Robert Went to Playgroup* (Hodder, 1984) k–3. Robert has his first introduction to school and goes on his first railroad journey. In school he has a mid-morning snack, the company of the family cat, the joys of painting and games. He also experiences chicken pox.

5780. ____. *When Robert Went to Stay* (Hodder, 1985) k–3.

5781. ____. *Robert's Playground Friends* (Hodder, 1986) k–3.

5782. ____. *Robert and Great Granny* (Hodder, 1987) k–3. Robert likes Great Granny, a lively old lady, and fun. He loves her stories and her naughtiness. He helps her get around, makes mince pies, and keeps her company. He gave her a frozen red and black lollipop he had kept in the freezer. She loved it.

5783. Rooke, Anne. *Lizzie and Friends* (Blackie, 1990) k–3. Lizzie goes through her first year at school, with minor crises arising from spilled paints and swallowed pebbles.

5784. ____. *How's School, Lizzie* (Blackie, 1990) k–3. An introduction to school life for five-year-olds. It deals with race differences and handicaps. Also some Hindu costumes like the celebration of Davali.

5785. Roos, Stephen. *Fair-Weather Friends* (Atheneum, 1987) 4–6. Kit and Phoebe are best friends but Phoebe is changing and is interested in boys. She and Kit will remain friends but on a different level. Phoebe likes Kit's brother, Derek.

5786. ____. *And the Winner Is* (Atheneum, 1989)

4–6. Phoebe's father has a financial set back and she believes she will lose her friends. Derek and Kit put on a talent show to raise money. Kit and Derek don't know about the selling of Phoebe's house.

5787. Roos, Stephen. *My Horrible Secret* (Delacorte, 1983) 4–6. Warren's secret is that he can't play ball. His brother is a superjock. He takes horse riding lessons, falls and breaks his arm. Now he can't play but the cast comes off before the big game. What now?

5788. ____. *Terrible Truth* (Delacorte, 1983) 4–6. Warren's class is now one year older but the enemy is still Claire. Shirley is trying to be friendly but manages to hurt her friend's feelings. Class rivalry runs rampant.

5789. ____. *My Secret Admirer* (Delacorte, 1984) 4–6. Claire is the main character in this story of Warren, Shirley and their classmates. She wants to win the Junior Achievement Award but when she gets a valentine from a "secret admirer" things change.

5790. Roos, Stephen. *Pet Lovers Club: Love Me. Love My Werewolf* (Delacorte, 1991) 3–5. Bernie befriends a small stray dog who proves to be invaluable around the house and is a hit at the Pet Lovers Club Halloween party.

5791. ____. *Pet Lovers Club: Crocodile Christmas* (Delacorte, 1992) 3–5. Unhappy that he is the only member of the Pet Lovers Club who does not have a pet. Lem, eight, gets carried away by his love of crocodiles and claims that he is getting one for Christmas.

5792. ____. *Pet Lovers Club: Cottontail Caper* (Delacorte, 1992) 3–5. Trying to raise money for a new animal shelter, the Pet Lovers Club holds a contest for new animals to represent Easter, but rabbit owner Erin is outraged because she was hoping her pet would lead the Easter parade.

5793. Roos, Stephen. *Dear Santa, Make Me a Star (Maple Street Kids)* (Hazleden, 1991) 3–5. Tara wants to be Mary in the Christmas play but can't because of her parent's A.A. meeting.

5794. ____. *My Blue Tongue (Maple Street Kids)* (Hazleden, 1991) 3–5. Rooney plays pranks that hurt other people and gets her in trouble. Her father gambles and the family suffers, but everyone denies it.

5795. Roose-Evans, James. *Adventures of Odd and Elsewhere* (Deutsch, 1971) 3–5. Odd, a toy bear and Elsewhere, a toy clown were left behind by a careless owner and have unusual adventures in London as they fend for themselves.

5796. ____. *Secret of the Seven Bright Shiners* (Rourke, 1972) 3–5. Odd and Elsewhere manage to exert their forceful and endearing personalities. The seven bright shivers are really six proud walkers…with neat tricks while on the job. Elsewhere foils them.

5797. ____. *Odd and the Great Bear* (Rourke, 1973)

3–5. Another story of Odd, the toy bear, and his clown friend, Elsewhere. Odd goes to Wales to search for a mythical relation and is chased by a vicious gang of treasure hunters.

5798. ____. *Elsewhere and the Gathering of Clowns* (Deutsch, 1974) 3–5. In this story of Odd and Elsewhere the reader gets a detailed description of the Clown's Gathering.

5799. ____. *Secret of Tippity Witchit* (Deutsch, 1975) 3–5. Odd is about to be crowned King of the Clowns. Coci the French clown is jealous. The old king teaches him Grimaldi's Secret of Tippity Witchit.

5800. ____. *Lost Treasure of Wales* (Deutsch, 1977) 3–5. Odd tries to massage Hallelujah Jones's spine by walking up and down on it. The Lost Tribe is a tribe of small bears just like Odd. Odd discovers he is Ursus Minor and Elsewhere is named King of the Clowns.

5801. ____. *Return of the Great Bear* (Rourke, 1982) 3–5. Odd is alone in the story—no Elsewhere. He is inside Bear Mountain. There the Great Bear is held prisoner by Malevil.

5802. ____. *Odd to the Rescue* (Rourke, 1983) 3–5. Odd helps the Great Bear out with the forces of evil.

5803. Rose, Madeline. *Witch Over the Water* (Angus, 1980) 4–6. When the Pitt siblings move to Australia with their parents, their granny follows on a broomstick.

5804. ____. *Witch in the Bush* (Angus, 1985) 4–6. Granny Enden is a witch. She whisks off the Pitt children, nine-year-old twins and their older brother and sister. Granny is a bossy witch and takes them to her isolated property in the outback.

5805. Rosen, Winifred. *Henrietta, the Wild Woman of Borneo* (Four Winds, 1975) 2–4. Henrietta's parents call her the "Wild Woman of Borneo," so she decides to have herself mailed there for a visit.

5806. ____. *Henrietta and the Day of the Iguana* (Four Winds, 1978) 2–4. Henrietta, a willful child, thinks she wants an iguana as a pet until she actually sees one.

5807. ____. *Henrietta and the Gong from Hong Kong* (Four Winds, 1981) 2–4. On a visit to her grandparents, Henrietta finds it difficult to be a Perfect Little Lady, especially when she knocks their gong from Hong Kong noisily down the stairs.

5808. Rosenbloom, Joseph. *Maximillian, You're the Greatest* (Lodestar, 1979) 4–6. Maximillian Augustus Adams cracks new cases in each chapter.

5809. ____. *Maximillian Does It Again* (Lodestar, 1983) 4–6. Maximillian, 12, helps Detective Walker of the New York City police department. An urban "Encyclopedia Brown" type series.

5810. Rosenstiehl, Agnes. *Mimi Takes Charge* (Advocacy, 1991) k–3. Mimi learns about herself through her imagination.

5811. ____. *Mimi Makes a Splash* (Advocacy, 1991) k–3. Mimi learns about herself as she swims, walks in the rain, washes and performs other activities with water.

5812. ____. *Mimi Moves Ahead* (Advocacy, 1992) k–3.

5813. Ross, Pat. *M and M and the Haunted House Game* (Pantheon, 1980) 2–4. When Mimi and Mandy try to scare someone as part of a game, they are the ones who are frightened.

5814. ____. *Meet M and M* (Pantheon, 1980) 2–4. Best friends Mandy and Mimi do everything together until they have a falling out.

5815. ____. *M and M and the Big Bag* (Pantheon, 1981) 2–4. New at reading Mandy and Mimi make their first trip to the grocery store alone, proudly carrying their grocery list.

5816. ____. *M and M and the Bad News Babies* (Pantheon, 1983) 2–4. Mandy and Mimi discover a way to make the unruly twins for whom they baby-sit into perfect angels.

5817. ____. *M and M and the Santa Secrets* (Viking, 1985) 2–4. Santa comes to the rescue when friends Mandy and Mimi need the perfect Christmas gift for each other.

5818. ____. *M and M and the Mummy Mess* (Viking, 1985) 2–4. Best friends Mandy and Mimi have a scary time when their eagerness to see mummies leads them to sneak into the new museum exhibit a week before it opens.

5819. ____. *M and M and the Super Child Afternoon* (Viking, 1987) 2–4. When best friends Mimi and Mandy turn out to be more talented at each other's special choice in a "Super Child" class, they decide to go their separate ways after school.

5820. ____. *M and M and the Halloween Monsters* (Viking, 1991) 2–4. Mandy and Mimi are preparing for Halloween. As they plan their costumes they see strange happenings in their apartment building: chains rattle, blood spots appear and they see a monster. The mystery is revealed and the girls find a new friend.

5821. Ross, Tony. *Hugo and the Wicked Winter* (Sedgwick, 1977) k–3. Hugo is a fat mouse who looks for Spring which is late. He is brave and rescues Summer from the clutches of Winter which requires all his courage. His allies are Redbreast and Snow Eagle.

5822. ____. *Hugo and Oddsock* (Rourke, 1978/1982) k–3. Little Hugo, a lardermouse, makes a sock horse to play with and soon finds himself in Lostsockland, where odd socks go to find their mates.

5823. ____. *Hugo and the Bureau of Holidays* (Rourke, 1982) k–3. When Hugo the mouse receives an Easter egg instead of a blackboard for a Christmas present, he goes to the Bureau of Holidays to see what can be done about the mix-up.

5824. ____. *Hugo and the Man Who Stole Colors* (Follett, 1977) k–3. Hugo, a mouse, and a fairy search for a person who is stealing colors.

5825. Ross, Tony. *Towser and Sadie's Birthday* (Pantheon, 1984) k–3. Sadie wants the moon for her birthday and Towser does his best to get it for her.

5826. ____. *Towser and the Water Rats* (Pantheon, 1984) k–3. Towser the dog outsmarts the Water Rats who try to take over his vacation house on the river.

5827. ____. *Towser and the Terrible Thing* (Pantheon, 1984) k–3. Towser the dog becomes a hero when he devises a way of ridding the kingdom of the Terrible Thing.

5828. Rounds, Glen. *Mr. Yowder and the Lion Roar Capsules* (Holiday, 1976) 2–4. Finding that the old lion he is given in trade is totally useless except for his roar, Mr. Yowder attempts to capitalize on that one asset.

5829. ____. *Mr. Yowder and the Steamboat* (Holiday, 1977) 2–4. A friendly card game becomes a disaster for a steamboat captain and his pilot.

5830. ____. *Mr. Yowder and the Giant Bull Snake* (Holiday, 1978) 2–4. The World's Bestest and Fastest Sign Painter teams up with a body-builder—Bull Snake—for a side-slapping tall tale.

5831. ____. *Mr. Yowder the Peripatetic Sign Painter* (Holiday, 1980) 2–4. Contains: "Mr. Yowder and the Lion Roar Capsules"; "Mr. Yowder and the Steamboat"; "Mr. Yowder and the Giant Bull Snake."

5832. ____. *Mr. Yowder and the Train Robbers* (Holiday, 1983) 2–4. Mr. Xenon Zebulon Yowder is a sign painter who has many misadventures.

5833. ____. *Mr. Yowder and the Windwagon* (Holiday, 1983) 2–4. Mr. Yowder tries to make his fortune by inventing a real prairie schooner from sails, a mast, a rudder, and an old wagon, but makes a mess instead.

5834. Rounds, Glen. *Whitey's Sunday Horse* (Grosset, 1941) 3–5. In this story Whitey takes unto himself a blind colt and finds a way to keep him against all odds.

5835. ____. *Whitey and the Rustlers* (Holiday, 1951) 3–5. Whitey wants a new saddle and when his two beef steers were taken by rustlers he was determined to catch them and get the reward. He does get his saddle but differently than expected.

5836. ____. *Whitey Takes a Trip* (Avon, 1954) 3–5. Old Uncle Torwal had sold a team of horses to the Crown W Ranch and there was nobody to deliver it except Whitey. The trip meant following a disused old freight road and camping overnight on the open range.

5837. ____. *Whitey Ropes and Rides* (Avon, 1956) 3–5. When Whitey and his cousin Josie decided to learn bronco and steer riding no young critter on the ranch had any peace until Uncle Torwal rigged up the Lone Tree killer.

5838. ____. *Whitey and the Wild Horse* (Holiday,

1958) 3–5. When Whitey and his cousin Josie find a trapped wild horse, they have a real problem on their hands to tame him.

5839. ____. *Blind Colt* (Holiday, 1960) 3–5. Relates the adventures of a blind colt as he roams with a band of mustangs and is eventually adopted and trained as a saddle horse by ten-year-old Whitey.

5840. ____. *Whitey's First Roundup* (Avon, 1960) 3–5. Whitey decided to go on the roundup—and then did everything wrong from the start. But once the grim morning was behind him, he buckled down and did the chores that came his way and wound up as a small hero.

5841. ____. *Whitey and the Colt Killer* (Avon, 1962) 3–5. Whitey and his cousin Josie set out from Rattle Snake Ranch in pursuit of the mean wolf who has attacked a pinto colt. Soon they are beset by double danger as a roaring fire sweeps across the range.

5842. ____. *Whitey's New Saddle* (Avon, 1963) 3–5. When Whitey decides to get himself a new saddle, he has a lot of trouble to cope with, including a prairie blizzard and rustlers. The young cowboy again proves himself to be a top hand.

5843. Routh, Jonathan. *Nuns Go to Africa* (Bobbs, 1971) k–3. Seven nuns are on vacation in Africa. There, gorillas steal the yellow car of two Father Christmases and they chase through the desert, past many animals, under waterfalls and up trees. The gorillas keep the car, then Santas get a bus and the nuns return on zebras.

5844. ____. *Nuns Go to Penguin Island* (Bobbs, 1973) k–3. Seven nuns go to an island and share their holiday adventures with ship wrecked penguins, whom they first mistake for long nosed nuns. And with a bear on stilts whom the penguins fear as a monster. They play games and musical instruments.

5845. Rubel, Nicole. *Sam and Violet Are Twins* (Harper, 1981) k–3. Twin cats try to show off how different they are from one another. They don't want to be viewed as one.

5846. ____. *Sam and Violet Go Camping* (Harper, 1981) k–3.

5847. ____. *Sam and Violet's Birthday Book* (Harper, 1982) k–3. Twin kittens turn seven and plan a surprise party for each other. They invite Plato Pig, dressed in shorts and shades; Rufus Rabbit who is in bed; Froggy in his lily-pad home. But their parents have a surprise party for both of them.

5848. ____. *Sam and Violet's Bedtime Mystery* (Harper, 19) k–3.

5849. ____. *Sam and Violet's Get Well Book* (Harper, 1984) k–3.

5850. Rubel, Nicole. *Goldie* (Harper, 1989) k–3. A tiny chicken causes big mischief when she goes shopping with her mother.

5851. ____. *Goldie's Nap* (Harper, 1991) k–3. Mis-

chievous Goldie doesn't want to take a nap at her day care center.

5852. Ruffell, Ann. *Dragon Fire* (Hamilton, 1980) 2–4. The dragon is a glum character called Gribble who spends most of his time trying to get rid of a bad cold in his head that is seriously jeopardizing his fire-breathing capacity.

5853. ____. *Dragon Earth* (Hamilton, 1982) 2–4. Gribble the dragon guards tin cans which he thinks is his treasure.

5854. ____. *Dragon Air* (Hamilton, 1989) 2–4. A story of an amiable dragon, Gribble, with a heart of gold who lives out an adventure among other dragons, trying to find his place in the world.

5855. ____. *Dragon Wanted* (Hamilton, 1989) 2–4. Gribble, a young dragon (only 150 years old), sees a notice "Dragon Wanted." A knight needs a dragon to fight and a princess to rescue. Gribble wants the job but he discovers that in this fight the dragon gets killed.

5856. Rush, Caroline. *Tales of Mr. Pengachoosa* (Crown, 1973) 3–5. While recovering from a long illness, a little girl is entertained by her pet hamster who tells her stories about his adventurous grandfather.

5857. ____. *Further Tales of Mr. Pengachoosa* (Crown, 1973) 3–5. The talking hamster is recaptured and recaged. The girl ignores his request for freedom and only pays attention to him when she is bored.

5858. ____. *Eight Tales of Mr. Pengachoosa* (Crown, 1974) 3–5. Hammy the hamster returns to his old home with more stories of his grandfather's adventures.

5859. Russ, Lavinia. *Over the Hills and Far Away* (Harcourt, 1965) 4–6. Peakie is shy and has a beautiful sister; these things make growing up even harder than normal but both the move and the boarding school help her conquer her fears.

5860. ____. *April Age* (Atheneum, 1975) 4–6. Peakie is now 18. She goes on a European trip, learns to dance, falls in love many times with a series of unsuitable men and rises and falls with each new romance.

5861. Russo, Marisabine. *Why Do Grown-ups Have All the Fun?* (Greenwillow, 1987) k–3. When Hannah is in bed unable to sleep, she imagines all the fun grown-ups are having—doing all the things she herself likes to do.

5862. ____. *Waiting for Hannah* (Greenwillow, 1989) k–3. Hannah's mother describes how she spent the summer she was waiting for Hannah to be born.

5863. Russo, Marisabine. *Only Six More Days* (Greenwillow, 1988) k–3. Becoming more and more annoyed as her brother Ben counts down the days until his birthday, Molly considers refusing to take part in the celebration.

5864. ____. *Where is Ben?* (Greenwillow, 1990) k–3. While Ben's mother makes a pie, Ben hides around the house.

5865. Rutherford, Meg. *Bluff and Bran and the Magpie* (Deutsch, 1986) k–3. Bluff is a cat; her friend is the teddy bear Bran. Bran fell in the pond and is hung up to dry. Magpie is attracted and Bluff goes to the rescue and takes Magpie's tail feathers.

5866. ____. *Bluff and Bran and the Snowdrift* (Deutsch, 1987) k–3.

5867. ____. *Bluff and Bran and the Birthday* (Deutsch, 1989) k–3. Bluff, a cat and Bran, a bear, ruin a girl's birthday party. They are sent out to the garden where they try to have their own party. All sorts of creatures are invited as guests.

5868. Ryan, John. *Pugwash and the Ghost Ship* (Phillips, 1968) k–3. Captain Pugwash buys luminous paint for his pirate ship. Tom, the cabin boy, suggests that the glowing *Black Pig* parade as a ghost ship and scare off rival pirates.

5869. ____. *Captain Pugwash* (Bodley, 1969) k–3. Tom sails with Captain Pugwash, as a cabin boy, aboard the *Black Pig*. Tom saves the day when Cut-throat Jake lured Captain Pugwash with a decoy treasure ship.

5870. ____. *Pugwash Aloft* (Bodley, 1970) k–3. Tom, a cabin boy, is the hero among an impossible pirate crew.

5871. ____. *Pugwash in the Pacific* (Phillips, 1973) k–3. Pugwash, an island dwelling pirate, manages to evade his captors after his archenemy Cut-throat Jake, is imprisoned in his stead.

5872. ____. *Pugwash and the Sea Monster* (Bodley, 1976) k–3. Captain Pugwash conceals himself and members of his crew in portions of the anatomy of a sea serpent. He sets off to frighten Cut-throat Jake away from the treasure hoard. He gets assistance from a genuine sea monster and the loot is captured.

5873. ____. *Captain Pugwash, the Smuggler* (Bodley, 1981) k–3. Captain Pugwash tries his hand at smuggling but finds himself involved with pirates and in trouble with excise soldiers. Tom, the cabin-boy, rescues him.

5874. ____. *Captain Pugwash and the Fancy-dress Party* (Bodley, 1982) k–3. Captain Pugwash plans a devious way of improving his fortune. He invites rich people to a fancy dress ball on board his ship, plotting to rob them at sea. Tom, the cabin boy, foils his plan.

5875. ____. *Pugwash and the Wreckers* (Bodley, 1984) k–3. Captain Pugwash is commissioned to deliver a load of silver bullion to the West Indies, but his old enemy, Cut-throat Jake, has plans to prevent that delivery.

5876. ____. *Pugwash and the Midnight Feast* (Bod-ley, 1984) k–3. A midnight feast on board the pirate ship, *Black Pig,* is interrupted by two sets of surprise visitors.

5877. ____. *Captain Pugwash: Battle for Bunkum Bay* (Bodley, 1985) k–3. Captain Pugwash and his men defeat Cut-throat Jake. The British and French fleets seize the treasure from a Spanish wreck.

5878. Ryan, Mary. *Dance a Step Closer* (Delacorte, 1984) 5–8. Katie wants to be a Broadway dancer, but her mother doesn't encourage her because she was a dancer and knows how hard it is. But Katie works hard, gets a boyfriend and adjusts to her family.

5879. ____. *I'd Rather Be Dancing* (Delacorte, 1989) 5–8. Katie wins a scholarship to Dance Academy. She faces stiff competition and sees more of the seedy side of show biz.

5880. Ryan, Mary. *My Sister is Driving Me Crazy* (S & S, 1991) 5–8. Tired of being an identical twin, Mattie, 13, seeks her own identity.

5881. ____. *Me, My Sister and I* (S & S, 1992) 5–8. Mattie, 13, seeks independence from her identical twin sister Pru by helping her mother manage the campaign of a candidate for city council.

5882. Rylant, Cynthia. *Henry and Mudge* (Bradbury, 1987) 2–4. Henry, feeling lonely on a street without any other children, finds companionship and love in a big dog named Mudge.

5883. ____. *Henry and Mudge in Puddle Trouble* (Bradbury, 1987) 2–4. For Henry and his big dog Mudge, spring means admiring the first show glory, playing in the puddles in the rain and watching the five new kittens next door.

5884. ____. *Henry and Mudge in the Green Time* (Bradbury, 1987) 2–4. For Henry and his big dog Mudge, summer means going on a picnic in the park, taking a bath under the garden hose, and going to the top of the big green hill.

5885. ____. *Henry and Mudge Under the Yellow Moon* (Bradbury, 1988) 2–4. In the autumn Henry and his big dog Mudge watch the leaves turn, meet with some Halloween spooks and share Thanksgiving dinner.

5886. ____. *Henry and Mudge in the Sparkle Days* (Macmillan, 1988) 2–4. In the winter Henry and his big dog Mudge play in the snow, share a family Christmas dinner and gather around a crackling winter fireplace.

5887. ____. *Henry and Mudge and the Forever Sea* (Bradbury, 1989) 2–4. Follows the seaside adventures of Henry, Henry's father and Henry's big dog, Mudge.

5888. ____. *Henry and Mudge Get the Cold Shivers* (Bradbury, 1989) 2–4. When Mudge gets sick unexpectedly, Henry does all he can to make him feel better.

5889. ____. *Henry and Mudge and the Happy Cat* (Bradbury, 1990) 2–4. Henry's family takes in a stray cat, the ugliest cat they have ever seen and an amazing relationship blossoms between it and their big dog Mudge.

5890. ____. *Henry and Mudge and the Bedtime Thumps* (Bradbury, 1991) 2–4. Henry worries about what will happen to his big dog Mudge during their visit to his grandmother's house in the country.

5891. ____. *Henry and Mudge Take the Big Test* (Bradbury, 1991) 2–4. Henry's dog, Mudge knows a lot of things but he doesn't know: Heel! Sit! Stay! So he is enrolled in Jack Papp's Dog School. Mudge is not a good student.

5892. ____. *Henry and Mudge and the Long Weekend* (Bradbury, 1992) 2–4. Mudge and Henry are so bored they can hardly stay awake but with a pair of scissors, some paint and thoughts of giant castles, brave knights, and dastardly dragons, the two cardboard boxes might become a kingdom.

5893. ____. *Henry and Mudge and the Wild Wind* (Bradbury, 1993) 2–4. Henry and his dog, Mudge try to keep busy inside the house during a thunderstorm.

5894. ____. *Henry and Mudge and the Careful Cousin* (Bradbury, 1994) 2–4. At first Henry's very neat cousin doesn't like the cookies under Henry's bed or Mudge's sloppy kisses, but when they all play Frisbee, she begins to enjoy her visit.

5895. ____. *Henry and Mudge and the Best Day of All* (Bradbury, 1995) 2–4. Henry and his dog Mudge celebrate Henry's birthday with a piñata, a party and a cake shaped like a fish tank, making May 1st the best day ever.

5896. Rylant, Cynthia. *Mr. Putter and Tabby Bake a Cake* (Harcourt, 1994) k–3. With his fine cat Tabby at his side, Mr. Putter bakes a Christmas cake for his neighbor Mrs. Teaberry.

5897. ____. *Mr. Putter and Tabby Pour the Tea* (Harcourt, 1994) k–3. Mr. Putter gets an old cat to share his life with him.

5898. ____. *Mr. Putter and Tabby Walk the Dog* (Harcourt, 1994) k–3. When their neighbor Mrs. Teaberry hurts her foot, Mr. Putter and his cat Tabby agree to walk her dog for a week, not knowing what they are in for.

5899. Sabin, Francene. *Secret of the Haunted House* (Troll, 1982) 2–4. The Maple Street Six club visit a haunted house and find a mysterious message.

5900. ____. *Mystery at the Jellybean Factory* (Troll, 1982) 2–4. Hoping to join their club, Jane tells the Maple Street Six she has witnessed a robbery, but because it is April Fool's Day, she is not believed.

5901. ____. *Great Easter Egg Mystery* (Troll, 1982) 2–4. After working hard to get them painted in time for the big Easter egg hunt, the Maple Street Six discover some of the eggs are missing.

5902. Sachar, Louis. *Wayside School Is Falling Down* (Lothrop, 1990) 4–6. More stories about the children and teachers in Wayside School and the non-sense that happens on the thirtieth floor of this strange school.

5903. ____. *Sideway Stories from Wayside School* (Knopf, 1990) 4–6. Humorous stories from the classroom on the thirtieth floor of Wayside School, which was accidentally built sideways with one classroom on each story.

5904. ____. *Wayside School Gets a Little Stranger* (Morrow, 1995) 4–6. Unusual things continue to happen in the classroom on the 30th floor of Wayside School which was accidentally built sideways with one classroom on each story.

5905. Sachar, Louis. *Marvin Redpost: Kidnapped at Birth?* (Random, 1992) 3–5. Red-haired Marvin is convinced that the reason he looks different from the rest of his family is that he is really the lost prince of Shampoon.

5906. ____. *Marvin Redpost: Is He a Girl?* (Random, 1993) 3–5. After Cassie tells him that if he kisses his elbow he will turn into a girl, Marvin, nine, experiments and finds himself very confused about his identity.

5907. ____. *Marvin Redpost: Why Pick on Me?* (Random, 1993) 3–5. A small incident during recess threatens to turn nine-year-old Marvin into the outcast of his third grade class.

5908. ____. *Marvin Redpost: Alone in His Teacher's House* (Random, 1994) 3–5. Mrs. North hires Marvin to dog-sit for beloved old Waldo while she is out of town, but despite his care Waldo dies. When Mrs. North comes back she reassures Marvin it wasn't his fault, pays him for the full week of pet-sitting and takes him to lunch.

5909. Sachs, Elizabeth. *Just Like Always* (Atheneum, 1981) 4–6. Courtney is interested in fantasy, secrets and chants, Janie is interested in baseball, Harold and is a tomboy. What they have in common is scoliosis. They meet in the hospital and become friends.

5910. ____. *Where Are You, Cow Patty?* (Atheneum, 1984) 4–6. Janie has been out of the hospital for over a year. Courtney comes for a visit and things don't always go well because of Harold's interest in Courtney but they remain close friends.

5911. Sachs, Marilyn. *Matt's Mitt* (Dutton, 1989) 2–4. The baseball mitt given at Matt's birth by his errant uncle possesses unusual qualities which shape his life.

5912. ____. *Fleet-footed Florence* (Dutton, 1989) 2–4. The fleet-footed star of the North Dakota Beavers meets her match when she encounters Yankee catcher, Fabulous Frankie.

5913. Saddler, Allen. *King Gets Fit* (Oxford, 1982) k–3. The king's attempts at getting fit enough to be an acrobat only make him sick.

5914. ____. *King and the Invisible Dwarf* (Oxford,

1983) k–3. A king longs to perform magic tricks, but succeeds only in making a fool of himself.

5915. _____. *King at Christmas* (Oxford, 1983) k–3. Grumpy King tries hard to change the Christmas traditions going on around him.

5916. _____. *Queen's Painting* (Oxford, 1984) k–3. When the Queen begins her painting she makes the King look fat and lumpy.

5917. _____. *Fishing Competition* (Oxford, 1984) k–3. The King held a fishing competition but forgot there were no fish in the moat. His people called him a cheat. He then summoned the magician to put fish in the moat. The King caught a fish, declared himself a winner and sent everyone home. The other fish grew and grew…

5918. _____. *Archery Contest* (Oxford, 1984) k–3. The archery contest is terminated by a king eager to sail his boat, but all he gets is wet feet.

5919. Sadler, Marilyn. *Alistair's Elephant* (Prentice, 1983) k–3. Alistair's life is never quite the same again after the day an elephant follows him home from the zoo.

5920. _____. *Alistair in Outer Space* (Prentice, 1984) k–3. When Alistair is kidnapped by a spaceship full of Goots from Gootula, his main concern is for his overdue library books.

5921. _____. *Alistair's Time Machine* (Prentice, 1986) k–3. Alistair's entry in a science competition takes him to many places and time periods, but unfortunately he can't prove this to the judges.

5922. _____. *Alistair Underwater* (S & S, 1990) k–3. Exploring an underwater cave in his homemade submarine, Alistair helps the frog people get rid of the dreaded monster Gooze.

5923. _____. *Alistair and the Alien Invasion* (S & S, 1994) k–3. When aliens invade from outer space, boy genius Alistair is the only person able to save the Earth.

5924. Sadler, Marilyn. *It's Not Easy Being a Bunny* (Beginner, 1983) k–3. Unhappy being a bunny, P. J. Funnybunny tries living with bears, birds, beavers, pigs, moose, possums and skunks.

5925. _____. *Very Bad Bunny* (Beginner, 1984) k–3. The Funnybunnies all think that P.J. is the worst bunny they have ever seen, until his cousin Binky comes for a visit.

5926. _____. *P.J., the Spoiled Bunny* (Random, 1986) k–3. P.J. Funnybunny finally learns that if he wants people to play with him he can't always have his own way.

5927. _____. *P.J. Funnybunny in the Perfect Hiding Place* (Western, 1988) k–3. When P.J. Funnybunny's little sister asks to play hide-and-seek with him and his friends, they run off and leave her until dinnertime when P.J.'s mother inquires where she is.

5928. _____. *Knock, Knock, It's P.J. Funnybunny* (Random, 1992) k–3. P.J. Funnybunny looks for new playmates behind the flaps of his book.

5929. _____. *P.J. Funnybunny Camps Out* (Random, 1993) k–3. Although P.J. and his friends refuse to let Donna and Honey Bunny go camping with them because "camping is not for girls," the girls follow and get proof that camping is hard work even for boys.

5930. Sadler, Marilyn. *Elizabeth and Larry* (S & S, 1990) 2–4. Elizabeth and Larry are contented best friends until Larry is scorned by neighbors for being an alligator.

5931. _____. *Elizabeth and Larry and Ed* (S & S, 1992) 2–4. A swamp animal moves in with an unusual couple when the animal loses his home to developers.

5932. Salten, Felix. *Bambi* (S & S, 1992) 5–8. The adventures of a young deer in the forest as he grows into a beautiful stag.

5933. _____. *Bambi's Children* (Random, 1960) 5–8. Relates how Bambi's son, Geno, gained self-reliance and saved his mother from the fangs of the winter wolf.

5934. Salvatore, R.A. *Woods Out Back* (Putnam, 1994) 4–6. A world of elves and dwarves, witches and dragons exist—in the woods behind Gary's house. Gary must become the land's lost hero, or else he can never go home.

5935. _____. *Dragon's Dragger* (Putnam, 1994) 4–6. Gary returns to the land of Fairie—but things have changed. Ware and revenge and a fiery dragon force Gary to traverse the enchanted world to battle the forces of darkness.

5936. Sampson, Pamela. *Mouse Family Album* (Rand, 1980) 2–4. A family album, put together from memorabilia found in an attic trunk, portrays the life of Amelia Woodmouse's family at the turn of the century.

5937. _____. *Incredible Invention of Alexander Woodmouse* (Rand, 1982) 2–4. Venerable inventor Professor Alexander Woodmouse acquires a new apprentice who proves to be very inventive indeed.

5938. Samuels, Barbara. *Fay and Delores* (Bradbury, 1985) k–3. Two young sisters agree and disagree, yet remain affectionate.

5939. _____. *Duncan and Delores* (Bradbury, 1986) k–3. Delores learns to curb some of her more smothering tendencies and wins the affection of her new pet cat, Duncan.

5940. _____. *Happy Birthday, Delores* (Orchard, 1989) k–3. Delores has a birthday party which is extremely boisterous but quite enjoyable.

5941. Sandberg, Inger. *Little Anna and the Magic Hat* (Lothrop, 1965) k–3. A tale of a baby-sitter who keeps saying "Hocus-Pocus- now you see a…Oh, no! I made a mistake this is a…"

5942. _____. *What Little Anna Saw* (Lothrop, 1966)

k–3. A story of what Anna saw when the big tall man invited her to sit on his green hat and view the world from the top of his head.

5943. ____. *When Little Anna Had a Cold* (Lothrop, 1966) k–3. Anna relies on her magic uncle for entertainment. Pink-nosed and bug-eyed in bed Anna sneezes away at her kind uncle so hard that things keep disappearing. But they are all brought safely back at the end.

5944. ____. *Little Anna's Mama Has a Birthday* (Lothrop, 1966) k–3. Anna has no money for her mother's birthday gift so she decides to make her a colorful present.

5945. ____. *Little Anna and the Tall Uncle* (Lothrop, 1973) k–3. Little Anna's tall uncle is amazingly tall. When he takes Anna sailing he has to have two boats so he can sit in one and put his feet in the other. He stretches his legs on the back of a whale.

5946. ____. *Where Is Little Anna's Dog?* (Lothrop, 1973) k–3. Anna and her tall uncle discuss a range of topics from the world's great inventions to the inverse ratio between size and the capacity to feel fear. Anna's uncle lives on the border between fantasy and reality because his height and accomplishments are impossible and exaggerated.

5947. ____. *Little Anna Goes Traveling* (Lothrop, 1983) k–3. Little Anna and her tall uncle travel by homemade saucer and inspect the natural and human phenomena of New Zealand.

5948. Sandberg, Inger. *Boy with 100 Cars* (Delacorte, 1968) k–3. Matthew was so fond of cars, his father wrote him a special story of a boy who had so many cars he got lost among them.

5949. ____. *Boy with Many Houses* (Delacorte, 1970) k–3. Five-year-old Matthew wants to build a house of his own but he can't seem to find a suitable place.

5950. Sandberg, Inger. *Dusty Wants to Help* (Farrar, 1987) k–3. Dusty wants to help his grandfather make pancakes, but only succeeds in causing problems for his grandfather.

5951. ____. *Dusty Wants to Borrow Everything* (Farrar, 1988) k–3. Dusty keeps his slightly flustered grandparents on their toes by borrowing all the interesting things in their house, from Grandma's glasses to Grandpa's hat to the big kitchen knife.

5952. Sandberg, Inger. *Nicholas' Red Day* (Delacorte, 1967) k–3. From the moment he pats the red bus and paints himself red, Nicholas has "red" experiences, even to coming down with red spots—the measles.

5953. ____. *Nicholas' Favorite Pet* (Delacorte, 1969) k–3. Nicholas and his father disagree on the advantages and disadvantages of various pets until his father surprises him with just the right one.

5954. Sandberg, Inger. *Little Spook Godfrey* (Dela-

corte, 1968) k–3. A little ghost, who can't do more than squeak, decides it's more fun to play with the prince than to scare him.

5955. ____. *Little Spook* (Methuen, 1969) k–3. Little Spook is a disappointment to his parents—he doesn't haunt well, he's scared, can't groan or chain rattle. The royal chambermaid takes pity on him and introduces him to a princeling.

5956. ____. *Little Spook's Baby Sister* (Methuen, 1978) k–3.

5957. ____. *Little Spook Haunts Again* (Methuen, 1979) k–3. In Morning Sun Castle, Little Spook and his companion Prince take over Father Spook's duties when he is seized by illness in color—he turns red and yellow. The two kids haunt with little impact. Father gets better and resumes his work.

5958. ____. *Little Spook and the Lost Doll* (Methuen, 1980) k–3. Spook plays with human children and loses a girl's favorite doll.

5959. Sandberg, Inger. *Johan's Year* (Methuen, 1971) 4–6. The problem of Johan: the relationship with his parents and grandparents, his near disastrous association with a young delinquent and the way he looks after his two-year-old cousin told with understanding.

5960. ____. *Johan at School* (Methuen, 1972) 4–6. Johan is allergic to animals and he longs for pets. He and his friend Knut start an animal hospital. They end up chasing biscuits on a timber raft in midstream.

5961. Sandberg, Inger. *Where Does All That Smoke Come From?* (Delacorte, 1972) k–3. Two children discover the town's air pollution problem is caused mainly by a dragon who smokes thirty cigarettes at one time.

5962. ____. *Let's Play Desert* (Delacorte, 1974) k–3. Two children make believe their sandbox is a desert.

5963. Sandman, Lilius. *Gold Crown Lane* (Delacorte, 1976) 4–6. The murder of a customs official in a small, late 19th century Finnish town has many repercussions for the townspeople, especially for the Halter family who become involved with the son of the suspected murderer.

5964. ____. *Goldmaker's House* (Delacorte, 1977) 4–6. A tiny Finnish town of Tulavall buzzes with speculation about Herr Turiam the alchemist, but only his housekeeper and Benadea the young maid servant know the true nature of his work.

5965. ____. *Horses of the Night* (Delacorte, 1979) 4–6. When life in a tiny Finnish village is disrupted by one unscrupulous man's schemes, vigilant spirits from long ago intervene.

5966. Sandwall-Bergstrom, M. *Anna All Alone* (Blackie, 1979) 4–6. Anna leaves the orphanage to stay with a lazy alcoholic mistress where she is overworked and dismissed when her usefulness ends.

5967. ____. *Anna at Bloom Farm* (Blackie, 1979) 4–6. Anna stays with a poor crofter family. She discovers her origin but her grandfather is a thoughtless, feudal landlord, unwise even in his attempts to establish her as his heir.

5968. ____. *Anna Keeps Her Promise* (Blackie, 1979) 4–6. Anna chooses to remain with the drunken crofter's family on their mother's death rather than fight for her inheritance.

5969. ____. *Anna at the Manor House* (Blackie, 1980) 4–6. Anna tries to make her grandfather accept the Karlberg children.

5970. ____. *Anna Wins Through* (Blackie, 1980) 4–6. Anna is almost burned to death rescuing the Karlberg children from a fire. She recovers in Dally-Pater's college and then returns to live in the manor. She persuaded grandfather to give the Karlberg children a home.

5971. ____. *Anna Solves the Mystery* (Blackie, 1980) 4–6. Regina tries to involve Anna in thefts which occur in the manor. Anna finds the thief and clears Matt's name.

5972. Saunders, Susan. *Patti's Luck* (Scholastic, 1987) 4–6. Stephanie invites Patti to the Friday evening sleepover she has with Lauren and Kate. Kate puts a curse on Patti and it seems to work.

5973. ____. *Patti Gets Even* (Scholastic, 1989) 3–5. Patti responds to the obnoxious Wayne Miller's bragging by betting that she can win more contests at the Winter Carnival.

5974. Saunders, Susan. *Mystery Cat and the Chocolate Trap* (Bantam, 1986) k–3. Mystery Cat story is told from a human point of view. There is a mystery to be solved. But where does the chocolate trap come in?

5975. ____. *Mystery Cat* (Bantam, 1986) k–3. Hillary and Kelly Ann are involved when Mystery Cat finds some counterfeit bills and the two girls decide to follow him back to the source. Hillary tracks the culprits down but walks into a trap. Mystery Cat and Kelly Ann must free her.

5976. ____. *Mystery Cat and the Monkey Business* (Bantam, 1986) k–3.

5977. Savage, Cindy. *Great Boyfriend Disaster* (Willowisp, 1988) 5–8.

5978. ____. *Let's Be Friends Forever* (Willowisp, 1989) 5–8. Krissy feels a rivalry with her younger sister Kitty who is a model. Krissy resents the T.V. crews, the tips given by Kitty and doesn't want to watch Kitty's screen test.

5979. ____. *Friends to the Rescue* (Willowisp, 1989) 5–8. Linda Jean lives with her father. One summer, she helps in a catering and a party planning business. Then her mother comes with a new husband and two stepchildren and a new interest in her daughter.

5980. ____. *Keeping Secrets, Keeping Friends* (Willowisp, 1989) 5–8.

5981. ____. *Friends Save the Day* (Willowisp, 1989) 5–8.

5982. ____. *New Friend Blues* (Willowisp, 1989) 5–8.

5983. ____. *That's What Friends Are For* (Willowisp, 1989) 5–8.

5984. ____. *More Than Just a Friend* (Willowisp, 1990) 5–8.

5985. Savitt, Sam. *Vicki and the Black Horse* (Doubleday, 1964) 5–8. Vicki, 13, loves her race horse Pat. She gets another horse Jesse whom she later sells but Pat misses Jesse more than anyone could believe.

5986. ____. *Vicki and the Brown Mare* (Dodd, 1976) 5–8. Sensing that her neighbor's thoroughbred has natural jumping abilities, a teenage girl tries to give the horse the training it lacks.

5987. Saxon, Nancy. *Panky and William* (Atheneum, 1983) 5–8. Panky is fat and new to school. William is a horse at the stable of her friend, Kathy. Panky befriends and reforms William.

5988. ____. *Panky in the Saddle* (Atheneum, 1984) 5–8. Panky trains William, a pony. She is ready to accept her father's job loss.

5989. ____. *Panky in Love* (Atheneum, 1985) 5–8. Panky thinks she is in love with one of the polo players at the club, but she doesn't like the way he and his friends treat their ponies.

5990. Scarry, Patricia. *Little Richard* (American Heritage, 1970) 3–5. Nine stories about Little Richard, the rabbit, and the many other animals that live in or near his house in the woods.

5991. ____. *Little Richard and Prickles* (American Heritage, 1971) 3–5. Relates the adventures of a little rabbit and his porcupine friend.

5992. Scarry, Patricia. *Waggy and His Friends* (Heritage, 1971) k–3. Sixteen bedtime stories record the adventures of David and his stuffed animal friends.

5993. ____. *More About Waggy* (McGraw, 1973) k–3. Ten short stories about a woolen dog and his friends who live in little David's room.

5994. Schatell, Brian. *Farmer Golf and His Turkey Sam* (Harper, 1982) k–3. A prize-winning turkey has a passion for pies.

5995. ____. *Sam's No Dummy, Farmer Goff* (Harper, 1984) k–3. Farmer Goff wants Sam to appear on television. But when he gets all the attention Farmer Goff gets into the act with disastrous results.

5996. Schealer, John. *Zip-Zip and His Flying Saucer* (Dutton, 1956) 4–8. Randy meets a strange boy in an old barn. He takes his older brother and sister to meet Zip-Zip who shows them his flying saucer.

5997. ____. *Zip-Zip Goes to Venus* (Dutton, 1958) 4–6. This time Zip-Zip takes the Riddle children to

Venus to rescue Zip's father. They are captured by the green people, gain their freedom and are captured again by desert dwellers.

5998. Schertie, Alice. *Cathy and Company and the Double Dare* (Children's, 1980) 2–4. Just when it seems that the Gunny Street Gang had gotten the best of them, the members of Cathy and Company received a little unexpected help.
5999. ____. *Cathy and Company and the Green Ghost* (Children's, 1980) 2–4. Three club members investigate a ghost who is mysteriously leaving them notes.
6000. ____. *Cathy and Company and the Nosy Neighbor* (Children's, 1980) 2–4. Cathy and Company observe the new neighbor's curiosity about them. Then they become the curious ones.
6001. ____. *Cathy and Company and Bumper the Bully* (Children's, 1980) 2–4. A member of a club was bothered by a bully while visiting a cabin in the woods.
6002. ____. *Cathy and Company and Hank the Horse* (Children's, 1980) 2–4. A club member befriends an old gray horse who longs for wide open spaces and green grass.
6003. ____. *Cathy and Company and Mean Mr. Meeker* (Children's 1980) 2–4. When their mascot has puppies in a mean neighbor's tool shed, the members of a club must find a way to retrieve the new family.

6004. Schmidt, Annie. *Bob and Jilly* (Methuen, 1976) 3–5. Bob and Jilly live next to each other. They play together, walk in puddles, eat apples, fight, play with toys and enjoy each other.
6005. ____. *Bob and Jilly Are Friends* (Methuen, 1978) 3–5. Bob and Jilly stories show accurately observed and often funny incidents. Very short text but each tale has a twist.
6006. ____. *Bob and Jilly in Trouble* (Methuen, 1980) 3–5. Bob and Jilly are normal five-year-olds who quarrel and make friends, have tantrums, overeats and get into mischief.

6007. Schmidt, Annie. *Dusty and Smudge Spill the Paint* (Methuen, 1977) k–3. Dusty, a little Dutch girl and her pup, Smudge, get into mischief, in this story with paint, in others with hair-cutting, water and typewriter ribbon.
6008. ____. *Dusty and Smudge and the Bride* (Methuen, 1978) k–3. Dusty is a tomboy girl who creates chaos wherever she goes with her dog, Smudge. She uses a typewriter ribbon as a lead for Smudge when she takes him to a wedding. Then Smudge wraps himself around the bride!
6009. ____. *Dusty and Smudge Keep Cool* (Methuen, 1978) k–3. Dusty is going to have her hair cut. She and her dog go to the hairdresser and she has her head shaved bald. She is at first teased by her friends but then they see the advantages of shaven heads.

6010. Schoch, Tim. *Creeps: An Alien in Our School* (Avon, 1985) 4–6. Jeff and Gwen befriend an unpopular, unusual new student until Jeff suspects her of being an alien from outer space.
6011. ____. *Summer Camp Creeps* (Avon, 1987) 4–6. Jeff and his friend Gwen take turns describing the rivalry between the boys and the girls one strange weekend at Camp Arrowhead, when a mysterious thief strikes repeatedly in the night.

6012. Schongut, Emanuel. *Catch Kitten* (Walker, 1983) k–3. A family of kittens explores the interior world of toys, prams and feeding bowls and the outdoors where they see rabbits, ducks, fish and others.
6013. ____. *Hush Kitten* (Walker, 1983) k–3. A family of kittens exploring the interior world of toys, prams and feeding bowls and outdoors, where they have their first encounter with rabbits, ducks, fish and other puzzling animals.
6014. ____. *Look Kitten* (Walker, 1983) k–3. A kitten lurks behind tall grass, watching as animals (puppy, bird, rabbit, duck, frog, fish) appear.
6015. ____. *Wake Kitten* (Walker, 1983) k–3. A family of kittens sleeps a lot but are very inquisitive when they do wake up.
6016. ____. *Play Kitten* (Walker, 1983) k–3. A family of kittens finds that play is a learning experience, an exercise and a source of fun.

6017. Schroeder, Binette. *Shop, Zebby, Shop* (Methuen, 1981) k–3. Zebby, the Zebra, acquires two pairs of boots. He is offered a dress and a green cape for it. But what he wants is a man's suit complete with bow tie and black boots.
6018. ____. *Zebby Goes Swimming* (Methuen, 1981) k–3. Zebby removes his black boots before going in for a dip. But over the horizon looms a lion who takes a fancy to the boots and dances around in them until he falls over.
6019. ____. *Zebby's Breakfast* (Methuen, 1981) k–3. Zebby eats all the flowers on one side of a chasm and then has a precarious journey (in black boots) across a tree trunk to the other side.
6020. ____. *Run Zebby, Run Run Run* (Methuen, 1981) k–3. Zebby rushes from page to page in his black boots pursued by the lion. He stops beside a fence with matching stripes and thereby disappears.
6021. ____. *Zebby Gone with the Wind* (Methuen, 1981) k–3. Zebby doesn't get blown away himself but his stripes do. He is left miserable (in black boots). The stripes are returned by the birds and he is happy again.

6022. Schroeder, Binette. *Tuffa and the Bone* (Dial, 1983) k–3. A rollicking dog searches for the perfect hiding place for her bone.
6023. ____. *Tuffa and the Snow* (Dial, 1983) k–3. Tuffa the dog and her owner enjoy a snowy day.
6024. ____. *Tuffa and the Ducks* (Dial, 1983) k–3. Wanting to play, Tuffa the dog chases some ducks.

6025. ____. *Tuffa and Her Friends* (Dial, 1983) k–3. A dog named Tuffa greets all her other dog friends.
6026. ____. *Tuffa and the Picnic* (Dial, 1983) k–3. A dog named Tuffa gets into trouble when she and a friend get into all the food on a picnic table.

6027. Schulman, Janet. *Jack the Bum and the Haunted House* (Greenwillow, 1977) k–3. A hobo goes to live in a haunted house, discovers a jewel thief hiding there, and is rewarded with a steady job.
6028. ____. *Jack the Bum and the Halloween Hand-out* (Greenwillow, 1977) k–3. On Halloween night, a hobo learns the meaning of UNICEF. He wins a prize for the best costume and donates it to UNICEF.
6029. ____. *Jack the Bum and the UFO* (Greenwillow, 1978) k–3. A clever bum finds an unusual way to prevent the children's pond and woods from being turned into a parking lot.

6030. Schultz, Irene. *Woodland Gang and the Hidden Jewels* (Addison, 1984) 4–6. Dave tells his new friends Bill, Sammy, and Kathy that their uncle had received a shipment of jewels by mail and hid them in the house.
6031. ____. *Woodland Gang and the Dark Old House* (Schultz, 1984) 4–6. Billy, Sammy, and Kathy meet Dave, a wheelchair victim, and form the Gang. They discover a tiny, 30-year-old man who has been hidden all his life. The doctor who protected him now considers sending him to medical school.
6032. ____. *Woodland Gang and the Two Lost Boys* (Addison, 1984) 4–6. Two homeless boys become the object of the gang's attention after one of the boys is found almost lifeless in the city park.
6033. ____. *Woodland Gang and the Missing Will* (Addison, 1984) 4–6. Four orphaned children and their housekeeper obtain valuable antiques for the national museum by uncovering a swindler's plot.
6034. ____. *Woodland Gang and the Stolen Animals* (Schultz, 1984) 4–6. Four orphaned children and their housekeeper help catch a gang of animal thieves who prey on zoos and circuses.
6035. ____. *Woodland Gang and the Old Gold Coins* (Schultz, 1984) 4–6. Four orphaned children and their housekeeper help discover an ancient buried Roman villa in England.
6036. ____. *Woodland Gang and the Mystery Quilt* (Addison, 1988) 4–6. Four orphans and their housekeeper solve two puzzles connected with an old patchwork quilt and save a wetlands as a nature preserve for their town.
6037. ____. *Woodland Gang and the Secret Spy Code* (Addison, 1988) 4–6. After buying several items at a garage sale, four orphans and their housekeeper find themselves harassed by a sinister bearded man of suspicious behavior.
6038. ____. *Woodland Gang and the Museum Robbery* (Addison, 1988) 4–6. Locked in the museum for the night, four orphans and their housekeeper try to foil a jewel robbery.

6039. ____. *Woodland Gang and the Ghost Cat* (Addison, 1988) 4–6. On a camping trip to Cave Park the Woodland Gang solve the mystery of their stolen food when they discover a "ghost cat" in a cave, which leads them to a family of Vietnamese refugees who are living in the cave.
6040. ____. *Woodland Gang and the Indian Cave* (Addison, 1988) 4–6. The Woodland Gang, Mrs. Tandy and Chief Hemster help search for a hidden cave on a friend's ranch.
6041. ____. *Woodland Gang and the Dinosaur Bones* (Addison, 1988) 4–6. A gang of orphans and their housekeeper help Dr. Justin search an Arizona canyon for fossilized dinosaur remains, despite sabotage and theft caused by greedy miners.

6042. Schumache, Claire. *Nutty's Christmas* (Morrow, 1984) k–3. A squirrel accidentally gets into a tree that is cut down and taken away to be a family's Christmas tree. He is in the trimmed tree when the family goes out; he opens the presents, nibbles the cookies and knocks things over. The family returns him to the forest.
6043. ____. *Nutty's Picnic* (Morrow, 1986) k–3. Nutty, the squirrel, forages a picnic basket and is taken aboard a sailboat and he is frightened. A human father returns the tired Nutty to his family.
6044. ____. *Nutty's Birthday* (Morrow, 1986) k–3. Nutty, the squirrel, and Tom both have a birthday. Tom's mother chases Nutty away from Tom's cake. Nutty climbs a tree to find his birthday present and rescues Tom's gift of a model airplane. Nutty's gift is a baby swing.

6045. Schwartz, Joel. *Upchuck Summer* (Delacorte, 1982) 5–8. Richie is having a bad time at summer camp. Then he finds he is the root of his problem.
6046. ____. *Upchuck Summer Revenge* (Delacorte, 1990) 5–8. Richie is now teaching youngsters at summer camp to play football. He avoids Chuck, his would-be friend and plots revenge on Jerry.

6047. Scott, Dustin. *Mojave Joe* (Knopf, 1950) 4–6. Mojave Joe is a coyote who is going to be put in a zoo. He escapes and heads for California and his old friend Mel, whose life he had once saved.
6048. ____. *Return of Mojave Joe* (Knopf, 1952) 4–6. Mojave Joe and Fleetfoot raise six young coyotes. Red-hair, the trapper is determined to kill Mojave Joe but Mel saves him and discovers gold in Mojave Joe's cave.

6049. Sefton, Catherine. *Ghost and Bertie Boggin* (Faber, 1980) 3–5. Bertie, too small to play with his brother and sister, finds that a ghost can be a very pleasant best friend.
6050. ____. *Bertie Boggin and the Ghost Again* (Faber, 1988) 3–5. The ghost is upset when a little baby sister comes to live in the house where ghost

lives in the coal bin. He packs up to leave but when he really meets the baby he changes his mind.

6051. Seibold, J. Otto. *Mr. Lunch Takes a Plane Ride* (Viking, 1993) k–3. Mr. Lunch, a canine bird-chaser extraordinaire, takes his first plane ride and finds adventure in the skies.
6052. ____. *Mr. Lunch Borrows a Canoe* (Viking, 1994) k–3. When Mr. Lunch, canine bird-chaser extraordinaire, sees a bear while canoeing, he paddles so fast and so far that he ends up in Venice.

6053. Seignobosc, Francoise. *Big Rain* (Scribner, 1961) k–3. Jeanne-Marie helps get farm animals to safety when rain floods come to their farm.
6054. ____. *Minou* (Scribner, 1962) k–3. The story of Nenette and her travels from one end of Paris to the other in search of her runaway cat.

6055. Selden, George. *Cricket in Times Square* (Ariel, 1960) 4–6. The adventures of a mouse who got transported to New York City in a picnic basket and the friends he makes, Mario, a boy, Tucker, a fast-talking Broadway mouse, and Tucker's pal, Harry the cat.
6056. ____. *Tucker's Countryside* (Farrar, 1969) 4–6. The further adventures of Chester Cricket, Harry Cat and Tucker Mouse come to Connecticut for a visit and help Chester with his problem of expanding housing.
6057. ____. *Harry Cat's Pet Puppy* (Farrar, 1974) 4–6. Harry brings her new friend, a puppy, to live in the subway with Tucker but he soon grows too big for that home and must find a new one.
6058. ____. *Chester Cricket's Pigeon Ride* (Farrar, 1981) 4–6. Lulu Pigeon takes Chester for a ride he will never forget. He views the Manhattan skyline at night. A slight story.
6059. ____. *Chester Cricket's New Home* (Farrar, 1983) 4–6. When two rather stout ladies sit on Chester Cricket's home in the Old Meadow, the worm-eaten stump collapses and Chester, aided by his friends is forced to look for a new home.
6060. ____. *Harry Kitten and Tucker Mouse* (Farrar, 1986) 4–6. A hungry mouse and a lonely kitten become friends and seek adventure and fortune together in the streets and subways of New York City.

6061. Seligson, Susan. *Amos: Story of an Old Dog and His Couch* (Joy Street, 1987) k–3. An old dog finds adventure when he discovers that his favorite couch has a motor and can be driven.
6062. ____. *Amazing Amos and the Greatest Couch on Earth* (Little, 1989) k–3. When Amos, who travels by motorized couch, makes friends with a group of circus performers, he finds himself unexpectedly in the limelight.
6063. ____. *Amos, Ahoy* (Little, 1990) k–3. When Amos, the dog, accidentally disturbs the neighborhood bully, he sets a high speed chase through town

with everyone from the dogcatcher to a used furniture salesman hot on his trail.
6064. ____. *Amos Camps Out* (Little, 1992) k–3. Amos, the dog who travels by motorized couch, discovers the joys and tribulations of camping.

6065. Selway, Martha. *What a Day!* (World, 1982) k–3. Confusion reigns through the day when the pig family oversleeps.
6066. ____. *Grunts Go on a Picnic* (World, 1982) k–3. Familiar picnic mishaps like ants, mud and a hostile bull is less awful in the end than the discovery that Pa has brought a bag of disposable nappies instead of the food.

6067. Shachtman, Tom. *Beachmaster* (Holt, 1988) 4–6. An account of the adventures of a sea lion, including his experiences with a man in a sea laboratory and his assumption of the role of beach master or head of the tribe.
6068. ____. *Wavebender* (Holt, 1989) 4–6. Further adventures of a sea lion as he wisely leads his tribe out of various dangers.
6069. ____. *Driftwhistler* (Holt, 1992) 4–6. At the head of a band of 13 different species of sea animals, Daniel the sea lion seeks to fulfill a legend and find Pacifica, the long-drowned, ancient home cove of their race.

6070. Shannon, Terry. *Dog Team for Ongluk* (Melmont, 1962) 2–4. Ongluk's dog has puppies and he undertakes the task of training them for his team.
6071. ____. *Wakapoo and the Flying Arrows* (Whitman, 1963) 2–4. The Chumash were peaceful people; hunting seals, fishing and playing at war. Then came the Eskimo fur hunters, sent by the Russians to rob and steal.

6072. Sharmat, Marjorie. *Nate the Great* (Coward, 1975) k–3. Nate the Great solves the mystery of the missing picture.
6073. ____. *Nate the Great Goes Undercover* (Coward, 1974) k–3. Nate the Great takes on his first night case and tries to solve the mystery of the garbage snatcher.
6074. ____. *Nate the Great and the Lost List* (Coward, 1975) k–3. Nate the Great interrupts his backyard vacation to find his friend's lost grocery list—before lunch.
6075. ____. *Nate the Great and the Stolen Base* (Coward, 1976) k–3. Nate the Great investigates the mysterious disappearance of the purple plastic octopus that his baseball team uses for second base.
6076. ____. *Nate the Great and the Phony Clue* (Coward, 1977) k–3. When he finds a torn piece of paper with only part of a word on it, detective Nate sets out to find the missing piece.
6077. ____. *Nate the Great and the Sticky Case* (Coward, 1981) k–3. Nate the Great and his dog

Sludge try to track down Claude's missing Stego-saurus stamp.

6078. ____. *Nate the Great and the Missing Key* (Coward, 1981) k–3. Nate the Great and his dog Sludge look for Annie's house key which has mysteriously disappeared.

6079. ____. *Nate the Great and the Snowy Trail* (Coward, 1982) k–3. When Rosemond's birthday gift for Nate disappears from her sled, the boy detective decides to unravel the mystery.

6080. ____. *Nate the Great and the Fishy Prize* (Coward, 1985) k–3. Though it means that Nate can't get his dog ready for the smartest pet contest, he agrees to search for the missing prize for the contest.

6081. ____. *Nate the Great Stalks Stupidweed* (Coward, 1986) k–3. Nate the Great searches for a missing weed after it disappears from a pot on Oliver's porch.

6082. ____. *Nate the Great and the Boring Beach Bag* (Coward, 1987) k–3. Nate the Great finds mystery at the beach when Oliver's beach bag vanishes.

6083. ____. *Nate the Great Goes Down in the Dumps* (Coward, 1989) k–3. When Rosamond looks into her crystal ball to read Nate the Great's future, she sees a new case for him to solve—her money box is missing and she wants him to find it.

6084. ____. *Nate the Great and the Halloween Hunt* (Coward, 1989) k–3. Nate and his dog Sludge try to solve a case on Halloween night and find themselves locked in a haunted house.

6085. ____. *Nate the Great and the Musical Note* (Coward, 1990) k–3. When Rosamond turns a phone message from Pip's mother into a music lesson with a secret meaning, Nate the Great steps in to solve the mystery.

6086. ____. *Nate the Great and the Tardy Tortoise* (Delacorte, 1995) k–3. In search of a lost tortoise's home, Nate the Great finds a messy yard with bits of flowers, grass and weeds strewn everywhere. "The yard has been bitten to death," he exclaims.

6087. Sharmat, Marjorie. *Mooch the Messy* (Harper, 1976) 3–5. Only for love does a very messy young rat clean up his hole to make his father's visit happier.

6088. ____. *Mooch the Messy Meets Prudence the Neat* (Coward, 1978) 3–5. A very messy rat worries about his friendship with his extremely neat new neighbor.

6089. Sharmat, Marjorie. *Rich Mitch* (Coward, 1983) 4–6. Mitch wins $250,000 in a sweepstakes and his greedy parents start spending it recklessly. Their normal routine life is shattered but Mitch humorously holds it all together.

6090. ____. *Get Rich Mitch* (Morrow, 1985) 4–6. Because of the popularity of the Rich Mitch doll Mitch is kidnapped but he escapes with his magnetic marble and the rival doll. Turnip Head outsells Rich Mitch and Mitch is again a non-entity.

6091. Sharmat, Marjorie. *Morris Brookside, a Dog* (Holiday, 1973) k–3. Mr. and Mrs. Brookside worry about Morris the dog's choice of friends.

6092. ____. *Morris Brookside Is Missing* (Holiday, 1974) k–3. After Mr. and Mrs. Brookside hurt his feelings, Morris, their dog, disappears.

6093. Sharmat, Marjorie. *Sophie and Gussie* (Macmillan, 1973) 3–5. Two squirrel friends spend the weekend together, exchange presents, plan a party and trade hats.

6094. ____. *Trip* (Macmillan, 1976) 3–5. Two squirrel friends prepare for a trip, clean house, listen to the rain, and care for a flower.

6095. Sharmat, Marjorie. *Great Genghis Khan Look-Alike Contest* (Random, 1993) 3–5. Fred enters his mean looking, but sweet dog, Duz, in a Hollywood contest that could lead to a movie contract, fame and fortune.

6096. ____. *Genghis Khan: A Dog Star Is Born* (Random, 1994) 3–5. Fred Shedd and his parents accompany their dog Duz to Hollywood where his new career as a movie star is almost ended before it begins when Duz is kidnapped.

6097. Sharmat, Marjorie. *Olivia Sharp, Agent for Secrets* (Delacorte, 1989) 2–4. Perfect Desiree seeks the help of wealthy problem solver, Olivia Sharp, in becoming princess of the school.

6098. ____. *Pizza Monster* (Delacorte, 1989) 2–4. Wealthy secret agent Olivia Sharp helps depressed Duncan find a friend.

6099. ____. *Princess of the Fillmore Street School* (Delacorte, 1989) 2–4. Olivia is an "Agent for Secrets." Her case involves Desiree who wants to be Princess of the Fillmore Street School. Desiree wants everyone to be as perfect as she is. Olivia solves this by telling Desiree she can't be perfect and bossy.

6100. ____. *Sly Spy* (Delacorte, 1990) 2–4. E.J. the spy tries to uncover a secret that Olivia is keeping for a client.

6101. ____. *Green Toenails Gang* (Delacorte, 1991) 2–4. Wealthy Olivia Sharp, agent for secrets, uncovers several secrets on a trip to Carmel, California to help a friend become a member of an exclusive club.

6102. Shaw, Janet. *Meet Kristen, an American Girl* (Pleasant, 1986) 3–5. Kristen, nine, and her family experience many hardships as they travel from Sweden to the Minnesota frontier in 1854.

6103. ____. *Kristen Learns a Lesson* (Pleasant, 1986) 3–5. After immigrating from Sweden to join relatives in an American prairie community, Kirsten endures the ordeal of a strange school through a secret friendship with an Indian girl.

6104. ____. *Kristen's Surprise* (Pleasant, 1986) 3–5. Kristen and her family celebrate their first Christmas in their new home on Uncle Olav's farm in mid–nineteenth century Minnesota.

6105. ____. *Happy Birthday, Kristen* (Pleasant, 1987) 3–5. On a Minnesota farm in the mid–1800s, the hard-working members of the Larson family find time to celebrate Kristen's tenth birthday.

6106. ____. *Changes for Kristen* (Pleasant, 1988) 3–5. A tough Minnesota winter brings many changes to Kristen's frontier life, including the new responsibility of helping her brother Lars set his traps and a move into a new house for her family.

6107. ____. *Kristen Saves the Day.* Kristen, ten, is excited when she finds a bee tree full of honey, one of the natural treasures of her Minnesota frontier world, but she exposes herself to great danger by trying to harvest the honey by herself.

6108. Shaw, Nancy. *Sheep in a Jeep* (Houghton, 1986) k–3. Records the misadventures of a group of sheep that go riding in a jeep. The jeep breaks down, the sheep give it a push, the driver doesn't look where he is going and the jeep ends up in a puddle.

6109. ____. *Sheep on a Ship* (Houghton, 1988) k–3. Sheep on a deep-sea voyage run into trouble when it storms and are glad to come paddling into port.

6110. ____. *Sheep in a Shop* (Houghton, 1991) k–3. Sheep hunt for a birthday present and make havoc of the shop, only to discover they haven't the money to pay for the things.

6111. ____. *Sheep Out to Eat* (Houghton, 1992) k–3. The sheep are off to a tea shop for some rollicking fun and, of course, disasters. When the mayhem gets to be too much and the sheep are asked to leave they don't have to look far to find the perfect place for lunch.

6112. ____. *Sheep Take a Hike* (Houghton, 1994) k–3. Having gotten lost on a chaotic hike in the great outdoors, the sheep find their way back by following the trail of wool they left behind.

6113. Shea, George. *ESP McGee to the Rescue* (Avon, 1984) 5–8. McGee tracks down a land developer's arson scheme.

(For other books on "ESP McGee," *see* Ernst, Kathryn F.; Lawrence, McMahan, Ian; Jim; Packard, Edward; Rodgers, Jesse.)

6114. Shearer, John. *Billy Joe Jive, Super Private Eye, the Case of the Missing Ten Speed* (Delacorte, 1976) 2–4. The best, bravest and smartest Private Eye in the world relates his latest adventure.

6115. ____. *Billy Joe Jive and the Case of the Sneaker Snatcher* (Delacorte, 1977) 2–4. Billy Joe Jive's culprit is a benchwarmer on the 100th Street Jets who steals the sneakers of the team's ace before the big game.

6116. ____. *Billy Joe Jive and the Case of the Missing Pigeons* (Delacorte, 1978) 2–4. Young detectives, Billy Joe and Susie, search the street for a pigeon thief.

6117. ____. *Billy Joe Jive and the Walkie-Talkie Caper* (Delacorte, 1981) 2–4. Two young detectives, Billy Joe and Susie, retrieve a pair of missing walkie-talkies.

6118. ____. *Billy Joe Jive and the Case of the Midnight Voices* (Delacorte, 1982) 2–4. Billy Joe and Susie investigate mysterious events at Camp Mountain Lake.

6119. Shefelman, Janice. *Paradise Called Texas* (Eakin, 1983) 4–6. Searching for a better life, Mina and her parents leave their German fatherland in 1845 and sail to Texas, U.S.A., where they find hardship, tragedy and adventure.

6120. ____. *Willow Creek Home* (Eakin, 1985) 4–6. A summer drought and epidemic illness in 1847 force Mina, Papa, and his new wife, Lisette, to move onto a larger land grant deep in Comanche territory.

6121. ____. *Spirit of Iron* (Eakin, 1987) 4–6. When Mina learns that Amaya, her Lipan Apache friend, has been kidnapped by a band of marauding Comanches, she disguises herself as a boy and follows the Texas Rangers to search for Amaya.

6122. Sheldon, Dyan. *Harry's Holiday* (Walker, 1992) 3–5. Sara Jane, 10, Lucy, 15, and Ben, 13, are siblings with a lot of rivalry. Harry is Sarah Jane's cat. There is to be a family camping holiday. It is magical Harry who arranges for them to have the same dream experience which solves the differences.

6123. ____. *Harry and Chicken* (Candlewick, 1992) 3–5. Chicken meets a talking cat, Harry. He was from outer space. She sneaks him home and in no time is in trouble. He eats the dessert, gets stranded up a tree and steals a pizza in the shopping mall. But Chicken keeps him anyway.

6124. ____. *Harry the Explorer* (Candlewick, 1992) 3–5. Chicken's cat Harry, who is actually an alien from the planet Arcana, takes her on an adventure that gets her into all kinds of trouble.

6125. ____. *Harry on Vacation* (Candlewick, 1993) 3–5. Harry, the cat-like alien, accompanies Chicken and her family on a camping trip.

6126. Sheridan, John. *Eric, the Wild Car* (Bobbs, 1978) k–3. Eric is a furry anthropomorphized car. Eric replaces private with public transport and rescues fish from oil polluted waters. When city inhabitants find the introduction of cars into their lives is destructive to their environment and makes them unhappy, Eric, a wild car, solves the problem.

6127. ____. *Eric and the Mad Inventor* (Bobbs, 1978) k–3. Eric, a wild car, and Mr. Flywheel, an inventor, cleans up a polluting oil spill and reminds a misguided scientist that he can't improve on nature.

6128. ____. *Eric and the Lost Planes* (Bobbs, 1978) k–3. An accident lands Eric, Granny Flywheel and Mr. Flywheel in a cave, where they discover some very hungry little lost planes which they attempt to rescue.

6129. Sherry, Sylvia. *Pair of Jesus Boots* (Puffin, 1969) 5–8. Rocky lives in a working-class subculture, on the fringe of respectable society, in which petty thieving, brushes with the police, alcoholism, illegitimacy and a diet of chips are the norm. He wears sandals (Jesus Boots), is a gang leader and wants to be like his jailed big brother, Joey.

6130. ____. *Pair of Desert-Wellies* (Puffin, 1985) 5–8. Rocky still leads the Cats gang in opposition to the gang run by Chick and Spadge. He trades his Jesus Boots for desert-wellies (training-shoes with ridged soles). Rocky faces, among other things, IRA bombers and nearly gets blown up.

6131. ____. *Rocky and the Ratman* (Cape, 1988) 5–8. Rocky, 12, tried to bring off a "real robbery." He lives as a lower class child. He escapes from a wrongful police arrest in order to rescue his sister Suzie from a fire. There is a happy ending.

6132. ____. *Rocky and the Black Eye Mystery* (Cape, 1992) 5–8. Rocky's brother returns, a local gang leader's vengeful plans for his brother and Rocky's own plans to rob a jewelry shop are all of great concern to Rocky. Rocky is bound for jail himself sooner or later.

6133. Shipton, Jonathan. *Horrible Crocodile* (Golden, 1995) k–3.

6134. ____. *No Biting Horrible Crocodile* (Golden, 1995) k–3. Flora acts like a horrible crocodile, biting all the other children in school, until one day she goes too far.

6135. Shire, Ellen. *Chicken Scandal at Number Seven Rue Petite* (Random, 1978) k–3. A competitor's attempt to discredit Jean-Pierre and Isabelle's restaurant backfires and the Rue Petite receives even more accolades.

6136. ____. *Mystery at Number Seven, Rue Petite* (Random, 1978) k–3. Isabelle and Jean-Pierre are curious about the locked room in the house of their employer, an antique dealer.

6137. Shreve, Susan. *Flunking of Joshua T. Bates* (Knopf, 1984) 3–5. Driving home from the beach on Labor Day, Joshua receives some shocking news from his mother: he must repeat the third grade.

6138. ____. *Joshua T. Bates Takes Charge* (Knopf, 1993) 3–5. Joshua, 11, worried about fitting in at school, feels awkward when the new student he is supposed to be helping becomes the target of the fifth grade's biggest bully.

6139. Shreve, Susan. *Family Secrets* (Knopf, 1979) 3–5. Five tales on serious subjects by a young boy named Sammy.

6140. ____. *Bad Dreams of a Good Girl* (Knopf, 1982) 3–5. Carlotta, a fourth grader, is a "good girl" in contrast to her three teenaged brothers. She deals with the "I Hate Lotty Club," gets closer to her fa-

ther and copes with her now working mother. She also ends the war with her oldest brother.

6141. Shura, Mary. *Chester* (Dodd, 1980) 4–6. Jamie, George, Eddie, Zach and Amy all have something special to brag about until Chester moves in the block and outdoes them all. But when he and his goat outwit the teenage bully all is forgiven.

6142. ____. *Eleanor* (Dodd, 1983) 4–6. Eleanor is Chester's sister and she, along with the gang at school, are designing a float for the Field Day parade.

6143. ____. *Jefferson* (Dodd, 1984) 4–6. Jefferson is Chester's brother. The gang is going to give him a birthday party. It is beset by one calamity after another.

6144. Sibley, Kathleen. *Adam and the F.A. Cup* (Dobson, 1976) 4–6. Adam was thrilled when his team wins the F.A. Cup. Together with his father he saw them return to their home ground. There is a theft by the Shadow. Adam finds his hideout and Shadow is caught by the police. Adam recovers the stolen F.A. Cup.

6145. ____. *Adam and the Football Mystery* (Dobson, 1980) 4–6. Adam likes football. He plays well with the new boy from the local fair. Suspicion is cast on two brothers who run a stall at the fair when certain footballs were used to hide valuable postage stamps. Adam and his friends are involved in bringing the stamp thieves to justice.

6146. Silcock, Ruth. *Albert John Out Hunting* (Viking, 1980) k–3. Albert John is a cat who has a lot of adventures.

6147. ____. *Albert John in Disgrace* (Viking, 1981) k–3. Albert John and his feline friend O'Flanagan are leaving home because their vocal efforts made them unpopular. They find unpopularity wherever they go.

6148. Sillitoe, Alan. *City Adventures of Marmalade Jim* (Robson, 1977) k–3. A racy account of a farm cat's adventures in the big city. Jim goes to market with the farmer's vegetables and soon is in trouble with Dustbin Dan, boss of the Alley Cat Gang.

6149. ____. *Marmalade Jim at the Farm* (Robson, 1980) k–3. Marmalade Jim meets a nasty gang of feline hooligans in the country. City brute force is defeated by rustic wit.

6150. ____. *Marmalade Jim and the Fox* (Robson, 1984) k–3. Dustbin Dan and his Alleycat Gang, enemies of Marmalade Jim had a tough winter and are starving. They search for food but are hampered by a fox. Marmalade Jim tells the gang there is food in the barn but not that the fox is in there, too. Dan and Jim part friends, but how long will it last?

6151. Silverstein, Shel. *Missing Piece* (Harper, 1976) 4–6. A circle has difficulty finding its missing piece but has a good time looking for it.

6152. ____. *Missing Piece Meets the Big O* (Harper, 1981) 4–6. A missing piece, looking for someone to carry it along, finally develops its own momentum.

6153. Simon, Seymour. *Einstein Anderson, Science Sleuth* (Viking, 1980) 4–6. Einstein is a brainy kid who likes to solve puzzlers. The reader gets the clues and a chance to solve the problem before the solution is given. A scientific "Encyclopedia Brown."
6154. ____. *Einstein Anderson Shocks His Friends* (Viking, 1980) 4–6. Einstein's father is a vet with a science background and he uses this knowledge to enhance his own solving ability. In this book he uses electricity, static, etc., to shock his friends.
6155. ____. *Einstein Anderson Makes Up for Lost Time* (Viking, 1981) 4–6. Einstein uses his scientific knowledge to solve the many puzzlers put to him, ranging from astronomy and zoology.
6156. ____. *Einstein Anderson Tells a Cornet's Tale* (Viking, 1981) 4–6. Einstein solves another series of puzzlers (with a few puns thrown in). The scientific basis for the solutions is clear and understandable.
6157. ____. *Einstein Anderson Goes to Bat* (Viking, 1982) 4–6. Einstein does use scientific logic to solve his puzzles, all of which can be tested. He still offers puns and riddles, and fun.
6158. ____. *Einstein Anderson Lights Up the Sky* (Viking, 1982) 4–6. Some aspect of science is used in solving these new problems. In this book meteorology and electrostatics are used.
6159. ____. *Einstein Anderson Sees Through the Invisible Man* (Viking, 1983) 4–6. Einstein is no longer just a solver of puzzlers but is a wit also. More puzzles to solve, more jokes and riddles to guess and more fun to be had.

6160. Simpson, Dorothy. *Honest Dollar* (Lippincott, 1957) 5–8. Janie wants to earn money for books because she can't afford to go to high school. The jobs she wants she can't get and the jobs she can get she doesn't want. But a happy solution is found.
6161. ____. *Lesson for Janie* (Lippincott, 1959) 5–8. Janie has a problem with the new girl, Myra. She appeared conceited and dull. They often quarreled instead of being friends. They competed daily. But a dangerous adventure showed Janie and Myra what the other one was really like.
6162. ____. *New Horizons* (Lippincott, 1961) 5–8. Full of bright expectations for the future, Janie, 14, leaves her island home to go to the mainland high school. But high school is a disappointment and her prospects for social life dim, until courage and character bring rich rewards.

6163. Simpson, J.B. *Awful Annie and Perfect Percy* (Macrae, 1986) 2–4. Annie adopts a stray terrier. She names him Perfect Percy. He scares a burglar away and is then accepted in the family.
6164. ____. *Awful Annie and the Nippy Numbers* (Macrae, 1987) 2–4. Mr. Trenchman gives Annie a

math machine called "Nippy Numbers" to help her improve her math grades. Annie loses the machine and while trying to find it she succeeds in catching a thief at the local Big House.

6165. Singer, Marilyn. *Fido Frame-Up* (Harper, 1983) 4–6. Sam Spayed recounts her invaluable assistance to her master as he searches for the thief of Lady Binghampton-Nugget's cameo.
6166. ____. *Nose for Trouble* (Holt, 1985) 4–6. Canine detective Samantha Spayed helps her master investigate industrial espionage at La Maison de Beaute, a woman's cosmetic company.
6167. ____. *Where There's a Will, There's a Wag* (Holt, 1986) 4–6. The owner of Pet Food has died and willed her fortune to a cat. Philip Barlowe, bumbling detective and Sam Spayed, his intelligent dog, find out she really left the money to Sam with Philip as trustee.

6168. Sinor, John. *Finsterhall of San Pasqual* (Joyce, 1976) 3–5. Amusing story of a local rabbit who finds himself enclosed in the boundaries of a wild animal park where strange creatures abound.
6169. ____. *Finsterhall Goes Over the Wall* (Joyce, 1978) 3–5. A story about a bunny who, after talking to other animals, decides to see what a Tasmanian Devil looks like. He takes another bunny along to the zoo and the two have exciting adventures.

6170. Sivers, Brenda. *Snailman* (Little, 1978) 4–6. Timothy had problems. He moved from the city, his parents are fighting and he is harassed by a bully at school. He befriends the town's hermit, a gentle man deformed by a car accident.
6171. ____. *Timothy and the Snailman* (Little, 1980) 4–6. Timothy is being bullied by the boys of the village where he just moved. He makes friends with a lonely weaver who has pet snails. The bullies taunt the snailman and his loom is broken and his snails destroyed.

6172. Sivers, Brenda. *Hound and the Witching Affair* (Abelard, 1981) 3–5.
6173. ____. *Hound in the Highlands* (Abelard, 1981) 3–5. Sherlock hound, a world famous dog detective, and Dr. Winston his companion go to visit Bogle, a noble dog who is unhappy and needs help.
6174. ____. *Hound and the Perilous Pekes* (Abelard, 1981) 3–5.
6175. ____. *Hound and the Curse of Kali* (Abelard, 1982) 3–5. Hound and Dr. John Winston, a sheepdog, are called by Sir Henry Barkerville, a greyhound, to solve a mystery. The reader will recognize the "Hound of the Baskervilles" theme.

6176. Slater, Jim. *Goldenrod* (Cape, 1978) 4–6. William Rod is blind but has other powers he uses to foil a plane hijack. Set in India, with an ayah and a fakir but also a vet, a police dog handler and an ophthalmic surgeon.

6177. ____. *Goldenrod and the Kidnappers* (Cape, 1979) 4–6. Goldenrod is a young boy with magical powers. He saves a Derby winner from an unmentionable fate.

6178. Slater, Jim. *Grasshopper and the Unwise Owl* (Holt, 1980) 3–5. Magic candy which causes him to shrink and the help of new animal friends make it possible for a boy called Grasshopper to save his mother's cottage from an unscrupulous landlord.

6179. ____. *Grasshopper and the Pickle Factory* (Granada, 1980) 3–5. The hero and his talking animals thwart a planner's scheme to site his factory in the woods, only to find his evil attention diverted elsewhere. Stumpy, the tailless squirrel, suitably disguised, is brought in to provide an ecological presence of such rarity that the plans are called off.

6180. ____. *Grasshopper and the Poisoned River* (Granada, 1982) 3–5. Graham Hopper, Grasshopper, can shrink in size to a few inches. He is carried by Jacob the owl. Graham and Jasper the rat bring the pollution criminals to justice.

6181. Slepian, Jan. *Hungry Thing* (Follett, 1967) k–3. The Hungry Thing comes to town and asks for tickles and feetloaf and other interesting things to eat while the townspeople try to figure out what he means.

6182. ____. *Hungry Thing Returns* (Scholastic, 1990) k–3. Hungry Thing and his daughter visit a school and ask for flameburgers, bellyjeans and blownuts to eat.

6183. ____. *Hungry Thing Goes to a Restaurant* (Scholastic, 1992) k–3. When the Hungry Thing orders bapple Moose, spoonadish and bench fries at a fashionable restaurant, who can guess what he really wants to eat.

6184. Sloan, Carolyn. *Mr. Cogg and His Computer* (Macmillan, 1979) 5–8. A story of Mr. Cogg, his cat Holly Mackerel and his computer Compie. Coggie wants a friend and Compie produces a large flying pepper-pot. Compie forges checks, produces wooly walking penguins; he really messes up Aunt Lacey. Between Coggie and Compie life is chaotic.

6185. ____. *Further Inventions of Mr. Cogg* (Macmillan, 1981) 5–8. Mr. Cogg and his computer produce situations that upset Aunt Lacey and the neighbors. A mynah bird and some cats are bothered too. And the Art Show was the end.

6186. ____. *Mr. Cogg and the Exploding Easter Eggs* (Macmillan, 1985) 5–8. Mr. Cogg is a hairbrained inventor. His cat's name is Holly Mackerel and his elderly aunt is Auntie Lacey. He has developed a computer with a mind of its own. The results are alarming; i.e., exploding eggs and runaway robots.

6187. Slobodkin, Louis. *Round Trip Space Ship* (Macmillan, 1968) 4–6. Eddie would like to visit Marty's home so, off they go to Martinea where things are strange indeed.

6188. ____. *Space Ship Under the Apple Tree* (Macmillan, 1971) 4–6. Eddie visits his grandmother on her farm and hardly expects a visit from Marty, the boy from outer space.

6189. ____. *Space Ship Returns to the Apple Tree* (Macmillan, 1972) 4–6. Marty returns from outer space and he and Eddie visit Washington and California by means of the Secret Power ZZZ.

6190. ____. *Three Seated Space Ship* (Macmillan, 1972) 4–6. Marty again visits Eddie while he's at his grandmother's farm. This time London and New York are the destinations in a new spaceship.

6191. ____. *Space Ship in the Park* (Macmillan, 1972) 4–6. Eddie's friend Marty from the planet Martinea, comes to visit and takes Eddie and Willie to Xonia to do research and solve a mystery.

6192. Slobodkina, Esphyr. *Pezzo the Peddler and the Circus Elephant* (Abelard, 1967) k–3. Pezzo the peddler takes his caps to the circus where an elephant's antics amuse the crowd and give Pezzo a temporary job under the big top.

6193. ____. *Pezzo the Peddler and the Thirteen Silly Thieves* (Abelard, 1987) k–3. When Pezzo, the cap peddler, has his wares stolen, he gets them back by shouting "Fire."

6194. Smallwood, Imogen. *Jane Telephones Her Friends* (Collins, 1986) k–3. Jane uses the telephone to talk to her friends; a step by step description of how she does this.

6195. ____. *Jane Shops at the Supermarket* (Collins, 1986) k–3. Jane makes out a shopping list for lunch, goes to the supermarket where she finds what she needs, pays for her purchases and returns home. She sets the table and prepares cheese and tomato on toast.

6196. Smith, E. Boyd. *Farm Book* (Houghton, 1982) 3–5. Bob and Betty learn about life and work on a farm during the summer vacation they spend with their Uncle John and Cousin Reuben.

6197. ____. *Railroad Book* (Houghton, 1983) 3–5. Bob and Betty learn about trains when the railroad opens up a line behind their garden.

6198. ____. *Seashore Book* (Houghton, 1985) 3–5. Bob and Betty learn about life and work at the seashore during a summer vacation with Captain Ben Hawes.

6199. Smith, Eunice. *Jennifer Wish* (Bobbs, 1949) 4–6. A family spends a summer on a farm. When it is time to leave the children can't bear the thought of being cooped up in the city. The farm is available for sale and the family buys it.

6200. ____. *Jennifer Gift* (Bobbs, 1949) 4–6. Jennifer's gift is one she meant for her family but gave to ill Sarabeth instead knowing that her family would not only understand but approve of her action.

6201. ____. *Jennifer Prize* (Bobbs, 1951) 4–6. Jennifer wins a prize for her written composition. She remains a likable girl in a very likable country family.

6202. ____. *Jennifer Is Eleven* (Bobbs, 1952) 4–6. Jennifer's pet is a bull calf and in spite of other activity on the Hill farm Jennifer's concern is her calf. She doesn't want to sell or give it up and accepts the responsibility of keeping it.

6203. ____. *High Heels for Jennifer* (Bobbs, 1964) 4–6. Jennifer is interested in art and horses. High Heels is a friend's horse that she cares for and rides. Her painting of him wins her a trip to Europe.

6204. Smith, Janice. *Monster in the Third Dresser Drawer* (Harper, 1981) 4–6. In a series of episodes a young boy must cope with a move to a new town, a new baby sister, a new tooth, a baby-sitter and his great-aunt Emily.

6205. ____. *Kid Next Door and Other Headaches* (Harper, 1984) 4–6. Two young boys who are best friends share different viewpoints about neatness, the best kind of pet, super heroes, horrible cousins, and what consideration an overnight guest is entitled to.

6206. ____. *Show and Tell War* (Harper, 1988) 4–6. Five stories relate the adventures and misadventures of Adam Joshua at school.

6207. ____. *It's Not Easy Being George* (Harper, 1989) 4–6. Adam Joshua shares problems with his "ordinary" dog George and lives through school events such as a pet show and an all-night sleepover in the library.

6208. ____. *Nelson in Love* (Harper, 1992) 4–6. Adam Joshua's Valentine's Day is extremely complicated and it doesn't help matters to know his best friend Nelson and his dog George are both in love.

6209. ____. *Serious Science* (Harper, 1993) 4–6. Devastated when his little sister and his dog George demolish his science project on the solar system, Adam Joshua becomes ingenious and inventive in coming up with a last-minute replacement.

6210. ____. *Baby Blues* (Harper, 1994) 4–6. Adam Joshua and his classmates' anxiety over the approaching maternity leave of their favorite teacher Ms. D. is heightened when they are each assigned an egg to be a substitute baby in a class project about parenting.

6211. Smith, Jim. *Frog Band and the Onion Seller* (Little, 1976) k–3. Eminent detective Alphonse Le Flic searches for a hidden casket containing treasure while being pursued by the enraged Frog Band.

6212. ____. *Frog Band and Durrington Dormouse* (Little, 1977) k–3. The Frog Band comes to the aid of Durrington Dormouse who wakes up in the 20th century following a Rip Van Winkle sleep to find his family being evicted from his property.

6213. ____. *Frog Band and the Mystery of Lion Castle* (Little, 1978) k–3. The Frog Band and the eminent

detective, Alphonse Le Flic, combine their efforts to solve the mystery of Lion Castle.

6214. ____. *Frog Band and the Owlnapper* (Little, 1980) k–3. Johann S. Frog and the Frog Band foil the kidnapping of young Olly Hoot and bring the notorious villain Nick Gristle to justice.

6215. Smith, Jim. *Nimbus and the Crown Jewels* (Little, 1981) k–3. Uncle Nimbus is a cat. He tells tales to his nephew kittens; his father vanishes on a balloon trip. Nimbus goes in search of him. He is invited to join a group of acrobats. Together they form a tower and see dad. Nimbus and his friends rescue him.

6216. ____. *Nimbus the Explorer* (Little, 1981) k–3. Uncle Nimbus relates his dangerous adventures near the Amazon River, where he encounters prehistoric animals and piles of precious stones.

6217. Smith, Ray. *Long Slide* (Macmillan, 1977) k–3. Jacko, Teddy and Barley climb the steps of a slide and in the climb they see the Concorde, a thunderstorm and some witches. On their race down the slide they go under a rainbow.

6218. ____. *Long Dive* (Macmillan, 1979) k–3. Barley the lamb, Jacko the monkey, and Teddy the bear go swimming in the Aegean and see schools of fish, a small submarine, a crab, an octopus and a seahorse. They surface, put on sunglasses and bake in the sun.

6219. ____. *Jacko's Play* (Macmillan, 1980) k–3. Barley the lamb acts as shepherdess in a blond wig; Teddy is the farmer who loses his sweetheart to Jacko, the photographer. A nice play put on by these three friends.

6220. Smyth, Gwenda. *Pet for Mr. Arbuckle* (Crown, 1984) k–3. Accompanied by a gingernut cat, Mrs. Arbuckle, who longs for a pet, travels the world over, interviewing exotic animals to find something suitable.

6221. ____. *Hobby for Mrs. Arbuckle* (Hamilton, 1989) k–3. Mrs. Arbuckle tries a series of hobbies each time with disastrous results. Mr. Arbuckle keeps the household going and cleans up her messes.

6222. Snape, Juliet. *Frog's Friends* (S & S, 1992) k–3.

6223. ____. *Frog's Odyssey* (S & S, 1992) k–3. When a construction project forces the frogs to lose their pond, they venture into the city to find a new home.

6224. Snyder, Carol. *Ike and Mama and the Once-a-Year Suit* (Coward, 1978) 3–5. Ike wants night-time blue for his once-a-year suit but when Mama takes him and 13 neighborhood boys shopping, he figures the chances of getting it are slim.

6225. ____. *Ike and Mama and the Block Wedding*

(Coward, 1979) 3–5. A story about growing up in New York in 1900.

6226. ____. *Ike and Mama and the Once-in-a-Lifetime Movie* (Coward, 1981) 3–5. Ike Greenberg and his friends appear as extras in a D.W. Griffith movie and surprise their families.

6227. ____. *Ike and Mama and Trouble in School* (Coward, 1983) 3–5. Ziggie the bully poses a problem for Ike at home as well as at school.

6228. ____. *Ike and Mama and the Seven Surprises* (Lothrop, 1985) 3–5. Ike is very skeptical when his mother promises that he will have seven surprises in the month before his Bar Mitzvah, especially with his father still hospitalized and the new arrival of a jobless cousin.

6229. Snyder, Zilpha. *Headless Cupid* (Atheneum, 1971) 5–8. When her mother remarries, Amanda's family moves into a house that is haunted. Amanda believes in the supernatural and uses this to justify her aloofness toward David and her new family. But....

6230. ____. *Famous Stanley Kidnapping Case* (Atheneum, 1979) 5–8. A gang of kidnappers run off with Amanda and the four Stanley children in Italy because of Amanda's boasting of her father's wealth.

6231. ____. *Blair's Nightmare* (Atheneum, 1984) 5–8. Blair really does see a dog at night but no one believes him. Finally the rest of the children see the dog, too, and complications begin. Can they keep the dog? Will David improve in school?

6232. Softly, Barbara. *Ponder and William on Holiday* (Young, 1968) k–3. Ponder and William are big on the other side of the pond; William is a human boy and Ponder is a talking Panda. They go to the seaside, a very British seaside, complete with Punch and Judy shows, shrimping and more, and paw-in-hand have a jolly good time.

6233. ____. *Ponder and William at Home* (Young, 1972) k–3. The setting is partly in the country with fishing and squirrels and partly in town with the subway and the zoo.

6234. ____. *Ponder and William at the Weekend* (Young, 1974) k–3. Ponder is a Panda. He and William are friends. They make a birthday present for cousin Winifred; have an egg and spoon race and "help" with spring cleaning.

6235. Solotareff, Gregoire. *Ogre and the Frog King* (Greenwillow, 1988) k–3. A frog tricks a giant ogre into believing the frog is the bigger and more powerful of the two so that the ogre will stop eating the forest animals.

6236. ____. *Never Trust an Ogre* (Greenwillow, 1988) k–3. A hungry ogre tries to trick the forest animals into coming over to his house for dinner.

6237. Sommer-Bodenburg, Angela. *Little Vampire* (Dial, 1982) 3–5. Tony, nine, meets a vampire called Rudolph. Tony is invited to the graveyard to meet Rudolph's parents. Tony then invites Rudolph and his sister to meet his parents.

6238. ____. *My Friend, the Vampire* (Dial, 1984) 3–5. A horror story fan, Tony Noddleman's life becomes more thrilling than anything he has ever read when he befriends a couple of vampires named Rudolph and Anna.

6239. ____. *Vampire Moves In* (Dial, 1985) 3–5. Banished by his family for making friends with a human, a little vampire comes to Tony, his only friend, takes up residence in the basement of his apartment building, and makes chaos of his life.

6240. ____. *Vampire Takes a Trip* (Dial, 1985) 3–5. Tony is not at all thrilled by the prospect of a week's vacation on an isolated farm until he convinces his beat friend, a little vampire, to come along.

6241. ____. *Vampire on the Farm* (Dial, 1989) 3–5. Tony and Rudolph are vacationing on a farm and Tony is still trying to keep Rudolph a secret while maintaining his friendship. Being friends with a vampire is not easy.

6242. ____. *Vampire in Danger* (S & S, 1991) 3–5. There are graveyards and vaults and tasty blood. The boy and the vampires are very similar. The vampires do some things better; the boy does others better.

6243. ____. *Vampire in Love* (Dial, 1991) 3–5. Tony's exciting friendship with several vampires is complicated when their creepy Cousin Olga comes to visit and pursues a crush on him.

6244. Sommerfelt, Aimee. *Road to Agra* (Criterion, 1961) 5–8. Lalu and Maya go to Agra hospital in order to save Maya's eyesight. It is a 300-mile journey in present day India. But the trip is harrowing and Lalu wonders if he did the right thing.

6245. ____. *White Bungalow* (Criterion, 1964) 5–8. Lalu has a chance to leave his poverty-stricken family and become a doctor but chooses to stay with his family, knowing that if he leaves they will starve since his father is so ill.

6246. Sonneborn, Ruth. *Seven in a Bed* (Viking, 1968) k–3. Papa meets the plane at the airport but there are seven ninos and Mama—four more than he expected. Where will everyone sleep?

6247. ____. *Friday Night Is Papa Night*. Papa's work takes him away from home through the week, but he comes home with money and gifts each Friday night.

6248. Spanner, Helmut. *Mouse's Train Ride* (Price Stearn, 1982) k–3. A rabbit is on the train and so are crayons and a feeding bottle.

6249. ____. *Where Is Mouse?* (Price Stearn, 1982) k–3. Mouse is hiding in a shoe, behind a cup, on top of a jar....

6250. ____. *Kitchen Mouse* (Price Stearn, 1986) k–3.

6251. Spanner, Helmut. *Teddy Bear's Day* (Methuen, 1983) k–3. Teddy Bear enjoys a bath, sits on potty, plays with bricks, waters flowers and tries out the telephone.

6252. ____. *Bear Goes Splash* (Price Stearn, 1986) k–3. A friendly, inquisitive bear finds water a total fascination.

6253. ____. *What's Teddy Bear Doing?* (Price Stearn, 1991) k–3. A friendly fuzzy bear rides a tricycle, waters his plants and sweeps up. A wordless picture book.

6254. Spinelli, Jerry. *Bathwater Gang* (Little, 1990) 2–4. Bertie's all-girl gang becomes involved in a harmless but heartfelt war with an all-boy gang, until Bertie's grandmother steps in with a perfect solution.

6255. ____. *Bathwater Gang Get Down to Business* (Little, 1992) 2–4. When the Bathwater Gang fails to make money with its pet-cleaning business, Bertie comes up with a slightly dishonest idea to ensure success.

6256. Spinka, Penina. *Mother's Blessing* (Atheneum, 1992) 5–8. Prequel. Before the birth of Four Cries, a wise man predicted that a baby would grow up to lead his people and unite three warring tribes. Four Cries is born but is a girl! She becomes a "New Woman" and leads her people.

6257. ____. *White Hare's Horses* (Atheneum, 1991) 5–8. White Hare is a young Chumash Indian girl living in the early 16th century in Southern California. Her grandfather dies and tells her she will need courage in future years. Her life is later threatened by Aztecs.

6258. Springstubb, Tricia. *Which Way to the Nearest Wilderness?* (Little, 1984) 5–8. As she watches her parents' marriage deteriorate, 11-year-old Eunice the sensible child in the family, wants to escape.

6259. ____. *Eunice Gottlieb and the Unwhitewashed Truth About Life* (Delacorte, 1987) 5–8. Eighth grader Eunice goes into the dessert catering business with her best friend Joy.

6260. ____. *Eunice (the Egg Salad) Gottlieb* (Delacorte, 1988) 5–8. In the midst of assorted crises, ten-year-old Eunice struggles to master the vault for her school's upcoming gymnastic exhibition.

6261. Springstubb, Tricia. *With a Name Like Lulu, Who Needs More Trouble?* (Delacorte, 1989) 5–8. Lulu caught a falling baby and became famous. She is shy and this incident brings a change to her life.

6262. ____. *Lulu vs. Love* (Delacorte, 1990) 5–8. Lulu, 11, explores the meaning of love as she struggles to accept the changes in her best friend Tilda, a teenage mother for whom Lulu baby-sits, when Tilda falls deeply in love.

6263. Stadler, John. *Hooray for Snail* (Crowell,

1984) k–3. Slow Snail hits the ball so hard during a baseball game that it flies to the moon and back. Will Snail have time to slide in for a home run?

6264. ____. *Snail Saves the Day* (Crowell, 1985) k–3. Snail's team may lose the football game unless he makes it to the stadium in time.

6265. ____. *Adventures of Snail at School* (Harper, 1993) k–3. Snail goes on three errands for his teacher and has amazing adventures.

6266. Stadler, John. *Cat at Bat* (Dutton, 1979) k–3. Presents 14 rhymed verses describing the activities of animals such as "A duck and his truck are stuck."

6267. ____. *Cat at Bat Is Back* (Dutton, 1991) k–3. Fourteen rhymed verses describe unusual activities of animals such as "A big pig tries a wig" and "A snake tries to bake a cake."

6268. Stahl, Hilda. *Elizabeth Gail and the Mystery at the Johnson Farm* (Tyndale, 1978) 4–6. Libby, 11, is happy in her new foster home, but it is clear that someone wants her to leave.

6269. ____. *Elizabeth Gail and the Secret Box* (Tyndale, 1979) 4–6. Happy in her new foster home, Libby is troubled when her father, whom she doesn't remember sends her gifts for her twelfth birthday.

6270. ____. *Elizabeth Gail and the Dangerous Double* (Tyndale, 1980) 4–6. While visiting her grandparents, Elizabeth Gail encounters a mystery, learns to love her enemies and grows up a bit.

6271. ____. *Elizabeth Gail and the Great Canoe Conspiracy* (Tyndale, 1991) 4–5. Elizabeth Gail struggles with her feelings of jealousy against her stepsister as she competes for the love of her stepfather.

6272. ____. *Elizabeth Gail and the Mystery of the Hidden Key* (Tyndale, 1992) 4–6. Libby, 12, learns how good it is to follow the example of her foster family when she helps two boys who are living in the shed behind her new father's store.

6273. ____. *Elizabeth Gail and the Secret of the Gold Charm* (Tyndale, 1992) 4–6. Libby, 12, is happy with her foster family, but she is reluctant to tell them about the gold unicorn charm she has found.

6274. Stahl, Hilda. *Kayla O'Brien and the Dangerous Journey* (Good News, 1990) 4–6. Kayla O'Brien and her brother Timothy expected to find happiness in the new land of America. But when their parents died during the voyage from Ireland, everything changed.

6275. ____. *Kayla O'Brian: Trouble at Bitter Creek Ranch* (Good News, 1991) 4–6. Kayla and her little brother Timothy are shipped west on an orphan train and go to live with the Larsen family on their ranch.

6276. ____. *Kayla O'Brian and the Runaway Orphans* (Good News, 1991) 4–6. The Larsens have never celebrated Christmas on their Nebraska mule farm, but this year, with the arrival of two orphans from the orphan train, will be different.

6277. Stahl, Hilda. *Chelsea and the Outrageous*

Phone Bill (Crossway, 1992) 4–6. Angry with her father for moving their family to another state, Chelsea, 11, disobeys him by making long distance phone calls to her best friend back home.

6278. ____. *Big Trouble for Roxie* (Crossway, 1992) 4–6. Angry and worried about her grandmother's illness, Roxie lies to her parents and risks losing her friend Chelsea.

6279. ____. *Kathy's Baby-Sitting Hassle* (Crossway, 1992) 4–6. Caring for her little sister becomes more disagreeable for Kathy.

6280. ____. *Hannah and the Special 4th of July* (Crossway, 1992) 4–6. Hannah struggles with her Native American heritage especially after her cousin comes to visit and questions her involvement with the King's Kids.

6281. ____. *Roxie and the Red Rose Mystery* (Crossway, 1992) 4–6. Roxie, 12, needs the support of her best friends when she starts helping Mary Harland with her entry in the local art contest and falls in love with Mary's older brother Dan.

6282. ____. *Kathy's New Brother* (Crossway, 1992) 4–6. With the help of her friends, Kathy, a sixth grader, learns to accept her foster brother and the trouble-making girl on the cheerleading squad that Kathy wants to join.

6283. ____. *Made-Over Chelsea* (Crossway, 1992) 4–6.

6284. ____. *No Friends for Hannah* (Crossway, 1992) 4–6. After God answers her prayers by giving her three new best friends, Hannah, 12, worries because they are suddenly too busy to stand by her, at a time when she is facing prejudice because she is an Ottawa Indian.

6285. ____. *Tough Choices for Roxie* (Crossway, 1993) 4–6. Competition over boys and a difficult new student threaten to break up the Best Friends, a group of girls who play and work together.

6286. ____. *Chelsea's Special Touch* (Crossway, 1993) 4–6. Chelsea works on two projects—getting an abused child to open up and trust her, and deciding whether to befriend the brusque and pushy Joan.

6287. ____. *Mystery at Bellwood Estate* (Crossway, 1993) 4–6. The Best Friends—Chelsea, Kathy, Roxie and Hannah—try to help Diane Brewster find out who's sneaking into the Brewster mansion and why.

6288. ____. *Hannah and the Daring Escape* (Crossway, 1993) 4–6. While attending a special art class, Hannah, 12, helps a frightened classmate who is certain that someone is after her.

6289. ____. *Hannah and the Snowy Hideaway* (Crossway, 1993) 2–6. Hannah, 12, wants to behave well as she deals with Alyson, a difficult neighbor, and Alyson's grumpy great-grandmother.

6290. ____. *Chelsea and the Alien Invasion* (Crossway, 1993) 4–6. Chelsea and the Best Friends help a frightened boy overcome his belief that aliens are going to destroy the world.

6291. ____. *Roxie's Mall Madness* (Crossway, 1993) 4–6. Roxie, 12, helps her sister Lacy and her brother

Eli, both of whom have been acting strangely, and may be in trouble.

6292. ____. *Secret Tunnel Mystery* (Crossway, 1992) 4–6. The Best Friends try to solve a dangerous mystery involving hidden tunnels, secret rooms, stolen antiques, and a family too scared to go home.

6293. Stahl, Hilda. *Sadie Rose and the Daring Escape* (Crossway, 1988) 5–8. Sadie Rose, carrying a heavy burden of guilt for her pa's death, meets with forgiveness and love.

6294. ____. *Sadie Rose and the Cottonwood Creek Orphan* (Crossway, 1989) 5–8. Sadie Rose has problems being the kind of girl she wants to be and has questions about a mysterious orphan. She finds wonderful answers.

6295. ____. *Sadie Rose and the Outlaw Rustlers* (Good News, 1989) 5–8. Sadie is trying so hard to be happy and to fit into her new family and friendships, while bravely facing the dangers of living in the Nebraska sandhills. Then Sadie's family must face the threats of three outlaws.

6296. ____. *Sadie Rose and the Mad Fortune Hunters* (Crossway, 1990) 5–8. Sadie Rose can't believe her eyes—the crazy Malda family has left two of their children in trade for Riley's colt. She and her brother try to straighten things out.

6297. ____. *Sadie Rose and the Double Secret* (Good News, 1990) 5–8. As Sadie Rose and her prairie family face robbery by Indians, a dangerous mountain man, and other perils, she attempts to guard a special secret and acquires courage.

6298. ____. *Sadie Rose and the Phantom Warrior* (Good News, 1991) 5–8. Sadie Rose sees an Indian warrior, runs into cousins from Michigan and searches for a missing friend.

6299. ____. *Sadie Rose and the Champion Sharpshooter* (Good News, 1991) 5–8. Sadie, 12, her family and her obnoxious cousin Gerda travel by wagon to the Vida Days celebration where Sadie enters the sharpshooting contest.

6300. ____. *Sadie Rose and the Secret Romance* (Crossway, 1992) 5–8. Sadie, 12, is visited by possible romance and possible danger in the form of a handsome con man.

6301. ____. *Sadie Rose and the Impossible Birthday Wish* (Crossway, 1992) 5–8. Sadie, 12, tries to resolve the running feud that develops between her and Barr, the orphan who has come to live with her Nebraska pioneer family.

6302. ____. *Sadie Rose and the Dangerous Search* (Crossway, 1993) 5–8. Sadie Rose, 12, and a runaway woman from Boston lost their way in a snowstorm and are taken captive by rustlers on the Nebraska frontier.

6303. ____. *Sadie Rose and the Mysterious Stranger* (Crossway, 1993) 5–8. Sadie and Opal find their way through an adventure at a Nebraska poor farm.

6304. Stahl, Hilda. *Sendi Lee Mason and the Milk*

Carton Kids (Good News, 1990) 2–4. Sendi, nine, helps her new friend Gwen search for stolen or missing children and the campaign threatens to reveal a big secret about Sendi's family.

6305. ____. *Sendi Lee Mason and the Stray Striped Cat* (Good News, 1990) 2–4. Though Sendi learns the stray cat she found really belongs to a lonely old woman, she decides to keep the cat anyway—but she finally does the right thing.

6306. ____. *Sendi Lee Mason and the Big Mistake* (Good News, 1991) 2–4. Sendi, nine, feeling a need to impress her newly found father with her math skills, cheats on a test.

6307. ____. *Sendi Lee Mason and the Great Crusade* (Good News, 1991) 2–4. While trying to get her parents to marry, Sendi, nine, tells a lie about a classmate.

6308. Stahl, Hilda. *Daisy Punkin* (Crossway, 1991) 4–6. Daisy adjusts to her new school and her mother's temporary absence.

6309. ____. *Daisy Punkin: Bratty Brother* (Crossway, 1992) 4–6. When she is teased by her older brother and a classmate and no longer spoiled by her mother, Daisy, nine, turns to her friends to help her grow up.

6310. Stahl, Hilda. *Great Adventures of Super J*A*M* (Crossway, 1989) 4–6. Jonathon Alex Michael Smith (J*A*M for short) learns from William Murray about real friendship.

6311. ____. *World's Greatest Hero* (Crossway, 1989) 4–6. A ten-year-old detective investigates her first case and makes an error in her quest to find an exciting story for the school newspaper.

6312. Standiford, Natalie. *Space Dog and Roy* (Avon, 1990) 3–5. When a spaceship crashes in his backyard, Roy gets what he always wanted, a puppy of his very own. Space Dog soon sets Roy straight, he is an explorer.

6313. ____. *Space Dog in Trouble* (Avon, 1990) 3–5. Roy's family is off to visit relatives. Space Dog promises to be good while they are gone. But while trying to avoid Alice's slobbering poodle, he runs out of the yard and into the arms of the dog catcher.

6314. ____. *Space Dog and the Pet Show* (Avon, 1990) 3–5. Roy enters Space Dog in a pet show to show Alice that Space Dog is better than her poodle. Space Dog agrees because Roy thinks it is important. But when he is taken to the dog salon for a makeover he nearly goes back to Queekrg.

6315. Stanek, Muriel. *Tall Tina* (Whitman, 1970) k–3. Tina is the tallest girl in her class. She is pleased until everyone teases her and she feels like a freak. But she works things out for the better.

6316. ____. *My Mom Can't Read* (Whitman, 1986) k–3. When Tina asks her mother for help in first grade reading, she discovers to her shock that her mother can't read. A concerned teacher helps them find tutors and they both learn to read together.

6317. Stanley, Diane. *Moe the Dog in Tropical Paradise* (Putnam, 1995) k–3. Moe is on vacation and shows the difference between sunny colored tropics and blue gray wintery scenes.

6318. ____. *Woe Is Moe* (Putnam, 1995) k–3. Moe wins the advertising contest at the Frozen Cow Ice Cream Factory. His life changes—a promotion, penthouse apartment, car phone and a trip to Paris. He has no time for Arlene until he finds no amount of fame can replace a friend.

6319. Stannard, Russell. *Time and Space and Uncle Albert* (Holt, 1990) 4–6. Gedanken's eccentric uncle sends her into outer space in a spacecraft to help him conduct a series of experiments regarding the law of relativity as it effects time and space.

6320. ____. *Black Holes and Uncle Albert* (Holt, 1991) 4–6. Gedanken is Uncle Albert's niece. They explain gravity, black holes, the big bang, bent light and colored light, all told with humor.

6321. Stanovich, Betty. *Hedgehog Adventure* (Lothrop, 1983) k–3. Hedgehog and his friend Woodchuck seek exciting adventure, decide where to plant flowers and wait out a storm.

6322. ____. *Hedgehog Surprises* (Lothrop, 1984) k–3. Hedgehog and his friend Woodchuck have many adventures including a surprise birthday party with more than one surprise.

6323. Steel, Danielle. *Martha's New Daddy* (Delacorte, 1989) k–3. Martha, five, is troubled by her mother's impending marriage, but talking things over with her understanding father helps her to view the situation with enthusiasm after all.

6324. ____. *Martha's New School* (Delacorte, 1989) k–3. When six-year-old Martha moves with her mother and new stepfather to Sausalito, she dreads going to a new school, but finds it a very pleasant experience after all.

6325. ____. *Martha's Best Friend* (Delacorte, 1989) k–3. A new girl from Paris arrives to spend the year at Martha's school and they become very good friends.

6326. ____. *Martha's New Puppy* (Delacorte, 1990) k–3. Martha, seven, learns a lesson about responsibility when daddy gives her a playful new pet.

6327. ____. *Martha and Hilary and the Stranger* (Doubleday, 1991) k–3. Hilary learns an important lesson in safety: never accept a ride from a stranger.

6328. Steel, Danielle. *Max and the Babysitter* (Delacorte, 1989) k–3. Unhappy with the baby-sitter he has, Max, four, is relieved when his parents find him a baby-sitter he likes very much.

6329. ____. *Max's Daddy Goes to the Hospital* (Delacorte, 1989) k–3. When his father is injured while rescuing three children from a fire. Max is very worried about him until he is finally allowed to visit him in the hospital.

6330. ____. *Max's New Baby* (Delacorte, 1989) k–3. Unsure about the prospect of having a new baby in the house, Max, four, finally decides that it might not be so bad after all when he sees his new twin sister and brother.

6331. ____. *Max Runs Away* (Delacorte, 1990) k–3. Jealous of the time his parents spend with his baby brother and sister, Max, seven, leaves home but soon learns the dangers of running away.

6332. ____. *Max and Grandma and Grandpa Winky* (Doubleday, 1991) k–3. Max is sad and lonely after a very sad phone call from Grandpa Winky. Grandma Winky dies. She was old and her heart was sick. Max's mom assures him that Grandma Winky is in heaven where she will wait for the rest of the family.

6333. Steel, Danielle. *Freddie's First Night Away* (Dell, 1992) k–3. Freddie, five, and freckled-faced, spends the night at a friend's house for the first time.

6334. ____. *Freddie's Trip* (Dell, 1992) k–3. Freckle-faced Freddie is five and he goes on a wonderful family vacation.

6335. ____. *Freddie and the Doctor* (Dell, 1992) k–3. Freddie, five, gets an early experience with the doctor and finds it is not too bad.

6336. Steele, Mary. *Crow and Mrs. Gaddy* (Greenwillow, 1984) 2–4. A crow and a farmer spend all their time playing tricks on each other and get nothing else done.

6337. ____. *Mrs. Gaddy and the Fast Growing Vine* (Greenwillow, 1985) 2–4. Mrs. Gaddy buys a fast growing vine that begins to take over her house, her animals and herself.

6338. ____. *Mrs. Gaddy and the Ghost* (Greenwillow, 1979) 2–4.

6339. Steig, William. *Doctor De Soto* (Farrar, 1982) k–3. Dr. De Soto, a mouse dentist, copes with the toothaches of various animals except those with a taste for mice, until the day a fox comes to him in great pain.

6340. ____. *Doctor De Soto Goes to Africa* (Harper, 1992) k–3. Expert mouse dentist Doctor De Soto is called suddenly to Africa to work on the sore tooth of a desperate elephant.

6341. Steiner, Barbara. *Oliver Dibbs to the Rescue* (Four Winds, 1985) 4–6. Beginning by painting his dog with tiger stripes, Ollie, ten, embarks on a series of sometimes disastrous moneymaking adventures to raise funds on behalf of wildlife preservation.

6342. ____. *Oliver Dibbs and the Dinosaur Cause* (Four Winds, 1986) 4–6. Lester, the bully, is jealous of Ollie and his ideas. This time his idea is to adopt a state fossil, namely a Stegosaurus. He also wants his class project to be the study of dinosaurs.

6343. Steiner, Barbara. *Foghorn Flattery and the Vanishing Rhinos* (Avon, 1991) 4–6. Carly and Foghorn are in Kenya where rhinos are being killed for their horns.

6344. ____. *Foghorn Flattery and the Dancing Horses* (Avon, 1991) 4–6. Carly, a fifth grader, and her genius brother Foghorn are in Vienna with their traveling parents and uncover a plot to steal a prize Lipizzan stallion.

6345. Stevens, Carla. *Hooray for Pig* (Seabury, 1974) 2–4. With the help of his friends, Pig finally overcomes his fear of the water and learns to enjoy swimming.

6346. ____. *Pig and the Blue Flag* (Seabury, 1977) 2–4. Pig just hates gym until a game of "Capture the Flag" proves his values to his teammates and to himself.

6347. Stevens, Kathleen. *Beast in the Bathtub* (G. Stevens, 1987) k–3. Lewis gets into mischief with an imaginary beast in the bathtub while his parents are watching television.

6348. ____. *Beast and the Babysitter* (G. Stevens, 1989) k–3. Lewis's companion, an enormous green beast, helps him entertain his baby sister while their baby-sitter is busy.

6349. ____. *Bully for the Beast* (G. Stevens, 1990) k–3. Lewis's monster friend the Beast helps him enjoy a day at the beach, building a fort in the sand and avoiding the unwelcome attentions of noisy Max.

6350. ____. *Beast at the Beach* (G. Stevens, 1991) k–3.

6351. Stevenson, Drew. *Case of the Horrible Swamp Monster* (Dodd, 1984) 5–8. Raymond and his friends see a "monster" in Lost Swamp. He and Huntly devise a plan to catch it. But a bank robbery interrupts them. Then the two events, the swamp monster and the bank robbery, are tied together.

6352. ____. *Case of the Visiting Vampire* (Dodd, 1986) 5–8. Raymond and his two buddies, Verna and Hunt, suspect a visiting Romanian actor of being a vampire and set out to prove it. (Hunt knows vampire lore.) Verna is the class bully but proves herself to be brave and a resourceful friend in need.

6353. ____. *Case of the Wandering Werewolf* (Dodd, 1987) 5–8. Chip tells Raymond that he saw a werewolf and together with J. Huntley English they hunt it down. They unravel the mystery and are almost killed.

6354. Stevenson, Drew. *One Ghost Too Many* (Cobblehill Books, 1991) 4–6. Clark and Frog reluctantly join Kate on an investigation to determine whether or not Maplewood Manor is really haunted.

6355. ____. *Toying with Danger* (Cobblehill Books, 1993) 4–6. With her friends, Clark and Frog, Sarah investigates some mysterious happenings at an isolated farmhouse where an eccentric toy inventor is working on a Frankenstein monster.

6356. ____. *Terror on Cemetery Hill* (Cobblehill Books, 1996) 4–6. Only super detective Sarah Capshaw could link the Wilsonburg Bank robbery with a monster sighted on Cemetery Hill.

6357. Stevenson, James. *Worst Person in the World* (Greenwillow, 1978) k–3. The meeting of the worst person in the world and the ugliest person in the world has some unexpected results.

6358. ____. *Worst Person in the World at Crab Beach* (Greenwillow, 1988) k–3. The worst person is having a terrible time on his vacation but he becomes even more miserable after he meets Miriam and her son.

6359. ____. *Worst Person's Christmas* (Greenwillow, 1991) k–3. The worst person particularly dislikes Christmas until his neighbor's kindness triggers a happy accident that forces him to participate in the holiday festivities.

6360. ____. *Worse Than the Worst* (Greenwillow, 1994) k–3. When he comes for a brief visit, Warren proves to be just as difficult to get along with as his great-uncle Worst.

6361. Stevenson, James. *No Need for Monty* (Greenwillow, 1987) k–3. Convinced that crossing the river on the back of Monty the alligator is too slow, the animals try to find a faster way to get their children to school.

6362. ____. *Monty* (Greenwillow, 1992) k–3. The rabbit, duck and frog find that they have no way to cross the river when their alligator friend, Monty, takes a vacation.

6363. Stevenson, James. *Yuck!* (Greenwillow, 1984) k–3. When two mean witches, Dolores and Lavinia, won't allow Emma to make a potion, she makes up her own special magic with the help of animal friends.

6364. ____. *Emma* (Greenwillow, 1985) k–3. With the help of her friends, and after a few false starts, a young witch named Emma learns to fly on her broom.

6365. ____. *Fried Feathers for Thanksgiving* (Greenwillow, 1986) k–3. Mean witches Dolores and Lavinia try to spoil Thanksgiving for everyone else but nice witch Emma and her friends outwit them.

6366. ____. *Happy Valentine's Day, Emma* (Greenwillow, 1987) k–3. Despite Dolores and Lavinia's nasty cards, Emma the witch and her friends have a wonderful Valentine's Day.

6367. ____. *Un-Happy New Year, Emma* (Greenwillow, 1989) k–3. Emma struggles with her New Year's resolution to be nicer to the other witches Dolores and Lavinia, as they continue being dreadful to her; their relationship climaxes in a dreadful revenge on New Year's Day.

6368. ____. *Emma at the Beach* (Greenwillow, 1990) k–3. Mean witches Dolores and Lavinia torment Emma and her friends and retreat to the cool comfort of the beach, but their victims strike back with a creative form of revenge.

6369. Stevenson, James. *That Terrible Halloween Night* (Greenwillow, 1980) k–3. Grandpa tells Louis and Mary Ann of the dreadful Halloween night that turned him into an old man.

6370. ____. *Worse Than Willy* (Greenwillow, 1984) k–3. Complaining to Grandpa that their baby brother is no fun, Mary Ann and Louie are surprised to hear that Grandpa's baby brother was the same way.

6371. ____. *Could Be Worse* (Greenwillow, 1977) k–3. Everything is always the same at Grandpa's house, even the things he says—until one unusual morning.

6372. ____. *Great Big Especially Beautiful Easter Egg* (Greenwillow, 1983) k–3. At Easter, a man tells his two grandchildren how he searched many years ago for a special Easter egg to give to his friend Charlotte.

6373. ____. *Grandpa's Great City Tour* (Greenwillow, 1983) k–3. Grandpa tours the city encountering animals and people whose names begin with a particular letter of the alphabet.

6374. ____. *That Dreadful Day* (Greenwillow, 1985) k–3. When Mary Ann and Louis return unhappily from their first day at school, Grandpa tells them about his own dreadful first day at school.

6375. ____. *No Friends* (Greenwillow, 1986) k–3. Worried that they won't make friends in their new neighborhood, Mary Ann and Louie listen to Grandpa reminisce about the new friends he and his brother made when he moved to another neighborhood.

6376. ____. *There's Nothing to Do* (Greenwillow, 1986) k–3. When Mary Ann and Louie are bored, Grandpa tells them what happened one day when he and his brother were bored.

6377. ____. *Will You Please Feed Our Cat?* (Greenwillow, 1987) k–3. When Mary Ann and Louie complain about the troubles they are having taking care of the neighbor's dog, Grandpa remembers the time he and his brothers took care of their neighbor's many pets and plants.

6378. ____. *We Hate Rain* (Greenwillow, 1988) k–3. Grandpa tells Mary Ann and Louie how he and his brother Wainey, coped with a massive rainfall when they were young.

6379. ____. *Grandpa's Too-Good Garden* (Greenwillow, 1989) k–3. Grandpa tells Mary Ann and Louie about a garden he had years ago that his brother Wainey "helped" him plant.

6380. Stevenson, Jocelyn. *Fraggle Rock* (Holt, 1983) k–3. Stories about Gobo, Wembley, Mokey and other inhabitants of Fraggle Rock.

6381. ____. *Red and the Pumpkins* (Holt, 1983) k–3. Hoping to make life easier for all the Fraggles,

Red steals and plants a pumpkin seed from the Gorg's Garden—but a horrible nightmare ensures.

6382. ____. *Best Friends* (Holt, 1984) k–3. Mokey, a quiet Fraggle, and her best friend Red, a noisy Fraggle, have very different experiences along the way to Brushplant Cave.

6383. ____. *Boober Fraggle's Giant Wish* (Holt, 1986) k–3. A magic wishing fork grants Boober's wish to be as big as Junior Gorg.

(For additional books on the Fraggles, Boober, Gobo, Mokey, Red or Wembley, *see* Brennan, Joseph; Calder, Lyn; Calmenson, Stephanie; Gilkow, Louise; Gilmour, H.B.; Grand, Rebecca; Muntean, Michaela; Perlberg, Deborah; Teitelbaum, Michael; Weiss, Ellen; Young, David.)

6384. Stine, Megan. *Three Investigators and the Case of the Weeping Coffin* (Random, 1985) 4–6. By making correct decisions, the reader assists the Three Investigators in solving a robbery at the strange Markels mansion.

6385. ____. *Three Investigators in the Case of the House of Horrors* (Random, 1986) 4–6. By making the correct decisions, the reader assists Three Investigators in determining whether the House of Horrors amusement park ride is really haunted.

6386. ____. *Three Investigators and the Case of Murder to Go* (Random, 1989) 4–6. The Three Investigators look into a rumor of poisoning in a fast-food chain.

6387. Stine, Megan. *Indiana Jones and the Dragon of Vengeance* (Random, 1985) 5–8. A swashbuckling archaeologist calls Hitler "a sawed off piece of Bratwurst."

6388. ____. *Young Indiana Jones and the Lost Gold of Durango* (Random, 1993) 5–8. In 1912, as Indy and a young Pueblo Indian friend search the cliff dwellings at Mesa Verde for the loot from a bank robbery, they encounter an eccentric old man who thinks he is one of the ancient Anasazi.

(For other books about the "Three Investigators," *see* Arden, William; Arthur, Robert; Brandel, Marc; Carey, M.V.; Les, Martin; West, Nick.)

6389. Stock, Catherine. *Sophie's Bucket* (Lothrop, 1985) k–3. On her first trip to the seashore, Sophie finds many things to put in her new bucket.

6390. ____. *Sophie's Knapsack* (Lothrop, 1988) k–3. Sophie accompanies her parents on an overnight hike to Purple Cloud Rock.

6391. Stone, Bernard. *Emergency Mouse* (Prentice, 1978) k–3. A young boy who is hospitalized discovers that a group of mice operate a hospital of their own in the wall of his room.

6392. ____. *Charge of the Mouse Brigade* (Pantheon, 1980) 2–4. The starving mice of Mouseville must recapture their stolen cheese from the Cats and thus a Mouse Brigade is formed.

6393. ____. *Inspector Mouse* (Holt, 1981) k–3. A distinguished detective apprehends a gang of robbers who have stolen a shipment of valuable Limburger cheese.

6394. ____. *Tale of Admiral Mouse* (Holt, 1982) k–3. The English mice go to war with the French mice over cheese, but after a fierce sea battle and a terrible storm, they all decide that cheese is better enjoyed at peace.

6395. ____. *Quasimodo Mouse* (Andersen, 1987) k–3. Quasimodo leaves Paris and heads for Cassis-on-sea. He saves Daisy, who is a beggar girl, from drowning and they both return to Paris as mouse and mousewife.

6396. Storr, Catherine. *Polly and the Wolf and Lucy* (Faber, 1969) 3–5. A book about sensible Polly and the frightening wolf.

6397. ____. *Adventures of Polly and the Wolf* (Macrae, 1970) 3–5. Polly always frustrates the dull-witted wolf who wants to eat her.

6398. ____. *Polly and the Wolf Again* (Faber, 1970) 3–5. Another story of sensible Polly and the frightening wolf.

6399. ____. *Clever Polly and the Stupid Wolf* (Macrae, 1980) 3–5. Polly outwits the wolf as he imitates the methods he will use to eat her.

6400. ____. *Tales of Polly and the Hungry Wolf* (Faber, 1981) 3–5. Eight more stories of Wolf and Polly. Wolf tries spells, special gifts, traps and an eating competition to catch Polly but she always outwits him. She finally sends him off to Persia on a piece of magic carpet.

6401. ____. *Last Stories of Polly and the Wolf* (Macrae, 1990) 3–5. Wolf wants to entrap Polly and eat her. He is disliked by all others and is pathetic in his attempts to get the better of Polly. But in this story he finally wins out.

6402. Storr, Catherine. *Marianne Dreams* (Faber, 1958) 5–8. Marianne, during a long illness dreams up a place, a house and a boy companion.

6403. ____. *Marianne and Mark* (Faber, 1980) 5–8. Marianne, 14, is bored and lonely. On vacation she is eager to make friends. She makes a date with a strange boy but then meets Mark.

6404. Storr, Catherine. *Lucy* (Prentice, 1968) 3–5. Before the boys would let a tomboy play with them, they tell her she must prove she is a fearless boy by catching a thief. Little do they suspect that she will.

6405. ____. *Lucy Runs Away* (Prentice, 1970) 3–5. Lucy, ten, runs away to a seaside resort in search of adventure. She rescues a drowning man by ringing an alarm bell. She is sent home and promises not to run away again until she is 12.

6406. Storr, Catherine. *Hugo and His Grandma's Washing Day* (Merimack, 1978) k–3. A cat decides to have her kittens in grandmother's washing machine.

6407. ____. *Hugo and His Grandma* (Merimack, 1981) k–3. Hugo's grandma knits a sweater but the sleeves are too long. Hugo looks for a wearer and finds a chimpanzee who enjoys the gift.

6408. Storr, Catherine. *Enter Wagga* (Belitha, 1984) k–3. This short story book Wagga, the dog, Nimmo the cat and their family of humans manage to sketch in life in a realistic urban terrace, single parent and all.

6409. ____. *Wagga's Magic Ears* (Belitha, 1984) k–3. Short storybook about Wagga the dog, Nimmo the cat and their family of humans, in a realistic urban terrace.

6410. ____. *Watchdog Wagga* (Belitha, 1984) k–3.

6411. ____. *Lost and Found Wagga* (Belitha, 1984) k–3.

6412. Stover, Marjorie. *When the Dolls Woke* (Whitman, 1985) 4–6. Long neglected dolls come awake and help their new owner and her elderly aunt find a treasure hidden in their dollhouse years ago.

6413. ____. *Midnight in the Dollhouse* (Whitman, 1989) 4–6. A family of dolls helps their owner, who has been left lame by an accident and finds a clue to hidden treasure.

6414. Stranger, Joyce. *Paddy Joe* (Collins, 1971) 5–8. Records the very surprising adventures of an orphan boy who runs away with his dog to save its life.

6415. ____. *Trouble for Paddy Joe* (Collins, 1973) 5–8. Paddy Joe, ten, spends his vacation with an elderly guardian on a Hebridean island, where he mingles with the wildlife. He loses his beloved dog.

6416. ____. *Paddy Joe at Keep Hollow Farm* (Collins, 1975) 5–8.

6417. ____. *Paddy Joe and Tomkin's Folly* (Pelham, 1979) 5–8. Deep Hollow has many animals and a few humans: a once ill-treated pony, a trapped falcon, and a stolen, running wild female dog and her puppies. A story of a boy's maturing.

6418. Strasser, Todd. *Help. I'm in the First Day of School* (Scholastic, 1995) 5–8. Being an eighth grader is not fun when you know what each day will bring. Is Jake doomed to relive the first day of school the entire school year?

6419. ____. *Help. I'm Trapped in My Teacher's Body* (Scholastic, 1995) 5–8. What happens when Jake the class trouble-maker, switches bodies with Mr. Dirkson, the horrible teacher with the nickname Mr. Dorkson? Worse yet, Mr. Dirkson doesn't want to change back. Will Jake ever be Jake again?

6420. ____. *Help. I'm in Obedience School* (Scholastic, 1995) 5–8. Jake, an eighth grader, his dog Lance and his best friend Andy are trapped in each other's body. Andy barks, eats dog food and chases squirrels.

6421. Streatfeild, Noel. *Gemma* (Dell, 1968) 4–6. Accustomed to a glamorous life as a famous young movie star, Gemma, 11, is horrified when, because of her mother's film career, she is sent to live with her "dull" and unknown cousins in a small industrial town.

6422. ____. *Good-bye Gemma* (Dell, 1969) 4–6. As her cousins find success singing and dancing on the stage, Gemma wins a coveted acting role in a local theater production but may have to give it up when her mother makes a startling announcement.

6423. ____. *Gemma Alone* (Dell, 1987) 4–6. Gemma finds the transition from being a glamorous child movie star to working as a student at a school for the performing arts, hard work, but she also joins her cousins in honing their musical, dancing, and acting talents for a competition on television.

6424. ____. *Gemma and Sisters* (Dell, 1987) 4–6.

6425. ____. *Gemma Abroad* (Dell, 1987) 4–6.

6426. Strete, Craig. *Paint Your Face on a Drowning in the River* (Greenwillow, 1978) 4–6. An Indian's desire to leave the reservation and live as white men do is complicated by the attempts of his grandparents and girlfriend to make him stay.

6427. ____. *When Grandfather Journeys Into Winter* (Greenwillow, 1979) 4–6. A young Indian boy struggles to accept his grandfather's rapidly approaching death.

6428. Strong, J.J. *Smith's Tail* (Evans, 1978) k–3. Smith, a cat that loves sun bathing, has a tail that grows very long, it tangles in furniture, almost strangles him and is very heavy. Then he learns to use it to his advantage.

6429. ____. *Smith Takes a Bath* (Evans, 1980) k–3. A cat discommoded by his long tail finds a way to deal with it.

6430. Strong, Jeremy. *Princess and Bungle* (Burdett, 1986) k–3. Relates how Bungle the cat saves Princess Miranda from the wicked magician Firescar.

6431. ____. *Bungle's Ghost* (Hodder, 1987) k–3. Bungle is Princess Miranda's pampered cat. When Prince Conrad and his mother Aunt Mildred come to visit, the cat runs for safety. Conrad chases him into the flour bin where the cook finds him the next day. He is ghostly white with green eyes and a pink tongue and scares the cook.

6432. ____. *Bungle to the Rescue* (Hodder, 1991) k–3. Hedgehog

6433. Strong, Jeremy. *Fanny Witch and the Boosnatch* (Hodder, 1985) k–3.

6434. ____. *Fanny Witch and the Thunder Wizard* (Hodder, 1987) k–3. A village is devastated by the benign vegetarian dinosaur conjured up by Fanny. He has more charisma than the scatty witch or the luckless inhabitants; he has bewildered dignity especially when he wears the barn as an overcoat. In the end he is turned to stone and peace is restored.

6435. Strub, Susanne. *Lulu Goes Swimming* (Viking, 1990) k–3. Lulu dreams about all the new things she will be able to do in the swimming pool once she has her birthday.
6436. ____. *Lulu on Her Bike* (Viking, 1990) k–3. Lulu dreams of all the new things she can do on her new bike.

6437. Sturgis, Matthew. *Tosca's Christmas* (Dial, 1989) k–3. Tosca the cat fears she is going to be left out of the celebration this Christmas, until she is on hand to witness Santa's visit.
6438. ____. *Tosca's Surprise* (Dial, 1991) k–3. Greatly in need of privacy for personal reasons, Tosca the cat searches the entire house and backyard before she finds the perfect spot.

6439. Sugita, Yutaka. *Caspar and the Lion Cub* (Evans, 1974) k–3. Caspar the crow frightens the zebras, pecks the hippopotamus and quarrels with the giraffe. But then he rescues the lost lion cub.
6440. ____. *Caspar and the Rainbow Bird* (Evans, 1975) k–3. Caspar, a crow, meets a parrot (Rainbow Bird) who is in a cage and has never seen natural flora and fauna. They fly away together to see the world.

6441. Sugita, Yutaka. *My Friend Little John and Me* (McGraw, 1972) k–3. Recounts the adventures of a St. Bernard and his master, Little John.
6442. ____. *My Friend Little John* (McGraw, 1982) k–3. Friendship is the theme where the gargantuan but submissive dog plays the role of the little boy's patient, and then his student and finally his pillow.

6443. Suhl, Yuri. *Simon Boom Gives a Wedding* (Four Winds, 1972) 2–4. Simon Boom thinks everything should be the very best for his daughter's wedding, with humorous results.
6444. ____. *Simon Boom Gets a Letter* (Four Winds, 1976) 2–4. Boom's love of gadgetry leads him to feed his younger brother's letter into a paper shredding machine which he mistakenly purchased as a letter opener.

6445. Sullivan, Silky. *Henry and Melinda* (Children's, 1982) k–3. Henry thinks that his sister Melinda is too small to play ball with him, but when he changes his attitude he's in for a surprise.
6446. ____. *Henry and Melinda Team Up* (Children's, 1982) k–3. When the three Harvey brothers move in next door, they think Melinda is too little to play basketball with them.
6447. ____. *B Street Five* (Children's, 1982) k–3. Melinda helps the B Street 5 beat the Kings at a basketball game, even though the Kings think that she is a boy.

6448. ____. *Kings on Court* (Children's, 1982) k–3. Melinda thinks her friend Long Sam should go to her brother's school and play on the basketball team with him.
6449. ____. *Roller Skates* (Children's, 1982) k–3. Melinda wants to wear her roller skates to school so that if she doesn't like her new teacher, she can skate away.
6450. ____. *Mystery at the Basketball Game* (Children's, 1982) k–3. Henry makes one mistake after another in the championship basketball game until Melinda notices that his feet look funny.

6451. Sundvall, Vineca. *Mimi and the Biscuit Factory* (Farrar, 1989) k–3. Adventures of Mimi and her friend Albert when they go on a field trip with their class to see Henry's Bread and Biscuit Factory and Mimi's loose tooth falls out.
6452. ____. *Mimi Gets a Grandfather* (R & S Books, 1991) k–3. Having no grandfather of her own, Mimi decides to adopt the owner of the town's shoe store.

6453. Sutton, Elizabeth. *Pony for Keeps* (Thomasson-Grant, 1991) 2–4. When Meg turns seven she takes riding lessons and receives her own pony.
6454. ____. *Pony Champions* (Thomasson-Grant, 1992) 2–4. Careless and rushed in her attempt to juggle her time between preparing for a pony competition and a tap dance recital, busy fourth grader Meg allows her pony Lady Jane to become very sick.

6455. Sutton, Larry. *Mystery of the Late News Report* (Carolrhoda, 1981) k–3. Jeff and his sister, Hollee, find clues, overlooked by adults, which may help locate a lost pilot.
6456. ____. *Ghost Plane Over Hartley Field* (Carolrhoda, 1981) k–3. Hollee and Jeff connect a mysterious airplane that flies at night with a stolen jewel found near the airfield.
6457. ____. *Case of the Trick Note* (Carolrhoda, 1981) k–3. Hollee and Jeff become suspicious when a stranger comes to pick up their friend's airplane before a big race.
6458. ____. *Case of the Smiley Faces* (Carolrhoda, 1981) k–3. When someone steals their tickets at Disney World, Hollee and Jeff think up a plan to trap the culprit.
6459. ____. *Mystery of the Blue Champ* (Carolrhoda, 1981) k–3. When their father's favorite airplane is discovered missing, Hollee and Jeff try to find out what has happened to it.

6460. Swallow, Pamela. *Melvin and Dewey in the Chips* (Bettering, 1986) 2–4.
6461. ____. *Melvin and Dewey in the Fast Lane* (Shoe Tree, 1989). 2–4. Wacky adventures ensue when students take the class gerbils home on weekends.

6462. Swede, George. *Case of the Seaside Buglaries* (Three Trees, 1982) 5–8. Sherlock, a hound, and Watson, a cat, are the pets of police inspector Holmes. They think like humans but are unable to communicate with their master.

6463. ____. *Case of the Moonlit Gold Dust* (Three Trees, 1981) 5–8.

6464. ____. *Case of the Missing Heirloom* (Three Trees, 1981) 5–8.

6465. ____. *Case of the Downhill Theft* (Three Trees, 1983) 5–8. This adventure is set in the Gengran Bay Ski Area. Inspector Holmes and his Sherlock and Watson face a challenging puzzle, with few clues. But the bloodhound with the help of Watson solves the mystery for inspector Holmes.

6466. Swindells, Robert. *Norah's Ark* (Wheaton, 1980) k–3. Norah comes from a large family. She equates the animals in the zoo with her own cramped quarters and sets them free. After several adventures she takes them back to their various habitats.

6467. ____. *Norah's Shark* (Wheaton, 1980) k–3. Norah acquired a ship and encounters a killer shark which the male sea captains have failed to subdue. She comes up with a way to rid the seas of the menace.

6468. ____. *Norah and the Whale* (Wheaton, 1982) k–3. Norah defeats Captain Lassen's illicit war on the threatened whale population.

6469. ____. *Norah to the Rescue* (Wheaton, 1982) k–3. Norah, eight, rescues the inhabitants of Turtle Island from volcanic eruption, where older ship masters have recoiled from danger.

6470. Szekeres, Cyndy. *Good-Night, Sammy* (Western, 1985) k–3. Sammy the fox has a terrible time falling asleep at bedtime until his parents come to soothe his troubles.

6471. ____. *Sammy's Special Day* (Golden, 1986) k–3. Sammy learns that toys are not fun but sharing them with a friend is fun.

6472. Szekeres, Cyndy. *Baby Bear's Surprise* (Golden, 1984) k–3. Baby Bear's surprise is a birthday party and a new red tricycle.

6473. ____. *Little Bear Counts His Favorite Things* (Golden, 1986) k–3. Little Bear describes some of his possessions from one chair to ten blocks.

6474. Szekeres, Cyndy. *Things Bunny Sees* (Golden, 1990) k–3. Bunny sees all sorts of things—blue, yellow, red, green and black—in and around his house.

6475. ____. *What Bunny Loves* (Golden, 1990) k–3. Bunny sees all sorts of things. The things he loves are what all bunnies (and children) love.

6476. Szekeres, Cyndy. *Puppy Too Small* (Golden, 1984) k–3. Puppy is too small for some things, but there are many things he can do that are nice for other people.

6477. ____. *Nothing-to-Do Puppy* (Western, 1985) k–3. While searching for members to join his Nothing-to-Do Club, a puppy plays with his animal friends.

6478. ____. *Puppy Lost* (Golden, 1986) k–3. Little Puppy and his mother become separated in the grocery store.

6479. ____. *Little Puppy Cleans His Room* (Western, 1993) k–3. A story emphasizing the need for orderliness for everyone.

6480. ____. *I Am a Puppy* (Western, 1994) k–3. A puppy describes its daily activities.

6481. Tannen, Mary. *Wizard Children of Finn* (Avon, 1981) 4–6. Fiono and Bran are transported in time to the Ireland of the Celts and Finn McCool.

6482. ____. *Lost Legend of Finn* (Knopf, 1982) 4–6. Determined to find out the truth about their father, Bran and Fiona use their uncle's magic book and go back in time to ninth century Ireland.

6483. Taro, Oda. *Panda the Doctor* (Hamlyn, 1982) k–3. Panda is ill and when he recovers he wants to bandage the dog, the cat and the goldfish bowl. He oils a toy robot, wraps up toy soldiers and puts his mother to bed.

6484. ____. *Panda the Explorer* (Hamlyn, 1982) k–3. Panda goes on a long journey with an apple to eat and a horse to ride on (a chair). They reach the desert and are thirsty but an oasis (refrigerator) is spied. Panda sits in his bathtub and paddles across the river and climbs a high mountain (the stairs).

6485. ____. *Panda the Racing Driver* (Hamlyn, 1983) With consoling mother in the background father absent driving a train, Panda enjoys role-playing with familiar objects, riding a broom-horse, fighting a dragon with a wooden spoon, and turning a chair into a boat.

6486. ____. *Panda the Train Driver* (Hamlyn, 1983) k–3.

6487. ____. *Panda the Wizard* (Hamlyn, 1983) k–3.

6488. ____. *Panda the Soldier* (Hamlyn, 1983) k–3.

6489. Tarr, Judith. *Isle of Glass* (Bluejay, 1985) 5–8. Alfred of St. Ruan abandons the secluded life of the abbey for the violence and intrigue of medieval English politics. He soon finds the outside world to be a confusing muddle of conflicting loyalties as three feuding kingdoms each stake claim on his allegiance.

6490. ____. *Golden Horn* (Bluejay, 1985) 5–8. Alfred of St. Ruan's goes to Constantinople during the Fourth Crusade. He is befriended by a Greek family but loses his ally, Thea, when crusaders sack the city.

6491. ____. *Hounds of God* (Bluejay, 1986) 5–8. Ex-monk Alfred, reconciled to his magical powers, is not only Chancellor of the Kingdom of Rhiyana but about to become a father. When the kingdom is attacked by the hounds of god, the king's son is slain;

Alfred's lover, Thea, and their newborn twins are carried off to Rome. Alfred follows them.

6492. Taylor Cora. *Julie* (Spindlewood, 1988) 3–5. Julie can see more than other people but doesn't know how to use it until her father's life is threatened. She learns how to direct her powers to save him.
6493. ____. *Julie's Secret* (Spindlewood, 1992) 3–5. A story of a young girl whose power of second sight isolates her from her family and community. Struggling to cope with being different, Julie is forced to use her gift to save her brother.

6494. Taylor, Judy. *Dudley Goes Flying* (Putnam, 1986) k–3. Dudley Dormouse goes flying through the air unexpectedly when he goes outside to unblock his chimney.
6495. ____. *Dudley and the Monster* (Putnam, 1986) k–3. Dudley Dormouse visits a nest of baby blackbirds and unwittingly saves them from a marauding cat.
6496. ____. *Dudley and the Strawberry Shake* (Putnam, 1987) k–3. Dudley Dormouse goes out to pick strawberries and finds it can be an alarming experience.
6497. ____. *Dudley in a Jam* (Putnam, 1987) k–3. Dudley Dormouse discovers that making plum jam is a very sticky business.
6498. ____. *Dudley Bakes a Cake* (Putnam, 1988) k–3. Dudley Dormouse bakes an unusual cake and enters it in a competition in order to win a bike.
6499. ____. *Adventures of Dudley Dormouse* (Putnam, 1991) k–3. The four books that took Dudley from spring to winter are bound here as one book.

6500. Taylor, Judy. *Sophie and Jack* (Philomel, 1982) k–3. Two hippopotamus friends go on a picnic and play hide-and-seek, but have trouble finding a place to hide, at first.
6501. ____. *Sophie and Jack Help Out* (Philomel, 1984) k–3. There are lots of surprises in store when two young hippopotamuses do the spring planting in the vegetable garden.
6502. ____. *Sophie and Jack in the Snow* (Philomel, 1985) k–3. Two hippopotamuses are enjoying winter indoors and out.
6503. ____. *Sophie and Jack in the Rain* (Philomel, 1989) k–3. Two bored hippopotamus children go to play in the rain on a fallen tree. Jack pretending to be an acrobat and Sophie as explorer. The sun comes out and they greet a rainbow with "Hip-hippo-ray."

6504. Taylor, Mark. *Henry, the Explorer* (Little, 1966) k–3. The day after a blizzard Henry and his dog Angus decide to go exploring and perhaps find a bear.
6505. ____. *Henry Explores the Jungle* (Atheneum, 1969) 2–4. Henry, in pith helmet, explores the "jungle" near his rural home. He takes a lunch and Angus, his dog. Henry does find a tiger escaped from

the circus and lures him into a cage thereby winning a ticket to the circus.
6506. ____. *Henry, the Castaway* (Atheneum, 1972) 2–4. While exploring for uncharted seas, Henry and his dog are castaway on an island.
6507. ____. *Henry Explores the Mountains* (Atheneum, 1975) 2–4. Henry's outing in the woods with his dog involves him in a dangerous forest fire, heroism and a helicopter ride.
6508. ____. *Case of the Purloined Compass* (Atheneum, 1985) 2–4. When Henry's compass disappears, dog detective Angus follows clues which lead him into danger and eventually to the thief, without Henry ever knowing how his property was recovered.

6509. Teitelbaum, Michael. *Cave of the Lost Fraggle* (Holt, 1985) k–3. Red Fraggle accepts a dare to explore the Cave of the Lost Fraggle, from which no Fraggle has ever returned.
(For additional books on the Fraggles, Boober, Gobo, Mokey, Red or Wembley, *see* Brennan, Joseph; Calder, Lyn; Calmenson, Stephanie; Gilkow, Louise; Gilmour, H.B.; Grand, Rebecca; Muntean, Michaela; Perlberg, Deborah; Stevenson, Jocelyn; Weiss, Ellen; Young, David.)

6510. Thaler, Mike. *What Could a Hippopotamus Be?* (S & S, 1975) k–3. Depicts some of the things a hippopotamus can't be—cowboy, secretary, ballet dancer—and suggests a perfect, if temporary, solution.
6511. ____. *There's a Hippopotamus Under My Bed* (Avon, 1978) k–3. A youngster befriends an escaped hippopotamus that sooner or later must return to the zoo.
6512. ____. *Hippopotamus Ate the Teacher* (Avon, 1981) k–3. A teacher takes her class to the zoo; while feeding the hippopotamus she is swallowed by him. The hippo returns to school with the class and proceeds to teach lessons. The students turn the hippo upside down and disgorge the teacher.
6513. ____. *It's Me, Hippo!* (Harper, 1983) k–3. With the help of his animal friends, Hippo builds a house, paints a picture, breaks out in spots and celebrates a birthday.
6514. ____. *Hippo Lemonade* (Harper, 1986) k–3. Hippo and his animal friends share a variety of adventures including making a wish, selling lemonade and telling a scary story.
6515. ____. *Seven Little Hippos* (Harper, 1991) k–3. Seven little hippos jump up on their bed. They get hurt and need a doctor but it does not stop them and they keep jumping until they literally bring the house down.
6516. ____. *Come and Play, Hippo* (Harper, 1991) k–3. Hippo and his jungle friends worry about Friday the 13th, start a band and enjoy a magic show.

6517. Thaler, Mike. *Bully Brothers Trick the Tooth*

Fairy (Grosset, 1993) k–3. When Bubba and Bumpo find out they can get money from the Tooth Fairy for any teeth they put under their pillows, they hatch a scheme to make themselves rich.

6518. ____. *Bully Brothers, Goblins Halloween* (Grosset, 1993) k–3. Bubba and Bumpo play a mean trick on the neighborhood boys and girls they invite to their Halloween party.

6519. Thesman, Jean. *Whitney Cousins: Heather* (Avon, 1990) 5–8. Heather's mother remarries and Heather finally has the family she thinks she has always wanted. But she has problems with her stepfather and stepsister. An understanding comes about for all.

6520. ____. *Whitney Cousins: Amelia* (Avon, 1990) 5–8. The story centers around the ugly aftermath of an attempted date rape. Amelia is flattered when Warren, a senior, asks her out. But she must fend off his advances and then wreaks a satisfactory revenge on Warren.

6521. ____. *Whitney Cousins: Erin* (Avon, 1990) 5–8. Erin, who buys her clothes at a thrift shop, is sent to live with cousin Amelia's family because her grandparents can't tolerate her behavior. Erin is still angry over her parent's death in a car crash and is confrontational.

6522. Thomas, Iolette. *Janine and the New Baby* (Deutsch, 1987) k–3. A little black girl is looked after by an aunt while her mother goes to have a baby. There are friendly neighbors in lively clothes as they busy themselves in an urban setting.

6523. ____. *Janine and the Carnival* (Deutsch, 1988) k–3. Dad takes Janine to the carnival and she gets lost. A policeman helps her to the Lost Children Tent where her mother is called and her dad is found.

6524. ____. *Princess Janine* (Deutsch, 1990) k–3.

6525. ____. *Mermaid Janine* (Deutsch, 1993) k–3. Janine, an Afro-Caribbean living in Britain, wants to swim like her cousins back home. She practices in the bath and mother must mop up. She joins a class and eventually achieves her goal.

6526. Thomas, J.B. *Dragon Green* (Abelard, 1976) 3–5. Little dragon looks for his mother, Gold Dragon. He meets a witch who cuts off his tail and then a magician who makes the tail grow again. He finds a friend in Sump the shark.

6527. ____. *Prince of the Dragon Green* (Abelard, 1976) 3–5. Dragon is grown up and living on an island where a princess has been put ashore as punishment for not marrying any young suitor. They fall in love and the kindly magician turns her into a little dragon.

6528. Thomson, David. *Danny Fox* (Puffin, 1966) 4–6. Danny Fox is crafty, sassy, and humorous but also kind and fatherly.

6529. ____. *Danny Fox at the Palace* (Puffin, 1976) 4–6. Clever Danny Fox tries to think of a way of rescuing his favorite princess from the dungeon where she has been shut up by the queen.

6530. Thomson, Ruth. *Peabody's First Case* (Lothrop, 1978) k–3. Peabody and his dog, Humbug, trap a bank robber in a parade in which he is carrying a drum but not playing it. The drum turns out to be full of loot.

6531. ____. *Peabody All at Sea* (Lothrop, 1978) k–3. Peabody and Humbug discover the island hideout of a gang of robbers. Peabody traps them on the island by towing their boat away.

6532. Thwaites, Lyndsay. *Super Adam and Rosie Wonder* (Deutsch, 1983) k–3. A brother and sister try to fly in their garden, despite their mother's admonition that children can't fly.

6533. ____. *Rosie's Wonderful Dances* (Deutsch, 1984) k–3. Rosie and her brother Adam, dancing ecstatically through the house, imagine themselves as washing machines, thunder and lightning, clouds and other fabulous apparitions in motion.

6534. ____. *Adam and Rosie Run Away* (Deutsch, 1985) k–3. A fantasy of running away to the jungle.

6535. ____. *Adam and Rosie and the Strange Planet* (Deutsch,) 1987. k–3

6536. Tibo, Gilles. *Simon and the Snowflakes* (Tundra, 1988) k–3. During a snowfall, a young boy tries to count the snowflakes.

6537. ____. *Simon and the Wind* (Tundra, 1989) k–3. Shows Simon playing different games in the wind.

6538. ____. *Simon Welcomes Spring* (Tundra, 1990) k–3. A little boy tries all sorts of ways to make spring come faster.

6539. ____. *Simon in Summer* (Tundra, 1991) k–3. Simon wishes the summer would never end. But summer must end and Simon's friends come back in the fall.

6540. ____. *Simon and His Boxes* (Tundra, 1991) k–3. Simon loves boxes. He makes homes for all the animals in the forest. But the animals prefer their own homes and don't even look at Simon's boxes. Jack-in-the-Box suggests he does something else with the boxes. He does.

6541. ____. *Simon in the Moonlight* (Tundra, 1993) k–3. Simon is trying to rescue the moon as it wanes down to a silver and then waxes again to a full moon.

6542. ____. *Simon Finds a Feather* (Tundra, 1994) k–3.

6543. Tinkler, David. *Scourge of the Dinner Ladies* (Andersen, 1988) 3–5. The children of Littlesprat Primary School have a teacher who lives up to her name, Mrs. Thrasher. The Dinner Ladies are a gang of professional villains. Granny Fang, their leader, kidnaps Caroline who is trying to expose them.

6544. ____. *Dinner Ladies Clean Up* (Andersen, 1991) 3–5.

6545. ____. *Revenge of the Dinner Ladies* (Andersen, 1992) 3–5. Granny Fang, Mrs. Slow, Batty and Mrs. Sludger are the Dinner Ladies. They were fired from Littlebampton School and now work at Blight Hall. After hours they are burglars. They are captured but will probably get away.

6546. Tison, Annette. *Barbapapa* (Walck, 1970) k–3. Barbapapa, an unusual animal, proves he is of great value to the community.

6547. ____. *Barbapapa's Voyage* (World, 1972) k–3. A search for a mate for Barbapapa to London, India, New York, and the outer space proves to no avail, but there is a surprise in the backyard.

6548. ____. *Barbapapa's New House* (Warne, 1972) k–3. The Barbapapa's house is no longer big enough for the family. They decide to build a kind of honeycomb-type house. When the road digging machines come, they defend their property and win.

6549. ____. *Counting with Barbapapa* (Warne, 1978) k–3. The Barbapapas shape 0 to 10 while 1 dog, 2 cats, 3 fish, 4 turtles, 5 birds are on an opposite page.

6550. ____. *Colour and Barbapapa* (Warne, 1978) k–3.

6551. ____. *Shape and Barbapapa* (Warne, 1978) k–3.

6552. ____. *Barbapapa's School* (Warne, 1979) k–3. The local school is in chaos. The children are uncontrollable; the teacher and parents are in despair. Barbapapa starts a school of his own using teaching methods which appeal to the children.

6553. ____. *Barbapapa's Theater* (Warne, 1979) k–3. The Barbapapas, who change themselves at will, change themselves into a brush. They then paste up notices that the circus will come to town. They become part of the circus, the animals, the seesaw and the roller coaster.

6554. ____. *Barbapapa's Winter* (Warne, 1982) k–3. Barbazoo was given a crate full of birds to keep his pet Toucan company. But Barbazoo lives in a cold climate and the birds cannot live there. Sweaters and fires didn't help so electricity was planned but failed. The birds must go back to a warm climate. Barbazoo got other animals who could stand the cold.

6555. Titus, Eve. *Anatole* (McGraw, 1956) k–3. Anatole lives in a mouse village near Paris with his wife and six children. He bicycles into the city to find food for his family. Suddenly he discovers people do not like mice and is unhappy.

6556. ____. *Anatole and the Cat* (McGraw, 1956) k–3. Anatole, the mouse, has a wonderful job in a French cheese factory. Then one night a cat appears and Anatole is faced with a problem that frightened mice before him—how to bell a cat.

6557. ____. *Anatole and the Robot* (McGraw, 1960) k–3. Monsieur Duval of the cheese factory gets

measles, and Larue the inventor is called in to take charge, he brings a cheese-tasting machine to replace Anatole. But Anatole proves that a robot can't replace an expert.

6558. ____. *Anatole Over Paris* (McGraw,1961) k–3. The giant kite which Anatole the mouse brings home sweeps him and his entire family sky-high over Paris into breathtaking adventure.

6559. ____. *Anatole and the Poodle* (McGraw, 1965) k–3. It's Anatole, mouse magnifique, to the rescue again, and this time its Juliette, the French poodle, who needs his help.

6560. ____. *Anatole and the Piano* (McGraw, 1966) k–3. Anatole, a music loving mouse, plays the miniature piano in the museum, saving a concert for the orphans of Paris by removing a broken string from the piano.

6561. ____. *Anatole and the Thirty Thieves* (McGraw, 1969) k–3. Anatole, a mouse, returns from vacation to find he is sorely needed to help solve the mystery of the Great Cheese Robbery which has closed his good friend's cheese factory.

6562. ____. *Anatole and the Toyshop* (McGraw, 1970) k–3. Desperate to have his family back with him, Anatole devises a plan to rescue them from the toyshop window where they are held prisoners to attract customers.

6563. ____. *Anatole in Italy* (McGraw, 1973) k–3. Official cheese taster, Anatole the mouse, is sent to Italy to save a cheese factory and discovers a lost masterpiece as well.

6564. ____. *Anatole and the Pied Piper* (McGraw, 1979) k–3. Anatole's mouse wife, Dourette, tries to rescue 24 schoolmice spirited away by Gussac, a flute player.

6565. Titus, Eve. *Basil of Baker Street* (McGraw, 1958) 3–5. A mystery story in which Basil, an English mouse detective whose idol is Sherlock Holmes, and Dr. Dawson solve one of Mousedom's most baffling cases.

6566. ____. *Basil and the Lost Colony* (Whittlesey, 1964) 3–5. Basil goes to Switzerland in search of the Lost Colony. He led an expedition of 32 mice up the towering mountain while he was pursued by Professor Ratigan, the sinister ruler of the mouse underworld. If it were not for Basil what would have happened to shaggy mouse (the Adorable Snowmouse)?

6567. ____. *Basil and the Pygmy Cats* (Pocket, 1973) 3–5. In search of the home of pygmy cats, intrepid mouse detective Basil encounters his enemy Ratigan plus numerous adventures, one involving a monster from Loch Ness.

6568. ____. *Basil in Mexico* (McGraw, 1976) 3–5. Basil, a mouse, plays the role of detective. The crime to be solved, Sherlock Holmes fashion, is the Case of the Counterfeit Cheese. The Mousa Lisa and Dr. Dawson are missing and the Mexican mice try their skills.

6569. ____. *Basil in the Wild West* (McGraw, 1982) 3–5. Headed for the Grand Canyon to investigate a mystery at a hotel, Basil finds himself involved in dangerous adventures as he tries to foil the schemes of a ruthless smuggler.

6570. Todd, H.E. *Bobby Brewster's Shadow* (Hodder, 1956) 2–4. Ashamed of Bobby's inexpert play, his boots practice secretly at night in the garden and ensure that his schoolmates look at him with more respect. Another book of the powers of inanimate objects.

6571. ____. *Bobby Brewster's Bee* (Brockhampton, 1972) 2–4.

6572. ____. *Bobby Brewster's Bookmark* (Brockhampton, 1977) 2–4. All about Bobby's latest adventures. An old favorite tale told by a gifted, caring father to his children with natural humor.

6573. ____. *Bobby Brewster's Tea Leaves* (Hodder, 1980) 2–4. Bobby Brewster plays cricket, finds a tea cup in the woods, is invited to a meal where the dog of the house eats the joint of meat, and gets an unexpected prize.

6574. ____. *Bobby Brewster's Lamp Post* (Hodder, 1982) 2–4. A lamp post with a view of his own, a somewhat didactic toothbrush, bells swinging on a Christmas card, pullover sweaters that resist borrowing—these and other items are in the daily life of Bobby Brewster.

6575. ____. *Bobby Brewster and the Magic Handyman* (Hodder, 1987) 2–4. The strange Handyman Hackentapp fixes a leaky tap and for a whole year strange things happen: garden tools dig on their own, the Brewsters learn music lessons very quickly, juice runs from the tap, and much more.

6576. ____. *Bobby Brewster's Hiccups* (Hodder, 1991) 2–4.

6577. Tolles, Martha. *Who's Reading Darci's Diary?* (Dutton, 1984) 4–6. Frantic when her secret diary suddenly disappears, Darci, 11, is convinced that her crush on the handsome Travis will be revealed to the whole school.

6578. ____. *Darci and the Dance Contest* (Lodestar, 1985) 4–6. Anxious to make friends in her new school, sixth grader Darci finds herself drawn into an uneasy relationship with the capricious Lisa and her circle of friends.

6579. ____. *Darci in Cabin 13* (Scholastic, 1990) 3–5. A summer camp story revolving around the competition among girls in two different cabins. A story of the Haves and Havenots.

6580. Torgersen, Don. *Troll Who Lived in the Lake* (Children's, 1978) k–3. The troll living at the bottom of the lake finally decides to do something about the children who are taking all the fish out of his lake and leaving a lot of debris behind.

6581. ____. *Girl Who Tricked the Troll* (Children's, 1978) k–3. Clever Karin thinks of a way to drive an enraged troll back into the forest.

6582. ____. *Troll Who Went to School* (Children's, 1979) k–3. A small boy longs to go to school with the other children but finds that his classmates laugh at him because of his unusual looks and habits.

6583. ____. *Scariest Night in Troll Forest* (Children's, 1979) k–3. Several children decide not to follow the safe path on their hike through Troll Forest and consequently experience a very scary night.

6584. ____. *Angry Giants of Troll Mountain* (Children's, 1980) k–3. Three boys disregard the many tales of sleeping giant trolls when they set off for an afternoon of skiing on a nearby mountain.

6585. ____. *Wicked Witch of Troll Cave* (Children's, 1980) k–3. Ravencraven, the wicked troll witch who terrorizes Tumble Town, keeps her enchanted gnomes busy making shiny gold coins.

6586. ____. *Huff and Puff and the Troll Hole* (Children's, 1982) k–3. Two mischievous gnomes try to outwit the three trolls who hold them captive.

6587. Tourneur, Dina. *Caspar's Hands* (Burke, 1977) k–3. Caspar uses his right hand to work with. His friend Jason uses his left hand. When they shake hands, they both use their right hand. Caspar uses his hands to eat, drink, wash and carry things.

6588. ____. *Caspar's Ears* (Burke, 1977) k–3. Caspar is a red-headed young boy. He hears strange noises, from the ice cream cart to footsteps on the stairs.

6589. Townsend, Tom. *Trader Wooly and the Secret of the Lost Nazi Treasure* (Eakin, 1987) 4–6. Wes and Trader Wooly, army brats, get involved in trying to find some stolen gold that was hidden in a forest that was mined. Ludwig was forced to hide the gold during World War II. Arty Sue is a friend who helps.

6590. ____. *Trader Wooly and the Terrorists* (Eakin, 1988) 4–6. Trader Wooly, seventh grader, and his friends, living on a military base in West Germany, stumble across a terrorists' plot to kill as many Americans as possible.

6591. Travers, Pamela. *Mary Poppins* (Harcourt, 1934) 5–8. Magical Mary Poppins is an extraordinary lady, full of fun and excitement. The children knew she was magical right from the beginning.

6592. ____. *Mary Poppins Comes Back* (Harcourt, 1935) 4–6. More adventures with the delightful baby-sitter. She said she would return and she did. She arrives at the end of a kite string.

6593. ____. *Mary Poppins Open the Door* (Harcourt, 1943) 5–8. Whimsical Mary is back with new adventures. This time she comes back as a falling spark and finds there is a new baby, Annabel.

6594. ____. *Mary Poppins in the Park* (Harcourt, 1952) 5–8. Mary Poppins brings Michael, Jane, the twins and Annabel the best in fun and enchanting adventures.

6595. ____. *Mary Poppins in the Cherry Tree* (Delacorte, 1982) 5–8. This book describes some of Mary's earlier adventures and is easier to read. It is more akin to *Mary Poppins from A to Z* and *Mary Poppins in the Kitchen.*

6596. ____. *Mary Poppins and the House Next Door* (Delacorte, 1989) 4–6. Luti, whom the formidable Miss Andrew brought from the South Sea to London in order to civilize, feels the need to go home again. So Mary Poppins helps him get back to his island by way of the Man-in-the-Moon.

6597. Traynor, Shaun. *Hugo O'Huge* (Methuen, 1984) k–3. A story of a giant who has been left behind when all his companions went away. A magic time happens when children find him much later. He told them many stories, but then disappeared. He reappears when the children climb the Hill of Dreams.

6598. ____. *Giants' Olympics* (Methuen, 1987) k–3. Hugo O'Huge and the details of the Giants' Eating Contest.

6599. Trimby, Elisa. *Mr. Plum's Paradise* (Lothrop, 1977) k–3. Mr. Plum has a nice backyard in a barren London rowhouse. Soon his neighbors follow suit and plant flowers and now the neighborhood looks like a park.

6600. ____. *Mr. Plum's Oasis* (Faber, 1981) k–3. Mr. Plum is a gardener who plans to bring water to the desert by towing an iceberg from the Antarctic so that he can create a beautiful garden for an Arab sheik's daughter.

6601. Tring, A. Stephen. *Penny Dreadful* (Goodchild, 1950) 4–6. Penny is a pony-mad schoolgirl. She notices that a brooch worn by a woman is much like the one stolen from a wealthy neighbor of Penny. She spots Captain Western in a shop where his dealings in stolen goods is confirmed.

6602. ____. *Penny Triumphant* (Goodchild, 1950) 4–6. Penny is now 12. She is intrigued with Miss Marchant's gardener. He is suspected of back-door dealing with Miss Marchant's produce.

6603. Tripp, Valerie. *Meet Molly* (Pleasant, 1986) 3–5. While her father is away fighting in World War II, Molly finds her life full of change as she eats vegetables from the victory garden and plans revenge on her brother for ruining her Halloween.

6604. ____. *Molly Learns a Lesson* (Pleasant, 1986) 3–5. During World War II, Molly, nine, goes to school and tries to aid in the war effort.

6605. ____. *Molly's Surprise* (Pleasant, 1986) 3–5. Even though he is away serving in an English hospital during World War II, Molly's father finds a way to make the family Christmas very special.

6606. ____. *Happy Birthday, Molly* (Pleasant, 1987) 3–5. When an English girl comes to stay at Molly's during World War II, she and Molly learn to bridge their differences and ultimately enjoy a wonderful, mutual birthday party.

6607. ____. *Molly Saves the Day* (Pleasant, 1988) 3–5. Molly conquers her fear of swimming underwater when she and the other campers at Camp Gowonagin divide into two teams to play Color War.

6608. ____. *Changes for Molly* (Pleasant, 1988) 3–5. Molly's excitement at performing in a big show is exceeded only by the announcement that her father is returning home from the war.

6609. Tripp, Valerie. *Happy Birthday, Samantha* (Pleasant, 1987) 3–5. A ten-year-old girl discovers the modern delights of turn-of-the-century New York City when she travels there with her grandmother to visit relatives.

6610. ____. *Samantha Saves the Day* (Pleasant, 1988) 3–5. While spending the summer at Grandmary's summer home on Goose Lake, Samantha and her twin cousins decide to visit the island where Samantha's parents were drowned during a storm.

6611. ____. *Changes for Samantha* (Pleasant, 1988) 3–5. When she discovers that Nellie and her sisters have been sent to an orphanage, Samantha, now living with her aunt and uncle in New York City, tries to help her friends as much as she can.

6612. Tripp, Valerie. *Meet Felicity* (Pleasant, 1991) 3–5. In Williamsburg in 1771, nine-year-old Felicity rescues a beautiful horse who is being beaten and starved by her cruel owner.

6613. ____. *Felicity Learns a Lesson* (Pleasant, 1991) 3–5. Shortly before the Revolutionary War, nine-year-old Felicity, who lives in Williamsburg, is torn between supporting the tariff-induced tea boycott and saving her friendship with Elizabeth, a young Loyalist from England.

6614. ____. *Felicity's Surprise* (Pleasant, 1991) 3–5. Christmas in Williamsburg means a dancing party at the Governor's Palace for Felicity, but her mother becomes very ill and cannot finish the special blue gown.

6615. ____. *Happy Birthday, Felicity* (Pleasant, 1992) 3–5. As her tenth birthday approaches, Felicity is excited by her grandfather's visit, but she is also concerned about the growing tensions between the colonists and the British governor in Williamsburg.

6616. ____. *Felicity Saves the Day* (Pleasant, 1992) 3–5. During a visit to her grandfather's plantation in Virginia during the summer of 1775, Felicity's loyalty is torn between her father and Ben, her father's apprentice who needs her help as he runs away to join George Washington's army of Patriots.

6617. ____. *Changes for Felicity* (Pleasant, 1992) 3–5. The outbreak of the Revolutionary War in 1775 brings drastic changes to Felicity's life in Williamsburg, affecting both her family and her friendship with Elizabeth.

6618. Tryon, Leslie. *Albert's Alphabet* (Atheneum, 1992) 3–5. Clever Albert uses all the supplies in his workshop to build an alphabet for the school playground.
6619. ____. *Albert's Play* (Atheneum, 1992) 3–5. Albert helps the children of Pleasant Valley School stage a play.
6620. ____. *Albert's Field Trip* (Atheneum, 1993) 3–5. Albert leads the third grade class on a memorable field trip to an apple farm, where they pick apples, watch apples being processed into apple juice and eat apple pies.

6621. Tsutsui, Yoriko. *Anna in Charge* (Viking, 1979) k–3. Anna is in charge of taking care of her little sister Katy; but Katy wanders off.
6622. ____. *Anna's Secret Friend* (Viking, 1987) k–3. Anna moves to a new house and someone leaves flowers and a letter for her. She is excited about her new home and sad about leaving her old one. The gift giver is a similar little girl, too shy to be seen.
6623. ____. *Anna's Special Present* (Viking, 1988) k–3. Even though Katy is a pest, Anna misses her when she is taken to the hospital. Anna thinks of the perfect little sister gift, the rag doll that Anna owns but Katy desires.

6624. Tully, Tom. *Little Ed* (Warne, 1980) 4–6. Ed is the editor of the Baker Street School Bugle. He has trouble finding stories that will sell his paper if he doesn't his paper will close down all together. He starts writing horoscope stories and a series of fortunate coincidences gives him the readers he desires.
6625. ____. *Little Ed at Large* (Warne, 1980) 4–6. Ed wants to make his private news-sheet, the Baker Street Bugle influential in the neighborhood. His copy provides the possibility of a Roman villa under Mr. Englefield's allotment, a hoax on local people preparing for a visitor, a haunted house and a dishonest Father Christmas.
6626. ____. *Look Out, It's Little Ed* (Warne, 1981) k–3. Ed is an obnoxious child who is editor of his school magazine. The head of the school is obsessed by the accuracy of Ed's horoscope readings. The reporters believe Ed's story of alien invaders.

6627. Turk, Hanne. *Surprise for Max* (Alphabet, 1982) k–3. Max the mouse finds a wrapped package waiting for him, and he wrestles with it until he has the satisfaction of discovering the treasure.
6628. ____. *Max Versus the Cube* (Alphabet, 1982) k–3. Max is a cheerful, persistent mouse ready to try anything even Rubik's infernal puzzle.
6629. ____. *Rope Skips Max* (Alphabet, 1982) k–3. Max a mouse who is willing to try anything such as an unwielding jump rope.
6630. ____. *Lesson for Max* (Alphabet, 1983) k–3. Max the Mouse takes up smoking hoping to look suave, but it only makes him sick.

6631. ____. *Rainy Day Max* (Alphabet, 1983) k–3. Max discovers the joy of walking in the rain.
6632. ____. *Max the Art Lover* (Alphabet, 1983) k–3. Max the Mouse visits an art gallery looking for just the right piece of art to buy.
6633. ____. *Max* (Alphabet, 1983) k–3. Max is a winsome mouse. He is brave and curious about everything around him.
6634. ____. *Merry Christmas Max* (Alphabet, 1984) k–3. Max burns his Christmas cookies then mysteriously receives a box of cookies at the door and happily walked away with them.
6635. ____. *Raking Leaves with Max* (Alphabet, 1984) k–3. An open-ended story with Max, the fun-loving mouse, with very humorous implications.
6636. ____. *Max Packs* (Alphabet, 1984) k–3. A story of Max and his frantic packing attempts which range from stuffing every last bit of clothing to finally taking only a toy, a camera and a large hat.
6637. ____. *Happy Birthday Max* (Picture Boo, 1984) k–3. Max is a dapper and imaginative mouse. Here he stages an elaborate birthday picnic for himself alone on a hill.
6638. ____. *Snapshot Max* (Alphabet, 1984) k–3. Max, an amateur photographer attempts to capture some engaging shots of himself while at the beach. End results: feet, ears and whiskers.
6639. ____. *Goodnight, Max* (Alphabet, 1984) k–3.

6640. Turkle, Brinton. *Obadiah, the Bold* (Viking, 1965) 2–4. A young boy's desire to be a pirate is quelled by his brothers and sisters during a game.
6641. ____. *Thy Friend, Obadiah* (Viking, 1969) 2–4. A seagull befriends a Quaker boy, much to his embarrassment, and it is not until he has helped the bird that he can accept its friendship.
6642. ____. *Adventures of Obadiah* (Viking,1972) 2–4. Because he is always making up stories, no one in the family believes Obadiah's adventure with the sheep shearing squantum.
6643. ____. *Rachel and Obadiah* (Dutton, 1978) 2–4. Rachel proves that girls, too, can do what boys have always done.

6644. Turner, Philip. *Steam on the Line* (World, 1968) 5–8. Taffy and Sarah discover a plan to derail the new train thereby saving passengers from death and the destruction of the transportation system.
6645. ____. *Devil's Nob* (Nelson, 1973) 5–8. Taffy is working in the slate mines of England. He is courting Sarah who, injured in a fall, must be rescued. He does so alone and cleverly. There is still competition between steam and horses.

6646. Tyler, Linda. *When Daddy Comes Home* (Viking, 1986) k–3. A young hippo is delighted when his father, who doesn't usually get home until his son is asleep, decides to set aside special evenings for the two of them to work together on special projects.

6647. ____. *Waiting for Mom* (Viking, 1987) k–3. A young hippo is worried and concerned when his mother, caught up in an unexpected delay, is late picking him up from school.

6648. Uchida, Yoshiko. *Sumi's Prize* (Scribner, 1964) 2–4. A kite contest was announced for New Year's Day in the village where Sumi lived. She was delighted and was going to make the most beautiful kite she could. However, she was in for a surprise.
6649. ____. *Sumi's Special Happening* (Scribner, 1966) 2–4. Sumi must think of something special to give her friend, 99-year-old Ojii Chan, for her birthday.
6650. ____. *Sumi and the Goat and the Tokyo Express* (Scribner, 1969) 2–4. Sumi, who is seven, has a friend, Ojii Chan, 99. Ojii has just received a new goat and Sumi takes it a welcoming gift.

6651. Udry, Janice. *What Mary Jo Shared* (Whitman, 1966) k–3. Everyone brought something to school to share—everyone but Mary Jo. Somehow everything Mary Jo planned was something somebody else had already chosen. Then Mary Jo had a wonderful idea. She had someone very special who belonged to her; she would share him.
6652. ____. *What Mary Jo Wanted* (Whitman, 1968) k–3. Mary Jo fulfills her promise to take full responsibility for the care and training of her long-desired pup.
6653. ____. *Mary Jo's Grandmother* (Whitman, 1970) k–3. When her grandmother is hurt in a fall, Mary Jo must get help to the remote farm where they live.

6654. Ungerer, Tomi. *Mellops Go Diving for Treasure* (Harper, 1957) k–3. Father and son go looking for treasure lost in the ocean by a Mellop ancestor. They find the treasure but have to pay most of their gain to the income tax bureau.
6655. ____. *Mellops Go Flying* (Harper, 1957) k–3. A family of pigs builds an airplane and fly away on a marvelous adventure, complete with Indians and an amazing rescue.
6656. ____. *Mellops Strike Oil* (Harper, 1959) k–3. The Mellops family—four boys, Mother and Father and the dog—are off on a new adventure. While on a picnic Mr. Mellop believes that oil could be found in the area. They rejoice over their good fortune but a terrible forest fire breaks out.
6657. ____. *Christmas Eve at the Mellops* (Harper, 1960) k–3. A family of winsome pigs tells how the four ingenuous piglets discover the secret of the "happiest Christmas ever."
6658. ____. *Mellops Go Spelunking* (Harper, 1963) k–3. A story about a family of French pigs. Father and son explore an underground cavern; unearth artifacts and discover paintings done by cavemen millions of years ago. The cavern is flooded and their rubber raft is punctured. They land in a smuggler's den.

6659. Updike, David. *Winter Journey* (Prentice, 1985) 2–4. Homer goes out at night into a snowstorm in search of his dog Sophocles and experiences some strange and thrilling adventures.
6660. ____. *Autumn Tale* (Pippin, 1988) 2–4. When Homer puts his jack o' lantern over his head like a helmet on the eve of Halloween, he gains access to a secret nocturnal meeting of the trees as they celebrate the arrival of the full moon.
6661. ____. *Spring Story* (Pippin, 1989) 2–4. Homer, his dog Sophocles, and Henry have fun riding an iceberg down the creek until rushing waters threaten to take them out to sea.
6662. ____. *Sounds of Summer* (Pippin, 1993) 2–4. During the long days of summer vacation, Homer realizes that his beloved Sophocles is no longer a young dog and that he may lose his companion soon.

6663. Ure, Jean. *Fright* (Orchard, 1988) 5–8. Catherine is a loner. A new girl with problems of her own, joins Woodside School. Recognizable, but complicated, series of events take place.
6664. ____. *Who's Talking?* (Orchard, 1988) 5–8. This story deals with tensions and misunderstandings in class; about cheating and owning up. It all takes place at Woodside School.

6665. Ure, Jean. *Wizard in the Woods* (Candlewick, 1992) 5–8. Ben-Mussy, a second-class junior wizard, bungles a spell during his junior wizard exams and ends up in Penny Woods where he meets Joel and Gemma and their adventures begin.
6666. ____. *Wizard in Wonderland* (Candlewick, 1993) 5–8. Joel and Gemma are enjoying a visit to Wonderland with their friend, junior wizard Ben-Mussy, when his magic broomstick is stolen by the Airy Fairies.

6667. Uttley, Alison. *Fuzzypeg's Brother* (Collins, 1971) k–3. The Hedgehog family has a new addition—Little Urchin. He sleeps in a rush-plaited hammock, plays games, goes to school and after winter hibernation he finds spring has garlanded his balloon with flowers.
6668. ____. *Fuzzypeg Goes to School* (Collins, 1982) k–3. Fuzzypeg's first day at school leads to a ducking in the river.
6669. ____. *Story of Fuzzypeg the Hedgehog* (Heinemann) k–3.

6670. Uttley, Alison. *Sam Pig Goes to Market* (Faber, 1965) k–3.
6671. ____. *Sam Pig Storybook* (Faber, 1971) k–3.
6672. ____. *Adventures of Sam Pig* (Puffin, 1976) k–3. Sam Pig is a gentle creature who has trouble staying out of mischief.
6673. ____. *Yours Ever, Sam Pig* (Faber, 1977) k–3.
6674. ____. *Sam Pig Goes to the Seaside* (Faber, 1978) k–3.
6675. ____. *Sam Pig and the Hurdy Gurdy Man*

(Faber, 1988) k–3. Sam, his sister Ann and brothers Tom and Bill along with their caretaker, Old Brock, the badger, fix the Hurdy Gurdy man's musical box.

6676. ____. *Sam Pig and the Cuckoo Clock* (Faber, 1989) k–3. Sam Pig breaks the family clock and sets off to find another.

6677. ____. *Sam Pig and the Wind* (Faber, 1989) k–3. Sam and his sister, Ann and his brothers Tom and Bill, are helped by their caretaker, Old Brock, the badger, to outwit the wind after it steals Sam's trousers.

6678. ____. *Sam Pig at the Theater* (Faber, 1989) k–3. Sam Pig brings his family to a play.

6679. ____. *Sam Pig and the Dragon* (Faber, 1989) k–3. Sam, Ann, Tom and Bill discover the problem of adopting a dragon.

6680. ____. *Sam Pig's Trousers* (Faber, 1989) k–3.

6681. ____. *Sam Pig and His Fiddle* (Faber, 1989) k–3.

6682. ____. *Sam Pig and the Scarecrow* (Faber, 1989) k–3.

6683. ____. *Sam Pig and the Christmas Pudding* (Faber, 1990) k–3.

6684. Uttley, Alison. *Hare Goes Shopping* (Collins, 1965) 2–4. The policeman says Hare "wouldn't harm a fly" but his capacity for mischief and idle pursuits is something else. He uses the Roman coins Moldy Wasp digs up to finance his sprees.

6685. ____. *Great Adventure of Hare* (Heinemann, 1968) 2–4.

6686. ____. *Hare and the Rainbow* (Collins, 1975) 2–4. Grey Rabbit lifts her paw and bows her head at the sight of the leaves after raindrops fall. A goddess steps out of a rainbow and distributes coins on the once-in-a-hundred-years Rainbow day.

6687. ____. *Hare and Guy Fawkes* (Collins, 1986) 2–4. Hare plans a special celebration for Guy Fawkes Day with the traditional bonfire and fireworks.

6688. ____. *Hare and the Easter Eggs* (Smithmark, 1990) 2–4.

6689. Uttley, Alison. *Squirrel, the Hare and Little Grey Rabbit* (Heinemann, 1929) 2–4. Grey Rabbit is a mother-figure whose care and concern help vain, pretty Squirrel and impetuous Hare when they get into difficulties.

6690. ____. *Squirrel Goes Skating* (Collins, 1934) 2–4. Pat breaks in Little Grey Rabbit's house while they were out skating and ate the lovingly prepared tea and leaving ugly footprints all over the floor.

6691. ____. *Little Grey Rabbit's Party* (Smithmark, 1936) 2–4. Wise Owl wants to eat everything. Even at Little Rabbit's party the hostess was under threat. In the game "Hunt the Thimble," Wise Owl ate the thimble.

6692. ____. *Little Grey Rabbit's Washing Day* (Collins, 1939) 2–4. Grey Rabbit allows herself to get enchanted once or twice by Gypsy Rabbit with her magic clothes pegs.

6693. ____. *Little Grey Rabbit and the Weasels* (Collins, 1947) 2–4. Little Grey Rabbit is abducted by the unscrupulous weasel family but is eventually rescued by Wise Owl.

6694. ____. *Little Grey Rabbit Makes Lace* (Collins, 1950) 2–4. With the help of her friends Grey Rabbit makes the lace she needs to trim the nightcap she is making for Mrs. Hedgehog. But she has to be careful that Wise Owl doesn't eat. It.

6695. ____. *How Little Grey Rabbit Got Back Her Tail* (Heinemann, 1968) 2–4.

6696. ____. *Little Grey Rabbit Goes to the North Pole* (Collins, 1970) 2–4. Little Grey Rabbit is looking after Hare and Squirrel and sharing their small adventure.

6697. ____. *Little Grey Rabbit's Spring Cleaning Party* (Collins, 1972) 2–4.

6698. ____. *Little Grey Rabbit and the Snow Baby* (Collins, 1973) 2–4.

6699. ____. *Little Grey Rabbit Goes to Sea* (Heinemann, 1976) 2–4.

6700. ____. *Tales of Little Grey Rabbit* (Heinemann, 1980) 2–4. Contains: "Squirrel, the Hare and Little Grey Rabbit"; "How Little Grey Rabbit Got Back Her Tail"; "Great Adventure of Hare"; "Story of Fuzzypeg the Hedgehog."

6701. ____. *Little Grey Rabbit's Christmas* (Collins, 1982) 2–4. Grey Rabbit and her friends celebrate a special Christmas.

6702. ____. *Grey Rabbit and the Circus* (Collins, 1982) 2–4.

6703. ____. *Little Grey Rabbit's Birthday* (Smithmark, 1982) 2–4.

6704. ____. *Little Grey Rabbit and the Wandering Hedgehog* (Collins, 1982) 2–4.

6705. ____. *Little Grey Rabbit's House* (Putnam, 1984) 2–4. A model home and cut-out characters for story recreation. The reader can move the cut-outs around a ready to assemble house.

6706. ____. *Little Grey Rabbit* (Collins, 1984) 2–4.

6707. ____. *Knot. Squirrel Tied* (Collins, 1985) 2–4. Wise Owl's advice to thieving Rat, whose knotted tail is making it hard for him to hunt for food, is that good deeds will cause the punitive knots to work themselves free, and so it turns out.

6708. Vacheron, Edith. *Here Is Henri* (Scribner, 1959) k–3. In three adventures a little French boy and his cat buy a fish, find an umbrella and learn what day of the week it is.

6709. ____. *Encore Henri* (Scribner, 1961) k–3. A story of the adventures of Henri and his cat, Michel.

6710. ____. *More About Henri* (Scribner, 1963) k–3.

6711. Van Der Beek. *Superbabe* (Putnam, 1988) k–3. A youngster relates the messy and mischievous antics of her baby brother.

6712. ____. *Superbabe II* (Putnam, 1989) k–3. Superbabe is the younger brother of the title of the story. It describes a visit to the park. The baby is obstinate and determined to be independent.

6713. ____. *Superbabe at the Park* (Putnam, 1989) k–3. Superbabe's visit to the park playground leaves everyone exhausted.

6714. Vander Els, Betty. *Bomber's Moon* (Farrar, 1985) 5–8. When Japan invades China, Ruth and Simeon, missionary children, are evacuated for safety's sake. They are not reunited with their parents for four years.

6715. ____. *Leaving Point* (Farrar, 1987) 5–8. Home from boarding school to spend Christmas with their missionary parents, Ruth, 14, and her brothers find the Communist Revolution brought restrictions that effect Ruth's friendship with a Chinese girl.

6716. Van Der Meer, Ron. *My Brother Sammy* (Hamish, 1980) k–3. A baby arrives and is sung to sleep. The story is to explain about babies to older siblings and persuade them not to be jealous. It also shows an active role of daddy.

6717. ____. *Sammy and Mara* (Hamish, 1980) k–3. These two books show a nice nuclear family, mother, father, Mara a new baby, Sammy, two curious cats, and a grandmother.

6718. ____. *Naughty Sammy* (Hamish, 1980) k–3.

6719. ____. *Sammy and the Cat Party* (Hamish, 1980) k–3.

6720. Van de Wetering, Janwillem. *Hugh Pine* (Houghton, 1980) 3–5. Hugh Pine, a porcupine genius, works with his human friends to save his less intelligent fellow porcupines from the deadly dangers of the road.

6721. ____. *Hugh Pine and the Good Place* (Houghton, 1986) 3–5. Hugh Pine, a porcupine, decides to live alone on an island in order to get away from all the problems the forest animals bring to him; but after a time he decides being alone isn't so wonderful after all.

6722. ____. *Hugh Pine and Something Else* (Houghton, 1989) 3–5. Hugh Pine, a porcupine, takes his first vacation when he accompanies his human friend, Mr. McTosh, to Brooklyn, New York.

6723. Van Leeuwen, Jean. *Tales of Oliver Pig* (Dial, 1979) 2–4. Five adventures of Oliver Pig with his family.

6724. ____. *More Tales of Oliver Pig* (Dial, 1981) 2–4. The further adventures of Oliver Pig and his family.

6725. ____. *Amanda Pig and Her Big Brother Oliver* (Dial, 1982) 2–4. Five stories about telling secrets, playing alone, and other activities in the lives of Oliver and Amanda who are sometimes known as Mighty Pig and Amazing Baby Pig.

6726. ____. *Tales of Amanda Pig* (Dial, 1983) 2–4. Amanda Pig, her brother Oliver, and their parents share a busy day, working and playing together from breakfast to bedtime.

6727. ____. *More Tales of Amanda Pig* (Dial, 1985) 2–4. More adventures of Amanda Pig and her family, in which noisy cousins come to visit and Father gets a stuffed toy for his birthday.

6728. ____. *Oliver, Amanda and Grandmother Pig* (Dial, 1987) 2–4. When Grandmother Pig comes for a visit, Oliver and Amanda learn just how much fun it is to have a grandmother in the house.

6729. ____. *Oliver and Amanda's Christmas* (Dial, 1989) 2–4. After joining his sister in wrapping presents, baking cookies, and picking a Christmas tree, Oliver tries to find a stocking big enough to hold the 22 toys he requested from Santa.

6730. ____. *Oliver Pig at School* (Dial, 1990) 2–4. During Oliver Pig's first day at school he builds with blocks, plays with his toy dinosaur and makes a new friend.

6731. ____. *Amanda Pig on Her Own* (Dial, 1991) 2–4. When her brother goes off to school, Amanda finds new things to do, including ballet dancing, cleaning her room and making a very sad, mad day go away, with the help of hugs from Mother Pig.

6732. ____. *Oliver and Amanda's Halloween* (Dial, 1992) 2–4. Oliver and Amanda Pig's Halloween activities include making their costumes, getting a pumpkin for a jack o' lantern, and going trick-or-treating.

6733. ____. *Oliver and Amanda and the Big Snow* (Dial, 1995) 2–4. Four stories about Amanda and Oliver and their parents who go outside to play after a big snowstorm.

6734. Van Leeuwen, Jean. *Great Cheese Conspiracy* (Random, 1969) 5–8. Tired of gangster movies and a steady diet of candy wrappers, three theater mice try to rob a cheese shop.

6735. ____. *Great Summer Camp Catastrophe* (Random, 1992) 4–8. Three mice who live in a department store are dismayed when they are accidentally shipped to a ten-year-old-boy at summer camp. But after joining in a few of the activities they find that they like camp life.

6736. Van Stockum, Hilda. *Mitchells* (Viking, 1945) 4–6. A story of a family of five children, living in Washington. Father is in World War II but mother and grandmother manage well and take in a boarder and rescue a shy war orphan.

6737. ____. *Friendly Gables* (Viking, 1960) 4–6. Twin boys are born to the Mitchells and they have a nurse called Miss Thorpe who is very straightlaced. But the Mitchells will always have fun.

6738. Velthuijs, Max. *Little Man Finds a Home* (Holt, 1985) k–3. Little Man loses the cardboard box in which he has been living and goes out among the animals of the world to find a new home.

6739. ____. *Little Man to the Rescue* (Holt, 1986) k–3. Little Man collects a group of animals to search for the sender of a "help" message in a bottle.

6740. ____. *Little Man's Lucky Day* (Holt, 1986) k–3. Despite a series of mishaps that befall him, Little Man is convinced that his four-leafed clover is bringing him luck.

6741. Velthuijs, Max. *Elephant and Crocodile* (Farrar, 1990) k–3. Crocodile's violin practice annoys his neighbor, Elephant, so much that he takes up the trumpet in self-defense.
6742. ____. *Crocodile's Masterpiece* (Farrar, 1991) k–3. Crocodile is inspired to even greater creative heights by Elephant's enthusiasm for his paintings.

6743. Velthuijs, Max. *Frog in Love* (Farrar, 1989) k–3. Frog is head over heels in love with Duck but too shy to tell her so. So, he paints her a picture, sends her flowers and jumps high to demonstrate his affection.
6744. ____. *Frog and the Birdsong* (Farrar, 1881) k–3. After carefully burying a dead blackbird, Frog and his friends realize that though life ends it is still wonderful to be alive.
6745. ____. *Frog in Winter* (Farrar, 1993) k–3. Frog's physiology does not permit him to enjoy winter, but his friends help him to make the best of the cold weather.
6746. ____. *Frog and the Stranger* (Tambourine, 1994) k–3. When a strange rat sets up camp in the woods, Frog's friends are very suspicious and unfriendly because he seems so different from them.
6747. ____. *Frog is Frightened* (Tambourine, 1995) k–3. Strange noises in the night frighten Frog and his animal friends.
6748. ____. *Frog Is a Hero* (Farrar, 1995) k–3.

6749. Velthuijs, Max. *Monsters from Half-Way to Nowhere* (Black, 1975) k–3.
6750. ____. *Monster and the Robbers* (Black, 1978) k–3. A docile, real, electricity-generating monster is stolen from the town he serves by a band of robbers who live in a hilltop fort. They didn't count on his strength or his fiery breath.

6751. Venture, Peter. *Sidney's House* (Granada, 1981) k–3. Sidney and his cat Mitzi lose their home to a bulldozer. But Sidney's tree is spared. In its branches is room for Sidney and Mitzi to live unnoticed.
6752. ____. *Sidney's Friend* (Granada, 1981) k–3. Sidney makes friends with a deep sea monster who scares the town and is captured, imprisoned and formally declared non-existent. Sidney smuggles it back from where it came.

6753. Verschoyle, Teresa. *Where Matthew Lives* (Penguin, 1977) 4–6.
6754. ____. *Matthew's Secret Surprises* (Penguin, 1989) 4–6. Matthew is cheered during a spell in bed with mumps when Daddy hangs peanuts outside the window and they attract birds. A birthday party, a

bonfire on the beach, a spring snow provide Matthew with many surprises.

6755. Vesey, Amanda. *Duncan's Tree House* (Carolrhoda, 1993) k–3. Duncan experiences the worst night of his life when he decides to stay overnight in his new tree house.
6756. ____. *Duncan and the Bird* (Carolrhoda, 1993) k–3. Duncan's attempts to feed the strange bird he has hatched in his tree house lead to disaster when it develops a taste for cake.

6757. Vestly, Anne. *Eight Children and a Truck* (Methuen, 1973) 4–6. A story of a poor, but happy family; the make-do-and-mend attitude of the truck driver's family, who live in a two-room flat, is both funny and touching. Granny comes for a visit; they visit the seaside and find a lost dog.
6758. ____. *Eight Children Move House* (Methuen, 1974) 4–6. A sequence of small domestic episodes in the lives of these eight children.
6759. ____. *Eight Children in Winter* (Methuen, 1976) 4–6. Eight children live with grandma—from Martha who is imaginative to Matt who is the toddler. A story of family life with warmth and security.
6760. ____. *Eight Children and Rosie* (Methuen, 1977) 4–6. A family does a kindness to the previous owners of their house, letting them use it for Christmas because their long lost son has returned from overseas. As a thank you they are given a cow named Rosie. There is no place for her outside in the winter so she is installed in the parlor. A group of friends build a proper stall and all is well.
6761. ____. *Eight Children and a Bulldozer* (Methuen, 1980) 4–6. Mary, Martin, Martha, Mark, Mona, Milly, Maggie and Matt live with their parents and Grandma and Rosie, the cow. The Council wants to destroy their farm to build a road. A happy solution is found.

6762. Vestly, Anne. *Aurora and the Little Blue Car* (Crowell, 1974) 3–5. A story of Aurora, her baby brother Socrates and her parents. They live in a high-rise flat. Father is working on his thesis and domestic duties while mother goes out to work. A good story.
6763. ____. *Hello, Aurora* (Crowell, 1974) 3–5. While mother works, Aurora, father, and baby Socrates, manage the household very well—something neighbors have difficulty understanding and accepting.
6764. ____. *Aurora in Holland* (Crowell, 1976) 3–5. A nice informative story of a Norwegian family on a trip to Holland.
6765. ____. *Aurora and Socrates* (Crowell, 1977) 3–5. While their parents are working full-time, Aurora and Socrates cope with their baby-sitter and vice versa.

6766. Vincent, Gabrielle. *Ernest and Celestine* (Greenwillow, 1982) k–3. Ernest the bear and Celestine the mouse lose Celestine's stuffed bird in the snow.

6767. ____. *Bravo, Ernest and Celestine* (Greenwillow, 1981) k–3. When the roof leaks, Ernest the bear plays his violin and Celestine the mouse sings in the street to earn money for repairs, but they find other uses for it.

6768. ____. *Ernest and Celestine's Picnic* (Greenwillow, 1982) k–3. The picnic day dawns rainy so Ernest and Celestine have a pretend picnic in a tent. They get an invitation from the owner of the land to his fine chateau.

6769. ____. *Smile, Ernest and Celestine* (Greenwillow, 1982) k–3. After he explains to Celestine why his collection of photographs does not include her, Ernest remedies the omission.

6770. ____. *Merry Christmas, Ernest and Celestine* (Greenwillow, 1984) k–3. Even though they have no money, Ernest and Celestine use their ingenuity to make a Christmas party for their friends, knowing that it is love and friendship and not money that really matters.

6771. ____. *Ernest and Celestine's Patchwork Quilt* (Greenwillow, 1982) k–3. Ernest and Celestine make a patchwork quilt, but when they realize only one can use it, they make another one.

6772. ____. *Breakfast Time, Ernest and Celestine* (Greenwillow, 1982) k–3. Ernest the bear is willing to help when his mouse friend Celestine breaks a cup, but she wants to take the responsibility for cleaning up her mess herself.

6773. ____. *Where Are You, Ernest and Celestine?* (Greenwillow, 1986) k–3. When Celestine momentarily loses Ernest at the museum, she fears that he prefers the paintings to her.

6774. ____. *Get Better, Ernest* (Macrae, 1988) k–3. Ernest, the bear, feels poorly so Celestine the mouse sends for the doctor who prescribes diet and rest. Celestine gets behind in her housework but amuses Ernest who is not the best of patients.

6775. ____. *Ernest and Celestine at the Circus* (Greenwillow, 1989) k–3. Ernest and Celestine go to a circus where Ernest was once a clown and take part in the show.

6776. Viorst, Judith. *Alexander and the Terrible, Horrible, No Good, Very Bad Day* (Atheneum, 1972) k–3. Alexander wakes up to a bad day and things get progressively worse as the hours wear on until he thinks he may escape it all and go to Australia.

6777. ____. *Alexander Who Used to Be Rich Last Sunday* (Atheneum, 1978) k–3. Alexander spends his dollar gift foolishly—penny by penny.

6778. ____. *Alex, Who's Not (Do You Hear Me? I Mean It.) Going to Move* (Atheneum, 1995) k–3. Angry Alexander refuses to move if it means having to leave his favorite friends and special places.

6779. Virin, Anna. *Elsa's Bears* (Harper, 1978) k–3. Little Elsa and her three toy bears go sledding.

6780. ____. *Elsa's Bears Learn to Paint* (Harvey, 1978) k–3. Elsa has fun with three cans of paint.

6781. ____. *Elsa's Bears in the Playground* (Harvey, 1978) k–3. Elsa goes bicycling and runs about barefoot in the playground. She goes out on a cold night without a robe.

6782. ____. *Elsa's Bears Need a Doctor* (Harper, 1978) k–3. Elsa's bears clamor for more of that tasty medicine.

6783. ____. *Elsa in the Night* (Harvey, 1978) k–3. Elsa cannot get to sleep until she finds her three bears and brings them to bed, too.

6784. ____. *Elsa Tidies Her House* (Harper, 1978) k–3. Elsa is seen scrubbing steps.

6785. Vivelo, Jackie. *Super Sleuth* (Putnam, 1985) 4–6. Given a list of clues and suspects the reader can start eliminating suspects until the crime is solved. Ellen, Beagle's partner, solves them in this manner.

6786. ____. *Beagle in Trouble* (Putnam, 1986) 4–6. The reader assists the two partners of the Beagle Detective Agency in solving a variety of cases including "The Big Pig Problem" and "Unmasking the Vandals."

6787. ____. *Super Sleuth and the Bare Bones* (Putnam, 1988) 4–6. Ellen and Beagle have found human bones buried many years ago, the disappeared college money and many other mysteries which the reader can solve from the information given.

6788. Wabbes, Marie. *Little Rabbit's Garden* (Atlantic, 1987) k–3. Little Rabbit samples some of the luscious things growing in his garden.

6789. ____. *It's Snowing Little Rabbit* (Atlantic, 1987) k–3. Little Rabbit enjoys a snowfall and makes a snow rabbit—just like himself.

6790. ____. *Happy Birthday, Little Rabbit* (Atlantic, 1987) k–3. Little Rabbit's birthday party features presents, games, good things to eat, and candles to blow out.

6791. ____. *Good Night, Little Rabbit* (Atlantic, 1987) k–3. A young rabbit's bedtime ritual.

6792. Wabbes, Marie. *Rose Is Hungry* (Messner, 1989) k–3. Rose is a pig without any supervision or intervention. She concocts a meal by herself.

6793. ____. *Rose is Muddy* (Messner, 1989) k–3. Rose is an unsupervised pig who goes her own way. She ends up very dirty.

6794. ____. *Rose's Bath* (Messner, 1989) k–3. No one supervises or interferes with Rose, the pig. She runs her own bath and prepares to bathe.

6795. ____. *Rose's Picture* (Messner, 1989) k–3. Rose is the unsupervised pig who is quite independent. She paints a self-portrait.

6796. Waber, Bernard. *Welcome, Lyle* (Houghton, 1969) k–3. Prequel. Takes us back in time to explain

Lyle's arrival in the Primm household. He is discovered in the bath, after the ominous sounds of "swish, swash, splash" heard from below, have puzzled the Primms.

6797. Waber, Bernard. *House on East 88th Street* (Houghton, 1962) k–3. Adventures of a pet crocodile (Lyle) who lives with a family in a New York brownstone.

6798. ____. *Lyle, Lyle, Crocodile* (Houghton, 1965) k–3. Lyle the crocodile wants to make friends with Loretta the cat. The Primm family copes, of course.

6799. ____. *Lyle and the Birthday Party* (Houghton, 1966) k–3. Lyle, that lovable crocodile, is helping the Primms prepare for Joshua's birthday.

6800. ____. *Lovable Lyle* (Houghton, 1969) k–3. Lyle, the crocodile, thought everyone loved him until the day he received a hate note from an anonymous despiser.

6801. ____. *Lyle Finds His Mother* (Houghton, 1974) k–3. Lyle scours the swamps for his long-lost mother.

6802. ____. *Funny, Funny Lyle* (Houghton, 1987) k–3. Lyle, the crocodile, experiences many changes in his life when his mother moves in with the Primm family and Mrs. Primm announces she is expecting a baby.

6803. ____. *Lyle at the Office* (Houghton, 1994) k–3. When Lyle the crocodile visits Mr. Primm's advertising office, he is almost recruited as the Krispie Krunchie Krackles cereal spokesperson.

6804. Waber, Bernard. *Ira Sleeps Over* (Houghton, 1972) k–3. When Ira is invited to sleep overnight at Reggie's house, he wants to go but should he or shouldn't he take along his teddy bear?

6805. ____. *Ira Says Goodby* (Houghton, 1985) k–3. Ira is surprised to discover that his best friend Reggie feels happy about having to move to a new town.

6806. Waddell, Martin. *Can't You Sleep, Little Bear?* (Candlewick, 1992) k–3. It's bedtime and Little Bear can't get to sleep. He's frightened of the dark, the dark all around, which not even Big Bear's largest lantern can light up. Big Bear finds a way to show Little Bear that there is no need to be afraid.

6807. ____. *Let's Go Home, Little Bear* (Candlewick, 1993) k–3. When Little Bear is frightened by the noises he hears while walking in the snowy woods, his friend Big Bear reassures him.

6808. Waddell, Martin. *Harriet and the Crocodiles* (Little, 1984) 3–5. At the loss of her pet snail, Harriet, a group of adults and classmates alike, decide to replace it with a crocodile.

6809. ____. *Harriet and the Haunted School* (Atlantic, 1984) 3–5. When Harriet hides a circus horse in the closet at school, its nocturnal wanderings start a rumor that the building is haunted.

6810. ____. *Harriet and the Robot* (Joy Street, 1987) 3–5. Harriet, who brings trouble wherever she goes, gives her dear friend Anthea a doll for her birthday—a large robot she has made herself.

6811. ____. *Harriet and the Flying Teachers* (Blackie, 1988) 3–5. "The two girls were standing in the main corridor of Slow Street primary school up against the fence and barbed wire and sandbags that marked the Harriet Free Zone. The zone extended on either side of the staff room and had been installed by Miss Granston, the headmistress, as a Teacher Protection Measure."

6812. Waddell, Martin. *Little Dracula's First Bite* (Viking, 1986) k–3. Big Dracula, Mrs. Dracula, Baby Millicent, Igor, Batty and Little Dragon make up the family. Little Dragon's first bite lands him in the dentist chair.

6813. ____. *Little Dracula's Christmas* (Viking, 1986) k–3. Baby Millicent has blood in her baby bottle and Igor finds a chopped off leg in his Christmas stocking.

6814. ____. *Little Dracula at the Seashore* (Candlewick, 1992) k–3. The inhabitants of Castle Dracula enjoy a variety of activities when they spend a day at the seashore.

6815. ____. *Little Dracula Goes to School* (Candlewick, 1992) k–3. Although he is apprehensive about starting school, Little Dracula finds that he loves it once he gets there.

6816. Waddell, Martin. *Little Obie and the Flood* (Candlewick, 1992) k–3. Through hardships and good times, Little Obie, Granddad, Effie, and newly adopted Marty grow to become a real family.

6817. ____. *Little Obie and the Kidnap* (Candlewick, 1994) k–3. When the old wild woman, Mrs. Jumping Joseph, adopts two orphans, Little Obie and his family come up with a plan to rescue them.

6818. Waddell, Martin. *Napper Goes for Goal* (Blackie, 1988) 3–5. A story of a small primary school setting up its own football team and beating its local rivals.

6819. ____. *Napper Strikes Again* (Blackie, 1988) 3–5. A football story about Red Row School Team. Miss Fellows, in charge of football, has failed to enter her team in the school's competition, so she has put them in the local youth league instead. The tale is told by a Red Row team member as they progress through the competition.

6820. ____. *Napper's Golden Goals* (Blackie, 1989) 3–5. This is Captain Napper's first season in the Primary Schools League. The story details the game of football. There is lots of action and almost no girls.

6821. Wahl, Jan. *Pleasant Fieldmouse* (Harper, 1964) 2–4. Pleasant Fieldmouse is the self-appointed fireman of the woodland creatures, and when not on duty he is busy trying to save his friends from various misfortunes.

6822. ____. *Six Voyages of Pleasant Field Mouse* (Delacorte, 1971) 2–4. Records the six eventful voyages of a fieldmouse who wants to know what is happening in the world.

6823. ____. *Pleasant Fieldmouse's Halloween Party* (Putnam, 1974) 2–4. Despite the costumed guests' scaring each other on the way to a party, Halloween is still celebrated in a festive and appropriate way.

6824. ____. *Pleasant Fieldmouse's Valentine Trick* (Dutton, 1977) 2–4. Pleasant, a mouse, has an idea for ending the unpleasantness of waiting for groundhog to tell if winter will continue. He celebrates Valentine's Day!

6825. ____. *Pleasant Fieldmouse Storybook* (Prentice, 1977) 2–4. Pleasant, a realistic mouse, wears a dried-grass scarf when he goes ice skating. As usual he acts in a reckless, trusting manner that things cannot remain unpleasant.

6826. Wahl, Jan. *Muffletumps* (Dell, 1966) k–3. Edward, Henrietta, Elsie and Maud, Victorian dolls get out of the trunks in the attic and live in the house while the Bediggians are on vacation. They play the piano, dance and sing. Henrietta cooks meals and when the Bediggians come back they return to the attic but cooking smells remain.

6827. ____. *Muffletumps' Christmas Party* (Follett, 1975) k–3. The four Muffletumps plot to brighten Christmas for a lonely old woman who comes to stay in their house while the family is away.

6828. ____. *Muffletump Storybook* (Follett, 1975) k–3. The adventures of four Victorian dolls who come out of the trunk in the attic while their owners are on vacation. This book contains several Muffletump stories.

6829. ____. *Muffletump's Halloween Scare* (Follett, 1977) k–3. Four forgotten Victorian dolls left in a cottage at the end of the summer celebrate Halloween.

6830. Wahl, Jan. *Doctor Rabbit* (Pantheon, 1970) k–3. Dr. Rabbit worked himself sick taking care of all the forest animals.

6831. ____. *Doctor Rabbit's Foundling* (Pantheon, 1977) k–3. Tiny Toad matures and leaves his foster parents to go out on his own.

6832. ____. *Doctor Rabbit's Lost Scout* (S & S, 1990) k–3. Dr. Rabbit and the scouts are camping when Spotty Squirrel sleepwalks away. A hunt party is formed and his cap is spotted. Spotty is found, asleep in a hole.

6833. Wahl, Jan. *Dracula's Cat* (Prentice, 1977) k–3. Life as Dracula's cat is spooky, but fun. Dracula does love his pet when he is not preoccupied with deciding who he is going to scare next.

6834. ____. *Frankenstein's Dog* (Prentice, 1977) k–3. Frankenstein's dog assists his master in helping the monster learn to walk. Together, pup and monster fetch sticks, dig for hidden bones and snuggle to sleep at night.

6835. Wahl, Jan. *Pipkins Go Camping* (Prentice, 1982) k–3. On the first warm day of spring the Pipkins spontaneously go on a camping trip and somehow manage, even though impractical and unorganized, to find their way home through an unexpected snowstorm.

6836. ____. *More Room for the Pipkins* (Prentice, 1983) k–3. The Pipkins decide that they all need space in their house, apart from anyone else, to pursue and enjoy their individual hobbies and interests.

6837. Wainwright, Sheila. *Freddie and the Star of Africa* (Methuen, 1985) k–3. The star of Africa is stolen from the Imperial Crown before the coronation of the King and Queen. Sergeant Freddie of the Royal Mouseguard vows to return it. With the aid of Charlie Brie, a French mouse he finds the hideout of Max the robber. The diamond is retrieved and returned before midnight.

6838. ____. *Freddie and the Bank of England Mystery* (Methuen, 1986) k–3. Sergeant Freddy Stilton, mouse detective, is called in to investigate why all the bank notes are suddenly blank. Max Kraft, the local rat, is responsible. He uses a chemical device that destroys all currency.

6839. Walker, David. *Rick Goes to Little League* (Carolina House, 1981) 3–5. Follows a boy's experiences through his first season of Little League baseball.

6840. ____. *Rick Heads for Soccer* (Caroline House, 1982) 3–5. Rick decides to play soccer instead of football after his new next-door neighbor introduces him to the game.

6841. ____. *Rick Tees Off* (Pro Golfer, 1985) 3–5. When Rick, 13, becomes interested in golf one summer, he discovers it is more than a slow game for sissies and old men.

6842. Walker, Frank. *Vipers and Company* (Macmillan, 1976) 4–6. A witch is married to a member of Parliament and plots to destroy London's old buildings and replace them with office buildings and parking garages.

6843. ____. *Pop Go the Vipers* (Macmillan, 1979) 4–6. Agatha and Lancelot, a wicked witch and her husband, want to murder music and provide food of Hate. Peter and Jane, hero and heroine, thwart the evil purposes.

6844. Wallner, Alexandra. *Adventures of Strawberry Shortcake and Her Friends* (Random, 1980) k–3. The Strawberry kids make an unusual scarecrow to frighten birds away from their crops.

6845. ____. *Strawberry Shortcake and the Winter That Would Not End* (Random, 1982) k–3. In their search for a stolen magic snow crystal on which the coming of spring depends, the kids and animals of Strawberryland come in contact with a lonely old badger.

6846. Wallqvister, Gun-Britt. *My Cat* (Harper, 1982) k–3. A young girl describes the habits and mischief of her little black cat, Miss.

6847. ____. *My Cat Has Kittens* (Harper, 1982) k–3. A young child describes the fun and surprises of a day with her cat Miss' four newborn kittens.

6848. Walstrip, Lele. *White Harvest* (Longmans, 1960) 4–6. Susan is a cotton picker who wants a permanent home and to have a chance to go to school. She gets her chance when her father accepts a New Mexico homesteading grant.

6849. ____. *Purple Hills* (Longmans, 1961) 4–6. Susan has new friends, a new life and new problems: ranch vs. settlers, feuds, and family squabbles.

6850. Walter, Mildred. *Lillie of Watts* (Ritchie, 1969) 4–6. Lillie, 11, was a black girl who was to "baby-sit" an expensive cat. She lets the cat out and is ordered to go find it or don't come back. She sees reality as she searches the streets for the cat.

6851. ____. *Lillie of Watts Takes a Giant Step* (Doubleday, 1971) 4–6. Lillie is going to junior high for the first time. She experiences jealousy, envy, friendship and all the things a shy, poor girl goes through in a black/white world.

6852. Walter, Mildred. *Mariah Loves Rock* (Bradbury, 1988) 4–6. As fifth grade comes to an end, Mariah, who idolizes a famous rock star, experiences many misgivings, as does every member of her family, about the arrival of a half-sister who is coming to live with them.

6853. ____. *Mariah Keeps Cool* (Bradbury, 1990) 4–6. Mariah, 12, envisions a great summer competing as a diver and planning a surprise party for her sister Lynn but half-sister Denise proves a cloud in Mariah's sunny summer.

6854. Ward, Sally. *Punky Spends the Day* (Dutton, 1989) k–3. Spending the day with her grandparents, Punky makes a hideout, rakes leaves and gets ready for a bedtime story.

6855. ____. *Punky Goes Fishing* (Dutton, 1991) k–3. A little girl spends the day fishing with her grandfather.

6856. Warner, Gertrude. *Boxcar Children* (Whitman, 1948) 4–6. The Alden orphans make their home in an abandoned boxcar. They are independent and resourceful. An understanding grandfather is discovered by the end of the book.

6857. ____. *Surprise Island* (Scott Foresman, 1951) 4–6. The Boxcar children spend the summer finding and exploring an Indian cave. They also find a previously unknown cousin.

6858. ____. *Yellow House Mystery* (Whitman, 1954) 4–6. The Boxcar children live with a wealthy grandfather and are involved in yet another mystery.

6859. ____. *Mystery Ranch* (Whitman, 1958) 4–6. Violet and Jessie begin an adventure when they journey to Centerville to keep Aunt Jane company on the family ranch.

6860. ____. *Mike's Mystery* (Whitman, 1960) 4–6. Henry, Violet, Jessie and Benny are spending the summer out west on a ranch. There they meet their old friend Mike. When Mike is blamed for starting a fire, the children know he is innocent. They must find out who is behind this false accusation.

6861. ____. *Blue Bay Mystery* (Whitman, 1961) 4–6. The Aldens find a castaway on a South Sea Island. How did he get there and who is he?

6862. ____. *Woodshed Mystery* (Whitman, 1962) 4–6. The Boxcar children are involved in a double mystery: one about Aunt Jane in her youth and the other going even farther back the early days of the Revolutionary War.

6863. ____. *Lighthouse Mystery* (Whitman, 1963) 4–6. Henry, Violet, Jessie and Benny now live with their grandfather and spend the summer in a lighthouse. Jessie sees a woman one night walking the grounds. Jessie's dog, Watch, wakes up growling. Henry finds a note in the sand. They finally solve these mysteries.

6864. ____. *Mountain Top Mystery* (Whitman, 1964/1992) 4–6. A family starts out on a one-day mountain climbing trip that becomes very exciting. In fact, it becomes an adventure for the former "boxcar" family and they unearth some mysteries and have a fine time in the process.

6865. ____. *Schoolhouse Mystery* (Whitman, 1965) 4–6. The Boxcar children are staying at an island fishing village. This time the mystery is about a crooked coin dealer. They also set up a school to teach the island children.

6866. ____. *Caboose Mystery* (Whitman, 1966) 4–6. The Boxcar children and their grandfather travel in what was once a circus train car. The mystery is about a lost necklace.

6867. ____. *Houseboat Mystery* (Whitman, 1967) 4–6. The Boxcar children are on a houseboat. A large black car roars through the village; horses who appear to be well cared for look starved. They help to capture two crooks and free the village of them.

6868. ____. *Snowbound Mystery* (Whitman, 1968) 4–6. A family, snowbound in a vacation cabin, discover adventures in surrounding wildlife, three children they find in the snow, and the search for a lost recipe.

6869. ____. *Tree House Mystery* (Whitman, 1969) 4–6. The Boxcar children help the new neighbor boys to build a tree house. They find a lost spyglass and a secret room in the attic.

6870. ____. *Bicycle Mystery* (Whitman, 1970) 4–6. The Boxcar children are on a bicycle trip to visit Aunt Jane. They stop and do some chores and stay in an abandoned house. They are followed by a stray dog that plays a big role in the mystery.

6871. ____. *Mystery in the Sand* (Whitman, 1971) 4–6. The Boxcar children are going to spend the summer in a beach house. They find a locket with a picture of a cat and initials R.L. They find information about the owner and the Tower House.

6872. ____. *Mystery Behind the Wall* (Whitman, 1973) 4–6. The Boxcar children and Rory follow clues from a sewing shop to a dollhouse to a clock where they find the treasure of coins.

6873. ____. *Bus Station Mystery* (Whitman, 1974) 4–6. The Boxcar children are on their way to a science hobby fair. There is a fight at the bus station about air pollution and a paint factory. They find a solution that is good for all.

6874. ____. *Benny Uncovers a Mystery* (Whitman, 1976) 4–6. Henry and Benny take summer jobs at a department store and strange letters and extra merchandise create a mystery that seems to point to the brothers.

6875. ____. *Haunted Cabin Mystery* (Whitman, 1991) 4–6. The Alden children travel on a Mississippi paddle-wheel steamer to visit an old family friend in his cabin near Hannibal and try to discover who is responsible for the mysterious activities near the house.

6876. ____. *Deserted Library Mystery* (Whitman, 1991) 4–6. At an old library, the Alden children discover a boy who needs their help and a stranger who is after a valuable object they found in the library.

6877. ____. *Animal Shelter Mystery* (Whitman, 1991) 4–6. The Alden children save an old woman's house, land and all the animals in her animal shelter from greedy contractors.

6878. ____. *Old Motel Mystery* (Whitman, 1991) 4–6. Someone is trying to put Aunt Jane's motel out of business, but the Alden children aren't going to let that happen.

6879. ____. *Mystery of the Hidden Painting* (Whitman, 1992) 4–6. The Alden children hunt for their late grandmother's necklace that has been missing for years.

6880. ____. *Amusement Park Mystery* (Whitman, 1992) 4–6. The Aldens search for carousel horses that have disappeared from the amusement park.

6881. ____. *Mystery of the Mixed-up Zoo* (Whitman, 1992) 4–6. The Alden children investigate various mix-ups at a zoo run by their grandfather's friend in an effort to save it, not only from pranksters but also from the town council.

6882. ____. *Camp-Out Mystery* (Whitman, 1992) 4–6. While on a camping trip with their grandfather, the Alden children try to find out about the loud music and missing food that threatens to scare away other campers.

6883. ____. *Mystery Girl* (Whitman, 1992) 4–6. While helping run Jerry Taylor's general store, the Alden children investigate his mysterious employee Nancy.

6884. ____. *Mystery Cruise* (Whitman, 1992) 4–6. While on a cruise with their grandfather, The Alden children help discover who is behind the mysterious troubles of the ship—disconnected phone lines, en-

gine trouble, a man overboard—and still have fun sightseeing, eating and swimming.

6885. ____. *Disappearing Friend Mystery* (Whitman, 1992) 4–6. At the same time that the Alden children's efforts to raise money for a new hospital wing are being sabotaged by nasty tricks, they find their attempts to befriend the new girl Beth frustrated by her strange behavior.

6886. ____. *Mystery of the Singing Ghost* (Whitman, 1992) 4–6. While helping fix up the old house their cousins have bought, the Aldens hear stories about it being haunted and find evidence suggesting that there may be a ghost there.

6887. ____. *Mystery in the Snow* (Whitman, 1992) 4–6. When the Alden children accompany their grandfather to the Snow Haven Lodge, a series of odd occurrences threaten to disrupt the annual winter games.

6888. ____. *Pizza Mystery* (Whitman, 1993) 4–6. When their favorite pizza restaurant almost goes out of business, the Alden children try to help their friends stay open while they find out who is behind all their problems.

6889. ____. *Mystery Horse* (Whitman, 1993) 4–6. When their grandfather arranges for them to spend two weeks at Sunny Oaks, the four Alden children enjoy settling into the routine of farm life but become suspicious about a mysterious horse locked in the stable.

6890. ____. *Mystery at the Dog Show* (Whitman, 1993) 4–6. The Alden children suspect someone of trying to sabotage the local dog show.

6891. ____. *Castle Mystery* (Whitman, 1993) 4–6. The Alden children have another mystery to solve when they visit a castle and must figure out which one of the quests has stolen the Stradivarius violin.

6892. ____. *Mystery of the Lost Village* (Whitman, 1993) 4–6. While visiting a Navaho Indian reservation, the Aldens try to save a forest under threat of development by proving it is the site of a lost buried village, but someone is sabotaging their dig.

6893. ____. *Mystery of the Purple Pool* (Whitman, 1994) 4–6. While staying at a hotel in New York City, the Aldens investigate a series of annoying pranks plaguing the management and guests.

6894. ____. *Ghost Ship Mystery* (Whitman, 1994) 4–6. While visiting the seaport of Ragged Cove the Alden children find the ship's log of the Flying Cloud, shipwrecked in 1869, supposedly during a mutiny.

6895. ____. *Canoe Trip Mystery* (Whitman, 1994) 4–6. While canoeing and backpacking near Timberwolf Lake, the Aldens receive strange warnings to stay away from the area and stumble upon clues to a missing cache of stolen coins.

6896. ____. *Mystery of the Hidden Beach* (Whitman, 1994) 4–6. While visiting the Florida Keys, the Aldens encounter suspicious characters, strange incidents at night and a plot to steal valuable coral.

6897. ____. *Mystery of the Missing Cat* (Whitman,

1994) 4–6. The mysterious disappearance of a reclusive neighbor's cat involves the Boxcar children in some complicated detective work.

6898. ____. *Mystery on Stage* (Whitman, 1994) 4–6. The Aldens become involved in a community theater production of "The Wizard of Oz," which is systematically and mysteriously being sabotaged.

6899. ____. *Dinosaur Mystery* (Whitman, 1995) 4–6. When the Aldens go to the Pickering Natural History Museum to assist with the opening of a dinosaur exhibit, their work is hampered by a series of mysterious happenings.

6900. ____. *Mystery of the Stolen Music* (Whitman, 1995) 4–6. The Alden children are thrilled when a famous orchestra comes to their town to perform and when the original Mozart score turns up missing, they solve the mystery of its disappearance.

6901. ____. *Chocolate Sundae Mystery* (Whitman, 1995) 4–6. The Boxcar children investigate when ice cream and other items start disappearing from their favorite ice cream parlor.

6902. ____. *Mystery of the Hot Air Balloon* (Whitman, 1995) 4–6. Benny wants adventure and finds it as he and the other Alden children help uncover the plan of those who would prevent ballooning from coming to Lloyd's Landing.

6903. ____. *Mystery Bookstore* (Whitman, 1995) 4–6. When their grandfather buys a bookstore at auction, the Alden children help clean it up and discover that several people seem to be obsessed with the store and its contents.

6904. ____. *Mystery of the Stolen Boxcar* (Whitman, 1995) 4–6. The Alden children plan to ride in their boxcar at the Greenfield Founders Day Parade, but the newly refurbished boxcar is stolen a couple of days before the big event.

6905. ____. *Mystery in the Cave* (Whitman, 1996) 4–6. While exploring the caves around Dragon's Mouth Cavern, a series of unusual and somewhat frightening events convinces the Alden children that someone does not want them around.

6906. ____. *Mystery on the Train* (Whitman, 1996) 4–6. The Boxcar children and Aunt Jane are heading to San Francisco by train. A woman's portfolio is stolen. She tells the Aldens that it contained valuable old movie posters she had inherited. Three are suspected: the porter, Mr. Reeves and a mysterious man in sunglasses.

6907. ____. *Mystery of the Lost Mine* (Whitman, 1996) 4–6. The Aldens are traveling in an RV in Arizona. They meet Luis Garcia and learn of the Lost Dutchman's Mine where a fortune of gold is hidden. Luis has stone pictures of the mine but they disappear and the Boxcar children have another mystery to solve.

6908. ____. *Guide Dog Mystery* (Whitman, 1996) 4–6. Mrs. Carter invites the Aldens to spend a week at the Greenfield Guide Dog School. Jason, the instructor, shows them how the dogs are trained. They meet Anna, a new student and her dog, Ginger. But Ginger is stolen and another mystery is to be solved.

6909. Warner, Gertrude. *Mystery on the Ice* (Whitman, 1994) 4–6. The Alden children investigate when Mrs. Murray's jewels are stolen during a party for the Starlight Skating Troupe.

6910. ____. *Mystery in Washington, D.C.* (Whitman, 1994) 4–6. The Alden children suspect that the other guests are somehow involved when things begin to disappear at the bed and breakfast where they are staying in Washington, D.C.

6911. ____. *Mystery at Snowflake Inn* (Whitman, 1994) 4–6. While staying at an eighteenth century inn the Boxcar children become curious about the mysterious "accidents" that keep plaguing the owners.

6912. ____. *Mystery at the Ballpark* (Whitman, 1995) 4–6. The Alden children uncover a plot to sabotage the Greenfield Bears baseball team.

6913. ____. *Pilgrim Village Mystery* (Whitman, 1995) 4–6. When the Alden children spend a week visiting a Pilgrim Village, they uncover a mystery behind the unusual happenings at the historic site.

6914. ____. *Mystery at the Fair* (Whitman, 1996) 4–6. The Boxcar children want to buy Grandfather a birthday present for $50.00. They try to earn money by entering their crafts, artwork and blueberry pie in a county fair contest. But someone is sabotaging the fair and the Aldens must find out who.

6915. Warren, Jean. *Huff and Puff on Halloween* (Warren, 1993) k–3. Two clouds play a Halloween trick on some trick-or-treaters.

6916. ____. *Huff and Puff on Thanksgiving* (Warren, 1993) k–3. Two clouds celebrate Thanksgiving with their family.

6917. ____. *Huff and Puff Around the World* (Warren, 1994) k–3. Two cloud characters travel around the world, seeing such sights as Big Ben, the Alps, the pyramids in Egypt, and China's Great Wall.

6918. ____. *Huff and Puff Go to School* (Warren, 1994) k–3. Two cloud characters go off to school in the fall and discover that learning shapes, colors and numbers is fun.

6919. ____. *Huff and Puff's April Showers* (Warren, 1994) k–3. Huff and Puff are two child-like clouds who strive to earn money to buy their mother a Mother's Day present. They end up giving her the gift of spring.

6920. ____. *Huff and Puff Go to Camp* (Warren, 1995) k–3. The cloud characters go off to Camp Milky Way where they eat around the campfire, learn to swim, and sleep in tents.

6921. ____. *Huff and Puff on Groundhog Day* (Warren, 1995) k-3. Huff and Puff cover the sun so that a groundhog can come out and enjoy an early spring day without worrying about seeing its shadow.

6922. Watanabe, Shigeo. *How Do I Put It On? Getting Dressed* (Collins, 1979) k–3. A bear demonstrates the right and wrong way to put on a shirt, pants, cap and shoes.

6923. ____. *What a Good Lunch! Eating* (Collins, 1980) k–3. Despite difficulties, a young deer eats his lunch all by himself.

6924. ____. *How Do I Eat It?* (Puffin, 1980) k–3. Baby Bear is trying out, with his usual excess of enthusiasm over success, the proper method of coping with problem foods like spaghetti.

6925. ____. *Get Set! Go!* (Philomel, 1981) k–3. Though Bear does not win the obstacle race, he demonstrates perseverance in getting through it.

6926. ____. *I'm the King of the Castle! Playing Alone* (Philomel, 1982) k–3. Using his shovel and pail, Bear constructs a land where he is king.

6927. ____. *I Can Ride It! Setting Goals* (Philomel, 1982) k–3. Not content to ride his tricycle or the two-wheeler, a bear attempts more difficult feats.

6928. ____. *Where's My Daddy?* (Philomel, 1982) k–3. A little bear asks passersby if they have seen his daddy.

6929. ____. *I Can Do It* (Philomel, 1982) k–3. Little Bear struggles with various wheeled vehicles. "I can roller skate." Crash! "I can eat." "I can dress myself." He grapples with the world around him with near successes.

6930. ____. *I Can Build a House* (Philomel, 1983) k–3. Bear perseveres until he finds just the right material for building the perfect house.

6931. ____. *I Can Take a Walk* (Philomel, 1984) k–3. Taking a walk all by himself, a young bear is glad to have his father join him on the way home.

6932. ____. *I'm Going for a Walk! Testing Limits* (Philomel, 1984) k–3. Little Bear, dressed in trousers, does all the things his human counterparts would do on a morning walk.

6933. ____. *Daddy, Play with Me* (Philomel, 1985) k–3. A young bear enjoys playing with his father.

6934. ____. *I'm Playing with Papa* (Philomel, 1985) k–3. Little Bear enjoys traditional activities such as piggyback, horse and rider, rough and tumble, cuddle and read until he and Papa are both exhausted.

6935. ____. *I Can Take a Bath* (Philomel, 1987) k–3. A young bear is reluctant to take a bath until he gets into the tub with his father and they have fun together.

6936. ____. *I'm Having a Bath with Papa* (Philomel, 1987) k–3. Little Bear plays in the sand, and needs to wash it off by sharing his bath with Papa. A nice family story.

6937. ____. *It's My Birthday* (Philomel, 1988) k–3. Bear's fourth birthday serves as an occasion for his family to go through the photo album commemorating his birth, his life as a baby and all his past birthdays.

6938. ____. *Ice Cream Is Falling* (Philomel, 1989) k–3. Bear and his friends have a wonderful time playing in the snow.

6939. ____. *Let's Go Swimming* (Philomel, 1990) k–3. Bear enjoys playing in the water, but he is not at all sure about learning to swim in the pool in the park.

6940. Watts, Marjorie Ann. *Crocodile Medicine* (Deutsch, 1977) k–3. Crocodile isn't the easiest patient in the hospital, nor are his friends the best behaved visitors; but he does make life in the children's ward much more fun.

6941. ____. *Crocodile Plaster* (Deutsch, 1984) k–3. Crocodile is in the hospital because of pains. The doctor finds nothing wrong. But his tail is broken in the door of the X-ray room and must be set in plaster.

6942. ____. *Crocodile Teeth* (Deutsch, 1987) k–3.

6943. Wayne, Jenifer. *Sprout* (McGraw, 1976) 3–5. A boy with a passion for elephants sets out to buy one, only to meet with disaster.

6944. ____. *Sprout and the Dogsitter* (McGraw, 1977) 3–5. Sprout joins a party of carol singers on Christmas Eve but before the evening is over loses both them and his new coat.

6945. ____. *Sprout and the Helicopter* (McGraw, 1974) 3–5. The desire to own a rubber dinghy ignites Sprout's characteristically strong sense of purpose.

6946. ____. *Sprout's Window Cleaner* (McGraw, 1976) 3–5. Sprout tries to grow an onion with the help of his friends: the window cleaner and the elephant lady.

6947. ____. *Sprout and the Magician* (McGraw, 1976) 3–5. Sprout attends his sister's birthday party looking forward to the food but little else. However, Meri, the magician has made Tilly's rabbit disappear and chaos takes over.

6948. Webb, Jackie. *Wilkes the Wizard* (Grofton, 1985) 4–6.

6949. ____. *Wilkes the Wizard and the S.P.A.M.* (Grofton, 1986) 4–6. While walking the Gram Tam bumps into Jay, a Texan, who sees the tourist potential of Diddlesdorf. Mr. Wilkes the Wizard, physicist and Peony Moondrop, the prime minister, are supportive. The idea is opposed by S.P.A.M.—Sensible People Against Magic.

6950. Weil, Lisl. *Melissa* (Macmillan, 1966) k–3. Melissa and her mother go to visit Aunt Bertha and Uncle Carol on their farm. Melissa thinks it will be a dull time. But aside from the animals and gypsies, Melissa gets her wish for an exciting adventure.

6951. ____. *Melissa's Friend Fabrizzio* (Macmillan, 1967) k–3. The last day of her vacation in Venice is full of romantic adventure for a little girl trying to stay clean and be good.

6952. Weilerstein, Sadie. *K'tonton on an Island in the Sea* (JPSA, 1976) 3-5. Adventures of a thumb-sized Jewish boy who must fend for himself when stranded on an island.

6953. ____. *Best of K'tonton* (JPSA, 1980) 3–5. Contains: "Adventures of K'tonton"; "K'tonton in Israel"; "K'tonton on an Island in the Sea."

6954. ____. *K'tonton in the Circus* (JPSA, 1981)

3–5. The adventures of a thumb-sized Jewish boy who joins the circus by mistake and celebrates Hanukkah with his circus friends.

6955. _____. *K'tonton in Jerusalem: Adventure in the Old City* (Chernak, 1988) 3–5.

6956. _____. *K'tonton on Kibbutz* (Chernak, 1988) 3–5.

6957. _____. *Visit with K'tonton* (Chernak, 1988) 3–5.

6958. _____. *K'tonton's Sukkot Adventure* (JPSA, 1993) 3–5. A small, thumb-sized boy is born to aging Jewish parents and has an adventure at the synagogue during the holiday of Sukkot.

6959. _____. *K'tonton's Yom Kippur Kitten* (JPSA, 1995) 3–5. After allowing a small kitten to take the blame for something he did, K'tonton, a thumb-sized young boy, feels guilty when he goes to services at the synagogue on Yom Kippur.

6960. _____. *K'tonton in Israel* (JPSA, 1988) 3–5.

6961. Weinberg, Larry. *Forgetful Bears* (Clarion, 1982) k–3. When the Forgetful Bear family decides to go on a picnic, they forget the food, the car, their grandfather and their own names, but they have a good time anyway.

6962. _____. *Forgetfuls Give a Wedding* (Scholastic, 1983) k–3. Confusion arises when a family of forgetful bears tries to plan a wedding.

6963. _____. *Forgetful Bears Meet Mr. Memory* (Scholastic, 1987) k–3. The Forgetful Bears cannot remember where they put the airplane tickets for their vacation, or even where they are going, until they get help from a wise old elephant named Mr. Memory.

6964. _____. *Forgetful Bears Help Santa* (Scholastic, 1988) k–3. When Mr. Forgetful Bear sees Santa's clothes and reindeer, he forgets who he is and delivers toys to children.

6965. Weir, Rosemary. *Albert the Dragon* (Abelard, 1961) 3–5. Albert's life is friendless and unexciting until he makes the acquaintance of Tony, who understands that even dragons need a little fun and companionship.

6966. _____. *Further Adventures of Albert the Dragon* (Abelard, 1964) 3–5. Albert, the vegetarian dragon, lives in a cave just outside a little fishing village. Tony is his true friend. They have fun together and also do brave deeds.

6967. _____. *Albert the Dragon and the Centaur* (Abelard, 1968) 3–5. Albert, a lonely dragon, wanted to be needed and in a short time became the guardian of a baby centaur that had run away from a cruel circus owner.

6968. _____. *Albert's World Tour* (Abelard, 1978) 3–5. Albert, a good natured, vegetarian dragon, finds his adopted children, the Dragonettes, a little too much for him. His friend Tony suggests a world tour. They set off and meet a unicorn, a helpful magician and also some lions. They arrive safely back home and Albert does not want to travel anymore.

6969. _____. *Albert and the Dragonettes* (Abelard, 1978) 3–5. Albert faces real human problems: a one-parent family with two spoiled kids and a cave that is too small for the three of them. There is also an unpleasant neighbor—a cowardly sea monster next door.

6970. Weir, Rosemary. *Uncle Barney and the Sleep-Destroyer* (Abelard, 1975) 2–4. Uncle Barney wants to invent something that does away with sleep (a real time waster). James is the guinea pig for all his (awry) inventions. The test of the success of his latest invention ends with Uncle Barney and James asleep in the police station.

6971. _____. *Uncle Barney and the Shrink-Drink* (Abelard, 1977) 2–4. Uncle Barney is an inventor. He wants to stop the pollution explosion by miniaturizing people. The Worleys are reduced successfully but the dolls' house fixtures don't work. The police are looking for this missing family. Uncle Barney leaves his nephew to clean up his mess.

6972. Weir, Rosemary. *Pyewacket* (Abelard, 1967) 4–6. The seven cats of Pig Lane make a truce with the rats and mice while they try to drive out their humans.

6973. _____. *Pyewacket and Son* (Abelard, 1981) 4–6. Chi Ki is a suave Siamese; Pete an excitable, mixed-up kitten with an unhappy childhood. Pyewacket is disreputable but a leader. They are the Official Rodent Exterminators at a cat food factory. Pigwiggin is accused of opening a crate of fish. Rats are not guilty; it is the Moggy Monsters and Whiskey Willis. Pigwiggins infiltrates the gang to learn about their entry.

6974. Weiss, Ellen. *Mokey's Birthday Present* (Muppet, 1985) k–3. Mokey Fraggle has a wonderful birthday but is in a dilemma when her best friend gives her a present that she doesn't like.

6975. _____. *Cotterpin's Perfect Building* (Muppet, 1986) k–3. After their assistant architect designs the "perfect building," the Doozers of Fraggle Rock stop building things and must cope with the resulting boredom.

(For additional books on the Fraggles, Boober, Gobo, Mokey, Red or Wembley, *see* Brennan, Joseph; Calder, Lyn; Calmenson, Stephanie; Gilkow, Louise; Gilmour, H.B.; Grand, Rebecca; Muntean, Michaela; Perlberg, Deborah; Stevenson, Jocelyn; Teitelbaum, Michael; Young, David.)

6976. Weiss, Nicki. *Maude and Sally* (Greenwillow, 1983) k–3. When her best friend Sally goes to summer camp, Maude finds she can become best friends with Emmylou also.

6977. _____. *Battle Day at Camp Delmont* (Greenwillow, 1985) k–3. While at camp together, Maude and Sally learn that they can play competitively against each other and still be best friends.

6978. Weiss, Nicki. *Weekend at Muskrat Lake* (Greenwillow, 1984) k–3. Pearl and her family spend a weekend at a lake and enjoy many activities including swimming, blueberry picking and fishing.
6979. ____. *Princess Pearl* (Greenwillow, 1986) k–3. Rosemary is mean to her younger sister Pearl until she sees Pearl's friend act mean toward her too.

6980. Welch, James. *Winter in the Blood* (Harper, 1974) 5–8. A young Indian is shadowed by childhood memories of his brother's death. Now in manhood, he indifferently faces obstacles in his daily path.
6981. ____. *Death of Jim Loney* (Penguin, 1987) 5–8. Jim Loney is alienated from society and his attempts at interpersonal relationships are not good.

6982. Wellman, Manly. *Ghost Battalion* (Washburn, 1958) 4–8. Clay goes to join the Confederates. He meets the Iron Scouts who work behind Union lines and helps them in many encounters. He is captured and jailed.
6983. ____. *Ride, Rebels* (Washburn, 1959) 5–8. Clay, a Confederate scout, is fighting for his life. There is lots of action and suspense about the end of the American Civil War.

6984. Wellman, Manly. *Rifles at Ramsour's Mill* (Washburn, 1961) 5–8. Zack is plagued by conflicting loyalties when the Revolutionary War breaks out. He decides to join the Rebels and becomes a spy for the Americans.
6985. ____. *Battle for King's Mountain* (Washburn, 1962) 5–8. Zack and Enoch are fighting in the Revolutionary War. There is much humor and a good feeling is experienced when you read how the war is felt by simple people.
6986. ____. *Clash on the Catawba* (Washburn, 1962) 5–8. Zack and his buddy Enoch are supporting the Rebels. There are humorous incidents in this tense story about the Revolutionary War and the divided loyalties of the people involved.

6987. Wellman, Manly. *Mystery of the Lost Valley* (Nelson, 1948) 5–8. Rand and Jeb are lost in Utah, trapped by a snowstorm. They learn how to survive the winter, hunt for food, make fire, get clothes and fight off hostile Indians.
6988. ____. *Wild Dog of Downing Creek* (Nelson, 1952) 5–8. Randy and Jeb solve the mystery of the wild dog pack that is stealing the stock and of the blind man that is leading them.

6989. Wells, Rosemary. *Max's New Suit* (Dial, 1979) k–3. Max figures out a new way to wear his hated new suit.
6990. ____. *Max's First Word* (Dial, 1979) k–3. Max learns a more sophisticated word than the ones his sister tries to teach him.
6991. ____. *Max's Toys* (Dial, 1979) k–3. Introduces the numbers one through ten as Max finally trades all his toys for his sister's doll.
6992. ____. *Max's Dragon Shirt* (Dial, 1979) k–3. On a shopping trip to a department store, Max's determination to get a dragon shirt leads him away from his distracted sister and into trouble.
6993. ____. *Max's Ride* (Dial, 1979) k–3. As Max's baby carriage careens unattended down a hill, the reader is introduced to nine words: go, down, stop, over, up, under, between and into.
6994. ____. *Max's Bedtime* (Dial, 1985) k–3. Though Max's sister offers him her stuffed animals, he cannot sleep without his red rubber elephant.
6995. ____. *Max's Breakfast* (Dial, 1985) k–3. Max's sister Ruby tries hard to get him to eat his breakfast egg.
6996. ____. *Max's Bath* (Dial, 1985) k–3. Ruby gives her brother Max two baths, but he winds up dirtier than ever.
6997. ____. *Max's Birthday* (Dial, 1985) k–3. Max's sister Ruby gives him a windup toy dragon for his birthday.
6998. ____. *Max's Christmas* (Dial, 1986) k–3. Despite his sister Ruby's admonitions, Max waits up on Christmas Eve to see Santa Claus coming down the chimney.
6999. ____. *Hooray for Max* (Dial, 1986) k–3.
7000. ____. *Max's Chocolate Chicken* (Dial, 1989) k–3. Max and his sister Ruby go on an egg hunt and vie with each other for the prize—a chocolate chicken.
7001. ____. *Max and Ruby's First Green Myth* (Dial, 1993) k–3. Ruby tries to stop her younger brother from sneaking into her room and snooping by reading him an altered version of "Pandora's Box."

7002. Wells, Rosemary. *Edward in Deep Water* (Dial, 1995) k–3. Edward, a shy young bear is not ready for birthday pool parties with high-spirited grade school bears.
7003. ____. *Edward Is Unready for School* (Dial, 1995) k–3. Edward a shy young bear is not ready for play school and feels out of place when surrounded by students who are ready, busy and happy.
7004. ____. *Edward's Overwhelming Overnight* (Dial, 1995) k–3. Edward's parents tell him that because of the snow he will have to stay overnight with his friend Anthony, but Edward finds this overwhelming.

7005. Wensell, Ulises. *Jackson Family: Mum and Dad* (Rand, 1977) 3–5. Mum has a part-time job as a dental receptionist. She makes breakfast, bathes the baby, shops at the supermarket and drives.
7006. ____. *Jackson Family: Smudge* (Rand, 1977) 3–5.
7007. ____. *Jackson Family: David* (Rand, 1977) 3–5.
7008. ____. *Jackson Family: Jenny and Steve* (Rand, 1978) 3–5. A story written about himself and his

older sister Jenny. They have unisex hair styles and unisex clothes.

7009. ____. *Come to Our House* (Rand, 1978) 3–5. A young brother and sister describe their family and their daily activities.

7010. ____. *Everyday Life* (Rand, 1978) 3–5. A book that shows daddy at the factory, Steve in school, a visit to a doctor's surgery and a film show at a neighbor's house.

7011. ____. *Our Home* (Rand, 1979) 3–5. In this book the emphasis is on the need for space and quiet for a happy family life.

7012. ____. *Uncle George and Auntie Mary* (Rand, 1979) 3–5. The young trendy Aunt Mary and Uncle George (he is an architecture student; she runs a dress shop) take the children to the museum, the airport and the fair. Mary and George live with Grandma and Grandpa Jackson.

7013. West, Colin. *King of Kennelwick Castle* (Lippincott, 1986) k–3. A cumulative tale relating how the king of Kennelwick castle receives a mysterious bundle from the Queen of Spain for his birthday present.

7014. ____. *King's Toothache* (Lippincott, 1988) k–3. Unable to find a dentist for the king's toothache, Nurse Mary tries a baker, a town crier, and a sailor before the poor man gets relief.

7015. West, Colin. *Monty, a Dog Who Wears Glasses* (Dutton, 1990) 3–5. Adventures of Monty, the dog who wears glasses to remind himself to stay out of trouble.

7016. ____. *Shape Up, Monty* (Dutton, 1991) 3–5. Relates the humorous adventures of Monty, a very clumsy dog.

7017. ____. *Monty Bites Back* (Dutton, 1990) 3–5.

7018. ____. *Monty: Up to His Neck in Trouble* (Dutton, 1992) 3–5.

7019. West, Nick. *Three Investigators and the Coughing Dragon* (Random, 1970) 4–6. When five dogs disappear from a seaside town and a dragon is sighted off-shore, the three investigators look into the situation.

7020. ____. *Three Investigators in the Mystery of the Nervous Lion* (Random, 1971) 4–6. Hired to discover why a wild animal farm's tame lion has become unpredictably nervous, three young detectives begin an investigation that uncovers a smuggling operation.

(For other books about the "Three Investigators," *see* Arden, William; Arthur, Robert; Carey, M.V.)

7021. Wheeler, Cindy. *Marmalade's Snowy Day* (Random, 1982) k–3. Marmalade, the cat, looks for a warm place to hide from the snow outside.

7022. ____. *Marmalade's Yellow Leaf* (Random, 1982) k–3. Marmalade, a cat, causes a commotion when he tries to retrieve a particular yellow leaf.

7023. ____. *Marmalade's Nap* (Knopf, 1983) k–3. Marmalade, the cat, looks for a quiet place in the barn to sleep, away from all the baby animals.

7024. ____. *Marmalade's Picnic* (Random, 1983) k–3. Marmalade, the cat, finds a satisfying way to accompany his owner on a picnic.

7025. ____. *Marmalade's Christmas Present* (Random, 1984) k–3. Marmalade, the cat, finds a very lively surprise waiting for him under the tree on Christmas morning.

7026. White, Diana. *Bother with Boris* (Dutton, 1989) k–3.

7027. ____. *No Bath for Boris* (Dutton, 1990) k–3. Boris, the little polar bear, needs a lot of persuasion to take his bath.

7028. Whitehead, Victoria. *Chimney Witches* (Orchard, 1987) 3–5. When Ellen, eight, meets the witches who live in the chimney of her house, she experiences the most exciting Halloween in her life.

7029. ____. *Chimney Witch Chase* (Orchard, 1988) 3–5. Ellen's efforts to get chosen for a school sports competition are complicated by the mischievous witch boy who lives in her chimney and likes to go for broomstick rides at the most awkward times.

7030. ____. *Witches of Creaky Cranky Castle* (Orchard, 1991) 3–5. The witches of Creaky Cranky Castle are under threat from Lady Darkella. They need help from a child in the Real World, so they send out junk mail. Trina wins a guided tour of the castle in one of these letters and she goes. There she writes the "Witches Weekly" and scares off Lady Darkella.

7031. Whitmore, Adam. *Max Leaves Home* (Burdett, 1986) k–3. Mortified because he has no tail, Max the cat leaves his home to wander through London in search of his missing appendage.

7032. ____. *Max In America* (Burdett, 1986) k–3. In search of his missing appendage, Max the tailless cat travels to New York City and then across country to San Francisco.

7033. ____. *Max in India* (Burdett, 1986) k–3. Max the cat's search for his missing tail takes him to India, where he befriends a tiger and has several dangerous adventures.

7034. ____. *Max in Australia* (Burdett, 1986) k–3. Max the tailless cat travels to Australia, where he searches for his missing appendage among the many unusual animals there.

7035. Whybrow, Ian. *Sniff Stories* (Bodley, 1989) 4–6. Ben, ten, has a dog named Sniff. He is always in trouble and Ben tries to ignore him. There are ten different crazy stories of Ben, his 2½-year-old sister and, of course, Sniff.

7036. ____. *Sniff Bounces Back* (Bodley, 1991) 4–6. Sniff, the dog, and his owner Ben put up with a nuisance little sister, a fussy mom and an immature dad.

7037. Wicks, Susan. *Katie and Orbie Pick Up Garbage* (Key Porter, 1991) k–3. Orbie is a sad-eyed orphan from a planet destroyed by ecological disaster, who is befriended by Katie, the little Earth girl who vows not to allow her planet to be similarly damaged. The following books cover other ecology topics.
7038. ____. *Katie and Orbie Plant a Tree* (Key Porter, 1991) k–3.
7039. ____. *Katie and Orbie Switch Off the Lights* (Key Porter, 1991) k–3.
7040. ____. *Katie and Orbie Save the Planet* (Key Porter, 1991) k–3.

7041. Wild, Robin. *Bears' ABC Book* (Lippincott, 1977) k–3. Three bears rummaging in a dump find an object for each letter of the alphabet.
7042. ____. *Bears' Counting Book* (Lippincott, 1978) k–3. While following the misadventures of three bears exploring an empty house, the reader is introduced to the numbers from one to ten and the numbers 20, 30, 40 and 50.

7043. Wild, Robin . *Spot's Dogs and the Alley Cats* (Lippincott, 1979) k–3. Two rival gangs play mean tricks and do good deeds.
7044. ____. *Spot's Dogs and the Kidnappers* (Lippincott, 1981) k–3. The Alley Cats, under ferocious Klaws, kidnap studious Arthur but his friends rescue him by disguising themselves as alluring (canine) females. The malice of the cats is exercised in two further plots before the disastrous boat race brings the rival gangs into temporary harmony.

7045. Wilhelm, Hans. *Bunny Trouble* (Scholastic, 1987) k–3. Ralph the rabbit prefers playing soccer to making Easter eggs until he is captured by a farmer.
7046. ____. *More Bunny Trouble* (Scholastic, 1989) k–3. When his baby sister crawls away while he is supposed to be watching her, Ralph and the other bunnies stop decorating eggs and search for her.

7047. Wilhelm, Hans. *Schnitzel's First Christmas* (S & S, 1989) k–3. A puppy can't think what he wants for Christmas, but Santa knows just the thing.
7048. ____. *Schnitzel Is Lost* (Scholastic, 1989) k–3. Schnitzel the dog becomes separated from his best friend Pretzel when he ventures from his backyard to chase leaves.

7049. Wilhelm, Hans. *Tyrone the Horrible* (Scholastic, 1988) k–3. A little dinosaur named Boland tries several ways of dealing with the biggest bully in the swamp forest, until finally hitting on a successful tactic.
7050. ____. *Tyrone, the Double Dirty Rotten Cheat* (Scholastic, 1991) k–3. Big, bad Tyrone the dinosaur

wins all the games at Swamp Island by cheating until he foils his own attempts to cheat in the treasure hunt.
7051. ____. *Tyrone, the Dirty Rotten Cheat* (Scholastic, 1992) k–3.

7052. Wilhelm, Hans. *Waldo and the Desert Island Adventure* (Random, 1986) k–3. Michael and his dog Waldo, walking along a rainy beach, pool their imaginations to share a possible adventure involving a band of pirates and several monsters.
7053. ____. *Waldo, One, Two, Three* (Gibson, 1989) 3–5. Michael and his dog Waldo, pool their imaginations to share a possible adventure involving counting.
7054. ____. *Waldo at the Zoo* (Gibson, 1989) 3–5. Michael and his dog Waldo, pool their imaginations to share a possible adventure involving animals at the zoo.

7055. Wilkes, Marilyn. *C.L.U.T.Z.* (Dial, 1982) 4–6. C.L.U.T.Z. is not in the best of condition but he is accepted by the Pentax family as their robot because Rodney likes him on sight. He is not as efficient as a newer model but he is likable.
7056. ____. *C.L.U.T.Z. and the Fission Formula* (Dial, 1985) 4–6. Rodney, Aurora, his dog, and C.L.U.T.Z. have many misadventures. They are accused of being spies when they try to get samples of soda pop whose secret formula is suspect.

7057. Willard, Nancy. *Island of the Grass King: Further Adventures of Anatole* (Harcourt, 1979) 4–6. Anatole goes to the island of the Grass King to find a cure for Grandmother's asthma.
7058. ____. *Uncle Terrible: More Adventures of Anatole* (Harcourt, 1982) 4–6. A boy's visit to Uncle Terrible, so named because he is so terribly nice.
7059. ____. *Uncle Terrible* (Harcourt, 1982) 4–6. Anatole is faced with the formidable task of retrieving the thread of death from the wizard Arcimboldo.
7060. ____. *Sailing to Cythera* (Harcourt, 1985) 3–5. Anatole tells three stories: To cross the river he exchanges his shirt and shoes for a raft; with the help of two ravens he aids a soldier with his memory; he befriends Blimlim, a monster.

7061. Williams, Susan. *Lambing at Sheepfold Farm* (Gollancz, 1982) 2–4. A story incorporating the account of farm lambing season. They move to lambing quarters, they plan, pack and rough it. There are emergencies and rescue operations.
7062. ____. *Summer at Sheepfold Farm* (Gollancz, 1983) 2–4. Spanning a shepherd's commitments from maggot treatment and clipping to dipping and marketing, Polly and Tim detect rustlers on their sheep farm.
7063. ____. *Winter Comes to Sheepfold Farm* (Gollancz, 1985) 2–4. Polly and Tim work on their farm. The ewes are threatened by fires. Tim manages to

curb a mystery dog who is bothering the sheep. There are sheep sales, Halloween festivities, a nativity play and harvest suppers.

7064. ____. *Year at Sheepfold Farm* (Gollancz, 1986) 2–4.

7065. Williams, Ursula. *Gobbolino the Witch's Cat* (Puffin, 1942/1965) 2–4. Gobbolino, apprenticed as a kitten to the witch on the Hurricane Mountains, had the heart of a common kitchen mouser and the witch cast a spell he needed to find a normal home.

7066. ____. *Adventures of the Little Wooden Horse* (Puffin, 1938) 2–4. Uncle Peder, who made the little wooden horse, had fallen on bad times and the brave animal set out to make a fortune to help his master.

7067. ____. *Further Adventures of Gobbolino and the Little Wooden Horse* (Puffin, 1985) 2–4. Gobbolino's life is interrupted when he gets a message from his sister, Sootica, who wants to be freed from witch servitude. He meets the little wooden horse who offers him a ride to relieve his bruised paws. Both serve the cause of goodness with courage and resource.

7068. Williams, Ursula. *Toymaker's Daughter* (Meredith, 1969) 4–6. Marta is a doll-girl made by the evil toymaker, Malkin. Niclo knows she is a doll not a human but Marta does try to act human. Her "real" self wins out and she leaves to go back where she belongs.

7069. ____. *Three Toymakers* (Meredith, 1971) 4–6. Malkin creates a walking, talking doll in a contest for the best toy, she is treated like a real child. The dollhouse and musical box presented by the other toy makers cannot compete.

7070. ____. *Malkin's Mountain* (Nelson, 1972) 4–6. Malkin, an exiled selfish toymaker, wants to remove the mountain which provides the trees that Rudi, the master toymaker requires for his livelihood. Rudi attempts to overcome Malkin's evil and is captured. He is later rescued by friends.

7071. Williams, Vera. *Chair For My Mother* (Greenwillow, 1982) k–3. A child, her waitress mother, and her grandmother save dimes to buy a comfortable armchair after all their furniture is lost in a fire.

7072. ____. *Something Special for Me* (Greenwillow, 1983) k–3. Rosa has difficulty choosing a special birthday present to buy with the coins her mother and grandmother have saved, until she hears a man playing beautiful music on an accordion.

7073. ____. *Music, Music for Everyone* (Greenwillow, 1984) k–3. Rosa plays her accordion with her friends in the Oak Street Band and earns money to help her mother with expenses while her grandmother is sick.

7074. Wilson, Robina. *Sophie and Nicky Go to the Market* (Heinemann, 1984) k–3. A small brother and sister enjoy the pleasures of independence with se-

curity behind them as they walk through the countryside to a village with their mother's shopping list.

7075. ____. *Sophie and Nicky and the Four Seasons* (Heinemann, 1985) k–3. Sophie made a seasons calendar at school: pink apple blossoms in spring, family picnics in summer; tints of colored leaves in autumn and snowballing in winter.

7076. Wilmer, Diane. *Daytime* (Macmillan, 1987) k–3. A young child moves through the house searching for and finding dad, mom, sister, brother and the family pets.

7077. ____. *Shopping* (Macmillan, 1988) k–3. Two of the older children go with their father to a bakery, a grocery store, a children's clothing store and then a bookstore.

7078. ____. *Nighttime* (Macmillan, 1988) k–3. Children observe first the town, then the street, the house, the room and at last the sleeping baby.

7079. ____. *My House* (Macmillan, 1988) k–3. This book is an introduction to all members of the family and the household setting.

7080. Wilmer, Diane. *Colors* (Aladdin, 1988) k–3. Nicky has five balloons of different colors which he gives away to various family members—including the cat.

7081. ____. *Counting* (Aladdin, 1988) k–3. At bedtime, Nicky and his sister put away their toys in groups of one to ten.

7082. ____. *Noises* (Aladdin, 1988) k–3. All kinds of sounds in and around a busy household defeat the family's attempts to keep the baby asleep.

7083. ____. *Big and Little* (Macmillan, 1988) k–3. As Nicky helps his little sister pack to spend an overnight with a friend, they choose from things that are too big, too little, and just right.

7084. ____. *Wet Paint* (Aladdin, 1988) k–3. When "Wet Paint" signs don't seem to work, Nicky finally solves the problem of keeping people from using the newly painted, still wet, front door.

7085. ____. *Down in the Shed* (Aladdin, 1988) k–3. Shortly after Mum packs up the family cat's favorite sweater to give to a jumble sale, the cat disappears.

7086. ____. *Over the Wall* (Aladdin, 1988) k–3. Nicky and Dan kick their ball across the wall into Mrs. Wood's garden and worry how to get it back.

7087. ____. *There and Back Again* (Aladdin, 1988) k–3. Nicky spends a wonderful day at the seashore with a friend Dan and his mother.

7088. Wilmer, Diane. *Benny: Story of a Dog* (Collins, 1986) k–3. Benny is mostly Old English sheepdog. There are facts about grooming, medical care and food for a large dog.

7089. ____. *Benny and the Jumble Sale* (Collins, 1986) k–3. Benny the dog is an English television character. Each book ends with a typical infant joke and each resolve a mildly frightening adventure with a smile.

7090. ____. *Benny and the Builders* (Collins, 1986) k–3.

7091. ____. *Benny and the Football Match* (Collins, 1986) k–3.

7092. ____. *Benny at the Fair* (Collins, 1986) k–3.

7093. Wilson, A.N. *Stray* (Orchard, 1987) 2–4. A proud old alley cat tells his life story to his grandson, including his adventures in a convent, in a feline commune and with his listener's grandmother.

7094. ____. *Tabitha* (Orchard, 1988) 2–4. Five episodes in the lives of Pufftail, father of many cats, his favorite daughter Tabitha the gray tabby, and the other cats of their neighborhood.

7095. ____. *Tabitha Stories* (Orchard, 1990) 2–4. Tabitha is the kitten saved by old Pufftail of *Stray*. From birth to motherhood Tabitha is true to life.

7096. Wilson, Bob. *Stanley Bagshaw and the Fourteen Foot Wheel* (Hamilton, 1981) k–3. Stanley, set to watch the bicycle wheel machine, falls asleep; the machine goes wrong and he has to chase the resulting wheel through the town.

7097. ____. *Stanley Bagshaw and the Twenty-Two Ton Whale* (Hamish Hamilton, 1983) k–3. Stanley and his friend Edward meet a 22-ton whale stranded in Huddersgate Canal. Stanley's efforts to guide the whale back to the Arctic result in a soaking for everyone—except Stanley and Edward.

7098. ____. *Stanley Bagshaw and the Mafeking Square Cheese Robber* (Hamilton, 1985) k–3. Stanley Bagshaw, on an errand for a neighbor, foils a robbery at the grocery shop.

7099. ____. *Stanley Bagshaw and the Short-Sighted Football Trainer* (Hamilton, 1986) k–3. Stanley cannot attend the Great Cup Final. He goes in the locker rooms, holds the goalie's gloves and hat and is sent in as a substitute to face Wayne Flacket of the Spurs.

7100. ____. *Stanley Bagshaw and the Rather Dangerous Miracle Cure* (Hamilton, 1987) k–3. Stanley's elderly friend, Ted, is in the hospital. Stanley loses his way in the hospital and ends up napping in the operating theater. He is mistaken for a patient about to have an eye operation. He awakens just in time.

7101. ____. *Stanley Bagshaw and the Mad Magic Mixup* (Hamilton, 1990) k–3. Stanley, in his voluminous shorts, triumphantly ruins a magician's show at the local Theater Royal.

7102. ____. *Stanley Bagshaw and the Ice Cream Ghost* (Hamilton, 1992) k–3. Offered a ticket by old Nell for the Townswomen's Circle visit to a stately home, Stanley gets from the public library essential historical misinformation. The visit itself turns into an adventure when two burglars try to steal the Poshington jewels.

7103. Wilson, David. *Elephants Don't Sit on Cars* (Chatti, 1977) 3–5. Jeremy James is not believed or paid attention to by his parents. He wants the can of mandarin oranges that is in the center of the bottom row of a ceiling high stack. They will not give him the beautiful shiny box in which they have just thrown away dead Great-Aunt Maud, among other things.

7104. ____. *Getting Rich with Jeremy James* (Chatti, 1980) 3–5. Jeremy takes what adults say literally and always gets into trouble. Since there can't be two Father Christmases, the local clergy must be an imposter and Jeremy says so.

7105. ____. *Beside the Sea with Jeremy James* (Chatti, 1981) 3–5. Jeremy James is on summer vacation and has to cope with a bad landlady, visits a high-class restaurant, rides a donkey and quarrels over a sand castle.

7106. Wilson, Gahan. *Harry, the Fat Bear Spy* (Scribner, 1973) 4–6. Harry, spy for Bearmania, is dispatched to the National Macaroon Factory to find out why all the macaroons are coming out a disgusting shade of green.

7107. ____. *Harry and the Sea Serpents* (Scribner, 1976) 4–6. Harry is a super spy bear who is asked to investigate the sighting of a sea monster.

7108. Winkler, Gershon. *Hostage Torah* (Judaica, 1981) 5–8. A fanatical band of student militants storms the Israeli embassy in a small Islamic nation and are holding 34 Jews as hostages. An American student on vacation has a plan that may save them.

7109. ____. *Egyptian Star* (Judaica, 1982) 5–8. Having promised to find a Nazi murderer in Cairo, two teenaged Jewish boys find adventure in both Egypt and Israel as they fall into the hand of Arabs.

7110. Winthrop, Elizabeth. *Bear and Mrs. Duck* (Holiday, 1988) k–3. Once he overcomes his initial fear, Bear has fun playing with his new baby-sitter, Mrs. Duck.

7111. ____. *Bear's Christmas Surprise* (Holiday, 1991) k–3. While playing hide-and-seek with his baby-sitter, Mrs. Duck, Bear peeks at his Christmas presents and feels terribly guilty afterwards.

7112. Winthrop, Elizabeth. *Lizzie and Harold* (Lothrop, 1986) k–3. Lizzie wants a best friend more than anything else, but, as she explains to Harold who would like to be her best friend, it must be a girl.

7113. ____. *Best Friends Club* (Lothrop, 1989) k–3. Lizzie learns to share her best friend and enjoy it, too.

7114. Wiseman, Bernard. *Morris Is a Cowboy, a Policeman, and a Baby-Sitter* (Harper, 1960) 2–4. Morris, a moose, tried his hand at being a policeman, a cowboy and a baby-sitter and is pretty successful—albeit in an unorthodox manner.

7115. ____. *Morris Has a Cold* (Dodd, 1978) 2–4. Morris the Moose has a cold and Boris the Bear tries various remedies to cure him.

7116. ____. *Morris Tells Boris Mother Moose Stories and Rhymes* (Dodd, 1979) 2–4. In order to help

Boris the Bear fall asleep, Morris the Moose tells his friend some familiar stories.

7117. ____. *Morris Goes to School* (Harper, 1983) 2–4. Morris the Moose has an exciting day at school learning the alphabet, counting, singing, spelling, and doing other things that make him a unique moose.

7118. ____. *Morris Has a Birthday Party* (Little, 1983) 2–4. Despite many misunderstandings, Boris the Bear and two children give a birthday party for Morris the Moose.

7119. ____. *Christmas with Morris and Boris* (Little, 1983) 2–4. Boris tries to explain Christmas to Morris but has little success until Billy and Laura invite them to spend Christmas Eve at their house.

7120. ____. *Morris and Boris at the Circus* (Harper, 1988) 2–4. Morris and Boris go to the circus as spectators and end up being part of the action.

7121. ____. *Morris the Moose* (Harper, 1989) 2–4. Determined to prove that the cow he meets is really a moose, Morris the Moose enlists the help of a rather confused deer and horse.

7122. ____. *Halloween with Morris and Boris* (Putnam, 1989) 2–4. Two friends, Morris the Moose and Boris the Bear, experience the frights and delights of Halloween.

7123. ____. *Morris and Boris* (Dodd, 1974) 2–4. Contains three stories about Morris and Boris: "Riddles"; "Tongue-Twisters" and "The Game."

7124. Wiseman, David. *Jeremy Visick* (Houghton, 1981) 5–8. Matthew moves back in time to 1852 when Jeremy was killed in a mine cave-in. The story moves between realism and fantasy.

7125. ____. *Fate of Jeremy Visick* (Houghton, 1983) 5–8. Matthew, 12, finds a tombstone "…Jeremy Visick, his son, age 12, whose body still lies in Wheal Maid." Matt is drawn to the past when Jeremy was alive. He goes into the mine where he is trapped. When he is found by rescuers, Jeremy's skeleton is also found and he then receives a decent burial.

7126. Wisler, G. Clifton. *Antrain Messenger* (Lodestar, 1985) 5–8. Scott is an alien from Antrain adopted by humans after being found when his parents' spaceship crashed. He decides he must leave them and return to his alien heritage but events change his mind.

7127. ____. *Seer* (Lodestar, 1988) 5–8. Scott creates a new identity for himself so he can use his special powers to help people. But he cannot find a real home and live "normally."

7128. ____. *Mind Trap* (Lodestar, 1989) 5–8. Scott knows he must escape from the research institute for psychic children where he has been kept against his will before the doctors discover that he is a telepathic seer from another planet.

7129. Wittman, Sally. *Pelly and Peak* (Harper, 1978) 3–5. A pelican and a peacock like surprises but they like each other better.

7130. ____. *Plenty of Pelly and Peak* (Harper, 1980) 3–5. Pelican and Peacock, friends, share four more adventures including losing a kite and finding a birthday.

7131. Wolde, Gunilla. *Betsy's Baby Brother* (Random, 1974/1990) k–3. Betsy helps take care of her baby brother.

7132. ____. *This is Betsy* (Random, 1975/1990) k–3. Scenes from the daily life of pre-school age Betsy as she dresses herself, eats, plays, and gets ready for bed.

7133. ____. *Different Peter and Betsy* (Random, 1979) k–3. Explains the concept "different" in terms of the child's own world.

7134. ____. *Betsy and the Chicken Pox* (Random, 1976) k–3. When she removes the red spots she painted on her face while pretending to have chicken pox, Betsy discovers that she has real red spots and the disease.

7135. ____. *Betsy's First Day at Nursery School* (Random, 1976) k–3. On her first day of nursery school Betsy tours the school and makes a new friend.

7136. ____. *Betsy and the Doctor* (Random, 1978) k–3. Betsy's fall from a tree results in a visit to the hospital emergency room to see a doctor.

7137. ____. *Betsy's Fixing Day* (Random, 1978) k–3. Betsy is gluing a doll's hair back on, sewing up a teddy bear's leg, nailing a wheel back on a carriage and bandaging her little brother's finger.

7138. ____. *Betsy and the Vacuum Cleaner* (Random, 1979) k–3. Betsy learns how to use a vacuum cleaner and what objects should not be vacuumed.

7139. ____. *Betsy and Peter Are Different* (Random, 1979) k–3. Explores the differences in Betsy and Peter, their home lives, and the things they enjoy.

7140. Wolde, Gunilla. *Tommy Cleans His Room* (Houghton, 1971) k–3. Tommy is looking for Bear. He finds everything else scattered about. He puts each one back into its proper place and is reunited with Bear. Tommy, Bear and Mother are pleased.

7141. ____. *Tommy Takes a Bath* (Houghton, 1971) k–3. A bare Tommy romps with Bear. They slosh around with sand and water. At grandmother's he plays near the sea and then takes a bath in her tiny tub, grooms himself and Bear and then they both go to bed.

7142. ____. *Tommy Goes Out* (Houghton, 1972) k–3. Tommy must wear warm clothes before going out: mittens, hat, sweater, etc. He gets confused while trying to put on each of these items properly.

7143. ____. *Tommy Builds a House* (Houghton, 1972) k–3. Tommy and Bear, without the help of his parents, manage to build up three walls and a roof. The windows were made by drilling holes in the walls. It was not well done but Tommy liked it.

7144. ____. *Tommy Goes to the Doctor* (Houghton, 1973) k–3. Tommy goes for a check-up. The doctor gives him a shot and he yells. Mother explains the shot is to keep him from getting sick. He gets a Band-Aid and goes home to explain this to his toy bear as he plays doctor.

7145. ____. *Tommy and Sarah Dress Up* (Houghton, 1973) k–3. Describes how two children, playing in the attic, put on each item of clothing, giggling at each other. Then take off the old clothes and they are Tommy and Sarah again.

7146. Wood, Lorna. *Dogs of Pangers* (Dent, 1970) 2–4. In this story dogs work together to capture a gang of jewel thieves.

7147. ____. *Panger's Pup* (Dent, 1972) 2–4. Panger's Pup is about a dog's club and the puppy who is blackballed by the club and later is rescued from kidnappers.

7148. Woodson, Jacqueline. *Last Summer with Maizon* (Delacorte, 1990) 4–6. Margaret, 11, tries to accept the inevitable change that comes one summer when her father dies and her best friend Maizon goes away to a private boarding school.

7149. ____. *Maizon at Blue Hill* (Delacorte, 1992) 4–6. Maizon must leave her best friend, Margaret, and Grandma behind on Madison Street when she gets a scholarship to boarding school. There are only five black students at Blue Hill and she is the only seventh grader.

7150. Wooley, Catherine. *Where's Andy?* (Morrow, 1954) k–3. A story of a game of hide-and-seek played by a mother and her young son.

7151. ____. *Andy Wouldn't Talk* (Morrow, 1958) k–3. Andy was shy about talking to anyone but his mother and his dog. One day he and his dog got lost but when anyone asked him his name and where he lived he wouldn't say a word.

7152. ____. *Andy and His Fine Friends* (Morrow, 1960) k–3. A baby bear, lion, kangaroo, and monkey came to visit Andy. Even though his mother couldn't see them she was polite and took them all shopping. No one could see his friends but he had a fine time playing with them.

7153. ____. *Andy's Square Blue Animal* (Morrow, 1962) k–3. Andy decided it wasn't exciting enough to tell mother he had just seen a squirrel, so he invented a strange creature. He wasn't sure of all the details as he began to describe it, filling them in as he went along.

7154. ____. *Andy and the Runaway Horse* (Morrow, 1963) k–3. Andy uses his knowledge of city traffic rules to stop a runaway horse.

7155. ____. *Andy and Mr. Cunningham* (Morrow, 1969) k–3. When a little boy decides to be Mr. Cunningham instead of Andy several problems arise. For instance, if Andy has gone away, how can he attend a birthday party on Saturday.

7156. ____. *Andy and the Wild Worm* (Morrow,

1954) k–3. Andy, pretending to be a worm, has his mother guess what wild animal he is.

7157. Wooley, Catherine. *Gus Was a Friendly Ghost* (Morrow, 1962) k–3. When the summer folks, the Scotts, had gone, the friendly ghost, Gus was lonely. He invited Mouse to share his house. In the spring when Mouse tried to scare away the Scotts, Gus became very angry with his friend Mouse.

7158. ____. *What's a Ghost Going to Do?* (Morrow, 1966) k–3. Gus's home is to be sold for demolition. But he manages to get the old house preserved.

7159. ____. *Gus Was a Christmas Ghost* (Morrow, 1970) k–3. Gus, the Christmas ghost, tries to help unfriendly Mr. Frizzle have a happy Christmas Eve.

7160. ____. *Gus and the Baby Ghost* (Morrow, 1972) k–3. Gus finds a baby ghost on his doorstep, takes it in and decides to keep it. Mr. Frizzle, the caretaker where Gus lives, is apprehensive until a visitor hears the baby coo and many more visitors come. Gus is now a happy foster father.

7161. ____. *Gus Was a Mexican Ghost* (Morrow, 1974) k–3. Adventures of Gus the ghost who takes a trip to Mexico.

7162. ____. *Gus Was a Gorgeous Ghost* (Morrow, 1978) k–3. Gus determines that ghosts needn't always wear white.

7163. ____. *Gus Was a Real Dumb Ghost* (Morrow, 1982) k–3. A ghost decides to go to school and learn to spell when a publisher returns his autobiography.

7164. ____. *Gus Loved His Happy Home* (Morrow, 1989) k–3. Gus the ghost neglects his housecleaning chores while Mr. Frizzle is on vacation and fears that his dereliction of duty will cause him and his animal friends to lose their home with Mr. Frizzle.

7165. Worchester, Donald. *Lone Hunter's Gray Pony* (Oxford, 1956) 4–6. A pony is stolen from a young Oglala Sioux boy by Kiowas. He recovers it and together he and the pony save their tribe from ambush.

7166. ____. *Lone Hunter and the Cheyennes* (Oxford, 1957) 4–6. Captured by the Cheyennes, two Oglala Sioux boys escape through a blizzard and are saved by a grizzly bear.

7167. ____. *Lone Hunter's First Buffalo Hunt* (Oxford, 1958) 4–6. Lone Hunter defies the law of his tribe to search out a herd of buffalo to keep them from starving.

7168. ____. *Lone Hunter and the Wild Horses* (Oxford, 1960) 4–6. Lone Hunter takes part in a foray into unknown country to capture wild horses for the tribe.

7169. Wormell, Mary. *Hilda Hen's Search* (Harcourt, 1994) k–3. Hilda Hen tries several different places before she finds the right spot to lay and hatch her eggs.

7170. ____. *Hilda Hen's Happy Birthday* (Harcourt, 1995) k–3. Hilda Hen finds birthday presents even in places her farm friends didn't intend.

7171. Worthington, Phoebe. *Teddy Bear Postman* (Warne, 1982) k–3. Teddy Bear Postman has a special mission on Christmas Eve. He does his best to make sure everyone gets letters and packages before the holidays.

7172. ____. *Teddy Bear Gardner* (Warne, 1983) k–3. Teddy Bear spends the morning clipping a hedge, mowing, raking and receives five pennies for his labor. Later he harvests flowers and veggies and sells them at market. Then home to dinner and bed.

7173. ____. *Teddy Bear Baker* (Puffin, 1985) k–3. Follows the industrious teddy bear baker through his busy day baking his goods and selling them to this customers.

7174. ____. *Teddy Bear Coalman* (Warne, 1980) k–3.

7175. ____. *Teddy Bear Farmer* (Viking, 1985) k–3. Teddy Bear Farmer works hard milking cows, feeding hens and a pig, tossing hay, and going to market; then relaxes with a cup of cocoa before bed.

7176. ____. *Teddy Bear Boatman* (Warne, 1989) k–3. Teddy Bear and his small sister Suzy worked their boat through a tunnel.

7177. ____. *Teddy Bear Friends* (Warne, 1990) k–3.

7178. Wright, Betty R. *Dollhouse Murders* (Holiday, 1983) 4–6. Amy finds a dollhouse in the attic. The dolls are in the position of Amy's aunt's grandparents when they were murdered. But a clue is there to solve the crime.

7179. ____. *Ghost in the Attic* (Holiday, 1985) 4–6. Amy, almost 13, is overwhelmed by her brain-damaged younger sister. She goes to an aunt who is cleaning out her grandparent's house. In the attic is a perfect doll's house with a family secret.

7180. Wright, Bob. *Mummy's Crown* (High Noon, 1989) 3–5. Tom and Ricky help track down the thieves when a valuable crown is stolen from an exhibit at the town's museum.

7181. ____. *Secret Staircase* (High Noon, 1989) 3–5. Tom and Ricky want to do a good turn for a neighbor. They offer to clean his yard. Mr. Bell's nephew arrives looking for hidden money. Events then lead to a secret staircase and a sum of gold.

7182. ____. *Red Hot Rod* (High Noon, 1989) 3–5. Tom and Ricky see a bag tossed from a red hot rod. Their dog, Patches, grabs the bag, runs away with it, and hides it. The two men in the hot rod later return and look for the bag. In the end Patches aids in their capture.

7183. ____. *Siamese Turtle Mystery* (High Noon, 1989) 3–5. Tom and Ricky set out to buy some turtles for a rock garden. The turtles they get have valuable gems hidden in their false shells. Their job is to outwit the smugglers.

7184. ____. *Video Game Spy* (High Noon, 1989) 3–5. Tom and Ricky chip in to buy a new video game. But it doesn't work right. Slowly the facts unravel; the game contains a code which has been used to send information from the video factory to a competitor.

7185. ____. *Gold Coin Robbery* (High Noon, 1989) 3–5. Eddie, best friend of Tom and Ricky, finds a valuable gold coin in his coat after he bumped into a big, fat man.

7186. ____. *Tree House Mystery* (High Noon, 1989) 3–5. Tom and Ricky build a tree house next to the creek. What a great place to use when they go fishing.

7187. ____. *Thief in the Brown Van* (High Noon, 1989) 3–5. Sergeant Collins gets Tom and Ricky to help him get the lost dogs home.

7188. ____. *Silver Buckle Mystery* (High Noon, 1989) 3–5. When Tom breaks his arm and leg and ends up in the hospital things start to happen.

7189. ____. *Falling Star Mystery* (High Noon, 1989) 3–5. Tom and Ricky set out to find a piece of a falling star.

7190. Wright, Dare. *Lonely Doll* (Doubleday, 1957/1986) 2–4. Mr. Bear and Little Bear show up at Lonely Doll's doorstep and she hopes she will never be lonely again. She and Little Bear misbehave and both are spanked by Mr. Bear.

7191. ____. *Holiday for Edith and the Bears* (Doubleday, 1958) 2–4. Edith and the bears go to the seashore where they climb dunes, gather seashells, explore an old shipwreck, visit a lighthouse, and much more. When they go to sea in a rowboat and lose their oars, they must be rescued by Mr. Bear.

7192. ____. *Doll and the Kitten* (Doubleday, 1960) 2–4. Edith is determined to take a farm animal home for a pet and Mr. Bear's negative attitude are upsetting until he, too, is won over by a kitten.

7193. ____. *Lonely Doll Learns a Lesson* (Random, 1961) 2–4. Edith spends all her time with her new kitten to the exclusion of her old friend Little Bear, who becomes sad and lonely. Mr. Bear helps her understand not to drop old friends for new ones.

7194. ____. *Edith and Mr. Bear* (Doubleday, 1965) 2–4. Edith lied about breaking a clock. She runs away but comes back and confesses.

7195. ____. *Gift from a Lonely Doll* (Random, 1966) 2–4. Story of a doll's present to a family of toy bears.

7196. ____. *Edith and Big Bad Bill* (Random, 1968) 2–4. Toys tell how the doll Edith and her teddy bear companions befriended the "big bad bear" in the dark woods.

7197. ____. *Edith and Little Bear Lend a Hand* (Random, 1972) 2–4. When Mr. Bear decides to move them out of the dirty city, Edith and Little Bear try to clean up the town so they can stay.

7198. ____. *Edith and Midnight* (Doubleday, 1978) 2–4. A doll and a teddy bear attempt to capture and tame their dream horse.

7199. ____. *Edith and the Duckling* (Doubleday, 1981) 2–4. Shows how Edith the doll and her teddy bear companions care for a duckling after its mother disappears.

7200. Wright, Geoff. *Charlie-Not-So-Good Plays*

Football (Coleman, 1985) 4–6. Charlie demonstrates an engaging lack of skill; he perseveres with coaching and practice, and eventually by a fluke scores the winning goal in his first match.

7201. ____. *Charlie-Not-So-Good Plays American Football* (Coleman, 1985) 4–6. Charlie gets mixed up with some young players on an American airbase and ends up scoring a touchdown while fleeing from an imagined pursuit by the Base Police.

7202. ____. *Charlie-Not-So-Good Goes Fishing* (Coleman, 1985) 4–6. Charlie catches a biggish sunfish but learns a lot of basic information about angling.

7203. ____. *Charlie Not-So-Good Goes Swimming* (Coleman, 1985) 4–6. Charlie starts off terrified of water and has to be coaxed into the learner pool by his dad.

7204. ____. *Charlie-Not-So-Good BMX Biking* (Coleman, 1985) 4–6. Charlie, in the middle of a field in the country, practices stunts on his BMX.

7205. Wright, Jill. *Old Woman and the Willy Nilly Man* (Putnam, 1987) k–3. When the old woman's shoes sing and dance all night and keep her awake, she goes to the scary Willy Nilly Man for help.

7206. ____. *Old Woman and the Jar of Uums* (Putnam, 1990) k–3. A little old woman and a naughty boy fall under the spell of a magic jar making them say "Uumm" and must go to the hideous Willy Nilly Man and get the charm lifted.

7207. Wright, Ralph. *Witch's Big Toe* (Methuen, 1983) k–3. Wendy is a schoolgirl who has various witchy adventures, with a cat, a hat and a broomstick of a sort.

7208. ____. *Witch's Funny Bone* (Methuen, 1986) k–3. It's Halloween night when the newly qualified Wendy Witch has her fortune told.

7209. ____. *Witch Goes for Gold* (Methuen, 1989) k–3.

7210. Wyatt, Woodrow. *Exploits of Mr. Saucy Squirrel* (Allen, 1976) 4–6. Saucy Squirrel lives in a beech tree on Mr. Waffle's land. He got a great deal of money as a reward when he found 112 gold sovereigns in an old barn. He spends a great deal of it on good causes.

7211. ____. *Mr. Saucy Squirrel!* (Allen, 1976) 4–6. Mr. Squirrel can talk, which helps him when he decides he wants to live in the style of humans for a while.

7212. ____. *Further Exploits of Mr. Saucy Squirrel* (Allen, 1977) 4–6. Relates the further adventures of a squirrel in the world of humans including the events surrounding his drey-warming party.

7213. Wyeth, Sharon. *Winning Stroke* (Skylark, 1996) 4–6. Kristy and Rosa join the swim team. She competes with Mary June. Her brother, also a swim-

mer, has won many medals. Can she be better than both Mary June and her brother?

7214. ____. *Human Shark* (Skylark, 1996) 4–6. Kristy is going to a three-day swimming meet. Mary June, her competitor, is planning on how to keep Kristy in the arcade instead of the pool. Can Kristy hold up her team and herself?

7215. ____. *Splash Party* (Skylark, 1996) 4–6. Kirk, 14, get a job as a lifeguard. He bosses everyone around, especially his sister, Kristy. Kristy has had it and thinks it's time to put her brother in his place. Then an accident threatens his summer job.

7216. ____. *In Deep Water* (Skylark, 1996) 4–6. Kristy is growing up and gets interested in boys. She joins a school play instead of the swim team. But a boy she likes is on a swim team. Even though she likes him she wants her team to beat his team.

7217. Wynne-Jones, Tim. *Zoom at Sea* (Harper, 1993) k–3. Zoom the cat realizes his lifelong dream of nautical adventures in the home of a mysterious woman with magical powers.

7218. ____. *Zoom Away* (Harper, 1993) k–3. Zoom and his friend Maria search at the North Pole for elusive Uncle Roy.

7219. ____. *Zoom Upstream* (Harper, 1994) k–3. Zoom the cat follows a mysterious trail through a bookshelf to Egypt, where he joins his friend Maria in a search for his Uncle Roy.

7220. Yektai, Niki. *Bears in Paris* (Orchard, 1987) k–3. Shows a multitude of bears, fat and thin, hairy and scary, with hearts and tarts, on their way to Mary's tea party.

7221. ____. *Hi Bears, Bye Bears* (Orchard, 1990) k–3. Each bear is hoping to be chosen by Sam, a young boy who can only purchase one.

7222. Yeoman, John. *Bear's Winter House* (World, 1969) k–3. Since his animal houseguests kept him awake during the winter, bear goes back to sleep when spring arrives.

7223. ____. *Bear's Water Picnic* (Atheneum, 1987) k–3. The pig, squirrel, hedgehog and hen join the bear for a picnic on a raft in the middle of the lake. Frogs want to join them, but they pole away. When they are stuck on a sandbar they must ask the frogs for help.

7224. Yeoman, John. *Old Mother Hubbard's Dog Takes Up Sport* (Houghton, 1990) k–3. When Old Mother Hubbard criticizes her dog for being lazy, he begins playing a variety of sports, creating havoc around the house and leaving Old Mother Hubbard exhausted.

7225. ____. *Old Mother Hubbard's Dog Learns to Play* (Houghton, 1990) k–3. When Old Mother Hubbard suggests her dog learn to play, rather than read all day, he takes her words literally, driving her crazy by enthusiastically playing a variety of musical instruments.

7226. ____. *Old Mother Hubbard's Dog Dresses Up* (Houghton, 1990) k–3. When Old Mother Hubbard complains to her dog about the ragged condition of his coat, he resorts to wearing a variety of disguises and drives her to distraction.

7227. ____. *Old Mother Hubbard's Dog Needs a Doctor* (Houghton, 1990) k–3. Old Mother Hubbard's dog feigns a series of illnesses to escape the threat of taking some exercise.

7228. Yep, Laurence. *Mark Twain Murders* (Four Winds, 1982) 5–8. A youthful Mark Twain and a sea urchin solve a mystery in the San Francisco of Lincoln's day.

7229. ____. *Tom Sawyer Fires* (Four Winds, 1984) 5–8. His Grace, the Duke of Baywater, Twain, a reporter and Tom Sawyer, a San Francisco fireman, try to find out who is setting fires. It turns out to be the same Confederate major from Book 1. This time he is finished off.

7230. Yolen, Jane. *Commander Toad in Space* (Coward, 1980) 3–5. The intrepid crew of the spaceship *Star Warts* lands on a water covered planet inhabited by Deep Wader, a horrible hungry monster.

7231. ____. *Commander Toad and the Planet of the Grapes* (Coward, 1982) 3–5. In search of new worlds to explore, Commander Toad and his crew land their spaceship *Star Warts* on the strange Planet of the Grapes.

7232. ____. *Commander Toad and the Big Black Hole* (Coward, 1983) 3–5. The spaceship *Star Warts,* commanded by Commander Toad, encounters a black hole which threatens the vehicle with doom.

7233. ____. *Commander Toad and the Dis-asteroid* (Coward, 1985) 3–5. Commander Toad and his spaceship *Star Warts* answers a mysterious call for help from a flooded asteroid.

7234. ____. *Commander Toad and the Intergalactic Spy* (Coward, 1986) 3–5. Commander Toad and the crew of *Star Warts* are asked to rout out Tip Toad Space Fleet's greatest and most elusive spy.

7235. ____. *Commander Toad and the Space Pirates* (Coward, 1987) 3–5. When Commander Salamander and his band of pirates capture the *Star Warts* spaceship, Commander Toad is forced to hop the plank.

7236. Yolen, Jane. *Spider Jane* (Coward, 1978) 2–4. Four episodes about a spider and a fly who become friends and decide to live together.

7237. ____. *Spider Jane on the Move* (Coward, 1980) 2–4. The adventures of Spider Jane as she moves, has a web warming, entertains a visitor and tries to find a web-sitter while she goes on vacation.

7238. Yolen, Jane. *Piggins* (Harcourt, 1987) k–3. During a dinner party, the lights go out and Mrs. Reynard's beautiful diamond necklace is stolen, but Piggins the butler quickly discovers the real thief.

7239. ____. *Picnic with Piggins* (Harcourt, 1989) k–3. A picnic in the country develops a mystery which turns out to be a birthday surprise.

7240. ____. *Piggins and the Royal Wedding* (Harcourt, 1989) k–3. Piggins, the butler at the Reynard household, solves the mystery of the missing royal wedding band.

7241. Yolen, Jane. *Giants' Farm* (Seaward, 1977) 2–4. A group of distinctly different giants have problems to solve when they decide to live together on a farm.

7242. ____. *Giants Go Camping* (Seabury, 1979) 2–4. Five giants share the fun and surprises of a camping trip to the mountains.

7243. Yolen, Jane. *Robot and Rebecca: Mystery of the Code-Carrying Kids* (Knopf, 1980) 4–6. Rebecca uses the robot she receives for her ninth birthday to solve a mystery in Bosyork, the biggest metroplex of the East Coast of America in 2121.

7244. ____. *Robot and Rebecca and the Missing Owser* (Random, 1981) 4–6. Rebecca and her mechanical companion investigate the mysterious disappearance of two rare, dog-like animals known as owsers.

7245. York, Carol. *Miss Know-It-All* (Watts, 1966) 3–5. Miss Know-It-All knows the shape of a hummingbird's nest and how to spell LLANFAIRFECHAN. Then Taffy asks "What's the biggest room in the world?" Miss Know-It-All didn't know. It is Mr. Not-So-Much the school controller who knows.

7246. ____. *Christmas Dolls* (Watts, 1967) 3–5. A box of repaired dolls comes to the Good Day Orphanage for Girls. Two are in very poor condition. Happily Tatty is the one girl who can talk to dolls and she rescues Florabelle and Lily before they are discarded. She sees to their restoration.

7247. ____. *Good Charlotte* (Watts, 1969) 3–5. The 28 girls that live on Butterfield Square are being looked after by a new Mrs. Singlittle. She played favorites, picking Charlotte (Tatty) as a model. Only Tatty knew the reason why!

7248. ____. *Good Day Mice* (Watts, 1968) 3–5. Big dog, little boys and 28 orphan girls add to the problems of Mother and Father Mouse after they move their family to the cellar of the Good Day Orphanage while attempting to rescue their son who has been captured by a little boy.

7249. ____. *Ten O'Clock Club* (Watts, 1970) 3–5. Esie May wanted to form a club with the 28 girls who live on Butterfield Square. But recruiting for the club has not been easy. When the club discovered a crystal ball, things begin to happen.

7250. ____. *Miss Know-It-All Returns* (Watts, 1972) 3–5. Miss Know-It-All returns to Butterfield Square to ask a favor of the 28 girls who live there. It is a strange favor but then again Miss Know-It-All is a strange person.

7251. ____. *Miss Know-It-All and the Wishing Lamp*

(Bantam, 1987) 3–5. One blustery October day, while cleaning out a closet at the Good Day Orphanage for Girls, Tatty, Phoebe, Mary and Little Ann find an old brass lamp—a wishing lamp!

7252. ____. *Miss Know-It-All and the Three Ring Circus* (Bantam, 1988) 3–5. The girls of Good Day Orphanage decided to produce a circus for neighbors and friends. It will be on Miss Plum's birthday. Miss Lavendar buys a vase as a gift and it is broken in the hectic preparations for the circus. However the girls and Miss-Know-It-All save the day.

7253. ____. *Miss Know-It-All and the Magic House* (Bantam, 1989) 3–5. A story about a house under a magic spell.

7254. York, Carol. *Doll in the Bakeshop* (Watts, 1965) 3–5. A kindly baker puts Julietta, the lost doll, in the window, hoping the owner will see her. However, it is Mr. Bib, his cat, who engineers Julietta's rescue.

7255. ____. *Revenge of the Dolls* (Dutton, 1979) 4–6. Alice visits Aunt Sarah and Grace in their old, eerie house. Sarah makes weird dolls. She makes one intended to kill cousin Paulie but Alice saves him.

7256. York, Sarah. *Budgie at Bendick's Point* (S & S, 1989) k–3. A little helicopter exhibits his bravery when he rescues two boys from a perilous boating situation.

7257. ____. *Budgie and the Blizzard* (S & S, 1989) k–3. Budgie the helicopter goes to the rescue when a blizzard traps a woman who is about to have a baby.

7258. ____. *Budgie, the Little Helicopter* (S & S, 1990) k–3. Budgie gets all the nastiest little jobs and wants to do something exciting. His wish is granted when a child is kidnapped and he must be the rescuer.

7259. ____. *Budgie Goes to Sea* (S & S, 1991) k–3. While delivering mail to a naval ship at sea, Budgie the helicopter performs a daring rescue of a man overboard.

7260. Young, Alida. *Terror in the Tomb of Death* (Willowisp, 1988) 5–8.

7261. ____. *Return of the Tomb of Death* (Willowisp, 1990) 5–8. Two boys find a magic amulet that enables them to see back in time to ancient Egypt. The boys and their grandfather discover a secret burial site where they are threatened by the mummy of an evil Egyptian priest.

7262. Young, David. *Marooned in Fraggle Rock* (Holt, 1984) 3–5. The big birthday party for Boober is shockingly held up when he and Red are trapped in a cave-in. They are rescued in the nick of time by friends who refused to give up hope.

(For additional books on the Fraggles, Boober, Gobo, Mokey, Red or Wembley *see* Brennan, Joseph; Calder, Lyn; Calmenson, Stephanie; Gilkow, Louise; Gilmour, H.B.; Grand, Rebecca;

Muntean, Michaela; Perlberg, Deborah; Stevenson, Jocelyn; Teitelbaum, Michael; Weiss, Ellen.)

7263. Young, I.S. *Two Minute Dribble* (Follett, 1964) 4–6. This is Bill Carson as a basketball player. In other books he is into baseball and football. His father is his trainer and he plays well.

7264. ____. *Carson at Second* (Follett, 1966) 4–6. Bill plays basketball but he is too small. He tries baseball and is good except he can't hit. He is liked by his teammates and the coach teaches him how to bunt.

7265. ____. *Quarterback Carson* (Follett, 1967) 4–6. Carson has everything in school, good grades, class officer, editor of the newspaper and quarterback for his team. But he knows it was his friends who painted the school walls.

7266. Young, Miriam. *If I Drove a Truck* (Lothrop, 1967) k–3. A youngster debates the fine points of the trucks he would like to drive; the snowplow, delivery truck, dump truck, and the fire engine.

7267. ____. *If I Flew a Plane* (Lothrop, 1970) k–3. A youngster tells of all the places he would go and things he would do as an airplane pilot.

7268. ____. *If I Sailed a Boat* (Lothrop, 1971) k–3. A little boy imagines the different adventures he would have on 14 different kinds of boats.

7269. ____. *If I Drove a Car* (Lothrop, 1971) k–3. A boy imagines what it would be like driving different kinds of cars when he grows up.

7270. ____. *If I Drove a Train* (Lothrop, 1972) k–3. A boy and his friends imagine themselves drivers of various kinds of trains.

7271. ____. *If I Drove a Tractor* (Lothrop, 1973) k–3. A young boy imagines himself driving a variety of tractors.

7272. ____. *If I Drove a Bus* (Lothrop, 1973) k–3. A young boy describes all the different kinds of buses he would like to drive.

7273. ____. *If I Rode a Horse* (Lothrop, 1973) k–3. A boy imagines the things he would do if he had different kinds of horses.

7274. ____. *If I Rode a Dinosaur* (Lothrop, 1974) k–3. A child fantasizes about riding different kinds of dinosaurs.

7275. ____. *If I Rode an Elephant* (Lothrop, 1974) k–3. A young boy imagines what it would be like to ride an elephant in a wedding procession in India, on a picture-taking safari, in a circus parade, and in many other situations and places around the world.

7276. Young, Miriam. *Miss Suzy* (Parents, 1964) k–3. Miss Suzy is a gray squirrel. Her home is usurped by some red squirrels. She moves to an attic where she finds a doll's house. She also finds five wooden soldiers who, after hearing her story, go off and scare away the red squirrels.

7277. ____. *Miss Suzy's Easter Surprise* (Parents, 1972) k–3. Miss Suzy loves her home dearly but the four orphan squirrels turn up that need love too.

7278. ____. *Miss Suzy's Birthday* (Parents, 1974) k–3. Suzy's children, Sylvester, Simon, Serena and Stevie are growing up. The other animals are deciding what to give Miss Suzy for her birthday. Stevie, because he is so young gives the secret away. But that doesn't spoil the fun.

7279. Zabel, Jennifer. *Miss Priscilla's Secret* (Warne, 1978) k–3.
7280. ____. *Miss Priscilla Strikes Again* (Warne, 1980) k–3.
7281. ____. *Miss Priscilla Scares 'Em Stiff* (Warne, 1982) k–3. A puppy is stolen by two evil-looking men. Miss Priscilla and her students go off to find it. Other dogs are reported missing. The thieves are at the haunted Neptune Inn. Miss Priscilla, acting as a ghost, puts the villains to flight.

7282. Zach, Cheryl. *Benny and the Crazy Contest* (Bradbury, 1991) 3–5. Seven-year-old Benny Holt enters a contest to win a new bicycle.
7283. ____. *Benny and the No-Good Teacher* (Bradbury, 1992) 3–5. Fourth grade gets off to a bad start for Benny—his friends are in a different class and he has the strict new teacher.

7284. Ziefert, Harriet. *Small Potatoes Club* (Dell, 1984) k–3. Four boys, two girls and a dog, Spot, make up a club. They build a clubhouse, hold meetings, play games and take trips.
7285. ____. *Small Potatoes and the Magic Show* (Dell, 1984) k–3. The Small Potatoes, a group of children, have a magic show as a fund-raiser.
7286. ____. *Small Potatoes and the Sleep-Over* (Dell, 1985) k–3. Small Potatoes, a group of kids, sleep overnight in their clubhouse. The next day one member does not keep an appointment. They go look for her and find her asleep.
7287. ____. *Small Potatoes and the Birthday Party* (Dell, 1985) k–3.
7288. ____. *Small Potatoes and the Snowball* (Dell, 1986) k–3. The members of the Small Potatoes Club go out to play in the snow but get into a snowball fight instead.
7289. ____. *Small Potatoes Busy Beach Day* (Dell, 1986) k–3.

7290. Ziefert, Harriet. *Baby Ben's Busy Book* (Random, 1984) k–3. Describes some of Baby Ben's daily activities.
7291. ____. *Baby Ben's Go-Go Book* (Random, 1984) k–3. Baby Ben plays with a train, a car, a truck and a plane. Each vehicle is fully illustrated.
7292. ____. *Baby Ben's Bow Wow Book* (Random, 1984) k–3. Baby Ben imitates the sounds of five baby animals.
7293. ____. *Baby Ben's Noisy Book* (Random, 1984) k–3. A jingle, a bang, a splash, and other sounds herald a lively baby's exploration of the objects in his world.

7294. ____. *Suppertime for Baby Ben* (Random, 1985) k–3. The reader discovers which foods Baby Ben and his animal friends enjoy.
7295. ____. *Baby Ben Gets Dressed* (Random, 1985) k–3. By lifting the flaps, the reader watches Baby Ben and Teddy get dressed and helps them spot their mistakes.

7296. Ziefert, Harriet. *Nicky's Christmas Surprise* (Puffin, 1985) k–3. Nicky, a kitten looks for ideas for his mother's Christmas present. He gets lots of suggestions from his animal friends. He likes all of them.
7297. ____. *Let's Watch Nicky* (Viking, 1986) k–3. Nicky is a small gray striped kitten. The kitten jumps, stretches, scratches and eats and then finally decides to "watch you."
7298. ____. *Nicky's Picnic* (Puffin, 1986) k–3. Nicky, a small, curious kitten gets acquainted with the sounds and smells of his surroundings.
7299. ____. *Nicky's Friends* (Viking, 1986) k–3. Nicky, the cat, has friends that include a baby, other kittens, two children, a man on a park bench, an elderly woman who feeds him on her porch and a puppy.
7300. ____. *Oh No, Nicky* (Viking, 1986) k–3. Nicky is a curious cat who gets into trouble—almost.
7301. ____. *Nicky's Noisy Night* (Puffin, 1986) k–3. An inquisitive kitten goes through the sounds and smells around him that occur during the night.
7302. ____. *Nicky Upstairs and Down* (Puffin, 1987) k–3. Nicky the cat runs upstairs and downstairs to hide from his mother.
7303. ____. *Where Is Nicky's Valentine?* (Puffin, 1988) k–3. See who is getting valentines from Nicky. But where is Nicky's valentine? Have his friends forgotten him? A surprise ending.
7304. ____. *Thank You, Nicky* (Puffin, 1988) k–3. Nicky the cat helps a lady dig in her garden, shares in the polishing of a man's car, picks up a dropped scarf, and engages in other helpful acts of kindness.

7305. Ziefert, Harriet. *New House for Mole and Mouse* (Viking, 1987) k–3. Mole and Mouse enjoy trying out everything in their new house where everything works "just fine."
7306. ____. *Clean House for Mole and Mouse* (Viking, 1988) k–3. Mole and Mouse work hard cleaning and tidying their house and spend the rest of the day outside so their house will stay clean.
7307. ____. *Car Trip for Mole and Mouse* (Viking, 1991) k–3. Mole and Mouse take an automobile trip to a flea market

7308. Ziefert, Harriet. *Good Night, Jessie* (Random, 1987) k–3. Before she gets into bed, Jessie must close her dresser drawer, check the window, rescue her slippers from the dog, and collect her clock, toys and blanket.
7309. ____. *Hurry Up, Jessie* (Harper, 1987) k–3.

Jessie prepares for a trip to the beach as her mother hurries her along.

7310. _____. *Dinner's Ready, Jessie* (Harper, 1990) k–3. Jessie has many things she wants to do before going in to dinner, but when her mother gives her a count of ten, Jessie becomes very speedy.

7311. _____. *Come Out, Jessie* (Harper, 1991) k–3. When Jessie's friend John shows up at her house to play, she stays inside, tells him to count to 50, and finally emerges with a surprise.

7312. Ziefert, Harriet. *Chocolate Mud Cake* (Harper, 1988) k–3. Molly and her little sister Jenny bake a make-believe cake out of mud, twigs, and berries when they spend the afternoon at their grandparents' house.

7313. _____. *Me, Too! Me, Too!* (Harper, 1988) k–3. Molly and her little sister have fun playing indoors and outdoors on a rainy day.

7314. Ziefert, Harriet. *Trip Day (Mr. Rose's Class)* (Little, 1987) 2–4. The class is off to a pond to collect water and mud samples for a microscope investigation back in class, observing and drawing what they see and setting up experiments.

7315. _____. *Pet Day* (Little, 1987) 2–4. Mr. Rose brings a variety of creatures to his rambunctious science class on Pet Day and teaches how to handle the little animals.

7316. _____. *Worm Day* (Little, 1987) 2–4. Mr. Rose brings his science class a cooler full of worms so that they can study the animals' characteristics first hand.

7317. _____. *Egg-Drop Day* (Little, 1988) 2–4. The students in Mr. Rose's science class have a contest to see whose wrapped egg can survive the drop from a window.

7318. _____. *Mystery Day* (Little, 1988) 2–4. Mr. Rose's class experiment in identifying "mystery powders" turns into a delicious chemistry lesson.

7319. Ziefert, Harriet. *Bear's Busy Morning* (Harper, 1986) k–3. Folded pages open to reveal Bear's activities on a busy morning.

7320. _____. *Bear Goes Shopping* (Harper, 1986) k–3. Folded pages open to reveal the purchases Bear makes as he goes shopping on different days.

7321. _____. *Bear All Year* (Harper, 1986) k–3. Folded pages open to reveal Bear's favorite activities at different times of the year.

7322. _____. *Beat Gets Dressed* (Harper, 1986) k–3. Folded pages open to reveal Bear's choice of clothing at different times of the year.

7323. Ziefert, Harriet. *I Won't Go to Bed* (Little, 1987) k–3. Unwilling to go to bed, Harry gets to stay up all night, only to discover it is not quite the treat he imagined it would be.

7324. _____. *Harry Takes a Bath* (Viking, 1987) k–3.

Harry Hippo takes a bath, plays in the water and cleans up afterward.

7325. _____. *Harry Goes to Fun Land* (Viking, 1989) k–3. Harry and his grandfather go to Fun Land, where he bravely faces a variety of scary experiences.

7326. _____. *Harry's Bath* (Bantam, 1990) k–3. Harry was sent upstairs to take his bath. All of a sudden, a bear appears and gets into the tub with him. Soon a dinosaur, a witch, and many more strange things were in Harry's bath. Quite a problem for Harry and his mother to solve.

7327. _____. *Harry Gets Ready for School* (Viking, 1991) k–3. Harry Hippo prepares for the first day of school. He visits the doctor, dentist, and barber; prepares pencils and a new outfit and gets a good night's rest.

7328. _____. *Harry Goes to Day Camp* (Viking, 1994) k–3. Harry Hippo goes to day camp, where he bravely deals with a great variety of new experiences, including making friends.

7329. Ziefert, Harriet. *Happy Easter, Grandma* (Harper, 1988) k–3. A rabbit tries to find out which bird lays Easter eggs so he can give one to his grandmother.

7330. _____. *Happy Birthday, Grandpa* (Harper, 1988) k–3. A rabbit, after trying to find the perfect gift for his grandfather, decides to grow a plant for the occasion.

7331. Ziefert, Harriet. *So Sick* (Random, 1985) k–3. In three episodes, Lewis is sick, plays doctor with his friend Angel, and sees him get sick from eating too many cookies

7332. _____. *So Hungry* (Random, 1987) k–3. Finding themselves extremely hungry, Lewis and Kate have fun making enormous sandwiches and eating them as fast as possible.

7333. Ziefert, Harriet. *Max and Diana and the Snowy Day* (Harper, 1987) k–3. Diana and Max play hide-and-seek indoors and build snow twins outdoors on a snowy day.

7334. _____. *Max and Diana and the Birthday Present* (Harper, 1987) k–3. Max and Diana go to the pet store to find a birthday present for themselves that will suit everybody in the family.

7335. _____. *Max and Diana and the Beach Day* (Harper, 1987) k–3. Twins spend a lovely day at the beach.

7336. _____. *Max and Diana and the Shopping Trip* (Harper, 1987) k–3. Twins Diana and Max go shopping with daddy.

7337. Ziefert, Harriet. *Sleepy Dog* (Random, 1984/1995) k–3. Portrays a small dog getting ready for bed, sleeping, dreaming and waking up.

7338. _____. *No More TV, Sleepy Dog* (Random, 1989) k–3. Sleepy dog thinks of many excuses why he cannot go to sleep at bedtime, but finally he does become sleepy enough to slip into slumber.

7339. Ziefert, Harriet. *Prince Has a Boo-Boo* (Random, 1989) k–3. There is excitement in the court when the little prince bumps his head and needs a Band-Aid.

7340. _____. *Prince's Tooth Is Loose* (Random, 1990) k–3.

7341. Ziefert, Harriet. *Play with Little Bunny* (Viking, 1986) k–3.

7342. _____. *Count with Little Bunny* (Viking, 1988) k–3. The reader is asked to help Little Bunny count her toys.

7343. _____. *Feed Little Bunny* (Viking, 1988) k–3. Readers can help Little Bunny choose just what she likes for breakfast, lunch, dinner, snack and even a party.

7344. _____. *Little Bunny's Noisy Friends* (Puffin, 1990) k–3.

7345. _____. *Little Bunny's Melon Patch* (Puffin, 1990) k–3.

7346. Zinnemann-Hope, Pam. *Let's go Shopping, Ned* (Macmillan, 1986) k–3. Ned and his dad try to buy a new sweater. Ned and his dog, Fred, would rather hop than shop and dad is in for a wild afternoon.

7347. _____. *Time for Bed, Ned* (Macmillan, 1987) k–3. Ned repeatedly eludes his mother as she tries to ready him for bed. He runs away, crawls under the doghouse and dives into the laundry basket.

7348. _____. *Find Your Coat, Ned* (Macmillan, 1987) k–3. Ned's search for his missing coat turns out to be a mischievous romp through the house.

7349. _____. *Let's Play Ball, Ned* (Macmillan, 1987) k–3. Ned and his dog, Fred, play ball indoors until Ned's father moves the game outdoors.

7350. Zion, Gene. *Harry the Dirty Dog* (Harper, 1956/1976) k–3. Harry hates baths, but one day he gets so dirty that even his owners don't recognize him.

7351. _____. *No Roses for Harry* (Harper, 1958/1976) k–3. Harry the dog gets a sweater knitted in a rose pattern by Grandma. He is not happy and tries to lose it but someone always returns it. Harry does not like his sweater, but he never expected a bird to solve his problem.

7352. _____. *Harry and the Lady Next Door* (Harper, 1960) k–3. Harry attempts to silence the lady singer who lives next door. When he fails he enlists the help of a cow, a parade musician, and even the wind. But finally his persistence gets him his way, and the singing lady is removed from hearing distance.

7353. _____. *Harry by the Sea* (Harper, 1965/1976) k–3. Harry sets off along the beach to find some shade and turns into a strange monster.

7354. Zistel, Era. *Thistle* (Random, 1967) 4–6. Thistle was found one day at the side of the road, a small, wet, very sick baby raccoon. She got better and played with a kitten and the mother cat. She eventually returns to the woods.

7355. _____. *Thistle and Company* (Little, 1982) 4–6. Thistle, a foundling raccoon, and two skunks share the inside and underside of a house.

7356. Zistel, Era. *Wintertime Cat* (Townsend, 1990) 4–6. Relates the wintertime activities of a cat and his family.

7357. _____. *Cat Called Christopher* (Townsend, 1991) 4–6. Christopher the cat loves his mistress and his home very much but must learn to share them, first with another cat and then with the man his mistress marries.

Index

References are to entry numbers.